AFRICA'S DEVELOPMENT IN HISTORICAL PERSPECTIVE

This edited volume addresses the root causes of Africa's persistent poverty through an investigation of Africa's *longue durée* history. It interrogates the African past through disease and demography, institutions and governance, African economies and the impact of the export slave trade, colonialism, Africa in the world economy, and culture's influence on accumulation and investment. Several of the chapters take a comparative perspective, placing Africa's developments alongside other global patterns. The readership for this book spans from the informed lay reader with an interest in Africa, to academics and undergraduate and graduate students, policy makers, and those in the development world.

Emmanuel Akyeampong is a professor of history and of African and African American Studies at Harvard University. He is the former editor of the *Journal of African History* and of *African Diaspora* and the author or editor of several books, including *Drink, Power and Cultural Change: A Social History of Alcohol in Ghana* (1996); *Between the Sea and the Lagoon: An Eco-Social History of the Anglo of Southeastern Ghana* (2001); *Themes in West Africa's History* (2006); and *Dictionary of African Biography* (six volumes) (2013).

Robert H. Bates is Eaton Professor of the Science of Government at Harvard University. His research focuses on the political economy of development, particularly in Africa, and on violence and state failure. Professor Bates has conducted fieldwork in Zambia, Sudan, Uganda, Kenya, Colombia, and Brazil. He currently serves as a researcher and resource person with the Africa Economic Research Consortium, Nairobi. Among his most recent books are *Analytic Narratives* with Avner Greif, Margaret Levi, Jean-Laurent Rosenthal, and Barry Weingast (1998); *When Things Fell Apart* (Cambridge University Press, 2007); and *Prosperity and Violence* (2009).

Nathan Nunn is a professor of economics at Harvard University. His primary research interests are in economic history, economic development, political economy, and international trade. He is an NBER faculty research Fellow, a research Fellow at BREAD, and a faculty associate at Harvard's Weatherhead Center for International Affairs. He is also currently coeditor of the *Journal of Development Economics.*

James A. Robinson is the David Florence Professor of Government at Harvard University. His main research interests are in political economy, comparative economic development, and economic history with a focus on sub-Saharan Africa and Latin America. He is the coauthor, with Daron Acemoglu, of *Economic Origins of Dictatorship and Democracy*, (Cambridge University Press, 2006), which was awarded the 2007 Woodrow Wilson Foundation Award by the American Political Science Association for "the best book published in the United States during the prior year on government, politics, or international affairs." He edited the book *Natural Experiments in History* with geographer and ecologist Jared Diamond in 2010. His most recent book, also written with Daron Acemoglu, is entitled *Why Nations Fail* and was declared one of the ten best books of 2012 by the *Washington Post.*

Africa's Development in Historical Perspective

Edited by

EMMANUEL AKYEAMPONG
Harvard University

ROBERT H. BATES
Harvard University

NATHAN NUNN
Harvard University

JAMES A. ROBINSON
Harvard University

CAMBRIDGE
UNIVERSITY PRESS

CAMBRIDGE
UNIVERSITY PRESS

University Printing House, Cambridge CB2 8BS, United Kingdom

One Liberty Plaza, 20th Floor, New York, NY 10006, USA

477 Williamstown Road, Port Melbourne, VIC 3207, Australia

4843/24, 2nd Floor, Ansari Road, Daryaganj, Delhi - 110002, India

79 Anson Road, #06-04/06, Singapore 079906

Cambridge University Press is part of the University of Cambridge.

It furthers the University's mission by disseminating knowledge in the pursuit of education, learning and research at the highest international levels of excellence.

www.cambridge.org
Information on this title: www.cambridge.org/9781107041158

First published 2014

A catalogue record for this publication is available from the British Library

Library of Congress Cataloging in Publication data
Africa's development in historical perspective / editors: Emmanuel Akyeampong, Harvard University, Robert H. Bates, Harvard University, Nathan Nunn, Harvard University, James A. Robinson, Harvard University.
pages cm
Includes bibliographical references and index.
ISBN 978-1-107-04115-8 (hardback) – ISBN 978-1-107-69120-9 (pbk.)
1. Economic development – Africa – History. 2. Africa – Economic conditions – History. 3. Africa – Politics and government. I. Akyeampong, Emmanuel Kwaku, editor of compilation. II. Bates, Robert H., editor of compilation. III. Nunn, Nathan, editor of compilation. IV. Robinson, James A., 1960– editor of compilation.
HC800.A57255 2014
338.96009–dc23 2014001822

ISBN 978-1-107-04115-8 Hardback
ISBN 978-1-107-69120-9 Paperback

Contents

Author Biographies

Emmanuel Akyeampong is a professor of history at Harvard University. He has written on social history and on the history of disease and the environment in West Africa. His more recent work has looked at trade and political economy, interests strengthened by his participation in the Harvard working group on "Understanding African Poverty over the Longue Durée." His recent articles in this area include: "Africa, the Arabian Gulf and Asia: Changing Dynamics in Contemporary West Africa's Political Economy," *Journal of African Development*, 13: 1 (Spring 2011), 73–105; and Emmanuel Akyeampong and Hippolyte Fofack, "The Contribution of African Women to Economic Growth and Development: Historical Perspectives and Policy Implications – Part I: The Pre-colonial and Colonial Periods," World Bank, Policy Research Working Paper, WPS 6051, April 2012.

Gareth Austin is a professor of international history at the Graduate Institute of International and Development Studies, Geneva. Previous employers include the University of Ghana and the London School of Economics. His research and teaching interests are in African, comparative, and global economic history. His primary research has focused on West Africa, especially Ghana and the precolonial kingdom of Asante. His publications include *Labour, Land and Capital in Ghana: From Slavery to Free Labour in Asante* (2005); "Resources, Techniques and Strategies South of the Sahara: Revising the Factor Endowments Approach to African Economic History," *Economic History Review*, 61: 3 (2008), 587–624; and (edited with Kaoru Sugihara) *Labour-Intensive Industrialization in Global History* (2013).

Robert H. Bates is Eaton Professor of the Science of Government at Harvard University. During the past decade, he has focused on conflict and state failure and, working with the Africa Economic Research Consortium, on the political economy of the "lost decades" following independence. In recent years, he has returned to the study of agricultural policy, focusing on political responses to international price shocks and policy responses to the enfranchisement of rural voters. He spends his summers in Ghana trying to figure out when the absence of violence transforms into the rule of law and peace becomes an institutionalized feature of political order.

Isaías Chaves is a PhD candidate in political science at Stanford University. His past research projects have examined the determinants of electoral fraud in 1920s Colombia and the divergent political consequences of civil war in Sierra Leone and Colombia. His current work in historical political economy studies the domestic political coalitions that drove British imperial expansion after the Great Reform Act. At the same time, he is pursuing projects in American politics that adapt techniques from empirical industrial organization to better understand the strategic behavior of legislators and campaign donors.

William G. Clarence-Smith is Professor of the Economic History of Asia and Africa in the School of Oriental and African Studies at the University of London. His major current research project is on Middle Eastern migrants in the colonial Philippines, who came mainly from "Greater Syria." This has taken him of late to Manila, Beirut, Madrid, and Washington, DC, and has involved probing the history of the global trade in embroidery and lace. He also works on tropical commodities and the manufacturing related to them, not only cotton, but also rubber, palm oil, hot beverages, masticatories, and large livestock. A third part of his research concerns the interplay between Islamic law and social history, notably in regard to slavery, sexuality, and technological change.

Christopher Ehret is Distinguished Research Professor in the Department of History at the University of California at Los Angeles. His research over the past four decades has dealt with a wide variety of African historical and cultural topics and a wide range of time periods. A major methodological focus in this work has been to develop the tools and techniques for reconstructing history, especially early African history, from the evidence of language and for correlating the evidence of language with other types of historical evidence. One long-running theme in his research has been the origins and early history of agriculture in Africa. A second major focus has been on understanding the ways cross-cultural interactions have shaped the courses of long-term social, cultural, and economic change across the continent. Recently he has embarked on a new course of research into the *longue durée* histories of African kinship systems, and he has also undertaken collaborative work with geneticists and biological anthropologists on the possibilities of correlating their findings with those of linguistics and archaeology.

Stanley L. Engerman is John H. Munro Professor of Economics at the University of Rochester. He is best known for his quantitative historical work along with Nobel Prize–winning economist Robert Fogel. His coauthored books include *Time on the Cross: The Economics of Slavery* (1974) with Robert Fogel and *Economic Development in the Americas since 1500: Endowments and Institutions* (2012) with Kenneth L. Sokoloff.

Linda Heywood is a professor and the director of African American Studies at Boston University. In November 2011, Heywood published an article entitled "Angola, the Violence Years: Civilian Casualties," and she has just completed her book *Queen Njinga of Angola/Matamba: A Biography.* During the summer of 2011, she spent three weeks in Angola working in the archives, where she collected materials for her Njinga project. She also visited the locations in Malange, Angola, where the people called Njingas live. There she conducted video interviews with the "king of the Njingas" and other officials who all claim to be the direct descendants of the Njinga dynasty and her followers. Heywood was allowed to visit the place where Njinga and other members of the Ndongo ruling elite are supposed to be buried. She was told that she was only the third outsider accorded this honor. Heywood has now turned her attention to the second part of the Njinga project, entitled "The Remaking of Njinga: Angola, Portugal and the African Diaspora."

Joseph E. Inikori is a professor of history at the University of Rochester. He was previously chairman of the Department of History, Ahmadu Bello University, Zaria, Nigeria. One of the pioneers of the study of Atlantic World history, he has published extensively on Atlantic World economic history. His most recent book in the field, *Africans and the Industrial Revolution in England: A Study in International Trade and Economic Development* (Cambridge University Press, 2002), won the 2003 American Historical Association's Leo Gershoy Award for "the most outstanding work in English on any aspect of the field of 17th- and 18th-century western European history," and also the 2003 African Studies Association's Herskovits Award. The book has been entered in the American Council of Learned Societies Ebook Project "dedicated to selecting and creating an electronic collection of important scholarly monographs that are expected to have continuing relevance in the field of history." His lifetime achievement honors include The Distinguished Africana Award from the African New World Studies Program, Florida International University (2007) and the Distinguished Africanist Award from the New York State African Studies Association (2008).

Patrick Manning is Andrew W. Mellon Professor of World History and director of the World History Center at the University of Pittsburgh. For many years, he has analyzed historical African populations, especially as they were influenced by enslavement, and he is near completion of a collaborative work with Scott Nickleach on African population from 1650 to 1950. He has written widely on migration in world history, most recently in *The African Diaspora: A History through Culture* (2009). His current project is a collaborative project, with historical linguist Christopher Ehret, on the history of migration and social change in early human communities (ca. 100,000–5,000 years ago) as seen through historians' reading of the evidence on language, genetics, archaeology, climate, plants, and animals.

Nathan Nunn is a professor of economics at Harvard University. Professor Nunn's research has focused on empirically examining the determinants of the long-term economic development of societies both within Africa and across the globe. His research traces the impacts of large historical events like Africa's slave trades, missionary activities in Africa, the transfer of food crops during the Columbian Exchange, plantation slavery in the Americas, historical state formation, historical conflict, and technology adoption. His ongoing research seeks to better understand exactly why many historical events have impacts that are persistent and continue to influence economic development today.

Ayodeji Olukoju is a professor of history at the University of Lagos and vice-chancellor, Caleb University, Lagos, Nigeria. He is the author of *The "Liverpool" of West Africa: The Dynamics and Impact of Maritime Trade in Lagos* (2004) and *Culture and Customs of Liberia* (2006). His other publications on maritime, social, economic, urban, and African history have appeared as authored and edited books, chapters in books, and articles in high-impact specialist and African journals. He serves on the boards of the *Journal of African History* and *History in Africa: A Journal of Method*. His latest contributions include "Food and Food Production" in Thomas Spear (ed.) *Oxford Bibliographies in African Studies* (2013) and a chapter on Lagos in Miguel Suarez Bosa (ed.), *Atlantic Ports and the First Globalisation, c. 1850–1930* (Cambridge Imperial and Post-Colonial Studies Series, Macmillan-Palgrave, 2014, chapter 6).

Jean-Philippe Platteau is a professor of economics at the University of Namur. Most of his work has examined the understanding of the role of institutions in economic development, and the processes of institutional change, especially under the joint impact of population growth and market penetration. The influence of noneconomic factors and various frontier issues at the interface between economics and sociology are a central focus of his research projects, hence his continuous interest in other social sciences than economics and his continuous emphasis on the potential contributions of sociology to the field of economics in general, and to economic development in particular. Recently, he has embarked upon two ambitious research projects. The first one deals with the transformation of farm-cum-family structures when land becomes more scarce and market integration increases. Field data of the panel type are collected in central Mali for the purpose of testing theoretical predictions. The second project concerns the interaction between the statutory law and the custom when the lawmaker wants to fight oppressive social norms and both informal and formal judges act strategically. Fieldwork in relation to the latter project is being carried out in Senegal, Guinea Bissau, and Guinea Conakry.

Richard Reid is a professor of African history at the School of Oriental and African Studies, University of London. He has recently completed a project dealing with long-term conflict in the Horn of Africa, which resulted in *Frontiers of Violence in Northeast Africa* (Oxford University Press, 2011). His thinking on African warfare more broadly has now been distilled into *Warfare in African History* (Cambridge University Press, 2012). While he continues to ponder the links between war and development in the making of modern Africa, he has also begun to travel in a slightly different direction, namely research on the role of historians and historical consciousness in African state and society during the nineteenth and twentieth centuries, using the case study of Uganda.

James A. Robinson is David Florence Professor of Government at Harvard University. He is currently on sabbatical in Colombia researching the origins of paramilitarism and how and why some paramilitary groups created state-like structures while others did not. He is also collecting data on elite networks in Haiti to investigate how elite control of the economy influences the development of the society. He has just finished an empirical project on the consequences of indirect rule for development in rural Sierra Leone and has been in the DRC, Uganda, and Rwanda researching the roots of delayed political centralization in Africa.

John Thornton is a professor of history and African American Studies at Boston University. He is primarily an Africanist, with a specialty in the history of West Central Africa before 1800. His work has also carried him into the study of the African Diaspora, and from there to the history of the Atlantic Basin as a whole, also in the period before the early nineteenth century.

David N. Weil is the James and Merryl Tisch Professor of Economics at Brown University. Most of Professor Weil's research examines long-run economic growth. Among the topics he has studied are technology transfer, population growth, accumulation of physical and human capital, and the transition from the Malthusian equilibrium to modern economic growth. Much of his recent work has looked at how population health affects the level of income in a country and how demographic changes such as declining fertility and population aging impact growth. In his latest completed research, he and his coauthors explore techniques for measuring economic growth using satellite observations of light that is visible at night. This method can be applied both in countries where standard national income accounts data are of low quality and to subnational or supranational regions for which no other data are available.

Warren C. Whatley is a professor of economics at the University of Michigan. His research interests include the economic history of Africans and African Americans – primarily African American workers in the twentieth century north and south of the United States, and the impact of the transatlantic slave trade and colonialism on African political and economic development. His articles have appeared in the *Quarterly Journal of Economics*, the *Journal of Economic History*, and the *Journal of Labor Economics*, among others. He is currently writing a book on the transatlantic slave trade and the political and economic development of West Africa.

Acknowledgments

This edited volume, *African's Development in Historical Perspective* comes out of the initiative of a working group on "Understanding African Poverty over the Longue Duree," funded by the Weatherhead Center for International Affairs at Harvard University. The working group organized a conference in Ghana in the summer of 2010, co-hosted by the International Institute for the Advanced Study of Cultures, Institutions and Economic Enterprise (IIAS), under the then director Professor Irene Odotei. We acknowledge the tireless assistance of Jaronica Fuller at Harvard and Sharon Okantey, Ebi Kanga Landry, and others from IIAS (Ghana), who made the Ghana conference a great success. We also express our deepest appreciation to all the scholars who participated in the Accra conference, and whose presence made this one of the most stimulating intellectual events ever.

Introduction

Africa – The Historical Roots of Its Underdevelopment

Emmanuel Akyeampong, Robert H. Bates, Nathan Nunn, and James A. Robinson

Africa poses the development challenge of our time. Once devastated by famine and mired in poverty, India and much of Asia are now growing economically. While Africa's economies too are now growing, in many African countries, people are just now returning to the levels of per capita income they enjoyed more than a half century ago.[1] The current poverty and the widespread economic decline following independence in Africa have led to a great deal of research by development economists and political scientists (Bates 1981; Easterly and Levine 1997; Ndulu et al. 2007; Sachs and Warner 1997). Yet this work is often very policy focused and does not place Africa within the larger processes that created the Great Divergence in the early modern and modern worlds (Pomeranz 2000).

This is somewhat odd, because the adoption of a much more historical approach has revolutionized research on comparative economic development in the past fifteen years. For example, the economic divergence that took place in the Americas during the nineteenth and twentieth centuries is now seen as deeply rooted in the different institutional structures created during the colonial period (Bruhn and Gallego 2012; Dell 2010; Engerman and Sokoloff 1997, 2011). It is commonplace, though not uncontroversial, to blame Africa's economic problems on its economic, political, and perhaps social institutions. It is less common to find studies that situate these

[1] In its focus on the historical roots of Africa's underdevelopment, this volume does not include contributions on more contemporary developments, such as the World Bank's structural adjustment programs or the current commodity boom, driven by rising Asian demand, among other factors (Mkandawire and Soludo 2003; World Bank 1994). On the current growth cycle in Africa, see IMF (2009) and Kasekende, Brixova, and Ndikumana (2010). See also Radelet (2010).

issues in a historical context and consider why they diverged from the rest of the world in the first place (see Austin 2008; Nunn 2008a; and Acemoglu, Johnson, and Robinson 2001, 2002; Acemoglu and Robinson, 2010, for exceptions).

The aim of this book is to trigger a research agenda of the type that has reoriented our understanding of the Americas (see Hopkins, 2009, for similar suggestions). Although scholars have published a rich literature on the economic history of Africa, contemporary approaches are yet to be integrated into the broader literature on its development, and for Africa we have nothing like the type of synthesis or consensus that has emerged for the Americas.

Attempts to provide grand narratives of African economic history are not new, of course, though they took some time to emerge. The economic problems of Africa were an intense subject of interest for European colonial officials. Colonial powers often justified their colonization of Africa on the basis of the continent's poverty, poor institutions, and backward technology. They put forth various explanations for African poverty. An example is the notion that the incidence of the tsetse fly limited the use of draught animals that impeded the adoption of the plow and wheeled transportation (see McPhee 1926). Yet colonial officials did not create a coherent view of the economic development of Africa and were typically content to argue that colonialism would lead to a straightforward dissemination of modern technology and institutions with immediate positive effects on African living standards.

As early as 1958, however, Suret-Canal provided a famous Marxist interpretation of African poverty by applying the notion of the "Asiatic mode of production." This approach took it for granted that Africa was relatively poor and explained this by the fact that Africa was trapped with precapitalist institutions. The research he pioneered long flourished in African studies (see Birnberg and Resnick 1975; Law 1978; Sender and Smith 1986) and triggered a fascinating debate over the role of feudalism in Africa (for example, Crummey 1980; Goody 1971). Another grand narrative emanated from anthropology, when the "substantivist school," also accepting Africa's historical poverty as given, argued that African societies were not based on market principles (though they did have marketplaces), and therefore did not respond to the economic incentives created since the Industrial Revolution in ways that generated prosperity (Dalton 1976; Polanyi 1966; Polanyi, Arensberg, and Pearson eds. 1957). The 1960s and 1970s also saw a great deal of work by dependency and world systems theorists who attempted to explain African underdevelopment not as a consequence of primarily internal dynamics, as in the Marxist and substantivist approaches, but as a consequence of its integration on unfavorable terms with the world economy (e.g., Amin 1974, 1976; Wallerstein 1974–2011). This literature has many variants; for example, Rodney (1972) developed an influential synthesis of Marxist and dependency theory approaches with a heavy emphasis on the impact of formal colonization. Other scholars pointed to specific features that were quantitatively so important as to become the dominant force shaping African economic history. For Goody (1971), this was the relative abundance of land and scarcity of labor. For Inikori (1992), it was the Atlantic slave trade. For Douglas (1962, 1963) and Vansina (1978), it was the historical dynamics of state formation in Africa. For Law (1981) and Miller (2009), it was the absence of the horse. For others, it was the impact of colonization (Palmer and Parsons 1977).

Common to this research was the acceptance of Africa's poverty relative to the rest of the world in the early modern period. In a seminal symposium based on the paper by Thornton (1992), those unconvinced by the historical evidence for Africa's poverty challenged this view. Other scholars also critiqued these early approaches for their overly static view of the African past (see Jerven 2010).

Alongside such grand narratives a large monographic literature developed focusing on specific themes. One focused on precolonial trade (Birmingham and Gray 1970; Bohannon and Dalton 1962; Meillassoux 1971). A second investigated the impact of the slave trade (Curtin 1975; Manning 1990; Miller 1996). These literatures have been surveyed by many (e.g., Austen 1987; Hopkins 1973; Wickens 1980, 1986).[2]

Yet while many of these early narratives linger (for example, the relationship between the substantivist school and Hydén's, 1980, 1983, "economy of affection") and have sparked productive and lively debates (for example, that between Hopkins, 1973, and Dalton, 1976, on the empirical applicability of substantivist claims and the book by Hill, 1963, arguing for the sophisticated economic rationality of Africans and the adaptability of traditional economic institutions), their conceptual frameworks have fallen out of favor. Political scientists focused much more on the politics of contemporary Africa. Anthropologists moved away from research on political and economic institutions. Economists studied contemporary development problems as if they were timeless, and conducted no research within the subfield of economic history in economics departments. The consequence is a relative void of convincing narratives of African economic history even in its own terms, let alone in a comparative context. For example, the big

[2] Austin (2008) provides a recent synthesis of much of this research.

debates in comparative economic history over the past twenty years have focused squarely on questions such as the divergence between Europe and Asia (Findlay and O'Rourke 2007; Jones 1981; Morris 2011; Pomeranz 2000; Rosenthal and Wong 2011; Van Zanden 2009; Wong 1997) or on why Britain diverged from Western Europe (Allen 2009; Mokyr 2009). In no study is there any reference to Africa or to its divergence from the other economies of the world. Why this occurred has never been one of the big questions in either economic history or comparative economic development.

Our book is a reflection of the fact that this situation of neglect is now changing. Allen (2011) has made a pioneering attempt to integrate Africa into his theory of the great divergence, and we hope that the chapters in this volume will provide stimulus to make further progress toward this goal.

At the same time as this nascent interest by comparative economic historians, economists who saw the economic problems of Africa as essentially those of any poor economy began to recognize the problematic nature of this view. As Africa emerged from colonialism in the 1960s, the first wave of development economists proposed simplified models of African poverty that either wrapped countries into general models of the problems of "backward economies," implying few differences between Africa and Asia, for instance, or proposed ahistorical models of the sources of poverty (see Killick, 1978, for a good overview). The starting point for this is easily seen by reading the characterization of African development problems by late colonial scholars such as Stamp (1953) and Batten (1954). Only with the successive failure of the models of development economics (see Easterly 2001) did a perception emerge that it is critical to understand the specificities of African society and institutions and where these came from in order to unlock the vast economic potential of the continent. There certainly were voices in the wilderness urging this (Hopkins 1986), but the larger intellectual reorientation over the past decade in comparative economic development toward a focus on historical long-run forces shaping institutional development has emphasized the need for completely rethinking the nature of African poverty.

The attempt to develop a convincing comparative account of African development is necessarily interdisciplinary. It involves absorbing not just the recent research in economic history and comparative development, but also the rich literature on the economic and political history and anthropology of Africa. It fact, it was historians, such as McGreevey (1971) and Coatsworth (1978), as much as anyone who initially framed the new questions that scholars began to ask about the comparative economic history of the Americas. The task is neither one of embedding Africa within some preexisting paradigm nor of developing some explanation for Africa's uniqueness. Rather, it is to refine and reevaluate the types of explanations that now reign in comparative economic history and development. The historical evolution and development of African political systems, economic institutions such as product and factor markets, or the nature of landownership provide an unrivaled chance to learn about economic history.

We do not pretend that this book can provide the type of synthesis to which we aspire. We can only hope that it marks the start. Its origins lie in a conference we organized in Accra, Ghana in July 2010, with the type of interdisciplinary group of scholars that seemed necessary for this venture. At the conference, we focused on several main questions: When did Africa become poor? Why did Africa become that way? What mechanisms made it so? And why did it stay that way?

While each of the chapters in this volume addresses the roots of Africa's poverty, they fall into four distinct categories. Contributors to the first category view Africa from a global perspective, asking "When did Africa become poor?" and comparing its development to that in other regions. In response to our next question, "Why did Africa become that way?," a second set of chapters focuses on institutions, both those that antedate the colonial encounter and the slave trade and those that were shaped by them. The third cluster of chapters highlights the values and practices of some of Africa's cultures and assesses the possibilities they open and the limitations they impose for better understanding long-term economic development. The last category of chapters addresses the impact of external forces, most notably the slave trade, colonialism, and global markets, in shaping African development.

AFRICA IN HISTORICAL PERSPECTIVE

The chapter by Christopher Ehret reaches far back in history – in some instances to 10,000 BCE – to argue that the level of economic development on the African continent was on par with that in the rest of the world. Agriculture, he contends, emerged sometime between 9000 and 6000 BCE in the southern part of the Eastern Sahara, which is comparatively early by global standards. Some of the earliest developments in ceramics took place in Africa around 9000 BCE, as did the domestication of cattle between 8500 and 7200 BCE by the Northern Sudanese in the Eastern Sahara. His reading of the evidence suggests that the people of this region also numbered among the first to cultivate crops. Far from lagging behind the rest of the world, African societies of this period were positioned at the technological frontier. Like all issues in early African economic history, the specific dating of developments is debated. Africa is far less studied archaeologically than the rest of the world, and the absence of written records and material remains means that a great deal of creativity has to be used, including such controversial techniques as glottochronology.[3] Yet it was just such innovations that put precolonial African history on the map in the 1960s.[4]

Ehret's chapter suggests that it is most likely that the economic divergence of Africa from Eurasia is a feature of the past millennium. Much other work points in this direction. Phillipson (1998), for instance, illustrated the compelling comparisons between the Kingdom of Axum and the Eastern Roman Empire at the start of the Dark Ages, and even pointed out how theories such as Piernne's "Mohammed and Charlemagne" applied equally to Ethiopia. Haour (2000) showed great continuities during the medieval period between the central Sahel and northwestern Europe.

Further evidence on these issues comes from David Weil's chapter, which manages to narrow down the timing of Africa's divergence to an even greater degree. He presents evidence on some proxies for Africa's prosperity relative to that of other regions, using such commonly employed measures as population density, city size, and technology.[5] His data suggest that at 1500 BCE, rather than being the poorest region of the world, Africa appears quite average. Population density, conditional on land quality, was higher in Africa than in the Americas and Oceania, but lower than in Europe and Asia. A similar picture emerges from the data on urbanization and technological choice: Africa was on par with the Americas, but significantly less urbanized and less technologically advanced than Europe and Asia. Weil also examines state development, measured from 1 to 1500 CE, using the State Antiquity Index developed by Chanda and Putterman (2007). Again, taken as a whole, Africa attained levels of state development that were lower than Asia and Europe, but higher than the Americas or Oceania.

As with Ehret's data, these estimates are conjectural. Population density, for example, has to be reconstructed by backward projection from early colonial censuses, and estimates of urban population may be even more speculative. The fact that different authors highlighted in this book marshal quite different numbers highlights this difficulty and the need for further

3 See Barker (2006) for a different assessment of what the evidence says about Africa, and see Vansina (2004) for a critique of the use of glottochronology.

4 See, for instance, Vansina (1985).

5 See Prados de la Escosura (2011) for a complementary exercise.

research. However, a great deal of qualitative evidence suggests that the end judgment is broadly accurate and unlikely to be overturned by further refinements in the data.

As Weil stresses, the average difference between Africa and the rest of the world masks significant heterogeneity within Africa, with the most developed parts being North Africa, West Africa, and Ethiopia. The measures Weil examined suggest that these parts of Africa had attained levels of development that were just below or even sometimes on par with Eurasia. Elsewhere, acephalous societies were common, for example, in the Horn of Africa or Southern Nigeria, and these places were probably quite a bit poorer and less technologically advanced. Moreover, even in the more advanced places, we know that there were important elements of technology that lagged behind technology in other parts of the world. While Ethiopia and North Africa had writing, the wheel, and the plow, West Africa did not.

To examine the trajectory of African development between 1650 and 2000 CE, Patrick Manning traces its demographic history. Total population both provides a proxy for economic development and is of interest for its own sake, particularly given the export of human beings during the slave trade. In many ways an update and extension of Manning (1990), the chapter argues that from the seventeenth century to the twentieth century, the continent's population was much larger in size yet growing at a slower rate than previously thought. The implication is clear: by 1650 Africa entered a period of sustained stagnation, one that lasted for two and a half centuries. Such a fact, if it holds up to further empirical scrutiny, is undoubtedly a big part of the story behind Africa's divergence since 1500.

Joseph Inikori takes a comparative perspective in his chapter and probes the relative development of West Africa and the Americas between 1400 and 1850 CE. Inikori examines estimates of city sizes and population densities, as well as the history of market development, trade, and specialization, and argues that, prior to 1500, the level of economic development was higher in West Africa than in the Americas, but that the economic development of the Americas thereafter increased dramatically while that in West Africa did not.

When Inikori turns to the causes of this reversal, he points to the transatlantic slave trade, which shipped between 11 and 12.5 million Africans to the Americas. The use of enslaved Africans enabled the growth of highly specialized plantation agriculture and mining: an advantage that accrued to the Americas rather than to Africa. In West Africa, participation in the transatlantic slave trade diverted effort from and actively hindered productive activity, thus contributing to Africa's stagnation and relative underdevelopment, he argues. See Inikori (1992) for a development of this view.

The chapters thus suggest that Africa's underdevelopment is not a historical constant or something inevitable. Regions within Africa – namely West Africa and Ethiopia – were once more highly developed than the Americas and Oceania and comparable to Europe and Asia. Not until after 1500 did Africa stagnate and lag behind, as measured by population, city growth, state development, or technological progress.

These chapters thus set the stage for our attempt to explain Africa's current underdevelopment. Because Africa's economic fortunes have varied, time invariant factors, such as natural endowments, are unable to explain its present underdevelopment. Rather, the authors turn to more malleable factors: institutions, culture, and relations with the outside world. It is easy to see that these things are likely interconnected. For example, one potential explanation for why Africa exported slaves given that it was labor scarce is that economic institutions within Africa were so poor that while physical marginal productivity was potentially very high, the appropriable product was low, thus making it relatively attractive to sell people into slavery rather than to exploit them on the continent (Robinson 2012).

INSTITUTIONS

Among the institutions examined in this book's chapters, the political receive the most attention. And among the most important institutions are the state and the regimes that governed it. Also critical, though less discussed in this book, are economic institutions.

Early accounts of Africa's interior often stressed the level of conflict and war making, which, some researchers claimed, helped to account for the continent's relative lack of development (a lucid nineteenth-century account with this flavor is Speke, 1863). Inspired by subsequent work in comparative history, some of the authors in this volume mount a counterargument. Early modern Europe, which experienced dramatic changes in political and economic institutions, was violent, Reid and Bates note in their chapters. But according to some (e.g., Bates 2001; Brewer 1988; Herbst 2000; Roberts 1956; Tilly 1975), the result was the emergence of the "fiscal-military" state: one that mobilized political power in support of economic development. Be it offensive or defensive, warfare is expensive – it must be financed – and those seeking to enhance the military capabilities of the state may therefore use their power to promote economic growth. In pursuit of this theme, Bates joins Reid in noting the protection states in Africa offered to trade routes and commercial centers, as well as states' provision of public goods: roads, pontoons, and peace in the market. Using data from the Standard Cross-Cultural Sample, Osafo-Kwaako and Robinson (2013) show that greater precolonial political centralization is indeed correlated with improved transportation infrastructure, greater occupational specialization, and the use of more advanced technologies. Heywood and Thornton, moreover, examine in their chapters attempts by embattled African rulers to promote technological change by securing trained artisans from abroad.

Thornton's chapter applies the paradigm of the fiscal-military state to Dahomey, which sent its armies out virtually every year. But, Thornton argues, these armies "may not have simply been economic instruments destined to shape the development of the state." He draws on the correspondence of Dahomean monarchs in the eighteenth and early nineteenth centuries (Agaja in the eighteenth century, Adandozan between 1810 and 1812, and others). Thornton underscores how in the letters the Dahomean monarchs refute the allegation that they went to war to capture slaves. Agongolo noted how, unlike England that was protected by the sea and had commerce everywhere, Dahomey was hedged in by other nations similarly armed, which was the cause of incessant conflict. We certainly can read the Atlantic trade as the backdrop to this militarization and constant wars, as the slave trade both militarized societies and absorbed the captives of wars. But for Thornton, the slave trade is not sufficient explanation for Africa's lack of industrialization. Thornton opines that the Industrial Revolution was not state run in Europe, but a private enterprise, often in spite of state interference and monopoly concessions. And it is this little understood dimension of precolonial African economies – the private sector – that may shed light on Africa's failure to industrialize.[6]

These works resonate with a long history in African studies that addresses the processes of state formation.[7] One tradition, recently surveyed by McIntosh (1999), argues that African states have developed along historical paths that differ from those traced by early states in Eurasian; by implication, it would reject the arguments of Bates and Reid.[8] The historical nature and dynamics of the state in Africa and its comparison with Eurasian states remains an important area for future research, particularly because recent empirical studies suggest that precolonial political institutions have left a

[6] See Law (1977) and Manning (2004) for discussion in the case of Dahomey.

[7] Going as far back as Evans-Pritchard and Fortes (1940).

[8] McIntosh (1988) for the Niger basin in West Africa and Sheriff (2010) for the East African coast stress the feature of heterarchy in inter-polity relations in early Africa, not hierarchy based on aggressive expansion.

long shadow in Africa (Gennaioli and Rainer 2007; Michalopoulos and Papaioannou 2013).

Early accounts by explorers, adventurers, and missionaries tended to stress the malevolence of Africa's rulers: their violent temperaments, their unbridled appetites, and their sadistic dispositions. But, Bates notes from the evidence we possess on Africa's traditional political institutions, while there certainly were despotisms, for example in the Kongo or Buganda, in many places political institutions existed that constrained such behavior (see also Beattie 1959). Even had these leaders been as benighted as European travelers held them to be, they would have found their actions checked by nonroyals who held high office or by independent councils. While travelers' accounts may stress the fearsome character of Africa's monarchs, then, the empirical record suggests a more nuanced portrayal: Africa's precolonial institutions were often imbricated with agencies of constraint. An important example of this theme is the literature that attempts to explain Botswana's extraordinary economic success since independence and that stresses the importance of precolonial institutions of accountability in the Tswana states in helping to create good governance (Acemoglu, Johnson, and Robinson 2003; Leith 2005).

In Africa as in Europe, there was warfare, of course; less obviously perhaps, Reid and Bates conclude, military insecurity appears to have fortified the hand of political leaders who sought to protect and promote economic activity. As Reid notes, in West Africa, most states possessed an urban core; in support of merchants and artisans, rulers employed the forces of the state to protect markets and to promote trade. In East Africa, he writes, such efforts were devoted to long-distance trade, which promoted regional specialization and "Smithian" growth, that is, increases in welfare resulting from specialization and exchange. By incorporating those who could pillage and destroy into administrative agencies subject to command and control, the formation of states demobilized banditry and transformed warfare into an instrument of public policy – sometimes for the worst, but sometimes too for the better.

The arguments of Bates and Reid suggest that rather than Africa diverging from Eurasia around 1500, the similarities were much closer until the past two hundred years. Indeed, both chapters suggest that African states were in many places during the early modern period evolving along similar lines to those in Eurasia, and only colonialism and the postcolonial international system blocked this path of institutional change. They both agree with Thornton (1992) that African economic divergence must have come much more recently.

The consequences of the strength and nature of the state and institutions of governance are crucial as well for understanding the nature of economic institutions in Africa. For instance, Douglas (1962, 1963) and Colson (1969) suggest that the absence of state authority in parts of precolonial Africa created disorder and insecurity of property rights. Yet just as some of the scholars featured in this book find parallels between African and Eurasian political institutions, others, for example, Hopkins (1973), found similarities between African economic institutions during the early modern and modern periods.[9] This thesis too is controversial.[10] It is clear, for example, that slavery was endemic in Africa until well into the twentieth century (Miers and Roberts 1988), and a potent source of economic inefficiency. Finley (1965) argues that slavery was the fundamental reason for the lack of technological change in the classical world, and the data surveyed by Lovejoy (2000) suggest that slavery in Africa was far more extensive as a percentage of the population than it was in ancient Greece or Rome. Finley's thesis might help us to comprehend the technological lag that Africa experienced (documented by Austen and Headrick 1983; Goody 1971; and Law 1980) and to resolve a long-standing puzzle: Why did African societies not adopt modern technologies of which they were clearly aware?[11] Recent research by Bezemer, Bolt, and Lensink (2012) has indeed found that the historical incidence of slavery in Africa is strongly associated with poor economic performance today.

CULTURE

Another set of chapters examines the importance of societies' values and cultural practices, something that resonates with the substantivist approach to African development. While aware of the existence of cultural diversity within Africa, Platteau identifies the existence of common cultural traits, while Olukoju, focusing on the culture of one society, the Yoruba, addresses themes of general significance. Each contributor stresses the significance of beliefs about the importance of equality and of resistance to hierarchy. Each points as well to the quest for social recognition. In so doing, they take

[9] Hopkins (1973) is the most famous statement.

[10] See Dalton (1976) for a critique.

[11] Other economic institutions of crucial importance being the way that land is owned, transferred, and allocated and the available evidence (Goldstein and Udry 2008) suggests very large economic inefficiencies in the way the system is currently organized, which itself reflects deep historical continuities in Africa (Colson 1971).

common aim at the ability of Africa's peoples to accumulate, to invest, and so to forge the means of production necessary for an industrial economy.

Reaching deep into his knowledge of Yoruba history, Olukoju marshals an array of instructive examples, some from the wars of the nineteenth century, others from the time of the foreign occupation of Lagos, and still others from the time of the creation of the cash crop economy. Olukoju's vivid portrayals confirm the entrepreneurial impulse that permeates Yoruba culture and the value placed on wealth. But he also points to the challenges facing those who might wish to conserve it or to invest. Those who are rich, he argues, are urged to celebrate their wealth, to display it, and to share it. Being wealthy is a social, not an individual, act. It has more – much more – to do with consumption than with investment. In Yoruba-land, one rarely encounters ascetic capitalists; nor does one often encounter capitalist institutions – firms or foundations designed to remain productive long after their founders have died.

One way of reading Olukoju's chapter is through the lens of sociologist Max Weber, who, when discussing social stratification, distinguished between class, status, and power. Viewed in this way, Olukoju is suggesting that Yoruba values lead people to trade wealth for status.

Platteau also underscores the importance of status and redistribution in Africa's cultures, but in so doing, illustrates the wide repertoire of defenses that the rich can deploy (see Baland, Guirkinger, and Mali, 2011, for an empirical study). Platteau illustrates how they can withdraw from the local cultures, forming communities of their own: thus his discussion of the industrial organization of commercial diaspora in West Africa. He also notes the role of conversion, leading to his discussion of Long's (1978) account of the use of religion as a defense against the "beer culture" of the Copperbelt in Central Africa and his discussion of Islam in Western Africa.[12] While offering an implicit critique of the arguments of Olukoju, in other respects, Platteau amplifies them, as in his discussion of witchcraft.

Nunn's chapter turns to the impact of early twentieth-century Christian missions on contemporary values. Controlling for possible alternative influences – some historical and others contemporary – Nunn finds that Africans from ethnic groups exposed to the influence of foreign missions achieve higher levels of educational attainment today. Interestingly, when Nunn examines the education effect along gender lines, he finds very different impacts for Catholic and Protestant missions. Although both had a similar

[12] Another classic discussion of the use of conversion to Islam to avoid traditional social exactions is Parkin (1972).

positive impact on long-run educational attainment, for Catholic missions the increased education was amongst males only, while for Protestant missions the impact was across both genders, and actually greater for females.

As with the chapters on the state, these chapters can be read as attempts to address the internal roots of Africa's underdevelopment. But clearly, cultural practices in other societies – particularly in societies that achieved growth – contributed to Africa's decline. One such force was Western science. The absence of writing throughout most of Africa may have played an important role in limiting the growth of science and therefore the growth of Africa's economies.

While the Enlightenment gave rise to a culture of skepticism and reason in Europe, it was the print revolution that underpinned organized science (Mokyr 2008). Printing made it possible for investigators to document the priority of "discoveries," while also disseminating them. Through correspondence and debate, ideas were shared and their merits subject to scrutiny. Reputations were thus made or lost; and with the invention of patents, fortunes were as well. Writing, record keeping, and communication enabled private efforts at innovation to yield financial reward, thereby strengthening the incentives to achieve scientific progress and promoting technical change (see also Goody 1986).

Africa too developed advanced technologies: its smiths forged iron of the highest quality, and its weavers, as recorded by Clarence-Smith in his chapter, produced superb textiles (see also Herbert 1993; Kriger 2006; and Thornton 1992). In East Africa, some societies also kept records and corresponded in writing, although often using Islamic scholars or Christian missionaries to do so. But without widespread literacy and a print industry to underpin it, Africa failed to generate widespread technical progress. It failed to produce an industrial revolution. Energetic, risk-taking, and appropriately celebratory of wealth, Africa nonetheless did not transform its economic foundations. Export agriculture, mining, services, transport: these industries existed in Africa. But while Europe and North America benefited from the harnessing of coal, petroleum, and other sources of energy for the production of goods, Africa did not.

Yet even an example as apparently simple as literacy is more complex than meets the eye. Chaves, Engerman, and Robinson show in their chapter that African societies knew about technologies such as the wheel but did not adopt them. Such was the case with writing. While we do not understand why Africa failed to widely adopt such technologies, the literature offers hints. Consider the work of Ewald (1988), for example, who argues that the use of writing was a political act, stripping power away from those who previously controlled oral knowledge and tradition.[13] Perhaps then the lack of literacy in Africa is but another product of its political economy.

EXTERNAL IMPACT

As noted at the outset, the preponderance of chapters suggests that Africa became relatively poor after the sixteenth century; until then, it occupied a middle position in the global rankings, as measured by technology, population, or power. What could explain the subsequent divergence? The arguments thus far stress the importance of institutions and cultures, but they are inconclusive. While some like Dalton (1976) or Acemoglu and Robinson (2010, 2012) argue that economic institutions in precolonial Africa were not conducive to development, others like Hopkins (1973), Thornton (1992), or Jerven (2010) dispute this. While Reid and Bates may argue that African states were developmental, this view is also hotly contested (Acemoglu and Robinson 2010). The inconclusive nature of these debates whets our appetite for an alternative explanation. For most, following the scholars of dependency theory, though emphasizing different mechanisms, the leading candidate is Africa's encounter with Europe. The date at which Africa's fortunes began to diverge, after all, marks as well the time of Europe's escape from the confines of the Mediterranean and the North Sea and its entry onto the global stage. The possibility therefore arises that Africa, like other portions of the globe, was itself subject to the great divergence.

Commerce and Agriculture

In some respects its encounter with Europe enriched Africa, promoting exchange, trade, and the growth of institutions that underpinned markets. And, as Akyeampong notes, its merchants, initially at least, grew prosperous from their participation in foreign trade during the nineteenth century. Drawing on the private papers of Gold Coast trading families such as the Ocanseys and the Caesars, examining the career of the young Christian Jacobson, and focusing on the major palm oil-exporting port of Ada, Akyeampong explores the impact of declining transport costs and rising foreign demand on the fortunes of merchants in West Africa. He studies as well the impact of global financial crises and the manner in which Gold Coasters interpreted them. Compiling detailed case studies, he explores

[13] Predating arguments more recently proposed by Feldman (2008) and Scott (2009).

the economic practices of families and firms – subjects that others, such as Platteau, theorize.

Focusing on agriculture rather than commerce, Austin's chapter also explores the impact of global markets on West Africa during the late nineteenth and early twentieth centuries. While doing so, he compares and critiques two major approaches: the "vent for surplus" school and the "dependency" school. The latter, he indicates, stresses the importance of coercion and views Africa's integration into global markets as implying a loss of welfare. While conceding that this interpretation might well fit the spread of cotton production in West Africa, Austin rejects it when applied to the spread of other cash crops: palm oil, ground nuts, or cocoa, for example. Nor does he fully embrace "vent for surplus" as a valid model. For while properly emphasizing, in Austin's view, the gains in income that resulted from the production of cash crops, the "vent for surplus" theory treated these gains as essentially free; they resulted, it was held, from the mobilization of slack resources. But, Austin notes, labor in fact had alternative uses. Put another way, the cash crop revolution in West Africa did not represent the birth but rather the restructuring of West Africa's economy.

Advancing this theme, Austin highlights the importance of that crucial period when slave labor became free, with the redistribution of income and the restructuring of contracts that must have accompanied that transition. His chapter thus bridges the precolonial and imperial eras in Africa, and our discussion of its economies during and after the slave trades.

The Slave Trades

For many, the answer to the question "Why did Africa become poor?" is obvious: the slave trades. Africa's slave trades did not merely subtract from the stock of labor, they also altered the way power and production were organized and the nature of African institutions (see Inikori 1992, 1994; Lovejoy 1989, 2000; Nunn 2008a). In short, the slave trades encouraged the creation of institutions that favored the extraction rather than the creation of wealth.

Were the standard models of international trade applied to Africa during the slave trade, they would have predicted economic gains on the part of exporters and importers alike. The evidence presented in this volume suggests that the standard models would have been wrong and that with the commencement of the slave trade, Africa's relative fortunes began to decline. What is suggested, then, is an approach that looks beyond the gains from trade to institutions and cultures. This, like the colonial period, may have shaped contemporary Africa, influencing the use of power and attitudes toward the production and accumulation of wealth. The analysis of the slave trade that emerges fits better with approaches advanced by, say, Brenner (1976), who stresses the role of power relations, rather than by, say, Postan (1937) or others who focus on the relative abundance of factors, prices, and the functioning of markets (see Acemoglu and Robinson, 2010, 2012, for a development of this approach).

Reid and Bates, echoing Fage (1969), note that the rise of some states in Africa was associated with the slave trade, though Nunn (2008a) shows empirically that the average effect of the slave trade on political centralization was negative. But while some of those who seized slaves may have forged states that encouraged trade, supplied public goods, and promoted the welfare of those they ruled, they did so at the expense of those they attacked and plundered. In addition, a major portion of the slaves withheld from export were assigned to plantations, where they grew food for members of the court, civil servants, and the military or for export abroad. As Inikori noted, plantation agriculture based on slave labor became a major form of production on both sides of the Atlantic: one that was privately profitable for slave owners, but that failed – in either region – to induce long-term growth (Engerman and Sokoloff 1997; Nunn 2008b).

The slave trade can thus be said to have launched Africa along a trajectory marked by slow growth and relative decline. It may also have impeded subsequent development by promoting ethnic fractionalization (Easterly and Levine 1997; Nunn 2008a). As Miguel and Gugerty (2005) show in their study of school committees in western Kenya and Habyarimana and colleagues (2007) reveal in their experiments on public good provision in Uganda, ethnic diversity makes it more difficult to share in the costs of providing public goods. It therefore leads to the under-provision of education, energy, roads and transport, and so forth that make economic development possible.

Of equal importance, although more difficult to measure, is the impact of slavery on economic institutions. Slavery involved extraction rather than the creation of value.[14] The slave trade may have led to the deterioration of economic institutions in Africa, a process that continued after the slave trade was abolished (see the essays in Law, 2002). Even more provocative is the finding of Nunn and Wantchekon (2011) of a relationship between slaving and modern levels of interpersonal and political distrust. Because

[14] As Lovejoy (2000) stressed, the evidence suggests that the rise of slave exports led to a large increase in the extent of slavery within Africa.

it is premised on labor repression, slavery presumes the existence of political forces capable of defending the claims of the slave-owning minority against those of the working majority. Its very existence therefore requires that power be employed to repress. This creates a rather different picture of Africa's historical states relative to the "developmental" one implicit in the fiscal-military hypothesis discussed by Bates and Reid. The nature and dynamics of precolonial African states is undoubtedly a crucially important area for future research.

The chapter by Warren Whatley explicitly tests for the impact of the transatlantic slave trade on political structure, measured by the form of succession of local headman. He does this by combining information from Murdock's Ethnographic Atlas, reporting ethnicity characteristics, with The Trans-Atlantic Slave Trade Database, reporting the total number of slaves shipped from each African port. His analysis shows that ethnic groups located close to ports that exported a large number of slaves were more likely to have hereditary succession; less likely to have succession based on influence, wealth, or status; and less likely to have succession determined by election or other forms of consensus. He concludes that the slave trade had a causal impact on succession, generating political structures that were more absolutist.

Whatley also provides evidence that the transatlantic slave trade not only impacted precolonial institutions, but also colonial institutions. Using data from Nunn (2008a), he documents a positive relationship, among British African colonies, between the intensity of the slave trade and British use of indirect rule (measured using data from Lange, 2004, 2009). Whatley argues that greater precolonial absolutism would have increased the efficiency of indirect rule for the British, making its adoption more likely.

The Colonial Period

When the external world intruded upon Africa, it took the form of the slave trade on the one hand. On the other, it assumed the guise of colonialism. The academic literature contains many channels via which colonialism could have created poverty in Africa (see Heldring and Robinson, 2013, for a survey), a claim made more plausible if one accepts the idea that Africa was not far behind the rest of the world during the early modern period.

Most who address the impact of colonialism focus not on the colonial period itself, but rather on the consequences of colonialism for the postcolonial period. Claims include those that the authoritarian nature of colonialism created despotism after independence (Mamdani 1996;

Young 1994); or left distorted "gate-keeper states" unable to promote development (Cooper 2002); or left arbitrary "nation-states" with no workable social contract, leading to low public good provision and to conflict (Engelbert 2000).

While the studies in this volume do not focus directly on these issues, Chaves, Engerman, and Robinson come close to doing so. In their chapter, they examine the economics of transportation, particularly those of the railways during the colonial period. In contrast to earlier revisionists who argue that the wheel was an "inappropriate technology" for Africa (Hopkins 1973), Chaves and colleagues argue that the introduction and use of wheeled transportation was in fact highly beneficial. Indeed, they show that the social rate of return on capital invested in the railways was huge, as much as 100 percent per year. If Africa was not isolated and therefore knew about these technologies (the Chaves, Engerman, and Robinson chapter contends that they did), and the technologies were economically efficient, why then were so few rail lines constructed in colonial Africa?

The authors provide evidence that the failure to adopt railways (if not other forms of wheeled transportation) was the result of efforts of the colonial powers to block their dissemination in some instances, and of the fears of African leaders in others. Illustrative is the fate of European investment in Ashanti in the 1890s. In this case, the Asante dispatched a mission to England in 1895 in search of the finances that would enable them to develop their economy through investments in mechanized gold mining and railways in partnership with European firms. But the project was blocked by colonial secretary Joseph Chamberlain, who instead ordered a military invasion (Wilks 1989). Rather than railways, Britain bound Ashanti with the coast through the use of force, invading Kumasi even while its delegation was in London. As Chaves and colleagues noted, in other instances – as in Ethiopia – local elites resisted the construction of railways, viewing them as a harbinger of colonial occupation. The latter response highlights an informative contradiction. In the precolonial era, those who ruled often sought to enhance political security by accelerating economic development. However, in the era of rapid colonization, rulers often sought to enhance it by retarding it. Thus did political calculations shape the pace and nature of Africa's development.

This chapter complements recent research by economic historians on colonial Africa. They have shown that in West African nations, where there were few European settlers, colonialism was consistent with rising living standards for Africans (Frankema and van Waijenburg 2012) and improving stature (Cogneau and Rouanet 2011; Moradi 2008, 2009). But where settler populations were large and intent upon mobilizing African labor, colonialism led to immiserization (the calculations in Heldring and Robinson 2013; Mosley 1983; Wilson 1972). While these chapters help to account for the level of development the colonial occupation bequeathed to independent Africa, they fail to inform us about the manner in which colonialism shaped institutions and values, and thus the future development of the continent. Important research is, however, beginning to look more precisely at these issues, for example, Frankema's (2011) work on colonial educational systems, and Gardner's (2012) work on systems of taxation. For additional evidence, we can turn to the works of scholars such as Anderson, Von der Mehden, and Young (1967), Young (1994), Firmin-Sellers (1995, 1996), and Boone (2003), who provide qualitative accounts and in-depth studies of the use of power in the colonial period. Important too is the recent research of Zaaruka and Fedderke (2010, 2011). Heldring and Robinson (2013) discuss the problems involved in assessing the impact of colonialism on African development (particularly the issues of the absence of clear counterfactuals), while nonetheless concluding that it is difficult to believe that colonialism stimulated development. Though Botswana has been an economic success since independence, it would surely have been a lot richer today had it not been colonized by the British (unless of course the counterfactual is that it would have instead been taken over by the British South Africa Company).

Colonialism did not just impede development, it also distorted it. The occupation of Africa resulted in a shift in control over war making, justice, taxation, and expenditures – that is, the core issues of politics – from the hands of the chiefs and headmen to those of the foreign occupier. As Bates and Reid argue, it also inserted colonial officials into the set of principals whom the local power holders needed to please to remain in office (see also Gluckman, Mitchell, and Barnes 1949). The first change weakened the incentives to invest effort in costly projects: traditional leaders now lacked the resources to mount them. The second expanded the opportunities for officeholders to advance their private agendas. When negotiating with one principal – say, the colonial office – a chief could plead pressure from the royal family. When arguing with indigenous power holders, in turn, he could cite directives from the occupier. The possibilities for self-serving maneuvering thus increased, enabling indigenous officeholders to gain privately even though their status and power had declined. In short, colonialism appears to have divorced political ambition from public service.

Pondering this argument, we can return to one of Bates's sources, the Standard Cross-Cultural Sample, which lists what it calls the "focal year" of the sources coded. For a given society, the "focal year" constitutes the central tendency of the annual distribution of the accounts from which the data were taken. Drawing from the Africa portion of this sample, we can compare data for societies that were observed during the nineteenth century with those observed during the twentieth: periods that roughly correspond to before and after the consolidation of imperial rule. When doing so, we focus on societies that possessed executives or centralized political institutions. We then find that during the nineteenth century, that is, before colonial rule, in 44 percent of societies with executives, the executives had to rule through councils. However, during the twentieth century, that is, during the colonial period, in only 25 percent of such societies were the executives similarly constrained. During the nineteenth century, moreover, 89 percent of the centralized societies possessed a judiciary. During the twentieth century, that is, after the introduction of colonialism, the percentage fell to 40 percent. These – and other – measures thus suggest that while Africa's political elites lost power while under colonial occupation, they were also freed of traditional impediments to the self-serving use of what powers they retained.

It is important to emphasize the scarcity of the data. The sample contains fewer than thirty societies in all. But the direction of the findings corresponds with the position taken in the qualitative literature: Africa's political institutions changed during the colonial period, and in a way that facilitated the self-interested use of power. Independence may therefore have found Africa governed by political institutions that had been rendered more authoritarian by colonial rule and people more inclined to view political elites as self-seeking (Cooper 2002).

CONCLUSIONS

The chapters in this volume offer rich insight into the nature and trajectory of Africa's development. If one thing unites them, it is the belief that an ahistorical understanding of Africa's current economic problems is of little value. Understanding Africa's relative standing in the global distribution of wealth entails understanding its development path and the legacies that shaped it. The absence of such an understanding undermines the efforts of practitioners to "save Africa," a point Hopkins (1986) lucidly made some time ago. And its presence will surely inspire new scholarship. By heightening interest in Africa among those with an interest in comparative historical development, we surely will induce creative insights, as those who study other regions encounter a history so different from their own.

Many important areas of African economic history have been well researched, and do not appear in this volume given our focus. One is the extent to which economic factors influenced the creation of colonialism and subsequently decolonization (Hopkins 1973; Austen, 1987, and Fieldhouse, 1986, 1994, 1999, review many of the theories, and see Milburn, 1977, and Marseille, 1984, as well as Cooper, 1996, 2005, for important monographs). This introduction and the chapters of this book also neglect the impact of Africa's economic development on Europe and the Industrial Revolution, an important theme since the work of Williams (1944). (Also see Acemoglu, Johnson, and Robinson 2005; Inikori 2002; Lynn 1997.) Labor issues, particularly the transition from slavery to free labor and the forms of labor coercion used during the colonial period, surface only transitorily (see Austin 2005; Cooper 1980, 1987). Important and vivid as well is the regional economic history of southern Africa (see Houghton, 1976, and Feinstein, 2005, for overviews), which includes important studies of mining (Worger 1987), business (Mager 2010), and labor (Bundy 1979; Van der Horst 1942; and Van Onselen 1982).

Our intention in putting together the conference and in editing this volume was not to provide a comprehensive guide to the enormous amount of high-quality research on many aspects of African economic history and development. It was rather to focus on the key themes we have stressed throughout and to inspire students and scholars to take this rich base of evidence and ideas and build it more effectively into a convincing comparative narrative.

References

Acemoglu, Daron, Simon Johnson, and James A. Robinson. (2001). "The Colonial Origins of Comparative Development: An Empirical Investigation." *American Economic Review*, 91(5): 1369–1401.

(2002). "Reversal of Fortune: Geography, Institutions in the Making of the Modern World Income Distribution." *Quarterly Journal of Economics*, 117(4): 1231–94.

(2003). "An African Success Story: Botswana." In *In Search of Prosperity: Analytic Narratives on Economic Growth*, edited by Dani Rodrik, 80–122. Princeton, NJ: Princeton University Press.

(2005). "Rise of Europe: Atlantic Trade, Institutional Change and Economic Growth." *American Economic Review*, 95: 546–79.

Acemoglu, Daron and James A. Robinson. (2010). "Why is Africa Poor?" *Economic History of Developing Regions*, 25: 21–50.

(2012). *Why Nations Fail*. New York: Crown.

Allen, Robert C. (2009). *The British Industrial Revolution in Global Perspective*. New York: Cambridge University Press.

(2011). *Global Economic History: A Very Short Introduction*. Oxford: Oxford University Press.

Amin, Samir. (1974). *Accumulation on a World Scale*, 2 vols. New York: Monthly Review Press.

(1976). *Unequal Development*. New York: Monthly Review Press.

Anderson, Charles W., Fred R. von der Mehden, and Crawford Young. (1967). *Issues of Political Development*. Englewood Cliffs NJ: Prentice-Hall.

Austen, Ralph A. (1987). *African Economic History: Internal Development and External Dependency*. London: Heinemann.

Austen, Ralph A., and Daniel Headrick. (1983). "The Role of Technology in the African Past." *African Studies Review*, 26: 163–84.

Austin, Gareth. (2005). "*Labour, Land, and Capital in Ghana: From Slavery to Free Labour in Asante 1807–1956*." Rochester: University of Rochester Press.

Austin, Gareth. (2008). "Resources, Techniques, and Strategies South of the Sahara: Revising the Factor Endowments Perspective on African Economic Development, 1500–2000." *Economic History Review*, 61: 587–624.

Baland, Jean-Marie, Catherine Guirkinger, and Charlotte Mali. (2011). "Pretending to Be Poor: Borrowing to Escape Forced Solidarity in Cameroon." *Economic Development and Cultural Change*, 60(1): 1–16.

Barker, Graeme. (2006). *The Agricultural Revolution in Prehistory: Why Did Foragers Become Farmers?* New York: Oxford University Press.

Bates, Robert H. (1981). *Markets and States in Tropical Africa*. Berkeley: University of California Press.

(2001). *Violence and Prosperity*. New York: W. W. Norton.

Batten, T. R. (1954). *Problems of African Development*. London: Oxford University Press.

Beattie, J. H. M. (1959). "Checks on the Abuse of Political Power in some African States." *Sociologus*, 9, 97–115.

Bezemer, Dirk J., Jutta Bolt, and Robert W. Lensink (2012). "Slavery, Statehood and Economic Development in Sub-Saharan Africa." African Economic History Network Working Paper no. 6.

Birmingham, David and Richard Gray, eds. (1970). *Pre-Colonial Trade: Essays on Trade in Central and Eastern Africa before 1900*. London: Oxford University Press.

Birnberg, Thomas B. and Stephen A. Resnick. (1975). *Colonial Development: An Econometric Study*, New Haven, CT: Yale University Press.

Bohannan, Paul and George Dalton, eds. (1962). *Markets in Africa*. Evanston, IL: Northwestern University Press.

Boone, Catherine. (2003). *Political Topographies of the African State: Rural Authority and Institutional Choice*. Cambridge: Cambridge University Press.

Brenner, Robert. (1976). "Agrarian Class Structure and Economic Development in Pre-Industrial Europe." *Past and Present*, 70: 30–75.

Brewer, John. (1988). *The Sinews of Power: War, Money and the English State, 1688–1783*. New York: Knopf.

Bruhn, Miriam and Francisco Gallego. (2012). "Good, Bad, and Ugly Colonial Activities: Do They Matter for Economic Development?" *Review of Economics and Statistics*, 94(2): 433–61.

Bundy, Colin. (1979). *The Rise and Fall of the South African Peasantry*. Berkeley: University of California Press.

Chanda, Areendam and Louis Putterman. (2007). "Early Starts, Reversals and Catch-Up in the Process of Economic Development." *Scandinavian Journal of Economics*, 109: 387–413.

Coatsworth, John H. (1978). "Obstacles to Economic Growth in Nineteenth-Century Mexico." *American Historical Review*, 83(1): 80–100.

Cogneau, Denis and Léa Rouanet. (2011). "Living Conditions in Côte d'Ivoire and Ghana 1925–1985: What Do Survey Data on Height Stature Tell Us." http://www.parisschoolofeconomics.eu/fr/cogneau-denis/.

Colson, Elizabeth L. (1969). "African Society at the Time of the Scramble." In *Colonialism in Africa, 1870–1960. Vol. 1: The History and Politics of Colonialism*, edited by Lewis H. Gann and Peter Duignan, 27–65. Cambridge: Cambridge University Press.

(1971). "The Impact of the Colonial Period on the Definition of Land Rights." In *Colonialism in Africa, 1870–1960. Vol. III: Profiles of Change: African Society and Colonial Rule*, edited by Victor Turner, 193–215. Cambridge: Cambridge University Press.

Cooper, Frederick. (1980). *From Slaves to Squatters: Plantation Labor and Agriculture in Zanzibar and Coastal Kenya, 1890–1925*. New Haven, CT: Yale University Press.

(1987). *On the African Waterfront: Urban Disorder and the Transformation of Work in Colonial Mombasa*. New Haven, CT: Yale University Press.

(1996). *Decolonization and African Society: The Labor Question in French Africa*. New York: Cambridge University Press.

(2002). *Africa since 1940: The Past of the Present*. New York: Cambridge University Press.

Cooper, Frederick. (2005). *Colonialism in Question*. Berkeley: University of California Press.

Crummey, Donald. (1980). "Abyssinian Feudalism." *Past and Present*, 89(1): 115–38.

Curtin, Philip D. (1969). *The Atlantic Slave Trade: A Census*. Madison: University of Wisconsin Press.

(1975). *Economic Change in Precolonial Africa: Senegambia in the Era of the Slave Trade*. Madison: University of Wisconsin Press.

Dalton, George H. (1976). "Review of A. G. Hopkins, Economic History of West Africa." *African Economic History*, 1: 51–101.

Dell, Melissa. (2010). "The Persistent Effects of Peru's Mining Mita." *Econometrica*, 78(6): 1863–1903.

Douglas, Mary. (1962). "Lele Economy Compared to the Bushong." In *Markets in Africa*, edited by Paul Bohannan and George Dalton, 211–33. Evanston, IL: Northwestern University Press.

(1963). *The Lele of the Kasai*. Oxford: Oxford University Press.

Easterly, William. (2001). *The Elusive Quest for Growth*. Cambridge: MIT Press.

Easterly, William and Ross Levine. (1997). "Africa's Growth Tragedy: Policies and Ethnic Divisions." *Quarterly Journal of Economics*, 112(4): 1203–50.

Englebert, Pierre. (2000). *State Legitimacy and Development in Africa*. Boulder, CO: Lynne Rienner Publishers.

Engerman, Stanley L. and Kenneth L. Sokoloff. (1997). "Factor Endowments, Institutions, and Differential Paths of Growth among New World Economies." In *How Latin America Fell Behind*, edited by Stephen Haber, 260–306. Stanford, CA: Stanford University Press.

(2011). *Economic Development in the Americas since 1500: Endowments and Institutions*. New York: Cambridge University Press.
Engelbert, Pierre. (2000). *State Legitimacy and Development in Africa*. Boulder, CO: Lynne Rienner Publishers.
Evans-Pritchard, E. E. and Meyer Fortes. (1940). *African Political Systems*. Oxford University Press.
Ewald, Janet. (1988). "Speaking, Writing and Authority: Explorations in and from the Kingdom of Taqali." *Comparative Studies in History and Society*, 30(2): 199–224.
Fage, John. (1969). "Slaving and the Slave Trade in the Context of West African History." *Journal of African History*, 10: 393–404.
Feinstein, Charles H. (2005). *An Economic History of South Africa*. New York: Cambridge University Press.
Feldman, Noah. (2008). *The Fall and Rise of the Islamic State*. Princeton, NJ: Princeton University Press.
Fieldhouse, David K. (1986). *Black Africa, 1945–1980: Economic Decolonization and Arrested Development*. New York: Routledge.
(1994). *Merchant Capital and Economic Decolonization: The United Africa Company 1929–1987*. Oxford: Clarendon Press.
(1999). *The West and the Third World: Trade, Colonialism, Dependence and Development*. New York: Wiley.
Findlay, R. and K. H. O'Rourke. (2007). *Power and Plenty: Trade, War and the World Economy in the Second Millennium*. Princeton, NJ: Princeton University Press.
Finley, Moses. (1965). "Technical Innovation and Economic Progress in the Ancient World." *Economic History Review*, 18: 29–45.
Firmin-Sellers, Katherine. (1995). "The Politics of Property Rights." *American Political Science Review*, 89(4): 867–82.
(1996). *The Transformation of Property Rights in the Gold Coast*. Cambridge: Cambridge University Press.
Frankema, Ewout. (2011). "Colonial Taxation and Government Spending in British Africa, 1880–1940: Maximizing Revenue or Minimizing Effort?," *Explorations in Economic History*, 48(1): 136–49.
(2012). "The Origins of Formal Education in Sub-Saharan Africa: Was British Rule more Benign?" *European Review of Economic History*, 16(4): 335–55.
Frankema, Ewout and Marlous van Waijenburg. (2012). "Structural Impediments to African Growth? New Evidence from British African Real Wages, 1880–1965," *Journal of Economic History*, 72(4): 895–926.
Gardner, Leigh. (2012). T*axing Colonial Africa: The Political Economy of British Imperialism*. Oxford: Oxford University Press.
Gennaioli, Nicola with Ilia Rainer. (2007). "The Modern Impact of Pre-Colonial Centralization in Africa." *Journal of Economic Growth*, 12(3): 185–234.
Gluckman, Max, J. C. Mitchell, and J. A. Barnes. (1949). "The Village Headman in British Central Africa." *Africa*, 19(2): 89–106.
Goldstein, Markus and Christopher Udry. (2008). "The Profits of Power: Land Rights and Agricultural Investment in Ghana." *Journal of Political Economy*, 116: 981–1022.
Goody, Jack. (1971). *Technology, Tradition and the State in Africa*. New York: Cambridge University Press.

(1986). *The Logic of Writing and the Organization of Society*. New York: Cambridge University Press.

Habyarimana, J., M. Humphreys, Daniel Posner, and Jeremy Weinstein. (2007). "Why Does Ethnic Diversity Undermine Public Goods Provision?" *American Political Science Review*, 101(4): 709–25.

Haour, Anne. (2000). *Rulers, Warriors, Traders, Clerics: The Central Sahel and the North Sea, 800–1500*. Oxford: Oxford University Press.

Heldring, Leander and James A. Robinson. (2013). "Colonialism and Development." In *Handbook on the Politics of Development*, edited by Carol Lancaster and Nicolas van de Walle. New York: Oxford University Press.

Herbert, Eugenia W. (1993). *Iron, Gender, and Power: Rituals of Transformation in African Societies*. Bloomington: Indiana University Press.

Herbst, Jeffrey I. (2000). *States and Power in Africa*. Princeton, NJ: Princeton University Press.

Hill, Polly. (1963). *The Migrant Cocoa Farmers of Southern Ghana: A Study in Rural Capitalism*. New York: Cambridge University Press.

Hopkins, Anthony G. (1973). *An Economic History of West Africa*. New York: Addison Wesley Longman.

(1986). "The World Bank in Africa: Historical Reflections on the African Present." *World Development*, 14(12): 1473–87.

(2009). "The New Economic History of Africa." *Journal of African History*, 50: 155–77.

Horst van der, Sheila. (1942). *Native Labour in South Africa*. London: Oxford University Press.

Houghton, D. Hobart. (1976). *The South African Economy*. 4th ed. Cape Town: Oxford University Press.

Hydén, Göran. (1980). *Beyond Ujamaa in Tanzania: Underdevelopment and an Uncaptured Peasantry*. Berkeley: University of California Press and Heinemann.

(1983). *No Shortcuts to Progress*. Berkeley: University of California Press and Heinemann.

IMF. (2009). "World Economic Outlook: Crisis and Recovery." In World Economic and Financial Survey, The International Monetary Fund.

Inikori, Joseph E. (1992). *The Chaining of a Continent: The Export Demand for Captives and the History of Africa South of the Sahara, 1450–1870*. Mona: University of the West Indies.

(1994). "Ideology versus the Tyranny of Paradigm: Historians and the Impact of the Atlantic Slave Trade on African Societies." *African Economic History*, 22: 37–58.

(2002). *Africans and the Industrial Revolution in England*. New York: Cambridge University Press.

Jerven, Morten. (2010). "African Growth Recurring: An Economic History Perspective on African Growth Episodes, 1690–2010." *Economic History of Developing Regions*, 25(2): 127–54.

Jones, Eric. (1981). *The European Miracle*. New York: Cambridge University Press.

Kasekende, Louis, Zuzana Brixova, and Leonce Ndikumana. (2010). "Africa: Africa's Counter-Cyclical Policy Responses to the Crisis." *Journal of Globalization and Development*, 1(1): Article 16.

Killick, Tony. (1978). *Development Economics in Action*. London: Heinemann.
Kriger, Colleen E. (2006). *Cloth in West Africa*. Lanham, MD: AltaMira Press.
Lange, Matthew. (2004). "British Colonial Legacy and Political Development." *World Development*, 32(6): 905–22.
(2009). *Lineages of Despotism and Development: British Colonialism and State Power*. Chicago: University of Chicago Press.
Law, Robin C. (1977). "Royal Monopoly and Private Enterprise in the Atlantic Trade: The Case of Dahomey." *Journal of African History*, 18: 555–77.
(1978). "In Search of a Marxist Perspective on Pre-Colonial Tropical Africa." *Journal of African History*, 19, 441–52.
(1980). "Wheeled Transportation in Pre-Colonial West Africa." *Africa*, 50: 249–62.
(1981). *The Horse in West African History*. Oxford: Oxford University Press.
Law, Robin C., ed. (2002). *From Slave Trade To "Legitimate" Commerce: The Commercial Transition in Nineteenth-Century West Africa*. New York: Cambridge University Press.
Leith, Clark J. (2005). *Why Botswana Prospered*. Montreal: McGill University Press.
Lovejoy, Paul E. (1989). "The Impact of the Atlantic Slave Trade on Africa: A Review of the Literature." *Journal of African History*, 30: 365–94.
(2000). *Transformations in Slavery: A History of Slavery in Africa*. 2nd ed. New York: Cambridge University Press.
Long, Norman. (1978). *Social Change and the Individual: A Study of the Social and Religious Responses to Innovation in a Zambian Rural Community*. Manchester: Manchester University Press.
Lynn, Martin. (1997). *Commerce and Economic Change in West Africa*. New York: Cambridge University Press.
Mager, Anne. (2010). *Beer, Sociability and Masculinity in South Africa*. Bloomington: Indiana University Press.
Mamdani, Mahmood. (1996). *Citizen and Subject: Contemporary Africa and the Legacy of Late Colonialism*. Princeton, NJ: Princeton University Press.
Manning, Patrick. (1990). *Slavery and African Life*. Cambridge: Cambridge University Press.
(2004). *Slavery, Colonialism and Economic Growth in Dahomey, 1640–1960*. New York: Cambridge University Press.
McGreevey, William P. (1971). *An Economic History of Colombia, 1845–1930*, New York: Cambridge University Press.
McIntosh, Roderick J. (1988). *The Peoples of the Middle Niger*. Malden: Blackwell Publishers.
McIntosh, Susan K. (1999). "Pathways to Complexity: An African Perspective." In *Beyond Chiefdoms: Pathways to Complexity in Africa*, edited by S. K. McIntosh, 1–30. Cambridge University Press.
McPhee, Allan. (1926). *The Economic Revolution in British West Africa*. London: George Routledge & Sons.
Marseille, Jacques. (1984). *Empire Colonial et Capitalisme Français*. Paris: A. Michel.
Metcalfe, G. E. (1964). *Great Britain and Ghana: Documents of Ghana History, 1807–1957*. London: T. Nelson for the University of Ghana.
Meillassoux, C., ed. (1971). *The Development of Indigenous Trade and Markets*. London: International African Institute.

Michalopoulos, Stelios and Elias Papaioannou. (2013). "Pre-Colonial Ethnic Institutions and Contemporary African Development." *Econometrica*, 81(1): 113–52.

Miers, Suzanne and Richard L. Roberts, eds. (1988). *The End of Slavery in Africa*. Madison: University of Wisconsin Press.

Miguel, Edward and Mary K. Gugerty. (2005). "Ethnic Diversity, Social Sanctions, and Public Goods in Kenya." *Journal of Public Economics*, 89: 2325–68.

Milburn, Josephine. (1977). *British Business and Ghanaian Independence*. London: Hurst.

Miller, Joseph C. (1996). *Way of Death: Merchant Capitalism and the Angolan Slave Trade, 1730–1830*. Madison: University of Wisconsin Press.

(2009). "Africa in World History: Lecture 1 History without Horses." W.E.B. du Bois Lectures Presented at Harvard University.

Mkandawire, Thandika and Charles Soludo, eds. (2003). *African Voices on Structural Adjustment*. Dakar: Codesria.

Mokyr, Joel. (2008). "The Institutional Origins of the Industrial Revolution." In *Institutions and Economic Performance*, edited by E. Helpman, 64–119. Cambridge, MA: Harvard University Press.

Mokyr, Joel. (2009). *The Enlightened Economy*. New Haven, CT: Yale University Press.

Monga, Celestin. (2006). "Commodities, Mercedes Benz and Structural Adjustment: An Episode in West African History." In *Themes in West Africa's History*, edited by Emmanuel Akyeampong, 227–64. Athens: University of Ohio Press.

Moradi, Alexander. (2008). "Confronting Colonial Legacies – Lessons from Human Development in Ghana and Kenya." *Journal of International Development*, 20: 1107–21.

(2009). "Towards an Objective Account of Nutrition and Health in Colonial Kenya: A Study of Stature in African Army Recruits and Civilians, 1880–1980." *Journal of Economic History*, 96(3): 720–55.

Morris, Ian. (2011). *Why the West Rules – For Now*. New York: Picador.

Mosley, Paul. (1983). *The Settler Economies: Studies in the Economic History of Kenya and Southern Rhodesia 1900–1963*. New York: Cambridge University Press.

Ndulu, Benno, Stephen A. O'Connell, Robert H. Bates, Paul Collier, and Chukwuma C. Soludo, eds. (2007). *The Political Economy of Economic Growth in Africa, 1960–2000*, 2 vols. New York: Cambridge University Press.

Nunn, Nathan. (2008a). "The Long-Term Effect of Africa's Slave Trades." *Quarterly Journal of Economics*, 23(1): 139–76.

(2008b). "Slavery, Inequality and Economic Development in the Americas: An Examination of the Engerman-Sokoloff Hypothesis." In *Institutions and Economic Performance*, edited by Elhanan Helpman, 148–80. Cambridge, MA: Harvard University Press.

Nunn, Nathan and Leonard Wantchekon. (2011). "The Slave Trade and the Origins of Mistrust in Africa." *American Economic Review*, 101(7): 3221–52.

Osafo-Kwaako, Philip and James A. Robinson. (2013). "Political Centralization in Pre-Colonial Africa." *Journal of Comparative Economics*, 41(1): 6–21.

Palmer, Robin and Q. Neil Parsons, eds. (1977). *The Roots of Rural Poverty in Central and Southern Africa*. Berkeley: University of California Press.

Parkin, David. (1972). *Palms, Wine, and Witnesses: Public Spirit and Private Gain in an African Farming Community*. San Francisco: Chandler Publishing Co.

Phillipson, David W. (1998). *Ancient Ethiopia*. London: British Museum Press.

Pirenne, Henri. (2001). *Mohammed and Charlamagne*. New York: Dover.

Polanyi, Karl. (1966). *Dahomey and the Slave Trade: An Analysis of an Archaic Economy*. Seattle: University of Washington Press.

Polanyi, Karl, Conrad M. Arensberg, and Harry W. Pearson, eds. (1957). *Trade and Market in the Early Empires: Economies in History and Theory*. New York: The Free Press.

Pomeranz, Kenneth. (2000). *The Great Divergence: China, Europe and the Making of the Modern World*. Princeton, NJ: Princeton University Press.

Postan, M. M. (1937). "The Chronology of Labour Services." *Transactions of the Royal Historical Society*, 70: 169–93.

Prados de la Escosura, Leandero. (2011). "Human Development in Africa: A Long-Run Perspective." University Carlos III, Working Papers in Economic History, WP 11–09.

Radelet, Steven. (2010). *Emerging Africa: How 17 Countries Are Leading the Way*. Washington, DC: Center for Global Development.

Roberts, Michael. (1956). *The Military Revolution 1560–1660: An Inaugural Lecture Delivered before the Queen's University of Belfast*. Belfast: M. Boyd.

Robinson, James A. (2012). "Why Did Africa Export Scarce Labor?" Unpublished.

Rodney, Walter. (1972). *How Europe Underdeveloped Africa*. London: Bogle-L'Ouverture Publications.

Rosenthal, Jean-Laurant and R. Bin Wong. (2011). *Before and beyond Divergence: The Politics of Economic Change in China and Europe*. Cambridge, MA: Harvard University Press.

Sachs, Jeffrey and Andrew Warner. (1997). "Sources of Slow Growth in African Economies." *Journal of African Economies*, 6: 335–76.

Scott, James C. (2009). *The Art of Not Being Governed: An Anarchist History of Upland Southeast Asia*. New Haven, CT: Yale University Press.

Sender, John and Sheila Smith. (1986). *The Development of Capitalism in Africa*. London: Methuen.

Sheriff, Abdul. (2010). *Dhow Cultures and the Indian Ocean: Cosmopolitanism, Commerce, and Islam*. Amsterdam: KIT Publishers.

Speke, John H. (1863). *The Discovery of the Source of the Nile*. London: William Blackwood and Sons.

Stamp, L. Dudley. (1953). *Africa: A Study in Tropical Development*. London: John Wiley & Sons.

Suret-Canale, Jean. (1958). *Afrique Noire, Occidentale et Centrale: Geographie, Civilisations*. Histoire, Paris: Éditions Sociales.

Thornton, John K. (1992). "Pre-Colonial African Industry and the Atlantic Trade, 1500–1800." *African Economic History Review*, 19: 1–19.

(1998). *Africa and Africans in the Making of the Atlantic World, 1400–1800*. Cambridge: Cambridge University Press.

Tilly, Charles, ed. (1975). *Reflections on the History of State Making. The Formation of Nation States in Western Europe*. Princeton, NJ: Princeton University Press.

Van de Walle, Nicolas. (2001). *African Economies and the Politics of Permanent Crisis, 1979–1999*. New York: Cambridge University Press.

Van Onselen, Charles. (1982). *Studies in the Social and Economic History of the Witwatersrand, 1886–1914*, 2 vols. New York: Longman.

Van Zanden, Jan Luiten. (2009). *The Long Road to the Industrial Revolution: The European Economy in a Global Perspective, 1000–1800*. Leiden: Brill Publishers.

Vansina, Jan. (1978). *The Children of Woot: A History of the Kuba Peoples*. Madison: University of Wisconsin Press.

(1985). *Oral Tradition as History*. Madison: University of Wisconsin Press.

(2004). *How Societies Are Born: Governance in West Central Africa before 1600*. Charlottesville: University of Virginian Pres.

Wallerstein, Immanuel. (1974–2011). *The Modern World System*, 4 vols. New York: Academic Press.

Wickens, Peter L. (1980). *An Economic History of Africa from the Earliest Times to Partition*. Cape Town: Oxford University Press.

(1986). *Africa, 1880–1980: An Economic History*. Cape Town: Oxford University Press.

Williams, Eric. (1944). *Capitalism and Slavery*. University of North Carolina Press.

Wilks, Ivor. (1989). *Asante in the Nineteenth Century: The Structure and Evolution of a Political Order*. Cambridge: Cambridge University Press.

Wilson, Francis. (1972). *Labour in the South African Gold Mines, 1911–1969*. Cambridge: Cambridge University Press.

Wong, R. Bin. (1997). *China Transformed: Historical Change and the Limits of European Experience*. Ithaca, NY: Cornell University Press.

Worger, William. (1987). *South Africa's City of Diamonds*. New Haven, CT: Yale University Press.

World Bank. (1994). *Adjustment in Africa: Reform, Results, and the Road Ahead*. New York: Oxford University Press.

Young, Crawford. (1994). *The African Colonial State in Comparative Perspective*. New Haven, CT: Yale University Press.

Zaaruka, Bernie P. and Johannes W. Fedderke. (2010). “Indicators of Economic and Political Institutions in Tanzania: 1884–2008.” ERSA Working Paper 231.

(2011). “Measuring Institutions: Indicators of Political and Economic Institutions in Namibia: 1884–2008.” University of Witswatersrand, Department of Economics, Working Paper 236.

PART I

LA LONGUE DURÉE

1

Africa in World History before ca. 1440

Christopher Ehret

1.1 THE AFRICAN ORIGINS OF HISTORY

Barely more than fifty thousand years ago, the ancestors of every single human being alive today lived in Africa. World history to that point *was* African history. That is now becoming accepted knowledge. Less generally understood is that, just because a few Africans left the continent around fifty thousand years ago and began to expand across the rest of the globe, history did not come to a halt in Africa. The Africans who stayed behind in our ancestral continent did not fall out of time into some kind of ahistorical stasis. They passed through the same great transitions of human history – from foraging to agricultural ways of life; from small-scale, local communities to societies of towns and states; and from localized, irregular exchanges of surplus to complex systems of formal, long-distance commerce – and they passed through those transitions *in the same broad periods of time* as did people elsewhere in the world.

1.2 THE FIRST GREAT TRANSITION

For thirty-five thousand years, human beings, wherever they spread in the world, continued to be gatherers and hunters of wild food. Then, separately in different parts of the world, the climatic shifts at the end of the latest ice age set off a long, episodic "First Great Transition" of human history, from foraging to food production – from the gathering and hunting of wild food to the deliberate tending and protection of animals and plants.

The author thanks Oxford University Press for permission to reuse several previously published passages in this chapter.

The initial warming of climate during the Bølling-Allerød interstadial, 12,700–10,900 BCE, brought increased rainfall and warmer conditions in many African regions. Three sets of peoples, speaking languages of the three language families that predominate across the continent today, probably began their early expansions in this period. Nilo-Saharan peoples spread out in the areas around and east of the middle Nile River in what are today the countries of Sudan and South Sudan. Peoples of a second family, Niger-Kordofanian, spread across an emerging east-west belt of savanna vegetation from the eastern Sudan to the western Atlantic coast of Africa. During the same era, communities speaking languages of the Erythraic branch of the Afrasian (Afroasiatic) family expanded beyond their origin areas in the Horn of Africa, northward to modern-day Egypt.[1]

This last point needs special emphasis, considering how widespread the notion is that the Afrasian family somehow originated in the Middle East. The linguistic, genetic, and archaeological evidence combines in locating the origins of this family far south in Africa, in Eritrea or Ethiopia, and not at all in Asia.[2] A complex array of lexical evidence confirms that the proto-Afrasian society belonged to the preagricultural eras of human history.[3]

None of these episodes of expansion proceeded into entirely empty lands. Other communities already lived in most areas into which the speakers of these three families of languages spread. An issue deserving of future historical attention is the question of what kinds of advantages each set of societies might have had that allowed their expansions into the lands of others. What little is known of the archaeology of that era in the middle Nile River regions suggests either or both of two developments may have contributed to the earliest spread of Nilo-Saharans. One would have been the expansion of grasslands northward toward the Sahara, opening up large new areas to the hunting of large herbivores. The other would have been the increased flow of the Nile, which would have enhanced the attractions of a more ancient regional economy based on the exploitation of aquatic food resources. In the case of the Afrasians, the reconstructed ancient Afrasian lexicon of subsistence indicates that they collected wild grains. The spread of grassland areas in the Red Sea hills and Egypt away from the Nile during the thirteenth millennium BCE would have opened up new areas to their kind of subsistence.[4] What subsistence advantages might have favored the

1 Ehret 2006, 2008, 2011, 2013.

2 Ehret and colleagues (2004) concisely summarize the convergent findings of these three fields.

3 Ehret (2006) provides a detailed exposition.

4 Ehret (2006); Ehret and colleagues (2004).

spread of the Niger-Kordofanians is a question the historical literature has yet to consider.

The return of colder, drier conditions in the Younger Dryas, 10,900–9500 BCE, would have brought these expansions to a halt and in some cases reversed them. At the same time, however, the period of climatic setback encouraged a new round of subsistence innovation before fully postglacial conditions took hold in the tenth millennium BCE. In a few areas of the world, people began the first protecting of plants or animals, in this fashion laying the earliest foundations for agriculture. From 9500 BCE onward, separately and independently in different parts of the world, the stage-by-stage developments toward agriculture quantitatively transformed the directions of human history. The deliberate tending of plants and animals multiplies by magnitudes the amounts of food potentially obtainable from the same amount of land. The growth of human populations from a few hundred thousand to billions, social stratification, urban life, states, and the development of complex technologies all rest on the creation of agriculture.

Africans actively contributed to these new directions in world history. In Africa, peoples of two distant parts of the continent's middle belt independently set in motion developments leading to agriculture, and they did so during the same broad era as did peoples in the Middle East, India, East Asia, New Guinea, and the Americas.

No later than the middle of the tenth millennium in the savannas of modern-day Mali, communities speaking the early daughter languages of proto-Niger-Congo, itself an offshoot of the Niger-Kordofanian family, began to intensively collect wild grains, among them probably fonio. Their Ounjougou culture is the earliest identified facies of the West African Microlithic,[5] the archaeological complex associated with the early Niger-Congo peoples.[6] Integral to their new subsistence system was their invention of one of the two earliest ceramic technologies in world history sometime before 9400 BCE. Rather than grinding whole grains into flour, the Ounjougou people made the grains edible by cooking them whole in pots.

When did the shift from gathering to the cultivation of grains begin among Niger-Congo peoples? The archaeobotanical evidence is as yet uncertain or unknown for the crucial periods. Provisional reconstructions of several early Niger-Congo verbs specifically connoting cultivation suggest, however, that the transition from collecting to cultivating grains in the grassland savannas of West Africa took place broadly in the

[5] Huysecom and colleagues (2009).

[6] Ehret 2002, 44.

period 9000–6000 BCE.[7] Black-eyed peas and African groundnuts (*Vigna subterranea*), along with grains, may have been the earliest protected plants of this incipient agriculture. Niger-Congo peoples domesticated both black-eyed peas and groundnuts by or before the fourth millennium BCE, earlier than can yet be demonstrated directly from the archaeology. The linguistic testimony shows that they were among the food crops the earliest Bantu took with them into the equatorial rainforests after 3000 BCE,[8] and both crops had spread all the way to East Africa equally early; we can reconstruct words for both in the proto-Southern Cushitic language of northern Kenya, spoken around the late fourth millennium BCE.

West African agricultural history entered a new stage around the sixth millennium BCE, with the cultivation of two new crops, Guinea yams and oil palms. The technological signature of this development was the adding of polished stone axes to the West African Microlithic toolkit.[9] The new crops and tools opened the way for communities of the Benue-Kwa branch of Niger-Congo to spread between 5000 and 3000 BCE into the rainforest zones of West Africa, from modern-day Côte d'Ivoire to Cameroon. With polished stone axes, they could clear forest for raising yams and oil palms, both of which require direct sunlight.[10] An additional technological innovation probably dating to this period was the Benue-Kwa invention of broadlooms for weaving raffia-cloth. After 3000 BCE, one offshoot of the Benue-Kwa group, the Bantu, carried the yam-based variety of West African agriculture farther southward and eastward through the equatorial rainforests of central Africa.

Far to the east, the Northern Sudanians, a Nilo-Saharan people of the southern eastern Sahara, took a very different first step toward agriculture. In the mid-tenth millennium BCE, a belated shift to wetter conditions spread Mediterranean climate, with cool-season rains and Mediterranean wild animals, most notably the cow, south to the middle of the Sahara. Contemporaneously, tropical grassland and steppe environments advanced north to the middle of the Sahara. The Northern Sudanians, following the climatic shift northward, encountered cattle at the interface of the two climatic regimes and, between 8500 and 7200 BCE, initiated the earliest herding of cattle in world history.[11] Like the Ounjougou people twenty-five hundred kilometers to the west, they collected wild grains, but, differently, they ground their grain into flour.

[7] Ehret 2010.
[8] Ehret 1998, 104–5.
[9] Shaw 1980.
[10] Ehret 2002, 84.
[11] Wendorf and Schild 1998.

Around 7200 BCE, a new development appeared in the eastern Saharan archaeology: neighborhoods of substantial homesteads, with thornbush cattle pens, round houses, and grain storage pits, and with sorghum as the notable grain.[12] The linguistic evidence in this case strongly backs these indirect archaeological indicators that the Northern Sudanians of this era had begun to cultivate. They had important contacts, too, with the contemporary Afrasian communities immediately east of them in the Red Sea Hills region. These communities spoke early daughter dialects of the proto-Cushitic language. In the second half of the seventh millennium, the northernmost Cushites, ancestral to the modern-day Bedauye (the Medjay of the ancient Egyptians), were the intermediaries in the diffusion of sheep from the Middle East to their Northern Sudanian neighbors. Even earlier, the Cushites began, like the Northern Sudanians, to raise cattle, and they either collected or cultivated sorghum.[13]

The Northern Sudanians of the ninth millennium, along with a closely related set of Nilo-Saharan peoples whom archaeologist J. E. G. Sutton called the "Aquatic Civilization of Middle Africa,"[14] participated in a second African invention of ceramic technology. The Aquatic societies responded in a different fashion to the mid-ninth-millennium climatic amelioration. They became specialist fishing and hippopotamus-hunting peoples along the new rivers and lakes of the Sahara, and in the later ninth millennium they spread this economy westward across the southern Sahara as far as the Hoggar mountains and the great bend of the Niger River.

Drier climates in the mid-Holocene then shrank many Saharan streams and lakes, shifting the balance of advantage away from the Aquatic communities. As a result, during the sixth millennium the descendants of the Northern Sudanians spread their agripastoral economy across the southern Sahara, displacing or assimilating many of the Aquatic communities. Where perennial water resources existed, such as along the Nile, the Aquatic livelihood persisted, but combined now with herding and probably cultivation. The inhabitants of the Khartoum Neolithic site of 5000 BCE along the Nile participated in a particularly notable invention, of cotton textile technology, attested by their possession of spindlewhorls.[15]

[12] Ibid.

[13] Ehret 2011.

[14] Sutton 1974.

[15] For published plates showing the spindlewhorls, see Arkell (1949). I am indebted to Merrick Posnansky for bringing these materials to my attention and explaining their significance.

As with ceramic technology, African societies were leaders in innovation in the early agricultural eras. The history of cotton provides a lesson as well, of wider relevance in history – that peoples with no knowledge whatsoever of each other can and do arrive at parallel inventions. The domestication of cotton as a fiber plant for textile production took place separately in three distant parts of the globe: the eastern Sudan of Africa, India, and the New World. In each region, the inventors of cotton weaving domesticated their own indigenous species of cotton. The evidence from Khartoum places this development as early in Africa as in India.

1.3 THE ERA OF AGRICULTURAL ELABORATION, 6500–3500 BCE

The long period from 6500–3500 BCE typically marks a second stage in the emergence of agricultural economies in world history. As in other world regions, in Africa these centuries were a time of growth in the variety of crops and animals that farmers raised, and a time of growth in the proportional contribution of agriculture to the diet. The women farmers of Niger-Congo civilization brought the two savanna legumes, the African groundnut (*Vigna subterranea*) and the black-eyed pea (*V. unguiculata*), into cultivation during this time. The Sudanic agripastoralists of the southern Sahara and the Sahel added, it appears, melons and gourds of several kinds to their original emphasis on sorghum, and they also began raising castor beans as a source of a nonedible oil. Niger-Congo farmers and Sudanic agripastoralists appear to have separately domesticated an additional major grain crop, pearl millet (*Pennisetum glaucum*). In the Ethiopian highlands, reconstructed early farming lexicon reveals that the Cushites during this time began to supplement their stock raising with two highland African grain crops, finger millet and t'ef, and probably a variety of gourds and calabashes.[16]

The seventh millennium to the fourth millennium BCE was also a period of world history during which crops and animals domesticated in one or another seminal region of agriculture first spread to other such world regions. In Africa between 6500 and 4000 BCE, Cushitic peoples domesticated the donkey, native to the Red Sea Hills and the arid foothills of the northern Ethiopian highlands.[17] Donkeys then spread via Egypt to the Middle East, where they became the earliest important beasts of burden in all of world history. Sheep and goats, of course, diffused in the opposite direction even

[16] Ehret 2011.

[17] Ibid.

earlier, during the second half of the seventh millennium, and rapidly became important animals in the Sudanic and Cushitic agripastoral traditions. From the Sudanic herders both goats and cattle spread west to the Niger-Congo societies of West Africa, again at a still uncertain period, but certainly well before 3000 BCE. Among the important early crop spreads, melons, gourds, and castor, brought under cultivation by Nilo-Saharan peoples of the Sudan belt and the southern Sahara, spread northward to the ancient Egyptians probably no later than the fourth millennium.

An especially interesting historical problem far from solved is the question of how three important grain crops domesticated in Africa, sorghum, pearl millet, and finger millet, reached India between 3000 and 1000 BCE[18] without passing through the Middle East first. Might seagoing trade have already connected northeastern Africa and India by that time? Sorghum soon spread even farther eastward, becoming a crop of northern Chinese agriculture before 1000 BCE.

What may surprise is that Egypt was not an initiating region of these seminal developments. The indigenous Afrasian communities of the Egyptian Nile in the seventh millennium still consisted of hunter-gathers. They gradually transformed their subsistence economy by adopting two staple crops, barley and wheat, along with sheep and goats, which diffused to them from the ancient Middle Eastern center of domestication. Melons, gourds, and donkeys reached them from the Sudanic agripastoralists to the south; surprisingly, cotton did not. Word borrowings in ancient Egyptian, along with recent archaeological discoveries, confirm that Sudanic herders also significantly influenced Egyptian beliefs and practices relating to cattle.[19]

1.4 THE SECOND GREAT TRANSITION: THE AFRICAN BEGINNINGS OF URBAN CENTERS AND STATES

By the fifth millennium BCE, the growing variety and productivity of agriculture brought about a growth in the size and density of human populations, such that a "Second Great Transition," from villages and tiny local political units to towns and states, began to take place in several world regions. Historians have long identified Egypt as an early locus of this transition in the African continent. But because of the dominant Western idea of Egyptian exceptionalism, historians have generally failed to note that the formative area of ancient Egyptian culture, southern Upper Egypt, was the

[18] Fuller 2006.

[19] Ehret 2001.

northern outlier of a wider nexus of emerging complexity in the fourth millennium. Predynastic Upper Egypt of the fourth millennium BCE did have encounters at a distance with a separate nexus of town and state development centered on the Fertile Crescent. But as recent archaeological discoveries reveal, the cultural and political world we identify as ancient Egypt grew out of institutions and ideas already present among its Nilo-Saharan neighbors in the fifth and early fourth millennia BCE. The southern eastern Sahara and eastern Sudan, though greatly neglected relative to Egypt by scholars, remained the locus of towns and cities and powerful states from the fourth millennium BCE until recent centuries.

The first evidence of emerging complexity in the fifth millennium appeared not along the Nile itself, but in the then steppe country west of northern Lower Nubia. Two hundred kilometers from the river, the inhabitants of Nabta Playa erected an extensive megalithic archaeoastronomical array. The associated burials, of both cattle and people, reveal a wealthy pastoral society, with a complex ritual basis, in existence centuries before similar complexity and before the same specific cultural features, such as cattle burial, appeared in Upper Egypt.[20]

A further progression toward social and political complexity followed in the fourth millennium BCE, this time along the Nile itself, with states and the first towns appearing between the Nile-Abbay confluence in the south and southern Upper Egypt in the north. Town life along the river grew in importance, even as the drying of the Sahara during the fourth millennium brought the Nabta Playa culture to an end. Because of the relative archaeological neglect of Nubia, just two excavated sites, Shaheinab and Qustul, provide most of our knowledge of this era south of Egypt. The two towns lay respectively at the far northern and far southern ends of a thousand-kilometer stretch of cultural commonality along the Nile. On sites of ritual importance, the people of this Middle Nile culture built large conical earthen mounds, reshaped since then by rain and wind into more formless-seeming tumuli. Ritual sites of this type represent a very long-lived cultural and political tradition, lasting in some cases until recent centuries.

Qustul was the capital of wealthy kings from the mid-fourth millennium BCE almost until to the unification of Egypt late in the millennium. Like the earlier Nabta Playa pastoralist sites, the Qustul sites include numerous cattle burials. Pictorial documents in the royal graves explicitly depict the kings of the Qustul state as having conquered Upper Egypt. There is no a

[20] Kobusiewicz and Schild (2005); Malville and colleagues (2008).

priori reason to reject these claims. If one sets aside the received notion of Egyptian exceptionalism, it is quite evident, as archaeologist Bruce Williams argues, that here was a kingdom every bit as significant as its late predynastic contemporaries in Upper Egypt.[21]

Behind the rise of the highly centralized kingship of dynastic Egypt may have been an additional factor, the adoption in late predynastic Upper Egypt of elements of the rituals and royal ideology of the Qustul kingdom. Early Egyptian royal tombs, before the shift to pyramid building in stone, were covered with a conical mound of earth, mimicking the practice known as early as the fourth millennium in Nubia and still prevalent two thousand years later in the kingdoms to the south. These outward resemblances accompany resemblances in ideology as well, from the special ritual significance accorded cattle to the claims of both Sudanic and Egyptian kings to a degree of personal sacredness unparalleled in the Middle East. Did Upper Egyptian rulers build their power in the later fourth millennium BCE by adopting legitimizing ideas from Nabta Playa and Qustul? The outward signs, at least, favor that proposal.

Two notable kingdoms persisted in Nubia through the Old Kingdom period. The more powerful state, Kerma, ruled the Dongola Reach in Upper Nubia and probably other lands farther south. The great fortifications at Buhen in Lower Nubia, built by the rulers of the Middle Kingdom (2040–1700 BCE) after their conquest of the northern Sai kingdom, suggest an Egyptian concern with the potential threat from Kerma farther south. The placement of Kerma's capital at the northern end of its territories, closest to Egypt, may imply a similar concern in Kerma about Egypt. Alternatively, it may indicate that the kings of Kerma wished to situate their court so as to better oversee and control trade with Egypt. The massive royal funerary sites at Kerma City give a sense of the power of this kingdom at its height. But as almost the sole major excavations relating to the Kerma state, they leave us little idea of urban life more generally in Kerma, and no knowledge of how much farther south Kerma's power might have extended.

In the late 1500s, Thutmose I accomplished something new, a conquest that extended Egyptian power into the Dongola Reach between the third and fourth cataracts and imposed a thoroughgoing colonial rule over the region. A common historical presumption is that this conquest destroyed the Kerma kingdom. But was that the case? With the decline of Egyptian

[21] Williams and Seele 1986.

power in Dongola Reach during the twelfth and eleventh centuries BCE, many features of material culture reminiscent of Kerma's high era reemerged in the archaeological record. Somewhere to the south, beyond the reach of Egyptian rule, the political and cultural traditions of Kerma apparently persisted.

In the ninth century BCE, there arose south of Egypt a new major kingdom, called *Kush* by Egyptians. Historians today give this kingdom two names, Napata during the period until the sixth century when its capital was at Napata City on the Dongola Reach, and Meroe after the sixth century, when the capital shifted to the southern city of Meroe. Around 750 during the reign of Piye, Napata conquered Egypt, and Piye's successors ruled large parts of Egypt for much of the next century. The future capital, Meroe City, already existed in the seventh century and surely lay within its southern territories.

The Western scholarly tradition of Egyptian exceptionalism obscures a startling fact. Piye's immediate successors ruled over an empire probably larger in territory than native Egyptian kings ever did, even at the height of the New Kingdom. In Egypt, they tailored their religious relations and political propaganda to appeal to their Egyptian subjects, and for their efforts got recognition, from the parochial perspective of the Egyptians, as Egypt's twenty-fifth dynasty. From the record they left behind in Egypt, it is nevertheless evident that the Napata-Meroe rulers understood themselves as ethnically different and were not hesitant to represent themselves as such in royal art. Nor were they hesitant to make changes in the relations of political to religious power, with lasting effects even after Egypt regained its independence in the seventh century.[22]

The Napatan rule in Egypt from the mid-eighth to the mid-seventh century was a conquest by a foreign power as much as were the subsequent Assyrian and Persian conquests. The foreign power did not fade away just because it eventually lost the conquered Egyptian lands. The lands from the first cataract to the Nile-Abbay confluence remained the territory of one Napata-Meroe empire from the eighth century BCE until the third or fourth century CE, a period of more than one thousand years. The empire became a manufacturing center of cotton textiles in its several cities along the Nile; Meroe City itself became a major iron-producing center by the fourth or third century BCE. The kings built dams and encouraged new irrigation techniques to enhance animal husbandry and cultivation, and the state began to keep written records in its own Meroitic language.

22 Gordon 2009.

1.4.1 Economy and Society in West Africa

A "Third Great Transition" in world history was the emergence of merchant-managed commerce, an economic changeover beginning in the later second millennium BCE that transformed the nature of economic transactions and created the earliest forms of the relations of capital and production that characterize the world today. More significant, these new kinds of relations began the long, drawn-out process of building global connections among human societies around the world. Over the later second millennium and the first millennium BCE, merchant enterprise of the First Commercial Revolution eventually brought into being a series of long-distance links extending from the Pillars of Hercules to the Indian Ocean, Southeast Asia, and China.[23]

What has not been understood until recently is that a separate West African commercial revolution was under way during almost precisely the same era of time. It began with the towns and manufacturing villages of Tichit during the middle second millennium BCE and grew into an extensive network of trade routes and commercial towns and cities all across the eastern and central Sudan over the course of the first millennium BCE. Sporadic contacts between the two commercial revolutions in the first millennium BCE changed into regular trans-Saharan trade by the early first millennium CE, bringing West Africans in as full participants and contributors to the networks of contact and movement of things and ideas from one end of the Eastern Hemisphere to the other.

In Tichit, located in modern-day southern Mauretania along a low escarpment with reliable water sources, a skein of large villages and at least one town flourished during the middle and second half of the second millennium BCE. Different settlements seem to have specialized in a particular product for trade: one produced grindstones, another arrowheads, still another beads, and so forth. At the middle of the skein lay one town larger than all the rest. Its location and greater size mark it out as the probable capital town of an early polity ruling over that skein of settlements.[24]

An additional region where the development of more complex polities appears to have been under way during the mid-second millennium was the Aïr Mountains of modern-day Niger. Archaeologist Augustin Holl argues for an independent invention of copper metallurgy in Aïr in the

[23] The characteristics and consequences of this "First Commercial Revolution" are described in Ehret 1998, 16–20.

[24] Augustin F. C. Holl, *Holocene Saharans* (London, New York: Continuum, 2004), pp. 122–137, 164–184.

period 2500–1500 BCE. Five large megalithic elite burial sites existed in the mid-second millennium in different parts of the region, indicative of the existence of five chiefdoms or small kingdoms, each associated with copper production and strongly pastoral in other aspects of economy.[25] Possibly these statelets formed provinces of an overarching larger polity.

Most intriguing, sub-Saharan Africans may have separately invented ironworking. Iron smelting dates to the eleventh and tenth centuries BCE in sites as far apart as Rwanda and Lake Chad, too early and too far south to be reasonably explained as having diffused from an origin just five hundred years earlier, three thousand kilometers away in Anatolia – especially as ironworking did not reach the intervening lands, such as Carthage, until *after* the tenth century BCE, and Egypt and Meroe until still later than that. Even earlier dates for African ironworking, extending well back into the second millennium BCE, come from new research sites in the present-day Central African Republic, which lies between two other early ironworking regions, the Lake Chad Basin and the Great Lakes.[26]

As early as the eleventh century, the centers of lasting urban development and commerce in West Africa shifted south to the better-watered Sahel belt. Central in the new developments was the Inland Delta of the Niger River in modern-day Mali. Well before 1000 BCE, peoples of this region specialized in different kinds of food production for trade. Farmers among the bayous of the Delta domesticated African rice (*Oryza glaberrima*) probably as early as the fourth millennium, while other communities became fishing specialists. Savanna farmers outside the Delta supplied sorghum and other savanna crops, along with domestic animals, to the Delta communities. By the early first millennium BCE, the growth of manufacturing turned these long-existing trade relations into an emerging commercial revolution, with merchants, regular market centers, and long-distance transport of goods by both boat and donkey.

Urban life in the western Sudan and Sahel evolved in a unique fashion. The towns and cities developed as market centers for earlier village clusters, in which each village had engaged in a different kind of production – cotton textile weaving in one village, potting in another, and leather working in still another. A fourth manufacturing specialization, ironworking, further diversified production during the first millennium BCE, while the importation of copper from Aïr and from new mines in the far western Sahara

25 Holl 2004, 122–37, 164–84.
26 Holl (2009); Zangato and Holl (2010).

greatly expanded the long-distance sector.[27] Another valued metal, gold, coming from upper Niger and Senegal River goldfields, further enhanced these trends by the late first millennium.

In the north-central parts of modern-day Nigeria, the new directions of economic change eventuated, between 900 and 400 BCE, in the emergence of the earliest significant state as yet known from West Africa, associated with the Nok culture. Around the central areas of this culture, excavators have unearthed many huge terracotta sculptures, broken and buried in the graves of high-ranking persons. From the distribution of its cultural remains, the Nok state appears to have been as large as any kingdom of more recent centuries in the region. Iron was a major product, and Nok was probably a center for tin mining as well.[28]

It is often assumed that the rise of the Garamantes in the Fezzan oases of the north-central Sahara after 900 BCE owed to their position as intermediaries between the First Commercial Revolution of world history and the West African commercial revolution.[29] The evidence for a direct Garamantes role is still sparse, but at least occasional contacts of some kind did exist between the Carthaginian and Inland Niger Delta commercial spheres: the peoples around the Delta acquired the Punic name for the horse, and thus presumably the animal, sometime during the first millennium BCE.

Regular trans-Saharan trading networks likely did not develop, however, until the establishment of camels as beasts of burden and primary food animals among the inhabitants of the northern Sahara. Timothy Garrard has proposed that the opening of the Roman mint at Carthage in the late third century CE reflects the arrival of West African gold from across the Sahara. Most telling, he shows that the system of gold weight measures West African merchants used until the nineteenth century preserved the particular system put into effect at the Carthage mint.[30]

1.5 EARLY TOWNS AND STATES IN THE HORN OF AFRICA

Urban centers also emerged in the Horn of Africa in the first millennium BCE. Differently from the endogenous rise of towns and cities in the western Sahel and Sudan, the founding of urban centers in the Horn owed in large part to the First Commercial Revolution. South Arabians from the

27 McIntosh 1998.

28 A planned twelve-year archaeological investigation of Nok, led by Peter Breunig of the Goethe Universität, Frankfurt, is currently under way.

29 E.g., Kea 2004.

30 Garrard 1982.

opposite shore of the Red Sea, like the Phoenicians who founded Carthage and the Greeks who founded Cyrene, came to Africa seeking new commodities and new sources for old commodities – initially frankincense and myrrh, but subsequently tortoise shell and ivory – and their settlements took the form, like Carthage and Cyrene, of city-states, planted amidst the indigenous Cushitic pastoral and farming populations of the northern Ethiopian Highlands.[31]

At first, the routes tying the Horn of Africa to the First Commercial Revolution of world history passed overland through South Arabia to the Levant. After 300 BCE, the Red Sea itself became the central conduit of trade between the Mediterranean and the expanding commercial networks of the Indian Ocean. Sea routes passed from the Gulf of Aden across the Arabian Sea to India and from India to Indonesia, and south down the East African coast at least as far as modern-day Dar-es-Salaam in Tanzania. The terminus of this latter route at the beginning of the first millennium CE was Rhapta, the earliest known East African town.

During the early first millennium CE, the kings of one far northern Ethiopian city-state, Aksum, brought all the towns and the countryside of the northern Horn of Africa under their rule. By controlling, protecting, and taxing commercial enterprise in the Horn and in the southern Red Sea, the Aksumite kingdom grew into a major regional power, with its hegemony periodically extending to South Arabia as well. A notable outcome of Aksum's dominant position along the main route linking the Mediterranean to the Indian Ocean was the spread of Christianity to Aksum, with King Ezana adopting it as the official religion about thirty years after Constantine had taken the same step for Rome.

The Sassanian conquest of South Arabia in the 570s undermined Aksum's predominance in the Red Sea trade, and the rise of the first Islamic empire in the 640s to 750s completed Aksum's isolation from the main lines of commerce. In establishing Damascus as their capital, the Umayyad caliphs shifted the pivotal commercial sea link between east and west to the Persian Gulf. For a century the Red Sea became a commercial backwater.

From a comparative world history perspective, the significant consequence was that the Aksumite kings built a new material basis for their state, feudal in character. The transformation of Aksum from the later seventh to the ninth century strikingly parallels the course of change in contemporary, early medieval Western Europe. Urban life collapsed, with even the city of Aksum shrinking to an episcopal center of perhaps a thousand

[31] Ehret (1988); Schmidt and colleagues (2008).

people. The kings created a horse-mounted military class by granting fiefs to their soldiers, with the peasants of each fief owing a portion of their product to their lord. The titles of provincial officials in late prefeudal Aksum became the titles of the higher nobility. Monasteries became the principal centers of education and literacy. Kings granted fiefs of land to the monasteries to support their activities as religious centers, and the monks often acted as missionaries in spreading Christianity into the outlying areas of the kingdom.

One notable difference distinguishes the feudalisms of Europe and the Ethiopian highlands. Rights to land in prefeudal Aksum were vested in the local peasantry, rather than in great landed magnates, as in the western Roman Empire. As a consequence, a fief in feudal Aksum – and in its successor states, the Zagwe kingdom of the twelfth and thirteenth centuries and the Solomonic kingdom from 1270 onward – gave the lord a right to a portion of the peasants' production and certain other manorial privileges, but left the local farmers not as serfs, but as free people, able to bequeath the land they worked to their relatives and descendants.

1.6 AN ERA OF EMPIRES, AN ERA OF CITIES AND COMMERCE

Even as the northern Horn of Africa was entering a long period of feudal governance during the later first millennium CE, in the savannas of western Africa an age of empires was beginning. Wagadu (Ghana), the earliest known large empire, rose to prominence before mid-millennium. Stretching from the Inland Delta of the Niger to Senegal, Wagadu lay athwart the key trade routes linking the goldfields far to the south to the merchant networks of the Sahara. In an age when cities as such did not exist north of the Pyrenees, urban life flourished not just in Wagadu, but all across the western and central Sudan belt.

A series of empires succeeded Wagadu during the centuries after its decline in the twelfth century: Susu from the mid-twelfth to the early thirteenth century, with its power resting on control of the actual goldfields[32]; Mali from the 1240s to the mid-fifteenth century, controlling access to both the gold sources and the northern outlets of the trade; and Songay from the mid-1400s to the late 1500s, commanding the major Sahel trading cities and the salt trade of the Sahara. In the Chad Basin, the Kanem empire built its wealth and power, from the ninth to the fifteenth century, on a similar

[32] Bühnen 1994.

control over the access of neighboring states to the main trade routes of the central Sahara.

The commercial interests of these empires gave them strong ties to the Muslim world of those times. Islam had become established initially across North Africa following the early Muslim conquests between 642 and 710 CE. During the next several centuries, it became the religion of the trans-Saharan trading networks. In the Wagadu and Mali empires as well, it became the religious allegiance of the merchants and the commercial centers. During the eleventh century, the rulers of the Takrur kingdom of the Senegal Valley and the Kanem Empire of Lake Chad converted to Islam. The rulers of the later Mali and Songay empires also professed Islam, but the rural majority population in all those areas continued to follow their older religions. Islam also spread with commercial relations along the East African coast, becoming integral to urban identity in the Swahili city-states by the twelfth century CE. In the Horn of Africa, the spread of Islam, again among merchants, but also among the Cushitic pastoralist populations of the eastern Horn, provided religious backing for the military jihad of Ahmad Gurey (1527–43) against the Christian Solomonic kingdom of the Ethiopian highlands.

In these various fashions, Islam linked large areas of Africa to major currents of world history between the seventh and fifteenth centuries. Timbuktu in the thirteenth century, for example, was not only a trade center intimately connected to the Mediterranean and Middle Eastern worlds, but a university town in the early sense of that term, with the university as a place where noted scholars gathered to write and teach.

West of the lower Niger River in today's Nigeria, a rich city-state-based urban life developed during the second half of the first millennium CE. Ife, an early Yoruba city-state, grew into a major commercial entrepôt, manufacturing glass beads and dealing in goods from the rainforest and from the savannas to the north. Home to a splendid sculptural tradition of brass casting, using the lost wax method, Ife became, as well, the leading religious and ritual center of the Yoruba. An equally notable contemporary of Ile-Ife was the Igbo city of Igbo-Ukwu, also an artistic center for brass sculpture and the capital of a state, whose highly ritualized kings ruled the lands across the lower Niger, east of the Yoruba.

1.7 FROM FARMING TO COMMERCE AND STATES: THE SOUTHERN HALF OF AFRICA

In the southern half of Africa, where agriculture did not arrive until five thousand years ago, the first appearance of towns and states, not surprisingly, lagged behind areas farther north. In the equatorial rainforests of west-central Africa, long-distance commerce on the rivers of the Congo Basin developed during the last millennium BCE out of an earlier trade in fish, farm products, products of the hunt, and stone tools among the Bantu societies, who had spread agriculture across the region from 3000–1000 BCE, and the ancient foraging peoples of equatorial Africa, the Batwa ("Pygmies"). By the mid-first millennium BCE, the spread of iron across the Congo Basin introduced a new manufacturing component to this trade. Other industries, notably raffia textile weaving and boat building, further fueled trade expansion. The Batwa carved out their own niche in the new economy by becoming specialist providers of honey, wax, skins, ivory, and other forest products.[33]

In the Great Lakes region of East Africa, iron-using Mashariki Bantu settlers set off a different chain of developments during the early first millennium BCE. Encountering Sudanic and Cushitic agripastoralist communities, the Mashariki added sorghum and pearl millet from the Sudanic tradition and finger millet from the Cushites to their previously yam-based farming. The new crops, which required less rainfall than yams, allowed the Mashariki peoples to scatter between 300 BCE and 300 CE across most of eastern and southern Africa. Iron technology spread with them, and the demand for iron helped stimulate new kinds of regional trade wherever they settled.[34]

Those Mashariki communities who arrived at the East African coast toward the close of the first millennium BCE soon came into contact with the Indian Ocean developments of the First Commercial Revolution. The most salient and lasting effect of this encounter came not from the merchants who frequented East Africa's earliest town, Rhapta, but from Indonesian immigrants, who followed the Indian Ocean trade routes to East Africa and settled for a time at the coast before moving on to Madagascar around 300 CE. These ancestral Malagasy brought along several Southeast Asian crops, most important bananas, well suited to the wetter African tropical environments.[35] Banana cultivation, which spread rapidly west to the Great Lakes and into the Congo Basin, was far less labor-intensive as well as more productive than yam raising. Historians Jan Vansina and Kairn Klieman have argued that the arrival of bananas in the Congo Basin fostered a major leap in commercial activity in those areas, because reliance on the new crop freed up time for people to engage in trade and in the production of trade commodities.[36]

33 Klieman (2003) explores this history in considerable detail.

34 Ehret 1998.

35 Ehret 1998, chapter 6; Ehret 2010; Gonzales 2009.

36 Klieman 2003; Vansina 1990.

In the Congo Basin, political growth followed on the heels of these developments, with chiefdoms emerging between 500 and 1100 and, after 1100, kingdoms. The two earliest known kingdoms of the deep interior, the Songye and Upemba states of the middle Lualaba River region, date to roughly 1100–1400.[37] In the lower Congo areas near the Atlantic coast, Kongo with its large capital city, Mbanzakongo, and several smaller provincial capitals flourished from around 1300 until 1665. Both regions lay along major routes of long-distance trade and close to prime copper- and iron-producing areas.

In the African Great Lakes region, the earliest large states also date to 1100–1400. Supported by great wealth in cattle rather than trade, the rulers built extensive earthworks in their capitals. Several thousand people lived in these capitals, with their residential areas scattered over several square kilometers, interspersed with fields and pasture. These dispersed towns undoubtedly attracted trade in salt, iron, and foodstuffs, but their primary function was as political and ritual centers.[38]

In contrast, Southern Africa's first town, Mapungubwe, which flourished in the Limpopo Valley during the eleventh and twelfth centuries CE, was both a royal capital, with large stone structures, and the central entrepôt connecting the source areas of ivory and gold in the interior to the sea routes of the Indian Ocean.[39] The establishment of the Zimbabwe Empire in the thirteenth century shifted the heartland of urban development north to modern-day Zimbabwe. The capital city of Great Zimbabwe, famous for its great stone buildings, had fifteen thousand to eighteen thousand inhabitants during the fourteenth century. Several provincial capitals in the empire, though smaller, appear also to have deserved the appellation of town.

1.8 AFRICA IN A GLOBAL HISTORICAL PERSPECTIVE

To view Africa over the very long term is to discover that the notable developments of Africa's past followed similar pathways and proceeded at similar paces as comparable changes elsewhere in the world. These developments affirm something historians more widely in the world, including unfortunately only too many historians of the African continent itself, have not yet assimilated – namely, the comparability in the timing and content of

37 Vansina (1990) shows that the Songye, although an oligarchic republic in recent centuries, most probably evolved out of an earlier monarchy. See also Ehret 2002, chapter 6.

38 Sutton 1998.

39 Thomas N. Huffman, *Mapungubwe* (Johannesburg: Witerwatersrand Press, 2005).

historical change in Africa to the timing and content of historical change elsewhere. Two great transitions of human history during the Holocene – from foraging to farming and, several thousand years later, from villages and informal governance to towns and states – not only were *not* late in emerging in Africa, but Africa was a continent of primary invention in those times.

Cultivation of crops and herding of animals began in Africa as early as anywhere else except the Middle East, and only slightly later than there. The first domestication of cattle in world history took place in the southern half of the eastern Sahara one thousand to fifteen hundred years earlier than the separate domestication of cattle around the eastern Mediterranean. West Africans living south of the Sahara were among the first peoples in the world to invent ceramic technology, *before* eleven thousand five hundred years ago. A probable second African invention of ceramics took place almost as early in the eastern Sahara. The independent inventions, by different African populations in different regions south of the Sahara, of cotton textile weaving seven thousand or more years ago, of raffia-cloth weaving and polished stone tools almost equally early, and probably of copper metallurgy in the Sahara by 2000 BCE and ironworking in north-central Africa before 1000 BCE, reaffirm something that historians have long understood – that particular advances in human technological capacities often arise more than once and in disparate parts of the world.

Within the overall progression of human history since the end of the latest ice age, the lag time between the earliest agriculture and the earliest towns and states in Africa accords with wider world history patterns. Typically, whether in the Middle East, Middle America, China, or Africa, the earliest urban centers and states came into being around four thousand to five thousand years after the first deliberate plant or animal tending. In the eastern Sahara, the initial stage of the First Great Transition, from foraging to cultivation and herding, began around the mid-ninth millennium BCE. The Second Great Transition in those areas, from localized political relations to states and from villages to towns, began as early as anywhere in the world – during the fifth millennium at Nabta Playa and during the fourth millennium along the Nile itself, at such places as Shaheinab and Qustul in Nubia and Naqada in southern Upper Egypt. In West Africa, the earliest towns and larger polities date to the second millennium. In those regions, the span between first farming and first towns may have been as much as six thousand or as little as four thousand years, depending on how early the shift from gathering to cultivating wild grains came about.

African history cautions, as well, against the mistake of attributing all invention to the early regions of cities and states – to the cultural complexes historians have traditionally called "civilizations." Ironworking, for instance, rapidly established itself as a key productive sector in the commercial towns of West Africa during the first millennium BCE. But the men who innovated this technology lived elsewhere, in regions where village-scale residence patterns long prevailed; and ironworking spread equally rapidly across the nonurbanized, nonstate parts of the continent. Civilization is not a thing; it is an evaluation, and only too often an evaluation that nonhistorians turn into a judgment on human worth. A historian's job is to seek to give historical ordering to and make historical sense of the changes societies and people have undergone, to the extent possible from the evidence available. When historians fall into the trap of defining some cultures as civilizations and others as not, they make a value judgment even if they mean not to. More to the point, they inevitably narrow the scope of their inquiry and, as a result, very often fail to recognize the more encompassing history that makes the culture they single out in this fashion worthy of attention in the first place.

The glorification of ancient Egypt is a prime illustration of the need to discard the fallacious Western idea that there really is something called "civilization." Putting Egypt back into Africa, where it has always properly belonged, is fundamentally important, but it is a bootless exercise if we perpetuate the equally fallacious Western attribution of everything notable in Africa to the ancient Egyptians. As important as Egypt was in the history of early state formation, it was not an initiating region in the crucial transitions of Holocene human history to food production, but rather a crossroads in the subsequent diffusion of crops, animals, and technology. The crucial early innovative areas in the continent lay in the Sudan belt and in West Africa. Even within the gyre of political history, Egypt's first large state, the Old Kingdom, took shape not at the center, but at one side of a wider nexus of early complexity that included Saharan pastoralists, Nubian town dwellers, and the Qustul state and probably other, as yet undiscovered small states farther south in Nubia. The major technological turning points of early African history, from the invention of ceramics to the invention of ironworking, did not originate in Egypt, but spread there from other areas.

The events of the Third Great Transition of the last millennium BCE, the First Commercial Revolution, and the developments of the first fifteen hundred years CE deepened and extended the ways Africans from many parts of the continent participated in the wider compass of global history. The Sudan belt and northern Africa had numerous urban centers already during the first millennium BCE, when the western and northern Europeans of the same period had none at all. During much of the first thousand years CE, the northern three-fifths of Africa, as well as the eastern coast and its hinterlands, were intertwined economically with other world regions to an extent that Europe north of the Pyrenees and Alps began to match only between 1000 and 1400 CE. The first millennium and a half CE, it can be argued, were times of economic development and advance overall for Africa, in which large parts of the continent contributed to the far-flung currents of historical change across the Eastern Hemisphere.

Through all the eras before the mid-fifteenth century, Africa did not follow behind or lie outside the main trends and pathways of human history. The great question that we as historians of Africa must grapple with is how and why the developments of the past one thousand years, and more particularly the past five hundred years, in the end so greatly redirected history across large parts of the continent. A fuller understanding of African history over the very long term casts in sharpest relief the salience and complexity of that problem for historians.

References

Arkell, Anthony John. (1949). *Early Khartoum: An Account of the Excavation of an Early Occupation Site Carried Out by the Sudan Government Antiquities Service in 1944–5*. London, New York: Oxford University Press.

Bühnen, Stephan. (1994). "In Quest of Susu." *History in Africa*, 21: 1–47.

Ehret, Christopher. (1988). "Social Transformation in the Early History of the Horn of Africa." In *Proceedings of the Eighth International Conference of Ethiopian Studies*, edited by Taddese Bayene. Addis Ababa: Institute of Ethiopian Studies 1: 639–51.

(1998). *An African Classical Age*. Charlottesville: University of Virginia Press.

(2001). "The African Sources of Egyptian Culture and Language." In *África Antigua: El Antiguo egipto, una civilizatión Africana*, edited by Josep Cervelló, 121–8. Barcelona: Centre D'estudis Africans.

(2002). *The Civilizations of Africa*. Charlottesville: University of Virginia Press.

(2006). "Linguistic Stratigraphies and Holocene History in Northeastern Africa." In *Archaeology of Early Northeastern Africa*, edited by Marek Chlodnicki and Karla Kroeper, 1019–55. Posnan: Posnan Archaeological Museum.

(2008). "Reconstructing Ancient Kinship in Africa." In *Early Human Kinship: From Sex to Social Reproduction*, edited by Nicholas J. Allen, Hilary Callan, Robin Dunbar, and Wendy James. Oxford: Blackwell.

(2010). "Linguistic Testimony and Migration Histories." In *Migration in World History*, edited by J. Lucassen, L. Lucassen, and P. Manning. Leiden, Boston, MA: Brill.

(2011). "A Linguistic History of Cultivation and Herding in Northeastern Africa." In *Windows on the African Past: Current Approaches to African Archaeobotany*, Vol. 3, edited by Ahmed G. Fahmy, S. Kahlheber, and A. C. D'Andrea. Frankfurt am Main: Africa Magna Verlag.

(2013). "Holocene Migrations as Determined from Linguistics in Sub-Saharan Africa." In *The Encyclopedia of Global Human Migration*, Vol. 1, edited by I Ness and P. Bellwood, Chapter 13. Malden, MA, and Oxford: Wiley-Blackwell.

Ehret, Christopher, S. O. Y. Keita, and Paul Newman. (2004). "The Origins of Afroasiatic." *Science*, 306: 1680–1.

Fuller, Dorian. (2006). "Agricultural Origins and Frontiers in South Asia: A Working Synthesis." *Journal of World Prehistory*, 20(1): 1–86.

Garrard, Timothy F. (1982). "Myth and Metrology: The Early Trans-Saharan Gold Trade." *Journal of African History*, 23(4): 443–61.

Gonzales, Rhonda M. (2009). *Societies, Religion, and History: Central-East Tanzanians and the World They Created, c. 200 BCE to 1800 CE*. New York: Columbia University Press.

Gordon, William. (2009). "Cultural Identity of the 25th Dynasty Rulers of Ancient Egypt in Context: Formulation, Negotiation and Expression." PhD dissertation, University of California at Los Angeles.

Holl, Augustin F. C. (2004). *Holocene Saharans*. London, New York: Continuum.

(2009). "Early West African Metallurgies: New Data and Old Orthodoxy." *Journal of World Prehistory*, 22: 415–38.

Huysecom, E., M. Rasse, L. Lespez, K. Neumann, A. Fahmy, A. Ballouche, S. Ozainne, M. Maggetti, Ch. Tribolo, and S. Soriano. (2009). "The Emergence of Pottery in Africa during the Tenth Millennium cal BC: New Evidence from Ounjougou (Mali)."

Kea, Ray. (2004). "Expansions and Contractions: World-Historical Change and the Western Sudan World-System (1200/1000 B.C.–1200/1250 A.D.)." *Journal of World-Systems Research*, 10: 723–816.

Klieman, Kairn A. (2003). *The Pygmies Were Our Compass: Bantu and Batwa in the History of West Central Africa, Early Times to c. 1900 C.E.* Portsmouth, NH: Heinemann.

Kobusiewicz, Michal and Romuald Schild. (2005). "Prehistoric Herdsmen." *Academia*, 3(7): 20–4.

Malville, J. M., R. Schild, F. Wendorf, and R. Brenner. (2008). "Astronomy of Nabta Playa." In *African Cultural Astronomy: Current Archaeoastronomy and Ethnoastronomy Research in Africa*, edited by Jarita C. Holbrook, Rodney T. Medupe, and Johnson O. Urama. Dordrecht, New York: Springer.

McIntosh, Roderick J. (1998). *The Peoples of the Middle Niger*. Malden, MA: Blackwell Publishers.

Schmidt, Peter R., Matthew C. Curtis, and Zelalem Teka, eds. (2008). *The Archaeology of Ancient Eritrea*. Trenton, NJ: Red Sea Press.

Shaw, T. (1980). "Holocene Adaptations in West Africa: The Late Stone Age." *Early Man News*, 3/4: 51–82.

Sutton, J. E. G. (1974). "The Aquatic Civilization of Middle Africa." *Journal of African History*, 15(4): 527–46.

(1998). "Ntusi and Bigo: Farmers, Cattle-Herders and Rulers in Western Uganda, AD 1000–1500." *Azania*, 33: 39–72.

Vansina, Jan. (1990). *Paths in the Rainforests*. Madison: University of Wisconsin Press.

Wendorf, Fred and Romuald Schild. (1998). "Nabta Playa and Its Role in the Northeastern African History." *Anthropological Archaeology*, 20: 97–123.

Williams, Bruce B. and Keith C. Seele. (1986). *The A-Group Royal Cemetery and Qustul*. Chicago: University of Chicago Oriental Institute.

Zangato, Étienne and Augustin F. C. Holl. (2010). "On the Iron Front: New Evidence from North-Central Africa." *Journal of African Archaeology*, 8(1): 7–23.

2

Reversal of Fortune and Socioeconomic Development in the Atlantic World

A Comparative Examination of West Africa and the Americas, 1400–1850

Joseph E. Inikori

The comparatively poor performance of the economies of sub-Saharan Africa in the current global economy has been a challenge to scholars and policy makers alike. Economic historians, economists, and political scientists have struggled to understand the puzzle of sub-Saharan African economic development with little success. Without helpful guidance from economic historians and economists, policy makers have often applied ill-informed policy prescriptions with disastrous outcomes. For a while, economic historians seem to have abandoned sub-Saharan Africa out of frustration (Hopkins 2009). Happily, there appears to be a turnaround; economic historians are returning to sub-Saharan Africa as the growing popularity of globalization has helped to focus attention, once again, on long-run historical processes as a source of knowledge for the understanding of contemporary situations (Inikori 2007a). We have begun to see imaginatively articulated articles seeking to explain long-run development processes in sub-Saharan Africa.[1]

This welcome development, however, appears unconnected, or at least not seriously connected, to a major historiographical development with much potential for a clearer understanding of the long-run development process in western Africa. As part of the growing globalization discourse, Atlantic world history is now one of the fastest growing fields of historical scholarship (Bailyn 2005; Canizares-Esguerra and Seeman 2007; Coclanis 2005; Eltis, Lewis, and Sokoloff 2004; Inikori 1979, 2002a; Mancke and Shammas

[1] Acemoglu, Johnson, and Robinson (2002, 2005a); Austin (2008a, 2008b); Inikori (2002b, 79; 2009a); Nunn (2007, 2008); Nunn and Wantchekon (2011).

2005; McCusker and Morgan 2000; O'Rourke and Williamson 1999; Solow 1991). Studying the Atlantic basin as a unit of historical analysis enables us to overcome the myopic view of long-run development processes in the major regions of the Atlantic basin as self-contained and isolated phenomena (Davis 1973, xi). The relational framework of Atlantic world history gives us a clear view of the interconnections between the long-run development processes in the individual subregions of the Atlantic basin. Recent research seeking to explain long-run economic development processes in western Africa has yet to fully incorporate this relational framework of Atlantic world history. Like mainstream European economic historiography (Inikori 2009b), the highly imaginative recent works generally lose sight of the fact that long-run economic development processes in western Africa during the formative centuries, 1450–1850, were essentially part of an integrated historical process in the Atlantic basin. If we are not fully conscious of this fact, we are unlikely to accurately identify the causal factors in the process, properly understand how they operated and interacted with other factors, and assign to them their correct causal weights.

This chapter attempts to show what we can learn when the economic history of western Africa during the critical period, 1450–1850, is studied with the perspective of Atlantic world history. It examines West Africa's long-run economic development process, 1400–1850, in the light of the clear view offered by the Atlantic world history framework. A discussion of the comparative levels of economic development in West Africa and the Americas in two "long years" – ca. 1400 and ca. 1850 – with emphasis on markets and the development of the market economy, is presented in the first part of the chapter.[2] This part of the chapter aims to establish a clear fact of reversal of fortune among the major regions examined. Emphasis on markets and the market economy arises from the fact that efficient market allocation of resources is critical to sustained growth of per capita income and the further development of resources. The degree of market development is, therefore, a good barometer for measuring the level of economic development at a given moment. The second part of the chapter presents currently available evidence to demonstrate the extent to which the reversal can be explained in terms of the transatlantic slave trade and the employment of enslaved Africans in the Americas to produce commodities for Atlantic

[2] The choice of West Africa as the appropriate region in Africa for this comparative study arises from the fact that it was the region firmly linked to the Americas in a single interconnected long-run development process that produced, over the period 1450–1850, an integrated Atlantic economy that was the nucleus of the current global economy. See Inikori (2007a).

commerce from 1500 to 1850. Because the end result of the developments in the Atlantic world during this formative period constituted the nucleus of the current global economy (Inikori 2007a), this chapter's findings have a significant bearing on our understanding of the historical origins of the relative position of West African economies in the current global economic order.

2.1 COMPARATIVE LEVELS OF ECONOMIC DEVELOPMENT IN WEST AFRICA AND THE AMERICAS

Global comparison of regional development levels in the distant past, when data for measuring Gross Domestic Product (GDP) are nonexistent, relies heavily on demography – its absolute size, density, and urbanization – as a proxy (Acemoglu et al. 2005b; Allen 2009, 16–21). For West Africa in the "long 1400," a combination of Arabic sources, archaeological evidence, and oral sources forms the basis for researchers' demographic estimates. The more heavily documented studies focus largely on micro-regions, particularly the Niger Bend – the inland delta of the Niger River from the modern city of Segu in the west to where the river enters modern Nigeria. Specialists generally agree that the Niger Bend subregion of West Africa was heavily populated, with very large cities, from the early centuries of the first millennium CE to the first half of the second millennium CE (Cissoko 1984; Hunwick 1999; McIntosh 1998, 2005, 2008, 31–43; Moraes Farias 2003; Niane 1984a, 1984b, 1984c). Niani, Jenne, Timbuktu, and Gao are among the best known cities in the region. Niane puts the population of Niani during the fourteenth century at one hundred thousand; based on a late sixteenth-century census, Cissoko estimates the population of Gao at one hundred thousand, that of Timbuktu at eighty thousand, and that of Jenne at thirty thousand to forty thousand; Hunwick's estimate for Gao, based on the same data as Cissoko's, ranges between thirty-eight thousand and seventy-six thousand (Cissoko 1984, 206; Hunwick 1999, xlix; Niane 1984a, 156). The Niger Bend had many other towns during the late fourteenth- to the late sixteenth-century period. In fact, Mahmud Kati, an Arab visitor to the region during the period, reported that there were four hundred towns in the Mali Empire (Niane 1984a, 156). The research of Roderick McIntosh and that of P. F. de Moraes Farias, among others, strongly support earlier arguments that the Niger Bend was a highly urbanized region in West Africa, with relatively large overall populations, from the last centuries of the first millennium CE to the late sixteenth century (McIntosh 1998,

2005, 2008; Moraes Farias 2003). To the east of the Niger Bend, in what is generally known as West Africa's Central Sudan, the Hausa city-states, such as Katsina and Kano, and the Kanem-Borno Empire in the Lake Chad region also had many large towns during the period. So, too, did the West African forest belt, with large urban centers such as Ile-Ife and Benin City.

Among modern researchers competent in combining Arabic sources, archaeological evidence, and oral sources, only D. T. Niane has ventured to estimate the total population of the African continent between the fourteenth century and the sixteenth century. Because his estimate has been generally overlooked in recent discussions of the continent's population, it is pertinent to present the basis of his informed guesstimate to give readers a proper context for a fair comparative assessment. After detailing the general sociopolitical and economic conditions in Africa between the twelfth and sixteenth centuries to support his contention that "Africa was not an under-populated continent" during the period, he offers regional specifics to reach his overall numerical statement:

> We have some indications of the population of certain regions. According to Mahmud Kati, Mali had 400 towns or large population centres; the farming villages stretched in a continuous line along the waterways. Agricultural production was very extensive. Professor Cissoko ... has drawn attention to the extent of rice production; for example, among the Songhay in the fifteenth and sixteenth centuries, a single *fanfa* or overseer, directing the work of tributaries, could supply the king with more than 1000 *sounu* (large leather sacks which held about 70 kg). The royal stocks of food were immense; we may gain some idea of them from the fact that the king of Gao had a regular army of 100,000 men, garrisons near the main commercial towns and a very large court, and that all these people were fed and maintained by the king almost entirely from the agricultural revenues. It is difficult to estimate the size of the population, but the large number of well-populated trading towns and constructions on the scale of the Great Zimbabwe monuments would suggest that the population was dense. Over the whole continent, at this period of commercial expansion, the towns perhaps accounted for 10 percent of the population.... At this time Africa must have suffered epidemics, periods of drought and major floods, but the documents available make little mention of famine. Arab travelers – for example, Ibn Battuta, the fourteenth-century globe-trotter – noticed the abundance of food on the east coast and in the Sudan. For the whole of the continent, the population in Ibn Battuta's lifetime [the fourteenth century] may be estimated at 200 million. (Niane 1984c, 683–4)

Based on the writings of contemporary Timbuktu historians and information from Portuguese explorers who made contact with the emperor of Mali in the mid-fifteenth century, Niane puts the empire's population in the mid-fifteenth century at 40–50 million (Niane 1984a, 156).

Like all demographic estimates for these early periods across the globe, we can all agree, Niane's estimates must have a large margin of error. In some important sense, it may be best to treat them as orders of magnitude instead of exact figures. But, comparatively speaking, it is difficult to understand why scholars in recent times appear to prefer estimates, including those by Angus Maddison, that are not better documented than Niane's (Benjamin 2009; Iliffe 1995; Maddison 2001, 2003; Manning 2006). Based on Carr-Saunders's 1934 work, Patrick Manning employs in his analysis a total population of 100 million for the African continent in 1500, one-half of Niane's figure, and 50–60 million for West and Central Africa (Manning 2006, 53). From what we know about West Africa and Central Africa, it seems reasonable to suppose that at least two-thirds, that is, 40 million, of Manning's upper figure can be assigned to West Africa. With an area of 2.4 million square miles, this gives a density of 16.7 persons per square mile for West Africa in 1500. Density in the Niger Bend could not have been less than 25 per square mile during the fifteenth and sixteenth centuries. Again, readers should treat these figures as orders of magnitude and base their reasoned judgment on evidence concerning sociopolitical organization, agricultural production, and land use.

Coming to the demography of the Americas in the "long 1400," the subject has been a matter of dispute since the first reports by explorers during the sixteenth century (Diffie 1945; excerpts in Hanke 1967, 193). More recent discussions center on the works of what has become known as the Berkeley school (Borah and Cook 1960, 1963; Cook and Simpson 1948). The Berkeley school has been severely criticized. Francis Brooks's criticism probably represents the most severe:

> Embedded in the received story of the "conquest of Mexico" are two questionable assertions. The first is that the population of Central Mexico in 1519 was approximately 25 million people. The second is that these people were struck in 1520 by smallpox and, possibly, by other diseases; and that as a result perhaps one-third of them died.... Every element of this received account is false, epidemiologically improbable, historiographically suspect, or logically dubious. The population of Mexico in 1519 was almost certainly nowhere near as large as 25 million. (Brooks 1993, 1–2)[3]

The controversy continues, but figures derived from the synthesis by William Denevan, 53,904,000 for all the Americas in 1492, are probably the best

[3] Brooks adds that "the conclusions of the physical anthropologists, derived from the carrying capacity of the available agricultural technology," suggest a total population of 5 million to 10 million for Mexico in 1500 (Brooks 1993, 4–5). The literature cited includes Newson (1985) and Denevan (1976).

currently available (Denevan 1992, xxix; Newson 2006, 148, table 5.1).[4] The bulk of the population was concentrated in two regions: Mexico, 17,174,000 (31.9 percent); the Andes (including the Andean highlands and coastal Venezuela, Colombia, Ecuador, Peru, and Bolivia), 15,696,000 (29.1 percent). Two other regions had relatively large populations in proportion to their geographical area: Central America, 5,625,000 (10.4 percent); and the Caribbean, 3,000,000 (5.6 percent). The huge geographical area of North America (what later became the United States of America and Canada), 7 million square miles, had only 3,790,000 (7 percent); Paraguay, Uruguay, and southern Brazil had 1,055,000 (2 percent).

In terms of density, extremely low population densities characterized the Americas in 1492. The regional distribution of Denevan's total figure of 53,904,000 implies an average density of approximately 6.3 persons per square mile for Latin America and the Caribbean, and 0.5 for North America. The large concentration in Mexico and the Andes suggests that density in most areas of Latin America and the Caribbean was less than one person per square mile in 1492. As would be expected, the few urban centers in the Americas were located in Mexico and the Andes (Prados de la Escosura 2006, 476–7, table 13.3).

The uncertainty concerning the population estimates for West Africa and the Americas between the late fourteenth and late fifteenth century (the "long 1400") notwithstanding, it is clear enough from the evidence that West Africa was by far more densely populated than the Americas. As we now propose to show, market exchange and the market economy also developed to a much greater extent in West Africa than in the Americas during the first half of the second millennium CE.

The subregions of West Africa had their own internal factors (in particular, population growth and natural resource endowments) that stimulated the growth of trade and the evolution of the market economy in the regions. But the growth of trade in the economies of the Niger Bend operated as a powerful growth pole for all the subregions. For more than one thousand years, from the mid-first millennium CE to the mid-second millennium CE, the Niger Bend enjoyed considerable geographical location advantages – the agricultural resources provided by the flood plains of the inland Niger delta; the long stretch of river transportation along the River Niger; the ease of movement in the open savanna (including draft animals for transportation); the trade links to the copper- and salt-producing economies of

[4] While some scholars do not accept the Denevan synthesis figures, they are the most widely and frequently cited figures in the current literature, both in scholarly works and in major textbooks.

the southern Sahara and to the commercial centers of the Mediterranean world – all this made the region the center of trade and manufacturing in West Africa until the middle centuries of the second millennium.

An important internal factor in the region was the growth of population and the emergence of large urban centers. The demographic evidence discussed earlier suggests strongly that the bulk of West Africa's population at this time was located in the region. Urbanization in the region arose from the combined effects of population growth and the expansion of commerce. As McIntosh has shown, the growth of urban populations in the Niger Bend was not associated initially with administration in centralized states or religious worship as was the case with early urbanism in other parts of the world. Urbanism emerged spontaneously in the Niger Bend and the urban centers were self-organizing before they became part of centralized, bureaucratic, and military states (McIntosh 1998, 2005, 2008, 32). This must mean that urbanism in the region was largely the product of demography and commerce, and the urban centers functioned principally as commercial centers. The subsequent rise of centralized state systems in the region simply provided further impetus for the growth and geographical extension of the commercial business of the cities' merchants.

Thus, the Niger Bend became the center of a merchant diaspora that connected all the subregions of West Africa in an integrated network of long-distance interregional trade (Inikori 2010). Niger Bend merchants distributed the region's manufactures and other products to the subregional trading centers in West Africa in exchange for the commodities of the subregions. In addition, the Niger Bend traders conducted a large entrepôt trade, re-exporting southern Saharan products (largely salt and copper products) and products of the Mediterranean trading world (especially cowries from Asia and European textiles) to the forest and savanna subregions of West Africa. Gold and kola nuts were the most important products imported from the subregions into the Niger Bend. Much of the gold was re-exported to the Mediterranean trading world to feed the commercializing process in the economies of the Mediterranean and Europe. The rising Middle Eastern and European demand for gold beginning during the fourteenth century expanded the gold trade greatly, West Africa and its famed "Island of Gold" being the source of about two-thirds of global gold supply at this time (Hunwick 1999, liii; McIntosh 1998, 269, 273–4). Niger Bend merchant diaspora colonies spread out across West Africa, linking the subregional trading centers to each other and to the Niger Bend commercial cities (in particular, Jenne, Timbuktu, and Gao) in an embryonic West African regional globalization process centered in the Niger Bend (Inikori 2010).

As a result of this embryonic regionally based globalization, a gradual process of interregional specialization and division of labor was in progress in West Africa by the sixteenth century. A major feature of the process was the general tendency of the coastal regions (from the Upper Guinea coast to southeastern Nigeria) and their immediate hinterlands to export largely primary products (gold, kola nuts, aquatic products, etc.) to the interior savanna in exchange for mainly manufactures from the latter (Inikori 2002b, 2009a). The combined operation of local, intraregional, and long-distance interregional trade stimulated sustained commercial expansion and widespread evolution of the market economy all over West Africa during the fifteenth and sixteenth centuries.

The extent of market development and the geographical spread of the market economy in West Africa during the fifteenth and sixteenth centuries is indicated by the scale and widespread use of well-established exchange currencies in the region. Both in magnitude and geographical spread, the cowrie currency was probably the most important (Hogendorn 2006; Hogendorn and Johnson 1986; Johnson 1970). The cowrie shells were gathered from the Indian Ocean Maldive Islands. Early imports into West Africa came through the Middle East. As would be expected, evidence shows the upper and middle Niger (Niger Bend) was where they were first used as early as the eleventh century CE, and remained in regular use in the commercial cities of the region (Jenne, Timbuktu, Gao) thereafter. They spread to ancient Ghana by the thirteenth century; and through the gold and kola nut trade, the cowrie currency reached the Gold Coast (southern modern Ghana), from where it expanded to Whydah, Ardra, and southwest Nigeria several decades before the arrival of Portuguese explorers in those regions (Johnson 1970, 32, 35–6, 332–3). The other major currency in use in West Africa before the arrival of European explorers and traders was copper currency, imported from the southern Sahara in the form of small copper rods weighing about one pound each. The main area of the copper currency was southeastern Nigeria, where a local metal currency in the form of small iron hoes (called *anyu*) also developed (Inikori 2002b, 64). The quantity and relative value of currency in the imports European traders brought during the early decades of their trade in West Africa provide unambiguous evidence of the extent and continuing expansion of the market economy in West Africa (Inikori 2007b). Thus, taking all the evidence together, it is clear that the development of markets and the evolution of the market economy in West Africa that had been on since medieval times had advanced greatly by the late fifteenth century. The predominance of products derived from West African labor and natural resources in the first one hundred fifty years of

European trade in the region further intensified this ongoing development and geographical spread of the market economy.

The story in the Americas is radically different. There was market exchange of goods in all regions of the Americas during the fifteenth century. But in all the sparsely populated regions, with one person per square mile or less, subsistence production (production for direct consumption by producers without market exchange) was overwhelmingly dominant. This was the case for all of North America and the larger part of South America where modern Brazil, Uruguay, Paraguay, and Argentina are located (Bakewell and Holler 2010; Carmack, Gasco, and Gossen 1996; Hanke 1967; Katz 1972; Lockhart and Schwartz 1983; Trigger and Washburn 1996). As Storey and Widmer (2006, 77) put it:

> In pre-Columbus Latin America, there were far more autonomous societies and cultures than in Europe at the time. Most of these societies had economies characterized by a "domestic mode of production." Economies on this scale were self-sufficient. Each family constructed, produced, and gathered all that it needed to survive, and each family was economically redundant with the next – it engaged in the same economic activities:

In the more densely populated regions with complex sociopolitical organizations – the Inca and Aztec Empires – market development was limited partly by physical geography and partly by political institutions. In the expansive Inca Empire, the high mountains running north-south impeded east-west movement; in the Aztec Empire, physical geography also made movement between the plains and the highlands, which separated the western from the eastern plains, extremely difficult.

Possibly in adaptation to the physical environment, the quasi-socialist organization of the Inca Empire (Baudin 1967; Katz 1972, 282–94; Metraux 1967) imposed the greatest limit on the development of markets and the market economy in the polity. The state parceled out land among the families in the communes to meet their subsistence needs. The members of the communes paid labor dues employed on state lands to produce for the state and the priestly nobility, as well as surpluses kept for emergency purposes. The state also employed the labor dues in its massive construction works – the extensive state roads, bridges, irrigations, temples, and so forth. Craftsmen worked only for the state and religious institutions. Members of the communes were allowed to exchange goods in their local communities. But only the state could distribute products from one province to another, from one ecological region to another. The famous Inca roads, running north-south for a total of thirty thousand to fifty thousand kilometers, were not built for commerce; only those traveling on state business were allowed to use them (Bakewell and Holler 2010, 58; Katz 1972, 287). As Friedrich Kantz wrote of the Inca state: "there is no other state in pre-Spanish America, in the ancient East or in European antiquity in which trade was so uniquely controlled by the state that not a single general article of barter served as currency" (Katz 1972, 293).

There was much greater private trading organized by a merchant class in the Aztec Empire. Commerce, therefore, developed to a higher level than in the Inca Empire. Even so, the development and geographical spread of the market economy was very limited. The vast majority of the population had little or no connection with the market. Somewhat similar to the Inca economy, production was organized around the needs of the state and its supporting nobility in a tributary system. Trading itself was largely dependent on the tribute system. At the time of the Spanish conquest, 371 towns spread across the thirty-eight provinces of the empire paid tribute (Storey and Widmer 2006, 100; Von Hagen 1961, 170). A large bureaucracy of tribute collectors connected the provinces to the capital city of Tenochtitlan (Katz 1972, 198–200). The amount of tribute goods brought to the capital yearly was immense. For example, the province of Cuauhnahuac sent annually twelve thousand eight hundred cloaks, sixteen hundred loin cloths, sixteen hundred women's tunics, eight warriors' costumes, thirty-two thousand bundles of paper, eight thousand bowls, and four bins of maize and beans. The province of Toctepec on the Gulf Coast sent, among other things, ninety-six hundred decorated cloaks, sixteen hundred women's tunics, sixteen thousand rubber balls, eighty handfuls of quetzal feathers, twenty-four thousand little bunches of feathers, one hundred pots of liquid amber, and three hundred loads of cacao (Storey and Widmer 2006, 100–1). The state redistributed these tribute goods among the nobility and state functionaries. Tribute recipients sold to the merchants what they did not need and bought from them what they needed. The merchants thus provided a reshuffling service that enabled recipients to secure the basket of goods they needed. Craft production was also linked largely to the tribute system. By law, the most important manufactures the craftsmen produced – feather ornaments, gold and silver, cotton clothing, and precious stones – could only be used by the tribute-receiving nobility; and they alone were allowed to live in two-story houses and palaces, the building of which needed the services of experienced craftsmen. Merchants and craftsmen were thus dependent largely on the state: "The majority of craftsmen by the end of the fifteenth century were either employed in the palaces and worked for the state or were maintained on the tributes exacted from various parts of the [capital] city" (Katz 1972, 218).

It is clear from the operation of the tribute system that the vast majority of producers in the Aztec economy were hardly touched by market exchange. As Katz wrote:

> The Aztec peasant did not in fact require any craftsmen to satisfy his needs in housing, clothing, and agricultural implements. The houses constructed of dried adobe bricks were built by communal labour by members of the *calpulli*, articles of clothing woven out of maguey fibre were mostly made by the women and the agricultural tool – the digging stick, called coa – was so simple to make that nobody was required for this purpose. As yet no real division of labour between town and country existed in Mesoamerica. The craftsmen manufactured essentially luxury goods for the nobility and helped to build great state buildings. (Katz 1972, 218)

Some writers have attempted to show that Mesoamerica constituted "a world system" at the time of Spanish contact (Carmack 1996, 83–6). In some sense, the case can be made that a regionally based globalization process, centered on the Aztec empire, was in progress at the time. But the integration process was more political and cultural than commercial; the economic links were based largely on tributes and much less on market-based division of labor. It should be stressed at this point that, unlike the cities of West Africa's Niger Bend, those of the Inca and Aztec kingdoms originated as religious and administrative centers. Thus, while the state systems of the West African Middle Niger – Ancient Ghana, Mali, Songhay – were merchant empires by definition, those of the Americas of the same period were not. It is significant that there is no evidence of commercial intercourse between the two great empires of the Americas, the Inca and Aztec (Bakewell and Holler 2010, 249; Hagen 1961, 580).[5] The chronicles of the Aztec merchants' proclamation that "commerce began in Mexico-Tenochtitlan in the year 1504"[6] should be understood in this context to mean the beginning of commercial expansion, not the actual beginning of commerce. There can be no doubt, therefore, that the market economy had developed to a much greater extent in West Africa than in any part of the Americas at the close of the fifteenth century. Taken along with evidence on agricultural technology and pastoral farming, it can also be guessed that per capita incomes in West Africa should be higher.

By the "long 1850," the situation had changed completely. The predominantly subsistence (nonmarket-oriented) economies of the "long 1400" had become fully commercialized and the market economy had taken hold

[5] As Bakewell and Holler put it, "Peru had never before [Spanish contact] dealt directly with Central America and Mexico; nor the Andean province of Charcas with the Rio de la Plata; nor the Greater Antilles with Panama" (Bakewell and Holler 2010, 249).

[6] Quoted by Hagen (1961, 174).

Table 2.1. *Commodity production for export and population in Latin America and the United States of America, 1850–1912*

	Latin America			United States		
	Exports (3-yr. average p.a. US$)	Population	Exports per head (US$)	Exports (3-yr average p.a. US$)	Population	Exports per head (US$)
1850	159,484,000	30,381,000	5.25	162,000,000	23,192,000	6.99
1870	344,123,000	38,628,000	8.91	400,000,000	39,818,000	10.05
1890	602,147,000	51,662,000	11.66	859,667,000	62,948,000	13.66
1912	1,580,534,000	77,456,000	20.41	2,307,000,000	94,569,000	24.39

Source: Computed from Victor Bulmer-Thomas, *The Economic History of Latin America since Independence*. 2nd ed. (Cambridge: Cambridge University Press, 2003), appendix 1, tables A.1.1 and A.1.2, pp. 412 and 413.

in all of the Americas. In Spanish America, cities founded on commodity production and commerce, as opposed to the pre-Columbian cities that originated from religious worship and administration of centralized, militaristic states, emerged, around which predominantly market-based domestic economies developed (Bakewell 1984, 150; Burkholder and Johnson 2004, 171–3; Hoberman 1991). Similar developments occurred in the plantation and mining economies of Brazil, the Caribbean, and North America. They dominated commodity production (raw materials, foodstuffs, and bullion) for Atlantic commerce, and provided the foundation upon which the integrated nineteenth-century Atlantic economy was built. The evidence in Table 2.1 makes this clear.

As the table shows, by 1850 the population of the Americas at 53,573,000 was just about equal to the more acceptable 1492 population (53,904,000).[7] But the distribution was very different. The sparsely populated regions of 1492 (the areas that became the United States and Brazil) had more people (United States, approximately 23 million in 1850 and 40 million in 1870; Brazil, 7 million in 1850 and 10 million in 1870) than the more densely populated regions of 1492 (Mexico, approximately 8 million in 1850 and 9 million in 1870; the Andean region, comprising Ecuador, Peru, Bolivia, and Chile, 6 million in 1850 and 7 million in 1870) (Bulmer-Thomas 2006,

[7] Bulmer-Thomas's Latin American population does not include the population of the non-Latin Caribbean (English- and Dutch-speaking Caribbean). The populations of Jamaica (1844), Barbados (1851), Trinidad (1851), St Kitts (1844), Nevis (1844), and the Bahamas (1851) add up to 643,248 (Watts 1987, 459, table 10.2).

412, table A.1.1). The populations of Mexico and the Andean region in 1850 were far below those of 1492. The regional distribution of the population was a function of the regional distribution of commodity production for Atlantic commerce, by far the most important development of the period from 1492 to 1850: the phenomenal expansion that started in the mid-seventeenth century and accelerated from 1850 to 1912 (evidenced by Table 2.1) was central to population movement (including the development of new urban centers) and socioeconomic development. Relative to the 1492 situation discussed earlier, it is clear that all regions of the Americas shared in the great economic transformation associated with the phenomenal growth of commodity production for Atlantic commerce. But the revolutionary impact was exceptional for one region – the United States of America – which had become an industrialized region by 1912 (Chase-Dunn 1980, 189–230; Engerman and Sokoloff 1997, 260–304; North 1961, 1965, 673–705; Theberge 1968).

Comparatively, West Africa had fallen far behind the Americas in domestic market development and in commodity production for Atlantic commerce by the "long 1850." The annual average value of West Africa's commodity production for Atlantic commerce in the 1830s was £821,337 and that of transatlantic captive exports was £976,173, making a total of £1,797,510 (Inikori 1986, 56–7). This combined total is about 24 percent of Atlantic commodity exports by Brazil alone in the late 1840s (Inikori 2002a, 181, table 4.4). During the last decade of the nineteenth century, West Africa's commodity exports to Great Britain (the region's overwhelmingly dominant trading partner at the time) was £2,357,900 in 1891 and £3,106,300 in 1899 (Inikori 2008, table 2). The 1891 figure would be about 2 percent of the Latin American figure for 1890. Even if we double the West African figures to allow generously for exports to other Atlantic markets, this still gives a mere 4 percent.

More significant, the development of markets and the market economy in the Americas by the "long 1850" far exceeded that of West Africa, where subsistence (nonmarket-oriented) production was extensive and dominant in the domestic economies. For this reason, West Africa's domestic economies were very weakly connected to the commodity production chain of the nineteenth-century Atlantic economy, in contrast to the domestic economies of the Americas. All this would suggest that West Africa's Gross Domestic Product (GDP) and GDP per capita were considerably less than those of the Americas at this time. Looking back at the relative positions of the two regions in the "long 1400," there can be little doubt that a reversal of fortune of immense proportions had occurred. The next section attempts to show the contribution of the transatlantic slave trade and the employment of enslaved Africans in large-scale commodity production in the Americas for Atlantic commerce to this reversal of fortune.

2.2 HISTORICAL ORIGINS OF THE REVERSAL OF FORTUNE

What factors explain the development path of the economies of the Americas, relative to those of West Africa, in the period 1492–1850? Clearly, the prime mover was not internal. Given the "rude state" (as the classical economists would say) of those economies in 1492, market development originating primarily from internal factors would have to depend on sustained long-run internal population growth, as opposed to migration from other regions of the globe. We know there was no internally generated population growth in the Americas during the period. On the contrary, the indigenous populations in all areas of the region experienced a phenomenal demographic catastrophe during the sixteenth century. The indigenous population of central Mexico fell by about 85 percent between 1520 and 1620; the situation in the Andean area was similar. The experience was replicated in the rest of the Americas that had been sparsely populated in 1492; in the Caribbean islands, the indigenous population virtually disappeared in the sixteenth century (Bakewell and Holler 2010, 196–7). Internal population growth was, therefore, not the source of market development and the evolution of the market economy in the Americas during the period. As we have already implied, commodity production for Atlantic commerce was the prime mover. Our first analytical task in this section, it follows, is to show the contribution of enslaved Africans and analyze the relationship between exports and the development of domestic markets and the market economy in the Americas.

In the period 1500–1850, commodity production in the Americas for Atlantic-wide commerce faced two major problems that were related at some point – transportation cost and the availability of labor for large-scale production far beyond the scope of family labor. Given the rudimentary nature of transportation technology of the period, the cost of moving bulky goods across the oceans was extremely high. To be able to move such goods across the Atlantic and still secure for them large markets that included not just the rich but the middle class and the poor, the cost of production in the Americas had to be very low, in the first instance. Without meeting this precondition, very little was likely to happen in this sphere.

The story of rice production in the Americas narrated by Peter Coclanis confirms the point. Before Columbus reached the Americas in 1492, the production of rice had been well developed in Asia, Africa, and Europe. When entrepreneurs found out that rice was in demand in the Americas, there was enough rice in Asia, Africa, and Europe that could have been shipped to the Americas. But this did not happen because of transportation cost. Instead, the Americas had to develop their own rice production. As the American producers achieved economies of scale and production cost fell in the seventeenth and eighteenth centuries, they were able to export their rice to Europe. Subsequently, the new transportation technologies of the Industrial Revolution in England allowed Asian producers to take over the European markets and threatened to do the same in the Americas, until high-tech rice production in Arkansas confronted Asian producers (Coclanis 2007).

The problem of labor for large-scale production in the Americas arose from factor proportions – the abundance of land in relation to population, evidenced by the generally low population densities shown earlier. The problem was compounded by the catastrophic decline of the indigenous population in the sixteenth century that left huge tracts of land vacant for European immigrants to occupy at little cost, politically and financially. This made large-scale production, with a gang-labor organization of legally free workers, virtually impossible, because such workers preferred to secure their own land and engage in small-scale independent production. What is more, the proletarianization (transformation of the masses into workers owning little or no property) process in Europe, Africa, and Asia was yet to generate the kind of pressure that pushed millions of voluntary migrants from Europe and Asia to the Americas during the late nineteenth and twentieth centuries. Yet small-scale production of the valued bulky commodities, such as sugar, coffee, raw cotton, rice, indigo, and so on, was high cost, and large-scale production was needed to secure extensive economies of scale. The importation of indentured servants from Europe was tried as a solution with very limited and unsatisfactory outcome, as these servants picked up land and became independent small-scale producers at the end of their five-year contract. Only the massive importation and enslavement of captives from western Africa proved an effective solution to the labor problem.

Between 1500 and 1820, five out of every six persons crossing the Atlantic to the Americas were African captives transported for enslavement (Manning 1990, 37). Our knowledge of the total numbers transported continues to improve. The "New Database" by Eltis and Richardson has revised their earlier confirmation of Curtin's 11 million to 12.5 million (Eltis and Richardson 2008, 40–1, table 1.6; 2004b, 182, table 1).[8] While the improved knowledge is important for our understanding of what happened in western Africa, as will be shown shortly, what is important for the Americas is the demographic evidence showing the dominance of African labor in the production of the major commodities that fueled the growth of Atlantic commerce during the period (Inikori 2002a, 156–214).

Brazil was the first large-scale producer of sugar in the Americas. Its sugar-producing regions were populated by Africans and their descendants from the seventeenth to the nineteenth century: in Pernambuco, they were 68.2 percent of the total population in 1798 and 64 percent in 1872; Bahia, 78.6 percent and 72.3 percent; Rio de Janeiro, 64.3 percent and 48.8 percent; for the gold-producing regions, Minas Gerais, 74.6 percent and 57.6 percent, and Mato Grosso, 80.4 percent (1798); for the coffee-producing region of Sao Paulo, 43.5 percent (1872). People of African descent were 61.2 percent of Brazil's total population in 1798 and 58 percent in 1872. Note that because enslaved Africans were the forced specialized producers in plantation agriculture and gold production, they constituted virtually the total labor force in those sectors during the period (Inikori 2002a, 189 and 190, table 4.5.A and table 4.5.B). For purposes of large-scale commodity production for Atlantic commerce, Brazil was an extension of Africa at the time.

During the eighteenth century, leadership in plantation agriculture devoted to production for Atlantic commerce shifted from Brazil to the Caribbean, where it exploded. With that explosion, a demographic transformation followed that made the Caribbean even more African than Brazil. By the late eighteenth century, enslaved Africans employed in plantation agriculture, mostly sugar plantations (with cotton, coffee, and indigo as minor crops), made up at least 80 percent of the total population of most islands. In the first half of the nineteenth century, the growth of raw cotton production in the southern states of the United States of America became the epicenter of the Atlantic economy (Inikori 2002a; North 1961). Again, the cotton plantations depended entirely on enslaved Africans for their gang labor. The only sector of production for Atlantic commerce in the economies of the Americas in which the labor of enslaved Africans was not overwhelmingly dominant during the period was bullion production in Spanish

[8] As I argued elsewhere, the problem of incomplete data, though now reduced, remains; the new database, like the old, "must be treated as a large sample, rather than a comprehensive listing, of all slaving voyages" (Inikori 2003a). With all the emotions and bad blood the controversy unnecessarily generated, readers may now be able to tell who won and who lost.

America. Here, the indigenous population supplied much of the labor in silver mining. Yet the labor of enslaved Africans was not insignificant. The mine census of 1570 listed thirty-seven hundred enslaved Africans in the mining camps of New Spain, making up about 45 percent of the laboring population (Inikori 2002a, 181–2). In 1590, enslaved Africans provided on average approximately 14 percent of the labor employed in the major silver mines of "Nueva Espana," Zacatecas, Guadalajara, and Guadiana (Tandeter 2006, 318, table 9.1). On the other hand, enslaved Africans completely dominated gold production in Spanish America during the period, the same way that they did in Brazil (Inikori 2002a, 184–5). As Michael Taussig noted, enslaved Africans, not "Andean Indians," provided the labor force in the chief gold-producing region of the Spanish American empire located in the Cauca Valley of Colombia (Taussig 1977, 397).

Thus, it is beyond reasonable doubt that enslaved Africans and their descendants overwhelmingly dominated the gang labor employed in large-scale commodity production in the Americas for Atlantic commerce between 1500 and 1850. The below-subsistence cost of African slave labor (the slaves produced part of their own subsistence in their provision plots worked during their limited free time) and the economies of scale in large-scale plantation agriculture brought down production cost greatly. Hence, those commodities sold at considerably reduced prices, the high cost of transportation across the Atlantic notwithstanding. For example, in the second decade of the seventeenth century the price of tobacco in England was twenty to forty shillings (sterling) a pound. The phenomenal expansion of plantation production in the third decade brought down the plantation price in the Americas to less than a penny a pound by 1630, bringing down the price in England to one shilling or less in the 1670s (Davis 1954, 80). In general, plantation production of the other commodities experienced similar developments during the period. The magnitude of the price reduction created rapidly growing markets for the American commodities in Europe, thereby fueling the rapid growth of Atlantic commerce from 1650 to 1850 (Davis 1967; Inikori 2002a).

The explosive growth of highly specialized plantation agriculture and mining propelled the growth and development of interregional division of labor and intra-American trade, which stimulated the development of markets and the geographical spread of the market economy across the Americas. In regions that had less than one person per square mile in 1492, and market development was, therefore, at an extremely low level, such as Brazil and North America, the developments were truly astonishing. In Brazil, the expansion of specialized, large-scale plantation agriculture and gold mining, all devoted to production for Atlantic markets, created large domestic markets for foodstuffs, draft animals, and other goods. Because the domestic demand for these goods was very large, it created the market opportunity for a second round of specialized production and pushed further the frontier of market-oriented production. The details of the process are beginning to emerge from research (Barickman 1998; Luna and Klein 2003, 2004). Particularly significant in the Brazilian case, enslaved Africans were also employed in the production of these products for the domestic market (Luna and Klein 2004).

In what became the United States of America that was very much like Brazil in 1492, the growth of specialized, large-scale plantation agriculture in the Caribbean islands from 1650 to 1800 offered the initial market opportunity for the growth of market-oriented production and the gradual evolution of the market economy. This was particularly important for New England and the Middle Atlantic colonies that were locked up in a subsistence production cul-de-sac, because they lacked the natural resources needed to compete effectively in the production of plantation commodities for Atlantic commerce.[9] The Caribbean market for foodstuffs, lumber, draft animals, and shipping and other business services offered them the first major opportunities to enter the evolving Atlantic economy. The phenomenal expansion of specialized, large-scale plantation agriculture in the southern states of the United States during the first half of the nineteenth century, particularly the spectacular growth of the cotton economy, multiplied the opportunities a hundredfold. Somewhat similar to the Brazilian case, but on a much larger scale, the interaction between the specialized southern plantation economy and the maritime trading and shipping economy of the northeast opened up a large domestic market for foodstuffs that stimulated the growth of commercial food production in the western region of the United States. Ultimately, this gave rise to the growth of complementary economies in the southern, western, and northeastern regions of the United States. This tripartite interregional division of labor, centered on the southern cotton economy, was central to the subsequent industrialization of the northeastern region, which, in the long-run, set the economy of the United States apart from all the others in the Americas. The latter development has given rise to arguments attempting to explain the United States' divergence

[9] While new and increasingly sophisticated research on the subject continues to grow, an extensive literature already exists, of which the following is just a sample (Inikori 2002b; Khan and Sokoloff 1993; McCusker and Menard 1985; North 1961; Shepherd and Walton 1972; Sokoloff 1988; Sokoloff and Khan 1990).

in a manner that fails to accurately identify the real prime movers in the long-run development of the U.S. economy. This is particularly the case for the factor endowments paradigm and the institutional framework.

The factor endowments argument classifies the economies of the Americas into three according to their factor endowments – those with climates and soils particularly suited for growing highly valued crops with extensive economies of scale, making the employment of gang slave labor economic; those with dense indigenous populations forced by European colonizers to provide coerced labor; and those with climates and soils unsuited for plantation agriculture employing gang slave labor and with no dense indigenous populations that could be forced to provide coerced labor. New England and the mid-Atlantic region of the United States (the northeastern region) belonged to the last category. Without an Atlantic perspective, the factor endowments paradigm explains virtually in isolation the industrialization of the northeastern United States strictly in terms of its factor endowments. The plantation and mining slave economies are presented, again virtually in isolation, as performing relatively poorly in the long run because they employed coerced labor (Engerman and Sokoloff 1997). The institutional framework Acemoglu, Johnson, and Robinson employed, though located within the broader context of the Atlantic world, also fails to show elaborately the causal links between the slave economies of the Americas and industrialization in the northeastern United States (Acemoglu et al., 2002; 2005a).

The factor endowments argument surprisingly overlooks (as does, in different ways, the institutional analysis by Acemoglu and his coauthors) the well-documented fact that the northeastern region's commercial exploitation of its natural resource endowments depended, in the first instance, on the market opportunities created by the specialized, large-scale plantation and mining economies of the Americas employing coerced labor: Without the market opportunities arising from the division of labor centered on the slave economies of the Atlantic world, New England and the mid-Atlantic economies would not have been able to escape from their subsistence production cul-de-sac at the time they did. This subject has been treated elaborately elsewhere (Inikori 2002a, 156–214, 2007, 75–9).[10] There is no compelling reason to repeat the details here. A summary treatment will suffice.

[10] A large and growing literature on the subject, a sample of which is presented in footnote 9, provides direct and indirect support for the argument, empirically and logically.

The comparative per capita income of the free population in the British American colonies around 1774 testifies to the general economic predicament of New England and the mid-Atlantic region at the beginning of the last quarter of the eighteenth century: New England, £38.2; mid-Atlantic, £45.8; southern mainland, £92.7; West Indies, £1,200.00. Consistent with the economic data, demographic evidence shows unambiguously that New England was not attractive to European immigrants between 1680 and 1780, as it suffered a net loss of thirty-one thousand during the period (Engerman and Sokoloff 1997, 266). Only after the market opportunities created by the slave-based economies of the Americas had become sufficiently large for the mid-Atlantic and New England economies to extensively exploit their factor endowments were they able to break out of their subsistence production cul-de-sac and create the conditions for industrial take-off between the late eighteenth and the mid-nineteenth century. Douglass North's central argument, that "an analysis of the United States economic development must necessarily be put into the context of the expansion of the Atlantic economy,"[11] is hard to fault.

Once the factor endowments analysis is appropriately located within the evolving Atlantic economy, the main arguments become more intelligible. While large-scale production and specialization in the slave-based economies of the Americas were central to the expansion of Atlantic markets, on the basis of which revolutionary developments occurred in the economies of Old England and New England, the pattern of income distribution associated with the exploitation of slaves and the political economy that developed with it over time tended to impose limits on the long-run development of those economies. One major factor behind divergent developments in the northeastern United States and the slave-based plantation economies of the Americas was the relative economic and political power of large landholders. The overwhelming dominance of large landholders in the plantation economies led to state policies that favored free trade at the expense of industrialization. In contrast, the economic and political power of merchants, maritime shipping entrepreneurs, financiers, and incipient industrialists in the northeastern United States, relative to planters in the

[11] As North put it, in the 1830s, "it was cotton that initiated the concomitant expansion in income, in the size of domestic markets, and creation of the social overhead investment (in the course of its role in the marketing of cotton) in the Northeast which were to facilitate the subsequent rapid growth of manufactures.... [W]hen income from cotton exports, including shipments to textile mills in our own Northeast, grew from $25 million in 1831 to $70 million in 1836, it set in motion the whole process of accelerated expansion which culminated in 1839" (1961, 66–9, 68–9).

south, led to state policies that provided incentives for the development of manufacturing.[12] Ultimately, as stated earlier, industrialization set the United States apart from the rest of the Americas on the eve of World War I. The division of labor between industrial and nonindustrial economies in the global economic system of 1914 would continue to hold back progress in the nonindustrial economies for decades after the two world wars. But the preponderance of evidence makes it abundantly clear it cannot be reasonably argued that the slave-based economies of the Americas would have been better off in 1850 without the labor of enslaved Africans. On the contrary, the evidence shows beyond reasonable doubt that all the economies of the Americas benefited immensely from the employment of enslaved Africans in large-scale commodity production for Atlantic commerce. Paradoxically, as the evidence makes clear, the nonslave economies of North America benefited even more in the long run.

One important comparative insight generally overlooked in Kenneth Pomeranz's study of China strengthens this point further. The region of China with the greatest potential for industrialization in the nineteenth century, the Yangzi Delta, failed to realize its potential because the other provinces of China, with resource endowments similar to those of the northeastern United States, had no economic reason to develop complementary economies with the Yangzi Delta (Pomeranz 2000). Robert Allen's recent argument, similar to that of North cited earlier, is also pertinent. Writing about the contribution of coal energy to the Industrial Revolution, he says:

> We habitually describe coal as a "natural" resource. It is true that there would have been no coal trade had there been no coal in the ground. That much was a fact of nature. But the mere presence of coal was not sufficient to cause the coal trade. It was only activated by the growth of the international economy. Coal was a social artifact as well as a natural fact. (Allen 2009, 90)

Examining the reversal of fortune as it concerns West Africa, the first question we need to answer is whether the export of captives and the employment of those captives to produce commodities in the Americas for Atlantic commerce had adverse effects on the competitiveness of West Africa's economies in the development of commodity production for Atlantic commerce during the period. This is an important issue, because

[12] Those policies were unsuccessfully resisted by planters in the southern United States, whose short-term interests, like their counterparts in the rest of the Americas who successfully blocked them, favored free trading of primary commodities for imported manufactures from Europe.

global trade in products was one of the major factors in the commercializing process in West Africa up to the sixteenth century. The other factor was demography. The interaction between these factors gave rise to the process of enlargement of state systems (especially in the Niger Bend), which, in turn, supported the commercializing process, as we saw in the earlier part of this chapter.

As the evidence shows, trade in products derived from West Africa's labor and natural resources was dominant during the first two hundred years of European commercial enterprise in the region. Apart from Senegambia, most West African regions traded almost entirely in products. With all the needed caution in using the available data, the indication is that there was practically very little or no slave trading in Sierra Leone, the Windward Coast, the Gold Coast, and the Bight of Benin until the mid-seventeenth century (Eltis and Richardson 2008, 46–7, table 1.7). During this period, West Africa's Atlantic commerce in products grew steadily. In the late 1530s, a Portuguese official, writing about Portuguese trade in western Africa, declared:

> I do not know in this kingdom [Portugal] any yoke of land, toll, tithe, excise or any other royal tax which is more certain in each yearly return than is the revenue of the commerce of Guinea. It is, besides, so peaceful a property, quiet and obedient, that – without our having to stand at the touch-hole of the bombard with lighted match in one hand, and lance in the other – it yields us gold, ivory, wax, hides, sugar, pepper, and it would produce other returns if we sought to explore it further.[13]

It is significant that the Portuguese official did not mention revenue from slave trading. Clearly, this was not an oversight. From Senegambia to southeastern Nigeria, the product trade was overwhelmingly dominant – gold, hides and skins, ivory, and pepper (the main products from Senegambia through the Upper Guinea Coast to the Windward Coast); gold, the main product from the Gold Coast (southern modern Ghana); red pepper and cotton cloths, the main products from the Bight of Benin; ivory, the main product from southeastern Nigeria (Bight of Biafra).

The early focus of European traders on product trade reinforced the commercializing process in West Africa that was ongoing before the European contact. The hides and skins trade in the Upper Guinea Coast stimulated the growth of stock breeding and cattle trade, which enriched the Fulani cattle rearers economically and empowered them politically in the Futa Jallon plateau (Upper Guinea Coast) (Barry 1988, 38–9, 1992, 265, 289).

[13] Quoted in Vogt (1979, 93).

Ultimately, the focal point of the product trade from the mid-fifteenth to the mid-seventeenth century was the Gold Coast. The gold and kola trade had made the region a major part of the globalization process led by the Niger Bend merchant diaspora. Having no textile industry of its own, it was a major market for textiles from other parts of West Africa before European contact. Thus, a specialist in early Portuguese trade on the Gold Coast, John Vogt, noted:

> Despite a large population concentration on the Mina coast [Gold Coast] since a very early period, animal and vegetable fibers with which to weave cloth remained in short supply. The small quantities of fabric imported into the region from the Sudanese empires or from Nigeria before the Portuguese arrival brought high profits. However, this pre-European trade never fully satisfied local demands. When the Portuguese arrived at Mina in the late 1460s, they discovered that a ready market awaited them for any cloth that they wished to carry there. (Vogt 1979, 67)

Further expansion of the gold trade by European traders extended and intensified the preexisting trade links between the Gold Coast and other West African regions, especially the trading area of the powerful Benin kingdom (southwest Nigeria), which exported to the Gold Coast cotton textiles ("Benin cloth" in European records) partly produced locally, but largely procured from northeastern Yorubaland (Akintoye 1965, 544–6; Inikori 2009a, 92). The European traders entered this intra-West African trade as carriers during the sixteenth and early seventeenth century, raising the volume of the trade considerably and stimulating the growth of Benin's long-distance trade with its northeastern neighbors (Ryder 1965, 203–4). The multiplier effects of the general growth of trade in products in the Gold Coast region during the period created favorable conditions for the Akan merchants (referred to in European records as Akani or accanists) to invest their growing profits from trade in commercial agriculture aimed at the expanding domestic market that was fueled by the growth of urban centers (Kea 1982, 85–91; Wilks 1977). To meet the expanding labor needs of these developments, the Gold Coast imported labor from other regions of western Africa during the sixteenth century and the first half of the seventeenth century, with European traders as carriers (Kea 1982; Vogt 1979, 59–92; Wilks 1977). The general expansion of domestic trade and the deepening of the market economy in all regions of West Africa at this time is reflected in the ratio of currencies in the imports brought by the European traders of the period (Inikori 2007b).

Then came a radical shift of European traders' demand from products to captives as the growth of demand for captives to be enslaved in the Americas grew manifold from the mid-seventeenth century. From this time period, the Gold Coast was transformed from a region that imported labor to one that exported captives. Captives exported from the Gold Coast to the Americas in 1651–1700 were about and forty-three times (in number) those exported in the one hundred and fifty years from 1501 to 1650 (Eltis and Richardson 2008, 46–7, Table 1.7). This was a general phenomenon across all regions of West Africa, although it was more in some than in others. There is a general consensus among historians, consistent with the evidence, that demand drove this development. But there is some confusion concerning factors explaining supply.

For economic historians who believe the needs of European colonists in the Americas for coerced labor able to withstand the epidemiological environment of the region explain the growth of demand, what has to be explained is the generally low prices African suppliers were willing to accept, prices that, after adding transatlantic transportation cost, still made it economic to employ enslaved Africans to produce commodities in the Americas for Atlantic commerce. A political economy explanation appears the most logical and persuasive, particularly when presented in a global perspective. The operating factor in this explanation is political fragmentation that exposed communities without the protection of relatively strong states to capture (at little cost) by individuals or organized groups responding to export demand. Under such conditions, the main determinant of export prices was internal transportation and bulking cost, and the level of competition among the European exporters. The empirical evidence for this in western Africa is strong; it is also consistent with the evidence showing the operation of the same factor in the rise and demise of captive exports in Europe, the global perspective (Inikori 2003b).

A competing explanation is based on the productivity of agricultural labor in western Africa. As Manning argued, "prices were low because the low level of agricultural productivity [in western Africa] set by hoe agriculture limited the value of labor even when it was scarce" (Manning 1990, 21). Gareth Austin has recently elaborated the point. Austin's argument is nuanced and painstakingly articulated. But, in the end, Austin believes: "Relatively low labour productivity was a premise of the external slave trades [in sub-Saharan Africa]" (Austin 2008b, 996), the explanation for which rests with the physical environment that makes intensive agriculture virtually uneconomic (Austin 2007, 2008a, 2008b. 2009). This environmental argument, presented in different ways by other historians (Iliffe 1995), ignores the comparative case of the rise and demise of captive exports in Europe. No historian has argued, for example, that low labor productivity in agriculture or manufacturing explains captive exports from the British Isles during medieval times. What is more, it is not based on scientific collection and analysis of empirical evidence. Soil scientists, studying tropical agriculture across the globe, who have done that, draw contrary conclusions. Their data show that intensive agriculture based on a high input of purchased fertilizers in sub-Saharan Africa is a function of factor ratios (population to land ratios) and access to markets, and not the physical environment (Vanlauwe et al. 2002, 12, 38–9). As will be concluded later, the factor proportions and the level of development of markets for agricultural products resulted from the adverse effects of the transatlantic slave trade.

Placed in an Atlantic world history framework, there is enough evidence (some of which we presented earlier) to uphold the proposition that the transatlantic slave trade and African slavery in the Americas adversely affected the competitiveness of West Africa, relative to the Americas, in the production of commodities for Atlantic commerce. Clearly, labor productivity in the pre-Columbian Americas, whether in agriculture or manufacturing, was not higher than it was in West Africa of the same period. Given the evidence presented earlier, and other available evidence,[14] there is no reasonable basis to argue that the Americas could have outcompeted western Africa in the production of commodities for Atlantic commerce without the employment of enslaved Africans made available by the transatlantic slave trade. Had all of western Africa experienced the same levels of state enlargement and military organization that protected citizens against capture and export as the late medieval and early modern European states did – as also did some of the states that emerged in West Africa during the crisis of the transatlantic slave trade (such as the Futa Jallon Islamic state, the Asante state, the Dahomean state, and the earlier Benin state in Nigeria (Inikori 2003b)) – the Americas would have had no enslaved Africans to employ and West Africa would have continued to develop its production of commodities for Atlantic commerce that began in the mid-fifteenth century (Inikori 1992, 44–53).

The Gold Coast (modern southern Ghana) best illustrates the consequences of aborting the development of commodity production for Atlantic commerce and the substitution of captive exports. Urban development was reversed, as was the division of labor between town and country (Kea 1982, 11–32, 53–5, 85–91, 105–7, 136–68). Interregional trade between the Gold Coast and other West African regions was also adversely affected as the middlemen slave traders got European and Asian manufactures from the

[14] For more details, see Inikori (1992, 39–53).

European traders in direct barter exchange for captives, and turned the coastal societies into enclave economies, only violently connected to their hinterlands as sources for captives forcefully procured without commercial intercourse, in the first instance. This happened in all the West African regions as their hinterlands became victim sources of captives rather than suppliers of manufactures for the coastal societies (Inikori 2009a).

The addition of the demographic and political impact of captive exports largely accounts for the low level of market development and the limited geographical spread of the market economy in West Africa by the "long 1850" noted earlier. As a general order of magnitude, there is now enough evidence to uphold the inference that, but for the impact of the transatlantic slave trade, the population of West Africa would have been at least twice what it was in 1850 (Manning 1990, 85).[15] The research of soil scientists on tropical agriculture across the globe shows unambiguously that the agricultural resources of the region were more than adequate to support the additional population. After the considerable growth of population since 1850, the soil scientists still hold that:

> Although some areas are densely populated, the overall pressure on the land in sub-Saharan Africa is low and the application of inputs is minimal.... The use of inputs is higher where the crops are grown for export.... Although improved fallows work well in the humid tropics of Cameroon there is no demand for them as land is plentiful and fertility is yet to be depleted. (Vanlauwe et al. 2002, 12, 38–9)

Thus, the evidence presented here supports strongly the conclusion that the reversal of fortune established earlier, and the lowly position occupied by West Africa in the nineteenth-century Atlantic economy, resulted from the adverse effects of the transatlantic slave trade and African slavery in the Americas on the competitiveness of West Africa in commodity production for Atlantic commerce, together with the demographic and sociopolitical impact of captive exports in the region.

References

Acemoglu, Daron, Simon Johnson, and James A. Robinson. (2002). "Reversal of Fortune: Geography and Institutions in the Making of the Modern World Income Distribution." *Quarterly Journal of Economics*, 117: 1231–94.

[15] Manning's view that the sub-Saharan African population in 1850 would have been 100 million instead of 50 million is based on Curtin's figure of 11 million for the entire transatlantic captive exports. The new estimate of 12.5 million mentioned earlier would make Manning's view a conservative one.

(2005a). "Institutions as the Fundamental Cause of Long-Run Growth." In *Handbook of Economic Growth*, Volume 1A, edited by Philippe Aghion and Steven N. Durlauf, 385–472. Amsterdam: Elsevier.

Acemoglu, Daron, Simon Johnson, and James A Robinson. (2005b). "The 'Rise of Europe': Atlantic Trade, Institutional Change and Economic Growth." *American Economic Review*, 95: 546–79.

Akintoye, S. A. (1965). "The North-Eastern Yoruba Districts and the Benin Kingdom." *Journal of the Historical Society of Nigeria*, IV(4).

Allen, Robert C. (2009). *The British Industrial Revolution in Global Perspective*. Cambridge: Cambridge University Press.

Austin, Gareth. (2007). "Labour and Land in Ghana, 1874–1939: A Shifting Ratio and an Institutional Revolution." *Australian Economic History Review*, 47(1): 95–120.

(2008a). "Resources, Techniques, and Strategies South of the Sahara: Revising the Factor Endowments Perspective on African Economic Development, 1500–2000." *Economic History Review*, 61(3): 587–624.

(2008b). "The 'Reversal of Fortune' Thesis and the Compression of History: Perspectives from African and Comparative Economic History." *Journal of International Development*, 20: 996–1027.

(2009). "Cash Crops and Freedom: Export Agriculture and the Decline of Slavery in Colonial West Africa." *International Review of Social History*, 54: 1–37.

Bailyn, Bernard. (2005). *Atlantic History: Concept and Contours*. Cambridge, MA: Harvard University Press.

Bakewell, Peter. (1984). "Mining in Colonial Spanish America." In *Cambridge History of Latin America*, Vol. II, edited by Leslie Bethell. Cambridge: Cambridge University Press.

Bakewell, Peter and Jacqueline Holler. (2010). *A History of Latin America to 1825*. 3rd ed. Chichester, UK: Wiley-Blackwell.

Barickman, B. J. (1998). *A Bahian Counterpoint: Sugar, Tobacco, Cassava and Slavery in the Reconcavo, 1780–1860*. Stanford, CA: Stanford University Press.

Barry, Boubacar. (1988). *Senegambia and the Atlantic Slave Trade*. Cambridge: Cambridge University Press, 1998; original French edition, 1988.

(1992). "Senegambia from the Sixteenth to the Eighteenth Century: Evolution of the Wolof, Sereer and 'Tukuloor.'" In *General History of Africa, V: Africa from the Sixteenth to the Eighteenth Century*, edited by B. A. Ogot. Oxford, Berkeley, Paris: Heinemann, University of California Press, UNESCO.

Baudin, Louis. (1967). "The Inca Empire was Socialistic." In *History of Latin American Civilization: Sources and Interpretations, Volume 1: The Colonial Experience*, edited by Louis Hanke, 101–10. Boston, MA: Little, Brown & Company.

Benjamin, Thomas. (2009). *The Atlantic World: Europeans, Africans and Their Shared History, 1400–1900*. Cambridge: Cambridge University Press.

Borah, Woodrow Wilson and Sherburne F. Cook (1960). *The Aboriginal Population of Central Mexico in 1548*. Berkeley: University of California Press.

(1963). *The Aboriginal Population of Central Mexico on the Eve of the Spanish Conquest*. Berkeley: University of California Press.

Brooks, Francis J. (1993). "Revising the Conquest of Mexico: Smallpox, Sources, and Populations." *Journal of Interdisciplinary History*, XXIV(1): 1–29.

Bulmer-Thomas, Victor, John H. Coatsworth, and Roberto Cortes Conde, eds. (2006). *The Cambridge Economic History of Latin America, Volume I: The Colonial Period.* Cambridge: Cambridge University Press.

Burkholder, Mark A. and Lyman L. Johnson. (2004). *Colonial Latin America.* 5th ed. Oxford: Oxford University Press.

Canizares-Esguerra, Jorge and Erik R. Seeman, eds. (2007). *The Atlantic in Global History, 1500–2000.* Upper Saddle River, NJ: Pearson.

Carmack, Robert M. (1996). "Mesoamerica at Spanish Contact." In *The Legacy of Mesoamerica: History and Culture of a Native American Civilization*, edited by Robert M. Carmack, Janine Gasco, and Gary H. Gossen, 83–6. Upper Saddle River, NJ: Prentice Hall.

Carmack, Robert M., Janine Gasco, and Gary H. Gossen, eds. (1996). *The Legacy of Mesoamerica: History and Culture of a Native American Civilization.* Upper Saddle River, NJ: Prentice Hall.

Chase-Dunn, Christopher. (1980). "The Development of Core Capitalism in the Antebellum United States: Tariff Politics and Class Struggle in an Upwardly Mobile Semiperiphery." In *Studies of the Modern World System*, edited by Albert Bergesen. New York: Academic Press.

Cissoko, S. M. (1984). "The Songhay from the 12th to the 16th Century." In *General History of Africa, IV: Africa from the Twelfth to the Sixteenth Century*, edited by D. T. Niane, 187–210. London, California, Paris: Heinemann, University of California Press, UNESCO.

Coclanis, Peter A., ed. (2005). *The Atlantic Economy during the Seventeenth and Eighteenth Centuries: Organization, Operation, Practice, and Personnel.* Charleston: University of South Carolina Press.

(2007). "Reorienting Atlantic History: The Global Dimensions of the 'Western' Rice Trade." In *The Atlantic in Global History, 1500–2000*, edited by Jorge Canizares-Esguerra and Erik R. Seeman, 111–28. Upper Saddle River, NJ: Pearson.

Cook, Sherburne F. and Lesley B. Simpson. (1948). *The Population of Central Mexico in the Sixteenth Century.* Berkeley: University of California Press.

Davis, Ralph. (1967). *A Commercial Revolution: English Overseas Trade in the Seventeenth and Eighteenth Centuries.* London: Historical Association.

(1973). *The Rise of the Atlantic Economies.* London: Weidenfeld and Nicolson.

(1954). "English Foreign Trade, 1660–1700." *Economic History Review*, 2nd series, VI.

Denevan, William M., ed. (1976). *The Native Population of the Americas in 1492.* Madison: University of Wisconsin Press.

(1992). *The Native Population of the Americas in 1492*, 2nd ed. Madison: University of Wisconsin Press. 1st ed. 1976.

Diffie, Bailey W. (1945). *Latin American Civilization: Colonial Period.* Harrisburg, PA: Stackpole Sons.

Eltis, David, Frank D. Lewis, and Kenneth L. Sokoloff, eds. (2004). *Slavery in the Development of the Americas.* Cambridge: Cambridge University Press.

Eltis, David and David Richardson. (2004). "Prices of African Slaves Newly Arrived in the Americas, 1673–1865: New Evidence on Long-Run Trends and Regional Differentials." In *Slavery and the Development of the Americas*, edited by David

Eltis, Frank D. Lewis, and Kenneth L. Sokoloff. Cambridge: Cambridge University Press.

(2008). "A New Assessment of the Transatlantic Slave Trade." In *Extending the Frontiers: Essays on the New Transatlantic Slave Trade Database*, edited by David Eltis and David Richardson. New Haven, CT: Yale University Press.

Engerman, Stanley L. and Kenneth L. Sokoloff. (1997). "Factor Endowments, Institutions, and Differential Paths of Growth among New World Economies." In *How Latin America Fell Behind: Essays on Economic Histories of Brazil and Mexico, 1800–1914*, edited by Stephen Haber. Stanford, CA: Stanford University Press.

Hagen, Victor Wolfgang Von. (1961). *The Ancient Sun Kingdoms of the Americas: Aztec, Maya, Inca*. Cleveland, OH: The World Publishing Company.

Hanke, Lewis. ed. (1967). *History of Latin American Civilization: Sources and Interpretations, Volume 1: The Colonial Experience*. Boston, MA: Little, Brown & Company.

Hoberman, Louisa S. (1991). *Mexico's Merchant Elite, 1590–1660: Silver, State, and Society*. Durham, NC and London: Duke University Press.

Hogendorn, Jan. (2006). "Cowries." In *History of World Trade since 1450*, Volume 1, edited by John J. McCusker, 176–78. Farmington Hills, MI: Macmillan, Thompson Gale.

Hogendorn, Jan and Marion Johnson. (1986). *The Shell Money of the Slave Trade*. Cambridge: Cambridge University Press.

Hopkins, A. G. (2009). "The New Economic History of Africa." *Journal of African History*, 50(2): 155–77.

Hunwick, John O. (1999). *Timbuktu and the Songhay Empire: Al-Sadi's Ta'rikh al-sudan down to 1613 and other Contemporary Documents*. Leiden, Boston, Koln: Brill.

Iliffe, John. (1995). *Africans: The History of a Continent*. Cambridge: Cambridge University Press.

Inikori, Joseph E. (1979). "The Slave Trade and the Atlantic Economies, 1451–1870." In *The African Slave Trade from the Fifteenth to the Nineteenth Century*, 56–87. Paris: UNESCO.

(1986)."West Africa's Seaborne Trade, 1750–1850: Volume, Structure and Implications." In *Figuring African Trade: Proceedings of the Symposium on the Quantification and Structure of the Import and Export and Long Distance Trade in Africa in the 19th Century (C. 1800–1913), St. Augustin 3-6 January 1983*, edited by G. Liesegang, H. Pasch, and A. Jones. Berlin: Dietrich Reimer Verlag.

(1992). *The Chaining of a Continent: Export Demand for Captives and the History of Africa South of the Sahara, 1450–1870*. Kingston, Jamaica: Institute of Social and Economic Research, University of the West Indies, UNESCO Project.

Inikori, Joseph E. (2002a). *Africans and the Industrial Revolution in England: A Study in International Trade and Economic Development*. Cambridge: Cambridge University Press.

Inikori, Joseph E. (2002b). "The Development of Entrepreneurship in Africa: Southeastern Nigeria during the Era of the Trans-Atlantic Slave Trade." In *Black Business and Economic Power*, edited by Alusine Jalloh and Toyin Falola. Rochester, NY: University of Rochester Press.

(2003a). "The Known, the Unknown, the Knowable, and the Unknowable: Evidence and the Evaluation of Evidence in the Measurement of the Trans-Atlantic Slave Trade." In *Ghana in Africa and the World: Essays in Honor of Adu Boahen*, edited by Toyin Falola, 535–65. Trenton, NJ: Africa World Press.

Inikori, Joseph E. (2003b). "The Struggle against the Trans-Atlantic Slave Trade: The Role of the State." In *Fighting the Slave Trade: West African Strategies*, edited by Sylviane A. Diouf, 170–98. Athens: Ohio University Press.

Inikori, Joseph E. (2007a). "Africa and the Globalization Process: Western Africa, 1450–1850." *Journal of Global History*, 2(1): 63–85.

Inikori, Joseph E. (2007b). "Changing Commodity Composition of Imports into West Africa, 1650–1850: A Window into the Impact of the Transatlantic Slave Trade on African Societies." In *The Transatlantic Slave Trade: Landmarks, Legacies, Expectations: Proceedings of the International Conference on Historic Slave Route held at Accra, Ghana on 30 August - 2 September, 2004*, edited by James Kwesi Anquandah, 57–80. Accra: Sub-Saharan Publishers, 2007.

Inikori, Joseph E. (2008). "Africa and Globalization: Transition from the Atlantic Slave Trade to Commodity Production for Export in West Africa." Paper Presented at the Conference, Orb and Sceptre: Global and Imperial Histories, The European University Institute, Florence, May 14–16.

Inikori, Joseph E. (2009a). "English versus Indian Cotton Textiles: The Impact of Imports on Cotton Textile Production in West Africa." In *How India Clothed the World: The World of South Asian Textiles, 1500–1850*, edited by Giorgio Riello and Tirthankar Roy, 85–114. Leiden: Brill.

Inikori, Joseph E. (2009b). "Atlantic Perspectives on European Economic History, 1650–1850." Paper Presented at the XVth World Economic History Congress, Utrecht, Netherlands, August 3–7.

(2010). "West Africa's Niger Bend in Global Perspective, 1000–1591 C.E." Paper Presented at the American Historical Association Annual Meeting, San Diego, CA, January 7–10.

Johnson, Marion. (1970). "The Cowrie Currencies of West Africa." *Journal of African History*, XI, Parts I and II.

Katz, Friedrich. (1972). *The Ancient American Civilizations*. New York: Praeger, original German ed., Kindler Verlag, 1969.

Kea, Ray A. (1982). *Settlements, Trade, and Polities in the Seventeenth-Century Gold Coast*. Baltimore, MD: Johns Hopkins University Press.

Khan, B. Zorina and Kenneth L. Sokoloff. (1993). "'Schemes of Practical Utility': Entrepreneurship and Innovation among 'Great Inventors' in the United States, 1790–1865." *The Journal of Economic History*, 53(2): 289–307.

Lockhart, James and Stuart B. Schwartz. (1983). *Early Latin America: A History of Colonial Spanish America and Brazil*. Cambridge: Cambridge University Press.

Luna, Francisco Vidal and Herbert S. Klein. (2003). *The Evolution of the Slave Society and Economy of Sao Paulo, from the 1760s to the 1850s*. Stanford, CA: Stanford University Press.

(2004). "African Slavery in the Production of Subsistence Crops: The Case of Sao Paulo in the Nineteenth Century." In *Slavery in the Development of the Americas*, edited by David Eltis, Frank D. Lewis, and Kenneth L. Sokoloff, 120–49. Cambridge: Cambridge University Press.

Maddison, Angus. (2001). *The World Economy: A Millennial Perspective*. Paris: Organisation for Economic Co-Operation and Development.

(2003). *The World Economy Historical Statistics*. Paris: Organisation for Economic Co-Operation and Development.

Mancke, Elizabeth and Carole Shammas, eds. (2005). *The Creation of the British Atlantic World*. Baltimore, MD: Johns Hopkins University Press.

Manning, Patrick. (1990). *Slavery and African Life: Occidental, Oriental, and African Slave Trades*. Cambridge: Cambridge University Press.

(2006). "African Connections with American Colonization." In *The Cambridge Economic History of Latin America, Volume I: The Colonial Period*, edited by Victor Bulmer-Thomas, John H. Coatsworth, and Roberto Cortes Conde, 43–71. Cambridge: Cambridge University Press.

McCusker, John J. and Russell R. Menard. (1985). *The Economy of British America, 1607–1789*. Chapel Hill: University of North Carolina Press.

McCusker, John J. and Kenneth Morgan, eds. (2000). *The Early Modern Atlantic Economy*. Cambridge: Cambridge University Press.

McIntosh, Roderick James. (1998). *The Peoples of the Middle Niger: The Island of Gold* Oxford: Blackwell.

(2005). *Ancient Middle Niger: Urbanism and the Self-Organizing Landscape*. Cambridge: Cambridge University Press.

(2008). "Before Timbuktu: Cities of the Elder World." In *The Meanings of Timbuktu*, edited by Shamil Jeppie and Souleymane Bachir Diagne. Cape Town, South Africa: HSRC Press.

Metraux, Alfred. (1967). "Despotism or Socialism?" In *History of Latin American Civilization: Sources and Interpretations, Volume 1: The Colonial Experience*, edited by Louis Hanke, 110–18. Boston, MA: Little, Brown & Company.

Moraes Farias de, P. F. (2003). *Arabic Medieval Inscriptions from the Republic of Mali: Epigraphy, Chronicles, and Songhay-Tuareg History*. Oxford: Oxford University Press.

Niane, D. T. (1984a). "Mali and the Second Mandingo Expansion." In *General History of Africa, IV: Africa from the Twelfth to the Sixteenth Century*, edited by D. T. Niane, 117–71. London, California, Paris: Heinemann, University of California Press, UNESCO.

(1984b). "Relationships and Exchanges among the Different Regions." In *General History of Africa, IV: Africa from the Twelfth to the Sixteenth Century*, edited by D. T. Niane, 614–34. London, California, Paris: Heinemann, University of California Press, UNESCO.

(1984c). "Conclusion." In *General History of Africa, IV: Africa from the Twelfth to the Sixteenth Century*, edited by D. T. Niane, 673–86. London, California, Paris: Heinemann, University of California Press, UNESCO.

Newson, Linda A. (1985). "Indian Population Patterns in Colonial Spanish America." *Latin American Research Review*, XX: 41–74.

Newson, Linda A. (2006). "The Demographic Impact of Colonization." In *The Cambridge Economic History of Latin America, Volume I: The Colonial Period*, edited by V. Bulmer-Thomas, John H. Coatsworth, and Roberto Cortes Conde, 143–84. Cambridge: Cambridge University Press.

North, Douglass C. (1961). *The Economic Growth of the United States, 1790–1860*. New York: W. W. Norton, 1966, first published by Prentice Hall, 1961.

North, Douglass C. (1965). "Industrialization in the United States." In *The Cambridge Economic History of Europe*, Vol. VI Part II, edited by H. J. Habakkuk and M. Postan. Cambridge: Cambridge University Press.

Nunn, Nathan. (2007). "Historical Legacies: A Model Linking Africa's Past to Its Current Underdevelopment." *Journal of Development Economics*, 83(1): 157–75.

(2008). "The Long Term Effects of Africa's Slave Trades." *Quarterly Journal of Economics*, 123(1): 139–76.

Nunn, Nathan and Leonard Wantchekon. (2011). "The Slave Trade and the Origins of Mistrust in Africa." *American Economic Review*, 101: 3221–52.

O'Rourke, Kevin H. and Jeffrey G. Williamson. (1999). *Globalization and History: The Evolution of a Nineteenth-Century Atlantic Economy*. Cambridge, MA: MIT Press.

Pomeranz, Kenneth. (2000). *The Great Divergence: China, Europe, and the Making of the Modern World Economy*. Princeton, NJ: Princeton University Press.

Prados de la Escosura, Leandro. (2006). "The Economic Consequences of Independence." In *The Cambridge Economic History of Latin America, Volume I: The Colonial Period*, edited by V. Bulmer-Thomas, John H. Coatsworth, and Roberto Cortes Conde, 463–504. Cambridge: Cambridge University Press.

Ryder, A. F. C. (1965). "Dutch Trade on the Nigerian Coast during the Seventeenth Century." *Journal of the Historical Society of Nigeria*, III(2).

Shepherd, James F. and Gary M. Walton. (1972). *Shipping, Maritime Trade, and the Economic Development of Colonial North America*. Cambridge: Cambridge University Press.

Sokoloff, Kenneth L. (1988). "Inventive Activity in Early Industrial America: Evidence from Patent Records, 1790–1846." *The Journal of Economic History*, XLVIII(4): 813–50.

Sokoloff, Kenneth L. and B. Zorina Khan. (1990). "The Democratization of Invention during Early Industrialization: Evidence from the United States, 1790–1846." *The Journal of Economic History*, L(2): 363–78.

Solow, Barbara L., ed. (1991). *Slavery and the Rise of the Atlantic System*. Cambridge: Cambridge University Press.

Storey, Rebecca and Randolph J. Widmer. (2006). "The Pre-Columbian Economy." In *The Cambridge Economic History of Latin America, Volume I: The Colonial Period*, edited by Victor Bulmer-Thomas, John H. Coatsworth, and Roberto Cortes Conde, 73–106. Cambridge: Cambridge University Press.

Tandeter, Enrique. (2006). "The Mining Industry." In *The Cambridge Economic History of Latin America, Volume I: The Colonial Period*, edited by Victor Bulmer-Thomas, John H. Coatsworth, and Roberto Cortes Conde. Cambridge: Cambridge University Press.

Taussig, Michael. (1977). "The Evolution of Rural Wage Labour in the Cauca Valley of Colombia, 1700–1970." In *Land and Labour in Latin America: Essays on the Development of Agrarian Capitalism in the Nineteenth and Twentieth Centuries*, edited by Kenneth Duncan and Ian Rutledge. Cambridge: Cambridge University Press.

Theberge, James D., ed. (1968). *Economics of Trade and Development*. New York: John Wiley.

Trigger, Bruce G. and Wilcomb E. Washburn, eds. (1996). *The Cambridge History of the Native Peoples of the Americas: Volume I, North America*, Part 1. Cambridge: Cambridge University Press.

Vanlauwe, B., J. Diels, N. Sanginga, and R. Merckx, eds. (2002). *Integrated Plant Nutrient Management in Sub-Saharan Africa: From Concept to Practice*. New

York: CABI Publishing in Association with the International Institute of Tropical Agriculture.

Vogt, John. (1979). *Portuguese Rule on the Gold Coast, 1469–1682*. Athens: University of Georgia Press.

Watts, David. (1987). *The West Indies: Patterns of Development, Culture and Environmental Change since 1492*. Cambridge: Cambridge University Press.

Wilks, Ivor. (1977). "Land, Labour, Capital and the Forest Kingdom of Asante: A Model of Early Change." In *The Evolution of Social Systems*, edited by J. Friedman and M. J. Rowlands. London: Duckworth.

3

The Impact of Malaria on African Development over the *Longue Durée*

David N. Weil

An extensive literature examines the impact of disease generally, and malaria in particular, on economic development in the world today. Malaria is especially a focus in Africa because of the high prevalence of the disease. There are some 300 million malaria cases annually on the continent, and it is the leading cause of under-five mortality. A widely quoted estimate is that malaria reduces growth of GDP per capita by 1.3% per year in the African countries most afflicted (Gallup and Sachs, 2001). Africa is also the historical home of malaria, and the region with a physical environment most supportive of the disease.

In this chapter, I ask how malaria influenced economic development in Africa in the period before European contact. In particular, I ask whether malaria played a role in holding back African development and whether malaria shaped the geographic pattern of development. Knowing the role of malaria is part of the much larger project of understanding the determinants for Africa's early development in comparison to other parts of the world and also understanding heterogeneity within the continent itself.

Answering the question I pose requires overcoming a number of very serious obstacles. The first is the the absence of data. How prevalent was malaria in Africa? Was it more or less important, in either absolute terms or relative to other diseases, than it is today? Our understanding of the role played by malaria in the contemporary world relies on data generated by government statistical agencies and NGOs as well as on field surveys by

David_Weil@Brown.edu. I am grateful to Fred Piel, Ronald D. Lee, Andrew Mason, and Gordon McCord for sharing data; to Emilio Depetris Chauvin, Federico Droller, Evan Friedman, and Scott Weiner for research assistance; and to Quamrul Ashraf, seminar participants at Indiana University and Pennsylvania State University, and participants at the Weatherhead Center for International Economics conference on "Understanding African Poverty in the Longue Durée" for helpful comments.

trained professionals. Even modern doctors cannot accurately differentiate malarial illness from numerous other tropical maladies without using microscopes or rapid diagnostic tests. No statistical compilations exist from the period before Europeans started coming to Africa, and what textual sources are available do not provide sufficient information to make a serious quantitative analysis.

Much of the contribution of this paper lies in trying to overcome this first obstacle, that is, to measure the extent of malaria in the pre-European period. Although there are no paper records, malaria left a lasting imprint in human genes that can be interpreted in order to gauge the extent of the disease. Specifically, I look at the prevalence of the gene that causes sickle cell disease. Individuals who carried one copy of this gene were afforded a significant measure of protection against malaria, but those who carried two copies died before reaching reproductive age. The equilibrium prevalence of the gene therefore depended on how severe the selective pressure of malaria was – more concretely, on the fraction of children who didn't carry the gene who died from malaria before adulthood. One can thus infer the severity of malaria from the prevalence of the sickle cell gene in modern populations. I carry out such calculations, and construct estimates of the severity of malaria in Africa in the period before European contact. I find that in the more afflicted regions, malaria lowered the probability of surviving to adulthood by about ten percentage points. The reduction in the rate of malaria mortality over the last 500 years has been of approximately the same magnitude as the reduction in mortality from other causes.

Even with an estimate of malaria's health impact in the pre-contact period, establishing how malaria affected African economic development is no easy matter. As will be seen below, economists do not agree on how malaria affects economic growth today, despite far superior knowledge of the extent of the disease, data on the productivity of workers who are ill or healthy, and concrete information on the functioning of the economy. Thus an assessment of how malaria affected African economic development 500 years ago is necessarily highly speculative. I use simple economic models and modern data to explore two channels through which malaria might have affected growth: through loss of life (mortality) and through its effect on the productivity of workers and the learning ability of children (morbidity). I find relatively little evidence that malaria would have had a very significant effect on economic outcomes through either of these channels. Because malaria mortality is concentrated among the very young, the cost to society from malaria deaths is not large. In the case of morbidity, we know from modern data that the burden of malaria among adults is relatively light compared to other conditions. It is also notable that some of the areas of highest development prior to European contact, such as West Africa and the Niger Bend, had environments that were especially supportive of malaria transmission.

The rest of this paper is organized as follows. In Section 13.1, I paint a picture of the level of development in Africa prior to the arrival of Europeans, using a variety of indicators. I also discuss different theories about the factors that influenced early development in Africa, with a focus on the role of disease. Section 13.2 discusses the impact of malaria today and the biology of the relationship between malaria and the sickle cell trait. In Section 13.3, I construct estimates of the historical burden of malaria, based on current prevalence of the sickle cell trait. Section 13.4 turns to an examination of the potential economic impact of the malaria burden estimated in the previous section. Section 13.5 concludes.

3.1 AFRICAN ECONOMIC GROWTH OVER THE *LONGUE DURÉE*

I begin with an examination of variation in the level of development, comparing Africa to the rest of the world as well as looking at variation within Africa itself. There is of course no single measure that summarizes the state of economic development, and there are notable problems with all of the data that are available. I thus look at a variety of indicators. I take as my point of reference the year 1500, at least to the extent that this is practical, to assess Africa's standing prior to interaction with Europeans.

3.1.1 Population Density

The first measure I examine is population density. Density can be used, within reason, as a measure of technological development of societies that are living close to subsistence, which is a fair characterization of pretty much the entire world during the period of interest. According to a simple Malthusian model (see discussion in Section 3.4.1), countries with more advanced agricultural technologies will not have better fed people, just more of them. Within a given country, changes in population density over time are a good measure of technological change (Kremer 1993).

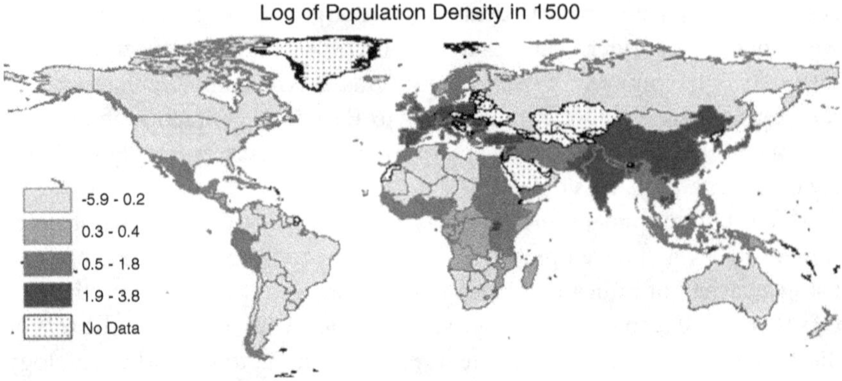

Figure 3.1. Population density in 1500.

Figure 3.1 shows a measure of population density. The data are from McEvedy and Jones (1978). The data have been mapped to the borders of current countries, most of which did not exist at the time. The map divides the countries into four groups of equal size (the underlying data are in the appendix to this chapter). The figure shows that the highest levels of population density were in the parts of Eurasia generally viewed as the most developed: Europe and Turkey, South Asia, China, Japan, and Indonesia. The second densest group of countries includes the Middle East, the Aztec, Maya, and Inca empires, and Egypt. Within sub-Saharan Africa, the countries that fall within this group include a large swathe of West Africa, and East Africa from Ethiopia and Sudan to Tanzania. Central Africa makes up most of the third most dense group, while the fourth most dense group is composed of the Americas (with the exceptions of the areas mentioned earlier), Australia, the countries of the Sahara, and the southern part of the African continent.

3.1.2 Land Quality

One obvious problem with using population density to measure the extent of development is that land quality may vary. For a given level of agricultural technology, population density will be higher, the more productive is the agricultural environment. Thus density will not be a good measure of the level of agricultural technology. To address this issue, I use data on the suitability of land for agriculture data from Ramankutty and colleagues (2002), which is in turn constructed from high-resolution data sets for croplands, climate, and soil characteristics. Their index represents the probability that a particular 0.5-degree grid cell (about 50 x 50 km at the equator) may be cultivated. Thus, each grid cell observation takes a value between zero and one. The authors assume that land suitability for cultivation is a function only of climate (temperature, precipitation, and potential sunshine hours) and soil properties (total organic components measured by carbon density and nutrient availability based on soil pH). Other biophysical and socio-economic factors such as topography and irrigation or market price and incentive structure are omitted. It is important to note that the index does not account for the productivity of a particular piece of land, but simply whether the characteristics of the land are favorable for crop cultivation. To give some sense of what these data look like, within the United States, the Midwest region has a mean of 0.77, the South 0.54, the Northeast 0.38, and the West (which includes Alaska) 0.22. The country with the highest value in the world is Uruguay, at 0.95. Within Africa, the highest levels of average land quality are found in Malawi (0.77), Lesotho (0.69), and Tanzania (0.64). The full set of values is available in the appendix.

To estimate the density of population conditional on the quality of land, I regress the country-level population density measures described previously on average land quality and the within-country variance of land quality. The results are shown in Table 3.1. I experiment with using both the level and the logarithm of population density as the dependent variable, although this seems to make little difference. The first and fourth columns of the results show mean density by continent, relative to Africa, which is the omitted category. Europe and Asia have significantly higher density, while Oceana and the Americas have lower densities. The second and fifth columns show that land quality has significant predictive power for population density. However, as the third and sixth columns show, adjusting for land quality has only a small effect on the continental measures of density.

3.1.3 Urbanization

Beyond population, a related measure of development over long historical periods is urbanization. The presence of large cities is taken as an indicator of the existence of a significant agricultural surplus, a developed transportation infrastructure, and/or an effective ruling entity. Cities served as loci for development in industry and knowledge. Finally, by their nature, cities are relatively well observed by contemporary travelers and historians.

Table 3.1. *Cross-country regressions for population density in 1500*

Independent	Pop density in 1500			Log of pop density in 1500		
Variables	(1)	(2)	(3)	(4)	(5)	(6)
Mean of Land Quality		9.440***	7.554***		1.682***	1.396***
		(2.22)	(1.95)		(0.56)	(0.50)
Variance of Land Quality		41.27**	28.12**		5.004	3.061
		(19.02)	(12.25)		(4.27)	(3.01)
Asia	6.578***		5.882***	1.153***		1.032***
	(2.09)		(1.94)	(0.27)		(0.24)
Europe	10.72***		9.265***	1.485***		1.248***
	(2.44)		(2.19)	(0.33)		(0.28)
Oceania	−2.515***		−3.088***	−1.949*		−2.016**
	(0.78)		(0.73)	(1.01)		(0.95)
America	−2.066***		−2.423***	−0.860***		−0.929***
	(0.69)		(0.88)	(0.27)		(0.28)
Constant	3.157***	0.436	−0.306	0.543***	−0.103	−0.0309
	(0.69)	(0.64)	(0.89)	(0.16)	(0.18)	(0.22)
Observations	145	145	145	145	145	145
R-squared	0.316	0.141	0.396	0.361	0.113	0.43

Robust standard errors in parentheses.
*** p<0.01, ** p<0.05, * p<0.1.

Table 3.2. *World city sizes by region in 1500*

	Sub-Saharan Africa	North Africa	Asia	Europe	N. America	S. America
20,000–49,999	22	17	28	78	19	4
50,000–199,999	2	3	58	19	4	2
200,000+	0	1	8	0	0	0

Source: See text.

I use a newly constructed database that combines data from six sources (although some borrow from others): Bairoch, Batou, and Chevre (1988), Chandler (1987), De Vries (1984), Eggimann (2000), Modelski (2003), and Rozenblat, Lennert, and Van Hamme (2011). The data are on population for historical cities, matched with their locations. I use data on all available cities in the year 1500.

Table 3.2 shows a breakdown of city sizes for the world as a whole. I divide Africa into sub-Saharan and northern regions. Figure 3.2 shows the geographic distributions of cities in Africa in 1500. By this metric, early development in Africa is strongly concentrated in the west of the continent: Mali, Niger, Burkina Faso, and most of all Nigeria. Outside this region,

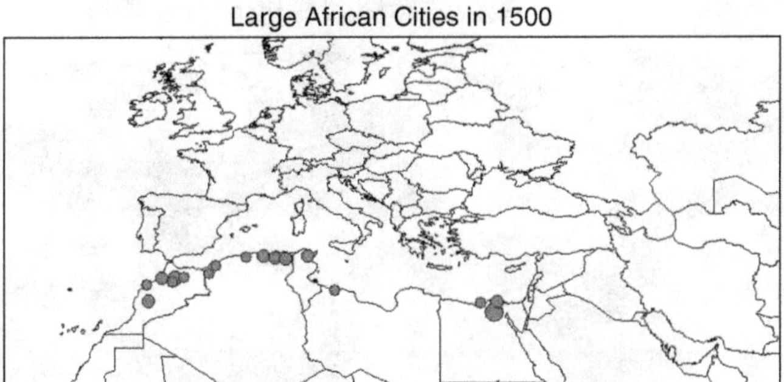

Figure 3.2. Distribution of cities in Africa in 1500.

extraordinarily few cities appear. Overall, the level of urbanization in Africa is similar to that of North America (where all but one city is in present-day Mexico or Guatemala). North Africa has roughly the same level of urbanization as sub-Saharan Africa (although in a much smaller area), while Europe has a significantly higher level and Asia higher still.

3.1.4 State Antiquity

While cities are an indirect measure of the existence of state power, one can also try to look at this dimension of development directly. Chanda and Putterman (2007) present an index of "state antiquity" that attempts to measure the degree of a country's political development. For every fifty-year period between the years 1 CE and 1500 CE, a country is awarded a score based on three factors: the existence of a government at a supratribal level, the proportion of the current territory of the country that the

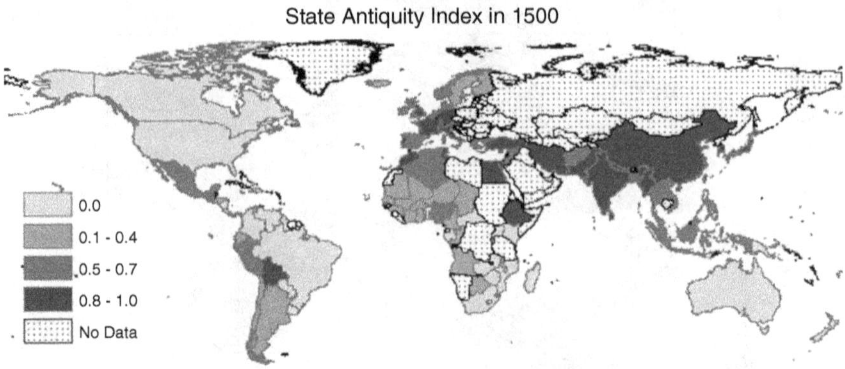

Figure 3.3. State history in 1500.

government controlled, and whether the government was indigenous or externally imposed. These half-century scores are then aggregated for the full fifteen-hundred-year period. The underlying sources for Chanda and Putterman's data are country entries in *Encyclopaedia Britannica*. Putterman and Weil (2010) show that the Chanda and Putterman index is a good predictor of modern economic development. One disadvantage of this data relative to other measures presented here is that rather than looking at a single point in time, it aggregates information from a millennium and a half. Further, to the extent that available documentary sources are slanted toward coverage of currently developed countries, the index will be similarly biased.

The data are presented in Figure 3.3, again broken down into four country groups – see the appendix for the underlying data. The highest group for this measure includes a broad arc in Asia from Japan and China through Iran, Turkey, Western Europe with the exception of Spain and Ireland, Bolivia, Peru, and, on the African continent, Egypt, Morocco, Tunisia, and Ethiopia. The second group includes much of Southeast Asia and Scandinavia, Mexico, Nigeria, Cameroon, Ghana, Botswana, and several states in the Sahara. The third group includes most of the rest of West Africa, while the lowest group in terms of state development includes America north of Mexico, the Amazon basin, Southern Africa, Australia, and New Zealand. It is also important to note that there are good number of countries for which there is no information at all for this index, although presumably there is a bias toward these being countries with relatively undeveloped states that left behind few records.

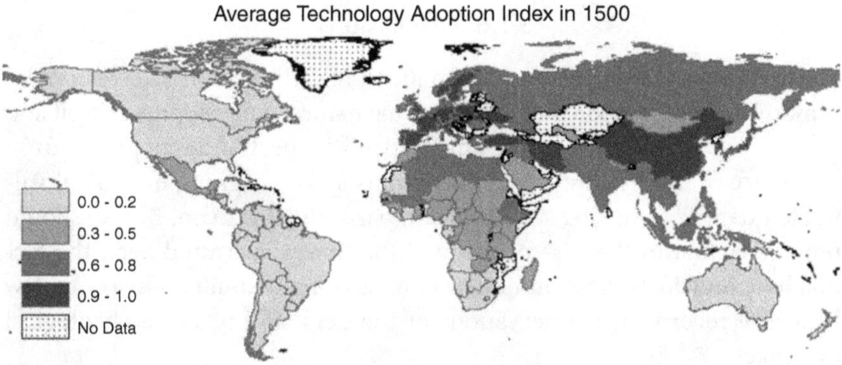

Figure 3.4. Technology in 1500.

3.1.5 Technology

As a final measure of development, I look directly at production technology. While observing actual quantities of production at a lag of five hundred years is close to impossible, historical sources are better suited to determine whether a particular piece of technology was used in a given area. Figure 3.4 shows an index of technology adoption in 1500, created by Comin, Easterly, and Gong (2010). Again, the underlying values are in the appendix. The index is an aggregate of five sub-indices in the areas of communications, agriculture, military, industry, and transportation. For example, in the agriculture sub-index, a country gets a score of four if the primary form of subsistence is plow cultivation, three if it is hand cultivation, two if it is pastoralism, and one if it is hunting and gathering.[1] In the transportation sub-index, points are awarded for possession of the wheel, horse-powered vehicles, the magnetic compass, and ships capable of crossing the Indian, Atlantic, and Pacific oceans.

The highest values in the technology index are those given to Japan, China, Turkey, and almost all of Europe. The second highest group includes South and Southeast Asia, the Middle East and North Africa, Ethiopia, Nigeria, Mali, and Burkina Faso. Most of the rest of Africa is in the third highest technology group, along with Mexico, Nepal, and Mongolia. The rest of the Americas, Australia, New Zealand, New Guinea, Botswana, and Namibia make up the lowest group.

1 However, Hopkins (1973) argues that environmental conditions made West Africa unsuitable to animal-powered plow agriculture. Thus the nonuse of plows is not necessarily a measure of available technology.

3.1.6 Discussion

The use of a variety of perspectives to measure early economic development is motivated both by the multidimensional nature of development itself and by the difficulties of measuring any particular aspect of development from a distance of five hundred years. Economists like assigning numerical values to quantities, making statistical comparisons, and so on. But we should remember that in the case of many of the things measured here, the factual base on which these numerical comparisons are built consists of a few historical records, the observations of travelers, and bits of archeological evidence.

Subject to these caveats, the overall picture painted by these data shows, first, a great deal of heterogeneity of development within Africa. Ignoring North Africa, which was generally part of the Mediterranean world, the highest levels of development by many indicators are found in Ethiopia (also relatively isolated geographically and culturally from much of the rest of the continent) and in the broad swathe of West African countries running from Cameroon and Nigeria eastward along the coast and the Niger River. In this latter region, the available measures show a level of development just below or sometimes equal to that in the belt of Eurasia running from Japan and China, through South Asia and the Middle East, into Europe. Depending on the index used, West Africa was above or below the level of development in the Northern Andes and Mexico. Much of the rest of Africa was at a significantly lower level of development, although still more advanced than the bulk of the Americas or Australia.

Several theories have been proposed to explain Africa's level of development on the eve of the modern era. Many of these have focused on sources of low agricultural productivity, which in turn prevented the accumulation of surpluses that could support urbanization, specialization, and technological advance. Diamond (1997) stresses the availability of plants and animals that could be easily domesticated (for example, sub-Saharan Africa had only four large seeded grasses that could be developed for cultivation compared to thirty-nine in Eurasia), and also the absence of Africa of a single large agro-climactic zone over which food production technologies could be shared. Other authors stress the impediments to agricultural productivity in tropical zones, including periods of torrential rain, leading to erosion of cultivated soil, and the absence of a temperate zone pattern of seasonal sunlight, which encourages development of easily stored seeds. Masters and McMillan (2001) point to the absence of frost, called "nature's great executioner" for its role in suppressing agricultural pests. Webb (2006) describes

West Africa as characterized by poor soils and low caloric yields from the principal grain crops. Looking beyond agricultural productivity, Gallup, Sachs, and Mellinger (1999) argue that African development was held back by lack of ocean-navigable rivers penetrating the continent and the location of population centers away from coastal lowlands, both of which impeded the development of waterborne trade.

Among the theories proposed to explain Africa's relatively low level of development, several authors have pointed to the continent's severe disease environment. As the historical cradle of humanity, African organisms that found humans to be congenial hosts had a significant head start over those in other parts of the world. Humans who migrated out of Africa left many of their parasites behind. In particular, two of the most significant tropical diseases, malaria and yellow fever, did not make the jump from Africa to the Americas until Europeans started sailing between the two areas (McNeill, 1977). Gallup, Sachs, and Mellinger (1999) find that beyond the expected effect of tropical location in predicting disease intensity, there is a further effect particular to sub-Saharan Africa. Discussions of the role of disease in shaping African development generally focus on two diseases in particular: malaria and trypanosomiasis (sleeping sickness). Webb (2006) describes these as the two "most significant of the microparasitic infections that influenced human settlement patterns and culture."

As discussed in Akyeampong (2006), much of our knowledge of health in Africa comes from accounts of travelers. Arab chronicler Al-Bakri, who wrote during the eleventh century, described a large town in northern Ghana as an area "where the inhabitants have yellow complexions because they suffer from fever and splenetis. There is hardly one who does not complain of one or the another." An enlarged spleen is a symptom of chronic malaria.

However, the theory that the health environment in Africa was particularly bad is not universally accepted. Premodern society was not healthy in any part of the world. People living in temperate zones, though freed from tropical parasites, faced many other health challenges brought on by climate, including nutritional deficiencies, diseases spread by being indoors, and diseases that made the jump from livestock with whom people were forced to share living quarters. Mabogunje and Richards (1985) point out that European travelers who described Africa's harsh disease environment may have been overly influenced by the terrible toll disease took on their own cohorts (who had none of the immunity acquired by Africans as children) as well as by the effects of new pathogens introduced by Europeans themselves. They conclude: "The grounds for supposing tropical Africa was any more badly affected by epidemic diseases in the past than, say, western Europe or North America are yet to be established."

3.2 MALARIA

3.2.1 The Impact of Malaria Today

In the World Health Organization AFRO region, which roughly corresponds to Africa south of the Sahara, in 2004 the annual death rate from malaria for children under five was 0.59 percent per year, implying that roughly 3 percent of children would die of malaria before their fifth birthday. Malaria accounted for 15.8 percent of the total mortality burden in this age group. Malaria deaths are highly concentrated among the young. After age five, people who live in malaria endemic areas have developed partial immunity to the disease (the exception is pregnant women, particularly women in their first pregnancy, who lose their immunity). Among people aged fifteen to twenty-nine, for example, the death rate from malaria was just 0.006 percent per year, and only 1.2 percent of deaths were due to malaria (Mathers, Fat, and Boerma 2008).

Beyond its effect on mortality, malaria also exacts a cost in terms of ill health and low productivity among those who survive. Table 3.3A shows data on the incidence, prevalence, and average duration of malaria in sub-Saharan Africa. Incidence is the number of cases per year, while prevalence is the fraction of the population that has the condition at any point in time. In the zero to four age group, there is an average of more than one case per child per year. Among adults, however, only 17.5 percent of individuals are afflicted each year, and because of the short duration of episodes, less than a quarter of one percent of individuals are ill at the average point in time.

Table 3.3B shows similar data for the neurological sequelae of childhood malaria. A small fraction of children who recover from cerebral malaria suffer from lifelong brain damage, including epilepsy, spasticity, and learning disabilities. Because the condition lasts a lifetime, the prevalence of these symptoms among the adult population is actually higher than the prevalence of episodic malaria.

Economic effects resulting from malaria may follow many channels. The direct effect is that adults are unable to work during episodes of the disease, and may be significantly weakened for a period afterward. Repeated infection with malaria is associated with anemia in children and adults. There are also effects on the human capital accumulation of children. Beyond the obvious effects in cases of neurological sequelae, children who suffer from

Table 3.3A. *Malaria episodes*

Age	Incidence (per 100,000)	Prevalence (per 100,000)	Average duration (years)	Death rate (per 100,000)
0–4	120,000	1,644	0.01	559
5–14	17,500	240	0.01	42
15–44	17,500	240	0.01	33
45–59	17,500	240	0.01	36

Source: Murray and Lopez (1996).

Table 3.3B. *Malaria – Neurological Sequelae*

Age	Incidence (per 100,000)	Prevalence (per 100,000)	Average duration (years)	Death rate (per 100,000)
0–4	164	365	37.1	0
5–14	0	701	–	–
15–44	0	617	–	–
45–59	0	474	–	–

Source: Murray and Lopez (1996).

malaria have reduced cognitive functioning and increased absenteeism from school. High childhood mortality from the disease may also induce parents to plan for extra births, and consequently invest fewer resources in each surviving child. Malaria may also affect the seasonal and spatial pattern of economic activity. Gallup and Sachs (2001) give examples of regions in Europe that were largely uninhabited prior to the eradication of malaria, and became productive agricultural regions afterward. The need to shift the harvest cycle away from seasons in which malaria is most prevalent may alter the distribution of crops that farmers plant away from those that would otherwise be the most profitable. Malaria also occasions direct use of resources. In heavily burdened countries, up to 40 percent of public health expenditures, 30–50 percent of inpatient hospital admissions, and 60 percent of outpatient health clinic visits are attributable to malaria (Aregawi 2010).

The overall magnitude of these economic effects of malaria is the subject of contentious debate. Most famously, the Abuja declaration of 2005, signed by fifty-three African heads of state claimed that "malaria has slowed economic growth in African countries by 1.3% per year as a result of which GDP for African countries is now 37% lower than it would have been in the absence of malaria." This conclusion is based largely on cross-country regression studies, particularly Gallup and Sachs (2001). Ashraf, Lester, and Weil (2008) argue that this sort of regression suffers from severe identification problems. Instead, they use a simulation model with key parameters based on well-identified microeconomic studies. Their conclusion is that eliminating malaria in sub-Saharan Africa would increase income per capita by a total of only 2 percent, with that benefit taking more than half a century to arrive.[2]

3.2.2 Malaria and Sickle Cell Disease

Malaria is caused by the plasmodium parasite, which is transmitted to humans through the bite of a female anopheles mosquito. Within the human body, the parasite follows a complex life cycle. In part of that cycle, plasmodium merozoites invade and multiply within the body's red blood cells, which eventually burst and release merozoites to infect new cells. Early symptoms of malaria include fever, chills, severe headache, and vomiting. In severe cases, these are followed by respiratory distress, severe anemia, or cerebral malaria. Infants are protected from the disease in the first few months of life by a combination of maternal antibodies and characteristics of the structure of fetal hemoglobin. In malaria endemic areas, most children have developed substantial immunity by the age of five.

Four types of malaria infect humans, of which the two most common are *Plasmodium falciparum* and *Plasmodium vivax*. *P. falciparum* is the most deadly. Africa accounts for 85 percent of world malaria cases and 90 percent of world malaria deaths. The geographical pattern of malaria's severity is largely determined by the climactic conditions that support mosquito breeding as well as by the mix of mosquito species present. There are significant differences in the vectorial capacity among the approximately twenty species of *anopheles* that transmit malaria, based on factors such as the mosquito's preferred targets, biting frequency, and lifespan. The most effective vector, *Anopheles gambiae*, is the principal vector in Africa.

Kiszewski and colleagues (2004) construct an index of "malaria ecology" that takes into account both climactic factors and the dominant vector species to give an overall measure of how congenial the environment is to the spread of malaria. The index does not take into account public health interventions such as swamp draining or differences among countries in economic development or health care infrastructure. In other words, it

[2] See Weil (2010) for a review of this literature.

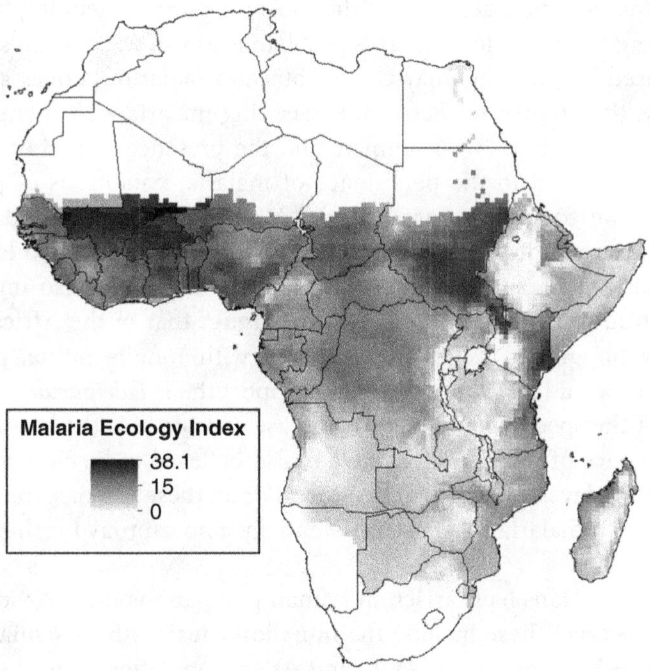

Figure 3.5. Malaria ecology in Africa.

represents the component of malaria variation among countries that is exogenous to human intervention. The index is calculated for grid squares of one half degree longitude by one half degree latitude. Average values of the index for countries are shown in the appendix. With the exception of New Guinea and some areas of Southeast Asia, Africa is the only part of the world in which the index reaches its highest levels. Areas in which malaria played a significant role historically but has now been eradicated, such as Greece, southern Italy, and the American South, all have relatively low values for the malaria ecology index. Even within Africa, there is substantial variation in the index, with peak values appearing in West Africa as well as in Chad and Sudan. Figure 3.5 shows values of the index at the grid-cell level in Africa. The mean value is 8.4 and the standard deviation is 9.7.

The current geographic distribution of malaria impact may not accurately represent the historical burden of the disease. Packard (2007) gives numerous examples of how human activity has changed the intensity of malaria. Clearing forests and introducing irrigation often produces the marshy environment needed for breeding of *Anopheles* mosquitoes. When a small number of landowners consolidate and control large tracts of land, people living on that land are often deprived of the tools for properly tending to it and for avoiding malaria infection. This problem is exacerbated when seasonal labor is used, as migrants may come from non-malarious zones and lack immunity, then return to these zones carrying malaria with them. As for Africa, he claims that "while climate and the presence of highly efficient vectors contributed to the persistence of malaria, conditions of production played an equal if not greater role." Webb (2008) similarly describes how the introduction of agriculture led to malaria endemicity in lowlands throughout the Eurasian landmass. Population density is also important to the nature of malaria burden. Packard argues that in the African contexts, low population densities associated with mobile hunter-gatherer populations would have been unable to support the *P. Falciparum* infection because of the speed with which the disease exits or kills the human host. The emergence of *Anopheles gambiae* is also believed to be closely associated with the development of agriculture. For all these reasons, the current distribution of malaria in Africa is potentially a poor proxy for the historical distribution.

Several mutations have arisen in human populations that provide resistance to malaria. These include the mutation causing thalassemia, which is present in Mediterranean, Arab, and Asian populations; the absence of the Duffy blood group in West Africa (which specifically blocks *P. Vivax*); hemoglobin E in Southeast Asia; and hemoglobin C in West Africa (Allison 2002; Nelson and Williams 2006). The most important such mutation is the one that causes sickle cell disease.

The sickle cell trait is a mutation in the gene that produces hemoglobin, the oxygen-carrying component in red blood cells. Individuals carry two copies of this gene, one received from each parent. Individuals who carry one normal copy of the gene (referred to as A type allele) and one copy with the sickle cell mutation (S type allele) are carriers of the disease. In individuals of the AS genotype, a fraction of the hemoglobin in their red blood cells has an abnormal structure. In individuals who have two copies of the sickle cell allele (SS genotype), almost all hemoglobin molecules are of the abnormal type.

In conditions of inadequate oxygen supply (hypoxia), hemoglobin produced by the S gene becomes rigid, leading to a characteristic sickle shape of red blood cells. Carriers of the sickle cell trait generally do not suffer many adverse effects.[3] However, negative consequences can arise from sickling

[3] Williams and colleagues (2005) show the absence of any significant effect of carrier status on a wide range of childhood diseases.

in conditions of low oxygen such as unpressurized airplane flights and extremely rigorous exercise (Motulsky 1964). In individuals of the SS genotype, such sickling of red blood cells is far more common, leading to acute episodes of disease in which abnormally shaped cells restrict blood flow to organs, cause severe damage to the spleen, and trigger anemia. In 1994, life expectancy for SS children in the United States was forty-two years for males and forty-eight years for females. In the absence of modern medical care, individuals of the SS genotype are not able to survive to adulthood.

The sickle cell mutation is relevant to malaria because infection of a red blood cell with the malaria parasite leads to hypoxia. In individuals of the AS genotype, such blood cells sickle and are then eliminated by the body's immune system, lessening the burden of infection. Carriers of the sickle cell trait are particularly resistant to severe malarial episodes; they are less resistant to mild cases. The mechanism by which AS carriers are protected from malaria is different than the acquired immunity that both AA and AS individuals achieve following repeated exposure to the disease.

The benefit that possessing a single copy of the sickle cell gene conveys counterbalances the biological cost incurred when homozygous SS children are stricken with sickle cell disease. An individual of the AS genotype is more likely to reach adulthood than is an individual of the AA genotype, but the former is also more likely to see his/her child die of sickle cell disease. This is known as a heterozygote advantage or balanced polymorphism. The stronger the pressure of malaria is on survival, the more advantaged are individuals who carry the S gene, and in equilibrium, the higher the percentage of the population who will be carriers.

Figure 3.6 shows data on the fraction of alleles that are of the S type among native African populations, using data from Piel and colleagues (2010). Because individuals have two alleles, the fraction of individuals who are carriers of the sickle cell trait (that is, the AS genotype) is slightly less than twice as large as the fraction of alleles that are of the S type.[4] The figure shows significant areas with an allele frequency of 15 percent or greater, implying that 25 percent or more of the population carries the sickle cell trait. According to Nelson and Williams (2006), the prevalence of AS hemoglobin in tropical Africa ranges from 16–29 percent in adults. Prevalence rates of up to 40 percent have been found in particular populations, for

[4] More precisely, if a fraction ρ of alleles are of the S type, then assuming no differential mortality, the fraction of people who are carriers will be $2\rho - 2\rho^2$. So, for example, 10 percent of alleles being of the S type would correspond to 18 percent of individuals being carriers. To the extent that mortality is higher for individuals of the SS genotype, the fraction of carriers in the population will be even closer to exactly 2ρ.

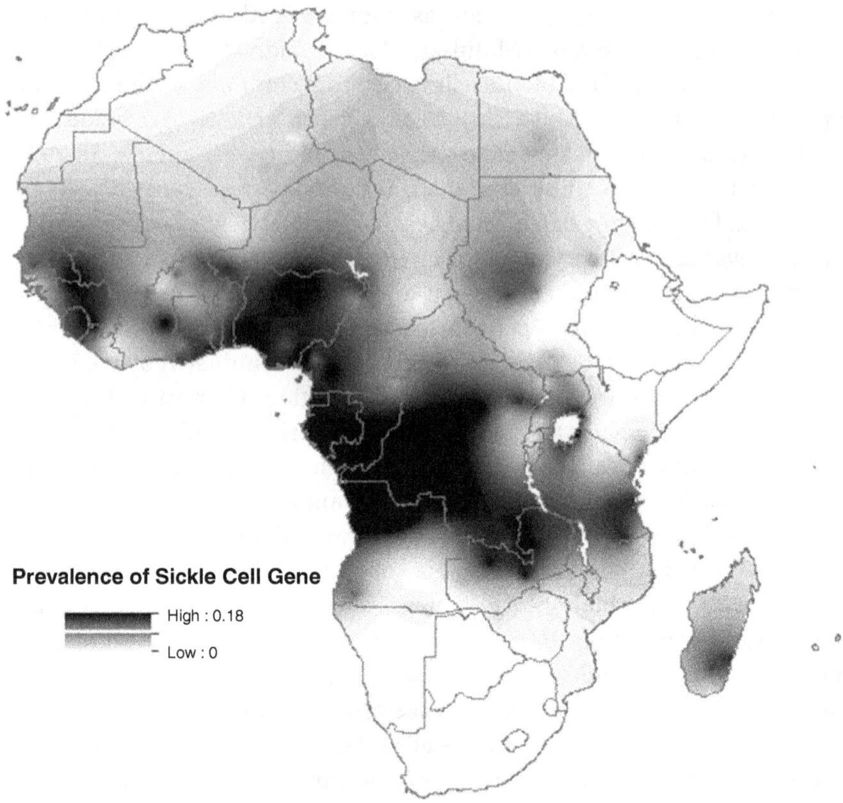

Figure 3.6. Frequency of the S Allele in Africa.

example in western Uganda and Tanzania south of Lake Victoria (Allison 2002). Figure 3.6 also shows a striking correlation of sickle cell prevalence with malaria ecology. Indeed, it was the correlation of high prevalence of the sickle cell gene and the presence of malaria that first led scientists to understand the protective role of the sickle cell mutation.

It is of interest to compare malaria ecology and sickle cell prevalence, on the one hand, to the indicators of early development discussed in Section 3.1, on the other. Notably, one of the regions with the highest level of early development, West Africa and the Niger Bend, also had one of the highest burdens of malaria, although this is not true of Ethiopia, which was the other locus of early development. The lack of a correlation between malaria burden and early development might suggest that malaria was not important in holding back development. However, such correlations must be interpreted cautiously, because many other factors that influence development are omitted.

3.3 MEASURING THE HISTORICAL BURDEN OF MALARIA USING DATA ON THE SICKLE CELL TRAIT

A related paper, Depetris-Chauvin and Weil (2013), presents a mathematical analysis of the historical impact of malaria as derived from data on sickle cell prevalence. The underlying logic, as described previously, is that the sickle cell trait is a double-edged sword: it protects against malaria, but raises the probability that a child will die from sickle cell disease. The fraction of children who will die from sickle cell disease depends on the fraction of adults who are carriers. The benefit from being a carrier depends on how severe the effect of malaria on noncarriers is and how much protection is offered by being a carrier. In equilibrium, the percentage of the adult population who are carriers of the sickle cell trait will depend on the severity of malaria in a region: the worse malaria is (in terms of the fraction of unprotected children who will die of it), the higher the fraction of adults who will be carriers of the sickle cell trait.

The bottom line measure of malaria's impact that I use is the relative survival into adulthood of carriers versus noncarriers. This reflects purely the protective effect of the sickle cell gene, because the available evidence is that carrier status has at most a trivial effect on survival from conditions other than malaria. Call this relative survival, which will be a number between zero and one, β. The lower β is, the more valuable the protective effect of carrying the sickle cell trait is. Depetris-Chauvin and Weil (2013) show how the value of β can be derived from the observed prevalence of the sickle cell trait in adult populations, which I label as π (which also ranges between zero and one). The value of β determines the equilibrium level of π. Thus, if one can observe the equilibrium level of π, one can back out how bad the selective pressure from malaria is, that is, β.[5] The second column of Table 3.4 shows the implied value of β for different values of π, which are shown in the first column. I consider values of adult prevalence ranging from zero to 40 percent, which is the highest level observed among specific populations. A prevalence of 20 percent, for example, implies that noncarriers are 89 percent as likely to live to adulthood as carriers.

One complication in using data on the frequency of the sickle cell trait to assess the historical burden of the disease is that most measures of the prevalence of sickle cell come from the past sixty years. By contrast, my basic analysis considers a population that is in equilibrium in terms of the

[5] The key equation is $\pi = (1-\beta)\Big/\left(1-\frac{\beta}{2}\right)$

Table 3.4. *Calculations based on prevalence of sickle cell trait*

Fraction of adults who are carriers (π)	Survival of noncarriers relative to carriers (β)	Probability of dying of malaria or sickle cell conditional on not dying of something else	Total death rate (preadult)	Probability of dying of malaria or SC (preadult)	Malaria and SC deaths as fraction of total (preadult)
0	1.000	0.000	0.444	0.000	0.000
0.05	.974	0.025	0.458	0.014	0.032
0.10	.947	0.050	0.472	0.030	0.064
0.15	.919	0.075	0.486	0.047	0.096
0.20	.889	0.100	0.500	0.064	0.128
0.25	.857	0.125	0.514	0.082	0.159
0.30	.824	0.150	0.527	0.100	0.190
0.35	.788	0.175	0.541	0.119	0.220
0.40	.750	0.200	0.555	0.139	0.250

selective impact of malaria and the prevalence of the sickle cell trait. Such a steady state presumably existed in Africa in the period before European contact. One might worry that modern prevalence rates are not the same as those that held historically, because the health environment has been changing over time. In practice, there is little reason to believe that contact with Europeans did anything to reduce the impact of malaria in Africa until the second half of the twentieth century, in which case prevalence rates would not have had much time to change before being measured. Depetris-Chauvin and Weil (2013) use the case of African Americans as a check on the basic model of selective pressure on the sickle cell trait. Slaves transported to what is now the United States found themselves in an environment in which the selective pressure of malaria was far lower. One would thus expect the prevalence of the sickle cell trait to fall over time. We show that the current prevalence of the trait among African Americans (approximately 8 percent) is consistent with sickle cell prevalence in the known source countries of the slaves who came to the United States and a time span of roughly ten generations since the average ancestor of current African Americans was removed from a highly malarious environment.

In calculating the burden of malaria and the protective effect of the sickle cell trait, one must also consider the cost from children who die from sickle cell disease. For example, if the prevalence of the trait among the adult population is 20 percent, then one in twenty-five children will have both parents be carriers, and of these children one in four will get two copies of the sickle cell trait – thus one percent of children will die from sickle cell disease before adulthood (if they do not die from something else first). More generally, if π is the fraction of adults who are carriers, then the fraction of children who suffer from sickle cell disease will be $\pi^2/4$. In the calculations presented later in this chapter, I measure the burden of malaria as constituting both deaths directly from the disease as well as deaths from sickle cell disease.

To turn estimates of relative survival of carriers into a measure of the overall burden of malaria, one needs a further piece of information. To see why, note that relative survival of 80 percent for noncarriers would be consistent with 0 percent of carriers and 20 percent of noncarriers dying of malaria, but it would also be consistent with 50 percent of carriers and 60 percent of noncarriers dying of malaria. Depetris-Chauvin and Weil (2013) discuss solving this problem by using data on the probability that carriers will die of malaria relative to noncarriers. Available data are sketchy, and further only apply to a modern health environment (where the probabilities of both carriers and noncarriers dying of malaria are lower than they were historically). These data show the relative death probability from malaria for carriers ranging from zero to 8 percent. In other words, the sickle cell trait is almost completely protective against a fatal case of malaria. For the calculations, I use a value of zero for this relative probability.

Beyond knowing mortality from malaria and sickle cell disease, to paint a complete picture of the burden of malaria, I also need to know the probability of dying from other diseases, or alternatively, the total rate of mortality. Part of the reason for this is that all of the previous calculations refer to the probability of dying of malaria or sickle cell disease *conditional* on not dying of something else. In a society in which there is more mortality from other sources, malaria deaths will necessarily be lower.

Systematic data on life expectancy in Africa is widely available only starting in the 1950s. For the period 1950–5, the United Nations estimate of life expectancy at birth in sub-Saharan Africa is 37.8 years (United Nations 2009). Acemoglu and Johnson (2007) date the beginning of the "international epidemiological transition," driven by more effective public health measures, the discovery of new chemicals and drugs, and international interventions, to 1940. Although the transition came late to Africa, it is very likely that the 1950–5 figure represents an improvement relative to previous decades. Clearly after 1955 the pace of change was rapid. The UN estimates that life expectancy in sub-Saharan Africa rose by two years in each of the subsequent five-year periods. Further evidence that health improvements were already under way by 1950 comes from data on total population size. Africa's population grew at a rate of 1.0 percent per year between 1900 and 1950, compared to a growth rate of 0.2 percent per year over the previous century (United Nations 1999).

Data for the period prior to 1950 are very sparse. Acemoglu and Johnson (2007, appendix C) pull together disparate sources to present a few estimates for the period before 1950. These are, Angola in 1940: 35 (both sexes); Mozambique in 1940: 45 (both sexes); Ghana in 1948: 38 (both sexes); and Mauritius, 1942–6: 32.3 (male) and 33.8 (female). Riley (2005) estimates that prior to the "health transition" that began in Africa in the 1920s (he uses a different definition than Acemoglu and Johnson), life expectancy at birth averaged 26.4 years.[6] In Asia, life expectancy prior to the health transition, which started there between 1870 and 1890, was 27.4. In Europe, the transition started in the 1770s, and prior to it life expectancy was 34.3.

Riley comments that available estimates of African mortality prior to the health transition all came from European colonies in Africa. There is a reasonable basis for thinking that life expectancy may have been higher prior to colonization, the arrival of Arabic-speaking merchants, and the dislocations produced by the slave trade. Unfortunately, little information for this period is available. Steyn (2003) looks at mortality during the precolonial period in northern South Africa through an examination of skeletal remains. She estimates life expectancy in the period 1000–1300 CE at 23.2, with the probability of surviving to age twenty being 48 percent. Remains for the post-1830 period show a slight decline in life expectancy after the expansion of European influence.

In the UN Model Life Tables for developing countries (1982), life expectancy at birth of thirty-five (general model, for females) implies that 61.4 percent of girls will survive to age twenty (and only 53.0 percent to age 30). The majority of premature deaths are concentrated at very low ages: 22.5 percent of girls would not reach age five. Unfortunately, the model life tables that are available, to the extent that they reflect African data at all, certainly do not reflect the pattern of age-dependent mortality that existed in the period before the modern health environment of both disease and treatment was in place. It is likely that the pattern of mortality,

[6] This is the mean of twelve estimates, which range from 22.5 to 31.0. Some representative values are Angola: 27 years in 1940; Egypt: 30–3 years in the 1930s; Ghana: 28 years in 1921; Kenya: 23.9 years in the 1930s; South African black population: 38.1–40 years in 1935–40; Tunisia: 28.8 in the 1920s; Uganda: 23.9 in the 1930s; Zimbabwe: 26.4 in the mid-1930s.

and in particular the ratio of deaths at different ages, differed from what is observed today, but a priori there is no basis for guessing the nature of this difference. Allowing for the fact that life expectancy at birth was almost certainly lower than thirty-five (the lowest value available in the UN model tables), and that "childbearing age" is not a single number but a range, a reasonable estimate for a value to use in our model is that 50 percent of births did not reach childbearing age.

My interest is in finding the fraction of people who do not live to reproductive age, which I call "preadult mortality." I make the assumption that the level of malaria mortality is uncorrelated with the level of non-malaria mortality. I also make the assumption that preadult mortality from malaria has the same approximate age profile as other sources of preadult mortality. I benchmark the model by assuming that in areas with sickle cell prevalence of 20 percent, total preadult mortality would be 50 percent. This allows me to back out the probability of death from non-malaria causes (in the case where an individual does not die of malaria), which turns out to be 44 percent.[7]

The last three columns of Table 3.4 use these assumptions about non-malaria mortality to paint a picture of the burden of malaria. For each value of sickle cell prevalence, π, I calculate the total rate of preadult mortality as well as the fraction of preadult deaths that would be due to malaria and sickle cell disease. The table shows that, going from an area where malaria was absent ($\pi = 0$) to one of reasonably high prevalence ($\pi = 0.2$), the overall preadult death rate rises from 44 percent to 50 percent. In the worst afflicted areas ($\pi = 0.4$), the probability of preadult death was 56 percent and fully 25 percent of deaths were attributable to malaria and sickle cell disease.

3.3.1 Comparison to Modern Malaria Mortality Rates

The death rate from malaria derived from the historical data can be compared to modern rates. As mentioned earlier, for the WHO AFRO region, the under-five death rate from malaria is 0.59 percent per year. In the 2008 World Malaria Report (data for 2006), the five most severely burdened countries are Niger (1.1%), Mali (0.98%), Burkina Faso (0.96%), Nigeria (0.88%), and Chad (0.87%). Multiplying these numbers by five gives an approximation of the probability of dying from malaria in the first five years of life, which is very close to the probability of dying from malaria before reproductive age. Although I cannot assign values of sickle cell prevalence

7 See Depetris-Chauvin and Weil (2013) for details.

(π) to particular countries, it appears that the malaria death rate in the pre-European contact period was about twice as high.

A different and somewhat cleaner way to do the comparison of historical malaria mortality to mortality today is to focus on the probability of dying of malaria (or sickle cell disease) conditional on not dying of something else. This is the measure constructed from historical data on prevalence, and although it is not generally reported, it can be constructed from modern data as well. Consider the case of Nigeria, which is a very heavily afflicted country. Annual malaria deaths for children under five are estimated to be 0.88 percent. This implies that roughly 4.4 percent of children will die of malaria before their fifth birthday. The life table for Nigeria for 2006 shows that the probability of a woman surviving to age twenty-five is approximately 0.75. From these two pieces of information, I can back out the probability of dying from malaria conditional on not dying of something else (see Depetris-Chauvin and Weil, 2013, for details). The result is 5.4 percent. Measured this way, the burden of malaria is far lower in Nigeria today than it was in countries with a sickle cell prevalence of 20 percent in the historical period, where, according to Table 3.4, the figure was 10 percent.

It is also of interest to compare the decline in malaria mortality to the decline in mortality from other causes. In the previous calculation, the probability of malaria death falls by slightly less than half. By contrast, the probability of dying of some other cause (conditional on not dying of malaria) falls from 44 percent to 20.7 percent – a decline of slightly more than half. Thus the probability of death from other causes has fallen slightly more than the probability of death from malaria, although the magnitudes of the two declines are close. Certainly, given the uncertainty in so many aspects of measurement, one cannot reject the possibility that the percentage of decline in malaria mortality has been the same as the decline in other types of mortality.

3.4 ASSESSING THE IMPORTANCE OF MALARIA TO EARLY AFRICAN DEVELOPMENT

Now that I have an estimate of how large a burden malaria imposed in terms of survival, I can turn to the question of whether malaria had a significant impact on African development. I divide my discussion into two parts, looking first at the effects of malaria deaths (mortality) and then at the effects of ill health among those who survived the disease (morbidity).

3.4.1 Direct Effect of Malaria Mortality

Current analyses of the burden of disease focus on measures such as years of life lost or disability-free life years lost. From this perspective, the death of a young child is particularly costly because he or she had so many potential life years. The ethical considerations regarding the allocation of scarce life-saving resources, and implicitly the cost of death and disease experienced at different ages, are quite complex (see Persad, Werthheimer, and Emanuael 2009). In assessing the role that disease played in affecting development historically, however, it seems reasonable to take a purely instrumental view of life and health, in which the primary considerations are how much society has invested in an individual and that individual's potential to produce services for society in the future. Under this sort of view, the most costly death is that of a young adult, who has consumed a good deal of resources (food, child care, education), and who has many years of potentially productive labor. The death of an infant or small child, by contrast, is far less costly, because fewer resources have been invested; and the death of an old person is similarly less costly because less productive potential is lost. Under this interpretation, malaria deaths are relatively low cost, with the exception of deaths of women in their first pregnancies, who are near the peak of their value as assets to society in terms of the balance between resources invested in them and services they can deliver.

To formalize this idea, consider a simple model of production and consumption with individuals of different ages. Let c_i be the consumption of an individual of age i, and similarly w_i be labor income. I ignore income from nonlabor sources, and assume that there is no storage of output between periods. Let N_i be the number of people in age group i. The social budget constraint is

$$\sum_0^T N_i(w_i - c_i) = 0$$

where T is the maximum lifespan. I assume that consumption at each age is determined by two things: a consumption level of individuals at some benchmark age (for example, prime age adults), which I call $\bar{c}$, and some age-varying relative consumption coefficient $\tilde{c}_i$.

$$c_i = \bar{c}\tilde{c}_i$$

The values of $\tilde{c}_i$ presumably reflect both changing biological needs for consumption over the course of the life cycle as well as the arrangements by which consumption is divided up among different groups in society. One would not necessarily expect the pattern of consumption to be the same in all societies at all times.

I assume that wages (or output produced via labor) at each age group are determined in a similar fashion:

$$w_i = \overline{w}\tilde{w}_i$$

Where $\overline{w}$ is the return to some standard unit of labor. Again, the pattern of relative labor input across age groups reflects both biological differences and differences among societies in the economic value of different characteristics (for example, strength versus wisdom versus manual dexterity).

Combining these equations, we can solve for the consumption level of the benchmark age group as a function of the age structure of the population as well as the relative wage and consumption weights.

$$\overline{c} = \overline{w}\frac{\sum_0^T N_i\tilde{w}_i}{\sum_0^T N_i\tilde{c}_i}$$

3.4.1.1 Consumption and Income Profiles

A number of sources provide data on the life cycle profiles of consumption and labor input. Mueller (1976) synthesizes data from nine societies practicing what she calls "peasant agriculture," by which she means agricultural systems that use primarily traditional methods of cultivation, small landholdings, and low capital inputs. Her data are primarily from South and Southeast Asia, from the middle of the twentieth century, but they may not be a bad approximation to the most developed parts of Africa in the periods of interest in this chapter. The profiles are shown in Figure 3.7. Note that Mueller's data on labor input apply to production of output as it would appear in measured GDP but exclude home production. Much of the latter is done by women, so in her data, productivity by prime age women is only 30 percent of the level of similarly aged males. Because I am interested in both sorts of output, I focus on the male profiles. For consumption, Mueller provides two profiles in which consumption of people at each age (and of each gender) is compared to males aged twenty to fifty-four. For the medium consumption profile, children aged zero to four have a value of 0.32; for the low consumption profile, the value is 0.12 (prime aged women get a value of 0.80). I use the medium profile. Lee and Mason (2011) show very similar-looking profiles for hunter-gatherer populations.

3.4.1.2 Population Age Structure

The other piece of data used in this equation is N_i, the number of people in each age group. In general, this will be a function of both the probability of survival to each age and the history of births or population growth. However, for the long historical periods that I am considering, population growth must have been very close to zero, which implies a constant number of births per year. We can thus approximate the age structure of the population with the fraction of survivors at each age from the life table.

My approach to assessing the role of disease in affecting consumption possibilities is to start with a baseline life table and then consider alternations that would result from eliminating or adding particular sources of mortality. To construct these alternative life tables, I use information on the age of death from different diseases. As my baseline, I use the United Nations (1982) model life table for a population with life expectancy at birth of thirty-five years (male and female combined).

To apply this framework to different diseases, one needs a profile of the mortality effect of the disease at different ages. Table 3.3 shows such data for malaria in Africa today. To model the effect of malaria on the historical life table, I proceed as follows. I start with the UN life table (life expectancy of thirty-five) discussed earlier. I take this as a benchmark. To this I add additional mortality at each age proportional to the current age profile of malaria mortality. Specifically, I take the current death rates from malaria (0.00559 for ages zero to four, 0.00042 for ages five to fourteen, etc.) and multiply them by a scaling factor, and add these death rates to the death rates in the UN life table. The scaling factor is chosen to match the magnitude of the change in malaria deaths I want to model. Specifically, I showed previously that for the case of going from zero malaria to the case where sickle cell prevalence is moderately high (π=.2), the total preadult death rate rose from 44 percent to 50 percent. In the UN data, the probability of living to age twenty-eight is .555, which is close enough to a 44 percent preadult death rate. (In the model "adult" is the age at which children are produced. In reality, there is no single age that is appropriate, but twenty-eight is roughly in the middle of the relevant range.) The scaling factor required

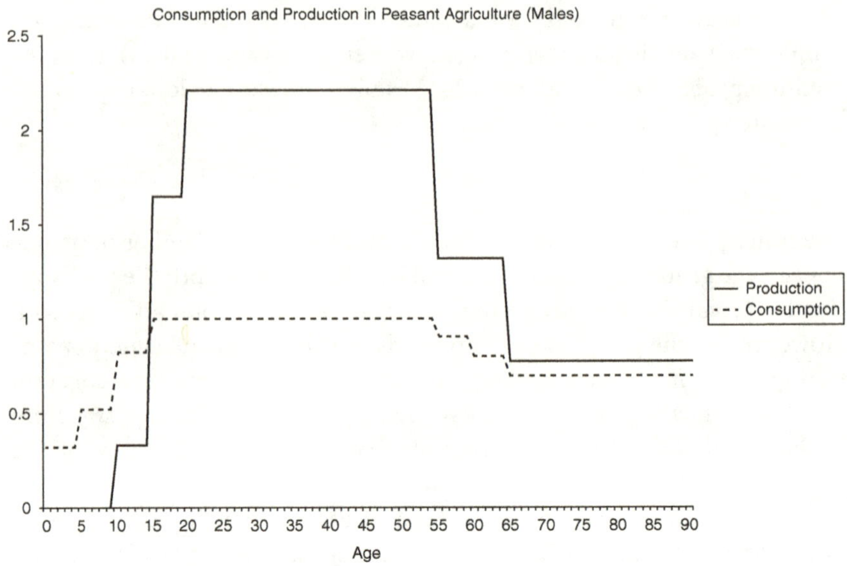

Figure 3.7. Production and consumption over the life-cycle.

to set survival to age twenty-eight equal to 50 percent is two.[8] Life expectancy falls by three and a half years from this additional malaria mortality.

This increase in malaria mortality lowers steady state consumption by only 0.63 percent. This is obviously an extremely small effect for such a large change in mortality. The reason is clear once one has seen Figure 3.7 and noted that malaria deaths are concentrated at very low ages. In this calculation, deaths beyond age five account for only one-third of the reduction in life expectancy due to malaria, but for two-thirds of the economic cost of the disease.

This analysis shows that, at least in terms of the extra costs associated with raising children who were subsequently going to die of malaria, the effect of the disease on the standard of living in Africa should have been relatively low. However, it is possible that there are other channels through which high malaria mortality may have mattered. Death from disease may impose an obstacle to economic development beyond the instrumental cost discussed here. Stone (1977) argues that in the face of high child mortality, premodern Europeans avoided forming emotional bonds with their

[8] Of course the UN table already includes deaths due to malaria. Another approach would be to take as the baseline a current life table stripped of malaria mortality, and then to add malaria mortality back in. This procedure would yield very similar results.

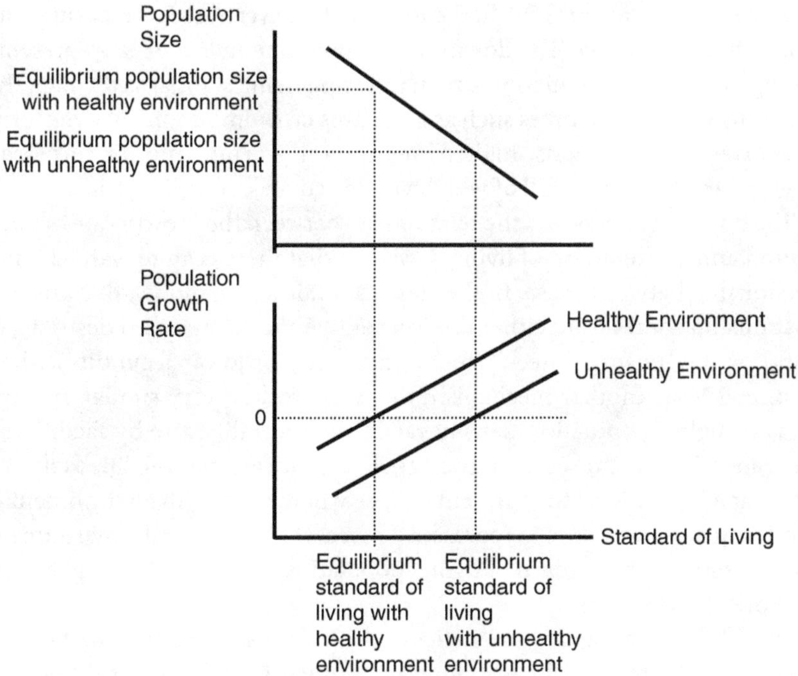

Figure 3.8. The Malthusian model.

young children, even to the point of giving the same name to two living children, expecting only one to survive. In such an environment, one might also expect to see less investment of tangible resources in the human capital (both health and education) of their children. Thus even if high child mortality from malaria were not important in the strict sense of draining resources from the economy, it might have contributed to reduced investment in children. Several recent theories of economic growth have stressed the importance of such investments to long-term development.

3.4.1.3 The Malthusian Perspective

This analysis takes the perspective that deaths are costly in social terms, because they represent the loss of potential productive workers. An alternative view points to a flip side of deaths, which is that they decrease the size of population and thus lower pressure on fixed resources.

Consider a simple Malthusian model, as represented in the two panels of Figure 3.8. In both panels, the horizontal axis measures the standard of living. In a modern economy, this would be GDP per capita, but the model should be applicable even in contexts where there are no markets or prices with which to measure GDP. In the top panel, the vertical axis measures the size of the population. The downward sloping line in the panel represents the effect of higher population size in reducing living standards through the crowding of fixed resources such as land. This crowding could take the form of shorter fallow periods, higher pressure on grazing land, or increased levels of animal disease, all of which would reduce per capita yields.

The bottom panel shows the relationship between the growth rate of population and the standard of living. I assume that there is an upward sloping relationship between these. In the classical Malthusian model, this positive relationship comes from either the "preventive check" (reduced desired fertility) or the "positive check" (higher mortality or lower fecundity) when income is low. Another mechanism that will produce very similar dynamics is if higher population density raises the mortality rate by facilitating the transmission of disease. In the panel, this upward sloping line is drawn twice, at a higher level to represent a place where the health environment is good, and at a lower level to represent a place where the health environment is bad. For a given standard of living, population growth will be higher in a healthier environment.

One of the defining characteristics of the Malthusian model is that it produces a steady state in which, as long as the quantity of land is constant and the production technology is fixed, population size is constant (or, more realistically, the population size and standard of living are mean reverting in response to stochastic shocks). The near constancy of human populations over long historical eras suggests that such a mechanism must have been operating in most places for most of human history (Galor and Weil 2000). Although there are clearly times when Malthusian constraints were lifted (such as the peopling of the Americas in prehistoric times), a simple analysis of the effect of compounding shows that most of the time, average population growth rates must have been quite close to zero. Without a homeostatic model of the Malthusian sort, it is vanishingly unlikely that such near constancy of population would obtain.

As the figure shows, a worse health environment leads to lower population and a *higher* standard of living in equilibrium. Thus malaria would have actually raised the standard of living in Africa. While counterintuitive, this conclusion is in line with the arguments in several recent analyses of growth. Voigtlander and Voth (2009) argue that in Europe before the Industrial Revolution, income rose as a result of increased mortality due to plague, urbanization, and warfare, and that this rise in income was instrumental in knocking the continent onto the path of industrialization. Acemoglu and Johnson, in their analysis of the worldwide epidemiological transition of the mid-twentieth century, find that countries that experienced greater increases in life expectancy saw slower growth in income per capita – a result that they attribute to the Malthusian effect of population growth. And Young (2005) claims that higher mortality and lower fertility due to HIV in South Africa will more than compensate for declines in worker productivity due to the disease, so that income per capita will actually rise as a result of the epidemic. Ashraf, Lester, and Weil (2008) examine the Malthusian channel as part of a broader analysis of how health improvements affect growth. They find that higher survival indeed pushes income lower through the Malthusian channel (as well as through capital dilution), although this effect is more than compensated for in the long run by higher labor productivity due to better health.

Whether this sort of Malthusian model applies to Africa in the period before European contact is unclear. Several authors stress that land shortage was not generally a problem in Africa. For example, Herbst (2000) argues that the abundant land was a persistent characteristic of African economies, as a result of which it was the control of people, rather than territory, that was of primary interest to rulers.

However, historians are often too quick to dismiss the Malthusian model without having another explanation for the near constancy of population over time. It is conceivable that, rather than land being the binding resource, the role of equilibrating population size was played by density-dependent disease. This would be consistent with the often-expressed view that labor, rather than land, was the binding constraint African economies faced. If so, the pressure from disease must have been extraordinarily high indeed, however, because human capacity to reproduce is very high. The levels of malaria indicated by the prevalence of the sickle cell trait would not be sufficient to hold down population growth in the absence of a land constraint, although it is possible that malaria in combination with other diseases did so.

It is also possible that malaria did indeed raise the standard of living in the short run by reducing population density, but at the same time low population density (due both to malaria and low agricultural productivity) prevented the development of large agglomerations that in other places were the loci of specialization, gains from trade, and technological advance.

3.4.2 Economic Effects of Malaria Morbidity

To pursue the question of how much malaria affects labor input of adults, I use data from the World Health Organization on Years Lost to Disability

(*YLD*s) from particular diseases. A country's *YLD* for a given disease is constructed as:

$$YLD = I \times DW \times L$$

where I is the number of incident (newly arising) cases in a period, DW is the disability weight attached to the disease, and L is the average duration of the disease until remission or death. The crucial parameter here is the disability weight, which is intended to be a cardinal measure of the severity of different diseases or impairments, on a scale from zero, indicating perfect health, to one, indicating death. Disability weights are constructed by panels of healthcare providers and medical experts using a "person trade-off" protocol, which establishes utility equivalences between years of life lived in different states of health. One year lived with a disability provides the same utility as (1-*DW*) years lived disability free (Murray 1996). Disability weights are therefore not primarily intended as a measure of labor supply. Nevertheless, these estimates provide at least some basis for comparing the effects of different diseases.[9]

To give an example of the interpretation of YLD: in the data presented later, the average YLD from all causes for Africa is 0.12. This means that in the average year, the average man suffers disease episodes that deprive him of the equivalent of 12 percent of a year's disability-free life. This could mean being fully disabled for 12 percent of the year, 50 percent disabled for 24 percent of the year, and so on. It could also mean suffering an incident that leaves him, say, 1 percent disabled for the next twelve years.

Table 3.5 shows the *YLD*s by disease type and age (for males) for the WHO's AFRO region (Mathers, Fat, and Boerma 2008). *YLD*s are counted at the age in which a disease incident occurs. Thus, for example, the neurological sequelae of malaria are counted as years lost to disability in the age zero to four age group, even though the actual years lost are spread through the individual's whole life. (Note that the "total" column is based on the distribution of the current population among age groups. Thus disabilities affecting the elderly, who are a very small percentage of the current African population, play a very minor role in determining the total figure.)

The table shows that overall, malaria accounts for only 5 percent of total years lost to disability. Further, almost all of these lost years were due to incidents in the first five years of life. Some of the years lost to disability in this

[9] Some examples of disability weights are blindness (0.600), deafness (0.216), HIV (0.136), AIDS (0.505), tuberculosis sero-negative for HIV (0.264), severe iron-deficiency anemia (0.093), malaria episodes (0.172), and neurological sequelae of malaria (0.473).

Table 3.5. *Years lost to disability per capita, WHO AFRO region*

	0–4	5–14	15–29	30–44	45–59	60–69	70–79	80+	total
All Causes	0.174	0.068	0.133	0.134	0.141	0.126	0.115	0.103	0.122
Communicable, maternal, perinatal, and nutritional conditions	0.112	0.028	0.040	0.037	0.021	0.015	0.013	0.010	0.046
Infectious and parasitic diseases	0.047	0.019	0.037	0.035	0.021	0.014	0.012	0.010	0.031
Tuberculosis	0.000	0.001	0.002	0.004	0.002	0.002	0.001	0.001	0.002
HIV/AIDS	0.000	0.000	0.017	0.015	0.004	0.001	0.000	0.000	0.007
Diarrheal diseases	0.004	0.002	0.001	0.001	0.000	0.000	0.000	0.000	0.001
Childhood cluster diseases	0.007	0.000	0.000	0.000	0.000	0.000	0.000	0.000	0.001
Malaria	0.027	0.001	0.002	0.001	0.001	0.001	0.001	0.001	0.006
Tropical cluster diseases	0.001	0.009	0.011	0.010	0.009	0.004	0.003	0.003	0.008
Noncommunicable Diseases	0.047	0.019	0.066	0.074	0.108	0.105	0.098	0.089	0.056
Injuries	0.015	0.021	0.027	0.023	0.011	0.006	0.004	0.003	0.021

Source: Global Burden of Disease, 2002 revision.

case affected adults, through the neurological sequelae of the disease, but much of the disability burden fell directly on children. Although disability (which in this case really just measures suffering) among children does not directly affect production, one could argue that it might have affected their accumulation of skills or human capital. In any case, however, the malaria burden is relatively small in comparison to that of other diseases.

As mentioned previously, another potential channel through which malaria might have affected economic development is through shifting population away from potentially productive areas. Gallup and Sachs give examples of this occurring in Europe. In the context of Africa, I do not know of evidence that particular regions were not settled because of malaria, and there is certainly evidence of people settling in areas of tremendously high malaria transmission. Given that malaria deaths were concentrated among the very young, and that mortality in this group was very high from other causes in any case, it is hard to see how malaria would have had a great influence on settlement patterns.

3.5 CONCLUSION

In this chapter, I set out to assess the role that malaria played in affecting African development in the period before Africans and Europeans came into contact. The largest contribution of this chapter is in assessing the health burden that malaria placed on Africans some five hundred years ago. I used data on the modern prevalence of the sickle cell mutation to estimate the intensity of malaria historically. In areas of high malaria transmission, 20 percent of the population carries the sickle cell trait. My estimate is that this implies that historically 10 percent of children died from malaria or sickle cell disease before reaching adulthood. Such a death rate is roughly twice the current burden of malaria in such regions. Comparing the most affected to least affected areas, malaria may have been responsible for a ten percentage point difference in the probability of surviving to adulthood. In terms of its burden relative to other causes of mortality, malaria appears to have been perhaps slightly less important historically than it is today, although I certainly can't rule out the decline in malaria mortality has been proportional to the decline in mortality from other diseases.

Thus malaria imposed a heavy mortality burden. Did it hold back economic development? As a starting point, it is worth noting that many of the areas with highest malaria ecology and highest prevalence of the sickle cell trait, most notably coastal West Africa, also had the highest levels of economic development by the various measures discussed in Section 3.1. Obviously the lack of correlation between malaria and low development is not firm evidence for a lack of a causal link. Those parts of Africa could have been well developed for other reasons, and were it not for malaria might have been more developed still. Nonetheless, simply looking at the locations of development and malaria suggests that malaria was not an insuperable obstacle to economic development within Africa.

My more detailed examination of the possible channels through which malaria might have affected economic outcomes also does not point to a strong role of the disease in holding back economic development. Malaria mortality occurs at very young ages, which implies a low social cost. In a Malthusian model, higher child mortality could even raise the standard of living. The morbidity burden of malaria on adults is low relative to other diseases. The fact that malaria bulked so large in the view of foreigners may be attributable to their lack of immunity, which Africans acquired as children.

My findings leave open several possibilities regarding the relationship between malaria and economic development in Africa. First, there may be some channel by which malaria affected precolonial development that is left out of my analysis. One possibility is that the overall disease environment, of which malaria was only a part, held back economic growth on the continent. If malaria was not, in fact, an important determinant of development before the arrival of Europeans, then could it have been important afterward? The analysis of Ashraf, Lester, and Weil (2008) suggests that the direct effects of malaria on productivity are not large enough to explain much of Africa's economic backwardness. However, it is possible that malaria held back growth through other channels during the colonial period. For example, Acemoglu, Johnson, and Robinson (2001) have famously suggested that malaria and other diseases had a negative effect on development in the tropics through their role in shaping the structure of institutions that Europeans established. Finally, of course, malaria may simply not be a part of the story of African underdevelopment.

APPENDIX

Country	Population Density in 1500	State Antiquity in 1500	Average Technology in 1500	Malaria Ecology	Average Land Quality
Afghanistan	3.08	0.63	0.62	0.03	0.23
Albania	6.67			0.01	0.81
Algeria	0.64	0.60	0.78	0.01	0.06
Angola	1.50	0.13	0.17	4.37	0.35
Antigua and Barbuda	1.25				
Argentina	0.11	0.01	0.03	0.07	0.45
Armenia				0.01	0.74
Aruba	1.25				
Australia	0.03	0.00	0.00	0.06	0.22
Austria	25.00	0.71	0.90	0.00	0.40
Azerbaijan				0.03	0.74
Bahamas	1.25			0.00	0.49
Bangladesh	23.70	0.42	0.63	6.11	0.82
Barbados	1.25	0.00			
Belarus				0.00	0.38
Belgium	41.67	0.68	0.90	0.00	0.59
Belize	1.54		0.23	0.71	0.76
Benin	4.23	0.00	0.17	17.46	0.49
Bermuda	1.25				
Bhutan				0.11	0.25
Bolivia	0.82	0.70	0.16	1.21	0.47
Bosnia and Herzegovina			0.83	0.00	0.64
Botswana	0.14	0.21	0.10	5.77	0.10
Brazil	0.12	0.00	0.13	1.93	0.36
Brunei Darussalam				3.25	0.38
Bulgaria	7.27			0.01	0.87
Burkina Faso	4.23	0.05	0.51	31.55	0.29
Burundi	25.00	0.00		1.57	0.52
Cambodia	8.33		0.75	8.57	0.58
Cameroon	1.50	0.24	0.17	13.18	0.39
Canada	0.02	0.00	0.13	0.00	0.06
Cape Verde Islands	0.50	0.02		3.04	0.01
Cayman Islands	1.25			0.00	
Central African Republic	1.50	0.00	0.23	17.99	0.36
Chad	0.60	0.18	0.40	21.46	0.15
Chile	0.79	0.02	0.16	0.00	0.14
China	11.46	0.91	0.88	0.30	0.35
Colombia	0.88	0.00	0.13	1.16	0.46

Country	Population Density in 1500	State Antiquity in 1500	Average Technology in 1500	Malaria Ecology	Average Land Quality
Comoros	5.00			4.77	0.37
Congo, Dem Rep	1.50		0.23	12.06	0.31
Congo, Rep	1.50	0.05	0.23	12.92	0.27
Costa Rica	1.54	0.00	0.13	0.04	0.63
Cote d'Ivoire	4.23	0.06	0.17	19.70	0.40
Croatia				0.03	0.85
Cuba	1.25		0.13	0.14	0.86
Cyprus	22.22	0.62		0.06	0.73
Czech Republic			0.83	0.00	0.55
Denmark	15.00	0.61	0.90	0.00	0.48
Djibouti				10.97	0.02
Dominica	1.25			0.13	
Dominican Republic	1.25	0.00			0.93
Ecuador	2.14	0.09	0.16	0.20	0.54
Egypt	4.00	0.76	0.78	1.73	0.00
El Salvador	1.54	0.00	0.23	1.05	0.90
Equatorial Guinea	1.50		0.17	12.96	0.32
Eritrea	2.00			4.71	0.05
Estonia				0.00	0.33
Ethiopia	1.67	1.00	0.53	2.03	0.50
Finland	0.29	0.14	0.69	0.00	0.04
France	27.27	0.74	0.93	0.01	0.74
French Guiana				1.91	0.54
Gabon	1.50	0.00	0.17	13.03	0.36
Gambia	4.23	0.00		15.56	0.53
Georgia				0.01	0.64
Germany	25.00	0.76	0.90	0.00	0.55
Ghana	4.23	0.21	0.38	23.33	0.43
Greece	7.69	0.52	0.93	0.02	0.81
Grenada	1.25				
Guadeloupe				1.50	
Guatemala	1.54	0.42	0.23	0.70	0.89
Guinea	4.23	0.09	0.40	18.68	0.60
Guinea Bissau	4.23		0.27	10.35	0.58
Guyana	0.21	0.00	0.13	3.00	0.54
Haiti	1.25	0.00		0.16	0.93
Honduras	1.54	0.13	0.23	1.04	0.72
Hong Kong	0.09	0.91	0.88	2.71	
Hungary	13.89		0.90	0.02	0.94
Iceland	0.60	0.21		0.00	0.00
India	23.70	0.69	0.76	0.11	0.59
Indonesia	5.17	0.55	0.66	3.18	0.41

(*continued*)

Country	Population Density in 1500	State Antiquity in 1500	Average Technology in 1500	Malaria Ecology	Average Land Quality
Iran	2.42	0.68	0.81	0.06	0.15
Iraq	2.27		0.78	0.16	0.13
Ireland	10.00	0.55	0.80	0.00	0.34
Israel		0.50		0.03	
Italy	33.33	0.70	0.90	0.07	0.76
Jamaica	1.25	0.00		0.15	0.50
Japan	45.95	0.83	0.83	0.00	0.58
Jordan	2.22	0.51		0.07	0.04
Kazakhstan				0.01	0.60
Kenya	2.63	0.00	0.23	4.80	0.35
Korea, Rep	18.18	0.90	0.85	0.00	0.77
Kuwait				0.23	0.00
Kyrgyzstan				0.01	0.26
Laos	1.67	0.58	0.75	2.63	0.43
Lebanon	7.50			0.01	0.90
Lesotho	0.47	0.00	0.17	0.00	0.69
Liberia	4.23		0.17	17.34	0.38
Libyan Arab Jamahiriya	0.28		0.78	0.02	0.01
Lithuania			0.85	0.00	0.44
Madagascar	1.19	0.00	0.33	5.03	0.50
Malawi	0.79	0.02		6.25	0.77
Malaysia	1.18	0.59	0.72	1.69	0.40
Mali	0.60	0.38	0.51	30.10	0.11
Malta			0.90		
Mauritania	0.60	0.31	0.17	4.17	0.01
Mauritius		0.00		6.82	0.00
Mexico	2.50	0.53	0.26	0.45	0.58
Moldova				0.01	0.97
Mongolia	0.38		0.41	0.00	0.08
Morocco	2.50	0.82	0.41	0.06	0.36
Mozambique	1.28	0.00		10.54	0.44
Myanmar	5.88	0.84	0.75	5.87	0.55
Namibia	0.14		0.10	3.72	0.07
Nepal	14.29	0.84	0.30	0.02	0.45
Netherlands	30.00	0.63	0.90	0.00	0.55
Netherlands Antilles	1.25				
New Zealand	0.37	0.00	0.13	0.00	0.32
Nicaragua	1.54	0.00	0.13	0.80	0.59
Niger	0.60	0.17	0.44	21.93	0.01
Nigeria	4.23	0.45	0.47	21.62	0.42
Norway	1.25	0.53	0.90	0.00	0.02

Country	Population Density in 1500	State Antiquity in 1500	Average Technology in 1500	Malaria Ecology	Average Land Quality
Oman	0.95			0.01	0.00
Pakistan	23.70	0.81	0.73	0.05	0.10
Panama	1.54	0.00	0.13	0.17	0.47
Papua New Guinea	1.53	0.00	0.13	9.57	0.51
Paraguay	0.49	0.00	0.00	2.33	0.61
Peru	1.55	0.66	0.16	0.54	0.36
Philippines	1.67	0.00	0.58	1.42	0.64
Poland	12.90		0.85	0.00	0.57
Portugal	13.89	0.72	0.97	0.05	0.62
Puerto Rico	1.25				0.27
Qatar				0.01	0.00
Romania	8.33		0.70	0.00	0.74
Russia	0.80		0.80	0.01	0.12
Rwanda	25.00	0.00		0.46	0.48
Sao Tome and Principe	1.50			8.42	0.23
Saudi Arabia			0.48	0.00	0.00
Senegal	4.23	0.40	0.33	15.34	0.25
Serbia			0.83		
Sierra Leone	4.23		0.17	16.72	0.45
Singapore	1.18	0.13	0.72	11.03	
Slovakia				0.00	0.62
Slovenia				0.01	0.58
Solomon Islands				4.86	0.01
Somalia	1.25			8.36	0.04
South Africa	0.47	0.00	0.17	0.97	0.28
Spain	13.00	0.56	1.00	0.10	0.73
Sri Lanka	15.15	0.90		0.04	0.77
St Kitts and Nevis	1.25				
St Lucia	1.25				
St Vincent and the Grenadines	1.25				
Sudan	1.60		0.38	19.12	0.27
Suriname	0.21			1.47	0.47
Swaziland	0.47	0.00		3.09	0.63
Sweden	1.78	0.31	0.90	0.00	0.07
Switzerland	20.00	0.68	0.83	0.00	0.34
Syria	7.50	0.56	0.70	0.06	0.32
Tajikistan				0.02	0.31
Tanzania	1.97		0.23	7.62	0.64
Thailand	3.92	0.53	0.75	6.30	0.48
Togo	4.23	0.00		21.14	0.57

(*continued*)

Country	Population Density in 1500	State Antiquity in 1500	Average Technology in 1500	Malaria Ecology	Average Land Quality
Trinidad and Tobago	1.25	0.00		0.21	
Tunisia	5.00	0.76	0.78	0.12	0.30
Turkey	8.18	0.81	0.83	0.02	0.79
Turkmenistan				0.07	0.09
Uganda	7.14	0.00	0.26	7.51	0.51
Ukraine			0.85	0.02	0.81
United Arab Emirates				0.01	0.00
United Kingdom	16.13	0.71	1.00	0.00	0.40
United States	0.09	0.00	0.13	0.06	0.41
Uruguay	0.00	0.00	0.00	0.00	0.95
Uzbekistan			0.45	0.05	0.24
Vanuatu				1.93	0.00
Venezuela	0.44	0.00	0.13	0.54	0.49
Vietnam	6.06	0.59	0.80	6.42	0.51
Virgin Islands US				0.12	
Yemen	4.69			0.79	0.01
Zambia	0.79	0.00	0.19	5.68	0.54
Zimbabwe	0.79	0.00	0.17	4.08	0.41

References

Acemoglu, Daron and Simon Johnson. (2007). "Disease and Development: The Effect of Life Expectancy on Economic Growth." *Journal of Political Economy*, 115: 925–85.

Acemoglu, Daron, Simon Johnson, and James Robinson. (2001). "The Colonial Origins of Comparative Development: An Empirical Investigation." *American Economic Review*, 91: 1369–1401.

Akyeampong, Emmanuel Kwaku. (2006). "Disease in West African History." In *Themes in West Africa's History*, edited by Emmanuel Kwaku Akyeampong, 186–207. Athens: Ohio University Press.

Allison, A. C. (2002). "The Discovery of Resistance to Malaria of Sickle-Cell Heterozygotes." *Biochem. Mol. Biol. Educ.*, 30: 279–87.

Aregawi, Maru. (2010). *World Malaria Report 2010*. Geneva: World Health Organization.

Ashraf, Quamrul, Ashley Lester, and David N. Weil. (2008). "When Does Improving Health Raise GDP?" *NBER Macroeconomics Annual*.

Bairoch, Paul, Jean Batou, and Pierre Chevre. (1988). *Population des Villes Europeennes de 800 la 1850*. Volume 2. Geneva: Droz.

Chanda, Areendam and Louis Putterman. (2007). "Early Starts, Reversals and Catch-up in the Process of Economic Development." *Scandinavian Journal of Economics*, 109: 387–413.

Chandler, Tertius. (1987). *Four Thousand Years of Urban Growth: An Historical Census* (revised edition). Edward Mellen.

Comin, Diego, William Easterly, and Erick Gong. (2010). "Was the Wealth of Nations Determined in 1000 BC?" *American Economic Journal – Macro*, 2(3): 65–97.

De Vries, Jan. (1984). *European Urbanization 1500–1800*. Taylor & Francis.

Depetris Chauvin, Emilio and David N. Weil. (2013). "Malaria and Early African Development: Evidence from the Sickle Cell Trait." NBER Working Paper 19603, October.

Diamond, Jared. (1997). *Guns, Germs, and Steel: The Fates of Human Societies*. New York: W. W. Norton and Co.

Eggimann, Gilbert. (2000). "La Population des villes des tiers mondes de 1500 la 1950." Universite de Geneve, Centre d'histoire economique comparee.

Gallup, John Luke and Jeffrey D. Sachs. (2001). "The Economic Burden of Malaria." *American Journal of Tropical Medicine and Hygiene*, 64(1, supplement): 85–96.

Gallup, John Luke, Jeffrey D. Sachs, and Andrew Mellinger. (1999). "Geography and Economic Development." *International Regional Science Review*, 22(2): 179–232.

Galor, Oded and David N. Weil. (2000). "Population, Technology, and Growth: From Malthusian Stagnation to the Demographic Transition and Beyond." *American Economic Review*, 90: 806–28.

Hopkins, A. G. (1973). *An Economic History of West Africa*. New York: Columbia University Press.

Kiszewski, Anthony, Andrew Mellinger, Andrew Spielman, Pia Malaney, Jeffrey Sachs, and Sonia Ehrlich Sachs. (2004). "A Global Index of the Stability of Malaria Transmission." *American Journal of Tropical Medicine and Hygiene*, 70(5): 486–98.

Kremer, Michael. (1993). "Population Growth and Technological Change: One Million B.C. to 1990." *Quarterly Journal of Economics*, 108(3): 681–716.

Lee, R. D. and A. Mason. (2011). "Generational Economics in a Changing World." *Population and Development Review*, 37: 115–42.

Mabogunje, Akin L. and Paul Richards. (1985). "The Land and Peoples of West Africa." In *History of West Africa*, volume 1, 3rd ed., edited by J. F. A. Ajayi and Michael Crowder. New York: Longman Publishing Group.

Masters, William A. and Margaret McMillan. (2001). "Climate and Scale in Economic Growth." *Journal of Economic Growth*, 6(3): 167–86.

Mathers, Colin D., Doris Ma Fat, and J. T. Boerma. (2008). *The Global Burden of Disease: 2004 Update*. World Health Organization.

McEvedy, Colin and Richard Jones. (1978). *Atlas of World Population History*. London: Penguin.

McNeill, William. (1977). *Plagues and Peoples*. New York: Anchor Books.

Modelski, George. (2003). *World Cities:-3000 to 2000*. Washington, DC: Faros2000.

Motulsky, Arno. (1964). "Hereditary Red Cell Traits and Malaria." *Am. J. Trop. Med. Hyg.*, 13 (Part 1): 147–58.

Mueller, Eva. (1976). "The Economic Value of Children in Peasant Agriculture." In *Population and Development: The Search for Selective Interventions*, edited by Ronald Gene Ridker, 98–153. Baltimore, MD: Johns Hopkins University Press.

Murray, Christopher J. D. and Alan D. Lopez. (1996). *The Global Burden of Disease: A Comprehensive Assessment of Mortality and Disability from Diseases, Injuries and Risk Factors in 1990 and Projected to 2020*. Cambridge, MA: Harvard University Press.

Nelson, Kennard and Carolyn M. Williams. (2006). *Infectious Disease Epidemiology: Theory and Practice*. 2nd ed. Jones & Bartlett Publishers.

Packard, Randall M. *The Making of a Tropical Disease: A Short History of Malaria*. Johns Hopkins University Press, 2007.

Persad, Govind, Alan Wertheimer, and Ezekiel J. Emanuel. (2009). "Principles for Allocation of Scarce Medical Interventions." *The Lancet*, 373: 423–31.

Piel, Frédéric B. et al. (2010). "Global Distribution of the Sickle Cell Gene and Geographical Confirmation of the Malaria Hypothesis." *Nature Communications*, 2(1): 104.

Putterman, Louis and David N. Weil. (2010). "Post-1500 Population Flows and the Long Run Determinants of Economic Growth and Inequality." *Quarterly Journal of Economics*, CXXV: 4.

Ramankutty N., J. A. Foley, J. Norman, and K. McSweeney. (2002). "The Global Distribution of Cultivable Lands: Current Patterns and Sensitivity to Possible Climate Change." *Global Ecology and Biogeography*, 11: 377–92.

Riley, James C. (2005). "Estimates of Regional and Global Life Expectancy, 1800–2001." *Population and Development Review*,31(3): 537–43.

Rozenblat, C., M. Lennert, and G. Van Hamme. (2011). "European Cities in Networks." United Nations – Habitat report.

Steyn, Maryna. (2003). "A Comparison between Pre- and Post-Colonial Health in the Northern Parts of South Africa, a Preliminary Study." *World Archaeology, Archaeology of Epidemic and Infectious Disease*, 35(2): 276–88.

Stone, Lawrence. (1977). *The Family, Sex and Marriage in England, 1500–1800*. New York: Harper & Row.

United Nations, Department of Economic and Social Affairs, Population Division. (1982). *Model Life Tables for Developing Countries*. New York: United Nations.

(1999). *The World at Six Billion*. New York: United Nations.

(2009). *World Population Prospects: The 2008 Revision*. New York. (advanced Excel tables).

Voigtlander, Nicola and Joachim Voth. (2009). "The Three Horsemen of Riches: Plague, War and Urbanization in Early Modern Europe," mimeo, UCLA.

Webb, James L. A. (2006). "Ecology and Culture in West Africa." In *Themes in West Africa's History*, edited by Emmanuel Kwaku Akyeampong. Athens: Ohio University Press.

Webb, James L. A. (2008). *Humanity's Burden: A Global History of Malaria*. Cambridge, UK: Cambridge University Press.

Weil, David N. (2010). "Endemic Diseases and African Economic Growth: Challenges and Policy Responses." *Journal of African Economies*, 19 (supplement 3): 81–109.

Williams T. N., T. W. Mwangi, S. Wambua, N. D. Alexander, M. Kortok, R. W. Snow, and K. Marsh. (2005). "Sickle Cell Trait and the Risk of Plasmodium Falciparum Malaria and Other Childhood Diseases." *Journal of Infectious Diseases*, 192(1): 178–86.

Young, Alwyn. (2005). "The Gift of the Dying: The Tragedy of AIDS and the Welfare of Future African Generations." *The Quarterly Journal of Economics*, 120(2): 423–66.

4

African Population, 1650–2000: Comparisons and Implications of New Estimates

Patrick Manning

New and comprehensive estimates of African population, at regional and continental levels, suggest that from the seventeenth to the twentieth century the continent's population was much larger in size yet growing at a slower rate than previously thought. In a project that is nearing completion, Scott Nickleach and I, with the assistance of Yun Zhang, Brian McGill, and Bowen Yi, are projecting African populations from 1950 back to 1650.[1] The analysis relies on a combination of methods that account for decennial and regional estimates of net growth rates, effects of various social and environmental factors, and especially the demographic impact of enslavement and the attendant migration and mortality. Two hypotheses – a dense early modern African population and a decline in African population because of slave trade – are linked tightly together.

The present chapter focuses on the social implications of this new demographic argument. It begins with a concise summary of the new estimates at continental and regional levels, a comparison with previously accepted figures, and a brief exploration of the plausibility of the new figures. The bulk of this chapter discusses global comparisons of African population estimates and focuses especially on the main economic and social implications of these new estimates for our understanding of African history.

4.1 SUMMARY OF THE DEMOGRAPHIC ESTIMATES

The analysis begins with the dependable figures for the late twentieth century and works stage by stage to earlier times. For this reason, the discussion of the overall results, summarized in Table 4.1, moves from the most recent period to earlier periods.

[1] Work in process is to appear as Manning and Nickleach (forthcoming).

Table 4.1. *Estimated African population by region, 1700–2000, in millions*

	West	Central	Southern	East	Northeast	Northern	Total
2000	226	93	50	172	112	154	807
1950	60	26	15	42	33	44	220
1890	41	19	10	26	20	29	145
1790	46	17	12	22	22	23	141
1700	50	22	10	20	19	17	138

The period from 1950 to 2000 was one of record-setting population growth, at net growth rates consistently more than 2.5 percent per year. This growth rate resulted especially from rapidly falling rates of mortality: from 1950 to 1990, the expectation of life at birth for the average African rose from thirty-five years to fifty years. This dramatic decline in mortality accompanied the accession of African nations to independence and substantial expansion in public health expenditures by the new governments and, in preceding years, by late colonial governments. In addition, a worldwide decline in mortality resulted from the spread of antibiotics and many other improved medical treatments. (Then, in a devastating change, average expectation of life decreased drastically in southern and eastern Africa during the 1990s as a result of the AIDS crisis, and declined to a lesser degree elsewhere on the continent.)

In the preceding sixty years, from 1890 to 1950 – the colonial era for most of Africa – African populations gradually shifted from stagnation to demographic transition. Populations rose at a very modest rate from 1890, then accelerated from 1920 to 1950. The most rapid decline in mortality rates took place at the end of this period in the 1940s, as DDT spraying reduced malaria incidence in many areas, enabling rapid population growth. African growth rates were much smaller than those assumed by colonial officials, however, so that the African populations were substantially larger than the estimates prepared by colonial regimes. Population growth was held down by the violence that continued on a substantial scale from 1890 to 1920: enslavement continued in the regions not yet under European control and the establishment of European control meant wars of conquest, repression of rebellions, and forced recruitment of laborers.

The era from 1790 to 1890 included the peaks of three waves of enslavement – the 1790s peak of the transatlantic slave trade, the 1870s peak of the trans-Saharan and Indian Ocean trades, and the 1850s peak in enslavement of people held within the continent. The combination of these factors created serious negative pressure on African regional populations – with the worst effects felt first in West Africa, then in Central Africa, then in East Africa, and finally along the northern savanna. Overall, African population remained stagnant slightly from 1790 to 1890.

From 1450 to 1790, the Atlantic slave trade grew irregularly. From 1650, the drain of enslavement became sufficient to reduce population size in various regions of the western coast of Africa, and by 1730, a general decline had begun in the population of coastal West and Central Africa, continuing until the 1850s. Because most of the captives sent across the Atlantic were male, a significant shortage of adult males developed within West and Central Africa and brought a substantial transformation in gender relations.

The methods used for these population estimates rely on projections backward in time. The projections start from 1950 and trace population for seventy regions of Africa corresponding to national and provincial boundaries of today, selected in such a way as to be representative of economic and social regions of earlier times. For the twentieth century, the projections rely on crude rates of growth drawn from study of a wide range of factors. For the nineteenth century and before, the analysis relies especially on a simulation that accounts for the age and sex composition of free populations and of those enslaved. The work includes new estimates of the volume and direction of the transatlantic slave trade, based on statistical analysis of the well-known "Voyages" dataset (Eltis).

4.2 NEW VERSUS PREVIOUS ESTIMATES

In general, the new estimates differ from previous estimates in that they were constructed through a comprehensive analysis. Previous studies took a piecemeal approach, investigating restricted regions, short periods of time, a limited range of social interactions, or simple continental guesstimates. Addressing the fuller scope of issues permitted the location of contradictions, lacunae, and errors in analysis. The effort to address the full range of issues in African population history has resulted in a more internally consistent argument. The groundwork for this analysis was the research performed on African populations under the auspices of the United Nations. For 1950–2000, the current decennial estimates of African population published by the United Nations Population Office are broadly dependable, thanks to years of review and analysis by demographers at the UN and elsewhere. The population totals for 1950 and 1960 are well above those first reported in censuses and surveys at the moment of African national independence. Thus, the true size of the African population in recent decades has only gradually come to be recognized.

Documenting African population for the years before 1950 will require an approach analogous to that successfully applied to the post-1950 years: large-scale, collaborative work, piecing together the many available shreds of evidence into a coherent global pattern. The program of estimation reported on here is an initial stage in the comprehensive analysis of the African demographic past that needs to be pursued.

Meanwhile, the literatures on African history, economic history, and demographic history have generally been skeptical of the notion that Africa had a large and dense population from early modern times, skeptical of the notion that African rates of population growth were lower than those of other regions, and skeptical of the notion that enslavement caused decline in African population. Thus this argument for the plausibility of the new estimates requires commentary on the preceding threads of skepticism about the idea of a dense pre-slave-trade African population.

An initial basis for skepticism about large early modern African populations arose from methodology – from the piecemeal approach of studies in demographic history. Perhaps understandably, scholarly studies from the 1960s through the 1980s worked on short periods of time and portions of the African continent, so they were never able to compare the figures they were using with continental figures. West Africanists studied the Atlantic trade; East Africanists, after a delay, studied the Indian Ocean trade; a continental picture did not yet exist.[2] For the precolonial era, analysts have given insufficient attention to the difference between the nineteenth century, when enslavement raged over most of the African continent, and the previous centuries, when the Atlantic slave trade was the main engine of the patterns of migration and social disruption that affected West and Central Africa most severely.

A second skepticism is based on a habitual reliance on colonial statistical records. During the years before World War II, it was widely assumed that the African continental population had risen from about 100 million in 1900 up to about 130 million in 1930 (Carr-Saunders 1936; Kuczynski 1934; Willcox 1931). It has only recently been noted that, to reach from

[2] And this despite the fact that continental estimates of African population had been advanced since the seventeenth century and were prominently published during the twentieth century. My 1990 attempt at a continental picture fell short in at least two ways: it was not linked to post-1950 populations and it did not enable readers to verify its calculations (Manning 1990).

130 million in 1930 to 220 million in 1950, Africa's population would have had to grow at 2.7 percent per year through depression and war. Global comparison shows that no large population worldwide was growing at such a rate before 1950 – the growth rate must have been lower and the earlier populations must have been higher. That is, African populations of the early twentieth century turn out to have been significantly underreported. Such underreporting is understandable from the viewpoint of African communities. Presumably, African communities had little incentive to present themselves for enumeration when the main results of enumeration were taxation and recruitment rather than provision of social services. Only from the 1950s, once social services began to appear in the national era – and when political representation began to be determined by population size – did the response to population surveys grow more positive.

A third basis for skepticism about the size of African populations and the effects of slave trade came from comparison with European migration. This was a comparison of European transatlantic migration (1850–1940) with transatlantic trade in African captives (mostly from 1650 to 1850). Because it was known that Europe, in the years after 1850, was able to grow in population even as large numbers of migrants left their home countries, it seemed to many observers that Africa ought also to have been able to avoid population decline. After all, Africa's 10 million emigrants compared to Europe's 50 million. Nonetheless, a detailed analysis shows that Africa's export slave trade was indeed sufficient to reduce the population of major regions and, for more than a century, of the continent as a whole. The negative factors that made the difference were the high general levels of mortality for Africa, the additional mortality brought by the violence of enslavement, the loss of young adult females and their offspring, and the high levels of maritime mortality in the days before steamships. For the reproduction of African population, the key group was fertile females, generally those in the age group from fifteen to forty-five. As soon as enough of them died or were exported, the result would be sufficient to halt population growth.

A fourth basis for skepticism, questioning the negative impact of enslavement on African population, argued that African nutrition improved with the arrival of American crops (maize, manioc, peanuts, etc.), and that African population therefore expanded. This argument – focusing on the era from the sixteenth to the nineteenth centuries – while plausible, has not yet come close to verification. That is, we have yet to verify when American crops became a significant portion of African diets, and have yet to verify that they were substantially more productive than the previous African crops (Manning 1982a; Wigboldus 1986).[3] It is possible, therefore, that Africans of the nineteenth century had a broader diet but consumed no more calories than their predecessors of the sixteenth century.

All of these reasons apply to the post-1450 period of Atlantic maritime voyages. An additional element of the overall African demographic debate is that of whether African population in earlier – "medieval" – times was dense or sparse. Some researchers claim that the population of coastal regions of West Africa and Central Africa had been extremely sparse in these times, and that they were settled from further inland only in early modern times. For instance, scholars have argued that the prevalence of malaria and other tropical diseases prevented population from becoming dense. This type of argument lacks plausibility because the presence of infectious disease, while a negative factor in the short term, is a clear indication that a dense population has existed in a region over the long term, as such a population was necessary to sustain the disease. Language distribution is another key to the historical depth and density of population: for West Africa in particular, the distribution of subgroups of the Niger-Congo language group indicates that populations have lived and migrated – in both the forested and savanna zones – for thousands of years, with a time depth far greater than that of populations in Europe (Williamson and Blench 2000, 11–42).[4] This does more to demonstrate that West African population was ancient than that it was dense, but it dismisses the notion that any regions of West Africa were unsettled (Figure 4.1).

Walter Willcox, A. M. Carr-Saunders, and R. R. Kuczynski, writing in the early 1930s, argued for a relatively static African population of about 100 million from 1650 to the late nineteenth century, and for a population of roughly 130 million in 1930 (Carr-Saunders 1936; Kuczynski 1934, 240–8; Willcox 1923). Caldwell and Schindlmayr argued forcefully against this vision, on the grounds that Africans had expanded into previously underpopulated areas from the sixteenth century, relying on new crops from the Americas.[5] Caldwell and Schindlmayr note approvingly "a collapse of the earlier African consensus" after 1970, as Durand, McEvedy, and Jones and

[3] On maize: (McCann 2005; Miracle 1966). These works, while highly valuable for the nineteenth and twentieth centuries, provide little dependable information on the initial adoption and spread of maize in Africa.

[4] For the methods of this analysis, see Christopher Ehret, *History and the Testimony of Language* (Berkeley: University of California Press, 2010).

[5] "Kuczynski was admittedly a demographic conservative, and as late as 1944 ... was arguing that Africa and probably most of the developing world was then not more populated than it had been 200 years earlier" (Caldwell and Schindlmayr 2002, 186). See also Kuczynski (1944).

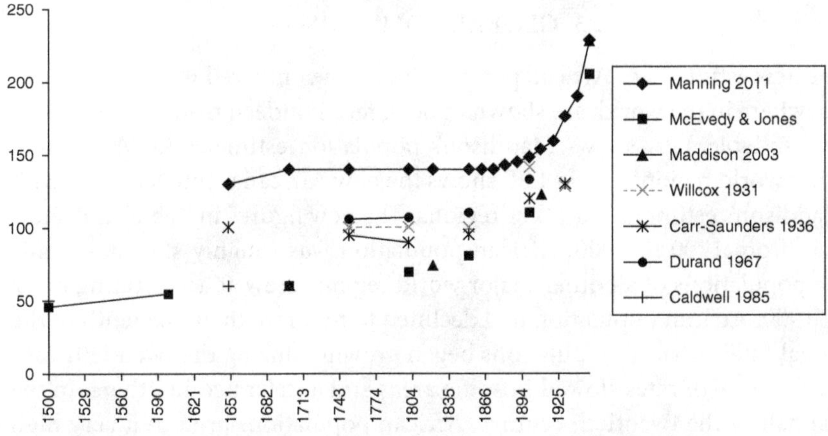

Figure 4.1. New and previous estimates of African population, 1500–2000.
Sources: Previous estimates from McEvedy and Jones (1978), Willcox (1931), Carr-Saunders (1936), Maddison (2001), Durand (1965), Biraben (1979), and Caldwell and Schindlmayr (2002).

Maddison each set African population at the much lower figure of about 50 million in 1500.[6] John C. Caldwell remains unsurpassed in his knowledge of African demography in late colonial and early postindependence Africa, and his analysis was crucial in unraveling the "consensus" among demographic historians that prevented an appropriate linkage among precolonial, colonial, and postcolonial demographic studies. But his willingness to treat Africans of the eighteenth century as just entering the Neolithic, combined with his neglect of the severity of enslavement throughout the continent, led him to assume rapid African population growth from the sixteenth through the nineteenth century when such growth was quite impossible.[7]

6 Caldwell and Schindlmayr argue an extreme version of this hypothesis, claiming that the loss to enslavement "probably did not translate into a comparable diminution of the rate of natural increase, and certainly not to a population decline, for three reasons. The first is that … the loss of some of the population probably allowed others to survive. The second reason is that only one-third of those transported as slaves were females.… The third point is that the period of slavery coincided with the spread of new foodstuffs introduced from the Americas, fostering slow but continuing population growth.… It is extremely doubtful whether either the absolute or relative decline of Africa's population ever took place" (2002, 196–7).

7 Caldwell and Schindlmayr argue that, "The spread of the Neolithic revolution in the form of hunting giving way to farming continued throughout the nineteenth and twentieth centuries and is still not complete." This argument that Africans were just reaching the Neolithic is particularly surprising given the ample evidence that the African iron age

4.3 GLOBAL COMPARISONS

The new estimates of African population, when compared with populations elsewhere in the world, are shown to be different indeed from previous estimates. Table 4.2A shows Maddison's population estimates for Africa and other world regions; Table 4.2B shows the new African estimates along with Maddison's estimates for other regions. The new figures in Table 4.2B show that, from 1700 to 1900, African population was roughly stagnant, while the populations of all other major world regions grew at accelerating rates: by 1900, African population had declined to no more than one tenth of the global total. African populations began growing during the twentieth century as growth rates slowed in some areas and accelerated in others. In the last half of the twentieth century, African populations grew at a very high rate, and by the time these growth rates began to decline, African population had again reached one seventh of the world total.

Along with the planetary comparison of Table 4.2, here are some additional comparisons of population size and density. Comparing Africa with Eurasia reveals a remarkable parallel in population density. Africa, in its surface area, has some 30 million square kilometers, while Eurasia has some 53 million square kilometers. Africa's current population is roughly one billion, while that of Eurasia is roughly four billion. Thus, Africa's population density is now just short of half that of Eurasia.[8] For 1700, Maddison shows Eurasian population at 530 million and African population at 60 million; the new estimates show an African population of 140 million in 1700. Thus the new estimates show an African population density that was half that of Eurasia – the same ratio as at present – while Maddison's figures propose an African population density in 1700 that was less than one fourth that of Eurasia. That is, the old estimates argue that Africa was consistently a sparsely populated continent until very recent times; the new estimates argue that Africa was not far behind Eurasia in density and has maintained

began at the same time as that of Eurasia, some two thousand years before the Atlantic slave trade expanded (Caldwell and Schindlmayr 2002, 197). Twenty years earlier, Caldwell had acknowledged the validity of my assertion that slave trade had the capacity to reduce African population, though at that time too he preferred the argument that American crops had overcome all obstacles to African demographic growth (Caldwell 1982); see also Manning (1981 and 1982b).

[8] This comparison in continental areas can be adjusted by accounting for underpopulated areas – the Sahara in Africa; Arabia and Siberia in Eurasia – yet the results tend to cancel out. Still another version of the comparison is to compare populations to areas of arable land for Africa and Eurasia – these too tend to show an African density about half that of Eurasia.

Table 4.2A. *Size and proportion of world population, 1700–1950 Maddison estimates by world region (showing % of global population)*

	1700	%	1820	%	1913	%	1950	%
Africa	**61**	10	**74**	7	**123**	6	**228**	9
Asia	402	67	710	68	978	55	1382	55
L. Am	12	2	21	2	81	5	166	7
Europe	125	21	224	22	497	28	572	23
W. offshoots	2	0	11	1	111	6	176	7

Table 4.2B. *New estimates for Africa, Maddison estimates elsewhere*

	1700	%	1820	%	1913	%	1950	%
Africa	**140**	21	**140**	13	**145**	8	**228**	9
Asia	402	59	710	64	978	54	1382	55
L. Am	12	2	21	2	81	4	166	7
Europe	125	18	224	20	497	25	572	23
W. offshoots	2	0	11	1	111	6	176	7

Source: (Maddison 2001, 175, 183). Maddison's "Western Offshoots" include the United States, Canada, Australia, and New Zealand; "Europe" includes the entire territory of the former Soviet Union. I calculated the growth rates shown.

or periodically regained its relative position in population density over the centuries.

Comparing Africa and Europe reveals a remarkable parallel in population size over the long term and shows both parallels and contrasts in the history of migration. European and African populations are roughly equal today, but Europe's population density is three times that of Africa; Europe (including Russia) is only 10 million square kilometers in area. The two regions had equal populations of some 140 million in 1700. European populations rose at a steady rate, however, while African population remained stagnant until the mid-twentieth century. In migration, Europeans outnumbered Africans as out-migrants from 1500 to 1600, Africans outnumbered Europeans as migrants from 1600 to 1850, Europeans outnumbered Africans again until 1960, and African migrants grew in number thereafter. Among other differences in the migratory patterns were that, in the era of slave trade, there were few slaves among European migrants, and European migrants were able to return home. After 1850, European migrants traveled on low-mortality steamships, while the ongoing African slave trade continued to exact a high toll in mortality. Some factors worked in the opposition direction. In monogamous Europe, the absence of males left women unmarried or marrying later in life, thus affecting their fertility. In polygynous Africa, the remaining women still had children in marriage or concubinage; indeed, it seems that the long-term shortage of males brought by slave trade expanded the frequency of concubinage (if not of formal marriage) in Africa.[9]

Africa and the Americas provide remarkable contrasts in population history. The Americas have 41 million square kilometers in area, but if one subtracts the 10 million square kilometers of sparsely populated Canada, the result is equal to the area of Africa. At present, the populations and therefore the population densities of Africa and the Americas are roughly equal. In 1700, however, the Americas had only some 13 million inhabitants (at least two million of them of African descent), so that the population density of the Americas was one tenth that of Africa.[10] Among the variations in patterns of population were that American populations declined sharply because of disease during the sixteenth and early seventeenth centuries, while from 1650 to 1850 African populations declined through slave trade as American populations rose through African immigration and recovery of the indigenous population. American populations grew rapidly through European migration after 1850 while African populations remained stagnant.[11]

4.4 AFRICAN IMPLICATIONS

The new demographic estimates for Africa, when combined with a reconsideration of the continent's economic, social, cultural, and ecological conditions, yield a substantially revised picture of African life. This section begins by laying out the main elements of the revised picture, then turns to explaining the logic of the new picture and providing recommendations on ways to pursue the reinterpretation of precolonial and colonial Africa.

[9] The large-scale, steamship-borne migrations from 1850 to 1940 transported migrants from other densely populated regions (Europe, East Asia, South Asia), but not from Africa. Only by 2000, when Africa had again become relatively densely populated, did overseas African emigration again become significant (McKeown 2004).

[10] Or an American population density one fourth that of Africa, using Maddison's population estimate.

[11] During the sixteenth and seventeenth centuries, African populations too may have been limited by the global circulation of diseases in that era.

African populations from 1500 to 1700 were relatively dense, linked with one another in various networks of exchange, relying on local moneys. Except along the fringes of the Eurasian commercial system, African states were small. A sort of "informal economy" enabled many to participate, if marginally, in the continental system of exchange. Mortality was high, many were poor, and reliance on external trade was minimal. Yet to treat this as a system of relatively dense population, we must assume that people were linked through networks of exchange rather than reliant on self-sufficiency in isolated households. From 1700 to 1900, slavery expanded in region after region of the continent, bringing violence, refugee life, increased mortality, new sorts of hierarchy (notably an expanded gender hierarchy), a growing proportion of the population in slavery, and the rise of states that relied significantly on warfare and enslavement. External trade – for which exports relied especially but not only on slaves – grew steadily from 1700 to 1900. From 1900 to 1950, African populations recovered from the pressure of enslavement and the shock of colonial conquest, and gradually entered an era of lower mortality. African economic growth (measured in terms of domestic product or external trade) remained relatively slow during the nineteenth and twentieth centuries except for occasional bursts of positive or negative growth; demographic growth became strongly positive from the 1940s to the 1990s.

As a framework for assessing African socioeconomic life, we may begin with that offered in 1973 by A. G. Hopkins, whose groundbreaking analysis of West African economic history crystallized the analysis of African economies through his distinction of "the domestic economy" from the "external trade" that crossed the desert and the ocean (Hopkins 1973). In these terms, African total output or Gross Domestic Product is the sum of the output of the domestic economy and the net value of external trade. Hopkins's two-sector model, although proposed for the interpretation of precolonial African economies, has in fact remained the default system for analyzing African economies from earliest times until the present. While this formulation is entirely logical, we will see that it has severe practical disadvantages. That is, while Hopkins proposed the two-sector model in an effort to draw attention to the size and diversity of the domestic economy, in practice, the historical and contemporary analysis of African economies has focused overwhelmingly on external trade. The domestic economy is commonly left out of discussion; further, it is widely presumed to have been homogeneous and rudimentary.

Viewed in this two-sector framework, the new estimates of African population imply a major rethinking of African economic structures. The new population figures suggest that the "domestic economy" was much larger than has been realized, and that "external trade" was a smaller proportion of GDP than previously realized. That is, the historical levels of sub-Saharan African external trade – across the oceans and desert – are known, within an order of magnitude. Now that we have new and higher estimates of African population, it is necessarily the case that estimates of output in the domestic economy for sub-Saharan Africa are larger than before, and that the ratio of intercontinental trade to GDP will appear smaller.[12]

For present purposes, therefore, the framework of the "domestic economy" appears vague and inadequate in that it avoids specifying the levels of exchange and economic interaction within the continent. The estimate of a larger population leads by demographic logic to the presumption of an expanded, continent-wide domestic economy. The same estimate of a larger population also leads, by the logic of economic productivity, to the presumption of substantial sectors of regional and local exchange networks. This expanded domestic sector is best treated in terms of a range of subsectors: self-sufficient production (including foraging), local exchange (with attention to occupational specialization), cross-regional and monetized commerce within sub-Saharan Africa, and the secondary and tertiary sectors of governance, knowledge, and cultural production. The "external trade" sector, the best-documented aspect of African economies, can then be linked more explicitly to the interacting subsectors of the domestic economy. In the paragraphs that follow, this expanded notion of sectors within the domestic economy is applied successively to the era from 1500 to 1700, the slave trade era from 1700 to 1900, and the colonial and neocolonial period of the twentieth century.

4.4.1 Rethinking Africa from 1500 to 1700

Such a framework should facilitate the creation of a new picture of Africa from 1500 to 1700, when African populations were presumably growing yet already dense. The elements of such a reconsideration proposed here include land-labor ratios, systems of money, the nature of ethnicity, the

[12] For an earlier discussion on the balance of the domestic economy and overseas trade in the Bight of Benin, see the works of Peukert and Manning: for the kingdom of Dahomey, Peukert assumed export value reached only 4 percent of GDP; for the larger Bight of Benin, Manning assumed export value reached 15 percent of GDP. Manning proposed a three-century series on export revenue and per capita export revenue, with rougher estimates of GDP (Manning 1982a, 2, 44; Peukert 1978).

functions of states, the role of poverty, and the contemporary notion of the "informal economy" as applied to precolonial times.

We need to rethink land-labor ratios for Africa. Should Africa before the twentieth century continue to be seen as a continent of land surplus and labor shortage? Or should it be viewed as a region of relatively dense population where land was better seen as a scarce resource than a free good? The interpretive choice, highlighted clearly by the new estimates, draws renewed attention to the old differences between Hopkins's assumption of African labor shortage, the Gemery and Hogendorn assumption of African labor surplus, and Ester Boserup's analysis of behavior change resulting from increased population density (Boserup 1965; Hopkins 1973; Gemery and Hogendorn 1974).[13] Regional and global comparisons of the labor intensity of production and the social organization of labor will surely reveal a need to study African labor more fully.

Study of the forms and dynamics of African money can facilitate the required rethinking of exchange in African markets. It is noteworthy that gold served as currency in the large portions of West Africa where it was mined, and gold also served as currency in southeast Africa and along the Swahili coast. Silver presented a contrast: silver was the main international currency from the late sixteenth century, but silver was little used as currency in sub-Saharan Africa. Partly this was a response to the scarcity of silver in Africa, but it also suggests that Africa was outside the main currents of global trade until the mid-nineteenth century, when silver coins became widely used in many parts of Africa. (An exception to this pattern is Ethiopia and northeast Africa generally – silver was traded and coined in that region, reflecting its integration into Middle East and Indian Ocean trading circuits.) Overall, a denser African population means a further magnified density in marketing. It means that there is much more to be learned about African currencies, credit, and other means of exchange.

We need to rethink the handling of ethnicity in Africa. Too often, analysis has focused on ethnic groups as if they were autonomous and self-sufficient groupings. Among the approaches to ethnicity that provide promise for developing an interactive approach to a multi-sector domestic economy is the work of Frederik Barth and Frederic Pryor. Barth's analysis of ethnic groups and boundaries, showing how families crossed ethnic boundaries at times when it was economically necessary, became useful in understanding

[13] The Gemery-Hogendorn interpretation of slave exports in terms of the "vent for surplus" theory was one of the few arguments of its time that land rather than labor was in short supply in the era of slave trade.

the response to drought in the central Sudan, as families shifted from agriculture to pastoralism and back (Barth 1994). Pryor's global study of peasant distribution systems, drawing on ethnographic accounts from the Human Relations Area Files, analyzed four types of distribution systems in peasant economies and found correlations suggesting surprisingly complex processes of economic choice and evolution (Pryor 1977).[14] As with ethnicity, so also with the spatial distribution of African population; attention to zones of high economic activity and high population density may reveal the African dynamics of interchange and division of labor that have been neglected in interpretations that have conceded too much to the notion of a poor, underpopulated, and backward African countryside.

The new estimates raise parallel questions about states and statecraft in Africa. While Africans had states throughout the continent, these states in general did not develop the bureaucracies, armies, and monuments of those in Eurasia. Indeed, the scarcity of such great states is one of the reasons scholars have tended to assume that African populations were sparse. Quite a different possibility is that African societies found ways to develop and nourish dense populations without giving such support to elite classes and state institutions.

Similarly, we should consider the issue of poverty in long-term perspective. It may be that significant insights will come from a rereading of John Iliffe's remarkably broad review, *The African Poor*. In this continental study of poverty in the nineteenth and twentieth centuries, Iliffe distinguished between the poor and the very poor, where the latter never escaped the fringes of hunger (Iliffe 1987). The question is how far into the past this analysis of poverty might be carried.

It is unlikely that new investigations will unearth previously unsuspected concentrations of great wealth and centralized power in Africa. We should look instead for an Africa of the past that can be linked to the Africa of the present – that is, societies with relatively dense populations, with considerable socioeconomic inequality, with an immense range of communities and activities, but in an environment of high mortality and widespread poverty. For instance, we should consider the benefits of extending to the more distant past the recently developed logic of the informal economy. A substantial literature has grown up centering on contemporary economic activity that takes place outside of the formal sector of wages, profits, and regulation – work and transactions that enable people to survive and sometimes prosper, but that escape formal economic accounting (MacGaffey

[14] A parallel study relying on HRAF records was that of Patterson (1982).

1991; Portes, Castells, and Benton 1989). The phenomenon of the informal economy, while generally treated as a spinoff of the globalizing capitalist economy, may instead be the current version of what was earlier the domestic and regional market of Africa. That is, the lessons learned from studying the contemporary informal sector might be applied to earlier times, and might help explain how a large African population could have sustained a lively regional economy that nonetheless had little interaction with global commerce.

4.4.2 African Social Dynamics, 1700–1900

The multi-sectoral approach to Africa's domestic economy can then be applied to the era from 1700 to 1900. During these two centuries, population stagnated overall and fluctuated up and down in most regions according to fluctuations in slave trade and other factors, and external trade expanded in tandem with domestic enslavement. The new population estimates provide a new basis for analyzing the main historical questions of this era. For instance, did the conditions of African life worsen in the era of slave trade? Did general mortality rates rise in West and Central Africa from the seventeenth to the nineteenth century and in nineteenth-century East Africa? It is certainly the case that enslavement, drought, famine, and epidemic reinforced one another periodically to the point that it becomes difficult to distinguish the various causes of misery (Miller 1982). The savanna regions of West Africa and Angola were particularly vulnerable to such downturns, but social tumult and the creation of refugee populations brought periodic turmoil to many African regions. Investigators of the emergence of the HIV virus in humans continue to explore the question of whether it was the social disorder of late nineteenth-century enslavement that led to the transfer of viruses among species and the formation of the human-carried version of HIV.

It may be that the character of African statecraft changed significantly as enslavement grew in significance. That is, the earlier focus of localized states on the welfare of the monarch's constituents (as in Ife and the Kuba kingdom) came to be replaced by more warlike and hierarchical states (such as Dahomey, Imbangala, and Segu). Meanwhile, the expansion of enslavement put a premium on effective defense and on the maintenance of refugee communities, which again undermined respect for large states.

What was the size of slave populations in Africa? This analysis has argued that the enslaved populations of Africa grew sharply in the eighteenth century and then grew again even more sharply in the nineteenth century. It seems certain that the worldwide peak in enslaved populations came in roughly 1850, and that those in Africa were the majority of those held in slavery. These are demographic projections, however, rather than descriptions of individual lives, so much more research will be necessary to verify the validity and the meaning of this assertion.

Another measure of the long-term effects of enslavement can be taken through comparison of the two-plus centuries of enslavement in West Africa with the one century of enslavement in East Africa. In eighteenth-century West Africa, transatlantic slave trade expanded steadily and trans-Saharan slave trade expanded to a lesser degree; eighteenth-century East Africa remained in a situation of relative autarky. In nineteenth-century West Africa, the Atlantic trade declined while the trans-Saharan slave trade expanded somewhat and enslavement within the region expanded as well. In nineteenth-century East Africa, Indian Ocean slave trade grew rapidly to a peak late in the century, then came almost to an end at the end of the century. In West Africa, the nineteenth-century decline in Atlantic slave trade coincided with a rapid growth in commodity exports; commodity exports from East Africa expanded considerably later. Overall, it appears that West Africa rebounded first from the negative demographic effects of slave trade, followed by Central Africa and then by East Africa. But the East African slave trade, though brutal in its impact, lasted for a shorter time than that for West and Central Africa, so the continuing social markers of the slave past seem clearer in West and Central Africa. In East Africa, Mozambique and Malawi are the regions that show the most after-effects of enslavement.

4.4.3 Twentieth-Century Africa

From 1900, enslavement had nearly stopped; those in slavery gradually achieved non-slave or ex-slave status. Export agriculture and expanding cities provided new opportunities for some, and refugee populations gradually came into the open. There were exceptions to this positive picture: for instance, the turmoil of the Congo basin and north Central Africa in the early colonial years, under King Leopold's Congo Free State and in the French Congo, each succeeding a period of several decades of intensive slave raiding. Whatever their growth rate, colonial African populations are now known to have been far larger than European rulers understood at the time. The inflection point was in the 1940s, when a world distracted by war left Africa in a near-autarkic situation. From that time, the population of Africa began expanding at an unprecedented and unrelenting rate until the present.

How long-lasting were the social effects of large-scale enslavement? Here is one suggestion that some effects may have been long-lasting indeed. Today, in the early twenty-first century, the African regions with the highest incidence of polygyny and the lowest level of female education are the same regions as those from which the export of male slaves was most consistent and longest lasting: West Africa and Central Africa (Tabutin and Schoumaker 2002). Can it be that centuries of slave exports and uneven adult gender balance created a self-reproducing system that continues to rely on the subordination of women?

To further test and document this line of argument, we need to expand research on long-term African population patterns, working especially in archaeology, linguistics, social and anthropological studies, and with written documents. For these demographic questions and for the accompanying social questions, it will take a while to clarify and document the implications of this new understanding of African population history.

4.5 AFRICA IN GLOBAL CONTEXT

The demographic analysis developed here contests sharply the notion – which has grown especially in the past forty years – that African population has consistently grown at a rate more rapid than the average of human population growth. Such a "rapid African growth" thesis has led to projections of a small African population base in medieval times and steady growth until the mid-twentieth century. This analysis also contests the colonial-era estimates of African population, because they were generally too low to be consistent with the earliest dependable African population figures during the 1950s and 1960s.

It is definitely the case that African population since 1950 has grown at rates higher than the average for humanity, but that pattern cannot reasonably be projected into earlier times, and for three main reasons. First, there is no reason to assume that African growth rates were among the highest in the world before, during, or after the era of the slave trade. Second, the effects of enslavement seriously reduced the ability of African populations to grow. Third, general African mortality was relatively high, so that precolonial and colonial African growth rates may well have been lower than for other regions. The old ideas about Africa's demographic past simply cannot stand up to a comprehensive and comparative analysis of African population in global context.

The African continent, viewed from the outside, appeared to have participated only to a modest degree in the global interactions and transformations of the era from 1500 to 1700, though the continent may have undergone major changes that are not yet fully understood – impact of disease is one possibility. Then, from 1650 to 1850, the continent was seriously drained in population through enslavement.[15] African migration continued after 1850 – as enslavement sent many captives to destinations within Africa and across the Sahara and into the Indian Ocean – though expanding migration from Europe and Asia overshadowed African migration after 1850. The adoption of American crops by African farmers is known to have taken place from 1500, but we do not yet have precise information on the pace of adoption or on the nutritional or demographic results of that agricultural change, and cannot simply assume that it overcame all other factors to generate steady population growth. From 1850 to 1950, Africa fell increasingly under European colonial rule, with its mix of repression, taxation, and economic transformation. Throughout these successive periods, African populations, though relatively dense, met consistent limits that prevented any long-term growth.

With independence after 1950, African nations experienced bursts of development in health, education, and economic growth, but fell into a pattern of neocolonial subordination to international organizations, as with the World Bank's structural adjustment programs. During this period, however, African populations escaped their previous limits and grew steadily at rates more than 2.5percent per year, a growth rate high enough to create its own problems.

While Africans overcame the limits on their demographic growth, the limits on African economic growth remained in place. From 1850 if not before, African prices and wages in international markets have been held at extremely low levels. Investment in the continent has been overwhelmingly out of domestic funds – yet the African funds available for investment were restricted by the low incomes that Africans gained in international transactions. Nevertheless, African economies have undergone transformations and even growth over the past century, a pattern that tends to argue that the domestic economy continues to have a viable mechanism of accumulation (Manning 1982a, 218–19). The population of the African continent is now – and presumably once again – near to one sixth of the total of humanity, and the distinctive long-term history of its demographic, economic, and social life may have important lessons for the continent itself and for regions beyond it.

[15] The guesses of Willcox and Carr-Saunders – that Africa remained in demographic stasis during the era of slave trade – are confirmed in general by this new research.

In sum, this assembly of evidence and analysis suggests that we should develop a modified perspective on the overall characteristics of African population from the sixteenth century through the colonial era. That is, we should envision African populations that were relatively dense, in comparison with others of their time. Their application of diversified technologies permitted relatively intensive exploitation of varying environments. They developed elites at local but not at imperial scales. Nonetheless, the disease environment kept mortality at a high level. The expansion of slave trade and a concomitant expansion in domestic slavery, in region after region of the continent, transformed and further marginalized this socioeconomic system but did not destroy it. It may be that the same pattern has been propagated into the present, though it cannot yet be said by what mechanisms the system was reproduced over time. As this pre-1950 demographic pattern clarifies, Africa should be compared more systematically with tropical South Asia and Southeast Asia, in both demographic and social terms. And Africa before 1950 should be compared systematically with Africa since 1950.

References

Barth, Fredrik, ed. (1994). *Ethnic Groups and Boundaries: The Social Organization of Culture Difference*. Oslo: Pensumtjeneste.

Biraben, Jean-Noël. (1979). "Essai sur l'évolution du nombre des homes." *Population*, 34: 13–25.

Boserup, Ester. (1965). *The Conditions of Agricultural Growth: The Economics of Agrarian Change under Population Pressure*. London: G. Allen & Unwin.

Caldwell, John C. (1982). "Comment on Manning, 'The Enslavement of Africans: A Demographic Model.'" *Canadian Journal of African Studies*, 16: 127–30.

Caldwell, John C. and Thomas Schindlmayr. (2002). "Historical Population Estimates: Unraveling the Consensus." *Population and Development Review*, 28: 183–204.

Carr-Saunders, A. M. (1936). *World Population: Past Growth and Present Trends*. Oxford: Clarendon.

Durand, John D. (1965). "World Population Estimates, 1750–2000." In *Proceedings of the World Population Conference, Belgrade, 30 August – 10 September 1965*, II: 17–22. New York: United Nations.

Eltis, David, ed. "Voyages: The Transatlantic Slave Trade Database." http://www.Slavevoyages.org/tast/index.faces.

Gemery, Henry A. and Jan S. Hogendorn. (1974). "The Atlantic Slave Trade: A Tentative Economic Model." *Journal of African History*, 15: 223–46.

Hopkins, A. G. (1973). *An Economic History of West Africa*. London: Longman.

Iliffe, John. (1987). *The African Poor: A History*. Cambridge: Cambridge University Press.

Kuczynski, R. R. (1934). "Population." In *Encyclopedia of the Social Sciences*, Vol. 12, edited by E. R. A. Seligman and A. Johnson, 240–8. New York: Macmillan.

(1944). "World Population Problems." *International Affairs*, 20: 449–57.

MacGaffey, Janet. (1991). *The Real Economy of Zaire: The Contribution of Smuggling & Other Unofficial Activities to National Wealth*. Philadelphia: University of Pennsylvania Press.

Maddison, Angus. (2001). *The World Economy: A Millennial Perspective*. Paris: Organisation for Economic Co-Operation and Development.

Manning, Patrick. (1981). "The Enslavement of Africans: A Demographic Model." *Canadian Journal of African Studies*, 15: 499–526.

(1982a). *Slavery, Colonialism and Economic Growth in Dahomey, 1640–1960*. Cambridge: Cambridge University Press.

(1982b). "Response to Comments by Caldwell and Inikori." *Canadian Journal of African Studies*, 16: 138–9.

(1990). *Slavery and African Life: Occidental, Oriental, and Atlantic Slave Trades*. Cambridge: Cambridge University Press.

Manning, Patrick and Scott Nickleach (forthcoming). African Population, 1650–1950: The Eras of Enslavement and Colonial Rule.

McCann, James. (2005). *Maize and Grace: History, Corn, and Africa's New Landscapes, 1500–1999*. Cambridge, MA: Harvard University Press.

McEvedy, Colin and Richard Jones. (1978). *Atlas of World Population History*. New York: Facts on File.

McKeown, Adam. (2004). "Global Migration, 1846–1940," *Journal of World History*, 15: 155–89.

Miller, Joseph C. (1982). "The Significance of Drought, Disease and Famine in the Agriculturally Marginal Zone of West-Central Africa." *Journal of African History*, 22: 17–61.

Miracle, Marvin P. (1966). *Maize in Tropical Africa*. Madison: University of Wisconsin Press.

Patterson, Orlando. (1982). *Slavery and Social Death: A Comparative Study*. Cambridge, MA: Harvard University Press.

Peukert, Werner. (1978). *Der Atlantische Sklavenhanden von Dahomey, 1740–1797*. Wiesbaden: Steiner.

Portes, Alejandro, Manuel Castells, and Lauren A. Benton, eds. (1989). *The Informal Economy: Studies in Advanced and Less Developed Countries*. Baltimore, MD: Johns Hopkins University Press.

Pryor, Frederic. (1977). *The Origins of the Economy*. New York: Academic Press.

Tabutin, Dominique and Bruno Schoumaker. (2002). "The Demography of Sub-Saharan Africa from the 1950s to the 2000s. A Survey of Changes and a Statistical Assessment." *Population*, 59: 457–555.

Wigboldus, Jouke. (1986). "Trade and Agriculture in Coastal Benin c. 1470–1660: An Examination of Manning's Early-Growth Thesis." *A.A.G. Bijdragen*, 28: 299–380.

Willcox, Walter F., ed. (1931) "Increase in the Population of the Earth and of the Continents since 1650." In *International Migrations, vol. 2, Interpretations*, edited by. W. F. Willcox, 33–82. New York: National Bureau of Economic Research.

Williamson, Kay and Roger Blench. (2000). "Niger-Congo." In *African Languages: An Introduction*, edited by Bernd Heine and Derek Nurse, 11–42. Cambridge: Cambridge University Press.

PART II

CULTURE, ENTREPRENEURSHIP, AND DEVELOPMENT

5

Redistributive Pressures in Sub-Saharan Africa: Causes, Consequences, and Coping Strategies

Jean-Philippe Platteau

5.1 INTRODUCTION

A widespread idea in the development economics literature of the past decades is that personalized relationships and social networks play an important role in the spontaneous evolution of institutions required for rapid growth, such as contract enforcement mechanisms and property rights (see, e.g., Aoki 2001; Bates 2001; Fafchamps 2004; Greif 2006; Hayami and Kawagoe 1993; North 1990; Platteau 2000). An intriguing question, which is rarely raised, is how to reconcile such a view with the well-known Weberian/Marxian thesis that the development of market societies is based on the rising autonomy of the individual and his (her) emancipation from the matrix of erstwhile social agencies.

This question has several aspects. Although personalized relationships allow good circulation of information, they do not necessarily create the best conditions for the impartial meting out of sanctions against rule violators, thereby undermining the effectiveness of reputation mechanisms (Baland, Somanathan, and Wahhaj 2013; Hoff and Sen 2005; Platteau 2000, chapter 6). Moreover, if traditional codes of honor prevail, even the informational advantage of personalized relationships can be disputed: thus, a lot of secrecy surrounds economic transactions if, in the event of rule breaking (think of loan delinquency), people are wary of not bringing shame on resident families with whom they are in continuous interaction, or if they are eager to conceal acts of malfeasance of which they have been the victims because such a revelation would undermine their reputation as strong persons (Platteau 2000, chapter 6). A cheated person may also refrain from leaking out the information if he (she) does not wish to protect other community members, say, because he (she) wants them to be harmed in the same way as he (she) has been. Finally, to the extent that norms based on values of generosity, sociability, and hospitality tend to prevail among closely related persons, relatively successful members of social groups or networks would face internal pressures to redistribute their incomes, which would create strong disincentives to apply effort, take risks, and accumulate capital.

The way out of this dilemma seems evident: kinship or place of origin should play little or no role in the formation of business and other social networks. This is what Arne Bigsten and his colleagues (Bigsten et al. 2000) actually found in their survey of indigenous trading and manufacturing firms located in a number of African countries. Note, however, that the implied process of emancipation still requires that entrepreneurial individuals are strong enough to withstand the redistributive pressures that are likely to be exerted from without by their kith and kin.

This is precisely the problem addressed in this chapter with special reference to lineage-based societies, from sub-Saharan Africa in particular. We argue that, indeed, personalized relationships are not the magical solution to contract enforcement problems that they are often portrayed to be. In the context of newly emerging economic opportunities, redistributive norms prevailing in the sphere of personalized relationships tend to undermine economic incentives and to slow growth. These pressures can nevertheless be overcome, at least partly, but always at a cost. Finally, we explore the difficult question of how to explain the pervasiveness and persistence of sharing norms in African countries compared with countries belonging to other continents.

Our endeavor clearly belongs to a strand of literature that stresses the role of culture for development and that has been out of fashion for a long time because of widespread criticisms against the excesses of the so-called modernization theory. This is perhaps the time to adopt a more nuanced view that recognizes that cultural factors cannot be assumed to be strictly endogenous – various ways lead to modernization, and they are influenced by historical and cultural factors – or that, at least, they are not so malleable as to rapidly evolve when the economic environment changes; social norms and codes of behavior are somewhat sticky (Basu 2000; Basu, Jones, and Schlicht 1987; Kuran 2011; Platteau 2011; Platteau and Peccoud 2011). The analytical perspective followed in this chapter does not rest on the view that African societies face cultural impediments that doom them to remain economically underperforming. Instead, it draws attention to specific obstacles that these societies encounter in their transition to what Simon Kuznets (1966) once called "modern economic growth," and that therefore shape their specific development path. In particular, it also helps us solve the following puzzle: Why is it that Senegalese people, for example, can be quite successful entrepreneurs in New York while being much more discreet in their own countries?

The remainder of this chapter is organized as follows. In Section 5.2, the various forms that acts of gift giving can take in lineage-based societies are reviewed with a view to highlighting the specific nature of the transfers that redistributive norms govern. In Section 5.3, attention is then focused on the nature of the sanctions that support these norms, while in Section 5.4 it shifts to the rationales underlying them. Section 5.5 then proceeds by distinguishing among the various disincentive effects redistributive pressures cause. In Section 5.6, individual strategies available to cope with these pressures are examined, whereas, in Section 5.7, it is the lack of broad-based forces to counteract them in the specific case of sub-Saharan Africa that is discussed in the light of the recent history of that region. Section 5.8 concludes.

5.2 GIFT GIVING AND REDISTRIBUTIVE NORMS

Gifts can obey different motives. A kind of gift that has received a lot of attention among social scientists, especially economists, during the past decades, are reciprocal, state-contingent transfers made on a voluntary basis (see, e.g., Coate and Ravallion 1993; Dercon and Krishnan 2000; Fafchamps 1992; Kimball 1988; Ligon, Thomas, and Worrall 2002; Morduch 1999; Townsend 1994; Udry 1994). They fulfill the function of informal mutual insurance and involve a quid pro quo inasmuch as, in the words of a renowned anthropologist, "everybody is thereby insured against hunger ... he who is in need today receives help from him who may be in like need tomorrow" (Evans-Pritchard 1940, 85).

Acts of symmetrical gift giving do not necessarily answer the need for protection against various types of risks in highly uncertain environments. As many anthropologists have stressed, they may also help to cement social ties and fashion alliances with strangers who are thereby transformed into surrogate relatives. These alliances or friendship relationships may fulfill different objectives, among which the building of trust required for economic exchanges is often mentioned. Masahiko Aoki (2001) has thus shown rigorously that the gift may serve both as a signal to communicate a willingness to cooperate to a potential partner, and as a commitment device because, once the gift has been made, the donator's interest is to abide by a contract provided that the partner also does it.

In these two instances, the gift and the counter-gift are a manifestation of enlightened self-interest, or of selfishness with foresight. In other words, they appear to be motivated by exchange rather than by altruism. Furthermore, they are made between equals, that is, persons occupying similar positions in the social structure and/or endowed with similar amounts of wealth. When we say that redistributive or sharing norms enjoin prosperous persons to share the fruits of their economic success with their kith and kin, we obviously refer to a different kind of gift: it is now wealthier people who transfer income to poorer ones and, to the extent that being more wealthy is not a transient state, a gift is unlikely to be reciprocated. Moreover, if the gift is voluntary, one may suspect it to be driven by noneconomic or non-tangible considerations that include symbolic advantages. When income is thus traded against social prestige or political power, the material gift is reciprocated by a demonstration of esteem, loyalty, allegiance, subordination, and devotion.

Gift exchanges of the latter sort can be termed asymmetrical, because they take place between persons of unequal wealth, rank, or social status. Insofar as generosity and hospitality are highly praised behaviors in traditional rural communities, successful individuals gain social prestige and esteem when they redistribute their surplus. There may be more at play, however, than the "warm glow" effect that gift giving sparks off among the attendance when made in public (Andreoni 1990). As we have learned from the works of many anthropologists (Belshaw 1965; Bourdieu 1990; Levi-Strauss 1969; Malinowski 1922; Mauss 1925; Polanyi 1944, 1968; Sahlins 1960, 1963, 1974), indeed, the whole point of the game of asymmetric exchange may actually consist for the dominant party of making sure that the tangible benefits or services that he renders (including insurance against the risk of hunger) can never be (fully) repaid. Being in his debt on the material level, the donee finds himself compelled to return the favor on another level, in ways that influence the donor's rank or status. Subordination is created and perpetuated because the obligation to reciprocate, which is a burden, cannot be relieved by means of a return gift equivalent to the initial gift (Offer 1997, 455). Upon this reading, social prestige and political power originate in asymmetric gift exchanges. Economists have recently enriched this approach by highlighting the conditions under which unequal rank or power positions may be permanently established through asymmetric gift exchange when a gift brings pride, social esteem, or power to the donor and shame or subordination to the donee (Gaspart and Seki 2003; Platteau and Sekeris 2010; Platteau and Seki 2007). This kind of asymmetric gift exchange is characteristic of class-based agrarian societies dominated by patron-client ties, such as are commonly found in large parts of rural Asia (Breman 1974; Scott 1976).

Transfers from rich to poor are also voluntary when they are governed by the desire to follow well-internalized norms of social solidarity. A central feature of lineage-based societies is, indeed, that other-regarding values are inculcated in every individual from early childhood and carefully nurtured all throughout his or her life; hence Albert Hirschman's (1958) characterization of them as "group-focused" societies.[1] Unlike what we find in the "Invisible Hand" doctrine, which is at the root of the market-based view of the economic system, the presumption is that the pursuit of selfish ends runs counter to the collective good in the general case. Evidence to the contrary must therefore be adduced before exceptions to this rule can be granted.

Other-regarding values and codes of conduct are stressed not only in each and every possible moment of ordinary life, but also under exceptional circumstances. Rituals and ceremonies during the course of which the unity and harmony of the group are strongly asserted and celebrated provide these exceptional moments (see, e.g., Godelier 1974). They are privileged occasions during which social norms and values stressing the collective good and the necessity for the individual to sacrifice his self-interest for the benefit of the community are put in the foreground and intensely felt through dances, songs in unison, and the sharing of abundant food and drinks (see, e.g., Gyekye 1996, 36). During such events, all participants are called on to manifest regularly and openly their concern for the collective good and their willingness to contribute to it. To the extent that such internalization of other-regarding values through nurturing and rituals succeeds, any reference to self-centered considerations tends to be suppressed from consciousness so that community members can think of themselves as moral individuals (Polanyi 1977, 60; Wright 1994).

Internalization processes are never complete, however, and this is why external reward and sanction mechanisms are needed to complement the work of collective rituals and education. Sanctions meted out to individuals who promote their own interest at the presumed expense of the group are probably becoming more important when a society is opened to new economic opportunities that certain individuals are more prompt than others to seize on. It is then, according to Arthur Lewis, that a member of an

[1] In Gambia, for example, the concept of *badingya*, which represents harmony, cooperation, and shared progress (or shared decline), is continuously emphasized in contrast to the concept of *fadingya*, which refers to selfish ambitions and competitiveness. Individualistic proclivities are accepted only to the extent that they are considered necessary for the advancement of the group as a whole (Von Braun and Webb 1989, 515–16; see also Sylla 1994, 170–6, for the Wolof in Senegal).

extended family system whose income increases "may be besieged by correspondingly increased demands for support from a large number of distant relations" (1955, 114). Transfers that are driven by redistributive norms in the sense meant in this chapter are arguably made under some degree of coercion. Coercion is directly exerted when, without warning, individuals settle down in the house of a prosperous relative so as to obtain free lodging and boarding for an indeterminate period of time; or when they drop some of their children into the house of such a relative, again for an indefinite time, without bothering to offer him (her) a compensation or leaving him (her) the choice to refuse to adopt these children[2]; or when they consistently evade repayment of their debts to close acquaintances. In many instances, redistributive norms are backed by severe sanctions, foremost among them ideological intimidation. The nature of these sanctions is highlighted later in this chapter with a special focus on countries of sub-Saharan Africa.

5.3 SANCTIONS IN SUPPORT OF REDISTRIBUTIVE NORMS

Norms that enjoin economically rising individuals to share their surplus with their kith and kin are justified by the belief that success is due to luck rather than to personal effort, risk taking, and talent. While transient luck is believed to result from the ordinary course of natural events, persisting or exceptional luck is attributed to the obscure manipulation of supernatural forces. This sort of accusation is extremely grave inasmuch as witchcraft is thought to cause the treacherous exploitation of other villagers and to jeopardize the survival of the entire group. Because they can easily degenerate into active hatred unless assuaged by corrective gifts, the aversive emotions of envy and jealousy are instrumental in bringing about a redistribution of income between (presumably) lucky and unlucky individuals. The hatred of fellow community members is something successful people try to suppress because it is liable to cause psychological oppression and physical harm (Jewsiewicki 1993).

In the words of an inhabitant of a South African village: "You build a beautiful house. They say that you are a witch. They come and burn it down. They say they are burning a witch's house. You buy a car. They come

[2] The author has collected stories of relatively well-to-do West Africans who upon their return from business travel found that the number of their "children" had suddenly increased. Exploiting their temporary absence, parasitic relatives (half-brothers or brothers-in-law, for example) had come to their house and entrusted the children whom they wanted to rid themselves of to the wife before disappearing to a rather distant location (typically, in a neighboring country).

and shoot you, just because you are working and they are not" (Golooba-Mutebi 2005, 947). The main problem with witchcraft accusations is that they are impossible to shake off because they are backed by a system of self-reinforcing beliefs and sanctions: "Even people who might be convinced of a person's innocence dare not come to his or her defense, lest they too be accused. Once accused, therefore, a person is shunned by all villagers, save for the most committed friends and kin" (Golooba-Mutebi 2005, 953).

Witch beliefs thus constitute a conservative force that helps sustain a rough egalitarianism, or a given distribution of ranks and status, by acting as a check on undue individual effort (Thomas 1973, 643–4, cited in Elster 1989, 261). As suggested by the example from South Africa, a rich man knows that if he is stingy with his relatives or fails to dispense generous hospitality to all, he is likely to be spoken of as a witch and to arouse suspicion that he has accumulated riches by robbing others (Elster 1989, 260). As Evans-Pritchard (1937) explained on the basis of his research on the Nuer tribe of Sudan, the evil "soul" of witchcraft is set to work by antisocial feelings such as envy, spite, jealousy, anger, and hatred. If these feelings are absent, the witchcraft remains "cool" and harms no one (see also Badini 1994, 141, for the Mossi of Burkina Faso). In rural communities of Rwanda (prefecture of Kibuye in the western part), according to a more recent account, only gifts can appease jealous feelings (*ishari*) and dismiss accusations of misplaced pride (*ishema*), which cause fear in prosperous individuals. Such fear is nurtured by the all-pervasive belief in poisonings (*uburozi*) that designate the many forms of baleful spells (Lame 1996, 182).

In Njombe district (Tanzania), prosperous traders and farmers were said to use secret powers to enrich themselves, in some cases by scattering the blood and flesh of victims on their farms so as to obtain plentiful harvests. The suspicion is that entrepreneurial people are ready to kill their own children and their relatives in the quest for riches. The truth is that individuals filled with greed, envy, hatred, and deep jealousy are busy day and night searching for poisons able to kill wealthy people so as to appropriate or inherit their wealth (Giblin 2005a, 198, 200).

Witchcraft accusations therefore appear as a powerful means of ideological intimidation aimed at suppressing deviance in general and economic self-advancement in particular. It is within the kinship group that witchcraft is summoned with special force, because jealous feelings are more intense as relations between people are closer: the gravest accusation against a successful individual is that he is ready to sell his parents in order to accumulate riches.[3] Repressive measures are also observed in tribal societies built on a ranked hierarchy of constituent groups and possessing a strongly centralized structure focused on the chief. According to many reports about life in African villages, the chief or the elders do not easily accept that the rank and file rise above them by acquiring new or ancient symbols of wealth and status. All efforts to accumulate such symbols are unavoidably viewed as conscious attempts to overturn the existing social order (in which chiefs and elders are richer but also stand as the main agents of redistribution), and they immediately arouse insinuations or open accusations of sorcery (Bruce 1993, 39–40; Colin 2004, 284–5; Geschiere 1995, 210; Peters 1994, 32). In Botswana, for example, someone a Tswana chief considered a dangerous competitor was accused of witchcraft and stripped of his property. In such cases, Pauline Peters argues, "the chief was able to justifiably 'eat' the miscreant" (1994, 32). Witchcraft accusations against social superiors are unthinkable, however, inasmuch as the latter are thought to be protected by powerful spirits able to launch effective counter-sorcery (Evans-Pritchard 1964, 243; Geschiere 1995, chapter 4).[4]

Evidence from anthropological writings converges to show that, far from diminishing, witchcraft accusations and practices continue to play an important role in repressing individual acquisitiveness and mobility in African (rural) societies, and the belief in occult forces is very common at different levels of education and among various religious affiliations (Kohnert 1996, 1348). For instance, René Bureau speaks about "a massive resumption of witchcraft accusations" (1996, 123–4) in the coastal area of Cameroon where the immense majority of those accused of being *balemba* (sorcerers) have an enviable place, function, fortune, or influence. In Cameroon, South Africa, Benin, and other African countries, as many new opportunities for economic differentiation arise, successful people are said to be sorcerers able to transform their victims into kinds of zombies whom they force to work at night in their invisible plantations in order to enrich themselves. The victims complain of waking up in the morning

[3] Sometimes, however, the feelings of jealousy, rivalry, and covetousness, which give rise to witchcraft, can nevertheless be considerably extended. For instance, they can affect the competition among tribes, clans, and villages for getting development projects. The belief is then that the tribe, clan, or village that wins a project does so because its spirits won a decisive battle against the spirits of rival tribes, clans, or villages (Geschiere 1995, 197–8; Harragin 2004, 310–11; Platteau 2000, 199–200).

[4] In the Green Valley (South Africa), for example, witchcraft accusations reinforced rather than challenged social privilege, because persons of relatively greater status and influence used them manipulatively to their own advantage (Niehaus 2001a, 198).

feeling extremely tired (Ardener 1970; Ellis and Ter Haar 2004, 123; Fisiy and Geschiere 1991; Geschiere 1994, 1995, 175, 192–8; Rosny 1981, 1992; Rowlands and Warnier 1988).[5]

In Rwanda, and also in Tanzania, Uganda, and Mozambique, we hear about the increasing incidence of spirit possession and poisoning threats as a result of social and economic differentiation or, to use the words of a Rwandese traditional healer (cited in Migeotte 1995), of "recent changes in economic conditions that arouse people's spite since nobody accepts that someone else surpasses him in wealth." Rich individuals are accused of possessing obscure powers and entertaining privileged relations with the invisible world, which enable them to appropriate wealth from others (Ellis and Ter Haar 2004, chapter 5; Lame 1996, 183; Platteau 2000, 202; Rennie 1984, 180–2). James Giblin has reported in detail the difficulties encountered in rural Tanzania by people who want to build a family business, and their accounts are particularly insightful. Economic success is invariably considered the result of exploitation of fellow villagers and "the proof that one uses witchcraft" (2005a, 199). Thus, when in the late 1950s, an individual from Njombe district obtained unusually abundant maize harvests from hybrid seeds, people said that he used *mkwego* to draw maize away from others (*mkwego* is a medicine used to capture for one's own use another person's ability to prosper), which eventually compelled him to share seeds with neighbors (Giblin 2005a, 198). Prosperous individuals know that behind the blame of maliciously using magic and witchcraft lies the grave accusation that they have violated the obligations of kinship (Giblin 2005a, 199).

In South Africa, witchcraft practices seem to be flourishing more than ever before, and social and economic differentiation provides fertile ground for suspicion and accusation "when the well-to-do fail to fulfill the expectations of poorer neighbours and kin for support." In Tiko village, witchcraft is feared by almost everybody, and it includes the use of poisons and other dangerous substances or "medicines" that bear a special local name (Golooba-Mutebi 2005, 939–44). Elsewhere, those named and killed as witches were often doing well – they had large numbers of cattle, or had

[5] Among the Douala, people believe that witchcraft powers are acquired in an ultrasecret society admittance to which is conditioned on the killing of a person, preferably a close relative such as a mother or a son. The most common way to harm people consists of removing their "soul of life" and to reduce them to slavery after their funeral. The victims then work for the sorcerer on the Coupé and Manenguba mountains. The sorcerer uses his flying powers to go to his secret plantation and collect the fruits of his slaves' labor (Bureau 1996, 107–8).

worked in the cities and earned a pension for their old age – jealousy appearing as the most common motivation for the killings (Niehaus 2001a, 2001b). Increasingly, young people, who were not traditionally allowed to accuse others of witchcraft, make accusations against older, typically richer persons (Ellis and Ter Haar 2004, 152).

The following accounts, one from Ramon Sarro (2009) for the Upper Guinea Coast (Guinea Conakry), and the other from Angelique Haugerud (1993) for central Kenya, provide two additional, vivid illustrations of the idea that witchcraft accusations have a tendency to increase with the rising economic differentiation that accompanies growth:

> A man asked his classificatory sister, who was living in Kamsar, to bring him new shoes from that city. She refused, and a few days later she died in Kamsar. People in the village thought she was killed by her envious brother.... Conrad ... [worked] for the Compagnie des Bauxites Guinéennes. He lived in Kamsar for several years, but always felt that his relatives in the village, only fifteen kilometres away, were very demanding, asking him far too often for money and goods from Kamsar. He opted to move further away to feel more at ease and therefore went to Conakry, where he was employed at the harbour.... He was very aware of the envy that his status could awake in the village ... every time he went to the village to spend some time building the house he took a fair largesse of money and presents to share among people from his and his wife's descent groups (most of the villagers helping him build the house were his in-laws, and were doing it for free).... In 1999, when the house was virtually finished ... Conrad died suddenly in Conakry. Despite all his efforts to avoid arousing envy while building his house, his death provoked all sorts of gossip and even a serious allegation of deser [witchcraft] against a young member of his own descent group who was accused of having killed his classificatory father out of sheer envy. (Sarro 2009, 156, 159)

> As opportunities to accumulate wealth grew in central Kenya, so too did the stakes for individual displays of "generosity" as opposed to "selfishness" ... enmities have arisen due to wealth. Several people spoke of the narrowing range of kin among whom one shares goats on ceremonial occasions, such as those associated with marriage and childbirth.... And an Embu man explained his decision not to open his own small shop, saying that such businesses often failed within one year, that customers asked for credit and called the owner "proud" if he or she refused to extend the credit, and that sorcery against the owner might follow. Less well-off individuals also termed "proud" wealthy individuals whom they believed did not assist others enough in finding jobs or places in secondary schools.... Treating visitors well includes preparing food for them rather than hoarding it for one's own family. Selfishness and social isolation, in contrast, may carry associations of witchcraft and sorcery, and at the very least invite negative gossip. Longstanding norms of sociality and patronage include the expectation that the less well-off will seek assistance from the wealthy, and that the latter indeed will respond with good will to such requests. (Haugerud 1993, 133–4)

5.4 THE RATIONALE BEHIND REDISTRIBUTIVE NORMS

The official reason invoked to justify redistributive norms is that when an individual becomes too successful economically compared to fellow group members, he (she) is likely to harm them: individual prosperity, according to this account, is bought at the expense of collective prosperity. Two mutually reinforcing rationales may underlie this assertion.

The first motive arises from the need to protect the group against the threat of erosion of its ability to shoulder risks. Indeed, if a prosperous individual were allowed to stop making gifts to fellow villagers, the size of the informal insurance network formed by the community would be reduced and the group's ability to spread risks would be correspondingly diminished.[6] Private wealth accumulation is perceived as antisocial behavior precisely because it is an attempt to break away from traditional solidarity networks, and the exit of the (best) members would make the rest of the kin group worse off (Fafchamps 1992, 160–3; Hoff and Sen 2005, 173; Platteau 1991, 160–1, 2000, chapter 5). According to Guy Hunter, we are dealing with "levelling societies, in which attempts by equals to gain individual advantage are constantly suspected and bitterly resented," and, at the root of this suspicious atmosphere, lies the "fear that the fundamental security of the village will slowly be lost if one individual after another can reach a platform of prosperity from which he might not need the help of the community and could therefore excuse himself from helping them" (Hunter 1969, 40).

Following the logic of this insurance-based argument, the establishment of sharing norms can be rationalized as the outcome of individual decisions by selfish community members. Assuming that idiosyncratic shocks are sufficiently severe or frequent and randomly distributed (and their effects are possibly amplified by collective shocks), and also assuming that community members are equally (or not too unequally) endowed in the initial situation, they will not only decide to join a mutual insurance scheme based on contingent reciprocal transfers, but they may also support the laying down

[6] Let us assume that individual incomes, which are independent and have identical variances ($=\sigma^2$), are entirely redistributed through a perfect pooling scheme. The variance of individual incomes after pooling is then simply equal to σ^2/n, from which it is evident that any reduction in the size of the pooling group ($=n$) increases the volatility of incomes for those who remain within it. Under our assumptions, indeed, the variance of aggregate income ($=Y$) is equal to the sum of the individual variances ($=n\sigma^2$), and the variance of individual incomes after pooling is, therefore, $Var(Y/n)= n\sigma^2/n^2= \sigma^2/n$.

of social norms. This implies that they will vote in favor of rigidly enforced rules aimed at preventing members from quitting when favorable circumstances make it worthwhile for them to do so (that is, when the expected payoff from participation becomes smaller than the payoff from nonparticipation). This is because, ex ante, they ignore what their income trajectory will be and they therefore fear the breaking down of the risk-pooling mechanism over time. "Forced mutual help," as Raymond Firth (1951) called it, is then used to maintain the status quo, which has the potential effect of discouraging exceptional individual performances on the grounds that they can only take place "at the expense of other members and of the cohesiveness of the group" (Hirschman 1958, 23).

The second motive underlying redistributive norms is of a quite different order: because the effort of any individual to improve his lot generates positional externalities that negatively affect the welfare of fellow villagers, redistributive norms that enjoin economically successful individuals to share their surplus appear as a form of taxation designed to curb positional race for status. This may be thought of as a desirable outcome if efforts to improve one's lot are mutually offsetting (everyone wants to "keep up with the Joneses"), and inefficient equilibria arise precisely because investment in status enhancement is more attractive individually than collectively (Congleton 1980; Frank 1985, 1998).

That the insurance-based explanation is insufficient to account for the pervasive presence of redistributive norms in lineage-based societies is evident from the aforementioned fact that the hierarchy of ranks may not be called into question. Typically, while one of their functions is to redistribute wealth toward the needy (see, e.g., Malinowski 1922; Sahlins 1960, 1963, 1972, the chief or the elders do not accept that commoners rise above them by acquiring old or new symbols of wealth and status (like cocoa plantations, mechanical devices, or roofs made of corrugated iron). All efforts to accumulate such symbols are unavoidably viewed as conscious attempts to compete with traditional leaders and to overturn the existing social order. As a consequence, they are strongly condemned and the prosperous commoner is immediately coerced into handing over to the chief his newly acquired riches. Thus, in a village Geschiere studied in Cameroon, a man who accumulated wealth and used part of it to buy a new local suit (a beautiful *boubou*) was severely rebuked by the local chief, to whom he was forced to hand over his new garment. This was done without any compensation, just on the ground that "he should not have displayed such a luxury while the chief had to go without it" (Geschiere 1995, 210, note). If the new symbol of wealth is a productive asset, the successful individual is badgered to either give it away to the chief or to use it for the latter's benefit, for example, by using his tractor to plow the chief's land (for other examples, see Platteau and Abraham 2002, 114–18 and Platteau and Abraham 2004).

The young generations often resent the situation as oppressive and may be prompt to seize any opportunity to oppose it. This is one of the central lessons to be learned from Ramon Sarro's analysis of the rebellion that spread through the villages of the Baga-speaking people of coastal Guinea during the colonial period. Initiated by a Muslim preacher (Asekou Sayon), this iconoclastic movement aimed at the destruction or abandonment of many customary ritual practices and objects perceived as negative for the development of the community. Educated people and war veterans who had been abroad (and many of whom converted to Islam) identified these animist practices with the despotic rule of local chiefs and elders, itself reinforced by the French colonial policy of appointing powerful canton chiefs. Chiefs and elders were, indeed, perceived as doing nothing "but drink the palm wine that youths had to tap for them" (Sarro 2009, 94), and customary ceremonies (the so-called masquerades), which involved a lot of hard work for the latter, were deemed far too numerous and costly. Under these conditions, writes Sarro, "it is not surprising that Islam, being a religious discourse that not only forbade masquerades and sacred bushes but also the tapping and drinking of palm wine, was increasingly attractive for the strata of society that felt (and were) abused by the elders" (2009, 95). Interesting, we are also told that the elders insisted on receiving gifts (including marriage payments) in the form of palm wine instead of money because palm wine being given in public and in large quantities, it could not be unduly appropriated by the recipient but had to be shared with other members of the ruling strata.

To sum up, lineage-based societies are prone to resist any differentiation process whereby relative status positions are modified. Social reshuffling is perceived as a dangerous force susceptible of jeopardizing the fragile social equilibria typical of small-group societies anchored in highly personalized relationships. As pointed out earlier, the redistributive pressures through which differentiation is repressed are often backed by powerful sanctions that include social pressures, constant harassment, and the use of effective mechanisms of ideological intimidation, most notably witchcraft accusations and practices. A direct implication of this analysis is that the phenomenon highlighted should not be restricted to sub-Saharan Africa, but be observed in all lineage-based societies dominated by personalized relationships. This prediction is supported by evidence from Asian villages, and even from Europe. In Malaysia, for example, James

Scott noted that the rich helped the poor "less from a spirit of liberality than as a response to the palpable pressures their neighbours and kin brought to bear upon them" (1985, 192). With reference to Europe, the presence of redistributive norms in Balkan villages is attested by the old Bosnian saying according to which: "If the whole society is prosperous, each of its members gains from it, but when one individual is too powerful, he harms his fellow members, whether he likes it or not. When a hand is too big, swollen and painful, it is because it has been bitten or invaded by bad spirits. In order to restore the health of the hand's owner, the swelling must be reduced or the hand will need to be cut off" (Karahasan 2000, 191, our translation).

The historical experience of Western Europe itself shows that redistributive pressures and the accompanying witchcraft accusations have become particularly widespread during the phase of transition from the egalitarian mutually dependent village community of preindustrial times to the more individualistic and socially differentiated structure of market-based societies. According to a British historian, "one of the major reasons for the rise of witchcraft accusations in the sixteenth century was the tension caused by a conflict between a traditional ethic of mutual responsibility and charity, the norms of self-contained and subsistence villagers, and the new acquisitive and individualistic spirit of capitalism and Protestantism" (Macfarlane 1978, 59).

Before looking at the various disincentive effects redistributive norms cause, it is worth emphasizing that the idea of redistributive pressures grounded in feelings of envy toward successful individuals has strong micro-theoretic foundations. The idea is that people's utility is influenced not only by absolute income levels, but also by their relative position in the (local) distribution of income, thus causing preferences to be interdependent (see Veblen, 1899, and Duesenberry, 1949, for the first formulations of this idea).[7] The component of the utility function that reflects the influence of an external reference point is interpreted as the "status return" from income, or the positional or conspicuous consumption aspect of income. Andrew Clark, Paul Frijters, and Michael Shields (2008) have recently concluded that the available evidence largely supports the hypothesis of relative income effects. In particular, works that

[7] This idea, coupled with the fact that people also compare their present income with their past income, is now used to explain the so-called Easterlin's Paradox – significant increases in real incomes in Western countries over the past fifty years have not been accompanied by corresponding rises in reported happiness levels (Easterlin 1974).

use a geographic approach to reference groups – social comparisons are made with people living in the same neighborhood – suggest that life satisfaction is totally relative to income. In rural China, for example, according to one survey based on ninety-two hundred households, 68 percent of individuals see their village as their reference group, while only 11 percent stated that their main comparison group consisted of individuals from outside of the village. Moreover, respondents who say that their income was much above the village average report far higher happiness than those who say that their income was much below that average (Knight and Song 2006, cited in Clark et al. 2008, 107, 112).

Perhaps more convincing, a study using respondent-defined (rather than assumed) reference groups reveals that individuals who associate with higher earners need more money to describe their income as good or adequate (Melenberg 1992, cited in Clark et al. 2008, 109–10). Another source of evidence on the importance of social comparisons to others in actual choice behavior may be found in the experimental economics literature, whether it deals with fairness (such as laboratory evidence on ultimatum games) or asks individuals to rank hypothetical outcomes. A series of papers using the latter approach have adduced evidence of strong positional concerns over income, in that individuals say that they are willing to give up absolute income to improve their relative position or gain status (Clark 2008; Clark et al. 2008, 120).

As hinted at previously, some economists refer to this kind of effect to advocate taxation of positional goods in all dynamic societies: because changes in rank have no social benefit even though they yield private benefits, and the additional benefit of positional goods to an individual leads to overconsumption of such goods at society level to the detriment of non-positional goods, the production of the latter type of goods needs to be encouraged through the taxation of the former type. If the positional good is equated to relative income and the non-positional good to leisure, there is thus a ground for income taxation to promote leisure (Frank 1985; Layard 2005).

The similarity between this position and the existence of redistributive norms in African countries is plain: to the extent that individual preferences are translated in utility functions in which absolute income and relative position are substitutes, a possibility to exert pressures on dynamic individuals to repress their upward income mobility may be used by less effort-prone or more-leisure oriented individuals even at the price of achieving a lower income than they could have otherwise received (say, because the growth generated by the efforts of the successful individuals may produce a trickle-down effect).[8] In other words, the availability of redistributive norms enables the individuals who do not want to forsake leisure to prevent the sparking of a chain reaction of emulating efforts.

5.5 THE DISINCENTIVE EFFECTS OF REDISTRIBUTIVE NORMS

The trade-off between absolute income and status, understood as a positional concern, is reminiscent of the well-known trade-off between equity and efficiency highlighted in the economic literature. Excessive taxation of the rich, by reducing efficiency too much, may result in lower incomes not only for the rich, but also for the poor. Efficiency losses are the outcome of various disincentive effects redistributive pressures cause. In the particular context of lineage-based societies, several such effects need to be distinguished.

First, redistributive pressures discourage effort. To make matters simple, just think of an individual who produces an output that is perfectly observable and anticipates that his (her) income will have to be shared with n kinsfolk. His (her) equilibrium level of effort will then be determined by the equality between the marginal disutility or cost of effort and the marginal productivity of effort divided by n. The effort applied will therefore be suboptimal, and the larger n the wider the gap between actual and optimal effort levels. Note incidentally that this disincentive effect is formally identical to that produced in an alternative situation in which output is collectively produced and perfectly observable, but individual effort is not. Joint output is then divided equally among the n participants who apply the same suboptimal amount of effort as that indicated earlier (under the assumption of constant returns to scale). In this instance, a dynamic individual who would like to improve his (her) lot would be prevented from doing so as a result of the so-called moral-hazard-in-team problem.

Second, redistributive pressures discourage entrepreneurship and risk taking. This is because these pressures operate in an asymmetrical manner: if the investment project fails, the risk taker will be the only one to bear

8 Think of a runner who has to choose between the two following situations: (a) another member of his team wins the race and transfers a (small) portion of the benefit earned to him; and (b) nobody in the team wins the race and the prize offered to the winner goes to another team. If the runner has the sort of preferences highlighted here, he will prefer (b) to (a): his absolute income is smaller than it could have been yet his relative position has not deteriorated (for a development-related illustration, see Abraham and Platteau, 2004, 220).

the burden of the ensuing loss, while, if the project is successful, the risk taker will have to share the benefits with his or her kith and kin. Given a certain degree of risk aversion, a dynamic individual will therefore refuse to embark on a risky project that he (she) would have attempted in the absence of redistributive norms. As a consequence, redistributive norms are likely to discourage savings and investment or to stimulate comparatively safe investments and invisible expenditures.

Third, redistributive pressures encourage misallocation of human resources. The dynamic individual subject to such pressures is typically compelled to hire relatives and friends when he (she) has reached an employer position (whether in the state bureaucracy or the private sector), a practice known as *nepotism*. There are two distinct reasons nepotistic behavior gives rise to inefficiencies. On the one hand, it amounts to favoritism toward relatives and friends that involves a cost in terms of the quality of employees hired (Hoff and Sen 2005, 175).[9] On the other hand, monitoring labor efforts and sanctioning bad behavior are particularly difficult for an employer or a manager who deals with people from his (her) own fold. This difficulty is actually reinforced if the employees believe they have a right to misbehave vis-à-vis a superior from whom they want to extract more benefits on the grounds that he (she) has not been sufficiently generous and "fair" with them (Platteau 2000, 313). The disciplining effect of the reputation mechanism that is made possible by the repeated, personalized nature of human interactions is then cancelled by the adverse effect of the attendant sharing norms.

Note that the third problem does not apply only to the sphere of labor relations, but to any kind of economic transactions in which a choice of partner is involved. For example, if the dynamic individual is a banker or a moneylender, or even a businessman, he (she) may be forced to extend credit to kith and kin who are unreliable borrowers. An almost natural experiment testifying to the importance of this nefarious effect was created by the short war between Senegal and Mauritania in 1989. Tension between the two countries led to the expulsion of all Mauritanian shopkeepers from Dakar, the Senegalese capital. Their shops were spread all throughout the city and were opened day and night to provide customers

[9] If there is competition among job seekers who have redistribution obligations toward relatives and those who do not, and if the former can be identified by employers who would bear the adverse consequences of their redistributive behavior (say, because the employee to be hired is a senior worker expected to choose junior workers for teamwork), they will suffer from discrimination in the modern sector labor market (Hoff and Sen 2005, 175–7).

with basic necessities. After their seizure by inhabitants of Senegalese origin, these businesses rapidly declined and became bankrupt until they were taken over by their previous Mauritanian owners when they were allowed to return to the country.

Two answers were given to me when I inquired into the reasons for the failure of the Senegalese experiment in shopkeeping. First, the shops were not opened in the evening and the night like they used to be when the Mauritanians ran them. Second, redistributive pressures compelled the Senegalese shopkeepers to sell on credit to their relatives and friends, and the loans were typically not returned. A common rationale for not returning overdue loans is that because the lender/shopkeeper is richer than the borrower, the latter has a perceived right to consider the loan taken as a (forced) gift. By contrast, Mauritanian shopkeepers followed strictly the rule of selling only against cash payments. Customers who did not comply were always rebuked. This explains why the presence of Mauritanian shopkeepers was both resented – they are doing well and are "selfish" – and felt necessary – their business is efficiently run and therefore provides a valuable service.

That such stories are not rare in sub-Saharan Africa is attested by the failures of Kenyans and Ugandans in their running of shops and businesses taken away from Indians. Regarding Kenya, we have the following account: "Within a short period of time a good many of the African businessmen who had taken over from the Asian shopkeepers had lost most of their capital and turned thriving shops into bars and lodging rooms instead. Others were inviting back previous owners and partners" (Himbara 1994, 89). In Congo-Brazzaville, the Popo fishermen from Benin, who were an active and economically successful community operating in Pointe-Noire, were harassed and, without any forward notification, eventually expelled by the Congolese government in September 1977 on the pretext that they did not have their formal stay permits. Their outboard engines were confiscated on the grounds that proper import authorizations were lacking. There quickly ensued a severe lack of fish in the markets in town, which forced the government to reverse its decision and recall the Popo, who slowly returned to Pointe Noire (Jul-Larsen 1993).

Finally, we may bear in mind the aforementioned account of Haugerud regarding the pervasive presence of redistributive pressures in central Kenya (see the citation provided at the end of Section 5.3), which implicitly testifies that such pressures may easily cause losses of efficiency, bankruptcies, and the forfeiting of growth opportunities. This is confirmed by another

African analyst who writes, with the experience of Kenya in mind, that "[African] entrepreneurs are expected to share their incomes with other members of the extended family. They are expected to come to aid in case of financial hardships and to employ relatives regardless of whether they are efficient. These considerations lead to a withdrawal of a substantial amount of capital from an enterprise and its eventual failure" (Kamau 1965, cited in Himbara 1994, 89).

5.6 INDIVIDUAL REDISTRIBUTION COPING STRATEGIES

Ordinary individuals are generally reluctant to start accumulating wealth and deviate from customary norms of behavior. This is especially so if they are afraid of being killed by envious local witches or of being accused and harassed as witches themselves (because they have acquired their wealth by using occult powers), a risk enhanced by the fact that the police are usually unable to investigate and punish witchcraft-related crimes because of the local people's refusal to reveal the names of the perpetrators (Golooba-Mutebi 2005, 951).[10] For those dynamic individuals who are strong enough, emotionally, to break from the traditional society, two strategies that involve distancing from the pressures of community life are nevertheless available: migration and religious conversion. For those who do not wish to take such a drastic step, a more defensive strategy consists of concealing incomes and assets. We start by examining the latter possibility before considering the other two, bolder strategies.[11]

5.6.1 Concealing Incomes and Assets

Concealing incomes and assets is the most evident way to escape demands for gifts emanating from relatives, friends, and neighbors. Yet it involves transaction costs that may turn out to be significant. In Burkina Faso, for example, affluent individuals may take wives and children outside of the home to eat so as to eschew the obligation to cater to unwelcome visitors (Platteau 2000, 210). In this instance, the cost of escaping redistributive

[10] A household survey conducted in urban Ivory Coast revealed that households who accommodate collateral kin dependents (defined as inactive people) are twice as wealthy as households who do not (Laiglesia and Morrisson 2008). Unfortunately, that study does not allow us to infer the direction of causality between wealth and accommodation of kith and kin.

[11] For the latter two subsections, I draw largely on Platteau (2009).

pressures takes the form of additional expenditures on transport and restaurants. The cost may also take the form of suboptimal allocation of wealth resulting from the need to opt for relatively inconspicuous uses of the savings accumulated. In Tanzania, we are thus told that better-off villagers avoid displays of wealth such as modern houses because the villagers believe a successful farmer is maliciously using supernatural forces (Giblin 2005a, 199).

Unfortunately, very few systematic empirical studies exist documenting redistribution-coping behavior in the context of sub-Saharan Africa. Two that I am aware of deserve close attention, one by Jean-Marie Baland, Catherine Guirkinger, and Charlotte Mali (2010) on Cameroon, and the other by Vincent Somville (2010) on Benin. While almost all the evidence presented thus far on the existence of redistributive pressures or norms in Africa has been drawn from the anthropological literature, these two studies have been produced by economists and offer us indirect evidence of this phenomenon.

The first study is based on a field survey of rural credit cooperatives belonging to the Cameroon Cooperative Credit Union League. Looking at the credit operations and deposits of the members of four cooperatives during the years 2004–6, Baland and colleagues (2010) uncovered a puzzling fact of what they term "excess borrowing" behavior. Around one-fifth of the loans taken from rural credit cooperatives are fully collateralized by savings available on the borrowers' savings accounts, and the amount of savings available to the borrowing member is on average twice as large as the amount of the loan. Still more intriguing is the fact that the behavior of these excess borrowers is costly because they could save on substantial interest payments by self-financing their investment projects. The authors adduce two kinds of evidence in support of the idea that the desire to escape redistributive pressures lies at the heart of the puzzle. The first kind of evidence is qualitative and consists of the explanations invoked by the excess borrowers themselves. Their statements can be summarized as follows: excess borrowing, and the consequent need to fulfill reimbursement obligations, are a way to signal financial difficulties to relatives in search of financial assistance. As a matter of fact, people believe that when an acquaintance takes a loan, it is because he (she) has no money. The explanation is credible: if the existence of savings accounts and credit contracts is common knowledge, the amount of the cooperative members' savings is unanimously hidden. Members actually report showing their credit book to suspicious relatives to prove their state of financial duress.

The second line of argument proceeds by dispelling competing explanations of excess borrowing. Thus, the authors show that there are no likely indirect benefits resulting from such a behavior. In particular, it is not true that the loan serves as a vehicle of risk diversification for risky investment projects under conditions of limited liability. The borrower's savings can be seized in the event of default, and there can be no risk sharing with the lender owing to full liability. In addition, the authors do not verify that excess borrowing is the outcome of time-inconsistent preferences, people engaging in illiquid saving to protect their money from their future selves while relying on credit to meet immediate cash expenses. In reality, local cooperatives explicitly allow their borrowers to draw on their savings accounts to pay back their loans.

In the second study, also based on firsthand data collection, Somville (2010) examines the role of so-called daily collectors in Benin. These operators, as their name suggests, collect small savings on a daily basis from their clients and keep them safe. In exchange for this service, they charge a monthly fee that is equal to the amount of one deposit. This fee is subtracted from the savings recovered at the end of each month by the client: amounting to 3.3 percent, it is equivalent to a negative annual interest rate of 54 percent. How to account for the people's willingness to use the services of such costly operators? One obvious answer is their desire to put their money in a safe place so as to protect it against the risk of loss, theft, or other hazards. According to the author, however, this explanation does not stand up to the scrutiny of the facts because it does not explain inter-individual variations in the use of daily collectors.

The need for protection against claims by household members and acquaintances is the motivation that appears to best match the two years of panel data collected in 2004 and 2006 in three different districts of the outskirts of Cotonou, the country's capital city. In particular, econometric testing bears out the hypothesis that, other things being equal, individuals use the services of a daily collector to contribute less to the household public goods and increase their own private consumption: men make smaller contributions to joint household expenditures such as electricity, house repairing and maintenance, and school expenses, while women contribute less to school expenses. Both men and women spend more on personal clothing when using the service. It also appears that these users transfer less money to those presenting requests considered as illegitimate, and more money to recipients of their own choice. Results thus show that women who use the services of a collector transfer less money to their husband but more to their children and their friends. As for men, they transfer less money to their spouse, their children, their friends, and the members of their own parish.[12]

In contrast to these two empirical studies, Jakiela and Ozier (2011) have conducted a controlled laboratory experiment in western rural Kenya to measure the economic effects of social pressures to share income with kin and neighbors. An important feature of the experiment is that the distribution of the sizes of the (variable) endowments given to the subjects at the start of the game is common knowledge, which creates an incentive for those receiving the larger amount to invest in a manner that keeps the size of their budget hidden. The authors found convincing evidence that women subjects are willing to reduce their expected income to avoid making investment returns observable to their kin. More precisely, women receiving the large endowment, who may wish to hide their advantageous position from the family, are significantly more likely to invest an amount no larger than the smaller endowment when returns are observable. Such an effect appears to be driven primarily by the behavior of women with relatives attending the experiment, who would be able to observe income from the experiment directly. Estimates indicate that these women invest much less when investment income is observable than when it is hidden. They are also significantly more likely to invest no more than the amount of the small endowment, suggesting that their strategy is designed to keep the size of their endowment hidden. Another stage of the experiment consists of offering the subjects the possibility, at a positive cost, to keep their investment returns secret. The results show that a significant proportion of those able to afford the cost of hiding income choose to do so.

[12] The problem is modeled as a two-step game. In step 1, both agents receive some income and simultaneously decide how much they deposit with the collector. They bring home whatever money is left. In step 2, they decide how much to contribute to a public good, given that each agent's contribution cannot exceed the income that the agent brought home. Finally, they recover part of their deposits and consume it as they wish. In this setting, the agents may make deposits with a view to reducing the amount of money taken back home, decrease their equilibrium contribution to the public good, and compel the other agent to increase his (her) contribution. The main result of the model is that because of the strategic interaction that takes place between them, the agents will follow the deposit strategy only if they receive similar incomes. If one agent receives a very low income compared to the other, he will not contribute to the public good in step 2. Simultaneously, the agent who received the high income is not making deposits either because the level of deposits that would be necessary to prompt the low-income agent to contribute is high, or the cost of the deposits is proportional to the level of deposits.

5.6.2 Migration and Estrangement

To escape the incriminatory and jealousy-ridden atmosphere that pervades many African villages, entrepreneurial individuals may choose to move a comfortable distance from their kith and kin. Yet even migration to cities will not necessarily enable them to start up a business and earn profits they can use for themselves rather than to support "an endless string of social parasites." They also need to sever their ties with relatives, neighbors, and friends so as to prevent them from settling in their new home and drawing on their incomes (Poewe 1989). Furthermore, they will seldom return to their native area, so as to evade customary rules of greeting and extended family pressures for showing generosity and compassion.

One account that deserves special attention here is drawn from the perceptive work on African capitalism by Paul Kennedy (1988). It is actually reminiscent of several points made in the previous section. According to Kennedy, few African firms can be labeled as genuine family businesses: there is, indeed, a marked reluctance on the part of African entrepreneurs to establish pooling arrangements with partners from the family for fear that relatives will seize opportunities to cheat. Any "disappearance" of their money into a common fund tends to be regarded as evidence that the main partner has squandered or stolen their assets. In addition, they are almost as unwilling to delegate authority to kin-related supervisors and managers as they are to share ownership, again because of deep distrust about people's honesty. Involving relatives in one's business undertakings, whether as supervisors or workers, gives rise to intractable problems and tensions.

On the one hand, relatives do not respond to the same discipline as other employees because they usually demand special treatment, causing discontent among the workforce. Also, jealous of the owner's success and resentful of his authority, they are more prone to dishonest and unreliable behavior in the workplace. On the other hand, the owner tends to be overwhelmed by continuous kinship obligations, such as requests for cash donations or gifts, demands to finance the education of nephews, nieces, and younger siblings, or obligations to provide more or less permanent support for widowed or deserted sisters. True, family connections may help in the early stages by providing start-up capital, yet these shortcomings largely outweigh this advantage. If they are strong enough, entrepreneurs will therefore resist demands to provide jobs for a wide range of kin, irrespective of their qualifications. They know that a business cannot grow unless a clear separation exists between the business and the kinship spheres (Kennedy 1988, 166–70; in the same vein, see also Beveridge and Oberschall 1979,

57–9; Ellis and Fauré 1995; Himbara 1994, 85–93; Marris and Somerset 1971, 131–45, 226–7; Nafziger 1977, 192–3).

Asians and Levantines, whose undertakings have typically taken the form of family firms, have apparently done much better than Africans (and, in the other way around, small native entrepreneurs from Central and West Africa have been successful in South Africa and even in New York).[13] Two factors explain their relative success. First, since colonial times, these two groups have lacked political power and occupied a position of social and cultural marginality, so that business offered them the only real opportunity to succeed in life. Much like the Levantines of West and Central Africa, the Asians in East Africa were willing to operate at low profit margins and had a high propensity to save. Many of them were also ready to live in rural outposts for long periods, taking the trouble to learn the vernacular and operating at low levels of turnover.[14] The second factor is more directly relevant for this discussion: by virtue of being strangers, Levantines and Asians are not subject to the institutions and customs that stifle the initiative of enterprising natives of their adopted country. In particular, they are not subject to extended family pressures for redistribution. Moreover, magical repression does not work against them, because they do not believe in the same spirits as the indigenous population. However, they tend to be widely resented by the local population, who sees them as strangers usurping the business opportunities that rightfully belong to indigenous people (Kennedy 1988, 47–9; Platteau 2000, 224).

The family firm provides foreign entrepreneurs in Africa with a low-cost, disciplined, and trustworthy labor force whose members all have a direct interest in the success of the joint endeavors (Kennedy 1988, 48). The fact that immigrants from the Middle East and Asia belong to small families (formed essentially around monogamous parents and their children) rather than to the extended kinship units typical of low-density African societies implies that the moral hazard-in-team and the incentive dilution problems that plague collective undertakings is relatively moderate in the former. This diagnosis has been largely confirmed by recent studies of indigenous

[13] Interesting, some of the mulatto descendants of European traders who operated from the ports and towns of the southern Gold Coast during the mid-nineteenth century were competing successfully with Europeans (Kennedy 1988, 34–5).

[14] As Kennedy pointed out, "where individuals or groups face a situation of multi-deprivation, strong personal motivations may generate an ascetic orientation towards economic activity … this asceticism and the energy, determination and rationality it sustained, did not stem from a set of shared cultural values existing in their own right, but originated as a response to the prevailing political, social and economic climate of inequality and power" (Kennedy 1988, 47–9).

and nonindigenous (immigrant) firms located in certain African countries, and based on detailed interviews of a sample of trading and manufacturing firms (see Fafchamps, 2004, for a synthesis of these findings). The central results are as follows.

(i) Kinship or place of origin play little or no role in the formation of business networks: individuals from the same village constitute a minute portion of the suppliers and clients reported by African manufacturers (Bigsten et al., 2000; Fafchamps 2002). Buying from and selling to family members is rare and, in a survey of fifty-eight firms in Accra and Kumasi (Ghana), no sales on credit to relatives were recorded (Fafchamps 1996, 2004, 454). This contrasts sharply with findings for Asia (Hayami and Kawagoe 1993). In Africa, the relationship between ethnicity and business networks is quite loose even when the latter are ethnically concentrated, in the sense of being located in areas dominated by one ethnic group (Fafchamps 2004, 307). More specifically, once networks are controlled for, the measured effect of ethnicity on access to supplier credit falls dramatically (Fafchamps 2000). In other words, business networks, which have strong returns,[15] essentially result from interaction among simple business acquaintances, and commercial relationships are nurtured through business meetings and socialization outside of work. Ethnic concentration "seems to result from nothing else than historical accident and socialization patterns that are reinforced by the practice of business itself" (Fafchamps 2004, 308; Fafchamps and Minten 2002). Such a conclusion also follows from the examples cited by Moore (1997), where it appears that successful African businessmen have used personal connections developed at an earlier stage of their professional career, yet outside the sphere of their kith and kin relations (often as salaried employees of European firms).[16]

(ii) Not only is trade with relatives and friends extremely rare in Africa, but, whenever it happens, it harms firm performance. Entrepreneurs complain that it is difficult to keep business with relatives within

[15] Typically, trust is based on repeated interaction. Continuing business with reliable suppliers with whom one has had satisfactory dealings in the past is the best way of avoiding problems. The same applies to trade loans (Fafchamps 2004, chapter 9, 1996; Fafchamps and Minten 2002).

[16] It is odd, therefore, that Moore uses those examples to criticize what he calls the "family/kin drag" thesis, thereby confusing kinship with other types of social connections.

the confines of an economic transaction. For example, it is hard to collect payment from relatives, whether for a loan or delivery of a good, typically because borrowers do not feel morally obliged to repay debts incurred from a prosperous relative. More generally, payment problems are frequent because friendship and family ties get in the way of exerting pressures on clients (Fafchamps 1996, 441, 2004, 104, 109, 173). In addition, firms buying from family and friends encounter more late delivery problems (Bigsten et al. 2000). The conclusion is that involving relatives in business is "the surest way to go out of business," while selling on credit to relatives and neighbors amounts to "signing the death warrant of the firm" and is therefore carefully avoided (Fafchamps 2004, 173).

(iii) Family background has some effect on start-up working capital, yet this effect is small, and no systematic effect of family networks on factor accumulation after enterprise creation can be discerned (Fafchamps 2004, 325–6; Fafchamps and Minten 1999). By the same token, relations based on family, friendship, or ethnicity/kinship make it easier for firms to solve disputes, yet they also raise the incidence of contract nonperformance. This may result from the Africans' preference for nonconfrontational methods of dispute resolution, which often end up in face-saving compromises.

(iv) There is no evidence of systematic mechanisms whereby information about clients' trustworthiness is shared among African manufacturing firms other than direct recommendation by common acquaintances (Fafchamps 2004, 173, 256–7, 295). Among agricultural traders, too, trust-based relationships constitute the dominant contract enforcement mechanism, implying that trust is established primarily through repeated interaction with little role for referral by other traders. Information on bad clients does not circulate widely, which severely limits collective punishments for opportunistic breach of contract (such as nonpayment). African-managed firms face more cases of nonpayment than other firms, and they also complain more frequently about deficient quality (Fafchamps 2004, 92, 109, 117, 135). Their transaction costs are consequently higher. Thus, the overwhelming majority of Malagasy traders (in Madagascar) and their clients respond to quality risk by inspecting each and every purchase, because the task is "virtually never delegated to family helpers, employees, or collecting agents" (Fafchamps 2004, 117; see also Fafchamps and Minten 1999). In other words, many African-managed firms fall back on a "flea market" mode of transacting: "inspect the good on the spot, pay cash and walk away with it" (Fafchamps 1996, 441–4). Firm size and firm growth are unavoidably restricted in such circumstances.

By contrast, within alien communities, information circulates rather freely and client referral is a common practice. As a result, nonindigenous firms operating in Africa are at an advantage. In Kenya, for example, it is only within the Indian community that first-time customers are able to obtain trade credit from the date of their first purchase. Moreover, indigenous firms (in Kenya and Zimbabwe) are less likely to socialize with suppliers, and they have more restricted knowledge about them and their supplies than do the immigrant firms, suggesting that ethnic barriers are more limiting for the former. Because better business contacts allow firms to enforce contracts and economize on screening costs, immigrant firms tend to be more profitable (Fafchamps 2004, 252–3, 258, 300).

(v) Foreign firms hesitate to enter into business relations with indigenous firms that they generally deem unreliable. In particular, they find fault with African managers for continuously trying to renegotiate delivery and payment terms ex post (Fafchamps 2004, 110). This bad reputation of unreliability and dishonesty seems to date back to colonial times (Kennedy 1988, 41, 46).

In the light of the finding reported under (iv), it bears emphasis that the multilateral reputation mechanism that, according to Avner Greif (1994), characterizes so-called collectivist cultures is conspicuously absent in sub-Saharan Africa. What we find, instead, is the bilateral reputation mechanism typical of "individualistic cultures." This is a rather paradoxical conclusion, yet it is perfectly congruent with our contention that in this region, kinship/ethnic ties and their associated obligations are more an impediment to private capital accumulation than a social capital susceptible of reducing transaction costs.

5.6.3 Religious Conversion

To escape the moral and social proscriptions against self-enrichment, willing entrepreneurs need not necessarily leave their native area physically. They can become "native outsiders" (Hagen 1975, 279) or "internal strangers," as converts or urban migrants (*ressortissants*) are termed in Guinea-Conakry (Sarro 2009, 160), that is, people who have chosen to distance themselves radically from their native network so as to be able to disregard the attendant obligations without much fear of hostility.[17] Such a transformation occurs when they symbolically adopt a kind of "stranger" status by converting to a different religion: "this places them effectively under an alternative set of obligations and links them to a spiritual community whose members encourage private accumulation and economic experimentation whilst providing resources such as technical knowledge, credit or labour" (Kennedy 1988, 141–2). In the new spiritual community, emphasis is put on virtues of self-restraint and consumption moderation (e.g., abstaining from drinking alcohol and gambling), and on the need to concomitantly do away with traditional feasts where lavish expenditures on food, drinks, and other goods are the rule.

In most cases, the necessary escape from community loyalty is secured through conversion to Islam or Christianity, the rise of which is paralleled by the decay of indigenous religions. These were, indeed, communal religions that could flourish only within local environments, and were doomed to retreat under the influence of increased market penetration, new social strains, and the development of modern communication means. Syncretic religions and independent churches combining faith in a High God with beliefs in magic and witchcraft that borrowed elements of Christian eschatology gradually supplanted them as they were better adapted to the new world of the Africans (Iliffe 2007, 234, 237). In particular, the churches "provided institutional models for people who had few relevant indigenous institutions" (Iliffe 2007, 235).

Especially successful in Africa (and other parts of the developing world, such as Central and South America) are charismatic churches that offer "places for retreat and personal transformation" while allowing people to engage in village life in new ways, opening up new career paths, and holding out good prospects for the forthcoming future (Jones 2009, 92, 97–8). Pentecostalism, for example, offers the individual "a chance to break with the past," and its various prohibitions – on alcohol, traditional medicine, and polygamy – "serve as outward signs of this inward rupture" (Jones 2009, 153). Presented here are a few examples destined to illustrate more vividly the transformation logic at work.

Among the Fra Fra people of northern Ghana, when successful individuals are unwilling to share their profits generously with members of

[17] In the Upper Guinea Coast of Guinea-Conakry, we are told: "More and more numerous are the young men who abandon their village for a nearby urban environment, where they hope to escape all control. Those who remain marry strangers, convert to Islam, and reject their former identity" (Sarro 2009, 97).

their ethnic group and simultaneously keen to avoid the grave accusation of being "swindlers," they convert to Islam or Christianity, which removes the need to move to an impersonal city (Hart 1975). In the Serenje district of Zambia, Jehovah's Witnesses were disproportionately represented in the commercial farmer and shopkeeper categories, although they were somewhat younger and had less urban experience than their economic rivals. They also tended to live outside the traditional matrilineal village in their own independent settlements, and in their spare time practiced such trades as bricklaying, carpentry, or tailoring from which they earned extra cash (Long 1968, 146). In addition, they systematically avoided hiring kinsmen-workers who did not share in the ownership of the farm or its equipment because their employment "is likely over time to lead to difficult farmer/worker relations which centre around the problem of reconciling the rights and obligations of matrilineal kinsmen with their role as workers on the farm." The fact of the matter is that Jehovah's Witnesses "have little interest in traditional status criteria and espouse an ethic which emphasizes the spiritual and moral dangers of associating too freely with non-believers, even if kin" (Long 1977, 138–9). In their struggles to disentangle themselves from the demands of the matri-kin, they can rely on religious justification, spiritual protection, and practical assistance provided by their church, thus improving their ability to concentrate on their business and nuclear family interests (Kennedy 1988, 142).

Parkin's study of the Giriama people of coastal Kenya (1972, chapters 2–5) provides another vivid illustration that shows, inter alia, how God can be summoned to defeat witchcraft. As Kennedy aptly summarized:

> [T]he conversion of some young entrepreneurs to the Islamic faith might follow a long period of psychological tension and physical illness induced by the possibility of conflict with the elders whose status and power were threatened by the younger men's activities. Such "illness" could be diagnosed as caused by powerful Islamic spirits whose appeasement required nothing less than the religious conversion of those unfortunate enough to become possessed. Once this had occurred, the Islamic ban on the consumption of alcohol and certain foods, as well as the need to follow a partly separate ritual and social life, all provided the opportunity for entrepreneurs to reduce their level of involvement in traditional society. Yet this behaviour no longer incurred community displeasure since it was now judged to be religiously determined rather than the result of selfish individualism. At the same time, the converts were still reasonably close to community affairs and so could use their social connections with the elders in order to gain access to land, reliable information, business contracts and so on. (Kennedy 1988, 142)

In eastern Uganda, the discourse and practice of "born-again" Christianity as they are observed within the Pentecostal Assemblies of God aim at helping church members to separate themselves from society. In the words of Ben Jones, "born-again Christians challenge accepted notions of community, kinship and tradition. Becoming 'born-again' means joining a new family, one bound together by faith. Within the community of the 'saved,' there is often a strong opposition to past relationships, as these relationships are often seen as a vehicle for sin or a sense of personal misfortune.... Church members are permitted to cut familial and kinship ties in the knowledge that they are leaving behind the worship of ancestors, gods or the use of traditional medicines. This leads to often radical social actions, precipitating some sort of retreat from wider society" (2009, 97–8). The same analysis of the role of Pentecostalism as a progressive force for the development of Africa has been made for other countries, such as Ghana (Meyer 1998, 2004) or Burkina Faso, to which our attention is now turned.

In Burkina Faso, a dynamic individual who had converted to the Pentecostal church expressed the view that: "If people see that someone is going to fare better, they use magic tricks to kill him, and this is something that inhibits our development because jealousy is great ... there are those who want to harm me, but I also know that, thanks to my love for God, they are made powerless since the power of God surpasses that of the evil local spirits" (Fancello 2006, 124). Conversion to Islam or to Assemblies of God also proved to be the most effective weapon available to a youth group who wanted to embark on a development project in their (*burkinabé*) village, but they were subject to threats of magical attacks manipulated by local elders (Laurent 1998, 108–9). Among the Orma pastoralists living near the Tana River (Kenya), likewise, it seems that the first shopkeepers and traders were young Islamic converts who chose to challenge the authority of the elders and who found in Islam codes of law and behavior particularly conducive to sound business relations (Ensminger 1992, 48–62). Poewe (1989) offers a similar analysis of the motives underlying the spread of evangelical churches in Zambia (see also Shillington 1989).

If the religious sodality or association serves as a business network, the convert enjoys a double advantage: besides becoming immune to the demands of kinsmen, friends, and neighbors, he (she) is able to economize on transaction costs because of the availability of effective contract enforcement mechanisms. This is because the sharing of the same faith ensures that people abide by the same codes of behavior, adopt the same rituals, and use the same language, resulting in a common identity grounded in the same symbolic universe. If the brotherhood is sufficiently small for information transmission to be effective, the mutual trust that it nurtures and the repeated interaction framework that it provides allow the members to solve many incentive problems (of the moral hazard and adverse selection kinds) arising in commercial relationships. Moreover, religion performs the function of signaling or identifying members. In fact, the religious association works as a club: entry into it involves a fixed cost (the initial fee) under the form, useless for outsiders and therefore not transferable, of learning the language as well as the doctrine and the rituals. It replicates a gift exchange relationship by a group of agents, and is effective to the extent that any violation of the standard of behavior (honest trading) within the club is punished by the termination of club membership (Aoki 2001, 64–7).

In West Africa, for example, long-distance trading communities or "trading diasporas" dating back to the thirteenth and fourteenth centuries have been built on elaborate and successful networks. An important feature of these networks is their openness to new entrants on the (obviously restrictive) condition that they shared or accepted the essential cultural requirements for participation in the moral community that distinguished the members from the host society: Islam and the appropriate trading language (Austin 1993, 115).[18] The adoption of Islam thus spurred the economic integration of West African regions and their integration into trans-Saharan trade thanks, in part, to increasing safety of the caravans and smaller contract enforcement costs (Brooks 1993, 117; Cohen 1969, 1971; Hopkins 1973, 58–65; Levtzion 1973). To enforce contracts and rules of commerce along the Juula and Hausa inland networks, as well as at the Sahelian entrepôts along the Niger bend, a parallel diaspora of clerical specialists, both judges (*qadis*) and legal scholars (*muftis*), was created. Interesting, however, they did not always demand strict religious adherence on the part of the local lay Muslim community (Lydon 2009; see also Launay 1992, 191, for the Dyula of Ivory Coast).

Especially worthy of note is the flexibility shown regarding the most growth-limiting Islamic rules, such as the law of commercial partnerships, which limited enterprise continuity and intergenerational persistence, and inheritance prescriptions, which encouraged wealth fragmentation and restrained capital accumulation.[19] Thus, according to Austen, descent could be manipulated so as to avoid dispersion of business assets by selecting one unique successor among slaves/clients (rather than relatives) recruited into the trading organization as junior partners. In fact, specific arrangements

[18] The nonfulfillment of this condition explains why European (French) merchants failed to make inroads in cattle trade within what is now the republic of Niger: they were unable to participate as equals in indigenous systems of guaranteeing credit and enforcing contracts that emphasize a common religion (Islam) and language (Hausa) (Austin 1993, 117).

[19] On these aspects, see Kuran (2003, 2004a, 2004b).

"depended almost entirely upon arrangements made within a modified version of the secular kinship idiom" (1987, 42–4).[20] The major social function of Islam was, in fact, "to provide merchants with an identity which reinforced their occupational role." Muslim merchants of Sudan acted as "representatives of a cult that had material and spiritual connections to a universe larger than the parochial world of local villages, or even savanna empires." This helped them to gain respect from other West African peoples. As is evident from the processes of formation of the Juula and Hausa groups, the Sudanic identity of Muslim merchants was based on multiple levels of ethnicity "beginning with their use of specific West African languages and receding into their consciousness of descent from various population groups strategically placed to enter the occupation of trade."[21]

The spread of Christianity and Islam may play a progressive role by overcoming traditional barriers to change in sub-Saharan Africa. Not only do the imported religions emphasize the need to fight against alcoholism, drug use, cheating at university exams, prostitution, corruption, nepotism, and delinquency (Fancello 2006, 103–4; Miran 2006, 447), but they also refuse to recognize ethnic identities and the customary obligations associated with them, especially when they involve lavish expenditures. In the words of Aboubacar Fofana, an influential reformist Muslim cleric of Ivory Coast, "what matters is not where an individual comes from, but what he or she does." Muslim brotherhoods put emphasis on personal merits and engagement, not on social status and ethnic identity: they are based on elective membership (Miran 2006, 450, 472–3). Generalized morality, without which an effective market and polity are hard to develop, precisely requires that the ability to see things from another's viewpoint becomes based on identity or loyalty feelings toward a large reference group accessible to all. To put it in another way, identity must be anchored in the abstract rather than the concrete other (Platteau 1994, 2000, chapter 7).

An important caveat must be mentioned. Acceptance of Islam may have been a collective, politically motivated move rather than an individual step of emancipation from erstwhile community control. Societies that are

[20] Sophisticated financial instruments, such as letters of credit and bank drafts, do not appear to have circulated farther away than the northern entrepôts of the Sahara itself, not a surprising finding because most Sudanic Muslim merchants remained functionally illiterate despite some training in Quranic liturgy (Austen 1987, 41, 43).

[21] The Juula groups were Soninké with a Mauritanian homeland. They took on their Manding linguistic identity during the height of the medieval Mali and Songhai empires. During the fourteenth and fifteenth centuries, they penetrated into the central Sudan, where they founded the first Hausa-speaking merchant lineages (Austen 1987, 42–3).

apparently Islamic may then have fundamentally retained their erstwhile kinship structure and organization, thus replicating the existing social structure under the new system. This outcome is more likely to be observed if religious conversion had been imposed on a people by foreign invaders. For example, strongly organized polities, such as the kingdoms of the Mossi, Dagomba, and Akan, in which central power was firmly based on the kinship organization of the people, resisted infiltration of Islam in the late eighteenth and early nineteenth centuries, and "continued to maintain the old Sudanic traditions of government which might use but which were never wholly committed to the new religion" (Fage 1995, 194–5).

Across the Hausa lands (in what is now northern Nigeria), the conquest by the Fulanis, who adhered to a rather strict version of Islam and possessed a highly developed class of Muslim clerics (*torodbe*), had quite different effects, depending on the strength of local political organizations and their ability to resist outside influences.[22] For example, after the Fulani conquest the Hausa peasantry remained submitted to the rule of powerful landlords, but because the new landlord class was, initially at least, an alien one less subject to the dictates of local custom, its erstwhile rights were less effectively protected. Yet "both landlords and peasants were now Islamised and operating within a framework of general law and principle, which militated against arbitrary oppression, and made for greater security and efficiency," hence the increasing prosperity of the trade and industries of the Hausa cities after the Fulani-led *jihad* (Fage 1995, 207–8).[23]

In the Songhai empire of Gao, bureaucracies might appear to have been Islamized, but the principles of Sudanic royal power remained pagan. The same holds true for the central Saharan Berbers, who, despite Islamization, still cling to their language and many of their customs, and have succeeded in absorbing the Arab groups as tributaries into their own tribal system. As for the Massassi (of mixed Soninke and Fulani descent), although they had Muslim clerics in their entourages, they acted in distinctly Islamic ways, but only when it suited their interests. Rather than pursuing the aim to

[22] With the general decline of Mande influence following the Moroccan invasion, Fulani clerics joined with those of the Tuareg in the leadership of Muslim scholarship in the Sudan (Fage 1995, 197).

[23] In the Futa Jalon, where the *jihad* actually started, Muslim Fulani leaders succeeded in completely overturning the existing sociopolitical structure. Indeed, local Jalonke chiefs initially had the right to tax Fulani herders and to control the allocation of land to them. By the middle of the eighteenth century, however, as a result of the Fulani Islamic upheaval, they had become tributary to Fulani overlords throughout the territory. Moreover, they ultimately converted to Islam and became accepted members of Fulani society (Fage 1995, 199–200).

propagate Islam (that is, to preach and establish the truth of the one God and of the universal brotherhood of man subordinate to his will alone), the Massassi actually wanted to convert the clan and age-grade structures of traditional Bambara society into associations of serfs and clients subordinate to their will as war leaders (Fage 1995, 187–9, 192, 194, 196–208).

When Islam was adopted as a result of a collective strategy of the dominant society or social group, appeals to strict interpretations of the faith may be the way disgruntled individuals or marginal groups chose to emancipate themselves from local customs and rules. A striking illustration is found in the attacks of Wahhabites on the relatively tolerant forms of Islam represented by the Sufi orders and practiced in the towns of Maradi (Niger) and Koko (Nigeria). The younger educated elite who espouse this puritanical version of Islam are attracted by its asceticism and its proclaimed rejection of any ostentatious redistribution of wealth. They want to set their members apart from the older Islamic community by rejecting the authority of local scholarly traditions and adopting distinctive behaviors and rituals (Cooper 1997, 130–4; Gregoire 1993, 109–10; Launay 1992, 104–31). The appeal of a strict Islam also seems to be strong for groups that were either excluded from the traditional sociopolitical structure, or felt that their position in it was, on the whole, disadvantageous. For these groups, indeed, pure Islam "provided a means by which the legality of the traditional system might be challenged," because this system could be shown to be "a denial of the essential brotherhood and equality of man, irrespective of his ethnic and social origins" (Fage 1995, 195).

The conditions under which Wahhabism rose in Ivory Coast are especially interesting: this puritanical doctrine started to spread during a period of increasing disruption of the traditional society as a result of quickly growing urbanization and migration movements after the Second World War. It attracted rich merchants, whom it supplied with an ideology that was both antiestablishment and bourgeois. Wahhabism was antiestablishment in the sense of being opposed to the feudal-like elite of the marabouts, who are at the heart of traditional Islam, but are viewed as impostors illegitimately interposing between God and the faithful. And it was bourgeois in the sense of being emancipated from the constraints of the traditional aristocratic system (Miran 2006, 250).[24] What bears most

[24] It is true that the egalitarian discourse of Wahhabism also appealed to low-caste people willing to liberate themselves from the yoke of the traditional system of hierarchy, but only in the 1980s did it start recruiting among the urban poor. For them, Wahhabism offered a partial response to their quest for social protection and spiritual advice in a context of urban economic precariousness (Miran 2006, 285).

emphasis is that behind the screen of religious antagonisms lay genuine social and political conflicts:

> [T]he battleground was less religious and doctrinal than social and political. As a matter of fact, the recourse to the religious sphere through wahhabite sectarianism allowed dissatisfied people to express differences that could not be overtly declared in the political realm. Accusations of intolerance, dogmatism and narrow-mindedness against the Wahhabites were therefore partly correct: since their separatism was grounded elsewhere, no discussion of a doctrinal nature was possible and no practical compromise could be reached with traditionalist Muslims. (Miran 2006, 259, my translation)

Clearly, the authenticity or depth of an act of religious conversion depends largely on the position of an individual or a group in the existing social and political structure, as well as on the opportunities and constraints for change that are perceived in particular historical circumstances. It is therefore not surprising that significant and robust relationship between religious affiliations and economic growth performance does not emerge from cross-country econometric studies, and that Islam, or Protestantism, sometimes appears to have a positive, sometimes a negative effect on growth. The complexity of historical processes and the crude manner in which religious affiliations are measured account for these disappointing econometric results (Platteau 2009; see also Austin 2008).

5.7 THE LACK OF BROAD-BASED COUNTERACTING FORCES IN SUB-SAHARAN AFRICA

If these highlighted strategies remain marginal attempts by a few individuals to escape redistributive pressures, the underlying social norm persists. If they are followed by a sufficiently large number of individuals, however, the norm of sharing is likely to fall into decay. Note that the same effect would be achieved, yet without incurring the cost involved in defensive or circumventing strategies, if a critical mass of deviant, "selfish" entrepreneurs could make a coordinated move to resist redistributive pressures (Platteau 2000, chapter 5). It is, indeed, reasonable to assume that the individual cost of being punished for noncompliance falls as the number of violators increases, so that there must exist a critical mass of violators above which this cost becomes smaller than the individual benefit from emancipation (assumed to be independent of the number of violators). Such a scenario seems to fit the situation observed in southern (yet not northern) Ghana today, where many rural migrants have not severed ties to their kith and kin. In fact, relationships with the latter are good enough to enable migrants to put up beautiful houses in their native villages without having to fear retribution for (partial) noncompliance with the norm of sharing.[25]

The overall picture nevertheless suggests that redistributive pressures remain a pervasive feature of many parts of Africa. This may be explained not only by the lack of coordinated moves by "selfish" entrepreneurs or the limited scale of religious conversions and tie-severing migrations, but also by the weakness of broad counteracting forces operating at the societal level. Following Karla Hoff and Arijit Sen, two types of drivers of cultural transformation can be distinguished: factors that tend to increase the market opportunities foregone as a result of the extended family system, such as the expansion of the domain of the market, on the one hand, and, on the other hand, factors that tend to lower the return to participation in this system, including a fall in non-covariate risk, an increase in mobility that raises the cost of enforcing kinship-based obligations, and exposure to new ideas that weakens the hold of supportive traditional norms and beliefs (Hoff and Sen 2005, 183). In the following discussion, attention is focused on two broad forces that are expected to yield these effects simultaneously, namely, the twin processes of industrialization and urbanization, and the emergence of nationwide ideological movements. They are examined in turn.

5.7.1 The Dilemma Born of the Lack of Industrialization

As Karl Marx rightly emphasized, the development of industrial capitalism and the accompanying concentration of a growing part of the workforce in large economic establishments go hand in hand with a process of social class formation epitomized by the rise of employers' associations and workers' trade unions. By creating new ties of solidarity and mutual help based not on the primordial ties of the family, village, and clan, but on work relationships woven in an alien environment, industrialization allows both the workers and the managers or capitalists to emancipate themselves from the web of reciprocal obligations inherent in their traditional universe. Social classes, as opposed to kin-based relationships, are wide reference groups, each with its own subculture. They provide their members with a new and enlarged vision of their own interests as well as a concrete basis on which to

[25] Noncompliance is only partial because among the Akan and the Ashanti ceremonials are still currently organized that are essentially aimed at containing successful migrants, prompting them to bring benefits to their native community (I thank Emmanuel Akyeampong for drawing my attention to this point).

anchor new patterns of brotherhood and socialization, as well as motivation for participating in society-level struggles.

A vicious circle is nevertheless set in motion if, as argued earlier, the existence of redistributive norms has precisely the effect of hampering the dynamic of capital accumulation, risk taking, and enterprise creation in the industrial sector, in particular. Such norms would then be self-supporting or self-reinforcing. Foreign direct investment, firm creation by ethnic or stranger communities, and/or the formation of a critical mass of indigenous entrepreneurs who have migrated or converted to a monotheistic religion are possible ways of breaking out of this nasty equilibrium. Yet the situation of sub-Saharan Africa is actually more intricate because other obstacles than redistributive norms are at work that discourage industrial investment and make for an economic landscape in which the overwhelming majority of African entrepreneurs operate very small businesses. Prominent among these additional obstacles are considerable transaction costs caused by poor physical infrastructure, lack of competition, and deficient macroeconomic management (Minten and Kyle 1999; Platteau 2000, chapter 2), lack of familiarity of African entrepreneurs with the conditions prevailing elsewhere both on the technological and institutional or organizational levels (Fafchamps 2010, 152–6), as well as political factors that include political instability, widespread state corruption and rent seeking, and subversion of political choices by ethno-regional forces (Bates 2008; Fosu 2008, 137–72; Ndulu and O'Connell 2008, 55–6; Platteau 2009, 671–8; Van de Walle 2001, chapters 3–4). All these factors point to the important role of politico-institutional factors for economic development, a role Jan de Vries underlined in the light of Western European history:

> The key to understanding the growing power of capital in the European economy is not to be found by searching for esoteric sources of capital; rather, it rests with the solution to the problem of preserving and keeping productive the capital stock already in existence. In other words, a major weakness of the European economy that had to be overcome was not the inadequacy of capital, but the misinvestment and dissipation of capital. (1976, 213–14)

5.7.2 The Lack of Deep-Rooted Nationalist Ideologies

We have seen earlier that the rapid rise of religions combining faith in a High God with beliefs in magic and witchcraft plays a progressive role in helping Africans to construct a collective identity based on the abstract rather than the concrete other. Social struggles, as has been pointed out previously, could generate the same effect of undermining particularized loyalties, yet they are still in their infancy in much of sub-Saharan Africa. Nationalist ideologies – in the sense of ideologies proposing a symbolic framework within which to give form and meaning to emerging nations, so as to create a diffuse sense of common destiny – could also broaden the Africans' vision of public purpose and image of social reality in which to anchor a new collective subject articulated to an independent state. In the words of Clifford Geertz, the formative stage of nationalism essentially consists of "confronting the dense assemblage of cultural, racial, local, and linguistic categories of self-identification and social loyalty that centuries of uninstructed history had produced with a simple, abstract, deliberately constructed, and almost painfully self-conscious concept of political ethnicity – a proper 'nationality' in the modern manner" (1973, 239). In any nation-building process, the new states, or their leaders, must contain or domesticate primordial attachments instead of wishing them out of existence or belittling them. This implies that they are able to reconcile them "with the unfolding civil order by divesting them of their legitimizing force with respect to governmental authority, by neutralizing the apparatus of the state in relationship to them, and by channeling discontent arising out of their dislocation into properly political rather than para-political forms of expression" (Geertz 1973, 277).

The problem is again that nationalist movements are of a rather recent origin in Africa, having started in the context of comparatively short anticolonial struggles. Moreover, political mobilization since independence has centered on competition for access to the privileges and rents associated with power, following a logic of patronage based on ethno-regional factionalism rather than on broad-based political movements and allegiances. These causes of ill development of nationalist ideologies in Africa are explored in two successive subsections.

5.7.2.1 Short-Lived Independence Movements

Compared to Latin America and Asia, sub-Saharan Africa has been subject to a rather short spell of colonial rule. This is largely the consequence of the fact that the African continent was swept along in the whirlwind of decolonization that surged throughout the world after the Second World War. Many African countries thus obtained their independence shortly after Asian countries that went through a much longer period of colonial domination. Unlike what was observed in Latin America and Asia, proindependence political movements in Africa had therefore little time to develop and consolidate. An important upshot of this situation is that they had to abruptly shift from the comparatively easy task of claiming national freedom and sovereignty by uniting against an external power to the much more complex task of building a nation in the aforementioned sense. A nation-building effort can succeed only if a sustainable compromise can be struck between the need of a country to modernize its social, political, and economic structures so as to adapt to the world environment, on the one hand, and the need to win a mass-based legitimacy and involve traditional interests that play on primordial attachments, on the other hand. The following diagnosis proposed by Geertz thus applies with especial force to sub-Saharan Africa:

> [T]he very success of the independence movements in rousing the enthusiasm of the masses and directing it against foreign domination tended to obscure the frailty and narrowness of the cultural foundations upon which those movements rested, because it led to the notion that anti-colonialism and collective redefinition are the same thing. (Geertz 1973, 239)

In many cases, the new African political leaders opted for a swift move to some form of top-down, centralized modernization policies heavily borrowed from the experiences of other continents or directly taken over from their own colonial models: import substitution, state planning, marketing boards, socialist cooperatives and consolidated village communities, and so forth. In other words, relying on a blend of African nationalism and some version of Marxism, the new educated elite gave little thought to the question of the suitability of these policies to the African context and to the importance of finding a common ground with local interests and traditional constituencies.

Tanzania is an interesting case to consider because the strength of the independence movement, the Tanganyka African National Union (TANU), was probably greater there than in any other African colonial territory. John Iliffe (2007) attributes the exceptionally widespread support TANU enjoyed to its use of the widely spoken Swahili language and the absence of strong tribal politics, conditions largely inherited from Tanganyka's nineteenth-century experience (Iliffe 2007, 256). Revealingly, Sir Richard Turnbull, governor of Tanganyka, confessed that he did not foresee that TEMO, the parliamentary caucus of TANU, would develop into "the monolithic, strictly disciplined structure" that it had become, and that the situation in Tanganyka was unique because he could not think of any other colonial territory where such a situation had occurred (Iliffe 2005, 189). The British authorities were still determined to refuse too quick an access of Tanganyka to independence both because this would trigger all other East African territories (Kenya, Uganda, Ethiopia, and Somalia) to follow suit, and because local human resources were deemed insufficiently developed to answer the needs of an independent state.

Under the growing influence of the radical wing of the TANU (especially after Oscar Kambona took its command in October 1959) to which even Julius Nyerere had to give in, the British were nevertheless forced to abandon their plan and concede independence to Tanganyka (in December 1961) although it was not ripe for it.[26] "The idea of a long pause between responsible government and independence" had become patently unrealistic in the eyes of British authorities overwhelmed by the fearful prospect of a combination of Mau Mau and Maji Maji rebellion (Iliffe 2005, 189, 192). It was considered wiser to try to maintain a good relationship with Nyerere to save the long-term interests of Britain in East Africa. In the words of Turnbull:

> We are, after all, under an obligation to make Tanganyka self-governing, and it would be better to reach the consummation too early with the people on our side than after a campaign with the people irrevocably against us. Our first interest must surely be to maintain peaceful conditions ... so that, when the final change comes about, Tanganyka will look to us and not to the Soviet bloc to keep the country supplied with technicians and as a source of manufactured articles.... It is essential for us to use Nyerere whilst he is still powerful; if we wait too long, he will be ousted by the extremists; and with him will go all hopes of an enduring European influence in Tanganyka. (Iliffe 2005, 190)

Strategic considerations born out of the Cold War context therefore prompted old European colonial powers to grant political independence to African countries that had too little time to evolve a genuine sense of nationhood.

5.7.2.2 Factionalism and Tribal Patriotism

If we follow the analysis of John Iliffe in his ambitious book *Africans – The History of a Continent* (2007, 239–41), a key feature of many tropical African colonies lies in the fact that they were purely European creations. They therefore lacked precolonial elites, which in North Africa, Asia, and Latin America were able to propose colony-wide perspectives and

[26] Radical leaders and activists of TANU, particularly of the Youth League, were remarkably effective in constructing a nationalist discourse and defining the content of a national identity and common destiny. In pursuing their aims they did not hesitate to openly blame the ruling clans for protecting unqualified officeholders and denying positions to educated individuals, for preventing appeals against the decisions of the chiefs' courts, and for perpetuating inefficiency, nepotism, and corruption (Giblin 2005b, 143–4; Monson 2005, 109–10).

implementation strategies. The modern politics of sub-Saharan Africa actually began at two levels, one above and the other below the territorial/national level. At the supra-territorial level, pan-African ideologies, such as that of *negritude* (which was born in the Caribbeans), inspired many African intellectuals, and pan-African political movements arose, such as the National Congress of British West Africa (NCBWA) with branches in the Gold Coast, Nigeria, Sierra Leone, and the Gambia. At the infra-territorial level, tribal patriotism prevailed. Africans strove to defend their locality against European intrusion, often resulting in the formation of innumerable local associations by traders, commercial farmers, teachers, clerks, and clergymen. Although their official purpose was to promote the development of the country, in actual practice they defended particularistic interests and did not hesitate to foster tribal identities to better achieve their objective.

Nationalism was therefore a veil behind which many parochial interests could conceal themselves. In the words of Iliffe, "as predominantly local people, most Africans saw nationalism in part as a new idiom for ancient political contests" (2007, 258). As a result, nationalist movements were frequently plagued by factional conflicts that put local issues in the forefront while minimizing the importance of national party affiliations. In these conditions, it is not surprising that "nationalism only partially aroused many of Africa's deepest political forces," and that "responses to it depended on local circumstances" (Iliffe 2007, 257). This said, it is precisely because nationalism was thus absorbed into local political rivalries rather than driven by broad social conflicts that it gathered the support needed to remove colonial rule. Unfortunately, for the same reason, after independence people continued to perceive national issues in terms of local interests and to judge their representatives and the state on the basis of their contributions to local advancement (Iliffe 2007, 258, 267).

Although less true than in other territories, this observation regarding the political motives underlying the anticolonial struggle was even verified in some districts of Tanganyka, such as in Mahenge, where people decided to join TANU in the hope of enlisting the support of the nationalist party in their "tribal" war. In particular, Ndamba activists hoped to obtain redress of a long list of grievances against the occupation of their (Ulanga and Kilombero) valleys by members of the Bena ethnic group. They became especially outraged when in the mid-1950s a Bena "big man" named Kiwanga required them to list their ethnicity as "Bena" in government books, which implied that they would have to abandon any claim to sovereignty over the valley (Monson 2005, 107–10).

In Uganda, a country much more subject than Tanzania to the divisive forces of local factionalism and tribal patriotism, it is impossible to understand the Teso rebellion if one overlooks the fact that its political dimensions were "parochial rather than regional in orientation" (Jones 2009, 50). Revealing, the rebels killed local "big men" (such as the village council chairmen, the parish chief, or the leaders of traditional associations) rather than district or regional officers, in spite of the rhetoric that their struggle was supposed to be fought against the central government. The fact of the matter is that the Teso insurgency was not a coordinated attack against the central government or an assault on the regional elite, but a local conflict opposing younger and older men. This conflict took center stage under harsh conditions where younger people felt threatened by the sudden fall of cattle stocks in the hands of the elders, thereby undermining the resources on which they depended for access to marriage and education (Jones 2009, 51–2, 61).

The famous Mau Mau revolt that erupted in central Kenya in the 1940s and 1950s was also driven by local interests, so much so that Kenyatta, president of the Kenya Africa Union (KAU) party, felt the need to denounce the movement's reactionary character in February 1951 (Kanogo 1987, 136–43). Violent acts committed by Mau Mau, such as the massacre of Lari (a village in the Central Province), were linked to land feuds that had their origins in the land alienation schemes for settlers. Local land conflicts in the Kikuyu region were actually the main force behind the Mau Mau revolt, and these conflicts were not necessarily ignited by land expropriation to the benefit of the British colonizer. A good part of rural tension also arose between families that had lost what they claimed were their ancestral lands and the new indigenous landed gentry who had acquired such lands through intimidation and corrupt means, including lengthy litigation processes and the associated payments of bribes. The loss of prestige of traditional elders as chiefs appointed by the colonial administration emerged as new centers of power, and the resulting severe clash of generations that caused the disintegration of traditional cultural obligations, were other critical factors in the chaotic situation epitomized by the Mau Mau movement (Maloba 1998, 27–34, 100–1).

Other examples readily come to mind. The Nigerian Youth Movement, which Iliffe considers the first truly nationalist program in tropical Africa, divided after a few years of existence (in the early 1940s) amidst rivalry between Yoruba and Igbo. It is telling that at that time British officials saw no danger in Africa of the nationalism threatening them in India. When elections were later granted by the Richards Constitution in 1946, fear of domination by the Igbo-led National Council of Nigeria and the

Cameroons (NCNC) led western and northern politicians to create regional parties, the Action Group, claiming to represent Yoruba, and the Northern People's Congress standing for the Hausa (Iliffe 2007, 242–3). In Ghana, the Convention People's Party of Nkrumah faced serious opposition in the mid-1950s from the National Liberation Movement. Both parties courted the support of Asante and Ahafo chiefs by taking sides in the rivalries that opposed them, particularly over the delicate question of the right to collect tribute from cocoa farmers. Like in Nigeria, "such strategies of political mobilisation served to link debates over customary jurisdictions and land rights to emerging patterns of party conflict, ensuring that the politicisation of rural property rights continued after the end of colonial rule" (Berry 1993, 124).

In Congo, the nationalist movement was hampered by deep divisions between small, unitarist ethnic groups and the large, federalist Kongo and Lunda groups. When political responsibilities were transferred to nationalist politicians (President Kasavubu and Prime Minister Lumumba) while control of the army and the civil service remained in Belgian hands, these centrifugal tendencies were cynically exploited by foreign powers (Belgium and the United States), and central power soon collapsed. Four regional armies came into being, and regional rebellions, millenarian movements, and tribal wars engulfed the whole country, creating an awful legacy of chaos, ethnic hatred, and violence (Berry 1993, 268).

The end outcome of these dynamics has been the emergence of societies stratified in complex ways, and where class alignments are crisscrossed by kinship, age group, ethnic and regional affiliations, as well as by patron-client relationships reflecting the Big Man syndrome (First 1970, 97, 103). Here is a world of factions understood as groups or networks that use parenthood, friendship, and clientelistic ties to conquer power and obtain material advantages (Redfield 1962, 42). The bureaucracies that emerged from independent African states were all to varying degrees patrimonial, in the sense that office was conferred in return for personal loyalty and service to the ruler. The regimes were typically held together by personal relationships among a small elite that coalesced into a single ruling group. Each member of this elite group stands at the apex of a patronage network typically based on ethnic or regional identities and linking him to a locality (Iliffe 2007, 269–70).

As for political parties, they have been aptly described by Jaindi Kisero, a Kenyan journalist in the *Daily Nation* (Nairobi, December 2000). According to him, indeed, they are "bereft of platforms and ideology and are no more than institutions whose only reason for existence is the intention to divide the spoils of state among the ethnic communities that support them. These attitudes are captured well by the Yoruba saying that 'an elder who is brought a plate does not lick it clean, or he will not find young ones to run errands for him.' … Instead of getting annoyed about cases of corruption, we Kenyans get more enraged when fruits of corruption are not shared out according to settled expectations" (cited in Berman, Eyoh, and Kymlicka 2004, 49). It follows that, despite often glaring social inequalities, social class identities do not emerge in societies with pervasive clientelism: by reproducing ties of reciprocity and allegiance across class lines, patron-client networks and factions reinforce ethno-regional identities and undermine the development of class consciousness and conflict (Bourdieu 1990, chapter 8; Chabal and Daloz 1999, 41–3; Van de Walle 2001). The aforementioned lack of urbanization and industrialization reinforces this process because it makes people strongly dependent on privileged and personalized links to patrons for their daily livelihood and protection against all sorts of misfortunes.

5.8 CONCLUSION

When dealing with the institutional prerequisites of an effective market system, economists typically focus their attention on property rights and contract enforcement mechanisms. Other social scientists, on the other hand, have put emphasis on the features of the social fabric needed to sustain the savings predisposition at the heart of the surge of capitalism. The Weberian distinction between *Gemeinschaft and Gesellschaft* is the classical approach to characterizing such social features. Because it deals with redistributive norms as they are applied in (traditional) societies dominated by highly personalized relationships, the present contribution clearly belongs to the second strain of thought, although it also points to the existence of interdependent links between the factors highlighted under the two approaches.

That redistributive pressures exist in sub-Saharan African countries is evident from a large body of anthropological observations documenting the widespread fear of ideological intimidation and more painful sanctions inflicted on successful people who refuse to share the fruits of their economic success with their kith and kin. Additional evidence is provided by the fact that when such pressures cannot be resisted bankruptcy tends to follow. Finally, there is solid ground to believe that African entrepreneurial individuals are ready to incur significant costs to escape the demands for help emanating from close and distant relatives. In the same line, it is striking that trade with relatives and friends is extremely rare in African countries, especially because of the risk of serious contract enforcement problems when a deal is made with an acquaintance. What needs to be emphasized is that the existence of redistributive or sharing norms has the effect of complicating these problems to the extent that customers or debtors can easily invoke them as an excuse for reneging on payment or repayment obligations. In other words, the disciplining effect of the reputation mechanism that is made possible by the repeated, personalized nature of human interactions is cancelled by the adverse effect of the attendant sharing norms.

That individuals attach a lot of weight to their relative income position seems to be an increasingly accepted fact, even in economically advanced countries. It has solid microeconomic foundations, too. Moreover, redistributive pressures exerted on prosperous individuals seem particularly strong in times of growing socioeconomic differentiation and when the degree of personalization of social relationships is high. The Weberian notion of *Gesellschaft*, which implies anonymous relationships and the use of rational, efficiency-based criteria, as opposed to the traditional world of the *Gemeinschaft*, takes on all its meaning here. What African people need is emancipation from the circle of kinship ties and the associated moral obligations. That is precisely what happens when they choose to migrate physically or symbolically out of their native universe.

When African entrepreneurs or traders avoid dealing with members of their family or clan, as pointed out earlier, it is typically because they have put a physical distance between them and their native area. Symbolic migration occurs when individuals become "internal strangers" vis-à-vis their own community as a result of conversion to a monotheist religion. This move enables them to escape their primordial attachments and loyalty obligations, as well as to adhere to new values more conducive to individual advancement. More precisely, the new converts can avail themselves of a formidable shelter against redistributive pressures emanating from kith and kin, while simultaneously practicing the virtues of frugality, honesty, and hard work that encourage saving, risk taking, and improved contract enforcement and flexibility.

Universal religions with a powerful God as figurehead have thus opened up to entrepreneurial Africans a way to fulfill the new expectations that they have themselves raised. It is a well-recognized fact, indeed, that education, which was pioneered by Christian missionaries, has provided the chief dynamic of colonial change: by bringing in new skills and securing opportunities for social differentiation, it became the main generator of both mobility and stratification. It expanded so quickly that most pupils were of relatively low status, even in strongly stratified precolonial societies. Therefore, and in contrast to India, for example, "African education at this time did more to foster social mobility than to entrench old privileged classes, largely because tropical Africa had no long-established literate elites except Muslim clerics" (Iliffe 2007, 230). Christianity's direct association with literacy and education, which included the learning of European languages and the acquisition of other skills required for employment in the state sector, explained much of its success during the first half of the twentieth century. The promise of social success and economic advancement was especially attractive for the young, the poor, and the female, who saw in it a refuge and an avenue for self-emancipation: like communism in twentieth-century Asia, Christianity represented an opportunity for generational revolt and a way out of the repressive customs of the precolonial society (Ellis and Ter Haar 2004, 138; Iliffe 2007, 232). Islam, on the other hand, has historically been associated with successful trading and a long tradition of Arabic education that gave rise to intellectual elites.

Universal religions in Africa do not only instill into people values and norms that violate customs with adverse effects on capital accumulation and entrepreneurship. They also nurture feelings of loyalty and identity toward a large reference group that exceeds ethnic boundaries, and by doing so they may help to gradually establish the basis for a generalized morality and an inclusive civic polity backed by pan-lineage and pan-ethnic institutions. In principle, this effect could also arise from other sources, in particular industrialization and urbanization, that lead to the creation of large companies, the formation of social class identities, and the unfolding of social struggles, or nationalist ideologies and movements that broaden the people's image of social reality and help fashion a new collective subject articulated to an independent state and belief in a common destiny. For complex reasons, however, these alternative mechanisms of emancipation from the web of obligations inherent in the traditional universe of social relationships could not be effectively used in most countries of sub-Saharan Africa. Various obstacles to investment in addition to redistributive norms and pressures, on the one hand, and the short duration of many independence movements and their domination by local and factional interests, on the other hand, help explain this situation.

A direct consequence of the failure of nationwide social and political movements or ideologies is that a big void is left for religions to fill up in Africa. It would nonetheless be a mistake to think that the recent rapid flowering of Pentecostal churches and other revivalist or charismatic movements born outside the ambit of established churches is necessarily a change that goes into the right direction.[27] It might just reflect the ability of unscrupulous and cynical entrepreneurs posing as inspired preachers or prophets to exploit the gullibility of poor, illiterate people who are especially vulnerable to charismatic leadership in times of prolonged economic and political crisis. Far from the ascetic morality that characterized mainline churches a few decades earlier, the new evangelists tend to be people who, by cunning and trickery, have succeeded in becoming immensely rich while deceptively promising to their followers that the same luck is soon going to befall them. Their success has much to do with their professed belief in the active presence of the Holy Spirit, and their alleged ability to cast out demons. Indeed, for people brought up in magical universes inhabited by spirits who are represented as real individual beings and with whom some form of effective communication is possible and essential, this feature offers almost irresistible attraction (Platteau 2009, 686–7).

Finally, it bears stressing that individual advancement does not require complete autonomization because the individual needs to join new networks of people (church parishes, religious sodalities, migrant or business associations) to effectively respond to the challenge of modernization and development. As pointed out previously, a process of individual emancipation from erstwhile kin-based circles and all the attendant obligations must take place. To promote rather than hinder modern economic growth, networks and associations must be freely formed and joined by individuals instead of being imposed on them.

References

Abraham, A. and J. P. Platteau. (2004). "Participatory Development: Where Culture Creeps In." In *Culture and Public Action*, edited by V. Rao and M. Walton, 210–33. Stanford, CA: Stanford University Press.

Andreoni, J. (1990). "Impure Altruism and Donations to Public Goods: A Theory of Warm-Glow Giving." *Economic Journal*, 100: 464–77.

Aoki, M. (2001). *Toward a Comparative Institutional Analysis.* Cambridge, MA and London: MIT Press.

Ardener, E. (1970). "Witchcraft, Economics and the Continuity of Belief." In *Witchcraft Confessions and Accusations*, edited by M. Douglas, 141–60. London: Tavistock Publications.

Austen, R. (1987). *African Economic History.* London and Portsmouth: James Currey and Heinemann.

[27] Today, more than 400 million Africans, about one-third of the whole African population, describe themselves as born-again Christians, compared to 17 million in 1970 (*The Economist* 2010, 35).

Austin, G. (1993). "Indigenous Credit Institutions in West Africa, c.1750-c.1960." In *Local Suppliers of Credit in the Third World, 1750–1960*, edited by G. Austin and K. Sugihara, 93–159. New York: St. Martin's Press.

(2008). "The 'Reversal of Fortune' Thesis and the Compression of History: Perspectives from African and Comparative Economic History." *Journal of International Development*,20: 996–1027.

Badini, A. (1994). *Naître et grandir chez les Moosé traditionnels*. Paris & Ouagadougou: Sépia-A.D.D.B.

Baland, J. M., C. Guirkinger, and C. Mali. (2011). "Pretending to be Poor: Borrowing to Escape Forced Solidarity in Credit Cooperatives in Cameroon." *Economic Development and Cultural Change*, 60(1): 1–16.

Baland, J. M., R. Somanathan, and Z. Wahhaj. (2013). "Repayment Incentives and the Distribution of Gains from Group Lending." *Journal of Development Economics*, 105: 131–9.

Basu, K. (2000). *Prelude to Political Economy – A Study of the Social and Political Foundations of Economics*. Oxford: Oxford University Press.

Basu, K., E. Jones, and E. Schlicht. (1987). "The Growth and Decay of Custom: The Role of the New Institutional Economics in Economic History." *Explorations in Economic History*, 24(1): 1–21.

Bates, R. H. (2001). *Prosperity and Violence*. New York: W. W. Norton & Company.

(2008). *When Things Fell Apart - State Failure in Late-Century Africa*. Cambridge: Cambridge University Press.

Belshaw, C. (1965). *Traditional Exchange and Modern Markets*. Englewood Cliffs, NJ: Prentice-Hall.

Berman, B. (1984). "Structure and Process in the Bureaucratic States of Colonial Africa." *Development and Change*,15: 161–202.

Berman, B., D. Eyoh, and W. Kymlicka. (2004). "Ethnicity and the Politics of Democratic Nation-Building in Africa." In *Ethnicity and Democracy in Africa*, edited by B. Berman, D. Eyoh, and W. Kymlicka, 1–21. Oxford: James Currey and Athens: Ohio University Press.

Berry, S. (1993). *No Condition is Permanent - The Social Dynamics of Agrarian Change in Sub-Saharan Africa*. Madison, Wisconsin and London: University of Wisconsin Press.

Beveridge, A. A. and A. R. Oberschall. (1979). *African Businessmen and Development in Zambia*. Princeton, NJ: Princeton University Press.

Bigsten, A., P. Collier, S. Dercon, M. Fafchamps, B. Gauthier, J. W. Gunning, A. Isaksson, A. Oduro, R. Oostendorp, C. Patillo, M. Soderbom, F. Teal, and A. Zeufack (2000). Contract Flexibility and Dispute Resolution in African Manufacturing. *Journal of Development Studies*, 36(4): 1–37.

Bourdieu, P. (1990). *The Logic of Practice*. Stanford, CA: Stanford University Press.

Breman, J. (1974). *Patronage and Exploitation: Changing Agrarian Relations in South Gujarat*. Berkeley: University of California Press.

Brooks, G. (1993). *Landlords and Strangers: Ecology, Society and Trade in Western Africa 1000–1630*. Boulder, CO: Westview.

Bruce, J. W. (1993). "Do Indigenous Tenure Systems Constrain Agricultural Development?" In *Land in African Agrarian Systems*, edited by T. J. Bassett and D. E. Crummey, 35–56. Madison: University of Wisconsin Press.

Bureau, R. (1996). *Le peuple du fleuve – sociologie de la conversion chez les Douala*. Paris: Karthala.

Chabal, P. and J. P. Daloz. (1999). *Africa Works: Disorder as Political Instrument*. Oxford: James Currey.

Clark, A. (2008). "Happiness, Habits and High Rank: Comparisons in Economic and Social Life." Paris School of Economics, mimeo.

Clark, A., P. Frijters, and M. A. Shields. (2008). "Relative Income, Happiness, and Utility: An Explanation for the Easterlin Paradox and Other Puzzles." *Journal of Economic Literature*, 46(1): 95–144.

Coate, S. and M. Ravallion. (1993). "Reciprocity without Commitment: Characterization and Performance of Informal Insurance Arrangements." *Journal of Development Economics*, 40(1): 1–24.

Cohen, A. (1969). *Custom and Politics in Urban Africa: A Study of Hausa Migrants in Yoruba Towns*. Berkeley: University of California Press.

(1971). "Cultural Strategies in the Organization of Trading Diasporas." In *The Development of Indigenous Trade and Markets in West Africa*, edited by C. Meillassoux, 266–81. London: Oxford University Press.

Colin, R. (2004). *Kénédougou – Au crépuscule de l'Afrique coloniale*. Paris: Présence Africaine.

Congleton, R. (1980). "Competitive Process, Competitive Waste, and Institutions." In *Toward a Theory of the Rent-Seeking Society*, edited by J. Buchanan, R. Tollison, and G. Tullock. Texas A&M Press.

Cooper, B. M. (1997). *Marriage in Maradi – Gender and Culture in a Hausa Society in Niger, 1900–1989*. Portsmouth: Heinemann and London: James Currey.

Dercon, S. and Krishnan, P. (2000) "In Sickness and in Health: Risk-Sharing within Households in Ethiopia." *Journal of Political Economy*, 108(4): 688–727.

Duesenberry, J. (1949). *Income, Saving, and the Theory of Consumer Behavior*. Cambridge, MA and London: Harvard University Press.

Easterlin, R. (1974). "Does Economic Growth Improve the Human Lot? Some Empirical Evidence." In *Nations and Households in Economic Growth: Essays in Honor of Moses Abramovitz*, edited by R. David and R. Reder, 89–125. New York: Academic Press.

Economist, The (2010). "Slain by the Spirit" (pp. 35–6). July 3.

Ellis, S. and J. Y. Fauré. (1995). *Entreprises et Entrepreneurs Africains*. Paris: Karthala-ORSTOM.

Ellis, S. and G. Ter Haar. (2004). *Worlds of Power. Religious Thought and Political Practice in Africa*. London: Hurst & Company.

Elster, J. (1989). *The Cement of Society – A Study of Social Order*. Cambridge: Cambridge University Press.

Ensminger, J. (1992). *Making a Market – The Institutional Transformation of an African Society*. Cambridge: Cambridge University Press.

Evans-Pritchard, E. E. (1937). *Witchcraft, Oracles and Magic among the Azande*. Oxford and New York: Oxford University Press.

(1940). *The Nuer: A Description of the Modes of Livelihood and Political Institutions of a Nilotic People*. Oxford: Clarendon Press.

(1964). *Closed Systems and Open Minds*. Chicago: Aldine Publishing Company.

Fafchamps, M. (1992). "Solidarity Networks in Preindustrial Societies: Rational Peasants with a Moral Economy." *Economic Development and Cultural Change*, 41(1): 147–74.

(1996). "The Enforcement of Commercial Contracts in Ghana." *World Development*, 24: 427–48.
(2000). "Ethnicity and Credit in African Manufacturing." *Journal of Development Economics*, 61: 205–35.
(2003). "Ethnicity and Networks in African Trade. Contributions to Economic Analysis and Policy." *Berkeley Electronic Press*, 2(1): Article 14.
(2004). *Market Institutions in Sub-Saharan Africa – Theory and Evidence*. Cambridge, MA and London: MIT Press.
(2010). "Markets and the Diffusion of Institutional Innovations." In *Culture, Institutions, and Development – New Insights into an Old Debate*, edited by J. P. Platteau and R. Peccoud, 143–59. London and New York: Routledge.
Fafchamps, M. and B. Minten (1999). "Relationships and Traders in Madagascar." *Journal of Development Studies*, 35: 1–35.
Fafchamps, M. and B. Minten. (2002). "Returns to Social Network Capital among Traders." *Oxford Economic Papers*, 54: 173–206.
Fage, J. D. (1995). *A History of Africa*, 3rd ed. London and New York: Routledge.
Fancello, S. (2006). *Les Aventuriers du Pentecôtisme Ghanéen*. Paris: Editions Karthala.
First, R. (1970). *The Barrel of a Gun – Political Power in Africa and the Coup d'Etat*. London: Allen Lane & the Penguin Press.
Firth, R. (1951). *Elements of Social Organization*. London: Watts.
Fisiy, C. and P. Geschiere. (1991). "Sorcery, Witchcraft and Accumulation: Regional Variations in South and West Cameroon." *Critique of Anthropology*, 11: 251–78.
Fosu, A. K. (2008). "Anti-Growth Syndromes in Africa: A Synthesis of the Case Studies." In *The Political Economy of Economic Growth in Africa, 1960–2000*, edited by B. J. Ndulu, S. A. O'Connell, R. H. Bates, P. Collier, and C. C. Soludo, 137–72. Cambridge: Cambridge University Press.
Frank, R. (1985). *Choosing the Right Pond – Human Behavior and the Quest for Status*. New York and Oxford: Oxford University Press.
(1998). "Social Norms as Positional Arms Control Agreements." In *Economics, Values, and Organization*, edited by A. Ben-Ner and L. Putterman, 275–95. Cambridge: Cambridge University Press.
Gaspart, F. and E. Seki. (2003). "Cooperation, Status Seeking and Competitive Behaviour: Theory and Evidence." *Journal of Economic Behaviour and Organization*, 51(1): 51–77.
Geertz, C. (1973). *The Interpretation of Cultures*. New York: Basic Books.
Geschiere, P. (1994). "Parenté et argent dans une société lignagère." In *La réinvention du capitalisme*, edited by J. F. Bayart, 87–113. Paris: Karthala.
(1995). *Sorcellerie et politique en Afrique – La viande des autre*. Paris: Editions Karthala.
Giblin, J. L. (2005a). *A History of the Excluded – Making Family a Refuge from State in Twentieth-Century Tanzania*. Oxford: James Currey, Dar Es Salaam: Mkuki na Nyota, and Athens: Ohio University Press.
(2005b). "Some Complexities of Family and State in Colonial Njombe." In *In Search of a Nation – Histories of Authority and Dissidence in Tanzania*, edited by G. H. Maddox and J. L. Giblin, 128–48. Oxford: James Currey, Dar Es Salaam: Kapsel Educational Publications, and Athens: Ohio University Press.

Godelier, M. (1974). "Anthropologie et économie. Une anthropologie économique est-elle possible?" In *Un domaine contesté: l'anthropologie économique*, edited by M. Godelier, 285–345. Paris: Mouton.
Golooba-Mutebi, F. (2005). "Witchcraft, Social Cohesion and Participation in a South African Village." *Development and Change*,36: 937–58.
Gregoire, E. (1993). "Islam and the Identity of Merchants in Maradi (Niger)." In *Muslim Identity and Social Change in Sub-Saharan Africa*, edited by L. Brenner, 106–15. Bloomington: Indiana University Press.
Greif, A., 1994. "Cultural Beliefs and the Organization of Society: A Historical and Theoretical Reflection on Collectivist and Individualist Societies." *Journal of Political Economy*, 102(5): 912–50.
Greif, A. (2006). *Institutions and the Path to the Modern Economy – Lessons from Medieval Trade*. Cambridge: Cambridge University Press.
Gyekye, K. (1996). *African Cultural Values – An Introduction*. Accra, Ghana: Sankofa Publishing Company.
Hagen, E. E. (1975). *The Economics of Development*. Homewood, IL: Richard D. Irwin.
Harragin, S. (2004). "Relief and an Understanding of Local Knowledge: The Case of Southern Sudan." In *Culture and Public Action*, edited by V. Rao and M. Walton, 307–27. Stanford, CA: Stanford University Press.
Hart, K. (1975). "Swindler or Public Benefactor? The Entrepreneur in his Community." In *Changing Social Structure in Ghana: Essays in Comparative Sociology of a New State and an Old Tradition*, edited by J. Goody. London: International African Institute.
Haugerud, A. (1993). *The Culture of Politics in Modern Kenya*. Cambridge: Cambridge University Press.
Hayami, Y. and T. Kawagoe. (1993). *The Agrarian Origins of Commerce and Industry: A Study of Peasant Marketing in Indonesia*. London: Macmillan and New York: St. Martin's Press.
Himbara, D. (1994). *Kenyan Capitalists, the State, and Development*. Nairobi: East African Educational Publishers.
Hirschman, A. O. (1958). *The Strategy of Economic Development*. New Haven, CT and London: Yale University Press.
Hoff, K. and A. Sen. (2005). "The Extended Family System and Market Interactions." In *The Social Economics of Poverty – On Identities, Communities, Groups, and Networks*, edited by C. B. Barrett, 171–87. London and New York: Routledge.
Hopkins, A. G. (1973). *An Economic History of West Africa*. London: Longman.
Hunter, G. (1969). *Modernizing Peasant Societies: A Comparative Study in Asia and Africa*. New York and London: Oxford University Press.
Iliffe, J. (2005). "Breaking the Chain at its Weakest Link – TANU and the Colonial Office." In *In Search of a Nation – Histories of Authority and Dissidence in Tanzania*, edited by G. H. Maddox and J. L. Giblin, 168–97. Oxford: James Currey, Dar Es Salaam: Kapsel Educational Publications, and Athens: Ohio University Press.
(2007). *Africans – The History of a Continent*. Cambridge: Cambridge University Press, first published 1995.
Jakiela, P. and O. Ozier. (2011). "Does Africa Need a Rotten Kin Theorem? Experimental Evidence from Village Economies." Working Paper, Department of Economics, Washington University, St. Louis and University of California.

Jewsiewicki, B. (1993). *Naître et Mourir au Zaïre – Un Demi-siècle d'Histoire au Quotidien*. Paris: Editions Karthala.

Jones, B. (2009). *Beyond the State in Rural Uganda*. Edinburgh: Edinburgh University Press.

Jul-Larsen, E. (1993). "The Micro-state of the Popo in Pointe Noire. An Analysis of Local Governance, State-Society Relations and Access to Resources." Centre for Development Studies, University of Bergen Norway, mimeo.

Kamau, J. (1965). "Problems of African Business Enterprise." Center for Economic Research, University of Nairobi, Discussion Paper N° 6.

Kanogo, T. (1987). *Squatters and the Roots of Mau Mau*. London: James Currey and Nairobi: East African Educational Publishers.

Karahasan, D. (2000). *L'âge de sable*. Paris: Robert Laffont.

Kennedy, P. (1988). *African Capitalism – The Struggle for Ascendency*. Cambridge: Cambridge University Press.

Kimball, M. S. (1988). "Farmers' Cooperatives as Behavior toward Risk." *American Economic Review*, 78(1): 224–32.

Kohnert, D. (1996). "Magic and Witchcraft: Implications for Democratization and Poverty-Alleviating Aid in Africa." *World Development*,24: 1347–55.

Knight, J. and L. Song. (2006). "Subjective Well-being and Its Determinants in Rural China." University of Nottingham, mimeo.

Kuran, T. (2003). "The Islamic Commercial Crisis: Institutional Roots of Economic Underdevelopment in the Middle East." *Journal of Economic History*,63: 414–46.

(2004a). "Cultural Obstacles to Economic Development: Often Overstated, Usually Transitory." In *Culture and Public Action*, edited by V. Rao and M. Walton, 115–37. Stanford, CA: Stanford University Press.

(2004b). "Why the Middle East Is Economically Underdeveloped: Historical Mechanisms of Institutional Stagnation." *Journal of Economic Perspectives*, 18(3): 71–90.

(2011). *The Long Divergence – How Islamic Law Held Back the Middle East*. Princeton, NJ and Oxford: Princeton University Press.

Kuznets, S. (1966). *Modern Economic Growth*. New Haven, CT: Yale University Press.

de Laiglesia, J. R. and C. Morrisson. (2008). *Household Structures and Savings: Evidence from Household Surveys*. OECD Development Centre, Working Paper N° 267.

de Lame, D. (1996). "Une colline entre mille ou le calme avant la tempête – Transformations et blocages du Rwanda rural." *Musée Royal de L'Afrique Centrale, Annales Sciences Humaines* 154. Tervuren (Belgium).

Launay, R. (1992). *Beyond the Stream: Islam and Society in a West African Town*. Berkeley: University of California Press.

Laurent, P. J. (1998). *Une association de développement en pays mossi*. Paris: Karthala.

Layard, R. (2005). *Happiness: Lessons from a New Science*. London: Allen Lane.

Levi-Strauss, H. (1969). *The Elementary Structures of Kinship*. London: Social Science Paperbacks (revised edition).

Levtzion, N. (1973). *Ancient Ghana and Mali*. New York: Africana Publishing Press.

Lewis, W. A. (1955). *The Theory of Economic Growth*. London: George Allen and Unwin.

Ligon, E., J. P. Thomas, and T. Worrall. (2002). "Informal Insurance with Limited Commitment: Theory and Evidence from Village Economies." *Review of Economic Studies*, 69(1): 209–44.

Long, N. (1968). *Social Change and the Individual.* Manchester: University of Manchester Press.

(1977). *An Introduction to the Sociology of Rural Development.* London and New York: Tavistock Publications.

Lydon, G. (2009). "A Paper Economy of Faith without Faith in Paper: A Reflection on Islamic Institutional History." *Journal of Economic Behavior and Organization*, 71(3): 647–59.

Macfarlane, A. (1978). *The Origins of English Individualism.* Oxford: Blackwell.

Malinowski, B. (1922). *Argonauts of the Western Pacific – An Account of Native Enterprise and Adventure in the Archipelagoes of Melanesian New Guinea.* London: Routlege (reprinted 1999).

Maloba, W. O. (1998). *Mau Mau and Kenya – An Analysis of a Peasant Revolt.* Oxford: James Currey and Bloomington: Indiana University Press.

Marris, P. and A. Somerset. (1971). *African Businessmen.* London: Routledge and Kegan Paul.

Mauss, M. (1925). *The Gift.* London: Routledge and Kegan Paul.

Melenberg, B. (1992). "Micro-econometric Models of Consumer Behaviour and Welfare." Tilburg University, mimeo.

Meyer, B. (1998). "Make a Complete Break with the Past: Memory and Post-Colonial Modernity in Ghanaian Pentecostalist Discourse." *Journal of Religion in Africa*, 27(3): 316–49.

(2004). "Christianity in Africa: From African Independent to Pentecostal-Charismatic Churches." *Annual Review of Anthropology*, 33: 447–74.

Migeotte, F. (1995). "Innovation institutionnelle et tensions sociales: le cas de l'intensification de l'élevage sur une colline rwandaise." Musée Royal d'Afrique Centrale. Tervuren (Belgium).

Minten, B. and S. Kyle. (1999). "The Effect of Distance and Road Quality on Food Collection, Marketing Margins, and Traders' Wages: Evidence from the Former Zaïre." *Journal of Development Economics*,60: 467–95.

Miran, M. (2006). *Islam, Histoire et Modernité en Côte d'Ivoire.* Paris: Editions Karthala.

Monson, J. (2005). "The Tribal Past and the Politics of Nationalism in Mahenge District, 1940–60." In *In Search of a Nation – Histories of Authority and Dissidence in Tanzania*, edited by G. H. Maddox and J. L. Giblin, 103–13. Oxford: James Currey, Dar Es Salaam: Kapsel Educational Publications, and Athens: Ohio University Press.

Moore, M. (1997). "Societies, Polities and Capitalists in Developing Countries: A Literature Survey." *Journal of Development Studies*, 33(3): 287–363.

Morduch, J. (1999). "Between the Market and the State: Can Informal Insurance Patch the Safety Net?" *World Bank Research Observer*, 14(2): 187–207.

Nafziger, E. W. (1977). *African Capitalism: A Case Study of Nigerian Entrepreneurship.* Stanford, CA: Hoover Institution Press.

Ndulu, B. J. and S. A. O'Connell. (2008). "Policy Plus: African Growth Performance 1960–2000." In *The Political Economy of Economic Growth in Africa, 1960–2000*, edited by B. J. Ndulu, S. A. O'Connell, R. H. Bates, P. Collier, and C. C. Soludo, 3–75. Cambridge: Cambridge University Press.

Niehaus, I. (2001a). *Witchcraft, Power and Politics: Exploring the Occult in the South African Lowveld.* Capetown: David Philips.

(2001b). "Witchcraft in the New South Africa: From Colonial Superstition to Postcolonial Reality." In *Magical Interpretations, Material Realities: Modernity, Witchcraft and the Occult in Post-Colonial Africa*, edited by H. L. Moore and T. Sanders, 184–205. London and New York: Routledge.

North, D. C. (1990). *Institutions, Institutional Change and Economic Performance*. Cambridge: Cambridge University Press.

Offer, A. (1997). "Between the Gift and the Market: The Economy of Regard." *Economic History Review*, 50(3): 450–76.

Parkin, D. J. (1972). *Palm, Wine and Witnesses*. London: Intertext Books.

Peters, P. E. (1994). *Dividing the Commons – Politics, Policy, and Culture in Botswana*. Charlottesville and London: University Press of Virginia.

Platteau, J. P. (1991). "Traditional Systems of Social Security and Hunger Insurance: Past Achievements and Modern Challenges." In *Social Security in Developing Countries*, edited by E. Ahmad, J. Drèze, J. Hills, and A. K. Sen, 112–70. Oxford: Clarendon Press.

(1994). "Behind the Market Stage Where Real Societies Exist – Part II: The Role of Moral Norms." *Journal of Development Studies*, 30(4): 753–817.

(2000). *Institutions, Social Norms and Economic Development*. London: Routledge.

(2004). "The Gradual Erosion of the Social Security Function of Customary Land Tenure Arrangements: The Case of Tribal Societies in SubSaharan Africa." In *Insurance against Poverty*, edited by S. Dercon, 247–78. Oxford: Clarendon Press.

(2009). "Institutional Obstacles to African Economic Development: State, Ethnicity, and Custom." *Journal of Economic Behavior and Organization*, 71(3): 669–89.

(2011). "The Role of Culture in Development: An Overview." In *Culture, Institutions, and Development – New Insights into an Old Debate*, edited by J. P. Platteau and R. Peccoud, 3–19. London: Routledge.

Platteau, J. P. and A. Abraham (2002). "Participatory Development in the Presence of Endogenous Community Imperfections." *Journal of Development Studies*, 39(2): 104–36.

Platteau, J. P. and R. Peccoud. (2011). "Revisiting the Role of Culture." In *Culture, Institutions, and Development – New Insights into an Old Debate*, edited by J. P. Platteau and R. Peccoud, 247–58. London: Routledge.

Platteau, J. P. and P. Sekeris. (2010). "On the Feasibility of Power and Status Ranking in Traditional Setups." *Journal of Comparative Economics*, 28(3): 267–82.

Platteau, J. P. and E. Seki. (2007). "Heterogeneity, Social Esteem, and Feasibility of Collective Action." *Journal of Development Economics*,83: 302–25.

Poewe, K. (1989). *Religion, Kinship, and Economy in Luapula, Zambia*. Lewinston: Edwin Mellen Press.

Polanyi, K. (1944). *The Great Transformation*. New York: Rinehart.

(1968). *Primitive, Archaic, and Modern Economics*. New York: Doubleday.

(1977). *The Livelihood of Man*. New York and London: Academic Press.

Redfield, R. (1962). *The Little Community*. Chicago: Aldine.

Rennie, J. K. (1984). "Ideology and State Formation: Political and Communal Ideologies among the South-Eastern Shona, 1500–1890." In *State Formation in Eastern Africa*, edited by A. I. Salim, 162–94. Nairobi, London, and Ibadan: Heinemann Educational Books.

De Rosny, E. (1981). *Les yeux de ma chèvre. Sur les pas des maîtres de la nuit en pays douala*. Paris: Plon.

Rowlands, M. and Warnier, J. P. (1988). "Sorcery, Power, and the Modern State in Cameroon." *Man*,23: 118–32.

Sahlins, M. (1960). "Political Power and the Economy in Primitive Society." In *Essays in the Science of Culture in Honor of Leslie White*, edited by G. Dole and R. Carneiro. New York: Crowell.

(1963). "Poor Man, Rich Man, Big Man: Political Types in Melanesia and Polynesia." *Comparative Studies in Society and History*, 5: 285–303.

(1972). *Stone Age Economics*. Chicago: Aldine.

Sarro, R. (2009). *The Politics of Religious Change on the Upper Guinea Coast – Iconoclasm Done and Undone*. Edinburgh: Edinburgh University Press.

Scott, J. C. (1976). *The Moral Economy of the Peasant – Rebellion and Subsistence in Southeast Asia*. New Haven, CT and London: Yale University Press.

(1985). *The Weapons of the Weak – Everyday Forms of Peasant Resistance*. New Haven, CT and London: Yale University Press.

Shillington, K. (1989). *History of Africa*. New York: St. Martin's Press.

Somville, V. (2010). "Daily Collectors & Public Good Provision in Non-Cooperative Households: Theory and Evidence from Urban Benin." Centre for Research in the Economics of Development (CRED), University of Namur, mimeo.

Sylla, A. (1994). *La philosophie morale des Wolof*, IFAN, Université de Dakar.

Thomas, K. (1973). *Religion and the Decline of Magic*. Harmondsworth: Penguin Books.

Townsend, R. M. (1994). "Risk and Insurance in Village India." *Econometrica*, 62(3): 539–91.

Udry, C. (1994). "Risk and Insurance in a Rural Credit Market: An Empirical Investigation in Northern Nigeria." *Review of Economic Studies*,61: 495–526.

Van de Walle, N. (2001). *African Economies and the Politics of Permanent Crisis, 1979–1999*. Cambridge: Cambridge University Press.

Veblen, T. (1899). *The Theory of the Leisure Class*. London: George Allen and Unwin.

Von Braun, J. and P. Webb (1989). "The Impact of New Crop Technology on the Agricultural Division of Labor in a West African Setting." *Economic Development and Cultural Change*, 37(3): 513–34.

De Vries, J. (1976). *The Economy of Europe in the Age of Crisis, 1600–1750*. Cambridge: Cambridge University Press.

Wright, R. (1994). *The Moral Animal – Why We Are the Way We Are: The New Science of Evolutionary Psychology*. New York: Pantheon Books.

6

Accumulation and Conspicuous Consumption: The Poverty of Entrepreneurship in Western Nigeria, ca. 1850–1930

Ayodeji Olukoju

The failure to develop a concept of business as an impersonal and long-term occupation helps to explain why, in spite of its many attributes, the African business community in Lagos was unable to produce a capitalist class capable of competing successfully with expatriate firms. (Hopkins 1964, 444)

6.1 INTRODUCTION

The underdevelopment of West African entrepreneurship, epitomized by the near-total absence of an indigenous capitalist class, alluded to here by Professor A. G. Hopkins, has been examined within the framework of divergent explanations – cultural versus structural.[1] In the same vein, Gareth Austin, pondering the "basic question … [of] the apparent rarity of transgenerational continuity of specific businesses in West Africa,"[2] suggested any of three possibilities for further investigation: the institutional (cultural issues, such as inheritance practices); the general instability of economic life (the vicissitudes and risks associated with enterprises); and the changes wrought by colonial intervention. Against the background of

I thank the editors of this volume and their anonymous readers, as well as Kenneth Nwoko, for comments on an earlier draft of this chapter.

1 Hopkins (1964, 1978, 1988) and Akeredolu-Ale (1975) examine the conflicting interpretations. Though reference will be made to "the poor" (*akuse, ol òsì*, and *tálíkà*), the subject of the John Iliffe-John Peel exchanges (see *Journal of African History*, 32, 1991, 495–500; 501–6) on poverty in nineteenth-century Yorubaland, this chapter focuses on the mercantile and political elite (*bòròkìní, olówó, olólà, gbajúmò*, etc.), rather than the "poor," to explain the poverty of development in the region. The underlying assumption in this chapter, which it seeks to demonstrate, is that Yoruba entrepreneurs, unlike their counterparts elsewhere, failed to seize the moment and drive the process of societal development to its logical conclusion.

2 Austin (2002, 122).

the propositions by Hopkins and Austin, this chapter argues, first, that the cultural context was as important as the constraining structure of British colonialism in explaining the underdevelopment of indigenous entrepreneurship, and, second, that both dynamics should be taken together in any meaningful explanation. The importance of the cultural dynamic, highlighted in this chapter, is anchored on indigenous Yoruba conceptions of accumulation, wealth, and social status.

First, the Yoruba distinguished among the poor (*akuse*, *olòsì*, and *tálíkà*), the rich (*olówó*), the wealthy (*olóró* or *olólà*), and the honorable person (*olólá*). Second, they esteemed the wealthy, who had property and assets (*olóró* or *olólà*) above the possessor of mere cash (*olówó*). Third, as society also prioritized honor, a person who combined honor and wealth with generosity – the *bòròkìní* or *gbajúmò* – was the ideal entrepreneur (Falola 1984, 71).[3] The profiles of nineteenth- and twentieth-century Yoruba entrepreneurs in Lagos and its hinterland show that, with few exceptions, the aspiring *bòròkìní* or *gbajúmò* eagerly sought to earn societal approval.

The second major concern of this chapter is the chronology of the decline of indigenous entrepreneurship. It attempts to show how, why, and when exactly this region missed the proverbial boat of development. It argues that the period 1880–1920 was critical to the failure of Yoruba entrepreneurs to take off to the stage of developmental entrepreneurship. That period was characterized by two concurrent developments: the transition to full colonial rule – with its constraints and opportunities – and at least two cycles of boom – 1906–14 and 1918–20. It was the failure to maximize the opportunities of this period and to surmount the institutional and structural disadvantages of the colonial context, coupled with anti-entrepreneurial societal expectations, that doomed Yoruba entrepreneurship under British rule. The lamentation of a boom-era observer while capital was being frittered away without sparing a thought for the future speaks volumes:

> Do we realize that whatever money we get now on our palm oil and palm kernels is our capital and that in spending it outright we are spending our capital? . . . [We] are frittering away with a hopeless want of foresight, rather characteristic of our people, that capital which alone can give us economic liberty in the future. . . . We sound the grave warning that our future position in this country will depend on how much of our own capital is invested in its development.[4]

[3] That such values and expectations were not peculiar to Yorubaland is indicated in Zakaria (1997, 63).

[4] *Lagos Weekly Record*, September 27, 1919, editorial: "Whither are we going?" There was an undercurrent of economic nationalism in this remark. A recent study is Olukoju (2010). See also Olukoju (2002b).

Against this background, this chapter examines the dimensions of the poverty[5] of indigenous entrepreneurship in western Nigeria, the homeland of the Yoruba, between 1850 and 1930. It details how chiefs, warriors, and traders (both male and female) accumulated and dissipated wealth (with particular emphasis on elite lifestyle and investment patterns). Though the politico-economic contexts were different – warfare in the first and colonialism in the second – this chapter highlights some striking parallels and contrasts.

In all, this chapter grapples with the following questions: Why did indigenous accumulation (admittedly in the face of local and external countervailing forces, especially domestic feudalism, oligarchic rule, and Western imperialism) fail to generate the societal transformation witnessed in, for example, pre-1952 Egypt, founded in part on mercantile enterprise? How did these entrepreneurs respond to changes in the local and wider political economy? What was the developmental and long-term impact of western Nigerian entrepreneurs on their society – against the demands of social obligations – in terms of diversification into noneconomic enterprises? Did the business elite really fail in view of the long-term consequences of their careers?

This chapter deals with these questions by analyzing case studies of notable entrepreneurs in the Yoruba urban and commercial centers of Ibadan, Ijaye, Abeokuta, and Lagos in their peculiar politico-economic settings.[6] It draws on official sources, contemporary newspapers, and private papers in the archives and libraries in Ibadan and Lagos. Newspapers and private correspondence provide contemporary insights into the issues and personalities examined in the rest of this chapter.

Business biographies provide valuable insights into the dynamics of entrepreneurship. Coupled with contemporary documentary and oral evidence, they help in understanding the contexts in which the protagonists operated, and how they coped with the challenges and utilized the opportunities available to them. This is amply illustrated by the career of Daniel Conrad Taiwo (1810s?–1901) (a.k.a. "Taiwo Olowo" – "Taiwo the Rich"), whose biographical sketch is one of the case studies that underpin this chapter. Of immediate importance is his striking epitaph in a Lagos newspaper:

[5] This refers to its failure to turn capital into an instrument of structural change in society and to build commercial houses with a record of intergenerational succession and transition from the precolonial or colonial past to the present.

[6] There are several biographical sketches and in-depth micro-histories of the business and sociopolitical activities of many of the selected personalities. They provide important source material for this chapter.

> Chief Taiwo … unquestionably wielded a greater influence than any other individual member of the community.… [He] was a true type of African "big man." *With him money became wealth in the fullest sense of the term, for he … utilized it* … and the result was that his name was a household word in all the surrounding country, while he was respected and revered far and wide.[7] (Italics added for emphasis)

The careers of Chief Taiwo and others cited in this chapter help to situate the central issue of the underdevelopment of indigenous entrepreneurship – how money was made and *utilized* – in the *longue durée.*

6.2 ENTREPRENEURSHIP IN THE CONTEXTS OF WARFARE AND POLITICAL COMPETITION IN NINETEENTH-CENTURY YORUBALAND

As is well detailed in the literature, the fall of Old Oyo, the rise of the successor states of Ibadan, Ijaye, and Abeokuta, and the protracted warfare among Yoruba states during the nineteenth century dovetailed into the British occupation of Lagos between 1851 and 1861 and culminated in the colonization of Yorubaland (the hinterland of Lagos) by 1893.[8] Initially, these were parallel processes, but both intersected in the fueling of the slave trade by the interstate conflicts in Yorubaland. Warfare between the southern emirates of the emergent Sokoto Caliphate (Ilorin and Bida) and the northern Yoruba successor states after the fall of Old Oyo, and the interstate wars among the Yoruba between 1820 and 1893 generated population movements and insecurity, and the massive export of slaves via the coastal ports, including Lagos and Badagry. The abolition of the transatlantic slave trade later provided a pretext for British intrusion into Lagos and, subsequently, the Yoruba hinterland. For our purpose, intermittent warfare in Yorubaland, including the Ibadan-Ijaye, Ibadan-Egba, and Ibadan-Ekiti Parapo wars, provided the context in which the processes of indigenous entrepreneurship unfolded between the 1820s and 1893. The internal and external trade in war captives, and the appropriation of the surplus generated by free and servile labor, underpinned the entrepreneurial activities of notable Yoruba political, military, and commercial leaders. Their wealth consisted in their slaveholdings and the exploitation of slave labor in agriculture, trade, and crafts to build up chiefly power.

7 *Lagos Weekly Record*, February 23,1901. This is a clear indication of popular perceptions and definitions of (the means and ends of) money, affluence and influence, and what it was to be a "big man."

8 See, among others, Akinjogbin (1998), Atanda (1973), and Babayemi (1990).

The careers of the leading Yoruba entrepreneurs of the nineteenth century – Kurunmi, the military autocrat of the short-lived state of Ijaye; the Ibadan war chiefs and two notable women entrepreneurs (Efunsetan Aniwura and Madam Tinubu, who also oiled the military machines of Ibadan, Abeokuta, and Lagos) – conflate issues of gender, militarism, power politics, and accumulation during the nineteenth century. In spite of the diversity of gender, origins, and circumstance, these personalities shared the following characteristics. First, they lived during the same epoch – the nineteenth century. Second, they were active players in the interstate warfare of the period. Third, they operated in the context of precolonial indigenous autonomy in the Yoruba hinterland. Fourth, they shared similar experiences of accumulation through slaveholding and through commercial and agricultural enterprise. Fifth, they all subscribed to the cultural ethos of utilizing social networks to build economic and political power.

In Ijaye, the autocratic leader, Kurunmi, and his chiefs amassed wealth in trade and farming. A British missionary, Henry Townsend, estimated that Kurunmi alone had extensive plantations that covered all of 100 acres.[9] Another contemporary observer, The Reverend S. H. Clarke, noted that farmlands stretched some ten to twelve miles beyond the city walls. Indeed, he rode on horseback for an hour through the farmlands cultivated in the direction of the Upper Ogun River. Such large-scale farming turned Ijaye into a food basket for the emerging megalopolises at Ibadan and Abeokuta, havens of large communities displaced by the wars of the 1820s and 1830s. Men and women engaged in the production of yam, corn, palm oil, vegetables, and fruits. Farming was complemented by weaving and cloth dyeing, carving, pottery, hunting, and, to a lesser extent, stock breeding. The products of these economic activities were fed into the local and regional commercial systems linking Ijaye with Ibadan, Oyo, Ogbomoso, Abeokuta, Ilorin, and Lagos. The regional market at Ijaye was the destination of more than twenty thousand people and caravans from the coast, which arrived three times during the week (Falola 1991a, 26, 1991b).

The foregoing narrative is intended to highlight the basis of accumulation in the indigenous Yoruba political economy during the nineteenth century. Although Ijaye was short-lived, it was typical of the successor states of Old Oyo (New Oyo, Ibadan, Ijaye, and the non-Oyo state of Abeokuta) in terms of how military and political leaders harnessed the resources of state to accumulate wealth. "On internal capital accumulation," Falola notes with reference to Kurunmi, "his strategy was to be the richest and weaken the

[9] See Falola (1991a, 24) for the details in this paragraph.

access of the other power elite to resources" (Falola 1991a, 27). His wealth derived from market dues and tolls on caravans, which were efficiently collected by his officials, war booty, heavy fines on offenders, gifts, heavy taxation, and tributes. All proceeds went into the central coffers that were under his personal control. He controlled the trade routes into the city-state and monopolized arms and ammunition, which also represented a form of wealth in material and military terms (Falola 1991a, 27–8).

Kurunmi was an atypical Yoruba military autocrat because he did not share power with chiefs who represented lineages and quarters as in other Yoruba kingdoms. But his style of accumulation paralleled that of Ibadan war chiefs of the nineteenth century. The latter also built their wealth on slaveholding, large-scale farming, control of trade, levying of tolls, tributes, and court fines. *Balogun* Ibikunle, the commander-in-chief of the Ibadan army in the 1850s, was reputed to be a rich man with extensive farmlands beyond the city walls, much like Kurunmi at Ijaye (Awe 1973, 67, note 4). Awe noted that "one of the distinctive [attributes] ... of any (Ibadan) war chief of repute was [the ability] ... to fight, farm and trade" (Awe 1973, 67, note 4). This was how they sustained the large body of men under arms and maintained large households in the metropolis. However, unlike Kurunmi, the Ibadan war chiefs had greater opportunities to accumulate and to build more enduring military and economic entities based on their lineages, military forces, and the control of subject territories because of the longer life span of the Ibadan state and the process of its expansion into the Ekiti-Ijesa territories. They employed the *ajele* system to administer and plunder the subject territories. But it was the system that underpinned the Ibadan state that also led to its fall as the excesses of the *ajele* (intendants) alienated the subject peoples of eastern Yorubaland and precipitated the protracted Ekiti Parapo resistance that sounded the death knell to the empire.

While virtually all the rulers of Ibadan were wealthy in slaves, property, and money, the case of a notable woman leader, Efunsetan Aniwura (1820s–74), the *Iyalode* (leader of the women), is particularly striking for its exceptionalism. She was the richest and most influential woman entrepreneur of her age, rivaled only by Madam Efunroye Tinubu (ca. 1805–87) of Lagos, Badary, and Abeokuta fame.[10] Both women were of Egba origins, amassed wealth in the context of warfare, and were deeply involved in the

[10] The only book-length account of Madam Tinubu's life, admittedly written by an amateur historian, is Oladipo Yemitan, *Madame Tinubu: Merchant and King-Maker*, Ibadan: University Press Limited, 1987. It contains some useful details.

power politics of their era, a male-dominated sphere in which they were given short shrift.

Married to Adele, a prince and later king (*Oba*) of Lagos, from 1835–7, Madam Tinubu was a notable trader in slaves, arms, and ammunition and a key player in succession politics in Lagos. She was also well established in her natal home of Abeokuta, where she had a thriving business managed by sixty slaves and a literate clerk (Awe and Olutoye 1998, 128). Such was the scale of her involvement in the defense of Abeokuta (against Dahomey) that she was made the first *Iyalode* of the Egba. Of direct relevance is Madam Tinubu's accumulation of wealth in land, material assets, and people. She had extensive landholdings on the island and mainland of Lagos, as well as in Abeokuta. Many of these holdings survive to this day or have been alienated by her descendants (her children died as minors). By 1855, Madam Tinubu reportedly sat atop a vast commercial network and "had few rivals among the traders in Lagos. She had vast properties and power" (Yemitan 1987, 24).

But she was heavily dependent on credit in the running of her business.[11] Hence, when her political stock fell and she was expelled from Lagos in 1856, she was indebted to the tune of £5,000, a huge sum of money at the time. One of her major creditors was Captain James Pinson Labulo (J. P. L.) Davies, to whom reference is made later in this chapter. He foreclosed her mortgaged properties on Lagos Island, but he too forfeited the land around modern Tinubu Square to the government when he became bankrupt in 1875. Such were the vicissitudes of commercial life in nineteenth-century Lagos and Abeokuta of which Tinubu, Davies, and others were victims. She and others made and lost fortunes to disasters like fire outbreaks, commercial slumps, and social debts. Tinubu's biographer stated that she "made money (from commercial enterprises) ... but she spent the money on people – never on herself alone" (Yemitan 1987, 28).

The details of Efunsetan's career can be found elsewhere,[12] but it is important to highlight some aspects of it that illustrate the processes of accumulation and consumption in nineteenth-century Yorubaland. A member of important aristocratic families in Abeokuta, Ife, and Ibadan, Efunsetan achieved some success as a trader in Abeokuta before moving to Ibadan. At Abeokuta, she traded extensively with Ibadan, Lagos, Badagry, and Porto Novo (modern Benin Republic). Efunsetan conducted trade with Portuguese and Brazilians, to whom she sold slaves, indigenous textiles,

[11] Ibid., for the details in this paragraph.

[12] The details in the following paragraphs are derived from Awe (2001).

ivory, and palm produce. In exchange, she procured tobacco, beads, a wide variety of textiles, and liquor, guns, and gunpowder. She also conducted a considerable internal trade across Yorubaland and with neighboring states, such as Ilorin and Nupeland, on the basis of the complementary needs and products of the different regions. Among these were foodstuffs, kolanuts, woven mats and cloths, natron, and livestock. These commodities were conveyed by river transport (on the Ogun) and head porterage.

Though unlettered and without a modern bookkeeping system, and operating in a milieu of traditional currencies and barter, Efunsetan built an extensive commercial enterprise, which included extensive farms on the outskirts of Ibadan. Her relocation to Ibadan demonstrated her keen business acumen, for the burgeoning war camp conferred strategic advantages – location on the forest-savanna fringe, extensive farmlands and production of agricultural surplus for export, and a booming market for guns and gunpowder and war captives. Efunsetan owned hundreds of slaves who served her in various capacities – as farm labor, retainers, and artisans. At her death in 1874, each of her three large farms contained 100 slaves, who planted yams, corn, and vegetables. Her male slaves traded on her behalf to as far as Bida (Nupe), manned her canoe fleet on the Ogun, and were pressed into battle as her contribution to the Ibadan fighting force. The female slaves wove *kijipa* (country cloth in great demand in the Yoruba and neighboring territories and in South America, where a large number of slaves had been transported) and mats, and cultivated indigo used for dyeing cloth. They also produced various indigenous cosmetics from camwood and palm kernel oil. Much of her commercial wealth derived from her virtual monopoly of the tobacco import trade. She mixed politics with business by extending generous credits in guns and gunpowder to the Ibadan war chiefs in return for war captives. Her political stature rose with her stupendous wealth and culminated in her appointment as *Iyalode* by either *Basorun* Ogunmola, who died in 1867, or *Aare* Latosa, who became Ibadan's supreme ruler in 1872. Not surprising, her political exposure and increasing assertiveness in a male-dominated society led to her clash with Latosa and her assassination in 1874. In addition to other issues, the huge indebtedness of Latosa and several Ibadan chiefs to Efunsetan and her refusal to grant them further credit in arms and ammunition made possible their common cause against her.

A significant point, to return to the idea of how wealth was utilized, was the use to which the war chiefs of nineteenth-century Yorubaland put their wealth in human and material resources (Awe 1973; Falola 1984). As autocratic as he was, even Kurunmi was wise to the use of wealth for political patronage – to sustain the support of his loyalists and to "placate the public" (Falola 1991a, 28). Like his counterparts in Ibadan, he maintained "a grandiose style of living" in consonance with his position in society. His conspicuous consumption and opulent lifestyle found expression in his vast compound that covered all of eleven acres, his harem of three hundred wives, and his holdings of one thousand slaves (Falola 1991a, 28). With her extensive farming, trading, and crafts enterprises, *Iyalode* Efunsetan Aniwura was extremely rich by the standards of the times. In addition to three large farms beyond the city walls, she had two cattle farms in the city managed by her Hausa slaves. As expected, she invested her wealth in an opulent lifestyle (expensive wardrobe and ornaments), in the Ibadan war effort, and in an elaborate political structure of her own to match her status as the female equivalent of the *Balogun* of Ibadan. First, she had a large collection of various types of expensive beads, silver trinkets and brass bracelets, and a rich wardrobe of the most expensive ceremonial cloth (*alari*, *sanyan*, and *etu*), in addition to the durable, everyday wear *kijipa*. Second, as the *mogaji* (head) of her lineage (*Basorun* Oluyole's), she was responsible for the upkeep of a large retinue of supporters and the funding of wedding, child naming, and funeral ceremonies in the compound. Finally, as *Iyalode*, her responsibility covered the entire community, which expected her to display opulence and generosity.

As illustrated by the careers of twentieth-century Ibadan entrepreneurs – Salami Agbaje and Adebisi Giwa – the community expected the wealthy to share their good fortune with the less privileged and to display their wealth on public occasions and in other forms of conspicuous consumption (Adeboye 2001). In the cases of the Ibadan war chiefs, Ijaye's Kurunmi and *Iyalode* Efunsetan, political power was accompanied by the dissipation of wealth in the community. In the event of a fall from grace – Kurunmi in Ijaye and Efunsetan in Ibadan – much of what was accumulated could be lost in a single orgy of looting ordered by the political establishment to obliterate a formidable adversary. In such cases, the wealth built up could not be passed on.

6.3 CIVIL ENTREPRENEURSHIP IN THE COLONIAL CONTEXT IN LATE NINETEENTH- AND EARLY TWENTIETH-CENTURY YORUBALAND

A complementary group of indigenous entrepreneurs in Lagos, Abeokuta, and Ibadan emerged from the mid-nineteenth century to the 1930s in the context of British colonialism. Fairly representative of the group were

Salami Agbaje and Adebisi Giwa of Idikan, both of Ibadan; and D. C. Taiwo (a.k.a. "Taiwo Olowo"), J. P. L. Davies, Peter Thomas, J. H. Doherty, S. H. Pearse, W. A. Dawodu, and Charlotte Olajumoke Obasa, who were based in Lagos. These entrepreneurs were prominent in different sectors of the economy, including shipping (Davies), urban transport (Dawodu and Obasa), farming (J. K. Coker and Davies), moneylending, and maritime commerce. The rest of this chapter traces their differential fortunes through the cycles of boom and bust during the period between 1850 and 1939. We shall see how they took advantage of openings in the colonial economy (in sectors where European and Levantine presence or interest was marginal) and the infrastructure of the colonial political economy – modern government and law enforcement, standardized currencies, road, rail, and maritime transport facilities, and banking services – to build their business enterprises. We shall also see how they were constrained by, and attempted to transcend, the structures of the colonial political economy.

D. C. Taiwo ("Taiwo Olowo") was typical of the rise of indigenous entrepreneurs in the context of the establishment of British rule.[13] Originally from Isheri, barely fifteen miles north of Lagos Island, he had come to Lagos in the early nineteenth century as a retainer in a chiefly family. He proceeded to amass considerable wealth from his investment in commerce, land, and people. Taking advantage of changes in land tenure as part of the new order imposed by British colonialism, Taiwo created a business enterprise based on trade, land acquisition, investment in real estate, and moneylending. Between the 1840s and his death in 1901, he steadily acquired land in strategic parts of Lagos Island and exploited the opportunities created by the transition from the slave trade to the so-called legitimate trade. It is significant that he utilized his contacts with influential indigenous peoples and the British to promote his commercial interests. He deployed credit advanced by European traders to develop a considerable export trade in palm produce and import business in textiles, especially during the 1890s, a period of extreme commercial conditions. Taiwo also supplied arms to Ibadan that were used in the Kiriji War.

Next, he took advantage of the issuance of Crown grants to buy and sell land and to use land as collateral for credit. He regularized the ownership of his existing land acquisitions and secured fresh ones under the new order. His huge investment in land is attested by the fact that he bought twenty-one properties in Lagos between 1870 and 1892. "Control of land and capital," Mann notes, "enabled the rising Lagosian to acquire wives, slaves, clients

[13] The section on Taiwo is based on Mann (1991).

and other dependants" (Mann 1991, 101). He also manipulated the legal system and his wealth to keep his subordinates in check, often by litigation. An adroit exploitation of the opportunities colonialism created enabled him to mobilize human and material resources for the advancement of his commercial and political interests. He did not acquire titles in Lagos, but assumed the paramount chieftaincy of his native Isheri. As his epitaph indicated, he was the most influential individual in Victorian Lagos on account of his stupendous wealth, access to British officials, and extensive networks among the local political elite.

Yet, like the traditional Yoruba entrepreneurs in Ibadan and Ijaye, Taiwo was careful to invest in people to maintain their loyalty and support. Such "extension of influence" in the community, Mann remarks, "consumed valuable resources" (Mann 1991, 101). In addition, Taiwo, like Salami Agbaje and Adebisi Giwa in colonial Ibadan, was expected to dispense financial favors and write off debts to secure the goodwill of the community. In the particular case of Taiwo, there were occasions when he waived his right to foreclose the property of loan defaulters for purely cultural reasons, as opposed to economic rationality. "He and other big men ... may sometimes have hesitated to foreclose for fear of alienating public opinion and losing followers" (Mann 1991, 96). But he (and his ilk) did not sustain a dead loss in such seemingly uneconomic transactions. First, indebtedness made the debtors beholden to him for life. "Indebtedness in general and mortgages in particular," notes Mann, "gave Taiwo great power over people" (Mann 1991, 96). Second, valuable contacts and networks of influence among Africans and Europeans enabled him to "increase trade, collect debts, protect property, and control subordinates" (Mann 1991, 102). By the 1880s, his influence extended beyond Lagos and the Yoruba hinterland to the middle Niger (Hopkins 1964, 41) and Kano in northern Nigeria, and beyond colonial boundaries to Porto Novo in French Dahomey. According to Cole, Taiwo was conferred with the sole privilege of presenting delegations from the hinterland to the British colonial officials (Cole 1975, 63, 170, 190).

A contemporary of Taiwo's, who also achieved commercial success and social influence in Victorian Lagos, was J. P. L. Davies (1828–1906).[14] Unlike Taiwo, Davies was a descendant of freed slaves who had returned to his ancestral homeland in Yorubaland. His checkered career witnessed his involvement in trade, agriculture, and shipping through the long nineteenth century until his death in 1906. He was credited with establishing the first commercially successful cocoa farm at Ijan on the outskirts of Lagos

[14] Details on Davies in this paragraph are sourced from Hopkins (1978, 83–96).

in 1880. Davies had experimented with coffee and cocoa that he obtained from a Brazilian ship and from the island of Fernando Po in 1879 and 1880, respectively. He subsequently pioneered the shipment of cocoa, which was to be the economic mainstay of western Nigeria from the 1920s. Davies had earlier been a successful trader and ship owner,[15] who was described as "the most prominent of the African merchants in Lagos in the 1860s and 1870s."[16] But his successes were punctuated by the economic turbulence of the 1880s and 1890s. Indeed, he ventured into agriculture to recoup his business losses with the aim of relaunching himself in the social life of Lagos, where he had enjoyed great prominence.

In addition to his pioneering role in cocoa farming and exports and attainment of mid-nineteenth century prominence in the commercial life of Lagos, Davies was also significant for his connection with the career of J. K. Coker, an important figure in agricultural entrepreneurship based at Agege about eighteen miles north of Lagos. For it was from Davies that Coker (whose brother married Davies' daughter) obtained the cocoa seedlings with which he started off his cocoa plantations at Agege, where his fifteen-hundred-acre holdings dwarfed Davies' two hundred acres at Ijan (Hopkins 1978, 88). Coker was the driving force behind the formation of the two-hundred-member Agege Planters Union (APU) in 1907. Like Davies, Coker veered into agriculture to make up for losses in his commercial enterprises in the late 1890s.

Though the APU was a collective, big planters like Coker who mentored the smaller holders dominated it. The foray of members of the union into agriculture had been induced by the economic downturn of the 1880s, when many of them lost their fortunes in the commercial fluctuations of the last quarter of the century. They were also keen to demonstrate the capacity of Africans to run large-scale business enterprises – a blend of pecuniary and nationalist motives. It can be argued that Coker and the APU succeeded in their enterprise not merely in terms of accumulation, but in the spread of the "gospel" of cocoa farming coupled with a brand of "African" Christianity into large parts of eastern Yorubaland. This was to be the economic foundation of the subsequent social and economic development of western Nigeria from the 1920s onward.

Other notable African merchants in Lagos during the opening decades of the twentieth century achieved social and commercial prominence beyond the agricultural sector and in spite of the commercial vicissitudes of the

[15] See Olukoju (1992, 259); Herbert Macaulay Papers, Box 30.

[16] See Hopkins (1978, 91) for this quote and information in the rest of the paragraph.

period. Most of them did not survive the severe depression of 1920–1, but it is important to highlight their careers for the insights they yield into the rise and decline of African entrepreneurship. Representative of this group are W. A. Dawodu, Nigeria's pioneer motor importer and automobile mechanic; S. H. Pearse; P. J. C. Thomas; and J. H. Doherty.

W. A. Dawodu has featured in the literature on aspects of the urban and economic history of Lagos for his pioneering role in the automobile import and repair business.[17] Scion of a notable Lagos business family, the Mabinuori Dawodus, his elder brother, B. C. Dawodu, was "one of the leading merchants in Lagos during the 1880s" (Hopkins 1964, 370). After his primary and technical education in Lagos, he taught for a few years before starting a bicycle sales and repair business in 1905. Foreseeing the prospects for motor transport as the colonial government embarked on road construction, he ventured into the motorcar import business and was helped by the generous credit facilities his American and English suppliers provided. This was the foundation of a business that encompassed the sale, hire, and repair of lorries, motorcars, and bicycles. Indeed, he enjoyed the sole agency of Ford cars and Humber cycles in the colony for a while.

The Dawodu automobile enterprise had a turnover of £26,000 on the eve of World War I and enjoyed a boom in the aftermath of the war. The range of Dawodu's operations extended beyond Lagos to the Yoruba hinterland and as far as Kano in northern Nigeria. Messrs W. A. Dawodu & Co. operated a transport service in Ilesha in central Yorubaland, where an expansion in the produce business in the context of the post–World War I boom stretched it to the limit. A report of September 1920 stated that its transport service had been "unable to cope with the transport business" in the locality.[18] Though the firm was acknowledged to have "done their best in the past," it was overwhelmed by the massive demand. Recourse was therefore made to the Railway motor service to make up for the shortfall in supply. At its height in 1921, the business had three retail outlets (showrooms) in Lagos and a large yard in Osogbo in the heartland of the Yoruba country and employed two hundred fifty persons. It declined steadily from the mid-1920s in the face of global economic adversity, competition from European firms, and his domestic crisis. By 1920, it had been joined in the motor import business by Miller Brothers (Ford cars – Touring and Runabout brands), John Holt (Willy's Knight Overland from the United States of

[17] Details of Dawodu's life and career in the following paragraphs are found in Hopkins (1964, 371–2).

[18] *Lagos Weekly Record*, September 11, 1920, Osogbo Notes & News.

America), L. Ambrosini, British American Produce Supply Company (Victor cars), and Thornton's Lagos Company. Other competitors were Nigerian Motors Limited and the African and Eastern Trade Corporation. The latter sold Dodge, Studebaker, and Reo cars and obtained its motor spares from Nigerian Motors Limited.[19]

Family sources were reticent about the details of the terminal crises of Dawodu's private and business lives.[20] An indication of the domestic crisis was the (probably forced) resignation of his first son, Alabi, as manager of Messrs W. A. Dawodu & Co. in August 1929. He was replaced by Mr. Frank Ade-John.[21] W. A. Dawodu himself died in January 1930, weeks after the death of his kinsman, James Patrick Dawodu, on December 31, 1929. The latter had been a "one time successful businessman in the Warri District," but had been "ousted by excessive competitions of firms with big capitals [*sic*]."[22] W. A. Dawodu's death finally ended his business enterprise, but he had lost the import of Ford cars to Nigerian Motors Limited well before then.[23] Described as "the Pioneer of the Motor Industry in Nigeria," and "a self-made ... and very shrewed [*sic*]" man, Dawodu was reported to have "conducted a very remunerative business *which became at last too big for him*."[24]

The scale of Dawodu's business enterprise can be deduced from the magnitude of assets that were auctioned to offset liabilities occasioned partly, according to oral sources, by mismanagement by his employees, including close kin. His business assets in Lagos were auctioned on June 28, 1930 after a newspaper advertisement invited engineers, mechanics, and general traders to make daily bids. The auctioneer, J. Aleshinloye Williams, listed the following items in stock: Brockway lorries, Hand tricks, crane, Willy's Knight cars, Federal lorries, Outer Boat engine, Ice chest, Indiana car engines, planks, iron bars, pieces of angle and flat irons, Go-cart springs, cutting and punching machines, portable lathe machines, machine driving lathes, emery machine, disc machine, band circular saw, playing machines, sawing machines, drilling machines, wooden window frames, corn mills, wooden chairs, iron plates, motor boat engine, rolling machine, iron anvils, fanning machine, pumping machine, motor engine,

19 *Lagos Weekly Record*, November 20 and 27, 1920.
20 Interview: Alhaji R. O. Dawodu, Mokola, Ibadan, 1984.
21 *Lagos Daily News*, August 26, 1929.
22 *Nigerian Pioneer*, January 10, 1930, Random Notes & News.
23 *Lagos Daily News*, May 19, 1930.
24 *Nigerian Pioneer*, January 10, 1930, Random Notes & News, italics added. It is not clear what the commentator meant by the remark in italics.

shafts, pulleys, three-face alternating current motor with starter, one motor boat under construction, circular saw with bench wood bending machine, new motor boat engine, propeller shaft, and "articles too numerous to mention."[25] In July 1930, the stock in his extensive warehouse in Osogbo was also auctioned.[26]

Another exceptional Lagos entrepreneur of the first third of the twentieth century was S. H. Pearse (1866–1953), who was described as "that rare type of African businessman, the produce merchant" (Hopkins 1988, 433). His career epitomized the vagaries of the maritime trade of Lagos and Nigeria as he experienced mixed fortunes in the export business. But it also demonstrated the flexibility and adaptability of African entrepreneurs to changing circumstances and challenging opportunities. Pearse reportedly took to business in emulation of his father's successful business friends – R. B. Blaize, J. P. L. Davies, and Z. A. Williams (Hopkins 1988, 434). He launched his own firm, Pearse and Thompson, in 1888 in partnership with a Sierra Leonean merchant after serving as a clerk in the European firm of W. B. McIver and Co. and as an apprentice under the African firm of Williams Brothers. Pearse's firm, however, folded in 1894 as a result of the trade depression of the 1890s and the Anglo-Ijebu war of 1892.

With a liability of £1,000, he briefly retired from business and spent some time in England, after which he became a Lagos agent of the African and Gold Coast Trading Company. In 1897, he entered into a new partnership in Calabar with a fellow Lagosian, E. O. Williams, who died only a year later. Pearse achieved commercial success by combining an export business in palm produce, ivory, and rubber with an import trade in various staple items. The profitability of the ivory trade in Calabar enabled him to pay off his old debt by 1902. His business expanded considerably to the point that he appointed an agent for his operations in Calabar and acquired an impressive head office on Broad Street, aptly named Elephant House in appreciation of the source of his wealth. Pearse conducted his European business through the Liverpool firm of Taylor and Company and diversified his business into other enterprises. He bought shares in three mining companies on the Gold Coast and opened the first hotel in Lagos in 1907 (Hopkins 1988, 435). By 1914, Pearse was already a man of considerable social and political influence in Lagos, in the mold of D. C. Taiwo, on account of his business success. Fitting, he became a member of the Nigerian Legislative Council in 1915.

[25] *Lagos Daily News*, June 27, 1930.
[26] *Lagos Daily News*, July 9, 1930.

On the outbreak of World War I, Pearse had accumulated wealth in property and liquid assets for his produce business. He also invested more than £10,000 in war bonds (Hopkins 1988, 436). However, he soon encountered difficulties owing to the decline of the ivory trade and the vicissitudes of the produce trade, both induced by wartime exigencies. The severe postwar slump of 1920–1 forced him to restructure his business by divesting in the hotel business and disposing of his war bonds. He then ploughed his capital into the rubber trade, where he also made a decent fortune until the outbreak of the Great Depression in 1929 practically decimated his business. Undaunted, Pearse diverted his capital and energy into the import of stockfish and the export of hides and skins. However, his prosperous business in these commodities was disrupted by the outbreak of World War II in 1939. A wartime accident incapacitated him and his business subsequently petered out well before his death in 1953.

Meanwhile, constitutional changes introduced in 1922 by Governor Hugh Clifford had been duly followed by the institution of the Legislative Council of Nigeria. Pearse was adopted by the *Alake* and Council as the representative of Egba Division in the Legislative Council. As a first step, he visited Abeokuta in April 1923 where the *Alake* gave a dinner in his honor and later installed him as the successor to the late *Oluwo* of Itesi Ake, whose stool had been occupied by Pearse's proxy that he had personally appointed and invested in Lagos in 1921. The *Alake* stated that Pearse had taken "great interest in his township" and often attended to the pressing needs of his people. He reasoned that, as Pearse "could not come home to fill the office himself, it was thought that he could better serve them in another capacity in Lagos by representing the Egbas on the Legislative Council at Lagos."[27]

This move generated a huge controversy as it was alleged that Pearse had procured a letter of introduction from the lieutenant governor to the resident of Abeokuta Province, which he used "to trick the Egbas into believing it (was) an instruction from the Government to get him appointed as their representative on the Legislative Council of Nigeria."[28] But this was refuted by the *Nigerian Pioneer*, which backed Pearse, by pointing out that he was indeed a native of Abeokuta domiciled in Lagos. "His trading successes which are evidently the result of foresight and care," the newspaper editorialized, "have brought him into prominence, and in religious, social and political life of this country, he is not obscure."[29] Pearse's other

[27] *Nigerian Pioneer*, May 4, 1923.

[28] N. Kuforiji, Abeokuta, letter to the editor, *Nigerian Pioneer*, May 25, 1923.

[29] *Nigerian Pioneer*, June 8, 1923, editorial: "Abeokuta Native Administration: Mr. S. H. Pearse, the Egba's Representative at the New Legislative Council."

engagements – as a representative at the local synod, member of the District (Church) Council, member of the Lagos Chamber of Commerce, member of the defunct Legislative Council, and member of unspecified "important Committees" – were also listed to buttress his suitability for the position. At the end of the day, he went on to occupy the Legislative Council seat. In 1929, Pearse became the *Odofin* of Itesi and in 1936 was granted the Member of the British Empire (MBE) by the British government.[30]

S. H. Pearse was the colonial-era gentleman par excellence. He lived in affluence and invested in the education and vocation of his children. Two of his daughters, Ayo and Remi, attended the Ryford Hall Ladies' College in England and excelled at violin and piano, respectively. Both were "highly commended," spent some time on the Continent, and were reputed to have been "the first from West Africa, Africans, whether male or female, who have flown in an Aeroplane."[31] The marriage of Ayo Pearse to Reverend S. C. Phillips on January 26, 1922 was celebrated in a major newspaper, which also published the full list of wedding presents and their donors.[32] Pearse's affluence earned him respect in business circles and made him one of the first Africans readmitted into the Lagos Chamber of Commerce when it was desegregated in 1921. His election was hailed by a Lagos newspaper for the valuable experience that he would bring to that body. It described Pearse as having "been in contact with the trade of Lagos, or for that matter Nigeria before some of the members of the present chamber were born." It urged the Chamber to consider the inclusion of Messrs J. H. Doherty and David Taylor at the "very earliest opportunity."[33] Pearse was unanimously elected vice president of the Chamber in 1922.[34]

Pearse's career was significant for several reasons. First, he remained in the export business much longer than any of his contemporaries, whose tenure often coincided only with the cycles of boom in the global economy.[35] Second, his career witnessed a succession of booms and slumps, including bankruptcy or near bankruptcy on several occasions. This made him counsel his son, who qualified as a medical doctor, not to dabble in business (Hopkins 1988, 437), a vocation that contemporary observers regarded

[30] *Nigerian Pioneer*, April 19, 1929; *Nigerian Daily Times*, June 26, 1936.

[31] *Nigerian Pioneer*, September 10, 1920, Random Notes & News.

[32] *Nigerian Pioneer*, January 27, 1922.

[33] *Nigerian Pioneer*, October 7, 1921, Random Notes & News.

[34] *Nigerian Pioneer*, April 28, 1922, minutes of meeting of Lagos Chamber of Commerce of April 11, 1922.

[35] A Lagos newspaper remarked caustically that "[w]ith the decline in the prices of Produce, we hope to see a great rush into clerical appointments." *Nigerian Pioneer*, June 11, 1920, Random Notes & News.

as nothing better than gambling.[36] Third, he was as active in politics and society as in business.

J. H. Doherty, another notable African entrepreneur, started on a small scale.[37] After serving as a clerk in one of the Lagos firms, he ventured into business in 1891 with a capital of £47. He then gained the confidence of a European firm that advanced him monthly credits ranging from an initial sum of £100 to £4,000. Through careful management of the business, Doherty was able to operate independently as a direct importer from 1898. He dealt in cotton and silk goods, hardware, and other imports. As his business expanded, he established branches in the hinterland of Lagos – Osogbo, Lokoja, Zaria, and Kano. A notable feature of Doherty's career was the investment in the education of his children, two of whom were sent abroad for university education: one to England for a degree in law and another to Fourah Bay College in Freetown, Sierra Leone (an affiliate of University of Durham in the United Kingdom) for a degree in the humanities to prepare him for succession to his father in the family business. Ultimately, this was an exceptional success story in business succession.

The final biographical subject considered in this survey is Salami Agbaje, an Ibadan-based entrepreneur of Iseyin (Oyo-Yoruba) parentage.[38] Born between 1865 and 1870, he migrated to Lagos with his Arabic teacher-father and trained as a tailor. Looking for greener pastures, he relocated to Ibadan, where he became a logger and, subsequently, a timber trader. He made his fortune as a timber contractor to the firm of Messrs Shelford and Sons, which constructed the railway from Lagos in the 1890s. Agbaje then diversified into the produce and import business on a commission basis as a middleman between producers and expatriate firms. He accumulated wealth by stockpiling cocoa during World War I and selling it at a substantial profit during the post-boom period.

His success derived from his ability to take risks, his extensive networks among and rapport with producers and European firms, and the operational strategies of advertising his business in the newspapers, especially the *Yoruba News*, engaging his own lorries and trucks to convey his produce,

36 The *Nigerian Pioneer*, June 18, 1920, noted that: "Trade is like a gamble; it has its chances." This apparently popular view was shaped by the severity of the slump and the harsh reversal of fortunes, rather than a carryover from the catastrophe of the slave trade era or precolonial politically induced business reverses of the likes of Madam Tinubu and Efunsetan Aniwura. It was reinforced by the constraining context of British colonialism and the calamity of the Great Depression, which finally doomed colonial-era indigenous commercial enterprises. See Olukoju (2002a, 176–98).

37 The entire paragraph is based on Macmillan (1993, 98–9).

38 The following paragraphs are based on Adeboye (2001).

and running a passenger transport service in Oyo Province and other parts of Nigeria. His entrepreneurial acumen in operating the transport service on "three important trade routes" was duly commended as "most progressive" by the resident of his province in 1921 (Adeboye 2001, 6). Agbaje established a mechanical garage to maintain his commercial fleet, but this soon developed into the largest commercial mechanical garage in the province, second only to that of the government's Public Works Department (P.W.D.). Even the P.W.D. referred cases to his garage because of the efficiency of his technicians, among them his own son, Seidu. The scale of Agbaje's business enterprises included small-scale manufacturing (mineral water and food processing) and commercial printing.

Salami Agbaje's career is significant for the following reasons. First, like Pearse, he diversified into several business lines, taking advantage of favorable circumstances (such as the postwar boom) and divesting where necessary from some business lines, such as the cinema business that he sold to the Levantines. Second, he adopted modern business methods – advertising his business in the newspapers, establishing a limited liability company (Salami Agbaje and Company), and joining forces with other entrepreneurs to form the Oke'Badan Trading Company in 1950. Third, Agbaje's business was transgenerational as his first son, Dr. Saka Anthony Agbaje, took over the commercial press and joined others to publish a newspaper, the *Western Echo*, in the 1940s. Fourth, like most other entrepreneurs, he was involved in the politics of his community and this involved dispensing patronage, which he refused to do. Hence, he was perceived as tightfisted, and this robbed him of his entitlement in the chieftaincy hierarchy in Ibadan.

Finally, on the important issue of how he utilized his wealth, Agbaje was in a class by himself. The scale of his enormous wealth was patent to all. The provincial report of 1922 stated that he owned "very large cement block houses on European lines" for his business and personal uses, "a very handsome dwelling for himself," and "a very large fleet of motors and a repair garage."[39] He had owned the first car in Ibadan as early as 1915, was the first to own a multistory cement block house, the first to connect electricity to his house, and the first private citizen to construct motorable roads in Ibadan (linking the city to his farms). Like Doherty, he invested heavily in the education of his children. His eldest son, the first Ibadan man to do so, qualified as a medical doctor in 1931. His children assisted him directly in running the business (as exemplified by Seidu) or offered him legal services (two sons, Mojeed and Ganiyu, qualified as lawyers). To this day, his family remains

[39] Cited in Adeboye (2001, 9).

influential in Ibadan (and western Nigeria) on account of the number of lawyers, judges, doctors, and other professionals among its scions.

6.4 CONCLUSION

This chapter has demonstrated that it was a combination of cultural and structural impediments to indigenous entrepreneurship in the context of colonialism and global economic dynamics that caused the nonemergence of a capitalist class in the mold of contemporary Asian enterprises. On the one hand, the colonial experience, while bringing modern transport, currency, credit, and banking facilities and thus creating an enabling environment for migrations and exchange, was equally constraining. The demonetization of precolonial currencies and the abolition of slavery effectively undercut the basis of the wealth and power of the category of entrepreneurs whose wealth had derived from the slave trade and the use of slave and indentured labor. Across West Africa, "businessmen and women lost much of the value of their assets as a result of colonial intervention" (Austin 2002, 135). In addition, colonial rule facilitated the ingress of European traders into the hinterland, thus reducing indigenous competitors to subsidiary operators given the overwhelming superiority of the former in capital, organization, and links with the imperial power. The loss of control over the hinterland stages of the emergent overseas trade proved fatal to the aspirations of indigenous entrepreneurs in the long run.

On the other hand, the weight of cultural values proved too heavy for sustained accumulation. For instance, societal expectations often made it too difficult for the entrepreneur to accumulate or act solely according to the profit motive. Nineteenth-century Ibadan epitomized the Yoruba conception of true wealth, entrepreneurship, and the ideal entrepreneur. Taiwo's epitaph cited at the beginning of this chapter confirmed the resilience of such views in colonial Lagos.

This was why Taiwo Olowo could afford to waive his right to foreclosure of mortgaged property for fear of earning a reputation for meanness. The failure to meet this societal expectation made the colonial Ibadan entrepreneur, Salami Agbaje, unpopular with "a large section of the predominantly illiterate populace … [which] dislike[d] him" (Adeboye 2001, 11). But Agbaje refused to bow to societal pressure and proceeded to expand his business and invest in the education of his children. According to his biographer, he "used his power derived from the modern economic sector without subjecting himself to the claims of tradition to which others bowed with the largesse of the big man" (Adeboye 2001, 11). In contrast, the

Dawodus of Lagos chose to conform in 1930. Even in the throes of the Great Depression, when two leading lights of the family (James Patrick Dawodu and William Akinola Dawodu) died in rapid succession in December 1929 and January 1930, respectively, the family undertook the opulent "reburial" of their long-dead forebear, Mabinuori Dawodu in June 1930![40] Economic rationality succumbed to social pressure even in the face of global distress.

On the whole, the survey of the selected leading entrepreneurs of nineteenth- and twentieth-century Yorubaland indicates that the constraining environment of warfare and colonialism provided a context for their ultimate failure to emulate their Asian counterparts. First, with the exception of Doherty and Agbaje, none had a clear succession plan within or outside the lineage. In addition, those who died intestate and even those who left a will hardly outlived their business as acrimonious disputes over sharing of assets effectively destroyed their legacies. Hence, the dissipation of assets and lack of cooperation among several branches of a typical polygynous family ruined many worthwhile businesses. Second, Yoruba entrepreneurs lacked a common focus and platform of action and were generally individualistic. Though Salami Agbaje collaborated with his Ibadan kinsmen to establish a joint stock company, this was the exception rather than the rule. Hence, there was no enduring indigenous chamber of commerce to advance their common interests. When these existed, they were short-lived and fractious. Instead, the leading lights of the indigenous entrepreneurial class strove to join the hitherto Europeans-only Lagos Chamber of Commerce. Third, the basis of their wealth was fragile – consisting of flimsy assets tied to the fluctuating economic circumstances. This made them vulnerable to the vagaries of global economic dynamics as happened during the interwar years. Fourth, the absence of a national bank for indigenous entrepreneurs during the period up to 1930, unlike in Egypt, denied the entrepreneurs a reliable source of capital for their business. The Egyptians established the wholly Egyptian Bank Misr in 1920 to supply capital to national industry. The charter of the bank limited shareholding and membership of board of directors to native Egyptians. Bank Misr accordingly "played a major role in mobilizing the savings of local people and using them to support a variety of projects including the establishment of a number of public companies" (Owen 1981, 5).

Finally, the concentration on commerce without a commensurate investment in manufacturing was the bane of African entrepreneurship. As observed with respect to Egypt, "[e]conomic nationalism was part and parcel

[40] *Nigerian Pioneer*, June 6, 1930.

of national ideology in Egypt from early on, and local industrialization was meant to be its most important project."[41] This policy focus of Egyptian, as opposed to Nigerian, nationalism was a critical issue in the divergence of their experiences. For the Egyptians used economic nationalism to drive the founding of their national bank, Bank Misr, and the promotion of indigenous manufacturing. Local manufacturers used advertisements to rally their fellow nationals to "Buy Egyptian" to show how patronage of local manufactures contributed to promoting Egyptian employment. But it must be admitted that the Egyptians, unlike the Nigerians, had room to maneuver as their country had gained "partial independence" by 1922, whereas the interwar years were the heyday of colonial rule in Nigeria, where indigenous capacity for freedom of action was highly circumscribed. In addition, Egypt was more culturally and politically coherent than was culturally and politically diverse Nigeria.

That said, several of the leading entrepreneurs invested in the education of their children, who sustained their legacy outside the mercantile sector. To that extent, the failure of indigenous entrepreneurship to sustain itself and to generate societal development was not totally unmitigated.

References

Adeboye, O. A. (2001). "Salami Agbaje: The Life and Times of an Indigenous Entrepreneur in Colonial Nigeria." *Lagos Historical Review*, 1: 1–15.

Akeredolu-Ale, E. O. (1975). *The Underdevelopment of Indigenous Entrepreneurship in Nigeria*. Ibadan: Ibadan University Press.

Akinjogbin, Adeagbo. Ed. (1998). *War and Peace in Yorubaland, 1793–1893*. Ibadan: Heinemann.

Atanda, J. A. (1973). *The New Oyo Empire*. London: Longman.

Austin, Gareth. (2002). "African Business in Nineteenth-Century West Africa." In *Black Business and Economic Power*, edited by Alusine Jalloh and Toyin Falola, 114–44. Rochester: University of Rochester Press.

Awe, Bolanle. (1973). "Militarism and Economic Development in Nineteenth Century Yoruba Country: The Ibadan Example." *Journal of African History*, XIV(1): 65–77.

(2001). "Iyalode Efunsetan Aniwura (Owner of Gold)." In *Nigerian Women: A Historical Perspective*, edited by Bolanle Awe, 63–82. Ibadan: Sankore/Bookcraft.

Awe, Bolanle and Omotayo Olutoye. (1998). "Women and Warfare in 19th Century Yorubaland: An Introduction." In *War and Peace in Yorubaland, 1793–1893*, edited by Adeagbo Akinjogbin, 121–30. Ibadan: Heinemann.

Babayemi, S. O. (1990). *The Fall and Rise of Oyo, c. 1706–1905*. Lagos: Lichfield Nigeria Limited.

[41] See Shechter (2008, 573) for this quote and the following discussion.

Cole, P. D. (1975). *Modern and Traditional Elites in the Politics of Lagos*. Cambridge: Cambridge University Press.

Falola, Toyin. (1984). *The Political Economy of a Pre-Colonial African State: Ibadan, 1830–1900*. Ile-Ife: University of Ife Press.

(1991a). "The Construction and Destruction of the Economy of Ijaye, c.1832–1862." *Afrika und Ubersee*, 74: 21–37.

(1991b). "The Yoruba Caravan System of the Nineteenth Century." *International Journal of African Historical Studies*, 24(1): 111–32.

Hopkins, Antony G. (1964). "An Economic History of Lagos, 1880–1914." PhD Diss. University of London.

(1978). "Innovation in a Colonial Context: African Origins of the Nigerian Cocoa-Farming Industry, 1880–1920." In *The Imperial Impact: Studies in the Economic History of Africa and India*, edited by Clive Dewey and A. G. Hopkins, 83–96. London: The Athlone Press.

(1988). *An Economic History of West Africa*, 2nd ed. London: Longman.

Macmillan, Allister. (1993). *The Red Book of West Africa*. Ibadan: Spectrum, reprint.

Mann, Kristin. (1991). "The Rise of Taiwo Olowo: Law, Accumulation, and Mobility in Early Colonial Lagos." In *Law in Colonial Africa*, edited by Richard Roberts and Kristin Mann, 85–102. Portsmouth, NH: Heinemann.

Olukoju, Ayodeji. (1992). "Elder Dempster and the Shipping Trade of Nigeria during the First World War." *Journal of African History*, 33(2): 255–71.

(2002a). "The Impact of British Colonialism on the Development of African Business in Colonial Nigeria." In *Black Business and Economic Power*, edited by Alusine Jalloh and Toyin Falola, 176–98. Rochester, NY: Rochester University Press.

(2002b). "'Nigeria or Lever-ia?': Nationalist Reactions to Economic Depression and the 'Menace of Mergers' in Colonial Nigeria." *Journal of Third World Studies*, 19(1): 173–94.

(2010). "Economic Nationalism and Decolonization: West Africa in Comparative Perspective." *Hagar*, 9(2): 137–56.

Owen, Roger. (1981). "The Ideology of Economic Nationalism in Its Egyptian Context: 1919–1939." In *Intellectual Life in the Arab East, 1890–1939*, edited by Marwan R. Buheiry, 1–9. Beirut: Center for Arab and Middle East Studies, American University of Beirut.

Shechter, Relli. (2008). "The Cultural Economy of Development in Egypt: Economic Nationalism, Hidden Economy and the Emergence of Mass Consumer Society during Sadat's *Infitah*." *Middle Eastern Studies*, 44(4): 571–83.

Yemitan, Oladipo. (1987). *Madame Tinubu: Merchant and King-Maker*. Ibadan: University Press Limited.

Zakaria, Yakubu. (1997). *The Cultural Context of Business: A Study of Firms in a Northern Nigerian Society*. Uppsala: Uppsala University Library.

7

Commerce, Credit, and Mobility in Late Nineteenth-Century Gold Coast: Changing Dynamics in Euro-African Trade

Emmanuel Akyeampong

7.1 INTRODUCTION

The nineteenth century represents one of the most fascinating and dynamic centuries in the history of West Africa in the second millennium in terms of West Africa's relations with the wider world. The century began with the abolition of the export slave trade and the substitution (a return to in some cases) of an export trade in primary products such as palm oil and groundnut oil. The simple technology behind African agriculture – the hoe, cutlass, and pick – and the centrality of the family as the social and economic basis of production and reproduction expanded the ranks of the economically active with the abolition of the slave trade. Chiefs and "big men," who dominated the slave trade as they had monopoly over the means of capture, remained major players in the era of "legitimate trade," deploying their capital and labor resources in new ways. It was a century of political revolution with Islamic jihads in the West African sahel and savanna and political experimentation along the coast based on the fusion of African and European ideas. In the social sphere, Christian missionary work and Western education from the 1820s created "new men and women," while kin and clan systems responded to the new opportunities of trade during the eighteenth and nineteenth centuries through social engineering in structures such as the "house system" in the Niger Delta. Technological advances added to the excitement of the century, and in mid-century, the introduction of the steamship and the demonstrated utility of quinine opened up West Africa

An early version of this chapter was presented at the July 2010 international conference in Accra on "Understanding African Poverty over the Longue Durée." I am grateful to Robert Bates for his insightful comments on earlier drafts.

to European traders and adventurers. Banks and commercial credit linked West African merchants with European merchant houses, and European commission houses served as brokers for West African traders, selling West African produce and purchasing European manufactured goods on their behalf.[1] Palm oil, palm kernel, and rubber from West Africa underpinned this buoyant trade during the nineteenth century. The enormous opportunities for social mobility these economic factors presented received a severe setback from the 1870s with a glut in the world market of fats and oils, the onset of economic crisis, and the constriction in credit facilities. The scramble for and partition of Africa would end a remarkable era of socioeconomic opportunity, and British imperial historian David Hargreaves noted with irony how European military force had been summoned to contain the socioeconomic revolution in West Africa that free trade had unleashed (Hargreaves 1986).

This chapter focuses on the last quarter of the nineteenth century (or the period from 1870), when the ground shifted under the feet of West African entrepreneurs and merchant houses collapsed. This followed two decades of economic prosperity in the 1850s and 1860s driven by European technological developments and financial investments that had a trickle down effect globally. Economists have argued that the period from 1873 to 1896 was technically not an economic "depression," as output increased considerably even as prices dropped. But 1873 marked a sharp economic downturn, initiating two decades of economic distress in industrial economies in Europe and North America. Adding to the confusion of the period, to "contemporaries, the nature of the problem was unclear" (Gourevitch 1986, 73). These closing decades of the nineteenth century witnessed bankruptcies on both sides of the Atlantic with dire implications for extensive commercial networks, introduced suspicion into relations between established Gold Coast and European merchants, and extinguished the hope of small

[1] *Commission houses*, sometimes referred to as *consignment houses*, were essentially brokers based in Britain or Europe, who for a commission of between 2 and 5 percent would receive produce from African traders on board steamships, sell the produce at prevailing market prices, and purchase European manufactured goods requested by the African traders and consign them to steamships bound for Africa. This facility had been made possible with the rise of steamship service to the western African coast from 1852, calling regularly at designated stops. It ended the monopoly of large expatriate traders who owned their own sailing ships, disconnecting trade and transport ownership. Small African traders were able to trade directly with Europe, bypassing expatriate merchants on the West African coast. Commission houses also extended credit to trusted clients. They kept accounts with their African clients. In the latter part of the nineteenth century, the more established commission houses had their own agents based in West Africa.

traders who aspired to the economic success of the "merchant princes," who also served as mentors for these small traders. Through the private papers of the established Gold Coast family businesses such as the Ocanseys and the Caesars of Ada, especially their correspondence with their European suppliers and brokers and the smaller African traders who depended on them for credit and supplies, I shed light on the local ramifications (economic, social, cultural) of shifts in the global economy, deepening an understanding of markets that transcend the abstract forces of demand and supply. I use the checkered career of Christian Jacobson, an aspiring young trader of Keta, to examine the closing of economic opportunities in the late nineteenth century and its impact on mobility and social aspiration. I draw on the insights of Pomeranz and Topik that markets are "socially constructed and socially embedded," and that "it is necessary to understand both the local specificity of a transaction or event as well as its international context to appreciate its importance" (Pomeranz and Topik 2006, xii–xiii). Access to information and credit was severely skewed against Gold Coasters and other West Africans during the nineteenth century, incorporated into commercial networks not of their creation, lacking the dispersed but connected international networks and solidarities of trading diasporas, and in the last resort lacking the military support of colonially minded European states that followed the interests of their merchants. Though West African chiefs were deeply invested in trade, their networks were local. Their combination of political and economic power would identify them as the major protagonists for European merchants. Colonial rule initially undermined chiefly power and enterprise, but a consolidated colonialism would in turn empower colonially endorsed chiefs, even seeking to establish them in business. At the end of the long nineteenth century, as the forces unleashed during the century played out into the immediate World War I era, it was the new hierarchy of colonial chiefs that remained standing in business with colonial backing.

7.2 NINETEENTH-CENTURY CONTEXT: THE INFRASTRUCTURE OF "LEGITIMATE" TRADE

7.2.1 Steamships and Quinine

In 1792, Denmark abolished the export slave trade for its citizens with implementation from 1803, becoming the first European power to abolish the Atlantic slave trade. Britain followed suit in 1807, and the motives for the British abolition have attracted scholarly attention over the twentieth century, beginning with Eric Williams's influential *Capitalism and Slavery* (1944).[2] A trade in cash crops such as palm oil and groundnuts, and older commodities like ivory and gold, was revived under the rubric of "legitimate trade" in contradistinction to the proscribed export trade in slaves. Palm oil was used in an industrializing Europe for greasing factory machines, lubricating new railway engines, and manufacturing soap and candles. Groundnut oil was used as cooking oil and in soap making. Palm oil trees grew wild in the West African forest from Sierra Leone to the Cameroons, with a dense concentration in the Niger Delta and its hinterland, earning the Delta the epithet of "oil rivers." British imports of palm oil from West Africa grew from 2,233 Cwt in 1807 to 213,467 Cwt in 1830, 315,458 Cwt in 1840, and 731,659 Cwt in 1854 (Lynn 1998, 13). The Senegambia was the groundnut basin in the second half of the nineteenth century, but Senegal exported virtually no groundnuts in the 1840s. These important developments intensified European interest in penetrating the interior of West Africa, an endeavor that united European statesmen, merchants, military men, explorers, and missionaries. The advent of the iron gun boat in the mid-nineteenth century was timely, and the British naval squadron that patrolled the West African waters to monitor the slave trade was instructed to make periodic forays up the Gambia and Niger Rivers to underscore British naval might and its commitment to protecting British merchants in these places.

It was the stranglehold of African chiefs and traders along the Niger Delta and their resistance to any attempts by foreigners to travel into the interior that the British hoped their Niger Expedition of the 1850s and 1860s would break. Touted as a scientific and exploratory mission, its economic implications were clear and profound. British trade ambitions coupled with scientific curiosity played itself out in West Africa first with the expedition of Mungo Park (1795–7) under the auspices of the Africa Association. Mungo Park's travels and the publication of his *Travels in the Interior Districts of Africa* (1799) became the basis for a domestic argument for an interventionist policy of setting up trade stations in West Africa backed by

[2] Williams probed the relationship between the West Indian plantation economy and the rise of British capitalism, and the subsequent elevation of wage labor over slave labor by the supposed beneficiaries of the plantation economy. Williams's thesis and the question of whether Britain was an economic beneficiary of abolition has elicited major works such as Anstey (1975), Drescher (1977), and Eltis (1987). More recent works on British abolitionism have highlighted how central the loss of the North American colonies was to British rethinking of empire, and how the British came to value the moral capital of abolitionism in the remaking of empire. See Brown (2006) and Jasanoff (2011).

military power (Marsters 2000). When Mungo Park revisited West Africa in 1805, it was under the sponsorship of the British government. In 1830, two other explorers, brothers John and Richard Lander, traversed the Niger Bend and discovered that the river continued to flow southward for another twenty-six hundred miles into the delta.

On their return to England, the Lander brothers were contacted by Macgregor Laird of the Birkenhead shipbuilding family. Together they created the African Inland Commercial Company with the objective of exploring and developing the commerce of the River Niger. Their ill-fated mission up the Niger in 1832–3 ended with heavy losses in life, but Laird retained his interest in Africa (Davies 1977). The 1832 expedition involved the first use of an iron steamer, *Alburkah*, on a West African river (Headrick 1981, 61). Subsequent expeditions up the Niger would be a partnership of the British government, mercantile, and missionary interests. The Rev. J. F. Schön and Samuel Crowther on behalf of the Church Missionary Society accompanied the 1841 expedition led by Dr. T. R. H. Thomson. The death rate among Europeans on the Niger Expedition of 1841 was equally horrendous. Thomson himself took regular doses of quinine on this trip and remained healthy, and his article in the *Lancet* in 1846 advocated the regular use of quinine in West Africa. The 1854 Niger expedition followed the medical prescription of quinine meticulously, and Dr. William Baikie, captain of *The Pleiad*, ensured that his crew took the appropriate dose daily. His ship stayed for one hundred twelve days on the Niger and returned with all its European crew intact (Headrick 1981, 68–9). The Niger expedition was contracted to merchant Macgregor Laird from January 1857, who received a British government subsidy to send a commercial steamship up the Niger annually with the backing of a British naval ship for a five-year period. A similar arrangement was already in place for the Gambia River.[3] Baikie also accompanied the 1857 expedition and became the embodiment of the Niger expedition through his death in 1864.

An Admiralty letter in 1862 summed up precisely what was at stake for the British in the Niger expedition. It pitted British mercantile interests against those of African trading chiefs and coastal merchants, insinuating – perhaps

[3] National Archives of Britain (NAB): FO 97/434. See Memorial to Viscount Palmerston, presented March 15, 1860. The memorialists were pleased by the government's arrangement with Laird and the presence of British naval ships on the Niger, and commented on how the similar presence of naval ships on the Gambia had been conducive for British commerce. Signatories to this memorial included the Earl of Shaftesbury, the Earl of Harrowby, Lord Viscount Middleton, the Lord Bishop of Oxford, Captain the Honorable F. Maud, and others.

rightly – that peasants in the interior would welcome direct British commerce and the removal of the centuries-old trade control by the chiefs.

> It has been shown by the reports received from Dr. Baikie and from the commanders of the several Expeditions that have at various times ascended the Niger that the Chiefs and People in the Upper part of the River are peaceably disposed and very anxious to trade with Europeans. The produce of the country is valuable and can be increased to any extent that there may be a demand for it, in fact the supply is only limited by the quantity of suitable European goods that can be brought into their markets. The river moreover is navigable for vessels of 300 tons further for a distance of upwards of 500 miles thus opening a highway into the very heart of Africa. It has been shewn also that from the regions visited by Dr. Baikie in the neighbourhood of the river, large caravans depart and arrive annually, carrying European goods that find their way up from the coast into the centre of Africa. In fact the trade that used to pass from the northern shores of the Mediterranean to central Africa is now being diverted to the Western Coast, sensibly diminishing the supply of slaves that used formerly to be taken to the Mediterranean Coast. If therefore it is found more profitable for the caravans to procure their supplies of European goods from the Western Coast, when these supplies have to be filtered through the hands of several chiefs and are enhanced in value by a long and dangerous land carriage how much more profitable would it be if the supplier they required were to be found in markets established in the upper banks of the Niger. But it is impossible that these markets should be established and the trade of the river developed as long as the navigation in the Delta is practically stopped by the hostility of some of the native chiefs. Render the navigation safe and our merchants will soon push their way up the river and establish trading posts.[4]

The display of hostility of towns along the lower Niger to British merchants was interpreted as the machinations of chiefly economic interest, and the British government and merchants recommended the use of naval force to protect British trade. Free trade was seen as a right for British traders and African peasants who supposedly yearned for that same right. British pioneers of the African frontier like Baikie painted a picture of numerous disparate "tribes" in the interior distrustful of each other, often speaking unintelligible languages and who would rather deal with Europeans than their neighboring Africans.[5]

Trade, then, was the key vision that drove British interest in accessing the West African interior from the early nineteenth century. This vision had been facilitated by technological innovations, and the advent of the steamship bore revolutionary consequences for the West African trade. In 1852, regular steamship service commenced between Britain and West Africa,

4 Ibid.
5 NAB: FO 2/20.

and under royal charter the African Steam Ship Co. was incorporated in August 1852 to transport mail to West Africa. This company was headed by Macgregor Laird. The African Steam Ship Co. would move its headquarters from London to Liverpool in 1856. A second shipping line would join the African Steam Ship Co. in 1869, the British and African Steam Navigation Co., which operated initially from Glasgow and Liverpool. From 1874, it operated only from Liverpool, which had emerged as the center of British shipping and palm oil trade with West Africa. By 1880, the age of sail was effectively over (Lynn 1989, 1998, 105–10).

These advances in technology, the expanding European economic vision in Africa, and other accompanying developments also created new social and economic opportunities for African producers and traders. So the period from the 1860s, for example, witnessed the increasing ranks of African small traders, who capitalized on the advent of regular steamship service, the proliferation of European consignment houses who represented the interests of African merchants in Europe for a small commission, and a growing familiarity with local consumer demand that often came through employment as clerks in European commercial firms. In 1866, barely a decade after the introduction of steamship service to West Africa, Charles Livingston, British consul, wrote from Fernando Po to Lord Stanley of the Foreign Office on how the era of the big commercial houses that had dominated the slave and ivory trade and the early palm oil trade was coming to an end.

> The monthly line of mail steamers has broken up the monopoly of the large traders on the West Coast of Africa. Business was formerly conducted on the principle of large profits and slow returns, but since the steamers furnished such facilities, great numbers of small black traders have sprung up whose motto evidently is small profits and speedy sales, many being satisfied with only 5% profit. The captain of one of the mail steamers informs me that a few years since a steamer used to bring 300 to 400 packages of goods to Sierra Leone all for white traders, but now each steamer brings 1500 to 1600 packages three fourths of which are for black traders and the same is true, he says, of Lagos and other parts of the coast.[6]

In the Gold Coast, major African merchants such as the Ocanseys of Ada at the mouth of the Volta River and John Sarbah with several trading posts along the coast emerged from the mid-nineteenth century. Both would enjoy remarkable success through the 1870s, and their trading networks would include several coastal and up-country traders who depended on these

[6] NAB: FO 2/47

African merchant princes for credit and supplies of European manufactured goods in return for palm oil and later palm kernel and rubber.

7.2.2 Credit and Trust in Euro-African Trading Networks

Lovejoy and Richardson in several works have underlined the centrality of pawnship or debt bondage in credit mechanisms that underpinned the slave trade in many parts of West Africa, and the city-states of the Niger Delta and the Gold Coast were two such areas (Lovejoy and Richardson 2001). Slaving privileged the political aristocracy in West Africa who possessed the means of capture, and chiefs were often big traders. In the Gold Coast, noted for its wealth in gold, which constituted another form of security in addition to human pawns, it has been observed for the eighteenth century that most credit advances Europeans gave were to people with political status. In Old Calabar, where gold was not mined, pawnship was the basis of European mercantile credit to African traders (Lovejoy and Richardson 1999, 333–55). In Bonny, where a strong monarchy existed, the state was the guarantor of credit (Lovejoy and Richardson 2004). The abolition of the slave trade and the rise of legitimate trade raised two key challenges where credit in Euro-African trading relations was concerned. First was the demise of pawnship as a means of security. Pawns represented ideal collateral for European merchants on the West African coast during the era of the slave trade, especially if the pawns were close relatives of West African merchants. These merchants then did everything within their means to redeem their kinsmen. Where pawns could not be redeemed, they became slaves and were carried away in the holds of slave ships. Indeed, ship captains noted that pawns, being insiders of coastal communities, were healthier and more inclined to survive the rigors of the middle passage than captives who had been marched from the interior to the coast. A second challenge related to the expansion of the ranks of African traders with several newcomers and the need for criteria to determine who could be trusted with credit.

Abolition meant that pawns were no longer acceptable security for British merchants. Emancipation in the last quarter of the nineteenth century and the abolition of pawnship forced a rethinking of the nature of labor. Old social networks provided some basis for trade and credit and provided a template for new social relations in business. Personal ties became an important basis of credit during the nineteenth century, and European merchants then used established African businessmen as references for new applicants for credit. Here there were continuities from the past. A perusal of the diary of Antera Duke from the late eighteenth century reveals the level of socializing between Efik merchants and chiefs and ship captains as both wined and dined each other (Duke 1956). It helped that a small group of merchants or mercantile families dominated trade in the Niger Delta city-states such as Calabar on both the British and African sides, embedding credit in social networks (Lovejoy and Richardson 1999). It is out of this context that British merchants such as Ambrose Lace brought the son of Robin John Ephraim (alias King George) of Old Town, Calabar, to Liverpool for schooling in 1767. The son spent two years in a school at Liverpool at Lace's expense before returning to the Niger Delta. Both sides expected such products to facilitate Euro-African trade to their mutual benefit. At the beginning of the nineteenth century, it was observed that several Africans from Calabar came to Liverpool expressly to learn English (Lovejoy and Richardson 1999, 342).

These strategies facilitated the transition to legitimate trade and the maintenance of credit networks. There were also novel developments during the nineteenth-century era of legitimate trade, and in Calabar in the 1820s it was noted that British ship masters had begun to join the Ekpe secret society that dominated political and economic social life. The society served as a guarantor of credit. Lovejoy and Richard see this innovation as an outcome of the palm oil trade and the changing political and commercial conditions after British abolition (Lovejoy and Richardson 1999, 349). They note how Ekpe served as a "merchants' guild." It is clear that over the eighteenth and nineteenth centuries merchants on both sides accumulated a body of knowledge of their opposite societies and cultures in the interest of the functioning of commerce. While this promoted commerce, it also had the potential to undercut the other side in trading. We have noted how increasing knowledge of the Niger Delta interior convinced British traders that interior peasants would rather deal directly with Europeans than through coastal middlemen chiefs. Likewise, African coastal merchants came to the conclusion that they could deal directly with Europe rather than through the European merchants on the West African coast, who profited through facilitating both African exports and imports. Consul Livingstone of Lagos had anticipated this development in 1866 in the same letter to Lord Stanley with his observations of the radical changes steamship service brought in West African trade.

> Another and greater change in the palm oil trade seems inevitable. The shrewd African chiefs, like those of Bonny will soon begin to ship oil themselves by steamer direct to Liverpool, there Commission Agents, for a small percentage, are ready to sell their oil and return by next steamer any kind of goods the natives may order. They offer likewise to insure the oil as soon as it is afloat, the natives in this way get

> 50% more for their oil and yet [are] able to sell it in Liverpool 50% cheaper than it is now sold.[7]

The extension of financial and brokerage services to West African traders by British commission houses, together with steamship service, reshaped trade in West Africa by leveling the ground in significant ways. It undercut the monopolistic advantages of the large expatriate companies that owned or chartered the sailing ships that brought goods to West Africa and took oil away from the coast.

Lynn notes how between 1830 and 1880 the number of British traders who dealt in West African palm oil at the ports of Liverpool, London, Bristol, and Glasgow increased from twenty-one to one hundred five.

> Numerous commission houses entered the palm oil trade in this period, of which Irvine and Woodward (later James Irvine & Co.) of Liverpool, John Holt's suppliers between 1867 and 1875, and John Walkden & Co. of Manchester, prominent in the 1870s and 1880s, were among the most notable. Even long-established firms like Tobins felt the pull of this trend: it became a commission house, the Company of African Merchants, in 1863. (Lynn 1998, 138)

Lynn comments on how the "increase in numbers of commission houses was simply a symptom of the emergence of smaller-scale palm oil traders that occurred during the third quarter of the century" (Lynn 1998, 138). Now West African traders could choose to use the long-established expatriate merchants on the coast or bypass them to send their produce direct to Europe and source their manufactured goods through commission houses. In the Gold Coast, the Ocanseys sometimes dealt with the firm of F & A Swanzy, an established mercantile company in the Gold Coast, and other times dealt directly with Liverpool using the commission house of Hickson and Sykes. John Sarbah used J. F. Hutton & Co. of Manchester and Grimsdale and Ridley as his commission houses (Lynn 1998, 141). It was to facilitate these developments that Alfred Jones – a former staff member of the African Steam Ship Co., who rose to become in 1884 the managing partner in the Elder Dempster shipping line in Liverpool – expanded into banking. In 1894, he set up the Bank of British Bank West, which dominated banking in West Africa until 1917, when the Colonial Bank (now part of Barclays) began operating in West Africa (Davies 1977, 13). Jones was deeply appreciative of how steamship service, banks, and cable could revolutionize West African commerce.[8] West Africa was linked to Europe by submarine cables in 1885 (Headrick 1981, 161).

[7] Ibid.

[8] Personal communication, Peter Davies, Liverpool, May 12, 2010.

7.3 BOOM AND BUST: THE COLLAPSE OF THE MARKET IN OILS AND FATS

These auspicious developments in the mid-nineteenth century concealed major contradictions in the commercial environment. Paradoxically, the seeds of West Africa's commercial decline in the late nineteenth century were embedded in the very processes that brought prosperity in mid-century. Just as the advent of iron steamships and steamer services had incorporated West Africa more deeply into European commercial networks as suppliers of raw materials for industrial purposes in Britain and elsewhere, so did these same processes incorporate other tropical sites in Asia into European networks as suppliers of oils and fats. West Africa had an initial advantage as an early supplier of oils, but not for long. Within West Africa itself, the huge expansion in supply depressed prices. While just about a dozen ports exported palm oil from West Africa to Britain in the 1830s and 1840s, in 1885 some one hundred thirty-three ports in West Africa were exporting oil to Britain (Lynn 1998, 240). Also, continued technological innovation generated the need for specialized oils for particular production processes, such as the manufacture of tinplate. For these specialized processes, an all-purpose oil like palm oil was unsuitable. The outcome was twofold: steamship service increased the number of palm oil suppliers from West Africa and Asia with a dampening effect on palm oil prices; competing oils emerged, such as Australian tallow (now made more accessible after the opening of the Suez Canal in 1869) and petroleum, discovered in the United States in 1859 with its by-product kerosene. Gradually, mineral oil displaced palm oil as the lubricant for machinery and railways from the 1860s (Lynn 1998, chapter 5). The 1850s peak of palm oil prices that galvanized trade in West Africa and Europe and underpinned the proliferation of commission houses thus marked the beginning of a downward trend in palm oil prices. The general prosperity of the 1850s and 1860s concealed this shift in the ground that became more apparent from 1873.

From a high point of £43.50 per ton of palm oil in the United Kingdom in 1855, palm oil prices dropped to £33.67 in 1873 and to £20.58 in 1897 (Lynn 1998, 112). German prices for palm oil continued to rise through the 1880s, but the German market was insignificant compared to the British one. The growth of an export market in palm kernels, a by-product of the oil palm, brought some relief from the 1860s. Palm kernel was used initially in soap manufacture, and increasingly in the making of margarine. Germany was the major importer of West Africa's palm kernels, explaining the broadening of the commercial networks of Gold Coast traders to include merchant houses in Hamburg. The Gold Coast's palm kernel exports from producers in Krobo and Akuapem went primarily to Germany (Lynn 1998, 125). Lynn concluded that the palm kernel trade moderated the worst effects of the slump from the 1870s, but it did not make up or compensate for the decline in palm oil prices on both sides of the Atlantic between 1870 and the 1890s (Lynn 1998, 126). In the Gold Coast, African producers would shift to rubber – which soon witnessed a similar glut on the world market – and eventually cocoa.

The pattern of technological innovation and investment in the mid-nineteenth century creating over capacity and then resulting in plummeting prices was repeated globally. The development of refrigeration meant that steamships could bring produce and meat from distant places, encouraging industrialized countries to specialize in high-end agricultural products such as dairy, meat, fruits, and vegetables, while depending on imports for their other food needs such as grains. The impact of the crisis of 1873–96 was varied in Britain. Among the four main sectors of the British economy in 1870 – agriculture, industry, banking and finance, and shipping – notable disconnections occurred that shaped how the crisis was experienced. Britain's agricultural sector continued to decline, especially as Britain as the pioneer industrialized nation believed it had comparative advantage in free trade. Britain's industries, such as iron and steel and textiles, remained profitable by cutting back investments in machinery, but lost their competitive edge after the crisis was over, setting the context for British decline in these industries. British banking and shipping in their international focus were to some extent disconnected from internal or national industries. Banking and shipping performed well in the crisis of the late nineteenth century, while several merchant houses collapsed (Gourevitch 1986, 76–83).

The British merchants Horsfalls, pioneers in the palm oil trade, exited West Africa in 1875. Other established companies that disappeared in the 1870s included R. & G. Benn, Tyson, Richmond and Jones, and Wilson and Dawson. The bankruptcies continued in the 1880s with John Capper and Co. (1880), Irvine and Woodward (1881), and Moritz Herschell (1886). Other commercial giants collapsed in the 1890s: the Gold Coast household name F & A Swanzy was taken over by Millers in 1894, Taylor, Laughland & Co. folded in 1896 and W. B. MacIver in 1900 (Lynn 1998, 147–8). Lynn notes that in a sense this was the end of the age of the older family businesses, which collapsed in spectacular fashion because of the economic pressures of the period or because the original founder had died. Those that survived merged to create joint-stock companies or found other ways of reorganizing such as through amalgamations. The collapse of these family businesses were replicated on the Gold Coast, and by the end of the nineteenth century, the Ocanseys, Ghartey, Sarbah, and other notable merchants who had emerged in the mid-century prosperity had also collapsed. Austen comments on the unwillingness of even the most successful Euro-African family businesses to adopt "the organizational and legal structure of modern European businesses" (Austen 1987, 90). The benefit of hindsight sheds light on the important need for these family businesses to have restructured; caught up in the uncertainty of the late nineteenth-century crisis, the causes of which remained unclear to contemporaries, the way out was not that clear cut. Their collapse underscores how invested they were in Euro-African trade, and how their commercial existence, like the European merchants operating in West Africa, had become dependent on the continuance of this commerce. Not all African merchants were able together with producers to "simply drop out of the market until conditions provided better incentives for commercial efforts" (Austen 1987, 102). Olukoju (Chapter 6, this volume) provides us with contrasting examples of African businesses that utilized the exit strategy described by Austen in southwest Nigeria. Here some Yoruba merchants, whose businesses collapsed in the economic crisis of the late nineteenth century, branched into agriculture and other ventures or local strategies of accumulation not so heavily dependent on Atlantic trade to recoup their losses and recapitalize for a more opportune reentry into commerce. But then Yorubaland was not annexed to British rule until the 1890s. Land and real estate represented important avenues of investment and diversification for merchants in the early colonial period.

Having sketched the context of boom and bust during the nineteenth century on both sides of the Atlantic within the global economy, it is time to examine the repercussions on commercial relations in the Gold Coast. The crisis marked the rise of tensions between Gold Coast merchants and their European counterparts, as they struggled to make sense of the continuous decline in palm oil prices compared to the stable prices of European imports; extended the impact of British bankruptcies to the Gold Coast; altered relations between large Gold Coast merchants and small traders in a period of trade constriction; and dashed the hopes of small traders for social mobility. We can now examine the local specificity of transactions and events and the social ramifications. How did merchants in the Gold Coast understand or interpret the economic crisis of 1873–96? It is noteworthy that the crisis began just before the commencement of colonial rule in the Gold Coast in 1874. Did merchants in the Gold Coast have sufficient information to understand the economics of the crisis and not to see the sudden adverse terms of trade as a product of the extension of colonial rule?

Trust was a central pillar of Euro-African trade. What was the impact of the crisis on trading relations? Can we discern the impact of the numerous bankruptcies in Britain from the 1870s on African businesses in the Gold Coast? And what was the impact of the economic downturn in the Gold Coast on the social aspirations of traders?

I have chosen to focus on the most notable trading family from Ada in southeast Gold Coast, the Ocanseys. With extensive trading relations to Britain and Germany, the Ocanseys were without a doubt the "merchant princes" of Ada. Ada was the outlet for Krobo palm oil producers, and this was the hub of the palm oil trade. Dumett counts the Ocanseys among the twenty-five or so large merchants that emerged in the Gold Coast between 1865 and 1900. The business documents – letter books, ledgers, and accounting records (invoices, cash and wage books, etc.) – relating to the Ocansey business have been deposited at the Public Records and Archives Administration Department (PRAAD) in Accra. Their sadly deteriorating state makes it difficult to follow developments for a continuous number of years from a single collection. Consequently, I draw on the correspondence of a second Ada trading family, the Caesars, though they did not operate on the grand scale of the Ocanseys. Correspondence between J. H. Caesar and Sons with their British partners illumines some of the questions raised on the local interpretation of a global economic crisis. And I draw on the private papers of a third trader, Christian Jacobson, who operated on a much smaller scale. Though based at Keta, a little to the east of Ada, he was very connected to the commercial world of Ada and was a protégé of the Ocanseys. Clearly knowledgeable about trade on the coast, as evident from a long line of former expatriate and Gold Coast employers and partners, Jacobson's futile attempts to set himself up during the 1880s and 1890s as an independent trader reflects the closing of the gates of opportunity in the late nineteenth century, compared to the prosperous 1850s and 1860s that had witnessed an explosion in the numbers of small, independent traders.

7.4 THE SOCIAL WORLD OF COMMERCE IN THE GOLD COAST

7.4.1 William Narh Ocansey of Ada: A Merchant Prince

Ada, at the estuary of the Volta River and an important trade artery into Krobo oil palm country and upcountry markets such as Kete Krachi, was the base of the prominent firm of William N. Ocansey and Sons in the second half of the nineteenth century.[9] Formerly part of the Danish sphere of influence on the Gold Coast, the Danes had withdrawn in 1850, selling their trading forts or lodges with the "spheres of influence" to the British. Ada thus came under British influence. That this transition coincided with years of prosperity in the palm oil trade, for which Ada was a major port, strengthened the place of Britain in the social world of Ada merchants and traders. Anlo territory to the east, with its leading trading town of Keta, had also been transferred from Danish influence to the British (Nørregård 1966).

William Narh Ocansey was born in the 1820s, and Dumett, who interviewed his son, described him as a "self-made man." Though illiterate, he built up an impressive business based on the export of palm oil to Britain and Germany and the import of European manufactures of cloth, liquor, and tobacco. Exploiting his strategic base at the mouth of the Volta, his canoes also sent local products of salt and fish to central and northern Ghana (Dumett 1983, 673). From the 1870s he was in correspondence with mercantile firms in London, Liverpool, Glasgow, and Hamburg, who valued his business and used him as a referee for other Gold Coast merchants in Ada, the lower Volta region, and east of the Volta who desired credit from European merchant houses. In 1877–8, a firm of Liverpool produce brokers, Hickson and Sykes, referred to William N. Ocansey and Sons as the "best traders on the coast" because of the firm's ability to buy palm oil cheaper than any other trader on the Gold Coast (Dumett 1983, 675). The nucleus of Ocansey's business seemed to have been in place even in the 1860s, when he is reported to have a network of twelve trading stations each with a store manager.

> At the height of its prosperity the Ocansey firm controlled branch factories at the towns of Keta, Beh Beach, and Danu [Denu] Beach on the eastern (Anlo) shore of the Volta estuary, as well as establishments at Agrave, Adidome, Battor, Weycoomabe, Amanor, Tolesem, Adafoa, Prampram, Akuse and Kpong in the western of Ada[n] gbe zone of influence. (Dumett 1983, 675)

The Ocansey papers help us to understand the infrastructure of commerce on the Gold Coast in the late nineteenth century.

9 Ghana Public Records and Archives Administration Department at Accra (PRAAD): SC 8: Ocansey Papers. Also important to this section are a number of pioneering articles written by Raymond Dumett during the 1970s and 1980s on Gold Coast entrepreneurs, such as the Ocanseys, and Gold Coast commercial history at the turn of the twentieth century (Dumett 1971, 1973, 653–79, 1983, 661–93).

The key exchange products were palm oil from the Gold Coast and the addition of palm kernels from the 1870s and textile, liquor, and tobacco imports from Europe with an assorted range of other minor items. William Ocansey shipped his palm oil direct to Europe, though he also shipped through the large European merchant houses such as the Basel Mission Factory and Alexander Miller (Dumett 1983, 675). In the Gold Coast, it has been noted that many of the major nineteenth-century merchants were from royal lineages or were affiliated to royal lineages in some way (Dumett 1983, 671, 680; see Dumett 1972). In nineteenth-century Anlo, several chiefs were prominent traders during the waning years of the slave trade and in legitimate trade (Akyeampong 2001, 58). Chiefs who were prominent traders in Anlo from the mid-nineteenth century included Chief Anthony of Addafia, Chief Amegbor of Klikor, Chief Hoku of Blekuso, Chief James Ocloo of Keta, and Chief Akolatse, who we will encounter again in the career of Christian Jacobson (Dumett 1983, 671). Though being a chief or coming from a chiefly family did not necessarily start late nineteenth-century Gold Coast merchants off with financial capital, they had enormous social capital that facilitated their hiring of local labor and their sourcing of produce. But membership in a chiefly family also had its exactions in terms of traders' personal wealth. In the legal disputes that marked chieftaincy in Ada during the colonial period, it was pointed out during one of the inquiries in the 1920s that the Ocanseys of the Kababiawe clan had provided the *manche* (king) of Ada for the preceding two hundred years (Sutton 1984, 53). William Ocansey was the younger brother to the king of Ada. Ada's most important natural resource was salt from the Songor lagoon. It is not surprising that William Ocansey and Sons was an important salt trader to markets upcountry. That the major oil producers of the Gold Coast, the Krobo, were situated in the lower Volta region and were Adangme speakers was an asset in Ocansey's ability to secure large quantities of palm oil at attractive prices (Dumett 1983, 673–4).[10]

Being a member of the royal family in Ada brought heavy financial impositions on William Ocansey in the 1860s and 1870s. As probably the wealthiest merchant in Ada and brother to its king, William Ocansey came to the support of his brother when the neighboring Anlo state attacked Ada in the 1860s. Ocansey reportedly lost £5,000 in this war, according to the personal account of his son John E. Ocansey. It is not clear whether this loss was a

[10] F. and A. Swanzy's agent Alfred Triggs spent a fortnight traveling in the interior of the Gold Coast in March 1870 going into Krobo country. He describes the "immense palm forests which afford us the staple of our palm oil supplies at Accra and Prampram" (The United Africa Company and Unilever Archives[UAC]: 2/33/AG/1/2/3, 1870).

contribution to the war effort or a result of damages to trade. And he almost lost his life from a gunshot wound in this very war (Ocansey 1989, 10).[11] Another "corporate" liability cost Ocansey $2,000 in 1875–6, when a ship of F & A Swanzy, prominent British traders in the Gold Coast, was wrecked off the coast of Ada. Swanzy's agent claimed that the wrecked ship was pillaged by the residents of Ada and sued the king of Ada in the colonial court for not protecting the ship. Awarded damages of $5,000, the residents of Ada paid $2,000 and refused to pay any more as they claimed the Ada agent for Swanzy (Charles Cassah) had removed goods from the ship before the ship sunk, hence they contested the value the agent had put on the goods aboard the ship. The colonial government put pressure on the king of Ada to make good the rest, and the king paid $1,000 and his brother the trader paid $2,000 (Ocansey 1989, 11–13). The war between Ada and Anlo took place before colonial rule was declared in the Gold Coast. The court case on the shipwreck showed how colonial rule had changed the operation of trade and understandings of liability. During the precolonial period, shipwrecks were considered fair game for looting. Residents in Ada found out just a year after colonial imposition that the rules of the game had changed.

7.4.2 Commerce and Credit in the Gold Coast in an Era of Economic Crisis

The boom years of the 1850s and 1860s had increased considerably the ranks of traders in the oil palm trade on both the European (Britain and Germany) and West African sides. As market prices declined from the 1850s, the investments European and African traders had made in their trade and their dependence on the trade made it difficult for them to pull out of the oil trade. European merchants continued to prime the pump, hopeful that expanded trade would make up for the decline in prices. This explains on the African side the expansion in the supply of palm oil – and later palm kernels – even in the face of declining prices. In the second half of the nineteenth century, African merchants on the Gold Coast had stations or stores in the interior with managers and agents who purchased produce such as palm oil, palm kernels, and rubber, and who sold an inventory of European manufactures. Such inland storekeepers advanced credit in goods to traders who dealt directly with producers, though store managers could also source produce directly from producers. Coastal merchants could sell their produce to European companies on the coast such as F. and A. Swanzy,

[11] Written by John E. Ocansey during his short stay in Liverpool, England in the year 1881.

Pickering and Berthoud, or Miller Brothers or send their produce directly to Europe to a consignment house via steamship service. These consignment houses then sold the produce on behalf of the African merchant, purchased and shipped their list of requested European manufactures, and kept an accounting of these imports and exports. Consignment houses charged between 2.5 and 5 percent commission on the net invoice value of goods they purchased and shipped to African merchants from Europe (shipping and insurance extra), and another 2.5 to 5 percent commission for selling palm oil, palm kernels, and rubber on behalf of these African merchants and traders (Dumett 1973, 664). Dumett notes the liberal extension of credit in the mid-nineteenth century by British consignment houses to small traders throughout the British Empire, and how this in turn eased local credit terms and facilities on the Gold Coast, providing a boost in general to trade (Dumett 1973, 655).

The role of large merchants such as William and John Ocansey as referees and guarantors for small traders needs to be emphasized as an important factor in the expansion of trade in the late nineteenth century, as European merchant houses utilized them as supervisors and even enforcers of goods given in trust, especially for traders these African merchants had recommended. As palm oil prices on European markets continued to drop, while prices for European manufactures remained constant or rose, many African merchants and traders were pushed into debt with consignment houses, breeding mistrust concerning European handling of African accounts. African merchants were often compelled to request an extension of credit from consignment houses, and the latter were willing to oblige at an added interest rate of about 8 percent per annum (Dumett 1973, 665–6).

John E. Ocansey, the literate adopted son of William Ocansey and married to Ocansey's daughter Salome, handled business correspondence on behalf of William N. Ocansey and Sons, and served as credit enforcer for minor merchants and African traders. He seemed to have guaranteed credit with consignment houses for Christian Jacobson of Keta, and for smaller Ada traders like J. T. Amenyar, Tetteh Dosoo, D. J. Adoajee, Theo Taye, and other members of the Ocansey family such as W. B. Ocansey and J. C. Ocansey.[12] The purchases of small traders were sometimes put on William N. Ocansey's bills of lading, which Ocansey and Sons would then deliver

12 See, for examples, PRAAD: SC 8, Ocansey Papers, Donner and Callenburg, 1889; PRAAD: SC 8, Ocansey Papers, Hart and Co., Oct. 1889; PRAAD: SC 8, Ocansey Papers, Hart and Co., Sept. 1888; PRAAD: SC 8, Ocansey Papers, Donner and Callenburg, 1888.

(PRAAD: SC 8/64, Edward Bros.). Christian Jacobson's business was struggling financially in the 1880s as discerned from the Ocansey correspondence. In August 1889, Jacobson acknowledged the accuracy of Donner and Callenburg of Hamburg's accounting that he owed them £217.1.4 [?]. Jacobson proposed a scheme by which he would gradually pay off his debt and improve on his business with the reduction in his liabilities (PRAAD: SC 8, Ocansey Papers, Jacobson). Donner and Callenburg forwarded a copy of Jacobson's letter to John E. Ocansey.

> Certainly we agree to this arrangement with Mr. Jacobson only when you prolongate your letter of guaranty given us for the debt of Mr. Jacobson to which no doubt you agree to. We enclose a letter for Mr. Jacobson and beg to hand it over to him when you agree to the above when you find it more advantageous to stop all business with him you will kindly return the letter to us. (PRAAD: SC 8, Ocansey Papers, Jacobson, Donner and Callenburg 1889)

Jacobson's account with Lionel Hart and Co in Liverpool was also bad, and the firm reminded John E. Ocansey in regard to Jacobson "that you personally in the first instance asked us to assist him for [your] sake we did so, now we must ask you to use your unlimited influence upon him to remit, or we will have to quarrel about his ac[count] and you only can prevent this unpleasantness happening" (PRAAD: SC 8, Ocansey Papers, Jacobson, Hart and Co., Dec. 1888). Eight months later, Lionel Hart and Co was blaming John Ocansey "for having introduced such a bad man to us" (PRAAD: SC 8, Ocansey Papers, Jacobson, Hart and Co., Aug. 1889).

Bad faith operated on both sides, as admitted in the letter of the Liverpool firm Fletcher and Fraser, as they made a bid for the business of Ocansey and Sons in 1887.

> We have no fear in saying that we should give you satisfaction, and of this be sure for every sovereign we might be fortunate to earn from you in the way of commission. Firms which shall remain nameless would extract five pounds by cutting your clothes, lowering the qualities, charging you for bags in which rice is shipped, not giving you the full price paid for your produce, and other [un]pleasant little *tricks* for which they are famous. (PRAAD: SC 8, Ocansey Papers, Jacobson, Fletcher 1887)

Mistrust clouded African interpretation of the economic crisis of 1873–96, and responsible European merchants did their best to allay the fears of their African partners that the decline in palm oil prices was not a result of price manipulation by European merchants.

Frequently in the 1880s, commission houses would dispatch together with the goods ordered by their African partners weekly produce prices on the European market to inform their clients of price fluctuations on the market. These dispatches also listed prices for competing oils and fats such as Australian tallow. Manchester merchants Pickering and Berthoud in their letter to J. H. Caesar and Sons on July 13, 1888, noted the long silence from their client in the Gold Coast.

> We trust we may soon hear again from you that we shall soon have further and regular remittances so there may be no delay with your orders. It is now some [time] since we had the pleasure of hearing from you, but the "Congo" from your front is now due and we look for news by her. We enclose the usual weekly produce prices current. Palm oil today is nominally about £16. 15/- per ton. Market inactive with buyers holding back. (PRAAD: SC 13/11, J. H. Caesar's Trading Papers)

As of September 21, 1888, when the Manchester merchants wrote again to J. H. Caesar and Sons, they still had not heard from their Gold Coast clients. They however reported a slight improvement in palm oil prices in the previous fortnight (PRAAD: SC 13/11, J. H. Caesar's Trading Papers: SC 8, Pickering Sept. 1888).

Pickering and Berthoud's letter to Caesar and Sons in October the following month acknowledged finally hearing from their Gold Coast clients and made suggestions on how to improve the efficiency of their business, including using the local agent of Pickering and Berthoud in the Gold Coast to make out orders for the firm instead of Caesar and Sons using their own clerks. The letter reflected the strained atmosphere of Euro-African trading relations during this period. In this particular instance, Caesar and Son's order for a surfboat through Pickering and Berthoud was yet to be fulfilled.

> *Surfboat*. On the 14th April last you sent us an order for this: on the 23rd idem you cancelled the order, and on the 28th of the same month you reordered it. Now this sort of thing is to say the least extremely confusing as we have an agent at your front whose duty is specifically to attend to the needs of our various clients. We cannot understand why you do not take advantage of his services.....
>
> We would however repeat the necessity of getting Mr. Vanderpuye to make out your orders as the manner in which this last indent is made out is very deficient and misleading, should any error in its execution be made by us, though being misled by your clerk. *You would no doubt [put] the whole blame on us, as you threaten, on certain conditions send the goods back to us.* [emphasis added] (PRAAD: SC 13/11, J. H. Caesar's Trading Papers, Oct 1888)

They reported an improvement in palm oil prices to £20. 5/ to £20. 10/ per ton for Ada quality, and that the market remained strong.

Part of the response of Gold Coast traders in this era of economic crisis was to search for other commission houses that would be more faithful in the conduct of business or provide better prices and services. Popkin notes how customer markets in produce (e.g., rubber) as distinct from auction markets (e.g., rice) tend to have higher middleman margins, so Gold Coast palm oil suppliers were not wrong in seeking better deals. But Popkin also emphasizes the importance of reputation in produce markets such as rubber – and by extension palm oil – in securing top value for quality produce. Hence, established traders with long relations with European consignment houses who trusted the quality of their produce were unlikely to switch brokers unless deeply provoked (Popkin 1981). Caesar and Sons began to explore from 1889 a new relationship with Radcliffe and Durant in Liverpool. Through their affiliate Christian Jacobson of Keta, who also operated in Ada, Akuse, and the River Volta district, Caesar and Sons sent palm oil on a trial basis to Radcliffe and Durant. The response of the Liverpool firm was enthusiastic: "We shall do all in our power to merit your confidence and hope by so doing we shall be able to do an extensive business with you to our mutual advantage" (PRAAD: SC 13/11, Radcliffe and Durant). Radcliffe and Durant from their correspondence seem to have worked hard to earn the trust of Caesar and Sons. Their correspondence addresses the volatility of the market in the Gold Coast in this time of crisis. Caesar and Son's attempt to cancel an order for guns and matchets in August 1890 as local demand had shifted could not be obliged as Radcliffe and Durant had already shipped the guns aboard the steamer *Africa*, and "the matchets are well in work and cannot now be cancelled" (PRAAD: SC 13/11, Radcliffe and Durant, Aug. 1890). In the insecure times of the late nineteenth century, a missed detail such as opting not to insure one's merchandise could be the tipping point to irrecoverable financial losses. Radcliffe and Durant were able to replace twenty cartons of headkerchiefs (scarves?) that Caesar and Sons had reported lost and had sent a certificate of loss.

> We have claimed on the insurance company for the value and no doubt we shall receive payment in due course. In the meantime we have enclosed another lot of 20 cts to be made and they will be shipped in a few weeks. (PRAAD: SC 13/11, Radcliffe and Durant, July 1890)

When the firm of Ocansey and Sons declined in the 1890s, it was a result of a combination of losses, including financial embezzlement by agents on the coast of West Africa, and bankruptcies suffered by partners in Europe. African businesses sought to reorganize in the crisis of 1873–96 to become more efficient. The ability to deliver produce safely to coastal ports from inland rivers was important, considering the rough surf that characterized the coast of Guinea. We noted earlier the attempt by Caesar and Sons to purchase a surfboat through Pickering and Berthoud. The success of the

Swanzys and George Watts on the west coast of Africa was partly based on their effective use of steam launches to open up new sources of palm oil (Lynn 1998, 146). A major financial blow was dealt to Ocansey and Sons when the Liverpool firm of Messrs. Hickson, Sykes & Co declared bankruptcy in 1881. William Ocansey had paid a substantial amount to Robert W. Hickson for the purchase of a steam launch for his business on Ada. It is the impact of bankruptcies in Britain on Gold Coast traders that we turn to in the next section.

7.4.3 Bankruptcies in England and the Gold Coast: Interconnectedness of Businesses

In 1878, Ocansey suffered a loss of £630 when forty butts of palm oil floated down the Volta River could not be stopped at the estuary at Ada and were lost to the sea because of rough surf. This incident – and the death of his son Gordon Samuel on April 20, 1880, who managed his upriver factory – lay behind Ocansey's decision to purchase a steam launch for his palm oil business on the Volta (Ocansey 1989, 14–15). The steam launch would improve the conduct of his business up the river, eliminate losses that resulted from floating palm oil casks down the river, and reduce dependence on agents who had cost him huge sums of money in the past through the extension of credit in goods. William Ocansey turned to Robert Hickson of the commission house of Messrs. Hickson, Sykes & Co. to purchase the steam launch estimated at about £2,200. Ocansey sent produce worth £2,678. 11s. 8d. to Hickson, who in his correspondence assured Ocansey that the launch would arrive in Ada by July or August 1880. The steam launch never arrived, and following a string of broken promises, Ocansey, suspecting foul play, sent his son John to Liverpool aboard the *Mayumba* in late April 1881 to ascertain the state of affairs.

John on arrival in Liverpool would discover that the firm of Hickson, Sykes & Co. had declared bankruptcy some months earlier, but lack of information had prevented Ocansey and sons from knowing this.

> On the day following my arrival, I made inquiries about Hickson, Sykes & Co., and then I found they had been declared bankrupt, and that the 17th of June had been appointed for the meeting of their creditors. This was terrible news. I felt my heart sink, and I could not eat for three days. I thought of dear father and the heavy loss he would sustain of £2,678, besides all the delay in the enlargement of his business for want of the steam launch, for which he had already paid, and which ought to be out and in full working order. I now found out that I could do nothing but wait and attend the meeting of the creditors. (Ocansey 1989, 26)

John E. Ocansey sued Robert Hickson, but the trial was delayed until the end of July, detaining him in Liverpool. In the interim, John visited business contacts in London, Manchester, and elsewhere, some of these meetings of which were arranged by a long-standing partner of his father's firm, Moritz Herschell.

The trial was a travesty of justice, as counsels for the prosecution and defense, Mr. Carver and Mr. Aspinall, seemed to have reached some private agreement not to press the more damning charge of defrauding the Ocanseys under false pretenses, though the correspondence between the two firms supported that charge. The judge's questioning led clearly to the fact that Hickson misled the Ocanseys into believing that the launch had been ordered and was on the way, when even the order for the launch had not been placed with the shipbuilders. Meanwhile, according to Hickson's defense, Mr. Aspinall, Hickson's produce broker appropriated the proceeds of the Ocansey shipments against debts owed him by Hickson. Justice Lopes's sentencing remarks sum up the case.

> Robert William Hickson, you have pleaded guilty to having misappropriated a large sum of money that had been entrusted to you as agent. You were also indicted for obtaining a very large sum of money by false pretences. No evidence was offered on that indictment, and you were acquitted. I desire to say that, if that indictment had been proceeded with, and you had been convicted, I should have felt it to be my duty to direct you to be placed in penal servitude for a considerable time, because the offence would be a most serious one. The offence to which you have not pleaded guilty is also a most serious one. Everything that can be said in your favour was urged by your counsel in palliation of the charge against you, and that charge is that you misappropriated something like 2,600. It has been said that you got into difficulties, and that you drifted into this act of dishonesty. It appears that in the month of May, 1880, you received special orders to purchase a steam launch for your employers in West Africa, and it also appears that you did not order it until December of that year. In the interval money enough had come into your hands to pay for it, the whole of which you did not apply to the purpose you were directed to apply it, but devoted it instead to your own purposes. I am desirous, as far as I possibly can, to give effect to any extenuating circumstances which I can find in your favour; but I cannot help saying that I find great difficulty in discovering any in this case, and I can pass upon you no other sentence than that you be imprisoned with hard labor for fifteen calendar months. (Ocansey 1989, 58)[13]

[13] (Ocansey 1989, 58). The huge disappointment to William Ocansey of this incident in the history of interracial, transatlantic trade relations has been reiterated in a recent book by Caryl Phillips on the Atlantic's historic connections (Phillips 2001).

Later that same decade, Moritz Herschell, who was a pillar of strength to John Ocansey in the latter's stressful visit to Britain, declared bankruptcy in 1886 (Lynn 1998, 148). At this moment I am unable to ascertain the impact of Herschell's bankruptcy on Ocansey's business, but this is a line of inquiry worth exploring as we can see in the case of Hickson.

These unfortunate incidents compelled William Ocansey and Sons to make changes in its conduct of business, including a decision that it would only ship produce on receipt of firm goods. The Hamburg firm of Wolber and Brohm complained to John in 1887:

> We know that your senior [William N. Ocansey] has made bad experience with certain Merchant firms, but who has not during his life and how much money is lost in Africa; we understand that since you have adopted a policy of expecting firm goods to be there, before shipping against their pay, not so much because you may require credits given to your good selves as with the open introduction, so to speak to be constantly on the safe side. This manner of business involves distrust, which misplaced, creates at once ill feelings. (PRAAD: SC 8/64, Wolber and Brohm)

And following the hard-nosed business practices of the consignment firms in Europe, who held John E. Ocansey partially liable for bad debts incurred by traders he had recommended, John also insisted on collecting commission on produce originating from traders he had recommended, such as Christian Jacobson and other Ocansey relatives who operated their own businesses (PRAAD: SC 8, Hart and Co., Nov. 1888).

By the end of the nineteenth century, the firm of William N. Ocansey and Sons was in decline and William Ocansey is said to have exhausted his wealth by the time of his death. Dumett explains the collapse of the impressive Ocansey business:

> The Ocansey firm's slow decline can be traced to a combination of natural disasters and external factors, including loss by fire, shipwreck, robbery, and involvement in warfare against the neighboring Anlo people. William Ocansey showed amazing resilience in rebounding from many of these misfortunes, but in the end succumbed to general loss from the declining palm oil trade coupled with default on credit by local middlemen and oppressive treatment by European competitors. (Dumett 1983, 676)

The liberal era of European trade credit to small traders throughout the British Empire that we have noted in the mid-nineteenth century had come to an end. The advent of colonial rule and the political economy of colonialism remapped the context and the nature of trade in West Africa. Not only were African merchants and traders displaced in Atlantic trade networks, regional long-distance trade systems that had predated colonial rule for generations were undermined. We look at the closing of these gates of opportunity for the career of young Christian Jacobson as we bring this section to a close.

7.4.4 Mobility Denied: The Frustrated Ambitions of Christian Jacobson, ca. 1880–1912

Christian Jacobson was by all accounts a talented young trader who in the 1870s and 1880s had a bright future in trade. Jacobson grew up during the prosperous 1850s and 1860s and had done the usual apprenticeship as an agent or a clerk for an expatriate mercantile company, the common route at this time for acquiring experience and knowledge in trade, as well as a network of both European merchants and African traders and producers. Young Jacobson was the agent or factor in charge of the lagoon shop of the Bremen Factory in Keta in the 1870s (PRAAD: SC 14/3). He certainly seemed to have made a favorable impression on many, and an established Anlo trader, Chief Akolatse, sought to woo Jacobson away from the Bremen Factory. Jacobson left the Bremen Factory in 1879 after five years employ to work with Chief Akolatse on terms that were unclear and would be disputed in an 1892 legal suit. What can be discerned from the court proceedings is that Akolatse lent Jacobson several large sums of money to go into business partnerships. Jacobson assumed that Akolatse was his partner. Akolatse argued that these were loans. In these arrangements, Akolatse managed to receive his imported goods through Jacobson's businesses at invoice prices, depended on Jacobson for his business correspondence, and even at one time rented one of his houses for Jacobson to be used as the premises for his business while retaining personal use of a section of the house. Clearly, Akolatse was an astute businessman who sought to benefit from the talents of the young Jacobson without being liable for any debts or losses Jacobson would incur in this volatile economic period.

The first major setback the young Jacobson suffered was the bankruptcy of the British commission house he used. Jacobson had been trading with Messrs. Taylor & Co. of 72 Virginia Street in Glasgow. He sent the firm African produce valued at £183 and the firm did not return the money or send the goods Jacobson had ordered. Rather, it declared bankruptcy, and unfairly instructed Jacobson to go and collect his money from its debtors in Grand Bassam in the Ivory Coast. Jacobson was John Ocansey's best friend when they were youths, and a relative of the Ocansey family. John Ocansey reflected on the impact of this early setback on the young Jacobson's trading career.

> Now, Mr. Jacobson is a young man just venturing out into trade; and it does seem very cruel that he should meet with such heartless conduct, and suffer so great a loss, on the doorstep of his life. To ask him, who lives at Quitta [Keta], to collect another man's account from the people of Grand Bassar, is adding insult to injury. (Ocansey 1989, 38)

Jacobson seemed to have followed the example of his friend John, who had gone to Liverpool in pursuit of the investment his father had made in a steam launch. Jacobson boarded a ship to Liverpool at the personal expense of £54 for his return ticket, with the intent to continue to Glasgow to collect his money from Messrs. Taylor & Co. John was still in Liverpool awaiting the outcome of his case against Hickson and was able to provide lodging for Jacobson. Jacobson wrote to the firm of Taylor & Co. from Liverpool and received a very duplicitous response.

> But they sent a letter back at once, saying they had nothing to do with their past affairs; that they had paid a part or composition to those who would receive it and as to his account they still expected it would be got from the people of Grand Bassar, and they would say no more as to the matter, but if Mr. Jacobson would send them any more produce they would do well for him. (Ocansey 1989, 39)

Jacobson returned empty-handed to Keta, saddled with a huge debt very early in his career that Chief Akolatse would insist was a loan and not a partnership. He set a historical record, though, as the first Anlo to have visited Europe, albeit under unhappy circumstances. Bankruptcies by British businesses worked against their African clients who often lacked even the information to know that bankruptcy had been declared and a settlement was to be reached with creditors.

Jacobson's subsequent string of unsuccessful business partnerships speaks to the unpredictable economic conditions of the 1880s. From 1880 to 1881, Jacobson went into partnership with Mr. Wood, agent for Edwards and Bros. Akolatse lent Jacobson £245 for this endeavor. Next came a partnership with a Mr. Bellois of Bremen from 1881 to 1883, and again Akolatse lent £201 for the business and received his imported goods at invoice prices. In addition he charged Jacobson and Bellois £10 a month for rent for the house from which they ran their business. Then came business with one Duncan, agent for Taylor and Co. Akolatse seemed to have retained Jacobson in some capacity between 1880 and 1886, and several witnesses, including trader Chief James Ocloo, attested that in their trade dealings with Akolatse, Jacobson had represented Akolatse (PRAAD: SC 14/3). As of 1892, Jacobson was still paying for the debts he had incurred to Akolatse from the early 1880s. Indeed, it appears that Akolatse even worked against the aspirations of his protégé. Jacobson recalled how he or the defendant had proposed around 1887 that they build a house for the business at the lagoon side, the house to be built under the supervision of Jacobson. Akolatse secured building materials on credit from the local agent of the Hamburg firm of Rotterman for the project. Jacobson recounted the demise of the project.

> It was to be a storey house but I only built the walls. One day deft. [Chief Akolatse] told me that he withdrew and transferred the house to me. He said a boy should not build a storey house. Then Rotterman sent a power of attorney to his nephew ... to demand from deft the amount for which he was surety for me. But W. N. Ocansey paid the debt for me. Deft. charged me £101.14.1 for the materials that he had got from Rotterman at Adda in '87 [1887]. (PRAAD: SC 14/3)

The traditional antagonism between chiefs or elders and young men had reared its head. In this instance, William Ocansey, the established merchant at Ada, had intervened to bail out his young relative by paying Rotterman the amount involved. Old Ocansey may also have discerned the manipulation of Chief Akolatse and his exploitation of young Jacobson, and instructed his son John to assist Jacobson in his business. John introduced Jacobson to British and German commission houses, serving as his guarantor. As the letters from British and German businesses to John indicate, these initiatives failed and they blamed John for recommending an unreliable trader to them. It is clear from the circumstances of Jacobson's career that the fault perhaps was due more to the unpredictable business environment than a character flaw.

A peeved Jacobson sued Chief Akolatse in the Supreme Court of the Gold Coast (Eastern Province) in 1892 for wages as Akolatse had not paid him wages for the five or six years that he served Akolatse in the capacity of a clerk. Jacobson's reasoning was that if he was not a partner to Akolatse, hence making Akolatse jointly liable for debts incurred, then he was an employee entitled to remuneration for his services. Akolatse in his defense argued that Jacobson left his employ in 1884, at which time he had given Jacobson a gift of $410. To be more precise, he reduced the amount Jacobson owed him by this amount. He also claimed that Jacobson wrote a single letter on his behalf to McIver of Glasgow in June 1884, but that was in the capacity of a friend and not a clerk. The case was dismissed with costs. As late as 1912, Jacobson was still struggling to find his feet in the world of commerce. In that year, he was appointed agent or representative for the

Volta River Districts of an American trading company based in Brooklyn, New York, the Akim Trading Company. This was probably an African American business. The times had certainly changed, but not the fortunes of Christian Jacobson.

7.5 DENOUEMENT: COLONIAL RULE AND THE DEMISE OF WEST AFRICAN MERCHANT PRINCES

The role of many European traders as advocates for European colonial rule in the late nineteenth century reflected their belief that they could dictate trading conditions and that their profits would increase under a political system in which they were dominant. Hopkins noted the importance of the economic downturn at the end of the nineteenth century in generating momentum for the colonization of Africa and of the 1930s depression in the decolonization of Africa (Hopkins 1973). Indeed, in many instances in West Africa, the treaties of protection that became the basis of formal European colonial rule had been entered into by European merchants with African chiefs on behalf of their national governments. George Goldie's treaties with chiefs of the lower and middle Niger was instrumental to the drawing of the colonial map of Nigeria. Big British traders like John Holt openly showed their displeasure when British tardiness resulted in the German annexation of the Cameroons (NAB, FO 84/1660). European merchants like Alexander Miller who believed that Jaja of Opobo in the Niger Delta had been treated unfairly in his defense of his political and economic sovereignty by his deposition and exile in 1887 were rare.[14] Colonial rule definitely changed the environment of trade. With the protection of colonial rule, European mercantile houses increasingly showed a preference for European agents on the West African coast. When Lebanese traders proved a suitable and cheaper alternative, they, not African merchants, would become the recipients of European credit, as racial lines hardened with the advent of scientific racism at the end of the nineteenth century (Akyeampong 2006; Bierwith 1999; Boumedouha 1990; Falola 1990; Van der Laan 1975).

[14] Jaja (1991) reproduces voluminous correspondence in which Miller Brothers petitioned the Foreign Office about the unjust manner in which Consul Johnston had treated Jaja, counseled Opobo chiefs on the right demeanor so as not to prejudice the Jaja case, and even ensured that Jaja was extended funds through F. and A. Swanzy while resident in Accra for his trial.

But the collapse of West African merchants in the late nineteenth century cannot be attributed only to the onset of colonial rule and economic discrimination. First, this chapter has shown that West Africans were incorporated into productive processes or systems in Europe based on technological developments beyond their control. The industrial processes that created a need for vegetable oils were based in Europe. Africans were happy beneficiaries of this development but not critical to its origin or sustenance. Second, it appears that coastal merchants in the Gold Coast had become overly dependent on Atlantic commerce compared to Yoruba merchants in the nineteenth century, who tapped into Atlantic commerce, but also farmed extensive acres to supply food to the large urban populations in Yorubaland. They were enmeshed in international, regional, and local markets, shifting their emphasis as economic circumstances demanded. Third, West Africans represented one supply source in an increasingly competitive market to supply Europe with oils. And palm oil, for that matter, was not indispensable to the productive processes for which it was required, increasingly becoming limited where specialized processes required nongeneric oils. Austen points to how at the end of the nineteenth century, the relative value of West Africa's trade within the Atlantic economy was already declining: "Within this market, the capacity of Africans to purchase the growing output of European products remained limited compared to more populous and accessible portions of the world" (Austen 1987, 112). The economic situation of West Africa at the end of the nineteenth century foreshadowed Africa's economic predicament in the twentieth century. As Dumett contemplated the decline of the African merchant princes at the end of the nineteenth century, he could not escape the conclusion that "[i]nherent distortions in the world market for tropical commodities plus biases in the political economy of colonialism, which favored Europeans, lie at the root of this discussion" (Dumett 1983, 693).

One feature of nineteenth-century trade in West Africa survived into the twentieth century and the political economy of colonialism: the prominence of chiefs in trade or business. In southern Nigeria and the Gold Coast, chiefs were prominent traders during the era of the slave trade, and moved their capital and control over labor into the export of cash crops during the era of legitimate trade. Colonial rule was initially inimical to chiefs, viewed as the major opponents to European rule. But as colonial rule became consolidated, the British shored up the authority of chiefs, whose collaboration became essential to the extension of European hegemony. Colonial administrations would even sponsor chiefs in business who lacked business acumen. So, during World War I, when wartime shipping shortage led to official restrictions on cocoa exports, the governor of the Gold Coast, Hugh Clifford, in 1917 gave export licenses to the notable paramount chiefs of Accra, Akuapem, and Akyem Abuakwa to export cocoa. That they sought to use their stools as collateral with the Colonial Bank to charter a ship perhaps reflects their lack of business savvy. The resulting outcry led to the destoolment of the paramount chief of Accra (Parker 2000, 211). In Lagos, "white cap" chiefs, or those who owned the land in Lagos, were instrumental in the establishment of British colonial rule. One study underscores the economic benefits that came out of this relationship as the white cap chiefs became the trading partners of the British during the colonial era, which positioned them as businessmen and captains of industry at the end of colonial rule (Oyo 1989). For other African traders in early colonial West Africa, the surest route to success was to be extended credit facilities by an expatriate company or to be made agent – particularly sole agent – to distribute an import that was in great demand. With the consolidation of European rule and the expansion of expatriate economic activities, these opportunities became more rare. Thus W. A. Dawodu's pioneering role in motor transport, his sole agency for a period of Ford cars and Humber cycles, and automobile servicing in the 1910s and 1920s brought him great wealth in his operations in Lagos and other major Yoruba cities, but he would fall victim to global economic adversity from the mid-1920s and fierce competition from expatriate firms with access to greater capital (Olukoju, Chapter 6, this volume). By the early twentieth century, land had become one of the most important sources of indigenous capital in a context of declining credit for Africans, facilitating the resurgence of chiefly wealth and influence. The century that began with the abolition of the slave trade and the advent of legitimate trade, a century that had witnessed ordinary commoners become economic producers and consumers, that had occasioned the flourishing of African merchants and traders, that had seen the political and economic foundations of chieftaincy challenged, ended with the chiefs in a new relationship with colonial rulers and being groomed as businessmen and the indigenous voice for the colonial agenda.

References

Akyeampong, Emmanuel. (2001). *Between the Sea and the Lagoon: An Eco-Social History of the Anlo of Southeastern Ghana c.1850 to Recent Times*. Oxford: James Currey.

(2006). "Race, Identity and Citizenship in Black Africa: The Case of the Lebanese in Ghana." *Africa*, 76(3): 297–323.

Anstey, Roger. (1975). *The Atlantic Slave Trade and British Abolition, 1760–1810*. Atlantic Highlands, NJ: Humanities Press.

Austen, Ralph A. (1987). *African Economic History: Internal Development and External Dependency*. London: James Currey.

Bierwith, Chris. (1999). "The Lebanese Communities of Côte d'Ivoire." *African Affairs*, 98(390): 79–99.

Boumedouha, Said. (1990). "Adjustment to West African Realities: The Lebanese in Senegal." *Africa*, 60(4): 538–49.

Brown, Christopher L. (2006). *Moral Capital: Foundations of British Abolitionism*. Chapel Hill: University of North Carolina Press.

Davies, P. N. (1977). "The Impact of the Expatriate Shipping Lines on the Economic Development of British West Africa." *Business History*, 19(1): 3–17.

Drescher, Seymour. (1977). *Econocide: British Slavery in the Era of Abolition*. Pittsburgh: University of Pittsburgh Press.

Duke, Antera. (1956). "The Diary of Antera Duke, an Efik Slave Trading Chief of the Eighteenth Century." In *Efik Traders of Old Calabar*, edited by Darryl Forde, 27–78. London: Oxford University Press.

Dumett, Raymond E. (1971). "The Rubber Trade of the Gold Coast and Asante in the Nineteenth Century: African innovation and Market Responsiveness." *Journal of African History*, 12(1): 79–101.

(1972). "Compilation of African Merchant and Traders' Agents of Major Towns in Ghana." *Transactions of the Historical Society of Ghana*, 13: 260–4.

(1973). "John Sarbah, the Elder, and African Mercantile Entrepreneurship in the Gold Coast in the Late Nineteenth Century." *Journal of African History*, 14(4): 653–79.

(1983). "African Merchants of the Gold Coast, 1860–1905 – Dynamics of Indigenous Entrepreneurship." *Comparative Studies in Society and History*, 25(4): 661–93.

Edward Brothers, Liverpool, to Messrs William N. Ocansey, March 17, 1887.

Eltis, David. (1987). *Economic Growth and the Ending of the Transatlantic Slave Trade*. New York: Oxford University Press.

Falola, Toyin. (1990). "Lebanese Traders in Southwestern Nigeria, 1900–1960." *African Affairs*, 89(359): 523–53.

Ghana Public Records and Archives Administration Department at Accra: SC 8, Accra.

Ghana Public Records and Archives Administration Department at Accra: SC 8, Schedule of Ocansey Papers.

Ghana Public Records and Archives Administration Department at Accra: SC 8/64, Accra.

Ghana Public Records and Archives Administration Department at Accra: SC 8/64, Accra, Letter Book.

Ghana Public Records and Archives Administration at Accra: SC 13/11, Radcliffe and Durant to Messrs. J.H. Caesar and Sons, Liverpool.

Ghana Public Records and Archives Administration at Accra: SC 14/3, Christian Jacobson Papers, Accra.

Gourevitch, Peter. (1986). *Politics in Hard Times: Comparative Responses to International Economic Crises*. Ithaca, NY: Cornell University Press.

Hargreaves, John. (1986). "The European Partition of West Africa." In *History of West Africa*, edited by J. F. A. Ajayi and Michael Crowder, 408–28. Essex: Longmans, 2nd edition.
Headrick, Daniel R. (1981). *Tools of Empire: Technology and European Imperialism in the Nineteenth Century*. New York: Oxford University Press.
Hopkins, Antony G. (1973). *Economic History of West Africa*. London: Longman.
Jaja, S. O. (1991). *Opobo since 1870: A Documentary Record with an Introduction*. Ibadan: University of Ibadan Press.
Jasanoff, Maya. (2011). *Liberty's Exiles: American Loyalists in the Revolutionary World*. New York: Alfred A. Knopf.
Lovejoy, Paul E. and David Richardson. (1999). "Trust, Pawnship and Atlantic History: The Institutional Foundations of the Old Calabar Slave Trade." *American Historical Review*, 1049(2): 333–55.
(2001). "The Business of Slaving: Pawnship in Western Nigeria, c.1600–1810." *Journal of African History*, 42(1): 67–89.
(2004). "'This Horrid Hole': Royal Authority, Commerce and Credit at Bonny, 1690–1840." *Journal of African History*, 45(3): 363–92.
Lynn, Martin. (1989). "From Sail to Steam: The Impact of the Steamship Services on the British Palm Oil Trade with West Africa, 1850–1890." *Journal of African History*, 30(2): 227–45.
Lynn, Martin. (1998). *Commerce and Economic Change in West Africa: The Palm Oil Trade in the Nineteenth Century*. Cambridge: Cambridge University Press.
Marsters, Kate Ferguson. (2000). *Travels in the Interior Districts Africa by Mungo Park*. Durham, NC: Duke University Press.
National Archives of Britain(NAB): FO 2/20. Dr. Balfour Baikie to the Secretary of the Cotton Suppliers' Association of Manchester, Lukoja, April 3, 1861.
NAB: London, FO 2/47. Consul Charles Livingstone to Lord Stanley, Fernando Po, October 1, 1866.
NAB: London, FO 84/1660. FO note by Lister, December 3, 1884.
NAB: London, FO 97/434. Niger Expedition, 1862–4.
Nørregård, Georg. (1966). *Danish Settlements in West Africa, 1658–1850*, Trans., Sigurd Mammen. Boston, MA: Boston University Press.
Ocansey, John E. and Kwame Arhin. (1989). *An African Trading; or The Trials of William Narh Ocansey of Addah, West Coast of Africa, River Volta*. 3rd ed. Accra: Ghana Academy of Arts and Sciences; First edition 1881, with Robert Hickson, Liverpool: J. Looney.
Oyo, Akinfe. (1989). "The White Cap Chieftaincy Institution of Lagos: A Historical Survey." BA Thesis, Department of History, University of Ibadan.
Parker, John. (2000). *Making the Town: Ga State Society in Early Colonial Accra*. Portsmouth, NH: Heinemann.
Phillips, Caryl. (2001). *The Atlantic Sound*. London: Vintage.
Pomeranz, Kenneth and Steven Topik. (2006). *The World that Trade Created: Society, Culture, and the World Economy 1400 to the Present*. New York: M. E. Sharpe.
Popkin, Samuel L. (1981). "Public Choice and Rural Development – Free Riders, Lemons, and Institutional Design." In *Public Choice and Rural Development*, edited by Clifford S. Russell and Norman K. Nicholson, 43–80. Washington, DC: Resources for the Future, INC.

Sutton, Inez. (1984). "Law, Chieftaincy and Conflict in Colonial Ghana: The Ada Case." *African Affairs*, 83(330): 41–62.
United Africa Company and Unilever Archives: Liverpool, UAC/2/33/AG/1/2/3, F. and A. Swanzy Papers, Alfred Triggs to Andrew Swanzy, Cape Coast, March 29, 1870.
Van der Laan, H. L. (1975). *The Lebanese Traders in Sierra Leone*. The Hague: Mouton Publishers.

8

The Textile Industry of Eastern Africa in the *Longue Durée*

William G. Clarence-Smith

8.1 INTRODUCTION

Historians are divided over the issue of the role of textiles in the economic development of eastern Africa, defined here as stretching from the Sudan to South Africa. Ravi Palat and Immanuel Wallerstein claim that India "deindustrialized" its Indian Ocean periphery by exploiting advanced textile techniques and cheap labor (Palat and Wallerstein 1999, 36–7). Similarly, John Mack and Pedro Machado contend that Indian imports fatally undermined a fragile textile sector in eastern Africa, long before Lancashire and New England cottons flooded in from the mid-nineteenth century (Machado 2005, 91–151, 2009, 167; Mack 1993, 303–4). Michael Pearson recognizes that Indian cloth penetrated deep into the markets of early modern eastern Africa, but he poses a crucial counterfactual question: Would the performance of African textiles have been better or worse without imports from South Asia? (Pearson 1998, 121–2).

The fact that textile production grew in South Asia's oceanic periphery from the mid-seventeenth to the mid-nineteenth century, including in eastern Africa, argues against the position adopted by Palat, Wallerstein, Mack, and Machado. Trade proved to have generally positive rather than negative consequences. While locally produced cloth was only episodically competitive overseas, it had substantial internal markets in Africa. South Asian artisans emigrated little, but they provided models to imitate. Specialized trade diasporas, often South Asian in composition, supplied information, credit, shipping, commercial facilities, and intermediate goods for further transformation, such as colored yarn and plain cloth (Clarence-Smith 2009, 2011). Thus eastern Africa was not a captive market for South Asia, but rather a partner in the development of textile production.

That said, eastern Africa's textile industry remained far weaker than that of South Asia, and there is absolutely no indication that any part of Africa was heading for an industrial revolution on European lines (Parthasarathi 2011). There is some evidence for tendencies toward proto-industrialization, marked by the specialization of workers, the creation of workshops, and market relations of a putting-out type. However, eastern Africa was very sparsely populated, with a few exceptions, and neither the productivity of agriculture nor per capita incomes were favorable to widespread proto-industry.

Colonial and postcolonial leaders usually failed to recognize the strengths of this budding artisanal sector, and their policies ensured that the proto-industrial path to economic development was even less likely to be followed. All their energies eventually went into developing modern mills that proved to be "white elephants." Nevertheless, rather surprisingly, the artisanal sector survived this misguided modernizing onslaught, and is at last being given some official attention in our own times.

8.2 ARTISANS OF EARLY MODERN MADAGASCAR

European newcomers in the sixteenth century considered Malagasy textiles to be the finest in the region (Grandidier 1928, 168; Rita-Ferreira 1999, 117–18). The great island displayed more diverse techniques, wove a greater variety of textile fibers, and employed a wider palette of colors than any other part of eastern Africa (Fee 2002; Mack 1987, 1989). Cotton cultivation dominated in the dry southwestern zone of Madagascar, while forested lowland zones were chiefly the domain of raffia. Wild silk prevailed in many places, and hemp, banana, spun bark, and plaited reeds played a minor role. Fibers were sent from the coastlands to the densely peopled central plateau for weaving, and cloth moved the other way (Campbell 2005, 31–2; Fee 2002, 40, map 2, 2005, 94).

Pedro Machado claims that South Asian competition was negatively affecting Madagascar's textile economy by the 1780s, citing sales of South Asian cloth on the central plateau at that time (Machado 2009, 168). However, the mere mention of markets for Indian textiles in the interior does not mean that local production was being undermined. Yemen may have ceased to purchase Malagasy cloth from the thirteenth century, but East Africa remained a significant external market (Baldry 1982, 17; Kent 1970, 69; Newitt 1995, 28). Moreover, European vessels took local cloth to the newly settled Mascarene Islands (Mauritius and Réunion) from the mid-seventeenth century (Ellis 1838, I, 68; Fee 2005, 98; Larson 2000, 52).

In any event, Madagascar's internal market for its own cloth showed no signs of weakening in the late eighteenth and early nineteenth centuries. Contemporary texts and oral traditions depict a flourishing and vital textile sector. A French traveler on the Malagasy central plateau in 1777 opined that women were so busy weaving that they left domestic chores to men, pointing to a growing division of labor. An 1826 report noted that local cloth was competing well with the imported variety, and that every woman in the country was busy weaving. Indeed, many women wove full time, ranging "from the King's wives to the slaves" (Fee 2005, 94; Larson 2000, 124, 128–9, 145). In 1838, one observer wrote about textiles as "the most general employment of the people," after rice cultivation, and gave a detailed description of spinning and weaving (Ellis 1838, I, 277, 282, 324–7).

Changing Malagasy attitudes toward rituals and politics boosted weaving. After Radama II had been murdered, partly for ordering his subjects to dress in Western clothes in 1861, it became mandatory to wear locally woven *lamba* for ritual occasions (Fee 2002, 61, 90, note 29). Burial ceremonies became more elaborate, involving greater quantities of cloth. In the Merina and northern Betsileo lands, there was a second solemn burial of dried remains of the deceased, which were wrapped in cloth. Only handspun and handwoven textiles appear to have been acceptable for these purposes (Bronson 2004, 166; Deschamps 1947, 121; Fee 2002, 62–3; Larson 2000, 128–9; Schaedler 1987, 428). Local cloth was also entrenched in the giving of gifts up and down the social hierarchy (Fee 2002, 64–7).

8.3 ARTISANAL TEXTILES IN EARLY MODERN NORTHEASTERN AFRICA

Northeastern Africa had a narrower range of products than Madagascar, almost entirely restricted to white cottons. However, these were of fine quality and were produced in considerable and growing quantities. Moreover, value was added by interweaving or embroidering with imported colored yarn.

The origins of cotton weaving were most ancient in Nubia, although cotton cultivation itself probably only dated from the beginning of the second millennium CE. Sudan's Blue Nile regions of Sennar and Damar were noted for their output of *dammar*, plain white cloth (Coquet 1993, 141–2; Lamb 2005, 107–8; Werbeloff 1987, 155). By the mid-nineteenth century, *dammar* was sold, given for marriage payments, paid as tribute, and used as currency (Ewald 1990, 72–3, 76, 87, 147–8). On the eve of colonial rule, women did the spinning, with Darfur enjoying a particular reputation, while men wove. The Jazirah (Gezira) region supplied *dammar* to Omdurman, where tailors turned it into the national costume. However, the best *dammar* was imported from Ethiopia, while printed cottons came from the wider world (Wingate 1986, 210, 380–2).

Ibn Battuta noted as early as the fourteenth century that Mogadishu's "unequalled" cotton textiles were exported "to Egypt and elsewhere" (Gibb 1962, 374). Although exports to Egypt had ceased by early modern times, Somalia's Benadir coast continued to send cotton wares to other parts of eastern Africa into the twentieth century. Exports by sea were estimated at three hundred sixty thousand to three hundred eighty thousand pieces a year in the 1840s, and much cloth also went inland into southern Ethiopia (Alpers 1983, 77–89; Reese 1996, 95–6). Mogadishu contained around a thousand weaving households in the 1840s, with smaller numbers in other Benadir towns, and raw cotton was imported from India. These textiles found their main market in southern Ethiopia, but were still regularly sent by sea to Mombasa and north Somali ports (Guillain 1856–7, II, 531–2, 535 and III, 148–9, 172, 323).

Highland Christian Ethiopia produced similar white cottons for its own densely settled territory (Pankhurst 1968, 257–60; Schaedler 1987, 93–9, 396–423). Gondar and Axum, in the north, were traditional centers of production, together with Adowa, Ankobar, and Harar (Lamb 2005, 108; Pankhurst 1968, 257). Reports of travelers from the sixteenth century suggest that cotton cloth was slowly becoming the normal form of dress, gradually replacing skins and hides. Men were said to have adopted cloth before women, and "Semitic" peoples before others (Simoons 1960, 186–7).

Ethiopia's plain white material was made into undergarments, shawls, and turbans, whereas more colorful and elaborate stuffs were typically imported from South Asia (Burton 1894, II, 16–17; Wylde 1901, 246–8). Although vegetable dyes were employed to a limited extent, Ethiopians commonly unraveled imported Indian cloths to obtain colored weft, which they used to decorate the borders of their cloth (Pankhurst 1968, 260). Europeans were impressed by the "closeness, warmth and durability" of this Ethiopian cloth. Male weavers did not usually grow crops, pointing to labor specialization (Darkwah 1975, 145–6). Women spun, as well as embroidering plain cloth (Pankhurst 1968, 32). By the 1840s, some six hundred women were spinning in the imperial palace to supply court weavers (Darkwah 1975, 146).

8.4 ARTISANAL TEXTILES IN THE "SWAHILI WORLD"

To the south, the production of cotton textiles and a little silk was best established in Swahili port cities, from Pate (modern Kenya) to Sofala (modern Mozambique) (Newitt 1987, 203, 206–7). Spindle whorls occur in the archaeological record of Muslim coastal settlements from the tenth century (Horton 1996, 337–41; Kjekshus 1977, 106). Portuguese documents suggest a growth spurt during the fifteenth century, and that even slaves wore a piece of locally woven blue or white cloth from waist to knees. The Portuguese also noted that imported Gujarati stuffs, especially blue ones, were unraveled to obtain colored yarn, for example in Sofala and Pate, although indigo dyeing was practiced in places (Newitt 2002, 31–3; Prestholdt 1998, 24–5, 33).

The Kirimba (Querimba) islands, off the coast of northern Mozambique, produced a *milwani* cloth that was dyed with local indigo, and cotton was sometimes mixed with imported silk yarn. *Milwani* cloth was sold widely in eastern Africa during the sixteenth century, and was one of the "cloths of the land" that Portuguese traders eagerly sought for local commercial operations. However, it was no longer mentioned in a report of 1634 (Newitt 1995, 189–92, 2002, 125, 127–30; Prestholdt 1998, 27–30). That said, its demise was probably due to raiding, provoking the migration of artisans (Newitt, personal communication). As weaving cotton in the wider Rovuma region continued, artisans simply seem to have moved out of the vulnerable islands (Kjekshus 1977, 107). This episode does not, therefore, prove the thesis of underdevelopment.

Offsetting collapse in one area was the rise of new industries elsewhere. Thus Zanzibar only became a center of textile production after the sultans of Oman moved their main residence to the island in the early nineteenth century (Guillain 1856–7, III, 342). Cotton weaving grew there from the 1850s, conducted in the open air. The wares of local weavers could be inspected on the pavements of the town in the 1860s (Kjekshus 1977, 105–6).

Most East African output was *machira*, which was made into hammocks, litters, blankets, cloaks, and belts (Davison and Harries 1980, 181–91, note 23). This was a coarse, unbleached cloth, a kind of cheap and durable homespun. Richard Burton criticized its "loose texture" and averred that "when it is dry it is rough and unpleasant, when wet, heavy, comfortless as leather, and it cannot look clean, as it is never bleached" (Burton 1860, II, 311, cited in Kjekshus 1977, 108). However, *machira* was widely traded, notably in exchange for gold dust on the Zimbabwean plateau (Alpers 1975, 24–5, 55; Newitt 1995, 28, 66, 75, 78, 94, 141, 214, 232, 239). The cloth was also used for currency, tax, bride price, and booty, and as an index of wealth and prestige (Davison and Harries 1980, 187).

Isolated tax figures suggest that the cost of *machira* roughly halved in the eighteenth century, pointing to increasing productivity (Rita-Ferreira 1999, 118). Portuguese reports indicate that output was rising, and that the cloth continued to find a ready market on the Zimbabwean plateau (Bhila 1982, 122, 131).

Most striking, *machira* production survived deliberate Portuguese attempts to suffocate it. From 1750, colonial officials considered that local weaving was reducing potential cloth imports from India, and thus negatively affecting tax revenues (Isaacman 1972, 66, 73–5, 199, 201). In 1750, the Junta do Comercio (Board of Trade) therefore suggested banning the cultivation of cotton in the lower Zambezi valley. This was judged to be unenforceable, as was an equally impractical scheme of 1753 to buy up all available raw cotton to sell it in India and China (Lobato 1957, 241–2; Machado 2005, 110). In the event, the Portuguese proved incapable of stifling the production and sale of *machira* cloth (Mudenge 1988, 187). Moreover, the mixed-race lords of the lower Zambezi's *prazo* estates undermined the stance of Portuguese officials, as they demanded *machira* cloth as tribute from their African "serfs" (*colonos*) (Isaacman 1972, 66; Newitt 1995, 232, 239).

In any event, *machira* cloth production was still flourishing in the *prazo* region in the mid-nineteenth century, when David Livingstone noted that it was preferred to imports for many purposes (Alpers 1975, 25, 35, note 86). Indeed, imported yarn, initially from North America, allowed artisans to weave "lighter and finer cloths." By the 1890s, imported colored yarn enabled the production of new intricately patterned designs, perhaps influenced by Malagasy traditions (Davison and Harries 1980, 181–3, 189; Mack 1993, 303–4).

Cotton in the interior of East Africa faced much competition from bark, raffia, leather, and skins (Alpers 1975, 16, 21; Beinart 1982, 24–5; Cuypers 2004; Darish 1989, 117–40; Gillow 2003; Picton and Mack 1989, 33–43, 83–90, 131; Vansina 1998). Nevertheless, there was patchy spinning and weaving of cotton, from the Great Lakes down to what are today the northern Transvaal and Natal. Wild cotton frequently provided the raw material, although there was some cultivation (Alpers 1975, 16, 21–2, 25; Davison and Harries 1980, 175–81, 187). Richard Burton reported in 1860 that he found looms in every village, and another traveler wrote that he found two to three looms in each village in 1891. Weavers in the center of today's Tanzania produced striped and checked materials in yellow and black. Around 1900, the Haya, to the west of Lake Victoria, had only just learned how to weave from their Nyamwezi neighbors, and were experimenting with new types of cloth (Kjekshus 1977, 107–9).

8.5 EARLY MODERN TECHNOLOGY AND PRODUCTION SYSTEMS

Textile technology remains the least researched aspect of the early modern story. The oft-repeated mantra that methods of production stagnated in Africa is clearly incorrect, even if economic historians find few or no mentions of techniques in documents, and archaeologists lament the perishable nature of wood. Technical change did not necessarily imply more intricate designs or weaves, the interest of art historians, but rather faster production, in greater quantities, more cheaply, and in more varied formats. However, such techniques required some investment and training, and the equipment generally became less portable.

Traders were one probable source of technical change. They specified designs, provided market information, controlled quality, purchased finished textiles, and shipped them to near and distant markets. Thus Indian and Portuguese traders commercialized *machira* together with Indian cottons (Antunes 1992, 127; Newitt 1995, 28; Prestholdt 1998, 283, note 111). Nyamwezi traders, from today's central Tanzania, were active over a wide area during the nineteenth century, spreading techniques of cotton weaving to new regions (Kjekshus 1977, 108).

There were occasional examples of putting-out arrangements, and of merchant-owned workshops. In sixteenth-century Madagascar, where Portuguese and Arab merchants competed keenly for local textiles, cloths were woven to order in individual homes in the north of the island (Kent 1970, 69; Newitt 1995, 28; Prestholdt 1998, 30). Wealthy Arab and Somali merchants of the Benadir coast owned textile workshops, although they were far from dominating production (Cassanelli 1988, 312).

Coerced labor was common in workshops. Slavery had advantages in terms of training and retaining skilled labor, and Muslim scholars frowned on other forms of compulsion (Clarence-Smith 2006). Slaves thus manned the royal workshops of Tasi, in the Sudan, in 1839 (Ewald 1990, 87).

However, slavery interacted with other forms of labor. Most Somali weavers in the 1840s were free, albeit of low caste, weaving full time and buying their food on the market, and assisted by slaves, family members, and clients (Alpers 1983, 81, 84; Guillain 1856–7, II, 531; Reese 1996, 96–8). Unlike spinning, a prestigious occupation, weaving in Christian Ethiopia was allocated to Muslims, Jews, and those of low caste (Levine 1974, 56–7;

Pankhurst 1968, 32, 40–1, 257–9). Men wove on the African mainland, whereas women did so in Madagascar, and women tended to dominate spinning everywhere (Kjekshus 1977, 109; Levine 1974, 113, 153; Mack 1989, 21; Schaedler 1987, 396–423).

Spinning wheels speeded up and cheapened the production of yarn, albeit at some cost in quality (Kuhn 1988). The evidence is sparse for eastern Africa, but the dynamism of Somalia's Benadir workshops was due partly to wheels, which produced four types of yarn in the 1840s. No date is given for their adoption, and they were probably simple spindle-wheels, lacking the crank, treadle, and flyer that enhanced the productivity of Saxon wheels (Guillain 1856–7, II, 532). As for Ethiopia, East Africa and Madagascar, they remained wedded to the hand spindle (Alpers 1975, 24–5; Grandidier 1928, 167; Kjekshus 1977, 106, 108; Pankhurst 1968, 258). In the Rukwa valley in 1899, in modern Tanzania, men spun with a "long spindled spool," rubbed between the palm of the hand and the thigh (Kjekshus 1977, 107–9). Christian missionaries tried to introduce spinning wheels to Madagascar in 1822, but the technique failed to take root after an English artisan returned home (Ellis 1838, I, 324, 327). Ambitious water-driven machines proved ill adapted to Malagasy conditions, and were rapidly abandoned (Fee 2002, 90, note 14).

Foot-operated treadles, lifting and lowering two fixed heddles, freed the weaver's hands to work more rapidly, and pit looms fitted with such treadles appeared in the settled communities of the Middle East and South Asia from around the beginning of the Common Era. Pits reduced the size of the wooden frame containing the loom and kept the yarn moist, thus less likely to break. As pit looms in northeastern Africa are generally of the Persian rather than Egyptian type, they probably came from the east (Lamb 2005, 98–107, 111–56; Roth 1977). Pit looms were standard by the nineteenth century in settled regions of northeastern Africa, spreading down into what is today northern Kenya (Alpers 1983, 80; Gillow 2003, 160–1; Lamb 2005, 107; Pankhurst 1968, 259–60; Roth 1977, 62–3).

King Tewodros (Theodore) of Ethiopia sought to improve looms, asking Queen Victoria to send artisans. A Protestant missionary arrived in 1855 for this purpose, and Swiss artisans followed (Bates 1979, 30, 55, 68). A photograph, taken in Gondar around 1900, depicts a large "tie-back" form of pit loom, typical of greater Syria and Egypt, which allowed for the weaving of longer and wider pieces (Lamb 2005, 107–10, 140, and plate 96). Such improved pit looms were probably introduced by diasporic traders rather than by European experts.

A kind of double-heddle loom was adopted in eastern Madagascar, seemingly in the eighteenth century. The northeastern coast employed such looms by around 1800, and the technique spread some way down the coast. Moreover, Merina weavers of the island's central plateau displayed knowledge of this technique of weaving at a later period, even though they no longer practiced it. When the Betsimisaraka of the east coast employed a single fixed heddle, they lashed it to the rafters, as in the Persian Gulf (Mack 1987, 84–5, 1989, 21–2, 29–31). A youth trained in England ran a guild that "wove cotton on mechanical looms" from 1826 on Madagascar's plateau, but this missionary initiative failed (Fee 2002, 88–90, notes 14–15).

East Africa, south of the Horn, as well as much of Madagascar, employed the simple horizontal ground loom, adapted from that of Middle Eastern Bedouins. With its fixed single heddle, it was quick and easy to disassemble (Hecht 1989, 61–5; Lamb 2005, 1–6, 62). Ground looms were not necessarily as rudimentary as they are sometimes depicted, however. When the White Fathers sought to revive weaving in the Great Lakes region, one difficulty they faced was that local looms were "very complicated and of a delicate construction" (Kjekshus 1977, 80). Moreover, ground looms wove cloths that were wider than those of West Africa (Davison and Harries 1980, 181–7; Lamb 2005, 31–3; Roth 1977, 40). Possibly reflecting the prevalence of raiding, miniature looms appeared in the interior of Central Africa, raised from the ground, and worked from the side (Lamb 2005, 32).

Other types of loom were occasionally found. Southern Madagascar had Southeast Asian looms, with the warp tensed by the use of a backstrap fitted on a seated weaver (Ellis 1838, I, 325; Fee 2005, 94; Grandidier 1928, 167; Mack 1987, 84–6, 1989, 22–32). Vertical or oblique looms, with a single heddle, existed in forested regions, generally confined to weaving raffia (Schaedler 1987, 65; Vansina 1998, 267).They may have been related to Egypt's vertical "Coptic loom," warp-weighted and with one fixed heddle (Lamb 2005, 61–3, 69, 72–3, 83, 86–8, 91).

Little colored cloth was produced outside Madagascar, but indigo dyeing was practiced in places, perhaps reflecting Arab traditions (Newitt 2002, 31–3; Prestholdt 1998, 24–5, 33). More significant, an anonymous author noted in the mid-eighteenth century that the Malagasy were imitating cloth from Bengal and the Coromandel Coast, suggesting incipient painting or printing (Peers 2004, 145).

8.6 THE PERSISTENCE OF ARTISANAL TEXTILES IN THE "AGE OF EMPIRE"

David Edgerton has argued persuasively that new technologies rarely simply displace old ones. Rather, novel techniques lead to resistance and adaptation

(Edgerton 2008). Tax policies led to the underreporting of Africa's artisanal output, while indirect rule and local rituals maintained a culturally protected niche for handmade textiles (Renne 1995, 128–43). Whereas hand spinning was adversely affected by imports of factory-made yarn, weavers, dyers, and tailors viewed imports of yarn, plain cloth, and chemical dyes as a godsend. Moreover, new modes of transport extended local markets (Johnson 1978; Munro 1984, 62–3). Intermediate goods for textile artisans only came from the West for a brief period. Favored by the provisions of the Congo Free Trade Zone set up in 1885, Indian yarn and cloth flooded into eastern African markets from the 1890s, followed by Japanese products after 1914 (Clarence-Smith 1989a, 176, 1989b).

New or reconstructed crafts emerged during the colonial period (Munro 1984, 63). Tailoring was not entirely novel, but it changed out of all recognition in response to treadle-powered and electric sewing machines, employed in households and workshops (Godley 2001). The embellishment of cloth by hand also flourished, as embroidery and lace came to be traded on a large scale around the globe (Clarence-Smith 2004, 449–51).

The Benadir coast of southern Somalia is the best-studied case of artisanal production in the Age of Empire. From around the 1880s, imported machine-made yarn, increasingly chemically dyed, became a significant intermediate good for local weavers (Alpers 1983, 87–92). Somalis still preferred locally woven to imported cloth in the 1890s, and weaving in Mogadishu was "flourishing," with substantial imports of yarn (Cattelani 1897, 67, 72–3, 88–9, 135; Robecchi-Bricchetti 1899, 618–20). South Asian yarn quickly replaced the Western product. Aden received nearly 2.5 million pounds of yarn from British India in 1894–5, much of which was redistributed along the Somali coast (Great Britain 1896, 46, 56). Exports of Benadir cloth continued, even as imports of European cloth grew (Chiesi 1909, 347–53).

Commercial disruptions caused by the First World War led to a renaissance in Somali weaving, with men taking up the craft in substantial numbers. India was the chief source of imported yarn, with Japan of growing importance (Alpers 1983, 87–93). A report of 1920 noted that "a few hundred" looms were active in Mogadishu alone, worked by men. Other towns along the Benadir Coast also produced cloth, notably Merka, and there were exports to Mombasa and Zanzibar. Furthermore, women could still be seen spinning, despite imports of machine-made yarn (Stefanini 1922, 39). As late as the 1950s, more than one thousand households wove on the Benadir coast. Local textiles had become prestige goods for special occasions. Merchants provided yarn in a putting-out system, decried by Marxists as rank exploitation (Alpers 1983, 93–7). Somalia also exported artisanal caps and shawls to neighboring countries (Administration Italienne 1954, 79–80).

From the late nineteenth century, India supplied yellow and blue yarns for Ethiopian weavers, while grey, unbleached cloth came sequentially from North America, India, and Japan (Pankhurst 1968, 261, 402–4, 407–8, 416). The sector remained buoyant after the devastation caused by the Italian occupation of 1935–41 (Levine 1974, 113). In the early 1950s, women of the northwest spun white cotton yarn with spindles, while colored yarn was imported. Male indigenous Muslims worked in pit looms, but there were also itinerant weavers, who carried a light loom on their shoulder (Simoons 1960, 187). In Jimma, in the southwest, plain white shawls for men and women were the main product, with weaving relegated to men of low caste (Lewis 2001, 53–4).

Sudanese weavers continued to produce plain white *dammar*. Indeed, the introduction of new strains of cotton, aimed at boosting exports of raw materials, may have had the unintended consequence of improving the quality of yarn for local weavers (Issawi 1966, 479, 484). Local cloth held its own despite rising imports of cotton textiles, which accounted for about a quarter of the colony's total import bill at the time of the First World War (Great Britain 1920, 136, 148).

French officials predicted the imminent demise of handweaving in Madagascar after the conquest of 1896, but some French people sought to revive local crafts. A school of applied arts, set up in 1925, preserved cloths that were no longer fashionable, and contributed to the prestige of handweaving (Fee 2002, 68–9, 74–5, 81). A revival of weaving during the interwar years also served the purpose of stocking colonial exhibitions (Peers 1995, 47). Simultaneously, wearing local *lamba* became a sign of opposition to Westernization (Fee 2002, 61). Malagasy weavers worked with imported yarns in the 1920s, as well as the locally spun article (Kusimba, Odland, and Bronson 2004, 34, introduction by Kusimba, citing Ralph Linton).

Various authors similarly proclaimed the death of handmade textiles in East Africa (Davison and Harries 1980, 189–91; Pearson 1969, 124; Silver 1984, 44–5; Swainson 1980, 26). However, Helge Kjekshus notes that Rukwa cotton textiles, in Tanganyika, "defied extinction largely through the patronage of the Christian missions." Officials also stimulated production to combat shortages of cloth during the Second World War (Kjekshus 1977, 109 (quote), and 80, 106–9). *Machira* cloth production persisted in the lower Zambezi valley, and photographic and descriptive evidence of weaving across the Central African plateau was common until the First World War and even later (Davison and Harries 1980, 181, 185). Moreover, Christian missionaries made considerable efforts to teach Western methods of spinning, weaving, and sewing, for example in Southern Rhodesia (Zimbabwe) (Jeater 2007, 105, 146, 158).

Indian mills became major suppliers of grey and bleached plain cotton cloth to eastern Africa from the 1890s (Pirio 1982, 174–5). From the 1890s, some of the plain cloth was locally printed, as South Asian merchants in Swahili towns employed wooden blocks, on the Indian model, to print popular *kanga*. These were two-piece rectangular wrappers for women, with written mottos (Fair 2001, 68, 80; Hilger 1995, 44–5; Zawawi 2005, 16). Printing blocks were increasingly consigned to museums after 1918, as foreign imitations of *kanga* flooded in (Fair 2001, 76–83). Nevertheless, old wooden blocks still exist in smaller settlements such as Lamu, where printed textiles have been produced until "quite recently" (Mack 1993, 304).

Embroidery also achieved a new prominence, with men, often Islamic scholars, embroidering skullcaps in coastal Swahili towns (Bhacker 1992, 134; Martin 1971, 538–41; Reese 1996, 94). However, these caps, "delicately worked with fine stitching," met severe competition from cheap imports in Dar es Salaam by the 1950s (Leslie 1963, 110).

South Asian immigrants initially dominated workshops making garments (Chauleur 1979, 111; Kilby 1975, 477). Some tailors had a background in textiles, notably Hindus from the Khatri caste of weavers (Enthoven 1920–2, II, 205; Morris 1968, 139–41). In 1952, five hundred seventy-five tailoring units were counted in Tanganyika, scattered around the territory. There were only forty-seven in 1961, but this reflected changing criteria for statistical purposes (Silver 1984, 44, 90, 94–5, 103).

The first tailoring "factory" in South Africa was recorded in 1907 (Werbeloff 1987, 139). Ashkenazi Jews from Lithuania exploited their skills as tailors and their knowledge of local markets as peddlers to develop a fragmented and small-scale garments industry, employing poor Afrikaner farm girls drifting into cities. They benefited greatly from protectionist South African import tariffs after 1925 (Saron and Hotz 1955, 362–5). They then extended their activities into Central Africa (Cinammon 2004). The Bulawayo Clothing Factory, which appeared in the records in 1920, may have been the pioneer (Wolfgang Döpcke, personal communication). Exports to neighboring territories were noted in 1930 (Mosley 1983, 209). In 1938, seventeen small clothing enterprises represented 3.2 percent of Southern Rhodesia's industrial output by value, and their production reached 17 percent of net imports of textiles and clothing (Mlambo, Pangeti, and Phimister 2000, 25; Southern Rhodesia 1946, 63–5). After 1945, modern industrial enterprises came to the fore in finishing South Asian intermediate imports (Kilby 1975, 483).

8.7 MODERN COLONIAL MILLS

Modern textile factories faced colonial hesitation rather than outright hostility (Kilby 1975). Metropolitan workers were perhaps those most consistently opposed to "exporting jobs" to the colonies, and they allied with small metropolitan textile entrepreneurs in declining regions, who feared the loss of protected markets. Colonial officials feared the social and political consequences of proletarianization and urbanization. In contrast, competitive Western textile firms were keen to cut costs by producing overseas. Moreover, metropolitan bureaucrats at times backed manufacturing for military reasons, or to appease nationalist leaders, and were increasingly prepared to grant a measure of tariff protection (Clarence-Smith 1985; Drummond 1974; Havinden and Meredith 1993; Marseille 1984).

Large modern integrated textile mills suffered from excessive protection, as well as diseconomies of scale. Skilled labor and capital were exceedingly costly in Africa, and even unskilled factory labor was expensive, as low productivity generally more than offset low wages. A supply of local raw fibers was a mixed blessing, because of poor quality and irregular deliveries. Entrepreneurs were chiefly attracted to the business by cheap land and hydroelectricity, and by high levels of tariff protection. Colonial regimes frowned on diasporic entrepreneurs, notably South Asians, while showering metropolitan firms with protectionist tariffs, quotas, licenses, and monopolies. These were double-edged swords, for any initial spur to investment came at the cost of structural inefficiency, most obviously reflected in a lack of exports beyond the region (Clarence-Smith 1989a; Kilby 1975).

The rising tide of Japanese imports into the Congo Free Trade Zone in the interwar years acted as a precocious spur to the establishment of modern mills (Austen 1987, 136). In 1925, two Belgian textile producers set up the Société Textile Africaine, or Texaf, in Léopoldville (Kinshasa), at the head of the Congo River navigation system into eastern Africa (Heyse 1938, 7–12; Lacroix 1967, 19–20). In 1927, Texaf obtained a concession to generate its own hydroelectric power, setting up a subsidiary for this purpose in 1930 (Heyse 1936, 329–34). This was a state-of-the-art integrated spinning and weaving mill. By 1930, the mill consumed about a fifth of the raw cotton grown in the Congo (Vellut 1985).

The impact of the early 1930s recession on Texaf was severe, but the company survived (Heyse 1938, 7–12). Texaf became a holding company in 1934, and the textile business was renamed Société Usines Textiles de Léopoldville, or Utexléo (Heyse 1938, 7–12). An unspecified Belgian bank acquired a controlling stake, and substituted labor for capital. Existing machines were not replaced, and real wages were compressed (Strihou 1961, 51–2, 62, 65, 78). Output went from 930 tons in 1931 to 1,640 tons in 1940, accounting for about a third of Congolese consumption (Belgium 1949, 576).

The Second World War inaugurated a period of rapid expansion in the Congo. Utexléo took on more workers, and acquired some good spindles and some indifferent secondhand looms in 1942–3. Production rose by 63.4 percent between 1940 and 1945, and the company imported foreign cloth to meet excess demand (Strihou 1961, 52–4). Utexléo's output reached 2,670 tons by 1945 (Belgium 1949, 576). After the war, Utexléo invested more and improved the quality of its finished goods (Strihou 1961, 53–5). Concurrently, Flemish industrialists established FILTISAF in Albertville (Kalemie) in 1946 (Vellut 1985).

The 1925 Belgian initiative sent shock waves through the Portuguese colonies. Although only northern Angola and northern Mozambique lay in the Congo Free Trade Zone, Léopoldville was the hub of a web of water and rail transport links across the continent. Expressing fears that the products of the Congolese factory would invade the Mozambican market, a leading Portuguese entrepreneur requested permission in 1926 to establish a similar industry in Mozambique. However, his plea was rejected (Macedo 1939, 280). Indeed, Antonio Salazar's conservative and authoritarian regime, shaken by the Great Depression, passed a decree in 1932, which guaranteed high fixed prices for colonial raw cotton in Portugal in return for formally prohibiting the creation of textile mills in the colonies (Clarence-Smith 1985, 84–6, 163–5).

Although British East Africa lay entirely within the Congo Free Trade Zone, and the proportion of textile imports from Japan rose to 70 percent during the interwar years, Britain failed to support initiatives to set up local textile mills. It was to no avail that imports had grown beyond a notional threshold for import substitution, and that a free trade area covered Kenya, Uganda, and Tanganyika from 1924. Nicola Swainson blames the Lancashire lobby for this outcome (Swainson 1980, 26–7, 43–5, 124).[1] In 1937, when an interdepartmental committee examined the question, the Colonial Office poured cold water on arguments for a protected "infant industry." Officials

[1] For the general British colonial position, see Havinden and Meredith 1993, 159, 168–74.

insisted on levying an excise tax on local production that would be equal to tariffs on imports (Drummond 1974, 441–2).

Shortages in the Second World War led to a British reappraisal. A restrictive licensing system, introduced in 1943, applied to cotton yarn, piece goods, and blankets. In 1959, a single textile mill had been authorized for Kenya and Uganda respectively, although several licenses were granted thereafter (International Bank 1962, 275; Swainson 1980, 116–21, 125). By 1963, the combined textile, apparel, and footwear sector employed 3,701 people in Kenya, and a further 3,250 in Uganda (Kilby 1975, 477–8). Uganda's Nyanza Mills, or Nytil, built in Jinja in 1954, integrated spinning, weaving, and finishing. It was built to consume cheap hydroelectricity from the Owen Falls dam, as well as local raw cotton (Elkan 1961, 5–7, 59–60; International Bank 1962, 275; Kilby 1975, 478; Pearson 1969, 125). A textile mill was set up in Thika, Kenya, toward the end of the 1950s, and exported within British East Africa (Mosley 1983, 212, 222; Swainson 1980, 125, 128). In 1952, Tanganyika had two dyeing firms employing eighty people and a cotton-weaving shed with thirty workers. By 1961, there were five weaving mills in the Dar es Salaam area, all small and processing imported yarn (Silver 1984, 74–5, 90–1, 94–5, 102–3. See also Werbeloff 1987, 163–4).

The British generally backed metropolitan capitalists against South Asian rivals, even though the latter had a proven historical track record in manufacturing (Clarence-Smith 1989b). Indians repeatedly asked for permission to manufacture textiles, for which much expertise existed in Gujarat, and the only textile mill in Kenya in the 1950s was a small Indian concern (Swainson 1980, 26–7, 125). Nevertheless, it was Calico Printers of Manchester who developed the large Jinja mill in Uganda. Despite benefiting from a local monopoly and cheap hydroelectricity, the firm lost so much money that the Uganda Development Corporation was obliged to buy the mill in 1957. Astonishingly, Calico Printers was retained as managing agent, turning a profit only because tariff protection was raised to a stiff 30 percent (International Bank 1962, 275; Kilby 1975, 478; Pearson 1969, 125–6). However, in 1963, during the decade of independence, the South Asian firm of Mehta was building a new textile mill, symbolically situated on the opposite bank of the Nile from the Jinja plant (Pearson 1969, 127).

Economic dislocation in the Second World War impelled Salazar to set up textile industries in Angola and Mozambique, mainly owned by metropolitan capitalists (Clarence-Smith 1985, 164–5). In 1950, a large textile factory was nearing completion in central Mozambique (Pitcher 1993, 163–4). Located at Vila Pery (Chimoio), on the railway inland from Beira, it was close to the frontier with Southern Rhodesia (Zimbabwe), and about twenty miles from an abundant source of cheap hydroelectric power on the Revue River. The skilled workers were immigrants from Portugal (Spence 1951, 83). In 1958, this factory consumed 1,774 tons of raw cotton for 14,500 spindles and 460 looms, and in 1960, it employed some 2,000 people. It was reputed to be the largest cotton textile factory in sub-Saharan Africa. In 1954, three textile establishments in Mozambique accounted for more investment than any other economic sector, apart from sugar (Bravo 1963, 82–5; Gersdorff 1958, 66–7). Artur Cupertino de Miranda's Banco Português do Atlântico, founded in 1942 on the basis of the remittance business from Brazil, provided much of the capital for the Sociedade Algodoeira de Fomento Colonial, with textile mills in both Mozambique and Angola. Concession companies, which purchased compulsorily cultivated colonial raw cotton, were junior partners (Clarence-Smith 1985, 169; Pitcher 1993, 163–5).

Some Western entrepreneurs functioned in a more diasporic mode. Roberto Barattolo, an Italian trader in Eritrea before the Second World War, was imprisoned by the British in 1941 and repatriated to Italy. He returned to Asmara to set up the Cotonoficio Barattolo in 1950. From an initial investment in spinning, he moved to weaving and finishing, and then to clothing, while simultaneously going upstream into raw cotton and ginning. By the time the Ethiopian Derg nationalized the enterprise in 1975, this was perhaps the most fully integrated textile company in eastern Africa. It had grown up gradually and organically, under the watchful eye of an entrepreneur who took a leading position in the resident Italian community.[2] In contrast, Somalia's Société de Manufactures Cotonnières Somalies, located in the capital Mogadishu (Muqdisho) and providing about a sixth of internal consumption in 1954, seems to have been owned by an Italian firm (Administration Italienne 1954, 81–2).

Southern African settlers wielded a political power that generally stimulated precocious industrial development, but textiles were an exception. British Central Africa's white miners and farmers opposed protection for consumer goods that might force up the wage rate and thus damage their export prospects. In addition, settler communities were determined to frustrate the economic advance of South Asian communities, most likely to prosper in the textile sector. Furthermore, Lancashire lobbied vigorously against protective tariffs (Brett 1973, 266–81; Mlambo et al. 2000, 12–13). At the imperial Ottawa Conference of 1932, the Southern Rhodesian regime made specific concessions on imports of British cotton piece goods

[2] http://www.quirinale.it/elementi/DettaglioOnoroficenze.aspx?decorato=612.

in return for British guarantees on Southern Rhodesian exports of mineral products (Cole 1968, 29).

The Southern Rhodesian government thus only intervened to encourage the cotton textile industry from 1941, as the war affected supplies. The authorities developed spinning at Gatooma from 1943, with 17,500 spindles installed by 1948. David Whitehead and Sons, from Lancashire, set up the first large weaving mill in 1951, with production starting two years later. A second spinning mill followed in 1952, with attached weaving and knitting units. The government privatized the Gatooma mill by 1960, seeing public ownership as a temporary aberration (Guillie 1995, 52; Kilby 1975, 483; Mlambo et al. 2000, 31). Exports were stimulated by free trade agreements with South Africa and by the market provided by the Federation of Central Africa from 1953 to 1963 (Mlambo et al. 2000, 37–8, 42–5; Mosley 1983, 212, 218–19). The textile and garments industries grew at an average annual rate of 20.8 percent from 1946 to 1953. By 1957–8, spinning and weaving employed 6,574 people in twenty-six establishments. Up to a third of Southern Rhodesia's textile output was destined for South Africa in the 1950s (Mlambo et al. 2000, 31, 45–7). By 1964, exports of textiles were worth roughly half as much as imports (Mosley 1983, 218–19).

Although South Africa industrialized early and extensively, textiles were not the leading sector. Secondary industries were a preserve for employing poor whites, but they were particularly costly to employ in textiles (Cronje 1952, 24–5; Saron and Hotz 1955, 364–5). A Cape blanket factory was founded in 1891, and woolen and cotton blankets were the country's only significant textile products for a long time. In 1933–4, there were twelve textile establishments employing 2,358 workers. Once again, the real boom came during and after the Second World War, with high levels of tariff protection, so that by around 1960 there were 104 factories and 29,142 workers (Beinart 1982, 24–5; Cronje 1952, 24; Du Toit 1978, 33, 37–8, 43). In 1967, 71,000 employees were recorded (Chauleur 1979, 113).

Fickle metropolitan capital came to the fore in this late spurt in South Africa. Textile firms from Britain, France, and Italy lacked electricity and other inputs at home to meet shortages due to the war in 1945, and relocated to South Africa. The low productivity of African labor was a disincentive, however, and investment fell drastically after 1951, as postwar global shortages turned to glut (Cronje 1952, 26–7; Kilby 1975, 483). Local Jewish concerns in the garments business, moving upstream to produce cloth, showed a more long-term commitment to the industry (Saron and Hotz 1955, 362–4).

8.8 THE ARTICULATION OF MODERN COLONIAL FACTORY PRODUCTION WITH ARTISANS

Modern textile factories in eastern Africa displayed little or no synergy with small producers (Pearson 1969, 124). Both Western and settler industrialists were unaccustomed to working with artisans. Indeed, many managers, isolated in their gleaming new factories and cosseted by officials, seem not to have realized that there were textile artisans at all. Discrimination on grounds of culture and race and weak or nonexistent representative institutions made it all the more difficult to bridge the cultural gap. The strongest linkages were in South Africa, where Jewish garment entrepreneurs and workers were legally deemed white.

Overall, entrepreneurs in Africa deliberately turned their backs on artisans, seeking out isolated hydroelectric sites where they could obtain cheap power and control the entire production process from start to finish. In particular, factories rarely supplied yarn to weavers, in stark contrast to the situation in Asia. Tellingly, the International Bank for Reconstruction and Development strongly criticized the Jinja mill in Uganda for not selling yarn or plain cloth within the colony. British managers seem to have feared competition from those who might purchase semi-manufactures from their mill (International Bank 1962, 275). That said, Utexléo's output of yarn rose twice as fast as that of cloth in the 1950s, suggesting that this Congolese enterprise may have been selling yarn to artisans (Strihou 1961, 55).

Clothing workshops had somewhat more positive links with modern mills, for integrated factories rarely extended to producing garments. Small workshops, making items of clothing mainly for the African market, thus purchased cloth locally (Döpcke 1992, 104–5; Mlambo et al. 2000, 25; Wilde 1971, II, 7, 3–4).

8.9 THE IMPACT OF INDEPENDENCE ON MODERN MILLS

Independence from around 1960 was accompanied by policies of import substitution, which were particularly ill suited to small extroverted economies (Chauleur 1979; Werbeloff 1987). Allied policies of modernization and state ownership made matters worse. Inefficient and corrupt independent governments interfered incessantly, whether they owned or regulated mills. Far from encouraging diasporic entrepreneurs, they sought to reduce their share of manufacturing (Morris 1968, 145).

From the 1960s to the 1980s, the general trend was thus for states to encourage large, integrated, and highly protected textile mills to meet the demands of restricted national markets. Thought was rarely given to exporting competitively within regions, let alone on the world market. Such factories seemed to be quite successful for a while, but only at the cost of ramping up protectionist tariffs, which already stood at an effective average of 269 percent for textiles in Tanzania in 1966. Foreign exchange shortages then throttled imports of inputs, fuel, and spare parts. Power shortages multiplied, labor discipline collapsed, maintenance ceased, productivity plummeted, location of new plants obeyed political criteria, debts ballooned, capacity utilization fell, and smuggled imports of foreign textiles soared. Private mills did better than state-owned ones, but only marginally (Chauleur 1979, 103–10, 109–13; Valk 1996, 146–52, 216–42; Werbeloff 1987).

As the "white elephants" of modernization theory and Marxism became increasingly discredited, export markets for textiles were created by multifiber agreements from 1973, and international agencies pushed strongly for export substitution on Asian lines from the 1980s. However, international agreements provided highly artificial stimuli, liable to sudden and devastating changes as international politics shifted. Foot-loose international entrepreneurs were then all too quick to move on to new pastures (Valk 1996, 107–10, 128, 137). The ending of the World Trade Organization's textile and clothing quota system in 2005 was a particularly heavy blow for Africa (Maliti 2005).

An alternative, albeit weak, reaction to the disastrous policies adopted at independence was to foster neglected and long-suffering textile artisans. This policy shift was aided by a glorification of precolonial "authenticity." However, this all too easily degenerated into folklore, which was desultorily marketed to sparse foreign tourists (Guillie 1995, 51; Polakoff 1982, 4–10).

After the Derg toppled Haile Selassie in Ethiopia in 1974, the "commanding heights" of the textile industry, at that time the third largest in sub-Saharan Africa, passed into the hands of the state-owned National Textile Corporation. In 1982, this body controlled twenty-one mills and employed some twenty-nine thousand people. Only some thirty small-scale knitting workshops and two small spinning and weaving enterprises fell outside the state's net. The sector suffered from poor and uneven productivity. Some two-thirds of total output came from the Diredawa mill, an old mill founded in 1943, but which was efficiently managed by a Japanese enterprise (Werbeloff 1987, 93–5).

A tale of two mills in Tanzania similarly indicates how state-owned textile plant could come in very different forms. Following the Arusha Declaration's call for economic self-sufficiency in 1967, the government set up two factories. Mwanza Textiles, only partially state owned, installed the most modern automated machinery that the West had to offer, at immense cost. The factory proceeded to lose money by the bucketful. In contrast, Friendship Mill, entirely state owned, was equipped with antiquated secondhand Chinese machinery, some of which had been designed in the 1930s. Employing far more workers, and thus soaking up urban unemployment, it was quite consistently profitable. Indeed, the Friendship Mill at times outperformed privately managed mills (James 1995, 35–6).

International sanctions constrained settler-ruled South Africa and Southern Rhodesia (Zimbabwe), but they obtained capital from Israel and Taiwan, and exported some of their output. By the mid-1980s, the Frame Group was South Africa's eighth largest company in terms of share capital, employed some twenty-two thousand people, and was allegedly the largest producer of blankets in the world. Not only did it spin, weave, and finish cloth, but it also produced garments, which was quite a common pattern in South Africa. The Tongaat Group, the country's second largest textile producer, even integrated upstream into cotton ginning (Werbeloff 1987, 140–2, 180). In contrast, Zimbabwe's textile sector declined rapidly after real independence had been achieved in 1980 (Valk 1996, 142–4; Werbeloff 1987, 181–2). Cone Textiles, the largest employer, went into liquidation in 1995, and David Whitehead, a Lonrho subsidiary, struggled to survive (Guillie 1995, 52).

The factory sector turned to copying imported finished cloth specially made for the African market, with Malagasy factories turning out brightly colored *kanga* with proverbs in Malagasy (Fee 2002, 69). Producers in Kenya, notably the integrated Rift Valley Textiles (Rivatex) of Eldoret, initially succeeded in ousting foreign *kanga* (Hilger 1995, 44). The same was true in Tanzania, but prices then rose above those of imports (Zawawi 2005, 29). Maurer Textiles of Switzerland managed Sotexki in Kisangani, in the eastern Congo, producing *chitenge* (*kitenge*), but political uncertainty and Asian copies undermined the enterprise (Guillie 1995, 51). Zambian factories developed "imiwax" in the 1970s to replace foreign copies of wax-dyed *batik* from Southeast Asia. However, by the 1990s, Mulungushi Textiles was under such pressure from imports that it switched to exporting undyed yarn and grey cloth (Guillie 1995, 51–2).

Imports of cheap, or even free, secondhand clothes from the West became a new and major threat to textile output in eastern Africa from the 1980s, although such imports were generally underreported or even unreported (Valk 1996, 116, note 25, 216). They undercut most kinds of local business, even if T-shirts, printed with topical local material, were able to compete (Guillie 1995, 52; Hilger 1995, 45). Zambian enterprises, unable to compete, sold their sewing machines for a song and witnessed the erosion of skills (Matheson 2000).

The alternative strategy promoted by multilateral organizations, namely export-substituting industrialization, remains to prove its worth. Italy's Zambaiti Group, an old textile company, bought Asmara's Cotonoficio Barattolo for the symbolic sum of one dollar in 2004. With experience of producing in China, the firm invested E13 million to revive the company. Integrated from spinning to clothing, Zambaiti Eritrea (Zaer) has 85 percent of its output earmarked for export.[3]

However, the experience of Mauritius casts a shadow on this strategy. The small island country experimented with Export Processing Zones from 1970, in order to lessen dependence on sugar. Liberal tax, customs, capital transfer, and labor regulations attracted foreign textile companies. They also obtained cheap water, electricity, and rents, as well as guarantees against nationalization. The policy was intensified from 1982, leading to a boom in the production of cloth and garments for export to the West, with about one hundred thousand workers employed by the mid-1990s. Unfortunately, this artificially generated sector could not stand up to growing Asian competition and global trade liberalization, and was in a serious crisis by 2003, which shows no signs of abating (Neveling 2010, 76–82; Valk 1996, 138–41).

8.10 THE PERSISTENCE OF ARTISANAL TEXTILES IN THE ERA OF INDEPENDENCE

Despite this official love-in with large integrated modern textile mills, the neglected and even despised artisans of eastern Africa survived (Valk 1996, 165). They also had to overcome major new hurdles, such as shortages of imported yarn, due to protectionism and foreign exchange crises, and outages in electricity supply (Renne 1995, 146). South Asian preponderance in tailoring, for example in Uganda, engendered additional official hostility (Wilde 1971, XII, 2, 6).

[3] http://www.eritreaeritrea.com/zambaiti_eritrea_plc.htm.

The Horn of Africa retained the healthiest artisanal sector. Ethiopia's weavers kept producing through the Marxist rule of the Derg after 1974, although makers of garments were forced into ineffective cooperatives (Werbeloff 1987, 94, 96). By the 1990s, weaving was in full swing again, with traditional double-heddle pit looms. Indeed, Ethiopia was declared an exception to the overall decline of artisanal textiles in eastern Africa (Gillow 2003, 157–60, 164).

Sudan was unusual in formally acknowledging the existence of an artisanal textile sector after independence in 1956. In addition to a program of modern mills, the government initiated weaving sheds containing up to 100 looms. In 1970, it was estimated that "handicraft producers" met about half the domestic demand for textiles, and the sector remained dynamic in the 1990s (Valk 1996, 103; Werbeloff 1987, 156). Tailoring was of further importance, often in the hands of West African immigrants (Yamba 1995, 98–9, 112, 140).

Tanzania's brand of humanistic socialism favored artisans, at least on paper. The National Small Industries Corporation was set up in 1967, providing subsidized rents for tailoring and other workshops, albeit with poor facilities and a reluctance to eject defaulting tenants (Wilde 1971, X, 3–7). By the 1980s, there was a conscious policy, largely borrowed from India, of developing small-scale textile manufacturing. On the one hand, there was to be a "decentralized" sector, typically consisting of "semi-urban" units, with knitting machines and ten to forty semiautomatic looms. On the other hand, there was to be a "manual" sector in rural areas. Three "handloom manufacturing units" were charged with distributing looms, of an unspecified type. Tanzania preached this model to fellow members of SADCC, but with indifferent success (Werbeloff 1987, 164, 166). Although it is unclear how these policies panned out on the ground, Gillow seems excessively pessimistic in asserting that handloom weaving has become merely a matter of "historical interest" (Gillow 2003, 158).

After an initial stress on modernization, Madagascar tipped the balance back toward supporting ancient traditions from 1992. Handweaving was concentrated in specialized quarters, small towns, and villages, especially in the highlands and the south. Weavers exported their wares to other parts of the island through middlemen, while regular fashion shows and sales to tourists helped to gain markets in the West. Output ranged from resurrected noble cloths to cheap loose weaves, the latter competing with imports to meet the needs of poor households. Men wove more often, at least in the capital city, breaking with the ancient gender division of labor. Tailors also worked to express ethnic identities in cloth. However, attempts to use handweaving to relieve extreme rural poverty failed, as did cooperatives, for some capital was needed for weaving, and fiercely independent households had little desire to cooperate (Fee 2002, 67–70, 74–86. See also Peers 1995, 46–7).

The revival of artisanal efforts in Madagascar was accompanied by technical adaptations, even if Valk criticized "outdated technologies" (Valk 1996, 100). Double-heddle treadle looms still existed in the northeast in the 1980s, and there were efforts to spread the technique, build larger looms, and introduce "European looms" (Fee 2002, 78; Gillow 2003, 214; Mack 1989, 31–2; Peers 1995, 47). The most expensive cloths were made with hand-spun yarn on old ground looms, and were colored with natural dyes. There were experiments with new natural fibers, for example a sisal warp. However, most artisans employed chemical dyes and factory-made yarn, including shiny imported synthetic fibers for cheaper wares (Fee 2002, 74–9, 85–6).

Davison and Harries consider that weaving and spinning skills were "almost forgotten" by the 1950s in southeastern Africa, although their own fascinating evidence clearly does not support this pessimistic conclusion. Thus, Shona and Chewa weavers of the 1970s, in Zimbabwe and Malawi respectively, wove belts for ritual purposes, such as spirit possession cults (Davison and Harries 1980, 175, 181, 185, 187–91). Similarly, weavers in Barue were producing *machira* as late as the 1970s (Davison and Harries 1980, 181–2; Lobato 1957, 242). As Africans gradually moved into textiles in South Africa, they embellished machine-made cloth with Ndebele and Zulu beadwork (Guillie 1995, 54).

8.11 CONCLUSION

Textiles formed a sector of modest dimensions in eastern Africa, and yet production persisted throughout the early modern and modern periods. Handicraft techniques progressed and proto-industrial structures emerged, although far too little research has been carried out on the artisanal sector. Modern mills appeared in the twentieth century, but were generally too capital-intensive, overly protected, and poorly articulated with artisanal production. That said, the mills of well-rooted diasporas, notably South Asian and Jewish, fared better than those of Western capitalists, white settlers, or independent governments.

This story gives the lie to extreme theories of underdevelopment, in which Africa was reduced to a source of raw materials and a captive market for foreign manufactures. In reality, South Asian textiles failed to deindustrialize early modern eastern Africa, probably because of rising African productivity. The model proposed here is that merchants reduced costs and uncertainties and spread best technical practice. Western and Asian textile industries more strongly affected the region from the late nineteenth century, but again without fulfilling Dependentista predictions. The existing artisanal sector did not die, not even hand spinning, and new workshops sprang up producing garments with sewing machines.

That said, the consequences of creating a disarticulated cotton textile sector were negative. Large mills had few or no moorings in civil society and were incapable of stimulating artisanal production. Once colonial or settler rule ended, such enterprises either lost the crutches of state support or became "white elephants," draining resources from the wider economy. This was an important factor holding back the emergence of "African tigers." Indeed, the bitter irony of independence has been that nationalists have been passionate about achieving industrialization, and yet have systematically killed the geese that laid the industrial eggs. For the historian, however, the era since independence is little more than the blink of an eyelid. The resilience of eastern Africa's artisanal textile sector in the past is a good augury for its prosperity in the future, and it should certainly act as a spur for better studying its history.

References

Administration Italienne de Tutelle de la Somalie. (1954). *Plans de développement économique de la Somalie, années 1954–1960*. Rome: Istituto Poligrafico dello Stato.

Alpers, Edward A. (1975). *Ivory and Slaves in East Central Africa*. London: Heinemann.

(1983). "Futa Benaadir: Continuity and Change in the Traditional Cotton Textile Industry of Southern Somalia, c.1840–1980." In *Entreprises et Entrepreneurs en Afrique, XIXe et XXe siècles* I: 77–98. Paris: L'Harmattan.

Antunes, Luis Frederico Dias. (1992). "A Actividade da Companhia de Comercio Baneanes de Diu em Moçambique, 1688–1777," MA Thesis, Universidade Nova de Lisboa.

Austen, Ralph. (1987). *African Economic History, Internal Development and External Dependency*. London: James Currey.

Baldry, John. (1982). *Textiles in Yemen: Historical References to Trade and Commerce in Textiles in Yemen, from Antiquity fo Modern Times*. London: British Museum.

Bates, Darrell. (1979). *The Abyssinian Difficulty: The Emperor Theodorus and the Magdala Campaign, 1867–68*. Oxford: Oxford University Press.

Beinart, William. (1982). *The Political Economy of Pondoland, 1860–1930*. Cambridge: Cambridge University Press.
Belgium (1949). Ministère des Colonies, *Plan Décennal Pour Le Développement Économique et Social du Congo Belge*, Brussels: De Visscher.
Bhacker, M. Reda. (1992). *Trade and Empire in Muscat and Zanzibar: Roots of British Domination*. London: Routledge.
Bhila, H. H. K. (1982). *Trade and Politics in a Shona Kingdom: The Manyika and Their African and Portuguese Neighbours, 1575–1902*. London: Longman.
Bravo, Nelson Saraiva. (1963). *A Cultura Algodoeira Na Economia do Norte de Moçambique*. Lisbon: Junta de Investigações do Ultramar.
Brett, E. A. (1973). *Colonialism and Underdevelopment in East Africa, 1919–1939*. London: Heinemann.
Bronson, Bennet. (2004). "Wrapping Up Malagasy Textiles." In *Unwrapping the Textile Traditions of Madagascar*, edited by Chapurukha M. Kusimba, J. Claire Odland, and Bennet Bronson, 164–9. Los Angeles, CA: Fowler Museum.
Burton, R. F. (1860). *The Lake Regions of Central Africa*. London: Longman, Green, Longman, and Roberts.
(1894). *First Footsteps in East Africa or an Exploration of Harar*. London: Tylston and Edwards, 2nd ed.
Campbell, Gwyn. (2005). *An Economic History of Imperial Madagascar, 1750–1895: The Rise and Fall of an Island Empire*. Cambridge: Cambridge University Press.
Cassanelli, Lee V. (1988). "The Ending of Slavery in Italian Somalia: Liberty and the Control of Labor, 1890–1935." In *The End of Slavery in Africa*, edited by Suzanne Miers and Richard Roberts, 308–31. Madison: University of Wisconsin Press.
Cattelani, G. (1897). *L'avvenire Coloniale D'Italia Nel Benadir*. Naples: F. Giannini e Figli.
Chauleur, Pierre. (1979). *L'Afrique Industrielle*. Paris: G. P. Maisonneuve et Larose.
Chiesi, Gustavo. (1909). *La Colonizzazione Europea Nell' Est Africa: Italia, Inghilterra, Germania*. Turin: Unione Tipografico-Editrice Torinese.
Cinnaman. John. (2004). "The Jews of Manicaland," http://www.zjc.org.il/showpage.php?pageid=155.
Clarence-Smith, William G. (1985). *The Third Portuguese Empire, 1825–1975: A Study in Economic Imperialism*. Manchester: Manchester University Press.
(1989a). "The Effects of the Great Depression of the 1930s on Industrialisation in Equatorial and Central Africa." In *The Economies of Africa and Asia in the Inter-War Depression*, edited by Ian Brown, 170–202. London: Routledge.
(1989b). "Indian Business Communities in the Western Indian Ocean in the Nineteenth Century." *The Indian Ocean Review*, 2(4): 18–21.
(2004). "Middle Eastern Migrants in the Philippines: Entrepreneurs and Cultural Brokers." *Asian Journal of Social Science*, 32(3): 425–57.
(2006). *Islam and the Abolition of Slavery*. London: Hurst & Co.
(2009). "The Production of Cotton Textiles in Early Modern South-East Asia." In *The Spinning World: A Global History of Cotton Textiles, 1200–1850*, edited by Giorgio Riello and Prasannan Parthasarathi, 127–42. Oxford: Oxford University Press.
(2011). "The Expansion of Cotton Textile Production in the Western Indian Ocean, c1500–c1850." In *Indian Ocean Worlds: Essays in Honour of Prof. K. N. Chaudhuri*,

edited by Stefan Halikowski-Smith, 84–106. Newcastle-upon-Tyne: Cambridge Scholars Publishing Ltd.

Cole, R. L. (1968). "The Tariff Policy of Rhodesia, 1899–1963." *Rhodesian Journal of Economics*, 2(2): 28–47.

Coquet, Michèle. (1993). *Textiles Africains*. Paris: Adam Biro.

Cronje, F. J. C. (1952). "The Textile Industry in the Union of South Africa." *South African Journal of Economics*, 20(1): 23–30.

Cuypers. Jan-B. (2004). *L'habillement du Rwanda Ancient*. Tervuren: Musée Royal de l'Afrique Centrale.

Darish, Patricia. (1989). "Dressing for the Next Life: Raffia Textile Production and Use among the Kuba of Zaïre." In *Cloth and Human Experience*, edited by Annette B. Weiner and Jane Schneider, 117–40. Washington, DC: Smithsonian Institution Press.

Darkwah, R. H. Kofi. (1975). *Shewa, Menelik, and the Ethiopian Empire, 1813–1889*. London: Heinemann.

Davison, Patricia and Patrick Harries. (1980). "Cotton Weaving in South-East Africa: Its History and Technology." *Textile History*, 11: 175–92.

Deschamps, Hubert. (1947). *Madagascar*. Paris: Berger Levrault.

Döpcke, Wolfgang. (1992). *Das Koloniale Zimbabwe in der Krise; Eeine Wirtschafts- und Sozialgeschichte, 1929–1939*. Hamburg: Lit.

Drummond, Ian. (1974). *Imperial Economic Policy, 1917–1939: Studies in Expansion and Protection*. London: George Allen and Unwin Ltd.

Du Toit, Bettie. (1978). *Ukubamba Amadolo: Workers' Struggles in the South African Textile Industry*. London: Onyx Press.

Edgerton, David. (2008). *The Shock of the Old: Technology and Global History since 1900*. London: Profile.

Elkan, Walter. (1961). *The Economic Development of Uganda*. London: Oxford University Press.

Ellis, William. (1838). *History of Madagascar*. London: Fisher, Son & Co.

Enthoven, Reginald E. (1920–2). *The Tribes and Castes of Bombay*. Bombay: Government Central Press.

Ewald, Janet. (1990). *Soldiers, Traders and Slaves: State Formation and Economic Transformation in the Greater Nile Valley, 1700–1885*. Madison: University of Wisconsin Press.

Fair, Laura J. (2001). *Pastimes and Politics: Culture, Community and Identity in Post-Abolition Urban Zanzibar, 1890–1945*. Oxford: James Currey.

Fee, Sarah. (2002). "Madagascar's Textiles through History." In *Objects as Envoys: Cloth, Imagery and Diplomacy in Madagascar*, edited by Christine M. Kreamer and Sarah Fee, 33–93. Washington, DC: Smithsonian Institution.

(2005). "*Ze Mañe Aze*: Looking for Patterns in Malagasy Cloth." In *Textiles in Indian Ocean Societies*, edited by Ruth Barnes, 85–109. London: RoutledgeCurzon.

Gersdorff, Ralph von. (1958). *Moçambique*. Bonn: Kurt Schroeder.

Gibb, H. A. R. (1962). *The Travels of Ibn Battuta, A.D. 1325–1354, Volume 2*. Cambridge: Cambridge University Press.

Gillow, John. (2003). *African Textiles: Colour and Creativity across a Continent*. London: Thames and Hudson.

Godley, Andrew. (2001). "The Global Diffusion of the Sewing Machine, 1850–1914." *Research in Economic History*, 20: 1–45.

Grandidier, Alfred and Guillaume Grandidier. (1928). *Histoire Physique, Naturelle et Politique de Madagascar, volume IV, Ethnographie de Madagascar, Tome quatrième*. Paris: Hachette.

Great Britain. (1896). "Statement of the Trade of British India with British Possessions and Foreign Countries for the Five Years 1890–1 to 1894–5." *Parliamentary Papers*, 1896, Accounts and Papers, C. 7997.

Great Britain, Foreign Office. (1920). *Anglo-Egyptian Sudan*. London: HMSO.

Guillain, Ch. (1856–7) *Documents sur L'histoire, La Géographie et Le Commerce de l'Afrique Orientale*. Paris: A. Bertrand.

Guillie, Jackie. (1995). "Southern African Textiles Today: Design, Industry, and Collective Enterprise." In *The Art of African Textiles: Technology, Tradition, and Lurex*, edited by John Picton, 51–4. London: Barbican Art Gallery.

Havinden, Michael and David Meredith. (1993). *Colonialism and Development: Britain and Its Tropical Colonies, 1850–1960*. London: Routledge.

Hecht, Ann. (1989). *The Art of the Loom: Weaving, Spinning and Dyeing across the World*. London: British Museum Publications.

Heyse, T. (1936). "Cessions et Concessions Foncières du Congo." *Congo*, 2: 329–38.

(1938). "Cessions et Concessions Foncières du Congo." *Congo*, 1: 7–12.

Hilger, Julia. (1995). "The Kanga: An Example of East African Textile Design." In *The Art of African Textiles: Technology, Tradition, and Lurex*, edited by John Picton, 44–5. London: Barbican Art Gallery.

Horton, Mark. (1996). *Shanga: The Archaeology of a Muslim Trading Community on the Coast of East Africa*. London: British Institute in Eastern Africa.

International Bank for Reconstruction and Development. (1962). *The Economic Development of Uganda*. Baltimore, MD: Johns Hopkins University Press.

Isaacman, Allen. (1972). *Mozambique: The Africanisation of a European Institution: The Zambezi Prazos 1750–1902*. Madison: University of Wisconsin Press.

Issawi, Charles. (1966). *The Economic History of The Middle East, 1800–1914: A Book of Readings*. Chicago: University of Chicago Press.

James, Jeffrey. (1995). *The State, Technology and Industrialization in Africa*. New York: St. Martin's Press.

Jeater, Diana. (2007). *Law, Language and Science: The Invention of the "Native Mind" in Southern Rhodesia, 1890–1930*. Portsmouth, NH: Heinemann.

Johnson, Marion. (1978). "Technology, Competition and African Crafts." In *The Imperial Impact: Studies in the Economic History of Africa and India*, edited by Clive Dewey and A. G. Hopkins, 259–69. London: Athlone Press.

Kent, Raymond K. (1970). *Early Kingdoms in Madagascar, 1500–1700*. New York: Holt, Rinehart and Wilson.

Kilby, Peter. (1975). "Manufacturing in Colonial Africa." In *Colonialism in Africa, Volume 4, The Economics of Colonialism*, edited by Peter Duignan and L. H. Gann, 470–520. Cambridge: Cambridge University Press.

Kjekshus, Helge. (1977). *Ecology, Control and Economic Development in East African History: The Case of Tanganyika 1850–1950*. Berkeley: University of California Press.

Kuhn, Dieter. (1988). *Science and Civilisation in China, Volume 5, Part IX: Textile Technology: Spinning and Reeling*. Cambridge: Cambridge University Press (section 31).

Kusimba, Chapurukha M. J., Claire Odland, and Bennet Bronson, Eds. (2004). *Unwrapping the Textile Traditions of Madagascar*. Los Angeles, CA: Fowler Museum.

Lacroix, Jean-Louis. (1967). *Industrialisation au Congo: La Transformation des Structures Économiques*. Paris: Mouton.

Lamb, Venice. (2005). *Looms Past and Present: Around the Mediterranean and Elsewhere*. Hertingfordbury: Roxford Books.

Landen, Robert G. (1967). *Oman since 1856*. Princeton, NJ: Princeton University Press.

Larson, Pier. (2000). *Becoming Merina in Highland Madagascar: History and Memory in the Age of Enslavement*. Oxford: James Currey.

Leslie, J. A. K. (1963). *A Survey of Dar es Salaam*. London: Oxford University Press.

Levine, Donald L. (1974). *Greater Ethiopia: The Evolution of a Multiethnic Society*. Chicago: Chicago University Press.

Lewis, Herbert S. (2001). *Jimma Abba Jifar: An Oromo Monarchy, Ethiopia, 1830–1932*. Lawrenceville, NJ: The Red Sea Press, 2nd ed.

Lobato, Alexandre. (1957). *Evolução Administrativa e Económica de Moçambique, 1752–1763*. Lisbon: Agência Geral Ultramarina.

Macedo, Alberto Cardoso Martins de. (1939). "Relações Entre a Indústria Nacional e a Agricultura Colonial." *Boletim da Sociedade de Geografia de Lisboa*, 57: 267–90.

Machado, Pedro. (2005). "Gujarati Indian Merchant Networks in Mozambique, 1777-c. 1830." PhD Thesis, University of London.

(2009). "Awash in a Sea of Cloth: Gujarat, Africa and the Western Indian Ocean, 1300–1800." In *The Spinning World: A Global History of Cotton Textiles, 1200–1850*, edited by Giorgio Riello and Prasannan Parthasarathi, 161–79. Oxford: Oxford University Press.

Mack, John. (1987). "Weaving, Women and the Ancestors in Madagascar." *Indonesia Circle*, 42: 76–91.

(1989). *Malagasy Textiles*. London: Shire Publications.

(1993). "Sub-Saharan Africa and the Offshore Islands." In *5000 Years of Textiles*, edited by Jennifer Harris, 295–305. London: British Museum Press.

Maliti, Tom. (2005). "Rise and Fall of African Textile Industry Provides Cautionary Tale." http://www.busrep.co.za/general/print_article.php?fArticleId+2447442&SectionId+552&fSetId=662 (consulted July 5, 2010).

Marseille, Jacques. (1984). *Empire Colonial et Capitalisme Français, Histoire d'un Divorce*. Paris: Albin Michel.

Martin, Bradford G. (1971). "Notes On Some Members of the Learned Classes of Zanzibar and East Africa in the Nineteenth Century." *African Historical Studies*, 4(3) 525–45.

Matheson, Ishbel. (2000). "Charity Killing Zambia's Textile Industry." BBC News Online. December 25.

Mlambo, A. S., E. S. Pangeti, and Ian Phimister. (2000). *Zimbabwe, a History of Manufacturing, 1890–1995*. Harare: University of Zimbabwe Publications.

Morris, H. S. (1968). *The Indians in Uganda*. London: Weidenfeld and Nicolson.

Mosley, Paul. (1983). *The Settler Economies: Studies in the Economic History of Kenya and Southern Rhodesia, 1900–1963*. Cambridge: Cambridge University Press.
Mudenge, Stanley I. G. (1988). *A Political History of Munhunmutapa, c. 1400 to 1902*. Harare: Zimbabwe Publishing House.
Munro, J. Forbes. (1984). *Britain in Tropical Africa, 1880–1960, Economic Relationships and Impact*. London: Macmillan.
Neveling, Patrick. (2010). "Von Nutzen der Geschichte, vom Wissen der Akteure und vom Nachteil der Multi-Sited Ethnography: Welthandel, Wirtschaftskrise und Standortwettbewerb in Mauritius Anfang des 21. Jahrhunderts." *Sociologus: Zeitschrift für empirische Ethnosociologie und Ethnopsychologie*, 60(1): 71–97.
Newitt, Malyn. (1987). "East Africa and Indian Ocean Trade." In *India and the Indian Ocean, 1500–1800*, edited by Ashin Das Gupta and M. N. Pearson, 201–33. Calcutta: Oxford University Press.
(1995). *A History of Mozambique*. London: Hurst.
(2002). *East Africa: Portuguese Encounters in the World in the Age of Discoveries*. Aldershot: Ashgate.
Palat, Ravi A. and Immanuel Wallerstein. (1999). "Of What World-System Was Pre-1500 'India' A Part?" In *Merchants, Companies and Trade: Europe and Asia in the Early Modern Era*, edited by Sushil Chaudhury and Michel Morineau, 21–41. Cambridge: Cambridge University Press.
Pankhurst, Richard. (1968). *Economic History of Ethiopia, 1800–1935*. Addis Ababa: Haile Selassie I University Press.
Parthasarathi, Prasannan. (2011). *Why Europe Grew Rich and Asia Did Not: Global Economic Divergence, 1600–1850*. Cambridge: Cambridge University Press.
Pearson, D. S. (1969). *Industrial Development in East Africa*. Nairobi: Oxford University Press.
Pearson, M. N. (1998). *Port Cities and Intruders: The Swahili Coast, India and Portugal in the Early Modern Era*. Baltimore, MD: Johns Hopkins University Press.
Peers, Simon. (1995). "Weaving in Madagascar." In *The Art of African Textiles: Technology, Tradition, and Lurex*, edited by John Picton, 46–7. London: Barbican Art Gallery.
(2004). "History and Change in the Weaving of Highland Madagascar." In *Unwrapping the Textile Traditions of Madagascar*, edited by Chapurukha M. Kusimba, J. Claire Odland, and Bennet Bronson, 142–53. Los Angeles, CA: Fowler Museum.
Picton, John and John Mack. (1989). *African Textiles*. London: British Museum, 2nd ed.
Pirio, Gregory R. (1982). "Commerce, Industry and Empire: The Making of Modern Portuguese Colonialism in Angola and Mozambique, 1890–1914." PhD Thesis, University of California at Los Angeles.
Pitcher, M. Anne. (1993). *Politics in the Portuguese Empire: The State, Industry and Cotton, 1926–1974*. Oxford: Clarendon Press.
Polakoff, Claire. (1982). *African Textiles and Dyeing Techniques*. London: Routledge and Kegan Paul.
Prestholdt, Jeremy G. (1998). *As Artistry Permits and Custom May Ordain: The Social Fabric of Material Consumption in the Swahili World, circa 1450 to 1600*. Evanston, IL: Northwestern University, PAS Working Paper No. 3.

Reese, Scott S. (1996). "Patricians of the Benaadir; Islamic Learning, Commerce, and Somali Urban Identity in the Nineteenth Century." PhD Thesis, University of Pennsylvania.

Renne, Elisha P. (1995). *Cloth That Does Not Die: The Meaning of Cloth in Bùnú Social Life*. Seattle: University of Washington Press.

Rita-Ferreira, António. (1999). *African Kingdoms and Alien Settlement in Central Mozambique, c. Fifteenth to Seventeenth Century*. Coimbra: Universidade de Coimbra.

Robecchi-Bricchetti, Luigi. (1899). *Somalia e Benadir; Viaggio de Esplorazione Nell'Africa Orientale*. Milan: Carlo Aliprandi.

Roberts, Edmund. (1972). *Embassy to the Eastern Courts of Cochin-China, Siam and Muscat in the US Sloop-of-War Peacock, during the Years 1832–3–4*. Wilmington, DE: Scholarly Resources Ltd., reprint of 1837 ed.

Roth, H. Ling. (1977). *Studies in Primitive Looms*. Bedford: Ruth Bean, 4th ed.

Saron, Gustav and Louis Hotz. (1955). *The Jews in South Africa: A History*. London: Oxford University Press.

Schaedler, Karl-Ferdinand. (1987). *Weaving in Africa South of the Sahara*. Munich: Panterra.

Silver, M. S. (1984). *The Growth of Manufacturing Industry in Tanzania: An Economic History*. Boulder, CO: Westview Press.

Simoons, Frederick J. (1960). *Northwest Ethiopia: Peoples and Economy*. Madison: University of Wisconsin Press.

Southern Rhodesia. (1946). *Report of the Committee of Enquiry into the Protection of Secondary Industries in Southern Rhodesia*. Salisbury: Government Printer (also known as the "Margolis Report").

Spence, C. F. (1951). *The Portuguese Colony of Mozambique: An Economic Survey*. Cape Town: A. A. Balkema.

Stefanini, Giuseppe. (1922). *In Somalia: Note e Impressioni di Viaggio*. Florence: Le Monnier.

Swainson, Nicola. (1980). *The Development of Corporate Capitalism in Kenya, 1918–1971*. London: Heinemann.

Strihou, Jacques van Ypersele de. (1961). "Variations des Coefficients de Fabrication dans Une Entreprise Congolaise, et Équilibre économique, 1931–1958." *Bulletin de l'Institut de Recherches Économiques de Louvain*, 27 (2): 47–96.

Valk, Peter de. (1996). *African Industry in Decline: The Case of Textiles in Tanzania in the 1980s*. Basingstoke: Macmillan.

Vandewalle, G. (1966). *De Conjuncturele Evolutie in Kongo en Ruanda-Urundi, van 1920 tot 1939, en van 1949 tot 1958*. Gent: Rijksuniversiteit te Gent.

Vansina, Jan. (1998). "Raffia Cloth in West Central Africa, 1500–1800." In *Textiles: Production, Trade and Demand*, edited by Maureen Fennell Mazzaoui, 263–81. Aldershot: Ashgate.

Vellut, Jean-Luc. (1985). "Originalités et Limites de L'industrie Manufacturière au Congo Belge, c.1920–1960." Unpublished longer version of a piece published under this title in *Les Belges à L'étranger: 150 Ans de Réalisations dans Le Tiers-monde*, catalogue for an exhibition held in Brussels March 21 to April 24.

Werbeloff, Arnold. (1987). *Textiles in Africa: A Trade and Investment Guide*. London: Alain Charles.

Wilde, John C. de. (1971). *The Development of African Private Enterprise*. Washington, DC: International Bank for Reconstruction and Development.

Wingate, F. R. (1986). *Ten Years' Captivity in the Mahdi's Camp, 1882–1892, from the original manuscript of Father Joseph Ohrwalder*. London: Darf, 2nd ed.

Wylde, Augustus B. (1901). *Modern Abyssinia*. London: Methuen.

Yamba, V. Bawa. (1995). *Permanent Pilgrims: The Role of Pilgrimage in the Lives of West African Muslims in the Sudan*. Washington, DC: Smithsonian Institute Press.

Zawawi, Sharifa M. (2005). *Kanga: The Cloth That Speaks*. New York: Azaniya Hills Press.

9

Explaining and Evaluating the Cash Crop Revolution in the "Peasant" Colonies of Tropical Africa, ca. 1890–ca.1930: Beyond "Vent for Surplus"

Gareth Austin

The fundamental economic change of the colonial era in the so-called peasant colonies of tropical Africa – those in which no major appropriation of agricultural land for use by European settlers or concessionaires occurred – was the massive expansion of export agriculture in areas with favorable land quality and location. The timing varied among and within individual colonies, but in general the fastest growth in the volume of agricultural exports took place during the early decades of colonial rule, ca. 1890 to ca. 1930, especially during the twenty years or so immediately preceding the First World War. In many areas, African agricultural exports had begun before the colonial occupation; in a few, such as northern Nigeria, with groundnuts (peanuts), it followed it. But even where it was already established, export agriculture expanded greatly during colonial rule. This expansion was associated with infrastructural innovation, especially the introduction of mechanized transport. It was also associated with institutional changes. The most important of these was the emergence of a migrant-labor system that channeled workers into the areas suited to export agriculture from the more distant and/or drier parts of the same or neighboring colonies.

The cash crop revolution is evidently a key episode in the economic history of Africa, defining the structure of most of the nonsettler economies. It is also particularly worthy of attention for students of comparative and

This chapter was written specifically for the July 2010 conference in Peduase, Ghana. In revising it, I have benefited from feedback there and on versions presented the same year to the Department of Economic History and Institutions, Universidad Carlos III, Madrid, and at the annual meeting of the African Studies Association of the United Kingdom, in Oxford.

long-term economic development. Sub-Saharan economies have often been thought of as static: at least before colonial rule, and perhaps during and since. Specialists know that there have been episodes of economic growth, albeit often sustained for just a few decades, in parts of the region during all these eras (e.g., Austin 2008; Berthélemy and Söderling 2001; Jerven 2010; Manning 1982). In this respect, the cash crop revolution is especially significant for several reasons. First, it was unusually widespread geographically. Second, in some areas for certain commodities, the speed of "takeoff" was dramatic. Third, production was carried out almost entirely by Africans; and, where they existed at all, European rivals failed in competition (e.g., Austin 1996). Thus research into this episode may be particularly useful as a means of testing long-term generalizations about the sources of stagnation or change in indigenous economic behavior.

The causes and effects of the expansion of African export agriculture became the subject of continuous research and lively controversy from the 1960s well into the 1980s. The "vent-for-surplus" (VFS) model(s), pioneered by Hlya Myint and Robert Seresewski at the London School of Economics, postulated that Africans expanded their output, in response to price incentives newly provided by overseas markets, by making fuller use of previously underutilized stocks of land and labor (Myint 1958, 1964/1973, 1977; Szereszewski 1965). Thus it means exporting without opportunity cost: production for domestic consumption (whether subsistence or marketed) is unaffected. In this perspective, African economic behavior was rational, but only minimally innovative. During the 1970s, dependency theory became popular in the academy, in Africa and beyond, with its radically pessimistic model in which, while Africans increasingly produced for export, they did so only because the colonial government prodded them into it, either through the direct coercion of compulsory cultivation and forced labor or through the indirect pressure of taxes that had to be paid in cash (Freund and Shenton 1977; Rodney 1972). The result was that the export growth had an opportunity cost in reduced subsistence output, because of the diversion of labor from food to cash crops. Both VFS and dependency interpretations became increasingly hard to sustain as research continued. Their accounts of the mechanisms and motives of the cash crop revolution were found, respectively, at best inadequate and at worst to a large extent wrong in the light of a series of studies of the creative and decisive role of African entrepreneurship in the faster and larger export expansions (see Berry 1975; Hill 1963, 1966; Hogendorn 1979, Hopkins 1973, 1978).

But in social science, even the most heavily criticized paradigms rarely lose all adherents, especially when intellectual markets are segmented by disciplinary and ideological boundaries.[1] Both VFS and dependency continue to attract occasional support (e.g., respectively, Teal 2002 and Thompson 2006). Indeed, when the debate went quiet in the later 1980s, it was not because the arguments had been definitively settled – certainly no new synthesis was established – but rather because the intellectual climate had changed. The hold of dependency theory on left-leaning scholars had been challenged by the critiques of a small but active group of heterodox economists sympathetic to the old Marxian expectation that, ultimately, colonialism could do no other than promote capitalist institutions, and thereby the potential for long-term economic expansion (Sender and Smith 1986; Warren 1980). Politically, the 1980s brought the ideal of the unfettered market "back in" at the level of policy, notably through "Structural Adjustment." Intellectually, the renewed interest in markets was animated by a concern with the institutional frameworks surrounding transactions (the seminal contributions, in the interdisciplinary study of Africa, being Bates 1981, 1983). Indeed, the trickle of studies of the cash crop revolution during the past quarter century was distinguished from the steady stream of the previous quarter century not only in frequency, but by a tendency to give more attention to institutional aspects (Austin 2005, 2007, 2009; Firmin-Sellers 1996; from a social history perspective, Fall 1993; Manchuelle 1997). This is not at all to say that recent work has completely overlooked issues of resources and technology, as is illustrated by Bassett's (2001) study of Ivorian cotton growing, and Ruf's (1995a, 1995b) exploration of the long-term dynamics of fertility and profitability in cocoa production. But an unmistakable shift of emphasis has taken place. An exception that "proves the rule" is Swindell and Jeng's work on groundnut production and trade in the Gambia. This gives a relative weight to resource issues that recalls an earlier generation of scholarship; and indeed, though completed recently, this important study had its roots in research that the authors began in the very different intellectual setting of the 1970s (Swindell and Jeng 2006).

On the causes of the cash crop revolution, given the general emphasis on institutional matters in recent economic historiography and related literatures, this chapter will take up the unfinished business of the sources and scale of resource inputs and how they were combined. The main discussion is organized in four sections. The first describes the growth of agricultural exports in more detail. The second section introduces the VFS approach, its variants, and the many lines of criticism directed at it from the 1960s

[1] What Hopkins called "the persistence of imperfections in the market for knowledge" (Hopkins 1987, 122; cf. Hopkins 1986, 1473).

to the early 1980s. The third section proposes a more nuanced framework for explaining the expansion. In what was a predominately labor-scarce region of the world, the issue turns on the mobilization, use, and productivity of labor. It will be argued that both VFS and dependency approaches fit at least part of the evidence from parts of the region, but that both miss a phenomenon that was both important at the time and significant for long-term economic development in Africa: expansion achieved by raising productivity.

The fourth section discusses the welfare consequences of the growth of export agriculture, and reflects on the long-term economic implications. The welfare outcomes were probably determined by the institutions as much as the size of income. On one hand, the capture of resource rents – by controlling access to the areas where export agriculture could most profitably be pursued – was a source of continuing inequality among different parts of the region. On the other hand, the transition from slavery to free migrant labor had more wide-ranging effects than previously recognized: it enabled welfare gains from increased purchasing power to be diffused, unevenly but much more widely than is usually supposed. Finally, this chapter will reflect, among other things, on the implications of colonial-era cash crop expansion for further structural and productivity change: on whether it was, as dependency writers argued and as VFS implied, a story of "growth without development,"[2] and one-off growth at that.

9.1 THE GROWTH OF AGRICULTURAL EXPORTS

The most striking characteristic of the expansion of export agriculture was its unevenness, over space as well as time.[3] Table 9.1 summarizes the growth of output of the major crops in the major centers of production in West Africa, which accounted for the majority of population and foreign trade in tropical Africa, and for the great majority of population and foreign trade from the "peasant" colonies. In contrast, central Africa included substantial foreign plantation sectors, while East Africa included a major "settler" colony, Kenya. Outside West Africa, the largest example of export agriculture was Uganda. In contrast to West Africa, there was apparently no precolonial cotton industry in Uganda. Following initial experiments in 1902–3,

[2] The phrase was used as the title of Clower, Dalton, Harwitz, and Walters (1966).

[3] This section briefly describes what subsequent sections try to explain. For fuller introductions, see Hopkins (1973, 167–236); Hogendorn (1975); and Harrison, Ingawa, and Martin (1987, 517–34).

Table 9.1. *Main agricultural exports from main producing colonies in West Africa, 1890–1910 (metric tons)*

Colony & Crop	1890	1900	1914
Senegal groundnuts	27,221	140,922	280,526
Gambia groundnuts	18,554	36,378	67,924
Ghana cocoa	0	0.5	53,746
Nigeria cocoa	6*	205	5,018
Nigeria palm oil	–	46,236	73,659
Nigeria palm kernels	–	86994	165050
Nigeria groundnuts	–	608	17,271

* Lagos only. For comparison, in 1900 Lagos accounted for 56 percent of the total (calculated from Berry 1975, 221).

Note: "–" means no figure available. In Nigeria during this period, exports of cocoa beans, palm oil (and palm kernels), and groundnuts came from the southwest, southeast, and (at least after 1912) north, respectively.

Sources: From Austin 2009, 5; Berry (1975, 221); Helleiner (1966, table IVA8); Hill (1963/1997, 177); Kay and Hymer (1972, 336); Martin (1988, 148); Searing (2002, 199); and Swindell and Jeng (2006, 23, 101, 149).

production rose to nearly six thousand metric tons in 1914–15 (Engdahl 1999, 51–3, 73).

Unevenness over time was manifest in the contrast between the relatively gradual multiplication of export volumes of certain crops from areas where they had already been produced for export for several decades (notably groundnuts in Senegambia and palm oil – and then also palm kernels – in southeastern Nigeria) and the rapid takeoff from nil exports in other cases (cocoa in Ghana, groundnuts from northern Nigeria, cotton in Uganda). The older export crop cultures went back to the transition from the Atlantic slave trade to "legitimate commerce" during the early and middle nineteenth centuries; groundnuts and palm oil were grown for export in areas not far from water transport, such as the Senegambian river basins and the Niger Delta. The dramatic new trades responded to the construction of railways to the interior (Uganda, northern Nigeria) and the new profitability of a relatively recently imported exotic crop, cocoa beans. The expansion of the area under export crops generally slowed greatly during the period from the middle of the First World War until at least the end of the Second World War, primarily because, while prices continued to fluctuate, they did so between lower bands than during most of the preceding quarter century (Martin 1989). It took a new era of higher prices to help induce a further major expansion of output during the last decade or so of colonial rule in most of tropical Africa: an episode beyond the scope of this chapter.

The unevenness over space was stark in its extremes: the contrast between the richest cash-cropping areas and the areas whose direct participation in the agricultural export economy never went much beyond the export of (mostly male, mostly migrant) labor to the production zones and marketing centers. The difference was a function of soils and transport costs.[4] The crops were not of equal value; cocoa beans were clearly the most profitable option where they would grow well, which was only in certain forest zones. The geographical variation, however, was graduated in two ways. First, colonial administrations generally encouraged, and – especially in the drier areas – in many cases tried to compel, savanna farmers to grow cotton. Despite compulsion, production in such areas remained relatively modest, as for instance in northern Côte d'Ivoire during this period (Bassett 2001). Hence migrant labor developed as a more realistic way by which the inhabitants could obtain the cash to pay tax and buy goods (Asiwaju 1976). Second, there were intermediate areas where crops were grown for export giving returns to labor that were high enough to avert any major exodus of labor but low enough not to attract an immigrant labor force. This was, for instance, the situation in much of the palm oil belt in southeast Nigeria.

9.2 VENT-FOR-SURPLUS MODELS AND THEIR CRITICS

By definition, VFS growth of exports occurs as result of putting to work a previously unused "surplus productive capacity" (Myint 1964, 321). It is growth with an unchanged production function: inputs are combined in the same proportions and using the same methods of production as for existing domestic markets. The only difference is that now they are applied for export as well. Though the intellectual lineage of the idea may be traced to Adam Smith, the VFS model proximately and decisively belongs to the same generation as W. A. Lewis's (1954) much more famous model of "economic development with unlimited supplies of labour." Like Lewis (from St Lucia in the West Indies), Myint was a native of a tropical colony (Burma) who became a professor in Britain. Like Lewis, he wrote in the classical rather than the neoclassical tradition, in that his model envisaged a stable equilibrium in which at least one factor of production was less than fully employed. Like Lewis, who had just written a important report on the (as

4 On the latter see Chaves, Engerman, and Robinson (Chapter 10, this volume); Jedwab and Moradi (2012); and Austin (2007, 100–3).

he saw it, not particularly encouraging) prospects for industrialization in Ghana (Lewis 1953), Myint was struck by the scarcity of labor relative to land in West Africa, as in his native Southeast Asia. Yet Myint postulated that labor was underemployed at the beginning of the growth of agricultural exports, in the sense that there was a "leisure" reserve. He envisaged an absolute deficiency of effective demand, such that Africans had no incentive to use even their very limited supply of labor, despite the availability of abundant cultivable land. The growth of agricultural exports was triggered by the arrival of mechanized transport, in the form of the steamship and then the railway, which greatly improved the barter terms of trade for African exporters (the ratio of units of imports they could obtain in return for one unit of exports). More than that, Myint envisaged the steamships bringing to Africa a range of new commodities, which greatly increased the desire of Africans to produce for export in order to be able to buy the expanded range of imports (Myint 1958, 1964, 1977).

Though the VFS idea is often referred to as "Myint's model," a series of other authors soon formulated different versions of it (notably Szereszewski 1965; Helleiner 1966; Elliott 1969). These revisions (none of whose authors were from the Third World, as it happens), were all in the neoclassical tradition. They replaced the underemployment equilibrium with a trade-off, but retained the fundamental proposition that export growth was achieved without reducing output for existing consumers. They did this by ascribing a positive value to leisure in the minds of producers, and in Elliott's case, also to risklessness. Thus the assumed initial idleness of part of the stocks of labor and land was the result of a trade-off between the incentive of possible but very limited rewards from trade (relatively expensive purchases) and the disincentive of losing leisure. While Elliott noted that farmers in some areas would risk their food supply if they went into export farming, he thought that, precisely for that reason, they would not want to do so. Where export agriculture took off, on his analysis, food supply was not at risk; though he recognized that the long gestation period of investment in cocoa trees made cocoa growing inherently high risk in terms of the effort and money involved (Elliott 1969).

The VFS approach drew a variety of criticisms. Some of the critics' observations could be accommodated in a modified version of the model; others were incompatible with it. One potential criticism was anticipated by Szereszewski himself: that, at least in the case of a tree crop like cocoa, the expansion involved capital formation on a wide scale. Thus one could hardly claim it was growth with the same production function as in "traditional" agriculture. Szereszewski proceeded to estimate the scale of capital formation involved, but noted that it consisted mainly of tree planting using simple tools, hence "the formation of cocoa capital was simply the capitalisation of current local labour" (1965, 75). Thus he argued that the production function was effectively a single-factor one, in that the size of output was essentially a function of labor inputs. Given this, the VFS framework could be retained, providing that its basic premise held: that land and labor were initially under used.

One obvious absence from the models was the important contribution of migrant labor to the expansion of the major centers of export agriculture. This falsified the notion of growth being achieved purely, or even largely, by the mobilization of previously idle hands. But it did so only at a relatively local level: the VFS model could still apply to the economic region concerned, if that is defined as comprising both the labor-importing area and the areas that supplied it with seasonal migrant workers.

Again, it was observed that cash crop zones became net importers of foodstuffs (e.g., Freund and Shenton 1977, 193). But the evidence for this comes from after export agriculture had already "taken off" in the area concerned. It is not surprising that a population swollen by seasonal migrants (both laborers and itinerant traders), and containing a high proportion of households whose purchasing power had been boosted by their involvement in the export economy, should provide a new market for foodstuffs from neighboring areas. Let us take a Ghanaian example. In Ejura district, in the savanna just to the north of the forest zone that had become the cocoa belt, commercial rice growing developed during the interwar years, supplying the market in Kumasi, the commercial center of Ashanti (the heartland of the former Asante kingdom),[5] which comprised the northern half of the Ghanaian forest zone (Austin 2005, 54–5, 470–1). This does not necessarily mean that food production within the cocoa belt actually declined, only that food consumption within it increased. That a cash crop center might eventually cease to be self-sufficient in foodstuffs does not contradict the basic VFS claim that the cash crop takeoff did not involve a reduction in production of foodstuffs within the area itself.

A criticism that posed greater difficulty for the model was that it erred by omitting any role of African entrepreneurship. The supply response envisaged in VFS models was purely responsive, requiring no innovation and amounting simply to doing more of the same thing. This stylized story took no account of the actual history of the adoption of cocoa cultivation. Cocoa was an exotic crop, and the people responsible for its initial spread in Nigeria

[5] Consisting of what are now the Ashanti and Brong-Ahafo regions of Ghana.

were not peasants but Creole merchants who, faced with difficult years in trade in Lagos, decided to venture a long-term investment in this novel tree crop. One of them, J. K. Coker, the leading figure in the Agege Farmers Union (founded 1907), also had a political motive: he and his colleagues spread what they apparently called "the cocoa gospel" so that others might join them in proving that Africans could be successful in "modern" activities without becoming European in outlook (Hopkins 1978). The adoption of the crop was not the only innovation of the early Nigerian cocoa planters. According to Agiri, the annual wage contract in Nigerian agriculture was pioneered on Agege farms (Agiri 1983–4, 102). In Ghana, though the Basel Mission had already been experimenting with cocoa growing, the colonial government recognized a blacksmith named Tetteh Quashie as its key pioneer. The most plausible version of the Tetteh Quashie story is that a young male dependent of his went to the Portuguese island of Fernando Po as a laborer on a cocoa plantation and smuggled cocoa pods back with him on his return. Quashie used them to establish a small cocoa nursery in Mampong on the Akwapim Ridge "from which he sold, or distributed, pods or seedlings to Akwapim farmers" (Hill 1963, 172–3). Hill documented the process by which cocoa farming in what became Ghana moved from an experimental stage on the Akwapim Ridge, to investment in the purchase of land in the Akim Abuakwa district, the planting of trees, and eventually the production of many thousands of tons of beans a year. As she emphasized, this was a story of risk taking and long-term investment (Hill 1963). Again, Hogendorn showed that the export trade in groundnuts from northern Nigeria began at the initiative of Hausa merchants. Confounding the expectations of British merchants and the hopes of the British government and Lancashire cotton textile manufacturers, well-capitalized Hausa merchants did not respond to the opportunity presented by the arrival of the railway at Kano by supplying cotton. Instead, Alhassan dan Tata and others responded by giving credit to peasants in return for promises to plant groundnuts that season to sell to the Hausa middlemen, who would sell them to the European buyers (Hogendorn 1979). The active role of African entrepreneurs does not necessarily conflict with the letter of the VFS models. On the other hand, the evidence of Africans as innovators, risk takers, and investors stands in contrast to the spirit of the VFS approach, with its depiction of the African role as purely responsive. Again, the likes of Tete Quarshie, Coker, and dan Tata are hard to reconcile with the VFS sketch of static, subsistence-dominated precolonial economies. Thus, the entrepreneurship issue suggests that VFS is at least insufficient as a framework for explaining the dynamics of the cash crop revolution.

Drawing together the available literature in the 1970s, Hopkins (1973, 231–6) and Hogendorn (1975, 1976) used VFS as their framework, but qualified and embellished it to take account of these kinds of criticisms. A major step toward refuting rather than just modifying the model was taken by Tosh, with a powerful argument restricting VFS to the forest zones. He noted that the assumption of a reserve of leisure was incompatible with the well-known brevity of the planting season in tropical savannas, which would have entailed a trade-off between the production of food crops such as millet for household subsistence and that of potential export crops such as cotton and groundnuts (Tosh 1980). While groundnuts were also part of the local diet, Tosh's point makes it hard to sustain the VFS premise that the export crop expansion involved no reduction in food crop output.[6]

During the 1970s and the early 1980s, writers attracted to dependency theory attacked the VFS approach wholesale for overlooking the role of colonial coercion. Forms of such coercion ranged from compulsory cultivation of cotton to the use of direct taxation, payable only in money, which obliged farmers to obtain more cash, either from their own farming or as migrant laborers (notably Freund and Shenton 1977; Mbodj 1980; Muhtar 1988; Watts 1983; and, earlier, Suret-Canale 1964/1971). Tosh's aforementioned argument clarified in principle why savanna farmers might be reluctant to respond to agricultural export markets, and why colonial administrations might therefore believe that coercion was necessary to induce them to do so. As a general framework for analyzing the agricultural export expansion in tropical Africa, an obvious weakness of dependency theory was (and is) that no serious reason exists to doubt that in many cases – including by far the largest cases – of export expansion, the decision to plant crops for export was voluntary. This applied to groundnuts, which was already the major export crop from the savanna before the colonial Scramble for Africa began in 1879. Groundnut exports expanded many times during the early colonial period. In southern Ghana (cocoa) and southern Nigeria (palm oil products and cocoa), there was not even any direct taxation during the early colonial decades. With coercion applicable to only some of the cases, the explanatory power of dependency theory is left to rely on the notion of unequal exchange.[7] Market economists and economic historians tend to be skeptical of this as a general explanation (particular monopolies excepted), to the extent that it relies on Marx's labor theory of value. Later I

6 Elliott noted the seasonal labor bottleneck, but did not consider that it applied as broadly as Tosh did (1969, 136–7).

7 For a brief discussion of the internal debate on this theory, see Frank (1978).

will consider briefly more limited versions of the idea of unequal exchange that do not rest on the labor theory of value.

Ironically, the ideological tension between the VFS and dependency interpretations of the colonial-period expansion of export agriculture overlay a partial similarity in their assessment of the dynamics of long-term economic development in Africa. Both agreed that the cash crop expansion constituted "growth without development," in the sense that the technologies and production functions remained the same. For the future, Myint envisaged two possibilities, once the land and leisure surpluses were exhausted. The optimistic scenario was a transition to what we might now call "Smithian growth": a process of rising specialization, with the export crops increasingly produced by farmers who produced nothing else, permitting higher allocative efficiency in the economy as a whole. But Myint also took seriously the pessimistic prospect of Geertzian agricultural involution: as the (in his view, exogenous) growth of population induced farmers to decrease production for the market in order to concentrate on growing enough food for the household's consumption on plots of gradually diminishing size. Thus, for Myint, the growth of export agriculture might prove to be either a bridge to structural change and further growth or an interval between a demand-constrained poverty amid underused resources and a supply-constrained poverty with increasing pressure on resources (Myint 1958, 329–31, 1964, 36–9).

In any case, by the mid-1980s, the accumulation of suggested supplements and partial refutations meant that the VFS approach had lost its initial aura of elegance and wide applicability across the various crops and places involved in the export agriculture "revolution." Dependency theory had proved even more flawed empirically. As noted earlier, the next step in the evolution of the literature was sideways: with some exceptions, scholarly interest shifted to other problems. The next section suggests ways in which we might take forward the unfinished business, especially in the light of research done on various precolonial and colonial contexts and themes over the past scholarly generation.

9.3 BEYOND "VENT FOR SURPLUS"

Rereading the writings of VFS authors, and indeed of dependency writers, I am struck by four assumptions that, whether reasonable or not at the time, have now been overtaken by later research. Let me begin from these.

First, the VFS models assumed that the starting point of the growth of export agriculture during the early colonial period was the ending of a more or less deep isolation from international trade. Of course, Myint and his colleagues were aware of the Atlantic slave trade, but in modeling what happened some decades after the beginning of the end of it, they made no allowance for the antiquity and continuity of Africans' commercial links with other continents, and for the growth of "legitimate" commerce in palm oil and groundnuts from the coast of West Africa, from well before the introduction of steamship services in the 1850s. Again, Uganda is often said to have been more removed from maritime trade, but that had changed greatly from the 1860s. A specific continuity from the external trade of these economies, from before until after colonization, is in the kinds of commodities that were imported. Cotton cloth, alcohol, and metal goods remained prominent.[8] To be sure, new products such as the bicycle arrived between colonization and the First World War, but their appearance came piecemeal rather than in one transformative moment. Thus the evidence for Myint's idea of the emergence of new consumer wants as an important motive for the growth of export agriculture is slight. On the contrary, colonial governments' imposition of their own currencies and restrictions on Africans' purchases of guns and gunpowder presumably constricted the demand for two of the main precolonial imports: materials for commodity currencies (such as cowrie shells) and firearms.

Second, the formulation of the VFS models, and the surrounding exposition and commentary, implicitly underestimated the extent of market activity within late nineteenth-century precolonial economies. This is not a criticism of the authors writing during the 1960s; that we can make this observation reflects other research that was under way then and synthesized soon afterward (Hopkins 1973), and augmented by subsequent work (including, for Uganda, on the Buganda kingdom in the nineteenth century: Reid 2002).[9] VFS writers, and their *dependista* critics, tended to treat commodity markets as if they had been pretty insignificant before colonization. Research has increasingly documented precolonial market exchange that was not only more widespread, but more important in the economic and social life of the populations than scholars previously recognized (Austin, forthcoming). A telling indicator of this is Inikori's observation that West Africans' importation of currency materials was intended not to facilitate trade with Europeans, but to lubricate intra-African trade: European merchants did not accept cowries and other commodity currencies back in

[8] For a convenient if rather inadequately disaggregated example, see the tables of imports in Kay and Hymer (1972, 327–31).

[9] Despite its title, Reid's book mainly concerns economic history.

payment; they were currencies only in internal markets (Inikori 2007, 84). For the precolonial decades of the nineteenth century, Lovejoy and others have shown that, besides the growth of "legitimate commerce" in place of the slave trade on the coast, there was also market expansion in the interior, centered on the Sokoto Caliphate (1804–1900) and its commercial hub, the city of Kano (e.g., Lovejoy 2005). The cotton textile industry and trade was central to the economy of the Caliphate and to West Africa as a whole. This means that the potential opportunity costs of export agriculture were incompletely realized in the VFS models.[10] Again, crops exported to other continents were not everywhere the first crops sold. Towns on the inner bend of the Niger river, in the latitude of the desert, had long depended on grains grown at a distance and brought by trading canoes.[11] In the Sokoto Caliphate, raw cotton and vegetable dyes, the raw materials of cotton textile manufacturing, were produced and sold from estates (e.g., Lovejoy 2005). Meanwhile on the other side of the continent, hundreds of miles from the ocean, the regional trade included such cash crops as sesame (Tosh 1978). In the Kigezi district of southwestern Uganda, before and during colonial rule, "food crops were cash crops" (Carswell 2007, 25).

The third, and perhaps starkest, of the implicit assumptions in the VFS literature about the starting point of the export takeoff is that the agricultural labor force comprised owner-cultivators and their families: no slaves or pawns, no labor market. The supposed absence of the latter follows from the underestimation of market activity: if commodity production was only a relatively small supplement to subsistence production, there would be no or negligible demand for extra-familial labor. Since the 1970s, research has cumulatively shown evidence of increasing use of slaves within West African economies, during the Atlantic slave trade and especially after it. The nineteenth century saw increased trading in slaves who stayed within West Africa, and were purchased primarily to produce commodities: whether for the maritime "legitimate commerce" or for intraregional trade (Austin, forthcoming). To a lesser extent, this also happened in parts of East Africa, including what became Uganda (Médard and Doyle 2007; Reid 2002). Slavery was not a marginal phenomenon during that century, especially toward the end of it. Klein estimates that

[10] In a very perceptive 1976 article, Sheila Smith considered the implications of including an existing handicrafts sector in the analysis (something of course omitted by the VFS models). But her article did not present enough evidence to convert her theory into an alternative historical interpretation (Smith 1976).

[11] The situation early in the colonial period was the subject of a report by a French official (Givieu 1911).

more than 30 percent of the population of French West Africa were slaves at the turn of century (Klein 1998, 252–6). Lovejoy and Hogendorn put the equivalent figure for the Sokoto Caliphate, the most populous precolonial state in West Africa, as "between a quarter and a half" (Lovejoy and Hogendorn 1993, 305). Pawning (debt bondage), too, was a major source of extra-familial labor recruitment in non-Muslim parts of West Africa (Lovejoy and Falola 2003).

The integral importance of slavery to most of the economies in which the cash crop revolution was to occur on a large scale is incompatible with the basic VFS proposition of surplus labor in the form of a prior leisure reserve. Again, the decline of slavery and pawning after colonization was often slow: colonial governments often, though not always, took immediate action against slave raiding and trading but in many cases were hesitant to take decisive measures against an institution on which they often considered chieftaincy and social control to depend. Not least, the economic conditions under which labor coercion was profitable to owners had not been abolished. Colonial governments acted on this when they used forced labor. Slave masters appreciated the point too. Hence, "'When the slaves left, the owners wept'" (Ohadike 1999). Before slaves ran away or walked out (as many, but far from all, did), they were often put to work establishing or expanding cash crop farms (Austin 2005, 240–2, 513–14, 2009; Salau 2010). Again, when credible state action was taken against slaveholding in south-western Nigeria, the supply of pawns proved remarkably elastic: pawn labor was substituted for slaves and for some years was the main source of labor on the Agege cocoa farms (Oroge 1985).

The final VFS assumption is not wrong, though it is too simple: the notion that land was relatively abundant, in the sense that the cost and availability of it was not a constraint on the expansion of output. I have reviewed this issue elsewhere in detail, over a much longer period (Austin 2008). Qualifications need to be made regarding the heterogeneity of land and the difficulty of reproducing soil fertility, especially where trypanosomiasis denied the opportunity to use animal manure. Even today, when chemical fertilizers exist (at relatively high cost in energy and money), the most efficient way to maintain fertility in much of West Africa seems to be the traditional one of fallowing (de Rouw 1995; Goldstein and Udry 2008). In the case of the most profitable of the early colonial cash crops, Ruf's long-term international comparisons and micro research have shown that the cost of producing cocoa when the trees are replanted, rather than planted on land newly cleared from forest, is high enough to have an often decisive influence on long-term profitability (Ruf 1995a, 1995b). But, for the first generation of cocoa farmers, that was not necessarily a problem (intergenerational trade-offs are considered in Austin 2005, 348–50, 533). Again, in Ghana perhaps more than anywhere, the adoption of cocoa stimulated buying and renting of land. While land was generally abundant, this was not so for farmers whose chieftaincies owned relatively little land suitable for cocoa farming. Such investors bought or rented, often in anticipation of future rather than current needs (Austin 2007; Hill 1963/1997). A final qualification is that land abundance may not have been true of the vicinity of Kano when the groundnut trade took off. Hogendorn conceded that additional groundnuts were grown on plots previously used for millet, though he maintained that land as such was not a constraint (Hogendorn 1979). His pioneering study focused on the groundnut trade; further research is needed on production.

We are now in a position to set out a range of forms taken by the growth of export agriculture, in the hope that this will provide a useful framework for thinking about it in the context of the weaknesses of both existing frameworks, VFS and dependency. Given that labor was generally the scarce factor, the most pertinent way to propose this is in terms of the use of labor.

First, there is at least one case the VFS framework still appears to fit: the oil palm belt of southeast Nigeria. There the growth of agricultural exports, at least until 1918, seems to have involved no opportunity cost: no reduction in existing forms of production, whether for export or domestic markets, according to Martin's study of Ngwa district, as well as Usoro's macro-level assessment (Martin 1988; Usoro 1974).

Second, there are many cases in the savannas of West Africa where the growth of exports constrained or would have constrained the planting of food crops. It is not entirely surprising that colonial governments and metropolitan textile manufacturers hoped that the African colonies would come to rival India, or even the southern United States, as suppliers of cotton: it was already very widely grown for the indigenous handicraft industry. But given that expanded production of output risked the food security of the producing households, it is also not surprising that there was reluctance and resistance. The use of terror to induce the collection of wild rubber in King Leopold's Congo had no parallel in the forests of Nigeria, Ghana, Côte d'Ivoire, and Guinea, where African producers and traders collected rubber freely (Arhin 1980; Dumett 1971; Fenske 2011; Osborn 2004). Even with cotton cultivation, the use of coercion by colonial authorities was more sustained and systematic in the concession colonies than in the "peasant" colonies (Isaacman and Roberts 1995, Likaka 1997). But in parts of the West African savannas, unlike with rubber collection in the forest, there were attempts at coercion by the administration. In northern Nigeria, as noted earlier, Hausa merchants interposed an alternative, groundnut exporting, which was so successful commercially that cotton ceased to be the priority for government revenue or for European merchants. In Uganda, it was different again. In Buganda, it appears that the plantain and banana diet could be supplied so efficiently, in labor terms, that the usual food security constraint on planting more cotton did not apply (Elliott 1969, 136–7). In western Uganda, the story was more complicated. Tosh reports that Lango farmers initially declined to expand their cotton output. But by the 1920s they changed their minds, partly because higher cotton prices increased the incentive, and partly because government measures to improve food security by establishing a system of communal granaries reduced the risk (Tosh 1978).

Third, there is at least one important case where cultivation for export was adopted at the expense, not of the farmers' food security, but of a local market. It seems that many of the Hausa peasants who planted additional groundnuts, to sell them into the export trade, found time and space to do so by reducing their planting of millet. Previously, they had sold millet in the Kano market to obtain cash for their own purchases and to pay tax (Hogendorn 1979). Note that the Sokoto Caliphate had a land tax payable in cash (cowrie shells) before the colonial conquest (Lovejoy and Hogendorn 1993, 165–6, 338). The trade-off between growing food crops for sale and growing groundnuts was one of the major sources of the 1916 famine in Kano (Watts 1983, 283–5). Further research may reveal other cases where export production created or contributed to food scarcities in local markets. The Lango farmers' eventual adoption of cotton was at the expense of reducing their cultivation of sesame seeds for regional markets (Tosh 1978). Carswell shows, however, that the failure of colonial attempts to promote export crops in Kigezi was to a large extent because farmers stuck to growing food crops, which they regularly sold but could also eat themselves if necessary (Carswell 2007, 24–48).

Finally, one major crop can be considered as a case of innovation and improved total factor productivity (Austin, in press, 2014). The adoption of cocoa farming in Ghana and southwestern Nigeria was new. As a "permanent" tree crop, its cycle was completely different from that of the annual crops that farmers were used to growing. Planting cocoa trees created capital goods. Its labor requirements in the harvesting and marketing phase extended through the dry season. This hugely increased labor productivity during the season in which, previously, there was very little to do in agriculture and therefore the opportunity cost of labor was very low (Austin 2005, 73–9, 475–6; Austin 2008, 609). It is not surprising that the story in both major cocoa-producing colonies (of this period) was one of African enterprise rather than colonial coercion. For in the supply of enterprise, and of cash to buy land (though much of that was on credit), pay rents, and support the workforce until the first cocoa trees came into bearing, Ghanaian and Nigerian producers reinvested the proceeds of earlier, precolonial market activities.

The adoption of cocoa entailed serious opportunity costs. It is often remarked that there was no risk to food supply, because West African farmers (especially women, in the Ashanti case) would plant tall food crops such as plantain to shade the young cocoa trees that they (and particularly their husbands) had planted. Once the cocoa trees formed a shade canopy, however, food crops could no longer survive on the farm. Farmers deliberately planted cocoa trees close together, because the shade also prevented weeds from growing. So once the cocoa stock stopped expanding, there was a risk to food security. This was why the Ashanti Confederacy Council of Chiefs came to ban new cocoa farms in 1938, for what proved to be eight years (Austin 2005, 325–36, 529–31). But more immediately, during the cocoa takeoff, existing forms of production for the market, rather than for subsistence, were dropped – at the choice of the producers – to make way for cocoa. Southwest Nigeria and much of the south of Ghana turned from palm oil production to cocoa farming (an option not available in southeast Nigeria). Further inland, in Ashanti, producers abandoned artisanal gold mining, again because cocoa paid better on average (Austin 2005, 78, 476).

Of the four categories of cases of export crop adoption or expansion, the VFS may well have been the least widespread. More commonly, the growth process involved opportunity costs. However, these varied. Where export agriculture expanded fastest, what was reduced was existing forms of production for the market: whether of food or gold. The overall implication is that the cash crop revolution of the early colonial period needs to be viewed in the context of the prior history of market production in West Africa and Uganda.

9.4 INSTITUTIONS, IMPLICATIONS, AND OUTCOMES

I have deliberately given priority to resources, products, and techniques, because their history has been neglected recently, compared to institutions. But politics and rule making is a necessary dimension of any explanation of economic change. The economic historiography written during the 1960s and 1970s was highly impressed with the flexibility and economic efficiency of indigenous institutions. Hill, above all, documented the social organization of collective land purchase by the stranger farmers in Akim Abuakwa, and pointed to its evident success (Hill 1963). This impression is supported by the account given earlier, with the difference that not all the institutions were good for everybody. In southwest Nigeria, pawning proved remarkably effective at quickly providing a supply of laborers when slavery was banned, but this flexibility evidently came at a cost to the pawns. Again, slavery was a major source of early cash crop labor in some areas.

Focusing on the colonial context, we have noted that the most prosperous "peasant" colonies were those where the colonial government did not impose direct taxation, still less compulsory cultivation. Again, where African farmers were left either free of European competition (as in Nigeria) or free to beat it without government interference (as in Ghana), the outcome was much more rapid growth of exports than where European settlers enjoyed privileged access to African labor through the French system of *corvée*, a form of forced labor. It is surely no coincidence that the Ivoirian cocoa takeoff began following the abolition of forced labor (Hopkins 1973, 218–19). The latter case shows what the former does not: that the European authorities did indeed have choice. It was politically possible to try to turn "peasant" economies into European planter colonies; and where that choice was taken, several decades passed before the policy was abandoned – after a campaign led by African capitalist cocoa farmers (Cooper 1996, 186–97, 527–31). For the British, the availability of settler colonies in Kenya and in the south may have reduced the demands on the administrators in West Africa and in London to concede to the demand of soap manufacturer W. H. Lever for large land concessions in Nigeria on which his company would produce palm oil. Given that degree of policy autonomy, the British in Ghana, in particular, could see how the "experiment" of African-led export agriculture worked out before they institutionalized it in the rhetoric of the "West Africa Lands Policy" (Austin 1996; Hopkins 1973, 209–16).

This is not to suggest that, even in British West Africa, colonial subjects were free to compete on fully equal terms with European firms. The European cartelization of the service sector of the export economy is well known, and on the whole was tolerated by the colonial governments (Austin and Uche 2007; Olukoju 1992, 2001–2). The attempts of European merchants to replace intense competition with price fixing often enjoyed some success, even though confounded in 1937–8 in Ghana by the most comprehensive and sustained of a series of cocoa "hold-ups" (Austin 1988; Miles 1978). Monopoly is one of the ways "unequal exchange" became reality, even though African brokers could occasionally exploit information asymmetries to extract economic rents from European firms (Austin 2005, 366–73, 535–6). Again, even when the markets were free of collusion,

Table 9.2. *Foreign trade of major West African economies, selected years (£ million, rounded down, at 2005 UK prices)*

	1897	1913	1919	1929	1932	1938	1945	1952	1960
Ghana	133	558	548	888	615	981	741	2,950	3,610
Nigeria	225	838	784	1,240	752	978	940	4,740	5,942
FWA	266	723	418	813	531	763	1,140	3,980	4,120
Uganda	n.a.	n.a.	n.a.	n.a.	n.a.	n.a.	n.a.	1,390	1,060

Key: FWA = French West Africa. The 1919 figure for FWA is actually for 1920. For the years marked "not available," the figures for Uganda's exports were not separated from Kenya's.
Source: Nominal data from Munro, *Africa*, Appendix 1, to two decimal places. Converted to real terms using Officer 2010. Accessed July 12, 2010.

W. A. Lewis's argument is surely valid, that the prices paid for African produce, as opposed to the prices paid for agricultural produce from the likes of Australia, were partly a function of the low average earnings of the rest of the economy (Lewis 1978).[12]

Even so, recent and current research suggests that the outcomes of the cash crop revolution, at least where it was on the kind of scale that might be considered revolutionary, were more positive than previously thought. Scholars have long recognized that export agriculture in "peasant" colonies multiplied the per capita import purchasing power. Whether the population of the colonies concerned more than doubled between 1900 and 1960, as has often been thought (a recent example is Tabutin and Schouemaker 2004, 590–1), or grew much more slowly as Manning (2010) argued, Table 9.2 suggests a major increase in foreign trade per head (even though the price index used, unfortunately, is the available but only loosely relevant UK retail price index).

But the distribution of this purchasing power was highly unequal, and there has been much debate about whether the migrant labor system diffused more than a very small proportion of it to the distant villages from which the seasonal workers came (Amin 1974b; Miracle and Bery 1970). Recently, Moradi has pioneered the use of anthropometrics as a means of studying changes in physical welfare during the twentieth century. Current work on the heights of African soldiers recruited to the Gold Coast Regiment provides strong evidence that people from all regions of Ghana (and beyond) tended to become taller during the colonial period (Moradi 2008). A paper on which Moradi, Austin, and Baten are currently engaged

[12] I thank Joseph Inikori for reiterating this in conversation.

includes evidence that the improvements in the average height of successive birth cohorts were correlated with cocoa income (output times price). This is consistent with an earlier finding that migrant laborers on Ashanti farms succeeded in obtaining gradually better terms of employment over several decades of the colonial period (and after) (Austin 2005, 316–21, 412–30, 528–9, 542–5). One cannot assume that the positive story revealed by the changing heights of African soldiers in Ghana will be replicated when the anthropometric spotlight shifts to African recruits in the French and Portuguese armies.[13] At least, given the resource poverty of much of French West Africa (the Ivorian forest zone and the Senegal groundnut belt excepted), it would be surprising if heights rose as much as in a cocoa economy – except insofar as migrant laborers from French West Africa were a major component of the hired labor force on Ghanaian cocoa farms.

The diffusion of cash crop income to migrant laborers, specifically via their capacity to obtain increasingly good terms from the owners of the cocoa farms, was made possible by a fundamental institutional change: the ending of slavery. The areas from which migrant laborers now came were often the same relatively poor places that had previously been the unwilling source of large numbers of slaves. But this institutional reform was not fully exogenous to cash cropping. Admittedly, the ideology of abolition was exogenous in this respect, and ultimately colonial administrations had no political alternative but to act – sooner or later – against the recruitment of new slaves, which in turn undermined the position of existing slave owners. But the areas where hired labor relatively quickly replaced slave labor were those where the advent of a lucrative cash crop, notably cocoa in southwest Nigeria and southern Ghana, enabled masters to afford to become employers. Simultaneously, even less profitable cash crops enabled former slaves to set themselves up as free peasants, paying their taxes and buying a modest range of items (Austin 2005, 236–49, 512–15, 2009).

Finally, let us reflect briefly on the significance of the cash crop revolution for long-term economic growth and structural change. "Peasant" economies, even when much of the output was really in the hands of small capitalists rather than peasants, tend not to provide the kind of linkages that facilitate early industrialization. The contribution of coffee profits to the origins of the Sao Paulo cotton textile industry before 1914 owed much to the concentration of those profits in the hands of large estate owners (Dean 1969). That was part of the logic – or at least, of the rhetorical rationale – for the later state "socialization" of export revenue through the

[13] The French data are currently being studied by Denis Cogneau and Alexander Moradi.

marketing board system, to usually disappointing economic effect. Cash crop earnings, private and public, however, paid for much of the formal education that the next generations received. They also expanded the market for manufactures. Recent work has shown that this included specialist African handicraft producers (Byfield 2002; Kriger 2006).

The cash crop revolution in tropical Africa was made possible by the industrialization of the West. The first industrial revolution created the mass markets for soap that made British and French merchants seek palm oil and groundnuts in the mid-nineteenth century. The "second industrial revolution" followed through with the rubber tire and milk chocolate. One thing the VFS approach got partly right is that, during the early colonial period, exporting had a very low opportunity cost for at least the more food-secure colonies, in the sense that producing cocoa or groundnuts for export usually delivered higher returns than did operating within purely domestic markets;[14] though this was not true of all crops everywhere, as we have seen. But the dynamic Western economies did not intersect with a purely static set of African economies. The cash crop revolution was a dramatic episode in the very long-term African path of responding to abundant but fragile lands with land-extensive agricultural techniques and a willingness to adopt innovations, notably exotic crops, providing they did not imperil the adopters' own food security (Austin 2008).

References

Agiri, B. A. (1983–4). "The Development of Wage Labour in Agriculture in Southern Yorubaland 1900–1940." *Journal of the Historical Society of Nigeria* 12(1&2): 95–107.

Amin, Samir. Ed. (1974a). *Modern Migrations in West Africa*. London: Oxford University Press for International African Institute.

(1974b). *Accumulation on a World Scale: A Critique of the Theory of Underdevelopment*, 2 vols. New York: Monthly Review Press.

Arhin, Kwame. (1980). "The Economic and Social Significance of Rubber Production and Exchange on the Gold and Ivory Coasts, 1880–1900." *Cahiers d'études africaines* 20: 77–8, 49–62.

Asiwaju, A. I. (1976). "Migrations as Revolt: The Example of the Ivory Coast and the Upper Volta before 1945." *Journal of African History* 14: 577–94.

Austen, Ralph A. (1981). "Capitalism, Class and African Colonial Agriculture: The Mating of Marxism and Empiricism." *Journal of Economic History* 41: 657–63.

Austin, Gareth. (1988). "Capitalists and Chiefs in the Cocoa Hold-ups in South Asante, 1927–1938." *International Journal of African Historical Studies* 21(1): 63–95.

[14] I thank Leandro Prados de la Escosura for this observation.

(1996). "Mode of Production or Mode of Cultivation: Explaining the Failure of European Cocoa Planters in Competition with African Farmers in Colonial Ghana." In *Cocoa Pioneer Fronts since 1800: The Role of Smallholders, Planters and Merchants*, edited by W. G. Clarence-Smith, 154–75. London: Macmillan.

(2005). *Labour, Land and Capital in Ghana: From Slavery to Free Labour in Asante, 1807–1956*. Rochester NY: Rochester University Press.

(2007). "Labour and Land in Ghana, 1879–1939: A Shifting Ratio and an Institutional Revolution." *Australian Economic History Review* 47(1): 95–120.

(2008). "Resources, Techniques and Strategies South of the Sahara: Revising the Factor Endowments Perspective on African Economic Development, 1500–2000." *Economic History Review* 61(3): 587–624.

(2009). "Cash Crops and Freedom: Export Agriculture and the Decline of Slavery in Colonial West Africa." *International Review of Social History*, 54(1): 1–37.

(in press, 2014). "Vent for Surplus or Productivity Breakthrough? The Ghanaian Cocoa Take-off, c.1890–1936," *Economic History Review*.

(Forthcoming). *Markets, Slaves and States in West Africa*. Cambridge: Cambridge University Press.

Austin, Gareth and Chibuike Ugochukwu Uche. (2007). "Collusion and Competition in Colonial Economies: Banking in British West Africa, 1916–1960." *Business History Review* 81: 1–26.

Bassett, Thomas J. (2001). *The Peasant Cotton Revolution in West Africa: Côte d'Ivoire, 1880–1995*. Cambridge: Cambridge University Press.

Bates, Robert H. (1981). *Markets and States in Tropical Africa*. Berkeley: University of California Press.

(1983). *Essays on the Political Economy of Rural Africa*. Cambridge: Cambridge University Press.

Berry, Sara S. (1975). *Cocoa, Custom and Socio-Economic Change in Rural Western Nigeria*. Oxford: Oxford University Press.

Berthélemy, Jean-Claude and Ludvig Söderling. (2001). "The Role of Capital Accumulation, Adjustment and Structural Change for Economic Take-off: Empirical Evidence from African Growth Episodes." *World Development* 29(2): 323–243.

Byfield, Judith. (2002). *The Bluest Hands: A Social and Economic History of Women Dyers in Abeokuta (Nigeria), 1890–1940*. Portsmouth, NH: Heinemann.

Carswell, Grace. (2007). *Cultivating Success in Uganda: Kigezi Farmers and Colonial Policies*. London and Nairobi: British Institute in Eastern Africa.

Chaves, Isaías, Stanley L. Engerman and James A. Robinson (2014) "Reinventing the Wheel: The Economic Benefits of Wheeled Transportation in Early Colonial British West Africa" (this volume)

Clower, Robert W., George Dalton, Michael Harwitz, and A. A. Walters. (1966). *Growth without Development: An Economic Survey of Liberia*. Evanston, IL: Northwestern University Press.

Cooper, Frederick. (1996). *Decolonization and African Society: The Labor Question in French and British Africa*. Cambridge: Cambridge University Press.

Dean, Warren. (1969). *The Industrialization of São Paulo, 1880–1945*. Austin: University of Texas Press.

De Rouw, A. (1995). "The Fallow Period as a Weed-Break in Shifting Cultivation (Tropical Wet Forests)." *Agriculture, Ecosystems and Environment* 54: 31–43.

Dumett, Raymond E. (1971). "The Rubber Trade of the Gold Coast and Asante in the Nineteenth Century." *Journal of African History* 12(1): 79–101.

Elliott, C. M. (1969). "Agriculture and Economic Development in Africa: Theory and Experience 1880–1914." In *Agrarian Change and Economic Development*, edited by E. L. Jones and S. J. Woolf. London: Methuen.

Engdahl, Torbjörn. (1999). *The Exchange of Cotton: Ugandan Peasants, Colonial Market Regulations and the Organisation of the International Cotton Trade, 19014–1918*. Uppsala: Uppsala University.

Fall, Babacar. (1993). *Le travail forcé en Afrique Occidentale française (1900–1945)*. Paris: Karthala.

Fenske, James. (2011). "'Rubber will not keep in this country': Failed Development in Benin, 1897–1921." Working paper.

Firmin-Sellers, Kathryn. (1996). *The Transformation of Property Rights in the Gold Coast*. Cambridge: Cambridge University Press.

Frank, Andre Gunder. (1978). "On Unequal Exchange." In *Dependent Accumulation and Under-Development*, edited by Andre Gunder Frank, 103–10. London: Macmillan.

Freund, W. M. and R. W. Shenton. (1977). "Vent-for-Surplus Theory and the Economic History of West Africa." *Savanna* 6(2): 191–6.

Givieu, I. H. (1911). "Etude commerciale sur les riz de la vallée du Niger." Dakar, March 25, unpublished: file Q.54, Archives national du Sénégal.

Goldstein, Markus P. and Christopher Udry. (2008). "The Profits of Power: Land Rights and Agricultural Investment in Ghana." *Journal of Political Economy* 118(6): 981–1022.

Harrison, C., T. B. Ingawa, and S. M. Martin. (1987). "The Establishment of Colonial Rule in West Africa, c.1900–1914." In *History of West Africa*, vol. 2, edited by J. F. Ade Ajayi and Michael Crowder, 485–545. Harlow, UK: Longman, 2nd ed.

Helleiner, Gerald K. (1966). *Peasant Agriculture, Government and Economic Growth in Nigeria*. Homewood, IL: R. D. Irwin.

Hill, Polly. (1963). *The Migrant Cocoa-Farmers of Southern Ghana*, 2nd edition with preface by G. Austin. Hamburg: LIT (1997 edition; 1963 edition, Cambridge).

Hogendorn, Jan S. (1975). "Economic Initiative and African Cash Farming: Pre-colonial Origins and Early Colonial Developments." In *Colonialism in Africa 1870–1960, vol. IV, The Economics of Colonialism*, edited by Peter Duignan and L. H. Gann, 283–328. Cambridge: Cambridge University Press.

(1976). "Vent-for-Surplus Models and African Cash Agriculture to 1914." *Savanna* 5(1): 15–28.

(1979). *Nigerian Groundnut Exports: Origins and Early Development*. Zaria: Ahmadu Bello University Press.

Hopkins, Antony G. (1973). *An Economic History of West Africa*. London: Longman.

(1978). "Innovation in a Colonial Context: African Origins of the Nigerian Cocoa-Farming Industry, 1880–1920." In *The Imperial Impact*, edited by Clive Dewey and Antony G. Hopkins, 83–96, 341–2. London: Athlone Press for University of London.

(1986). "The World Bank in Africa: A Historical Perspective." *World Development* 14(12): 1473–87.

(1987). "Big Business in African Studies." *Journal of African History* 28(1): 119–40.

Inikori, Joseph E. (2007). "Africa and the Globalization Process: Western Africa, 1450–1850." *Journal of Global History* 2(1): 63–86.

Isaacman, Allen and Richard L. Roberts. Ed. (1995). *Cotton, Colonialism and Social History in Sub-Saharan Africa*. Portsmouth, NH: Heinemann.

Jedwab, Rémi and Alexander Moradi. (2012). "Revolutionizing Transport: Modern Infrastructure, Agriculture and Development in Ghana." Paper presented at the Modern and Comparative Economic History Seminar, London School of Economics.

Jerven, Morten. (2010). "African Growth Recurring: An Economic History Perspective on African Growth Episodes, 1690–2010." *Economic History of the Developing Regions* 25(2): 127–54.

Kay, G. B. and Stephen Hymer. (1972). "Statistical Abstract." In *The Political Economy of Colonialism in Ghana*, edited by G. B. Kay, 305–419. Cambridge: Cambridge University Press.

Klein, Martin A. (1998). *Slavery and Colonial Rule in French West Africa*. Cambridge: Cambridge University Press.

Kriger, Colleen E. (1954). "Economic Development with Unlimited Supplies of Labour." *Manchester School of Economic and Social Studies* 20: 139–91.

(1978). "The Factorial Terms of Trade." In *The Evolution of the International Economic Order*, edited by W. A. Lewis, 14–20. Princeton, NJ: Princeton University Press.

(2006). *Cloth in West African History*. Lanham, MD: AltaMira Press.

Lewis, W. Arthur. (1953). *Report on Industrialisation and the Gold Coast*. Accra: Gold Coast Government.

Lewis, W. Arthur. (1954). "Economic Development with Unlimited Supplies of Labour." *The Manchester School*, 22(2): 139–91.

(1978). *The Evolution of the International Economic Order*. Princeton, NJ: Princeton University Press.

Likaka, Osumaka. (1997). *Rural Society and Cotton in Colonial Zaire*. Madison: University of Wisconsin Press.

Lovejoy, Paul E. (2005). *Slavery, Commerce and Production in the Sokoto Caliphate of West Africa*. Trenton, NJ: Africa World Press.

Lovejoy, Paul E., and Toyin Falola. Eds. (2003). *Pawnship, Slavery, and Colonialism in Africa*. Trenton, NJ and Asmara: Africa World Press.

Lovejoy, Paul E. and Jan S. Hogendorn. (1993). *Slow Death for Slavery: The Course of Abolition in Northern Nigeria, 1897–1936*. Cambridge: Cambridge University Press.

Manchuelle, François. (1997). *Willing Migrants: Soninke Labor Diasporas, 1848–1960*. Athens OH: Heinemann.

Manning, Patrick. (1982). *Slavery, Colonialism and Economic Growth in Dahomey, 1640–1960*. Cambridge: Cambridge University Press.

(2010). "African Population: Projections, 1851–1961." In *The Demographics of Empire: The Colonial Order and the Creation of Knowledge*, edited by Karl Ittmann, Dennis D. Cordell, and Gregory Maddox, 245–75. Athens: Ohio University Press.

Martin, Susan M. (1988). *Palm Oil and Protest: An Economic History of the Ngwa Region, South-Eastern Nigeria, 1800–1980*. Cambridge: Cambridge University Press.

(1989). "The Long Depression: West African Export Producers and the World Economy, 1914–1945." In *The Economies of Africa and Asia in the Inter-War Depression*, edited by Ian Brown, 74–94. London: Routledge.

Mbodj, Mohamed. (1980). "Sénégal et dépendance: le Sine-Saloum et l'arachide, 1887–1940." In *Sociétés paysannes du tiers-monde*, edited by Catherine Coquery-Vidrovitch, 139–54. Lille: Presses Universitaires de Lille.

Médard, Henri and Shane Doyle. Eds. (2007). *Slavery in the Great Lakes Region of East Africa*. Oxford: James Currey.

Miles, John. (1978). "Rural Protest in the Gold Coast: The Cocoa Hold-ups, 1908–1938." In *The Imperial Impact: Studies in the Economic History of Africa and India*, edited by Clive Dewey and Antony G. Hopkins, 152–70, 353–7. London: Athlone.

Miracle, Marvin P. and Sara S. Berry. (1970). "Migrant Labour and Economic Development." *Oxford Economic Papers* 22 (n.s.): 1, 86–108.

Moradi, Alexander. (2008). "Confronting Colonial Legacies – Lessons from Human Development in Ghana and Kenya, 1880–2000." *Journal of International Development* 20(8): 1107–21.

Muhtar, Mansur. (1988). "Vent for Surplus Critique and the Development of Export Crop Production in Northern Nigeria – Towards a Socio-Economic Interpretation of History." In *Topics on Nigerian Economy*, edited by I. A. Kiyawa, D. S. Hegde, M. Sagagi, and S. Yahaya, 1–18. Kano: Bayero University, Department of Economics, Occasional Papers 1.

Myint, Hla. (1958). "'The Classical Theory' of International Trade and the Underdeveloped Countries." *Economic Journal* 68(2): 317–37.

(1964). *The Economics of the Developing Countries*. London: Hutchinson, 1973 reprint.

(1977). "Adam Smith's Theory of International Trade in the Perspective of Economic Development." *Economica* 44: 231–48.

Ohadike, Don C. (1999). "'When the slaves left, the owners wept': Entrepreneurs and Emancipation among the Igbo People." In *Slavery and Colonial Rule in Africa*, edited by Suzanne Miers and Martin A. Klein, 189–207. London: Frank Cass.

Olukoju, Ayodeji. (1992). "Elder Dempster and the Shipping trade of Nigeria during the First World War." *Journal of African History* 33(2): 255–71.

(2001–2). "'Getting too great a grip': European Shipping Lines and British West African Lighterage Services in the 1930s." *Afrika Zamani* 9 &10: 19–40.

Oroge, E. Adeniyi. (1985). "*Iwofa*: An Historical Survey of the Yoruba Institution of Indenture." *African Economic History* 14: 75–106. Reprinted in *Pawnship, Slavery, and Colonialism in Africa*, edited by Paul E. Lovejoy and Toyin Falola, 325–56. Trenton, NJ, 2003.

Osborn, Emily Lynn. (2004). "'Rubber Fever,' Commerce and French Colonial Rule in Upper Guinée, 1890–1913." *Journal of African History* 45(3): 445–65.

Reid, Richard. (2002). *Political Power in Pre-Colonial Buganda: Economy, Society and Warfare in the Nineteenth Century*. Oxford: James Currey.

Roberts, Richard. (1996). *Two Worlds of Cotton: Colonialism and the Regional Economy in the French Soudan, 1800–1946*. Stanford, CA: Stanford University Press.

Rodney, Walter. (1972). *How Europe Underdeveloped Africa*. London: Bogle-L'Ouverture.

Ruf, François. (1995a). *Booms et crises du cacao: les vertiges de l'or brun*. Montpellier: Ministère de la Coopération CIRAD-SAR and Karthala.

(1995b). "From Forest Rent to Tree-Capital: Basic 'Laws' of Cocoa Supply." In *Cocoa Cycles: The Economics of Cocoa Supply*, edited by François Ruf and P. S. Siswoputranto, 1–54. Cambridge: Woodhead.

Salau, Mohammed Bashir. (2010). "The Role of Slave Labor in Groundnut Production in Early Colonial Kano." *Journal of African History* 31(2): 147–65.

Searing, James F. (2002). *"God Alone Is King": Islam and Emancipation in Senegal: The Wolof Kingdoms of Kajoor and Bawol, 1859–1914*. Portsmouth, NH: Heinemann.

Sender, John and Sheila Smith. (1986). *The Development of Capitalism in Africa*. London: Methuen.

Smith, Sheila. (1976). "An Extension of the Vent-for-Surplus Model in Relation to Long-Run Structural Change in Nigeria." *Oxford Economic Papers* 28(3): 426–46.

(1980). "The Ideas of Samir Amin: Theory or Tautology?" *Journal of Development Studies* 17(1): 5–21.

Suret-Canale, Jean. (1971). *French Colonialism in Tropical Africa 1900–1945*. London: Pica Press, (French original, 1964).

Swindell, Kenneth and Alieu Jeng. (2006). *Migrants, Credit and Climate: The Gambian Groundnut Trade, 1834-1934*. Leiden: Brill.

Szereszewski, R. (1965). *Structural Changes in the Economy of Ghana, 1891–1911*. London: Weidenfeld and Nicolson.

Tabutin, Dominique and Bruno Schoumaker. (2004). "La démographie de l'Afrique au sud du Sahara des années 1950 aux années 2000: Synthése des changements et bilan statistique." *Population* 59: 521–620.

Teal, Francis. (2002). "Export Growth and Trade Policy in Ghana in the Twentieth Century." *World Economy* 25(9): 1319–37.

Thompson, Alvin O. (2006). *Economic Parasitism: European Rule in West Africa 1880–1960*. Cave Hill, Barbados: University of the West Indies.

Tosh, John. (1978). "Lango Agriculture during the Early Colonial Period: Land and Labour in a Cash-Crop Economy." *Journal of African History* 19: 415–39.

(1980). "The Cash-Crop Revolution in Tropical Africa: An Agricultural Reappraisal." *African Affairs* 79: 314, 79–94.

Usoro, E. J. (1974). *The Nigerian Palm Oil Industry*. Ibadan: Ibadan University Press.

Warren, Bill. (1980). *Imperialism: Pioneer of Capitalism*, edited by John Sender. London: NLB.

Watts, Michael. (1983). *Silent Violence: Food, Famine and Peasantry in Northern Nigeria*. Berkeley: University of California Press.

10

Reinventing the Wheel: The Economic Benefits of Wheeled Transportation in Early Colonial British West Africa

Isaías Chaves, Stanley L. Engerman, and James A. Robinson

10.1 INTRODUCTION

Today sub-Saharan Africa is the poorest part of the planet. Though scholars and researchers debate just when the gap between Africa and the rest of the world developed, it is clear that Africa lagged behind Eurasia in terms of many of the key building blocks of economic growth. One can see this in the factors that go to determine income, for example literacy and human capital, but it is perhaps most evident in technology. The basis of the modern economic growth that emerged in Britain in the late eighteenth century was technological innovation, and the Industrial Revolution had itself built on a long incremental series of innovations in agriculture, transportation, and elsewhere in the economy. Many of these innovations did not take place in Africa. For example, outside of Ethiopia, no African country innovated the plow. Similarly, systems of writing were largely restricted to the same region, though also encompassing the Sudan and Somalia. Also absent was the wheel.

Department of Economics, Stanford University, 579 Serra Mall, Stanford, CA 94305–6044. E-mail: ichaves@stanford.edu.

University of Rochester, Department of Economics and Department of History, Harkness Hall, University of Rochester, Rochester, NY 14627. E-mail: enge@troi.cc.rochester.edu.

Harvard University, Department of Government, IQSS, 1737 Cambridge Street N309, Cambridge, MA 01238. E-mail: jrobinson@gov.harvard.edu.

We are particularly grateful to Gareth Austin, Emmanuel Akyeampong, Joel Mokyr, and Bill Summerhill for their detailed comments and suggestions. We also thank seminar participants at the WCFIA Conference on African Development in the Longue Durée at Akwapim, Ghana, and the Harvard Economic History Seminar, particularly Toke Aidt, Joseph Inikori, Noel Maurer, Joseph Miller, and Peter Temin. We also thank María Angélica Baustista and Leander Heldring for their invaluable research assistance.

The fact that wheeled transportation was not used in sub-Saharan Africa until the early colonial period is paradoxical because it is well established that African societies knew about the wheel from the early modern period onward.[1] They did not have to reinvent the wheel, only adopt it. Law (1980) documents many cases where Europeans gave gifts of wheeled transportation to different African kings. Wheeled carriages were in use in Dahomey from at least the eighteenth century and were even produced there. Nevertheless, wheeled vehicles did not spread out of ceremonial uses with the exception of a small amount of military use.

Why did African societies not adopt a technology that seemed to promise huge economic benefits in terms of reduced costs of transportation?[2] That such cost savings existed was certainly believed by early colonial officials and Europeans of the nineteenth century who noted this failure to adopt the wheel. In the absence of wheeled transportation, the majority of goods were transported by head porterage. British colonial diplomat Sir Gerald Portal noted in 1903:

> As an animal of burden man is out and out the worst. He eats more, carries less, is more liable to sickness, gets over less ground, is more expensive, more troublesome, and in every way less satisfactory than the meanest four-footed creature that can be trained, induced, or forced to carry a load. (Quoted in Clifford 1920, 151)

The consensus view about the absence of wheeled transportation on the development of West Africa is well summed up by the 1926 report that Secretary of State for the Colonies William Ormsby-Gore made to Parliament. Commenting on transportation difficulties in various parts of Nigeria where he visited, Ormsby-Gore wrote:

> The Province of Ogoja contains an estimated population of between 600,000 and 700,000 people who are producing little or nothing for export, and a low standard of life obtains. Until Ogoja is opened up by a network of roads ... there can be little trade with its consequent stimulus to production, and the real development of the Province has not yet begun. (Ormsby-Gore 1926, 24–5)

[1] See Piggott (1983) for a history of the use of wheeled transportation and Bulliet (1975) for how the introduction of the camel into the trans-Saharan trade led to the abandonment of the use of wheeled transportation on that route.

[2] As Goody (1971) and Austen and Headrick (1983) point out, this does not exhaust the puzzles surrounding the non-adoption of the wheel in Africa because neither potters' wheels nor spinning wheels were adopted either.

Later he noted:

> In British West Africa there is still too much of the most obsolete and expensive form of transport. I refer to the wide use of head porterage. (Ormsby-Gore 1926, 29)

Indeed, as recently as 1980 one could read in a textbook treatment:

> At first, head porterage had to be used for carrying imports; and palm oil was sent to the coast by the curious and expensive method of barrel-rolling. Porterage was a social evil, a political danger and an economic waste. (Church 1980, 152)

The use of such an incredibly labor-intensive system of transportation seems all the more puzzling when one considers that Africa has historically been very labor scarce (Austin 2008; Herbst 2000). Portal's view was widely shared by early colonial officials, who not only took it for granted that the absence of wheeled transportation was disastrously inefficient, but also routinely produced numbers to prove it.

Most of these officials gave no explanation for why Africans chose not to adopt a technology that they regarded as massively superior to the alternatives in use. The first attempt to provide such an explanation appears to be McPhee (1926). Though Portal noted how unhealthy human porters were, McPhee in essence argued that, at least in the forest zone of Africa, draught animals could not be used because of the presence of the tsetse fly. This, he claimed, made wheeled transportation, which would normally have depended on draught animals, uneconomical. His argument is rather equivocal, however, because the relevant chapter of his book attempts to show in some detail that road and rail transportation were far superior to head porterage. He seemed to take it for granted that Africans could not have built motorable roads or railways. He also explicitly pointed out, on the basis of Lugard's 1919 report on the amalgamation of northern and southern Nigeria for northern Nigeria, that:

> Strangely enough, although there are over 3,000,000 cattle, 176,000 donkeys, 113,000 horses and 4,000 camels, yet such a thing as a cart may be said to be unknown. (McPhee 1926, 121)

Therefore, though the argument about the tsetse fly is obviously relevant, it can at best only be a very partial solution to the puzzle. McPhee's discussion was augmented by Hopkins (1973), who argued that the cost of building roads through the forest zones was so high that this also made wheeled transportation uneconomical. Ogunremi (1975) also claims that head porterage was economically efficient because labor was not really scarce, and he claims that the calculations made by Lugard and others are misleading because they ignore the huge capital costs involved in constructing railways. In essence, McPhee to an extent, but certainly Hopkins and Ogunremi, respond to the puzzle of the non-adoption of wheeled transportation by asserting that it is not a puzzle and that in fact it was an economically rational decision given the circumstances.[3]

These existing explanations present obvious problems. First, none of them is based on any real calculation or what was or was not economically rational. Second, while it is clearly correct that the impact of the tsetse fly made it difficult to use draught animals in large parts of central Africa,[4] wheeled transportation was not used in areas where there was no tsetse either. This is true not just in southern Africa, but also in the Sahel or northern Nigeria. Third, as Portal's remark notes, humans were very unhealthy as well, so what is relevant is the health of animals compared to humans, not the absolute health of animals in the tsetse zone. Finally, Hopkins's claim that wheeled transportation was not adopted in the forest zone because roads were uneconomical to build runs into the problem that African polities in the forest zone did indeed build such roads. Most notably, Wilks (1989) discusses in detail the great roads of the Asante Empire in the Gold Coast in the first half of the nineteenth century,[5] and Reid (2002) does the same for the roads built by the Buganda state. Yet neither the Asante nor the Buganda states used wheeled transportation.

In this chapter, we conduct the first attempt, to our knowledge, at bringing systematic evidence to bear on the question of whether wheeled transportation was economically rational in sub-Saharan Africa. We focus on the three British West Africa colonies of the Gold Coast, Nigeria, and Sierra Leone, largely because the British colonial state recorded in great detail the costs of constructing and maintaining different transportation systems in these colonies. Though we examine the efficiency of various types of wheeled transportation, including carts and motor vehicles, the bulk of our analysis focuses on railways. Railways of course embody not just wheels, but also

[3] See Basu and Weil (1998) and Acemoglu and Zilibotti (2001) for formalizations of the idea of appropriate technology.

[4] Witness, for instance, the enormous and costly lengths to which the Oyo Empire had to go to keep its cavalry safe from the ravages of tsetse (see Law 1977).

[5] The early colonial officials who deplored the backward state of transportation in Africa seem not to have been aware of these roads. In his discussion, McPhee, for example, notes: "At the beginning of the last century no proper roads existed anywhere in West Africa.... The earliest roads, not much better than rough tracks which were liable to be obliterated within a year by forest growths, were military roads. Thus Sir Garnet ... Wolsley constructed a road into the heart of Ashanti during the War of 1873–1874. Throughout the whole century very little progress was made" (1926, 106–7).

other technologies, such as iron smelting and casting and steam engines. Our focus is motivated by the fact that we have from colonial records very comprehensive information on the amount of goods and passengers that the railways carried, which we do not have for any other method of transportation. We also know a great deal about the capital expenditures associated with railway building, the neglect of which has been used as a critique of earlier estimates that head porterage was inefficient. In addition, this focus allows us to make comparisons with the rich literature in economic history that has examined the economic impact of railways. Our methodology is the canonical one based on that of Fogel (1964).[6]

Our basic findings are very contrary to the conventional wisdom. First, all forms of wheeled transportation were economically rational in the sense that they generated positive social savings, that is, that their adoption would have increased national income. In the case of railways, the social savings for goods traffic as a percentage of GDP range from a low of 0.8 percent in the Gold Coast in 1909 to a high of 7.8 percent for the same colony in 1934–5. For passenger traffic, the numbers are smaller, basically zero. Second, and more important, the social rate of return on railway construction was incredibly high, a calculation that explicitly takes into account the capital expenditures. This rate of return was around 100 percent in Nigeria, implying that the social savings in any year were equivalent to the entire capital outlays until then. Elsewhere they were lower, but were close to 50 percent for both the Gold Coast and Sierra Leone for much of the period. Our estimates therefore contradict the idea that wheeled transportation was not adopted in sub-Saharan Africa because it was an inappropriate technology.[7] Indeed, quite contrary to the conventional wisdom that railways were not appropriate because they were too expensive to build in African conditions, we find that they were cheap to build – their cheapness, in fact, causes the astonishing social rates of return calculations we present. This is consistent with the recent findings of Jedwab and Moradi (2011), who find that colonial railway construction in the Gold Coast had a powerful effect on exports and development.[8]

6 Tsey (1986), in his analysis of the expansion of railways in the colonial Gold Coast, observed that one could undertake such an exercise but he chose not to do so.

7 At some level this is not very surprising. Technological differences today, as captured by total factor productivity, are at the heart of differences in income per capita between Africa and the rest of the world (Acemoglu, Johnson, and Robinson 2001; Hsieh and Klenow 2010; Hall and Jones 1999), but few believe that such differences are efficient.

8 See also the innovative work by Donaldson (2010), who finds large positive effects of colonial railroads in India using a general equilibrium model.

If wheeled transportation was economically efficient and generated very high social rates of return, why did Africans not adopt it? For the case of railways, we can identify three types of explanations. The first is the obvious point that it was very difficult to construct such large public works as railways without sufficient political centralization. We illustrate this argument in Sierra Leone. The second comes from thwarted attempts by a mission from the Asante state in Ghana to contract British engineers in London to build a railway in 1895: European powers had an interest in restricting technology adoption by African polities. Asante's attempt to build a railway, part of a larger program of modernization embarked on after 1874, was blocked by British colonial secretary Joseph Chamberlain. The likely explanation is that Britain did not want autonomous modernization of African polities. African states considering adopting railways invariably needed to rely on foreign capital, engineers, and expertise. This was normal during the nineteenth century: railways in Latin America and the Middle East were built with foreign capital and expertise. But at the time of the Scramble for Africa, European powers wished to control this type of technology adoption by African polities because it made them harder to control, a kind of incentive that was absent in Latin America and the Middle East. The third explanation comes from the rich evidence on the one independent African polity that actually built a railway, Ethiopia. Namely, African polities that could have profitably adopted railway technology had a political incentive not to because doing so might hasten the loss of sovereignty to Europeans. Here the evidence clearly shows that the Ethiopians were very concerned that constructing a railway from Djibouti up to Addis Ababa would precipitate a process of colonial domination and conquest. Similar mechanisms were at work elsewhere, for example in the Sultanate of Zanzibar.

This chapter proceeds as follows. In the next section, we discuss some of the estimates of the costs of transportation that colonial officials and administrators made during the early twentieth century. This evidence, which certainly suggests that head porterage was inefficient, is typically very incomplete, because it is not clear exactly what is involved in the calculations or how representative any of the information is. In Section 10.3, we discuss the data that are available to undertake cost and benefit calculations in the British colonies of the Gold Coast, Nigeria, and Sierra Leone. Section 10.4 then uses this data to provide estimates of the social savings from the introduction of the railways in these three colonies, and it also provides more speculative estimates of the social savings associated with simpler forms of wheeled transportation. Section 10.5 then focuses on the social rate of return of the railways. Section 10.6 discusses in more detail, and presents evidence for, our explanation for why African states did not adopt economically superior transportation technology during the nineteenth century. Section 10.7 concludes.

10.2 CONTEMPORARY DISCUSSION AND EXISTING EVIDENCE

British colonial officials did not doubt that the lack of wheeled transportation was a major impediment to economic progress in West Africa. To demonstrate this, they produced a whole range of different numbers, which were then constantly repeated over the years. Some of these are summarized in Table 10.1.

Unfortunately, in all the cases we have found, it is never clear exactly how these estimates were constructed or what considerations went into them. Ormsby-Gore's numbers, for example, were introduced by noting that:

> At Zaria, in Northern Nigeria, I was provided with some carefully compiled figures regarding the cost of different forms of transportation per ton-mile. Head porterage in an area where labour is plentiful and cheap works out at 2/6 per ton-mile; motor transport at 1/- per ton-mile; donkey transport at 11d; camel transport at between 9d and 10d; while the railway takes baled cotton from Zaria to Lagos at under 2d per ton-mile. (1926, 29–30)[9]

These numbers were widely reproduced, for example in Hailey's famous survey (1938, 1540). Yet Ormsby-Gore provided no further information about who gave him these figures or what sources they used to calculate them. Clearly, taken at face value, these numbers suggest that head porterage was extremely inefficient. According to these numbers, while the cost of shipping freight by railway was two pence per ton-mile, the cost of head porterage was two shillings and six pence, or fifteen times more!

Sir Frederick Lugard similarly regarded head porterage as extremely inefficient:

> For uncounted centuries the African has been his own beast of burden, and a simple calculation shows that the cost of land transport by such means with a wage rate of 9d. per day is about 3 shillings per ton mile. (1922, 461)

This number is also very widely reproduced. In a footnote, Lugard noted that this calculation was based on assuming that a porter carried sixty-five pounds and could walk twelve miles a day and was then adjusted upward to

[9] The notation d. means pence, s. means shillings; there were twelve pence in a shilling and twenty shillings in a pound.

Table 10.1. *Contemporary estimates of the relative cost of different methods of transportation (cost in shillings and pence per ton-mile)*

	House of Commons (1909)	Ormsby-Gore (1926)	Ogunremi (1982)
Cask Rolling	1s.21/2 d. – 1s.11d.		
Hand Trucks	1s. 10d		
Head Porterage	3s.1d – 5s.	2s.6d.	1s.10d. – 2s.
Motor Lorry	1s.8d.	1s.	
Railway		2d.	
Donkey		11d.	9d. – 10d.

allow for sickness and supervision. He also observed that "for bulky loads the cost is much more." Elsewhere Lugard remarked that "a railway train of average capacity and engine power will do the work of 13,000 carriers at one twentieth of the cost" (1922, 462–3).

Other calculations suggest similar things about the relative efficiency of different forms of transportation. For example, the numbers taken from the House of Commons (1909) come from an extensive survey of methods of transportation in the entire British Empire undertaken by the secretary of state for the colonies. In this survey, carried out in 1907, the governors of the different colonies were requested to provide information to a standardized set of questions about the nature of transportation in their colonies. The information provided for the Gold Coast, presented by E. F. W. Wilkinson, acting director of public works, suggests that transportation by head porterage cost between three shillings and one pence to five shillings per ton-mile (House of Commons 1909, 43). These figures are as much as twice those for Zaria, perhaps indicating the relative labor scarcity of the Gold Coast during that period. They are, however, consistent with Lugard's numbers.

For our purposes at the moment, the most interesting comparison is between head porterage and the railways.[10] These oft-quoted numbers suggest that head porterage was about fifteen to twenty times as costly as the railway. Yet it is not clear how these numbers were constructed. Most crucially, it is not clear whether they factor in the large fixed cost of constructing

[10] Forms of transportation other than head porterage were very important in different precolonial contexts. For instance, Hill (1972) describes how tobacco produced in Katsina in northern Nigeria was shipped as far south as Ilorin using donkeys, and the great kola trade between Nigeria and Ghana was carried out mostly by donkey (Lovejoy 1980).

the railway or whether they are based just on the variable cost. Because it is precisely the large cost of constructing modern transportation systems in West African conditions that Hopkins (1973) argues made them economically irrational, we need to assess the efficiency of different systems of transportation properly taking these costs into account – something we will do by calculating the social rate of return.

10.3 THE DATA

10.3.1 Railways

The surveys for railway construction were carried out at different dates in British West Africa. For Sierra Leone, they were undertaken in 1893–4, and for Lagos, they were undertaken in early 1893 during the tour of Governor Sir Gilbert Carter. Construction on the Sierra Leone and Lagos railways started in 1896, while construction on the Gold Coast Railway started in 1898 (see Shelford 1920). The Sierra Leone railway ran southeast from Freetown and reached Pendembu in 1908. The first railway in the Gold Coast went inland from the port of Sekondi toward the Asante goldfields, and it reached Kumase in 1903. The second line, linking Kumase to Accra, was started in 1909 and completed in 1923. The first railway line in Nigeria started at Lagos and reached Jebba on the Niger river in 1909. The second railway linked Kano to the port of Baro on the Niger, and it was completed in 1911. All the lines were built and operated by the colonial governments.[11]

Our main source of data on the costs of constructing, maintaining, and running the railway, the amount of freight hauled, the number of passengers carried, and the revenues generated from freight and passengers is the various reports of the colonial governments to London, particularly the reports of the railways and transportation departments. We focus on three dates, 1909 (1911 for Sierra Leone because earlier reports did not present the appropriate data), 1924/25, and 1934/35. The financial year for all colonies started on January 1 for 1909/11, but it switched to April 1 for the Gold Coast and Nigeria during the 1920s and 1930s – whence the fact that for our latter two colonies and dates, the data on railways straddles two years. Our basic data on railways for the Gold Coast comes from the 1909 "Report of the General Manager upon the Government Railways," and the Gold Coast Railway Administrative Reports for 1924–5 and 1934–5. For Nigeria, we have the "Lagos Railway Annual Report 1909," the "Nigerian Railway

[11] For a contemporary discussion of the pros and cons of government versus private ownership and operation of the railways, see House of Commons (1924).

and Udi Coalmines Administrative Report for the Year ending 31st March 1925," and for 1934/35 the "Annual Report on the Government Railway and Colliery of Nigeria for the Financial Year ending 31st March 1935." Finally, for Sierra Leone, we have the "Report on the Transport Department for the Year 1911" and the Administrative Reports of the Railway for 1925 and 1935.

These sources of information give us extensive data to calculate the amount of freight and passengers the railways carried in these three years. The reports also provide information on current receipts and expenditures, as well as capital outlays to date on railway construction and maintenance.

A potentially important and obvious advantage of the railway is that it moved people much faster than they could have moved by walking. We can estimate the social savings associated with this change, because for most years the railway reports tell us the total number of passenger miles traveled. We can estimate how long it took to travel this number of miles if we know how fast the trains went, and also how fast it took to walk. Unfortunately, we have only discovered a railway timetable for Nigeria in 1921 (Burns 1921), but not for either the Gold Coast or Sierra Leone, and the reports of the Railway Department never mention how long it took trains to travel between stations (though they do assiduously report the percentage that were late). The data in Burns (1921) implies an average speed of fifteen miles per hour. As a reality check, a rough calculation of the speed of the trains can be backed out of the travel account of Alldridge (1910), who visited Sierra Leone in the early twentieth century. Alldridge traveled on the train from Freetown to Bo leaving at seven in the morning and arriving at five in the evening. Because the distance between the stations is 136 miles, we can say that the average speed in Sierra Leone was 13.6 miles per hour. This appears to be very slow, but it is partly justified by the fact that the Sierra Leone railway had a narrow gauge, which possibly meant that it had to go slower than one would have expected. We have no comparable account of travel from the Gold Coast or Nigerian railways. These used broader gauges, so the fifteen miles per hour in Nigeria seems completely reasonable. Thus we choose fifteen miles per hour as a conservative estimate. For an estimate of how fast someone could walk in this region, we use Wilks (1989, chapter 1), who has an extensive discussion of travel times between different parts of Asante during the nineteenth century. All his estimates are close to fifteen miles per day, which is the modal estimate of how far a head porter could walk, and we shall take this as the relevant travel speed for passengers on foot. This implies a speed of two miles per hour.

To value the time saved by travel on the railway, it is natural to take the wage rate as the opportunity cost of time. Exactly what the correct wage to use is depends on who the traveler was. For example, in 1924–5 in the Gold Coast, of the 1,487,164 passengers who traveled by train, 14,851 traveled first class, 21,988 traveled second class, and the rest traveled third class. We do not have the information necessary to decompose the total passenger miles into components of different groups, so we could assume instead that the passenger miles were allocated in proportion to the numbers of each class (i.e., on average each type of person traveled the same distance). This implies that of the 41,751,573 total passenger miles, 416,936 (1%) were first class passenger miles, 617,305 (1.5%) were second class passenger miles, and the rest (97.5%) were third class passenger miles. To value the time saved by the introduction of the railway, we need to impute some opportunity cost of time to these different groups. For third class passengers, we could choose the unskilled wage rate of 9d. per day or 1d. per hour, assuming a nine-hour workday. Skilled wages in the Blue Books range from 2s.6d. to 5s. To calculate the value of time for first and second class passengers, we value the hours saved at the rate of 5s. per day. Unfortunately, this (1924–5) is the only time for which our sources document the breakdown among the different classes of passengers. And yet, as is evident, first and second class travel was relatively so unimportant that year-to-year changes in the composition of passenger miles are unlikely to drive our results. Therefore, we proceed with the simple assumption that time can be valued at the unskilled wage rate. This is 9d. per day for all the colonies for the first two dates and then 12.d., 8.d., and 11.d. in the mid-1930s for the Gold Coast, Nigeria, and Sierra Leone, respectively.

10.3.2 Head Porters

To compare to the cost of using head porters, we need data on how much a head porter could carry and the rate of pay. Though information on this is much less systematic than the data from the railways, the consensus seems strong on what the right numbers are. Ormsby-Gore notes:

> [T]here is a considerable body of labour temporarily employed on road and railway construction. The supply of voluntary labour for the latter purposes has always proved inadequate in Nigeria, and recourse is had to compulsory or "enlisted" – sometimes called "political" – labour for these essential public works and services. All the railways and most of the roads in Nigeria have involved the use of this compulsory labour.... Such compulsory labour is recruited by the native authorities. It is only called upon to work for a definite period, usually, and never more than, one

month at a time. It is paid, usually at a rate of 9d. per day.... Unpaid compulsory labour legalized under the Roads and Rivers Ordinance of Northern Nigeria is only used for keeping clean roads and rivers within local boundaries when called upon to do so by the Resident. (1926, 133)

Nine pence a day is the figure that is widely quoted from all over British West Africa for the cost of a head porter from around 1910 until the middle of the 1920s, though head porterage was surely much less prevalent in 1925. Ormsby-Gore reported a higher number from his visit to Sierra Leone: 1s.3d. per day in the Colony (the capital Freetown and its environs) and 1s. per day in the Protectorate (the hinterland and interior of what is now Sierra Leone) (1926, 58).

Just as there is a consensus on wages in the primary sources, there is also a consensus that a head porter could carry about sixty pounds. Indeed, this seems to have been more or less the official load colonial officials used when they hired porters for government work (Ogunremi 1975, 47). The numbers on how far a fully loaded porter could walk in a day do vary, with perhaps fifteen miles being the consensus. For instance, in the Sierra Leone case, Ormsby-Gore reported that a porter usually carried forty-five to fifty pounds of weight and could walk twelve to fifteen miles per day (1926, 58). A command paper from the House of Commons on mechanized transportation suggested that in the Gold Coast:

The motor lorries carry about 1 ton to 2 1/2 tons; a cask of palm oil weighs 17 3/4 cwt.; a cask of cocoa weighs about 12 cwt.' a hand truck carries from 15 to 20 cwt with 6 to 8 men to a truck; head loads are about 60 lbs. (House of Commons 1909, 42)

Moreover, "casks, hand trucks and head loads get over 20 miles per day." The chief commissioner for the Northern Territories of the Gold Coasts reported that, although "native rates [are] impossible to gauge," the government paid "10d. a day for loads of 50 to 60 lbs., 1d. a day of which goes to the chief who provided the carriers." As for how far a porter could walk, the commissioner noted, "At present natives are content to do 10 to 15 miles a day." Northern Nigeria presents a similar situation, with sixty pounds mentioned as the normal head load and wages for hammock men listed at nine pence and those for a laborer at nine pence to one shilling per day (House of Commons 1909, 22–3). In Sierra Leone, "Head loads 60 to 100 lbs. Hand carts 1 ton to 30 cwts" (House of Commons 1909, 102). Though this report provided no information on the wage paid to head porters in Sierra Leone, it noted that a barrel roller, a similarly unskilled worker, was paid one shilling per day. This figure is identical to the wage Ormsby-Gore recorded for a head porter.

To judge if these wage rates are reasonable, we can compare them to other readily available information. For example, Oyemakinde notes that workers who were recruited by compulsion to build the railways in northern Nigeria between 1911 and 1915 were paid nine pence per day, while in Yorubaland, where workers freely took up such employment, they were usually paid one shilling per day (1974, 318). The House of Commons command paper detailing the costs of railway construction in the Gold Coast, Nigeria, and Sierra Leone does report the daily wage rate of unskilled workers used in railway construction (House of Commons 1904). These were ten pence a day in Sierra Leone, one shilling a day in Lagos, and one shilling three pence a day in the Gold Coast.

All in all, these scattered numbers are quite consistent with each other, and for the period around 1909 they suggest that Lugard's number of three shillings per ton-mile is a reasonable figure for the cost of head porterage, at least to the extent that he corrected it for the health of the porters, which would explain why the cost is higher than other simple calculations. Ormsby-Gore's 1926 figures suggest that this number is reasonable for 1924–5 as well. For our 1935 estimates, we do not have contemporary information on the rates of pay of head porters. However, the Blue Books for the colonies report unskilled workers' wages. Because the wage rates we have for head porters in earlier periods correspond closely to the wages for unskilled workers as stated in Blue Books, we can use the latter data to get a counterfactual wage for head porterage in 1935. In the Gold Coast, this wage ranged from nine pence to fifteen pence; in Nigeria, the range three pence to one shilling per day is given; and in Sierra Leone, unskilled workers' wages are reported as eleven pence. We therefore used the wage rates of twelve pence for the Gold Coast, eight pence for Nigeria, and eleven pence for Sierra Leone.

Rather than use Lugard's three-shilling estimate, we assume in our calculations for 1909/11 and 1924/25 that head porters could walk fifteen miles in a day, carry sixty pounds, and were paid nine pence in all the colonies. These numbers imply a cost of one shilling and ten pence per ton-mile for head porterage. For 1934/35, this cost increases in the Gold Coast by one third to two shillings and six pence per ton-mile, it falls to one shilling and eight pence per ton-mile in Nigeria, and it increases to two shillings and three pence per ton-mile in Sierra Leone.

An important issue that can limit the applicability of the social savings approach to colonial Africa is the nature of the labor market. Coerced labor (or "political" labor, as colonial officials called it) was used extensively to build roads and railways; at the same time, slaves were also commonly used as head porters, and some of these slaves were no doubt supplied by chiefs to help railway and road construction as well. In the Gold Coast in particular there appears to have been a great labor shortage at the time the British were building the railway, and the supply of Africans that were forthcoming at the wages that the British were prepared to pay was insufficient to get the work done. Colonial officials therefore induced local chiefs to provide labor (see Akurang-Parry 2000; Mann 1995; and Thomas 1973 for studies of forced labor, and Mason 1978 and Swindell 1992 for specific studies in the context of railway construction all in the context of British West Africa). One could argue that because labor could be coerced either to build and run railways or to work as porters this should not influence the relative benefits of the two methods of transportation. Nevertheless, because head porterage is much more labor intensive than railway construction, a natural conjecture would be that the ability to repress labor would bias downward the social savings from railways. We return to this when we discuss the West African colonies in comparative perspective. We note, however, that coerced labor was not everywhere used for head porterage. For example, in East Africa, Rockel (2006) shows that there was a basically free labor market for head porterage, so this problem may be much more important there (see Coquery-Vidrovitch and Lovejoy, eds. 1985 for comparative studies).

10.3.3 GDP Estimates

To get some sense of how big the cost differences between different methods of transportation were, it is useful to have something to compare the costs to. The most obvious normalization is with respect to GDP, and this is the standard approach in the social savings literature. However, to our knowledge, with the exception of Szereszewski's (1965) pioneering construction of GDP estimates for the Gold Coast in 1891, 1901, and 1911, no estimates of GDP for the colonies of interest exist for this period. Szereszewski's approach was based on colonial Blue Books, which contain extensive information about imports and exports and the public sector. He used a number of assumptions to construct estimates of consumption and capital formation. Most speculatively, he also constructed estimates of the consumption and investment made by the "native economy," of which there are only population estimates during this period. Nevertheless, Szereszewski's approach uses the existing information in a very creative way and produces quite believable estimates. We therefore used it to construct from the Blue Books estimates of nominal GDP for the three colonies, for all of the relevant periods. These calculations may be of independent interest, and we discuss them in detail in the appendix to this chapter.

10.4 WERE THE RAILWAYS ECONOMICALLY EFFICIENT? A SOCIAL SAVINGS APPROACH

Though the calculations discussed previously are interesting, they fall very short of a systematic treatment of the issue. Moreover, one could easily imagine that colonial officers, anxious to legitimize their "civilizing mission" in Africa, may have been inclined to overemphasize the technological backwardness of Africa and therefore the advantages of "modern" methods of transportation.

The conventional method for tackling the issues broached in this chapter is that of social savings introduced by Fogel (1964) and Fishlow (1965). The social savings of a given method of transportation, such as the railways, is the difference between the actual cost of shipping the goods and people by that method of transportation and the cost of shipping them without that method of transportation. As Fogel (1979) points out, the social savings associated with a particular efficient method of transportation is the loss of national income associated with the substitution of an inefficient method of transportation for the efficient one. In our case, we focus on the social savings associated with using railways rather than head porterage to move goods and people.

This approach has been heavily criticized, requires strong assumptions about the nature of the economy, and fails to capture important impacts of transportation innovations (see Crafts 2004; Fogel 1979; Leunig 2010; O'Brien 1977; and Summerhill 2003 for extensive discussions of the pros and cons of this approach). For our purposes, one central problem with this method is that it requires the assumption that one is studying a perfectly competitive industry in long-run equilibrium, so that price (average revenue) is equal to long-run average cost. Obviously railways, which involve a huge fixed cost, cannot be in such an equilibrium. Moreover, in all the West African colonies the prices charged for freight and passengers were not determined by perfect or imperfect competition; they were set by the colonial administration.[12] Furthermore, basic social savings calculations cannot incorporate the potentially large externalities created by the construction of the railways. It is clear from contemporary discussions that

[12] Indeed, it is not just that the colonial administration regulated ton-mile prices; it also regulated other activities in ways that heavily influenced the profitability of the railways. For example, in 1936 the Gold Coast government passed Ordinance 38, which prevented the carriage by roads of key export goods (such as cocoa) and key imports because road transportation was diverting traffic from the railways. Sierra Leone adopted a similar measure the following year (Ordinance 6 of 1937) (see Hailey 1938, 1559–60 and Church 1956).

colonial officials strongly believed these externalities were real and significant. Harry Johnston, an avid colonizer of Africa, noted in 1889 that:

> There is no civiliser like the railway, and to build a railway through an uncivilized country is to centuple its existing trade, or to create commerce if none exists: the railway saps race prejudices and dissolves fanaticism. (quoted in McPhee 1926, 111)

British observers in many places echoed his views. McPhee argued that:

> Slavery in Northern Nigeria found its chief buttress in the demand for cheap transport in a region where animal transport was not feasible on account of the tsetse fly … the Government built railways, and slave carriage died a natural death, because it became uneconomical. (McPhee 1926, 126–7)

Lugard observed about the construction of the railway in Nigeria that "it has killed the slave trade" (1922, 463). Knowles extensively discussed positive externalities flowing from railway construction (1928, 138–52).

Despite these caveats, in the absence of sufficient data to calibrate a general equilibrium model, the social savings methodology does present us with a simple method of looking at the economic impact of the railways; and because these caveats would apply to all such studies, the comparison between our results and those of others is in itself interesting. To apply this methodology, we follow the simplest approach of Fogel (1964) in assuming a zero elasticity of demand for transportation services. Maybe more important in the present context, we assume that, in the counterfactual scenario where the freight hauled by the railways is carried instead by head porterage, there is no impact on the labor market; with this assumption, we can use the observed wages to calculate the counterfactual cost of moving the freight by head porterage. Hence, we are assuming that labor supply is completely elastic.

10.4.1 Results from the Gold Coast

Table 10.2 presents basic data on the Gold Coast railways for the three dates of interest. In 1909, only 168 miles of track were open in the colony, from Secondi on the coast up to the Asante capital of Kumase. By 1924–5, the railroad had expanded to 394 miles, because by then a line linked Kumase to the colonial capital of Accra, and by 1934–5 it had grown to 500 miles, as the grid had been extended to a number of smaller feeder railways (Gould 1959 gives a good overview). Between 1909 and 1924–5, the amount of freight hauled expanded dramatically, with the number

Table 10.2. *Basic data on the Gold Coast railways*

	1909	1924–5	1934–5
Mile of Track Open	168	394	500
Total Freight Hauled (Tons)	56,454	796,888	730,382
Total Freight in Ton-Miles	3,763,552	43,170,885	42,952,026
Total Passengers Moved	215,729	1,487,164	1,822,093
First Class		14,851	
Second Class		21,988	
Third Class		1,450,325	
Total Passenger Miles		41,751,573	44,704,654
Total Freight Revenues (£)	146,845	850,238	633,525
Total Passenger Revenues £)	38,565	214,703	150,840
Total Expenditures (£)	73,914	568,012	487,530
Total Capital Outlays (£)	1,808,323	7,419,086	9,241,698

of ton-miles growing by more than 1,000 percent. From that point until 1934–5 there was a contraction, which no doubt reflects the impact of the Great Depression; the economic collapse in Britain and elsewhere severely restricted the demand for tropical exports. The data for total passenger miles is unfortunately incomplete and does not exist for the earlier date (or dates near it), and we only have the breakdown of passenger traffic into different classes for the period 1924–5. We also record in Table 10.2 total freight and passenger receipts, which rose sharply but then fell quite significantly between 1924–5 and 1934–5. Finally, we record total capital outlays to date for the three dates.

Table 10.3 contains our three sets of estimates of social savings from freight for 1909, 1924–5, and 1934–5. In all columns, the first set of calculations relates to our direct measure of the relative costs of the different methods of transportation. The first row reports total ton-miles of freight transported in the different years; these numbers are taken from Table 10.2. The second row contains the information from Table 10.2 on total freight revenues. The third row shows how much it would have cost to move the observed ton-miles of railway freight with head porters, given our assumptions that a head porter walked fifteen miles a day and could carry sixty pounds (there are 2,240 lbs in a British ton). As discussed earlier, for the first two columns we assume a wage rate of nine pence per day, increasing to twelve pence a day in 1934–5. The social savings from railways are then simply the difference between lines 3 and 2. In all cases, these are positive,

Table 10.3. *Estimates of social savings from freight in the Gold Coast*

	1909	1924–5	1934–5
Total Freight Ton-Miles	3,763,552	43,170,885	42,952,026
Total Freight Revenues (£)	146,845	850,238	633,525
Total Cost of Head Porterage (£)	344,992	3,957,331	5,369,003
Social Saving (£)	198,147	3,107,093	4,735,478
GDP (in current £)	26,266,269	53,108,142	61,068,569
Freight Social Saving (as a % of GDP)	0.8	5.9	7.8

suggesting that the introduction of the railways did indeed increase national income. To get some relative quantitative sense of how big these numbers are, we record our estimates of nominal GDP in row 5, and then we present measured social savings as a percentage of GDP in row 6. In 1909, as the railway was getting under way, social savings were negligible, but by 1924–5 they were up to 5.9 percent of nominal GDP, with the number increasing further in 1934–5 to 7.8 percent of GDP. This latter increase shows up in the data mostly as a consequence of the assumed rise in head porter wages over time. The numbers are not disproportionately large but are nevertheless significant.

In Table 10.4, we calculate the social savings from passenger transportation. For 1924–5 and 1934–5, the colonial sources record the total passenger miles traveled. The second row then calculates the total time used up in moving these passengers by rail based on the assumption that trains moved at fifteen miles per hour. We then compare this to the amount of time it would have taken for passengers to walk this far on foot, rather than travel by train, on the assumption that they could walk at two miles per hour. The third row shows how long it would have taken by foot – clearly much longer than it would have taken by rail. To calculate the social savings, we then price the time difference between the two modes of travel using different wage rates, 1d. per hour for 1909 and 1924–5 and 1.33d. per hour for 1934–5, as we mentioned previously. Row 5 shows the value of the time saved by moving people by rail instead of having them walk. To calculate the social savings, we compare this to total passenger revenues in the next line. It is clear that revenues were actually greater than the value of the time saved, suggesting that the benefit of moving people by rail did not compensate for the extra cost of doing so. Hence the social savings are negative.

Table 10.4. *Estimates of the social savings from passengers in the Gold Coast*

	1909	1924–5	1934–5
Total passenger miles		41,751,573	44,704,654
Total time required to travel by rail (at 15 miles per hour) (hours)		2,783,438	2,980,310
Total time required to travel by foot (at 2 miles per hour) (hours)		20,875,786	22,352,327
Travel time saved (hours)		18,092,348	19,372,017
Value of Time Saved (£)		85,939	118,653
Total Passenger Revenues (£)	38,565	214,703	150,840
Passenger Social Saving (£)		−128,764	−32,186
GDP (in current £)	26,266,269	53,108,142	61,068,569
Passenger Social Saving (as a % of GDP)		−0.24	−0.05

Table 10.5. *Basic data on the Sierra Leone railways*

	1911	1925	1935
Mile of track open	255.5	338	341
Total freight hauled (tons)	55,540	72,298	71,628
Total freight in ton-miles	5,971,693	9,437,472	10,569,611
Total passengers moved	339,332	587,944	450,707
Total passenger miles		11,047,266	11,377,080
Total Freight Revenues (£)	82,086	167,687	107,868
Total Passenger Revenues (£)	22,644	52,305	28,383
Total Expenditures (£)	69,503	176,482	128,862
Total Capital Outlays (£)	989,194	1,359,680	6,994,715

10.4.2 Results from Sierra Leone

Table 10.5 mimics for Sierra Leone the structure of Table 10.2. By 1911, the railway grid in Sierra Leone was 255.5 miles in length, longer than the amount of track open at the time in the Gold Coast, but it grew much more slowly than the Gold Coast's thereafter. Row 3 shows that the growth in freight haulage was also much smaller in Sierra Leone. Though in 1911 the Sierra Leone railway hauled more freight than the Gold Coast railway, by 1925 it was hauling less than a quarter of the amount hauled by the Gold Coast railway. This is a reflection of the rapid expansion of the cocoa economy in the Gold Coast over this period, a development that had no analogy in Sierra Leone. The Sierra Leone railway also moved far fewer passengers,

Table 10.6. *Estimates of the social savings from freight in Sierra Leone*

	1911	1925	1935
Total Freight Ton-Miles	5,971,693	9,437,472	10,569,611
Total Freight Revenues (£)	82,086	167,687	107,868
Total Cost of Head Porterage (£)	547,405	865,102	1,189,081
Social Saving (£)	465,319	697,415	1,081,213
GDP (in current £)		25,444,186	32,818,287
Social Saving as a % of GDP		2.7	3.3

about one-third by the mid-1920s, a pattern that, like the relative freight haulage, continued into the 1930s. Unsurprisingly, freight revenues were much lower in Sierra Leone.

These differences partially show up in Table 10.6, in the sense that total social savings in pounds are considerably lower by the mid-1920s in Sierra Leone and also make up one-half the size relative to GDP (we do not have estimates for GDP in Sierra Leone in 1911) as compared to the Gold Coast.

In Table 10.7, we move to the social savings for passengers in Sierra Leone. The findings here are very similar to those for the Gold Coast. Social savings are negative but hardly distinguishable from zero, as was the case in Table 10.4. The methodology is identical in both cases, except that we apply the wage rate of 1.22d. per hour to the last column to reflect the increase in nominal wages between the mid-1920s and the mid-1930s.

10.4.3 Results from Nigeria

Table 10.8 then records the basic data from Nigerian railways. Though in 1909 the length of track open in Nigeria was slightly larger than that in Sierra Leone and around two-thirds greater than that in the Gold Coast, it is already evident that Nigerian railways were much more active. The freight ton millage, for example, is about three times greater and freight revenues about double that of Sierra Leone. This divergence becomes more stark by 1924–5. The amount of ton-miles of freight is more than twenty times that of Sierra Leone and more than five times that of the Gold Coast. Moreover, this gap is even bigger by 1934–5. By this time there were 2,184 miles of track open in Nigeria, more than four times the amount in the Gold Coast and about six and a half times the amount in Sierra Leone.

Table 10.7. *Estimates of the social savings from passengers in Sierra Leone*

	1911	1925	1935
Total passenger miles		11,047,266	11,377,080
Total time required to travel by rail (at 15 miles per hour) (hours)		736,484	758,472
Total time required to travel by foot (at 2 miles per hour) (hours)		5,523,633	5,688,540
Travel time saved (hours)		4,787,149	4,930,068
Value of Time Saved (£)		19,946	25,061
Total Passenger Revenues (£)	22,644	52,305	28,383
Passenger Social Saving (£)		−32,359	−3,321
GDP (in current £)		25,444,186	32,818,287
Passenger Social Saving (as a % of GDP)		−0.13	−0.001

Table 10.8. *Basic data on Nigerian railways*

	1909	1924–5	1934–5
Mile of Track open	272	1,220	2,184
Total freight hauled (tons)	165,150	680,107	866,681
Total freight in ton-miles	16,024,024	218,427,093	293,186,018
Total passengers moved	285,202	1,922,580	5,080,016
Total passenger miles	13,353,158	92,283,840	148,165,399
Total Freight Revenues (£)	154,126	1,736,194	1,721,825
Total Passenger Revenues (£)	46,387	290,639	230,270
Total Expenditures (£)	131,820	970,446	1,038,758
Total Capital Outlays (£)	1,377,284	14,978,225	23,014,851

Table 10.9 reports the basic social savings calculations for Nigerian freight. In absolute terms, these are much larger than those of the Gold Coast or Sierra Leone, but expressed relative to GDP they are quite similar. For example, in 1909 they are 1.2 percent of GDP and after that the numbers are very close to those of the Gold Coast.

Table 10.10 examines the social savings associated with passenger travel. The findings here are very similar to those from the Gold Coast and Sierra Leone, though for 1934–5 we do find positive, but very small, social savings on passenger transportation.

Table 10.9. *Estimates of the social savings from freight in Nigeria*

	1909	1924–5	1934–5
Total Freight Ton-Miles	16,024,024	218,427,093	293,186,018
Total Freight Revenues (£)	154,126	1,736,194	1,721,825
Total Cost of Head Porterage (£)	1,468,869	20,022,480	24,432,170
Social Saving (£)	1,314,743	18,286,286	22,710,345
GDP (in current £)	105,316,616	300,260,499	300,859,733
Social Saving as a % of GDP	1.2	6.1	7.5

Table 10.10. *Estimates of the social savings from passengers in Nigeria*

	1909	1924–5	1934–5
Total passenger miles	13,353,158	92,283,840	148,165,399
Total time required to travel by rail (at 15 miles per hour) (hours)	890,211	6,152,256	9,877,693
Total time required to travel by foot (at 2 miles per hour) (hours)	6,676,579	46,141,920	74,082,699
Travel time saved (hours)	5,786,368	39,989,664	64,205,006
Value of Time Saved (£)	24,109	166,624	238,094
Total Passenger Revenues (£)	46,387	290,639	230,270
Passenger Social Saving (£)	−22,277	−124,015	7,824
GDP (in current £)	105,316,616	300,260,499	300,859,733
Passenger Social Saving (as a % of GDP)	−0.02	−0.04	0.003

10.4.4 A Comparative Context

To give some comparative context, Table 10.11, adapted from Leunig (2010, 791, table 1), records benchmark estimates of the social savings of railways in different countries of the world using the methodology that we have used here. In particular, these are estimates that assume zero elasticity of demand for transportation services, so that the actual amount of passengers and freight moved by the railways is taken as the amount that would have been moved by the less efficient method of transportation in the absence of railways. Table 10.11 shows that the types of numbers we have found are fairly normal for the social savings literature. They are, however, much smaller than the numbers Summerhill calculated for 1913 Brazil, where social savings were not less than 18 percent of GDP and quite likely more, and much smaller than the even larger numbers Coatsworth (1979) found

Table 10.11. *Estimates of social savings for various countries*

Belgium		
1846	Freight and passenger	1%
1865	Freight and passenger	2.5%
1912	Freight and passenger	4.5%
Brazil		
1913	Freight	18%–38%
	Passengers	4.6%
China		
1933	Freight and passenger	0.5%
Colombia		
1924	Freight	4.8%
England and Wales		
1865	Freight	4.1%
1890	Freight	29.1%–31.6%
1843–1913	Passengers	1.5%–14%
France		
1872	Freight	5.8%
	Passengers	1.7%
Germany		
ca. 1900	Freight	<5%
Mexico		
1910	Freight	24.9%–38.5%
Russia		
1907	Freight	4.6%
	Passengers	1.6%
Spain		
1878	Freight	7.5%
1912	Freight	11%
United States		
1859	Freight	3.7%
1859	Passengers	1.6%
1890	Freight	4.9%
1890	Passengers	4.8%

for Mexico in 1910. Both of these scholars attributed the large social savings to the very inefficient alternative means of transport in their countries of study. Because neither Mexico nor Brazil had a canal system like the United States', freight had to be moved by very inefficient (according to their calculations) mule cart in the non-railroad counterfactual world. Fogel himself argued that in the nineteenth-century United States, social savings might have been as high as 30 percent of GDP, were it not for the relative efficiency of the American canal system. Now, especially in light of all the remarks by colonial officers complaining about head porterage, one would have anticipated that the same argument that worked for Mexico and Brazil would apply to West Africa: head porterage, a highly inefficient pre-railway method of transportation (even more so than mule carts), would imply large social savings from railway adoption. As we described, however, we find small social savings, which is quite surprising. One likely reason for this is the ability of both precolonial African rulers and colonial governments to coerce labor into head porterage at below market prices (something strongly suggested by the historical record). This coercion would then make head porterage seem cheaper in our data than it would have been if wages had been set at normal market clearing levels. There were no mechanisms of this type in Brazil and Mexico that could artificially keep down the costs of alternative methods of transportation.

10.4.5 Social Savings from other Forms of Transportation

Having made these calculations for the railways, we can make simpler calculations for other forms of transportation. From Table 10.12, we do have estimates of the cost per ton-mile of freight carried with simpler methods of transportation, in particular barrel rolling, handcarts, and motor lorries. Using the data from the 1909 Parliamentary Report on these issues, we can investigate the social savings of using these other "wheeled" methods of transportation as opposed to head porterage. We do this just for the Gold Coast. For comparability, therefore, we take the data for the cost per ton for head porterage from this report, which gives 48.5d. per ton-mile (the midpoint of 3s.1d. and 5s.), which is significantly higher than our own estimates based on the information we have. To calculate the social savings associated with cask rolling, for example, we take the midpoint of the estimate presented in the Parliamentary Report on the cost per ton-mile of cask rolling and assume that all of the freight moved by the railway was moved by cask rolling (with the usual zero elasticity of demand for freight and zero supply of labor assumptions). We then compare the cost of moving all of this freight by cask rolling to the cost of moving it by head porterage. These simple calculations suggest that all forms of wheeled transportation created positive social savings though the numbers are modest expressed relative to GDP.

Table 10.12. *Implied social savings relative to head porterage of different methods of transportation in 1909 in the Gold Coast*

Total freight carried by the railways (in ton-miles)	3,763,552
GDP (in current £)	26,266,269
Total Cost of Head Porterage (£)	760,551
Total Cost of Cask Rolling (£)	258,744
Social Savings of Cask Rolling (£)	501,807
Relative to GDP (%)	1.9
Total Cost of Hand Trucks (£)	344,992
Social Savings of Hand Trucks (£)	415,559
Relative to GDP (%)	1.6
Total Cost of Motor Lorry (£)	313,629
Social Savings of Motor Lorry (£)	446,922
Relative to GDP (%)	1.7

10.5 THE SOCIAL RATE OF RETURN

We now turn to a different way of looking at this issue. Instead of asking what the social savings associated with the construction of railways was, we ask what the social rate of return from these projects was. We can do this in the case of railway construction, because we have detailed knowledge of the capital expenditures involved in building the railways. This methodology has the advantage that it explicitly takes into account the capital costs associated with the construction of the railways; the fact that social savings calculations ignore this has often been cited as a major drawback of this approach. The construction of the numbers needed here is straightforward; the social rate of return of the railways in any particular year is simply the social savings in that year plus the net railway revenues, as a percentage of the capital outlays to date. While results using this method are not necessarily reflective of the relevant decision margins, that is, they are not marginal social rates of return for an additional unit of capital, they serve the key purpose of illustrating the magnitude of the railways' effect on the economy.[13] The findings of this calculation, reported in Table 10.13, are very striking. They show that the social rate of return was remarkably high in these West African colonies, even exceeding 100 percent in Nigeria: in

[13] For a different approach to measuring social rates of return, with a critique of the current method, see Mercer (1970).

Table 10.13. *Social rates of return %*

	1909/1911	1924–5	1934–5
Gold Coast	11.0	41.9	51.2
Sierra Leone	48.0	51.3	15.5
Nigeria	95.5	122.0	98.7

other words, the social savings in a single year were sufficient to cover the entire capital outlays until then. To give some sense of how large this rate of return is, we present in Table 10.14 some estimates of social rates of return for railroads in other countries.[14] Estimates of social rates of return for historical railways are less common than social savings calculations, so we cannot be as certain in our comparative assertions about West Africa as we were in Table 10.11. Nonetheless, as Table 10.14 makes clear, the social rate of return in West African railways was, at its lowest, significantly larger than the largest recorded social rate of return for Western European economies. Even in the Brazilian example, which Summerhill (2003, 2005) has convincingly argued shows a much larger effect of railway adoption than that in the United States and Western Europe on account of the country being a "small, laggard economy," the social rate of return was between 17 and 23 percent, depending on various assumptions about the extent of social savings. Only Coatsworth's calculations for Mexico approach the magnitude of our estimates, and even then they are at their highest half the size of the rates of return we find in Nigeria.[15]

How could it be that while social savings in West Africa were so modest, the social rate of return was so high? The obvious answer is that, quite contrary to the argument that it was expensive to build railways in the forest zone of West Africa, building railways there was remarkably cheap by international standards. This is not entirely surprising. Though building these lines did require cutting down trees, West Africa is mostly very flat, and in the three cases we consider, railway construction did not face the

[14] For England and Wales, we use Hawke's estimates of gross social returns without passenger comfort considerations (1970, 406, table XV.01, column 5) combined with Kenwood's capital expenditure figures, net of depreciation, and maintenance expenses (1965, 322, column 1), rather than Hawke's own. Kenwood's capital expenditure data have the advantage of stretching back to 1825 and are separated into net and gross categories.

[15] These rates of return we find are also outsized in comparison to other forms of infrastructure investment. For instance, in a related calculation outside of the railway context, Maurer and Yu (2011) showed that the social rate of return on the construction of the Panama Canal oscillated between 3 percent and 16 percent, depending on the year.

Table 10.14. *Estimates of social rates of return (%) for various countries*

Country/ year	Social Rate of Return (%)	Source
Brazil		
1913[a]	17.9–23.1	Summerhill (2005, 87, table 7).
England and Wales		
1854[b]	13.58	Constructed from Hawke (1970, 406, table XV.01, column 5) and Kenwood (1965, 322, column 1).
1855	13.68	ibid.
1856	14.61	.
1857	14.54	.
1858	13.98	.
1859	15.15	.
1860	16.07	.
1861	15.77	.
1862	15.51	.
1863	15.98	.
1864	16.67	.
1865	16.46	.
1866	17.18	.
1867	17.62	.
1868	17.91	.
1869	18.43	.
1870	19.68	.
Mexico		
1881[c]	1.8	Coatsworth (1972, 141, table IV.12).
1882	10.4	ibid.
1883	14.2	.
1884	9.7	.
1885	18.8	.
1886	14	.
1887	15.3	.
1888	18.9	.
1889	20.3	.
1890	26.6	.
1891	35.9	.
1892	34.9	.
1893	27.2	.
1894	25.3	.
1895	29.1	.
1896	30.3	.
1897	31.6	.
1898	33.4	.
1899	52	

(continued)

Table 10.14. (*continued*)

Country/ year	Social Rate of Return (%)	Source
USA		
1859	15	Fishlow (1965)
1890[d]	12.3–15.8	David (1969, 522–3), social savings from Fogel (1964)
1890[e]	15.8–20.4	ibid.

Notes: a) Uses demand elasticity of -1. b) See text. c) Refers only to the largest railroad company. d) Returns net of maintenance expenditures. e) Returns gross of maintenance expenditures.

problem of bridging large rivers (the railways skirted or went around what large rivers there were, such as the Volta or Niger). In the United States and the British isles, the relative abundance of good waterways that made the railways less appealing also made them more expensive to build. This topic deserves further investigation.

10.6 WHAT STOPPED TECHNOLOGY ADOPTION?

If wheeled transportation, particularly railways, was economically efficient, why did African societies not adopt it? Part of the explanation for this stems from the nature of African polities. Most of the continent had relatively low levels of political centralization and consolidation, which would make it difficult to implement public works projects with such a large fixed cost. In Sierra Leone, for example, Abraham (2003) shows how the south of the country, Mendeland, was divided into a system of nine competing and warring states in the second half of the nineteenth century. He makes a distinction between territorial states, such as the Sherbro, Lugbu, Gallinas, Bumpeh, and Kpaa-Mende states, which had well-defined territories and which were not identified with a single person, and the Hegemonies, such as the Tikongoh state of Makavoray and the Luawa state of Kai Londo, which were. Nevertheless, even the territorial states were not bureaucratized and did not collect systematic taxes from their inhabitants, though they did collect tribute and organize compulsory labor and armies. It is difficult to imagine that these states could have cooperated sufficiently to create large-scale public works like a railway, even if they had been able to raise the capital and attract the expertise. This lack of political centralization in much of sub-Saharan Africa is plausibly part of the explanation for why railways were not built (though it does not explain the failure to adopt much simpler wheeled technologies).

Nevertheless, this explanation can hardly apply to larger, more bureaucratic, and consolidated African states such as Asante and Ethiopia (see Hopkins 2000a, 2000b; Warner 1999). In both these historical cases, we have direct evidence relevant to the issue of railway adoption; Asante made a belated attempt to construct a railway to Kumase, and Ethiopia did in fact build a railway before its colonization. We also have evidence for Zanzibar, where a similar project to build a railway was started by the independent sultan and then collapsed.

In the case of Asante, Wilks notes, "from the reign of Mensa Bonsu onwards, the Asante government began to explore the possibilities of utilizing European capital and skills to create a railroad system in Asante" (1989, 41). Asantehene (king) Mensa Bonsu came to the throne in 1874 and ruled until being deposed in 1883. Agyeman Prempe took the throne in 1888. Prempe's chief of his "foreign affairs bureau" was John Owusu Ansa, who took up the task of developing a railway. To this aim, he proposed setting up the "Ashanti and Prah Mining and Trading Company." On April 26, 1892, the Asantehene signed an agreement with Dr. J. W. Herivel to start the company, which was to finance and manage the construction of railroads in cooperation with the Asante government; the government even agreed to immediately supply four hundred laborers to begin laying track. As Wilks notes:

> Governor Griffith of the Gold Coast viewed the project with considerable alarm, and deemed it expedient to deter Herivel from pressing forward with a scheme which might greatly have strengthened the Asante economy. In 1893 the actual agreement between the Asantehene and Herivel was impounded by the High Court of the Gold Coast, and Herivel was harassed by the Customs Department until finally in 1894 he was obliged to abandon the scheme. (1989, 636)

This setback did not deter the Asantehene, however. In early 1895, he sent an embassy headed by Ansa to London. In October of that year, the Asante entered into an agreement with George Reckless, giving him "a Charter for the opening up of Ashantee to British enterprise and skill" (Wilks 1989, 650). Part of what Reckless agreed to do was to build a railway from the coast to Kumase. As Wilks puts it, "Chamberlain's reaction was to refuse to accept the validity of the concession" (1989, 652). Ansa responded by hiring a barrister, and Chamberlain was forced to concede the charter was legal. Nevertheless, even before Ansa was on the boat back to West Africa, Chamberlain had cabled Governor Maxwell to inform him that the "expedition must go [to] Kumasi at all events" (Wilks 1989, 655). British military intervention blocked any chance of autonomous adoption of the railway.

The evidence from Asante suggests that one reason that African states did not adopt railways during the nineteenth century was perhaps precisely because they were economically efficient. European powers, embarked on colonial expansion, had an interest in blocking the diffusion of technology to places they considered valuable colonies. The modernization of Asante would have made it more difficult to colonize, which explains why the British opposed it. This mechanism seems likely to have operated quite widely during the nineteenth century.

The case of Ethiopia is just as revealing about the mechanisms that prevented African states from building railways during the nineteenth century, and it independently paints a picture that is very consistent with the evidence from Asante (see Gilmour 1906 for an entertaining contemporary account). Plans to build a railway from the coast to the capital city of Addis Ababa moved forward the moment that Menelik II came to the throne in 1889. In February 1893, Menelik empowered one of his advisers to create a company, and Leon Chefneux, a French trader who had been living in Ethiopia since 1882, was sent to Europe to look for capital to build a railway between Djibouti, in French Somaliland, and Addis Ababa. By this time, the Italians had declared Ethiopia a protectorate of Italy, which made it difficult to raise capital and also made the French government reluctant to allow the construction of a railway across French territory. However, the military defeat of the Italians by the Ethiopians at the battle of Adowa in 1896 solved these problems. There was a great deal of internal opposition to the railways, however. Ras Makonnen, a leading aristocrat, told Menelik, "When the railway reaches Harar, Harar will no longer be yours and when it reaches Addis Ababa, Shoa will no longer be yours" (Pankhurst 1968, 307). Gleichen, a British diplomat, recorded that "a large number of the chiefs … strongly object to such a new fangled idea … on the grounds that it would introduce into the country the all-pervading white man" (Pankhurst 1968, 308). Work began on the line in October 1897, though it took until July 22, 1901 for the first train to run. At that point the track going inland from Djibouti was 106 kilometers long and had just passed into Ethiopian territory at Dire Dawa. The British, whose colony of Somaliland was just next to Djibouti, disliked the fact that a French private company ran the railway. With the encouragement of the colonial office, British investors began buying up shares in the company, and in response the French government effectively nationalized it in 1902. In the process, the French unilaterally rewrote the concession violating both the original details and the spirit of the deal signed with the Ethiopian monarch. Menelik was incensed: "the Emperor, arguing that his original concession had been violated, withdrew various priviledges [*sic*] ... [and he] refused to grant permission to start on construction of the line between Dire Dawa and the capital" (Pankhurst 1968, 323). He announced that, while he still wanted the railway, "he would not permit the line to be built by a foreign government or by a company controlled by a foreign government" (quoted in Pankhurst 1968, 323). In response to this crisis, various schemes were proposed; British and French interests, for example, suggested the internationalization of the railway, while Menelik attempted to raise the needed capital himself, directly from international financial markets. The reasoning behind the French takeover of 1902 surfaced in a remarkably frank debate in the French Senate on April 1, 1905, when the Comte d'Aunay remarked:

> [W]e were able to cherish the finest hopes for our position in Abyssinia. We had the monopoly of the railway, which gave us a precious instrument of penetration; one could say that the Empire of Menelik would become a colony for us from which we could gather the benefits without assuming any of the responsibilities. (Quoted in Pankhurst 1968, 327)

In mid-1906, an exasperated Menelik began the construction of the railway from Addis Ababa to Dire Dawa. Regardless, by 1908, Chefneux's company went bankrupt. Menelik, unable to build the railway himself without external financing, gave a second concession to the French, who agreed that this concession would again be a private company run through the Banque de l'Indo-Chine. The new company was charged with extending the line up to Addis Ababa, which it reached in 1917 after the death of Menelik and during the regency of Ras Tafai (later Haile Selassie).

The evidence from the Ethiopian case makes clear that a key obstacle preventing African polities from adopting the modern technology of the railway was that they feared this adoption would accelerate colonization.

Finally, we see similar, if not identical, political pressures affecting the decision of African polities to introduce railways in the Sultanate of Zanzibar. The Sultanate of Zanzibar was descended from the Arab monarchy that ruled Oman, which had established political supremacy along the East African coast before the massive entry of European interests into the region. After the abolition of slavery in the British colonies, when British efforts to eliminate the slave trade shifted to East Africa, the British refrained from extending any formal political authority in the region, leaving the Sultanate's sovereignty intact. Moreover, colonial officers tried to strengthen the monarchy and its state apparatus, and then relied on informal influence to pressure Zanzibari rulers into curbing the trade in their domain. Thus, by the 1870s, the Sultanate of Zanzibar claimed suzerainty over wide swathes of the land extending from the coastline of modern Tanzania, Kenya, and Somalia into the East African interior as far as southern Sudan and the Great Lakes, making it one of the largest political entities in Africa at the time.

Secondary sources describe strategic reasoning by the Sultan of Zanzibar that strongly resembles the considerations facing Menelik in Ethiopia, when proper allowances are made for the very different nature of the two kingdoms. In the 1870s, the Egyptian Khedive's plans to expand his empire deep into the Sudan threatened the territorial claims of the Sultan. At the same time, the East African interior had begun to attract the interest of William Mackinnon, a politically connected British shipping magnate (Galbraith 1972). In 1876, Sultan Bargash therefore seriously considered giving a concession to a British company led by Mackinnon where, in exchange for the right to function almost as an autonomous government (taxing, regulating trade in arms and liquor, garrisoning troops) in the Sultan's inland domain, the company committed to constructing roads and railroads on the Sultan's behalf and upholding his sovereign claims over the area. The decision was far from straightforward. As Coupland described, the Sultan reasoned that:

> If he called European capital and enterprise to his aid, he would profit financially, all going well, from the increase in duties in the mainland trade, and he would profit politically by the establishment of effective control in the interior. The financial and commercial interests he enlisted in his service would be mobilized to prevent any more attempts like [the Khedive] Ismail's to question his authority and violate the integrity of his domains. But there was an obvious risk. His servants might become his masters. Those European pioneers might prove to be more than philanthropists and business men. They might be converted into instruments of national aggrandisment; and, once they had got a firm grip on the interior in the Sultan's name, they might coolly hand it over to their Government. (Coupland 1939, 305)

Coupland argues that Bargash was willing to face this risk because the alternatives were quite likely the loss of sovereignty to the Khedive or eventual colonization where none of his sovereign rights would be recognized. The negotiations advanced considerably, with the Sultan demonstrating strong commitment to the project, and in fact this proposal received approval at the highest levels of the British government. Disagreement exists in the historical literature on why exactly the negotiations collapsed, but at least part of the reason was that "[Bargash's] advisers remonstrated against his inclinations to transfer his rights, even his sovereign power, to a European company. The Europeans would preempt trade with the interior, and the Arabs would be deprived of their livelihood" (Galbraith 1972, 67). Thus, in this case as well, the benefits of technology adoption were weighed against the political risks arising from the threat of colonization and European control.

10.7 CONCLUSIONS

In this chapter, we have undertaken preliminary calculations to examine the economic benefits of introducing modern methods of transportation into the British West African colonies of the Gold Coast, Nigeria, and Sierra Leone during the early twentieth century. We did this in the context of an academic literature that has argued that the reason that Africans did not adopt modern technologies, such as wheeled transportation, was that they were not appropriate technologies given the underlying factor endowments and circumstances. The bulk of this chapter focused on the introduction of railways. Though this is not the cleanest case for examining the economic rationality of wheeled transportation, it is facilitated by the very rich data that the British colonial state collected on the construction and operation of the railways. The main question we ask is whether constructing the railways was economically rational compared to moving goods by head porterage and moving passengers by foot. We tackle this issue in two ways, first by using the social savings approach of Fogel (1964) and second by calculating the social rate of return. Our results are very contrary to the conventional wisdom. Though it is true that the social savings railways created were modest compared to estimates of national income, the more interesting concept, the social rate of return on capital, was very high. In the case of Nigeria, it averaged around 100 percent per annum, suggesting that the social savings in one year were sufficient to cover the entire capital expenditures until then.

We would also argue that in a sense these calculations almost certainly underestimate the economic impact of the adoption of the railway. This is for the simple reason that the British colonial government built the railways not simply as an economic activity, but also as part of a strategy of extending colonial rule. For instance, Tsey (1986) points out that the first railway built in the Gold Coast, though it headed north into the Asante goldfields, which seems economically sensible, was extended to Kumase to allow the British to extend their military domination into the heart of the Asante state, not from any obvious economic motive. Similarly, in the case of Sierra Leone, when construction of the first railway started, the original plan was for the tracks to run from Freetown to the north of the country. In 1898, however, a massive rebellion, the "Hut Tax Rebellion," (known in modern Sierra Leone as the Bai Bureh War) broke out. Though it started in the north, it was most intense and lasted the longest in Mendeland in the south. After they defeated the rebellion, the British changed the planned route of the railway line, and instead of building it to the north, they built it to the south, right into the heart of Mendeland. To the extent that military and strategic factors were important in determining the routes the railways took, and to the extent that the relevant economic fundamentals were not perfectly correlated with the political fundamentals that made some places harder to govern, the railways could not have been built in the most economically optimal places for them. Therefore our findings surely underestimate the economic potential for railway construction.

Nevertheless, the fact that railways were economically efficient but not adopted by Africans does not imply in any sense that Africans were irrational or not able to ascertain the relevant costs and benefits. In fact, in the case of railways, we showed that three circumstances inhibited African polities from adopting such technologies. First, there was little political centralization (so that private costs and benefits diverged from social costs and benefits); second, technology adoption was blocked by potential colonial powers who did not want autonomous African development; third, the African polities feared that railway construction would in itself accelerate colonization.

APPENDIX: RECONSTRUCTING COLONIAL GDP

This appendix describes the procedure we followed to reconstruct the GDP for the Gold Coast, Sierra Leone, and Nigeria. To the best of our knowledge, no other systematic attempts to reconstruct GDP for the prewar era have been constructed for these countries, except for the pioneering work of Szereszewski (1965). We largely follow his method, which we outline for the Gold Coast together with our deviations from his method. We present a full result for the Gold Coast in 1909 in Table 10.A2. Finally, we briefly discuss differences between reconstructing Gold Coast GPD and GDP for Sierra Leona and Nigeria.

Szereszewski's Work

Szereszewski tries to understand the structure of the Ghanaian economy to investigate the process that transformed the Gold Coast from an

Table 10.A1. *Components of colonial GDP*

Symbol from (1)	Category
C	(2) Private Consumption of Imported Goods
	(4) Consumption of Public and Related Services
	(6) Traditional Consumption
G	(3) Consumption of Government Services
I	(5) Gross Capital Formation
E	(1) Export Production
M	(7) Imports of Goods and Non-factor Services

agricultural society into the largest cocoa exporter in the world in 1911. For 1891, 1901, and 1911 (coinciding with census years), he constructs three "successive accounting models which would assess quantitatively the structural changes of the economy over the two decades and the magnitude of its growth" (1965, 128). He considers an *introduced* and an *indigenous* sector, broadly corresponding to the coastal area and the hinterland in Ghana (and the Colony and Protectorate in Nigeria and Sierra Leone).

Data and Methodology

All data are taken from the so-called Blue Books, which are colonial reports submitted to the British government (Government of the Gold Coast, 1909, 1926, 1935; Government of Northern Nigeria, 1909; Government of Southern Nigeria, 1909; Government of Nigeria, 1925, 1935; and Government of Sierra Leone, 1909, 1925, 1935). These reports contain, aside from a short descriptive part, data on imports and exports and on government activity. From these data we constructed an estimate of GDP following a standard GDP from expenditure formula:

$$Y = C + G + I + E - M$$

where Y stands for GDP, C for consumption, G for government expenditure, I for investment, E for exports, and M for imports. We break this formula down into two building blocks, the introduced part of the economy (G, I, (E-M) and the introduced part of C) and the traditional (indigenous) consumption (the indigenous part of C). The letters in the equation correspond to categories in our GDP calculation (see Table 10.A2). Table 10.A1 lists the inputs in the equations and their equivalents in our calculation. The names of the equivalents have been chosen to conform to Szereszewski (1965) and to match closely to the Blue Books.

Table 10.A2. *Estimated Expenditures on GDP – Gold Coast 1909 – in pounds*

Category from Table A1		Total
(1) Export Production		2,656,000
Seaborne	2,656,000	
(2) Private Consumption of Imported Goods		3,490,178
Spirits	775,200	
Textiles	1,048,000	
Tobaccos	158,400	
Provisions	779,850	
Miscellaneous	728,728	
(3) Consumption of Government Services		746,000
(4) Consumption of Public and Related Services		199,000
Post and Telegraph	5,000	
Education	12,000	
Railway	182,000	
(5) Gross Capital Formation		746,240
Buildings and construction	820,000	
Equipment	512,400	
Cocoa	0	
Net accumulation of specie	133,000	
Changes in stock of imported goods	8,000	
(6) Traditional Consumption		20,646,650
(7) Imports of Good and Non-factor Services		2,217,800
Seaborne	2,205,000	
Services other than insurance and freight	12,800	
New imports of specie	133,000	
GDP is the total of categories 1–5 minus 7.		
GDP including (6)		26,266,270
GDP excluding (6)		5,619,618
	Total Population	Unskilled wage (pence)
	1,696,985	8

The indigenous consumption part (category (6)) accounts for the contribution of the indigenous population to GDP. Szereszewski computes a typical consumption basket for the Gold Coast and multiplies this by the population to arrive at the money value of traditional consumption. This measure is hard to replicate, and it isn't easily transferable across countries. Therefore, we assume that the minimum unskilled labor daily wage rate is set such that the population was made indifferent between subsistence farming and unskilled day labor. We then find the minimum day labor wage from the Blue Books and multiply this with the population to arrive at a measure of the traditional expenditure on GDP. The other components of our analysis, the categories in Table 10.A1, will be dealt with later in this appendix.

Export Production

Because exports are paid for from abroad, they add to GDP. The total figures for exports, including imports duties and c.i.f. (cost, insurance, and freight) costs, in one particular year can be taken directly from the Blue Books. Overland exports were usually not measured in any coherent way. Therefore, we confine ourselves to seaborne exports.

Private Consumption of Imported Goods

Szereszewski computed ratios between the import and the consumption of different classes of goods. With these ratios and the import figures from the Blue Books we can compute domestic consumption of these goods. In the Blue Books, all imported commodities are listed with their respective import value and are taken from the "home consumption" categories in the Blue Books. We have aggregated the individual commodities into five categories; Spirits, Textiles, Tobacco, Provisions (food, paper, candles, etc.), and Miscellaneous (tools, fuel, medicine, etc). From Szereszewski we take the following conversion factors:

Spirits, 1.7
Textiles, 1.6
Tobacco, 1.6
Provisions, 1.5
Miscellaneous, 1.4.

This means that, for instance, in the Gold Coast in 1909 total spirit imports were worth 456,000 pounds and total consumption of spirits was worth 775,200 pounds.

Consumption of Government Services

This category records the expenditures of the government, given directly in the Blue Books. To this have been added the expenditures of the local governments such as, in the case of the Gold Coast, the governments in Accra,

Cape Coast, and Secondi. Traditional government is not included. Also, government expenditure on construction is considered separately.

Consumption of Public and Related Services

This category records consumption of the services offered by the postal service and the railway services. Both quantities can be recorded directly from the Blue Books. For the Gold Coast in 1909, we were able to include expenditure on missionary schools as well.

Gross Capital Formation

As a means of accounting for investment, several capital formation categories are computed.

Buildings and construction. We have used government expenditure on construction works as a measure of the capital investment in building and construction. Szereszewski uses the money value of the imports of building and construction materials times a "construction coefficient" meant to capture the relation between the money value of the imports and the eventual investment value for GDP. He estimates this coefficient at four. We have used this methodology only for the Gold Coast in 1909, lacking detailed government expenditure data. To the government expenditure on buildings and construction, the government expenditure on railway plant and rolling stock is added.

Equipment. Spending on equipment is constructed from the import lists in the Blue Books. However, only for the Gold Coast in 1909 and Sierra Leone in 1925 could detailed figures on equipment imports be found. For other country/years the ratio between construction spending and equipment spending (0.26) for the Gold Coast in 1909 has been assumed constant and has subsequently been applied to the construction figures to generate the data for the equipment category.

Agriculture. Although all agricultural output was created by labor inputs, there is one category, the establishment of new cocoa farms, that deserves attention. We measure the investment/expenditure on GDP by the extra acreage of cocoa planted. The acreage we get from the tonnage of cocoa exported, which is mentioned in the Blue Books. Using the average yield formula from Szereszewski of four hundred twenty pounds per acre we can compute the total acreage that was used for growing the exported tonnage of cocoa. This is subsequently multiplied by the number of days it takes to bring an acre of cocoa to bearing age (170 days; sources are in Szereszewski). Finally, we use the unskilled labor wage rate to assign a money value to these days worked. This gives the money value of the investment needed to grow the exported quantity of cocoa. This investment is recorded in the year of export, although it was actually invested seven years before, which is the time it takes for cocoa to grow to maturity. However, we record expenditures as they enter output, so the data of the year of inquiry can be used to "trace" the original investment and assign it to the current year. No other crops or agricultural investment can be assessed in a similar way.

Accumulation of specie. The category records the difference between the imports and exports of specie (foreign currency).

Changes in stocks of imported goods. This category records the difference between total imports and the imports cleared through consumption (in the "home consumption" categories in the Blue Books). The difference represents the goods stock in warehouses in the ports and includes mainly spirits and textiles and can be seen as an stockpiling investment.

Traditional Consumption

This category records the traditional consumption as outlined earlier. It uses the population figures and unskilled wage figures from the Blue Books to assess the money value of the traditional consumption. We assume that the unskilled wage rate was set such that people were made indifferent between (subsistence) farming and unskilled labor.

Imports of Goods and Non-Factor Services

This category records the money value of imports which are to be deducted from total GDP because the money to pay for the imports in added to the exporting country's GDP. Also, the imports of specie are deducted here because the domestic currency to pay for the foreign currency accrues to the other nation's GDP. As a last element, the remunerations for services performed by firms abroad are added here (f.i., the treatment of soldiers/officers in hospitals in England).

Table 10.A2 gives a complete reconstruction using the aforementioned methodology for the GDP of the Gold Coast for the fiscal year 1909. This same methodology can be applied, mutatis mutandis, to Sierra Leone and Nigeria. Their total GDP figures, together with the remaining figures for the Gold Coast, are given in Table 10.A3.

Table 10.A3. *Colonial GDP for the Gold Coast, Nigeria and Sierra Leone, in pounds*

	(Fiscal) Year	GDP with traditional consumption	GDP without	Population	Unskilled wage rate (pence)
Gold Coast	1909	26,266,270	5,619,620	1,696,985	8
Sierra Leone	1909	2,330,890	1,398,250	76,655*	8
Nigeria (North)	1909	94,832,020	29,336,230	6,714,038	9
Nigeria (South)	1909	10,484,600	9,937,100	60,000*	6
Nigeria (Total)	1909	105,316,620	39,27,330	6,774,038	
Gold Coast	1924/25	53,108,140	21,913,280	2,279,077	9
Sierra Leone	1924/25	25,444,1890	4,419,280	1,536,066	9
Nigeria	1924/25	300,26,500	14,561,340	18,900,391	9
Gold Coast	1934/35	61,068,570	17,969,230	3,163,568	9
Sierra Leone	1934/35	32,818,270	3,233,090	1,768,480	11
Nigeria	1934/35	300,859,730	28,225,050	19,918,516	9

* Population without Protectorate (Colony only).

Nigeria and Sierra Leone

The main differences between the analysis for the gold coast and Sierra Leone and Nigeria come from two sources. The first source, which applies only to Nigeria, is that Nigeria was for administrative purposes split into Northern and Southern Nigeria in 1909. GDP figures for both colonies plus a total are given in Table 10.A3. By 1925 the colonies had merged. The second source, which applies to both countries, has to do with population figures. In 1909 the population figures in the Blue Books give only the population figures for the Colony and not for the Protectorate, causing an underestimation of total GDP.

Extra References for the Appendix

Government of the Gold Coast. (1909). "Blue Book." Accra: Government Printers Office.

Government of the Gold Coast. (1926). "Blue Book." Accra: Government Printers Office.

Government of the Gold Coast. (1935). "Blue Book." Accra: Government Printers Office.

Government of Northern Nigeria. (1909). "Blue Book." Lagos: Government Printers.

Government of Southern Nigeria. (1909). "Blue Book." Calabar: Government Printers.

Government of Nigeria. (1925). "Blue Book, Colony & Protectorate of Nigeria." Lagos: Government Printer.

Government of Nigeria. (1935). "Blue Book, Colony & Protectorate of Nigeria." Lagos: Government Printer.

Government of Sierra Leone. (1909). "Blue Book." Freetown: Government Printing Office.

Government of Sierra Leone. (1925). "Blue Book." Freetown: Government Printing Office.

Government of Sierra Leone. (1935). "Blue Book." Freetown: Government Printing Office.

References

Abraham, Arthur. (2003). *An Introduction to the Pre-Colonial History of the Mende of Sierra Leone*. Lewiston: The Edwin Mellor Press.

Acemoglu, Daron, Simon Johnson, and James A. Robinson. (2001). "The Colonial Origins of Comparative Development: An Empirical Investigation." *American Economic Review*, December, 91(5): 1369–1401.

Acemoglu, Daron and Fabrizio Zilibotti. (2001). "Productivity Differences." *Quarterly Journal of Economics*, 116: 563–606.

Akurang-Parry, Kwabena O. (2000). "Colonial Forced Labor Policies for Road-Building in Southern Ghana and International Anti-Forced Labor Pressures, 1900–1940." *African Economic History*, 28: 1–25.

Alldridge, T. J. (1910). *A Transformed Colony: Sierra Leone as It Was, and as It Is, Its Progress, Peoples, Native Customs and Undeveloped Wealth*. London: Seeley and Co. Limited.

Austen, Ralph A. and Daniel Headrick. (1983). "The Role of Technology in the African Past." *African Studies Review*, 26: 163–84.

Austin, Gareth. (2008). "Resources, Techniques, and Strategies South of the Sahara: Revising the Factor Endowments Perspective on African Economic Development, 1500–2000." *Economic History Review*, 61: 587–624.

Basu, Susanto and David N. Weil. (1998). "Appropriate Technology and Growth." *Quarterly Journal of Economics*, 113: 1025–54.

Bulliet, Richard W. (1975). *The Camel and the Wheel*. Cambridge, MA: Harvard University Press.

Burns, A. C. (1921). *The Nigeria Handbook Containing Statistical and General Information Respecting the Colony and Protectorate*. Lagos: Government Printer.

Church, R. J. Harrison. (1956). "The Transport Pattern of British West Africa." In *Geographical Essays on British Tropical Lands*, edited by R. W. Steel and C. A. Fisher, 30–61. London: G. Philip.

(1980). *West Africa : A Study of the Environment and of Man's Use of It*, 8th edition. New York: Longman.

Clifford, Sir Hugh. (1920). *The Gold Coast Regiment in the East African Campaign*. London: J. Murray.

Coatsworth, John H. (1972). "Impact of Railroads on the Economic Development of Mexico, 1877–1910," PhD Dissertation: Department of History, University of Wisconsin.

Coatsworth, John H. (1979). "Indispensable Railroads in a Backward Economy: The Case of Mexico." *Journal of Economic History*, 39(4): 939–60.

Coquery-Vidrovitch, Catherine and Paul E. Lovejoy, eds. (1985). *The Workers of African Trade*. Beverly Hills, CA: Sage Publications.

Coupland, Sir Reginald. (1939). *The Exploitation of East Africa, 1856–1890: The Slave Trade and the Scramble*. London: Faber and Faber Ltd.

Crafts, Nicholas F. R. (2004). "Social Savings as a Measure of the Contribution of a New Technology to Economic Growth," London School of Economics, Department of Economic History, Working Paper No. 06/04.

David, Paul A. (1969). "Transportation Innovation and Economic Growth: Professor Fogel On and Off the Rails." *Economic History Review*, 22: 505–26.

Donaldson, Dave. "Railroads of the Raj: Estimating the Impact of Transportation Infrastructure." forthcoming in the *American Economic Review*.

Fishlow, Albert. (1965). *American Railroads and the Transformation of the Antebellum Economy*. Cambridge, MA: Harvard University Press.

Fogel, Robert W. (1964). *Railroads and American Economic Growth: Essays in Econometric History*. Baltimore, MD: Johns Hopkins University Press.

(1979). "Notes on the Social Saving Controversy." *Journal of Economic History*, 39: 1–54.

Galbraith, John S. (1972). *Mackinnon and East Africa, 1878–1895: A Study in the "New Imperialism."* Cambridge: Cambridge University Press.

Gilmour, T. Lennox. (1906). *Abyssinia: The Ethiopian Railway and the Powers*. London: Alston Rivers Ltd.

Goody, Jack. (1971). *Technology, Tradition and the State in Africa*. New York: Cambridge University Press.

Gould, Peter R. (1959). *Transportation in Ghana*. Northwestern University, Studies in Geography No. 5.

Government of the Gold Coast. (1909). "Report of the General Manager upon the Government Railways," Accra: Government Printers.

(1926). "Gold Coast Railway Administrative Report for the Year 1924–1925," Accra: Government Printers.

(1935). "Gold Coast Railway Administrative Report for the Year 1934–1935," Accra: Government Printers.

Government of Nigeria. (1909). "Lagos Railway Annual Report 1909," Lagos: Government Printers.

(1925). "Nigerian Railway and Udi Coalmines Administrative Report for the Year Ending 31st March 1925," Lagos: Government Printers.

(1935). "Annual Report on the Government Railway and Colliery of Nigeria for the Financial Year Ending 31st March 1935," Lagos: Government Printers.

Government of Sierra Leone. (1911). "Report on the Transport Department for the Year 1911," Freetown: Government Printers.

(1925). "Sierra Leone Railway Administrative Report for the Year 1925," Freetown: Government Printers.

(1935). "Sierra Leone Railway Administrative Report for the Year 1935," Freetown: Government Printers.

Hailey, Lord. (1938). *An African Survey*. London: Oxford University Press.

Hall, Robert E. and Charles I. Jones. (1999). "Why Do Some Countries Produce So Much More Output per Worker than Others?" *Quarterly Journal of Economics*, 114: 83–116.

Hawke, G. R. (1970). *Railways and Economic Growth in England and Wales, 1840–1870*. Oxford: Clarendon Press.

Herbst, Jeffrey I. (2000). *States and Power in Africa*. Princeton, NJ: Princeton University Press.

Hill, Polly. (1972). *Rural Hausa: A Village and a Setting*. New York: Cambridge University Press.

Hopkins, Anthony G. (1973). *An Economic History of West Africa*. New York: Addison Wesley Longman.

(2000a). "Asante and the Victorians: Transition and Partition on the Gold Coast." In *Imperialism, Decolonization, and Africa*, edited by Roy Bridges, 33–57. London: Palgrave Macmillan.

(2000b). "Quasi-States, Weak States, and the Partition of Africa." *Review of International Studies*, 26: 311–20.

House of Commons. (1904). "Papers Relating to the Construction of the Railways in Sierra Leone, Lagos, and the Gold Coast," Cd. 2325.

(1909). "Mechanical Transport in the Colonies," Cd. 4589.

(1924). "Private Enterprise in British Tropical Africa," Cmd. 2016.

Hsieh, Chiang-Tai and Peter J. Klenow. (2010). "Development Accounting." *American Economic Journal: Macroeconomics*, 2(1): 207–23.

Jedwab, Remi and Alexander Moradi. (2011). "Transportation Technology and Economic Change: The Impact of Colonial Railroads on City Growth in Africa." http://home.gwu.edu/~jedwab/Jedwab_Moradi_Oct2013.pdf.

Kenwood, A. G. (1965). "Railway Investment in Britain, 1825–1875." *Economica*, 32: 313–22.

Knowles, Lilian C. A. (1928). *The Economic Development of the British Overseas Empire*. London: George Routledge & Sons.

Law, Robin C. (1977). *Oyo Empire, c.1600-c.1836: West African Imperialism in the Era of the Atlantic Slave Trade*. New York: Oxford University Press.

(1980). "Wheeled Transportation in Pre-Colonial West Africa." *Africa*, 50: 249–62.

Leunig, Timothy. (2010). "Social Savings." *Journal of Economic Surveys*, 24(5): 775–800.

Lovejoy, Paul E. (1980). *Caravans of Kola: The Hausa Kola Trade, 1700–1900*. Zaria: Ahmadu Bello University Press Ltd.

Lugard, Frederick. (1922). *The Dual Mandate in British Tropical Africa*. London: William Blackwood and Sons.

Mann, Kristin. (1995). "Owners, Slaves and the Struggle for Labour in the Commercial Transition at Lagos." In *From Slave Trade to "Legitimate" Commerce: The Commercial Transition in Nineteenth-Century Africa*, edited by Robin C. Law, 144–71. New York: Cambridge University Press.

Mason, Michael. (1978). "Working on the Railway: Forced Labor in Northern Nigeria." In *African Labor History*, edited by Peter C. W. Gutkind, Robin Cohen, and Jean Copans, 56–79. Beverly Hills, CA.

Maurer, Noel and Carlos Yu. (2011). *The Big Ditch: How America Took, Built, Ran and Ultimately Gave Away the Panama Canal*. Princeton, NJ: Princeton University Press.

McPhee, Allan. (1926). *The Economic Revolution in British West Africa*. London: George Routledge & Sons.

Mercer, Lloyd J. (1970). "Rates of Return for Land-Grant Railroads: The Central Pacific System." *Journal of Economic History*, 30: 602–26.

O'Brien, Patrick K. (1977). *The New Economic History of the Railways*. London: Croom Helm.

Ogunremi, Deji. (1975). "Human Porterage in Nigeria in the Nineteenth Century." *Journal of the Historical Society of Nigeria*, 8: 37–45.

Ogunremi, Gabriel. (1982). *Counting the Camels: The Economics of Transportation in Pre-Industrial Nigeria*. New York: Nok Publishers International.

Ormsby-Gore, W. G. A. (1926). *Report by The Hon. W.G.A. Ormsby-Gore, M.P. on His Visit to West Africa during the Year 1926*. London: H. M. Stationary Office.

Oyemakinde, Wale. (1974). "Railways Construction and Operation in Nigeria, 1895–1911: Labour Problems and Socio-Economic Impact." *Journal of the Historical Society of Nigeria*, 7: 303–24.

Pankhurst, Richard. (1968). *Economic History of Ethiopia 1800–1935*. Addis Ababa: Haile Selassie I University Press.

Piggott, Stuart. (1983). *The Earliest Wheeled Transport from the Atlantic Coast to the Caspian Sea*. Ithaca, NY: Cornell University Press.

Reid, Richard J. (2002). *Political Power in Pre-Colonial Buganda: Economy, Society, and Warfare*. Oxford: James Currey.

Rockel, Stephen J. (2006). *Carriers of Culture: Labor on the Road in Nineteenth-Century East Africa*. Portsmouth, NH: Heinemann.

Shelford, F. (1920). "Transport in Africa by Road, Rail, Air, and Water." *Journal of the African Society*, 19: 165–75.

Summerhill, William R. (2003). *Order against Progress: Government, Foreign Investment, and Railroads in Brazil, 1854–1913*. Stanford, CA: Stanford University Press.

(2005). "Big Social Savings in a Small Laggard Economy: Railroad-Led Growth in Brazil." *Journal of Economic History*, 65: 72–102.

Swindell, Ken. (1992). "The Struggle for Transport Labor in Northern Nigeria, 1900–1912: A Conflict of Interests." *African Economic History*, 20: 137–59.

Szereszewski, R. (1965). *Structural Changes in the Economy of Ghana, 1891–1911*. London: Weidenfeld and Nicholson.

Thomas, Roger G. (1973). "Forced Labour in British West Africa: The Case of the Northern Territories of the Gold Coast 1906–1927." *Journal of African History*, 14: 79–103.

Tsey, Christian E. (1986). "Gold Coast Railways: The Making of a Colonial Economy, 1879–1929," PhD thesis, University of Glasgow.

Warner, Carolyn M. (1999). "The Political Economy of 'Quasi-Statehood' and the Demise of 19th-Century African Politics." *Review of International Studies*, 25: 233–55.

Wilks, Ivor. (1989). *Asante in the Nineteenth Century*, 2nd edition. New York: Cambridge University Press.

11

Mbanza Kongo/São Salvador: Culture and the Transformation of an African City, 1491 to 1670s

Linda Heywood

Since it is necessary to write many times about the city of São Salvador ... Your Excellency should not be led to believe that it is a city like those of Europe; I have no doubt that in the past it was a lot better, given the ruins that exist.[1]

11.1 INTRODUCTION

During the early decades of the Atlantic slave trade, slaving ports located on the Atlantic coast of Africa and localities far removed from the coast served as centers of trade as well as cultural contacts between Africans and Europeans. Although the economic impact of the trade in human beings has been the subject of numerous scholarly studies, less is known about the cultural dimensions of the trade. In fact, in no place in Atlantic Africa were the cultural ramifications as pronounced and different as in the kingdom of Kongo. Recent works by Kristin Mann on Lagos and Robin Law on Whydah (Kristin 2007; Law 2004) have contributed significantly to this issue as they have brought into focus the social dynamics that led to the rise and transformations of these two important Atlantic slave ports. Law's use of the concept of the "middleman community" to explore the place of port cities in the Atlantic world is a good starting point for the study of Mbanza Kongo, and it also was a slave trade center. In some respects, however, Law's "middleman community" does not fully represent the complexity of the social and cultural dynamics of Mbanza Kongo as the city not only served as an entrepôt for the slave trade with the Portuguese, but was also the capital of the kingdom.

[1] Informazione sul regno del Congo di Fra Raimondo da Dicomano (1798), ed. Arlindo Correia, http://www.arlindo_correia.com/121281.html, note 3.

Unlike Lagos and Whydah and other port cities whose character was informed by the trade in slaves, Mbanza Kongo was the administrative and political capital of one of the most centralized states in Africa at the time. For more than a century after the arrival of the Portuguese in 1487, Kongo kings and nobles were guided not so much by the demands of the trade in slaves, but by imagining Mbanza Kongo as a new city. The ideas that they implemented transformed Mbanza Kongo into their version of the "Christian city." During this period, they collaborated with a host of Portuguese religious and cultural personnel sent by the kings of Portugal and missionaries coming from Rome to give Mbanza Kongo a new life and identity. Over time, they so transformed the physical and cultural landscape of the court that the city came to possess European-style churches, the city supported a wide range of cultural institutions that the churches promoted, and the life of the African elite as well as commoners came to be defined by the rhythms of the Christian religious calendar. In essence the presence of churches, other Christian institutions, and a cultural life dominated by mixed Kongo-Christian observances and rites marked Mbanza Kongo as a unique cultural space in Atlantic Africa. During the period that the city flourished as an Atlantic city, Mbanza Kongo was not a replica of a medieval European city nor did its cultural life mimic that of European Christian cities. Even though the kings and nobles who lived in the city requested priests and Christian ritual objects from Europe, developed literacy in European languages with Portuguese as the language of instruction in the schools and convents they built, conducted European-style court proceedings, underwent Christian baptism, and adopted Christian names and feudal titles, the European aspects of this new life were in many ways grafted on to Kongo religious ideas, political apparatuses, and preexisting cultural norms. The Kongo experiment remained under Kongo direction because the kings and nobles defrayed the economic cost. In the end they created a unique Atlantic African Creole culture where free and slave and noble and peasant were proud to assert the Christian Kongo identity of the city. The experiment, however, did not last as toward the end of the seventeenth century the city crumbled under the weight of civil war and neglect. Dependent on European technical expertise, the model of the "Christian city" was perhaps unsustainable in the long run. Exploring the social investments that the Kongo elite put into the project might offer early lessons for *longue durée* understandings of wealth and poverty in the Atlantic during the era of the slave trade.

11.2 MBANZA KONGO AND ITS EARLY TRANSFORMATION

The Portuguese were the first Europeans to establish some of the early cultural centers in Atlantic Africa – Elmina in 1482 and Luanda in 1575. Although the Portuguese visited African courts like Benin City in the 1470s and Mbanza Kongo in 1483, the transformation of the city only began in 1491. When the first Portuguese visitors arrived in Mbanza Kongo, which means city (or large central place) of Kongo in Kikongo, the locality served as the court of Nzinga Nkuwu, the reigning Kongo king. Mbanza Kongo's roots go back to the fourteenth century when Nzinga Nkuwu's predecessors conquered it. Oral traditions identify Mbanza Kongo as the first place that the conquerors of what became the Kongo Kingdom settled once they crossed the River Zaire.[2] The invaders chose Mbanza Kongo because of its strategic location, for it is situated on a flat, well-watered mountaintop some ten miles in circumference. From the time of its original occupation until the kingdom became part of Portuguese Angola in 1914, Mbanza Kongo (called São Salvador from the 1570s) served as both the real and the symbolic capital of the Kongo Kingdom.

Mbanza Kongo already had a distinctive layout, which the earliest visitors to the area noted. The first description of the physical appearance of the capital comes from a 1491 letter of the ambassador of Milan to Lisbon, which noted that the king of Kongo had "a terra [land] encircled by a wall as large as Evora and is inland, some 60 leagues from the sea, all full of houses better than are found in all of Guinea."[3] Because Évora was the second largest city in Portugal, the fact that Mbanza Kongo was compared to it suggests that Portuguese visitors were impressed by Mbanza Kongo's size and appearance.

We know little more of the physical layout of the capital or of the religious, political, or economic life of the residents in the period before King Nzinga Nkuwu greeted the first Portuguese visitors who arrived at his court. Mbanza Kongo, however, underwent significant physical transformation from 1491 when the king and members of his court were baptized in a lavish religious ceremony at his residence to celebrate their conversion to the Catholic faith. By 1548, when we have the first estimates of the density of the population of Mbanza Kongo and the rural population it supported,

[2] For the events leading to the establishment of Mbanza Kongo as recorded in modern oral traditions, see Cuvelier (1934, 65, 85). For earlier traditions and for how these modern traditions developed, see Thornton (2001, 112, 119).

[3] Letter of Milanese ambassador in Lisbon, November 6, 1491, in Adriano Capelli, "A Proposito di Conquiste Africane." *Archivo Storico Lombardo* (1896, 416).

the population numbered about sixty thousand people. From 1491 to 1678, when the city was temporarily abandoned, Kongo kings oversaw a physical transformation of the city that in some respects made it appear to have more in common with Portuguese Luanda than with the capitals of other African court cities such as Benin City or with port cities such as Whydah and Lagos. The city's physical transformation was most noticeable in the new materials used to rebuild the wall around the court, in the new stone palace, and in the many stone structures that were built. The density of the city also increased as new settlements grew up around the court. In addition to its physical transformation, Mbanza Kongo became a political and religious ritual center as churches and institutions connected to them replaced or were built in places that had served as the administrative and religious centers in precontact Mbanza Kongo (Thornton 2000, 67–85).

Mbanza Kongo's physical transformation began immediately after the first Portuguese cultural mission arrived early in 1491. This mission brought Portuguese religious teachers and skilled workers, including carpenters, masons, bakers, Christian women, and "farmers with their tools and a bell for the church." In the months following, the king and his nobles mobilized thousands of Kongo laborers to build a Christian church of stone, the first major public work project in the city after their conversion. Thousands of Kongo laborers worked under the supervision of Portuguese craftsmen and were able to complete the project in record time. They began on May 6 and completed the building by June 1. The church, dedicated to Our Lady, was the first European-like structure in the city, and thousands of stones and pounds of mortar were used to build it.[4] Before this project, the people in Mbanza Kongo had never used stone or mortar to construct their houses or public buildings but instead used wattle and daub and thatch. A rich trove of letters penned by Kongo officials, Portuguese residents, and visitors to the city beginning in the early 1500s describes the continuing physical transformation of the city as more churches and other stone structures went up in the following years. The most spectacular of these was the stone wall built around the court, and the construction of a stone palace that the laborers began to build for Kongo's most famous Christian king, Afonso I (1509–42). During Afonso's reign, many more stone houses were constructed for the Portuguese who called the city home.[5]

[4] Rui de Pina, Crónica d'El D. João II, Cap. 61 in Carmen Radulet, *O Cronista Rui de Pina e a "Relação do Reino de Congo"* (Lisbon, 1992).

[5] King Afonso to Manuel I, October 5, 1514, *Monumenta Missionaria Africana* (*MMA*) [Ser. 1, 15 vols. Lisbon, 1952–88] 1:294–323; King Afonso to Manuel I, June 13, 1517, *MMA* 1:410–11.

The city's physical transformation was really the brainchild of King Afonso, who implemented elaborate plans for reconstructing the city during his long reign. He largely financed the building as well as helped recruit or gave money to the craftsmen to recruit Kongo laborers, who he intended would work alongside the Portuguese craftsmen and learn new skills. In 1509, for example, he welcomed masons and carpenters, who King Manuel of Portugal had sent to build churches, as well as materials and other products that came from Portugal with the several Portuguese cultural missions that included Portuguese farmers, teachers, and skilled workers such as stone masons and carpenters. Moreover, he paid for upkeep of the skilled workmen who also came from Portugal to rebuild his residence so that stone buildings could replace the thatched ones. One of the most impressive results of this Kongo-Portuguese cultural and technical collaboration was the building of a mile-long stone wall, twenty feet high, that separated the royal residences from the rest of the city. Although in 1514 Afonso complained that the masons had not completed his stone residence despite the money he paid them because they were more interested in trading in slaves, he pushed for the building of more stone structures in the city. For example, to make sure that his relatives and other nobles in his household were exposed to the new knowledge the priests from Portugal brought, he "gathered together all our brothers and children and cousins and the children of our criados in such a way that there were 400 young men and children and … we ordered a great wall made with many thorns on top so they could not climb it and flee and we entrusted the fathers with teaching them, and we also ordered other walls made … for the fathers to live together."[6] In addition, he ordered the construction of walled enclosures for priests and a large walled enclosure with houses for the "1,000 sons of nobles with their teachers and dependants so that the priests could teach them reading, writing, grammar and the things of our holy faith."[7] In fact, Afonso was so concerned that the Kongo students he had recruited to study under the Christian foreigners found ways of escaping from the walled enclosures that he asked the king of Portugal to turn over to him the island of São Tomé so he could have schools built there where he could send "male and female" Kongo students who could study and would not have the incentive to run away and return to their families.[8]

6 King Afonso to Manuel I, October 5, 1514, *MMA* 1:299–306.

7 "De Algumas Coisas que Tocam ao Rei do Congo," 1516, *MMA* 1:374.

8 King Afonso to Manuel I, October 5, 1514, *MMA* 1:299–306.

Figure 11.1. Garcia II with the Dutch (1668) depicting the 1641 meeting.

Construction of stone buildings was not limited to Afonso's palace; he also gave permission to the Portuguese to build a somewhat smaller wall around the stone houses that they were building. As a result of Afonso's building initiatives, the physical landscape of the city was rapidly changing. For example, between the walled enclosures that he had built he left a large open space in the city "where the principal church was built." Later every nobleman would build his own city residence, although each of them would also have villas in the villages outside the city (Pigafetta, Lopes, and Grassi 1591, 39–40). Afonso was very concerned about the upkeep of these buildings, and in 1517 and again in 1526 he asked the king of Portugal to send him more stonemasons and carpenters to complete the churches that were under construction. For example, in 1526, when only one carpenter remained in the city, he wrote to King João III requesting five masons and twenty carpenters to finish one of the churches, called Nossa Senhora da Victoria. He noted that he only had one carpenter left who "who can repair and cover the churches"[9] (Figure 11.1).

[9] King Afonso to João III, August 25, 1526, *MMA* 1:475, 479.

The basic layout of the city would remain the same in the decades following Afonso's reign, although later kings built additional churches, schools and convents, cloisters, and other buildings for the missionaries and nobles built residences to ensure that they had a place in the center of power. By the late 1500s, Mbanza Kongo (by then known as São Salvador) contained several churches, the most prominent being the Cathedral built in 1549 and located in the large square where outdoor masses were held to accommodate thousands of parishioners. The central place that the churches and other religious institutions occupied set the city apart from other port cities in Atlantic Africa. Mbanza Kongo's physical transformation continued in the 1600s. In the early 1600s, for example, land was set aside to build a monastery for the Dominican missionaries, while in 1632 Alvaro IV gave the Jesuits, who were beginning their work in the city, a site for a college as well as "other lands for their upkeep." He requested that they build "a church for the college that can be visited any time and continuous alms that the people could give."[10]

Afonso, and the kings after him, allocated funds not only for the building of the stone structures and the payment of the workers, but for the upkeep of the churches and other buildings they had constructed. The income to maintain these buildings and their staffs increased as the number of churches grew. At the end of Afonso's reign in 1542, there were already between six and eight churches in the city, while by the late 1590s the number had risen to twelve. In 1595, Antonio Viera, the Kongolese ambassador to Lisbon, noted that although there were only six churches in the city, many nobles kept their own private chapels.[11] These churches were all dedicated to Christian saints and were located throughout the city. Both the Church of St. James and the Church of Our Lady of the Conception were located within the palace grounds, while the Nossa Senhora de Ajuda Church was located in the Portuguese quarters. The Jesuits also had three unidentified churches and a cloister in the part of the city that they occupied. By 1642, when a Dutch embassy visited the city, they were able to list by name at least ten churches, although some were already in ruins and others in need of repair. At that time four of the churches – St. James Church, the Church of the Holy Ghost, the Church of St. Michael, and the Church of St. Joseph – were located within the palace walls while the others – the Cathedral, the Church of Our Lady of the Conception, the Church of Victory, the Church

10 Alvaro IV to General of the Company of Jesus, October 25, 1632, *MMA* 8:199–200.

11 "Interrogatorio de Statu Regni Congensis Facta Ulissipone. Anno Domini 1591" *MMA*, 3:503.

Figure 11.2. Dapper São Salvador (1668) situation in 1641.

of Seven Lamps, and the Church of St. Anthony – were located in various parts of the city. Walls also separated some of the churches from the surrounding area. For example, the Church of Our Lady of the Conception was surrounded by a stone wall in an area that also contained two very large residences built with thatch, giving the appearance of a convent.[12] The city by this time had named streets as well. Some, like St. James Street, took their names from the churches that stood on them, while another street called Bacas de las Almadias (Gulf of the Canoes) was located near a river (Ogilby 1670, 525). Olfert Dapper's engraving of the city as it appeared in 1641–2 depicted several of the prominent features of the city, including the Cathedral, the two-story palace, the wall, and several other churches (Figure 11.2).

The lifestyle of city residents also changed as celebrations connected to the Christian religious calendar came to dominate city life. As the social experiment continued, all aspects of life in the city, from politics to economics and recreation, created demands for trained personnel and for the goods required to support the activities of the church. Church personnel from Europe, along with the religious items that informed church life, were

[12] Relacão Dos Carmelitas Descalços (1584), *MMA* 4:396.

Figure 11.3. Kongo clothing – Olfert Dapper (1668) depicting the situation in 1641.

high in demand, and the kings spared no effort in acquiring the wherewithal to pay the expenses of the European and African church personnel that staffed the churches and for the variety of Christian ritual objects that came from Europe. As the city grew, it became increasingly divided into two social groups. On the one hand was the king, his court, nobles who were recognized by their mixed European African clothing, their literacy, and their memberships in the various religious institutions; on the other hand was a large population (almost half of the city residents) who were slaves and freemen only marginally integrated into the new lifestyle. Although in many ways the social distance between the two groups diverged, in many ways the social experiment brought slaves and freemen closer to the members of the nobility. The European missionaries and secular European (mainly Portuguese merchants) and church personnel who lived in the city also added another social dimension to city life. They had their own quarter with a wall as well (Figure 11.3).

The city's position as an Atlantic Creole center was evident in the prominent role the Kongo Catholic Church and the institutions connected to it had in the life of the residents of the city. Church services and rituals connected with the Christian calendar dominated the culture of the city. Weekly services and celebrations connected to saints' days attracted large numbers of the city's residents as did the yearly celebration associated with St. James Day, which by 1584 had become Kongo's national day. In fact, a 1619 a report commenting on the life of the Christians in São Salvador noted that so many people wished to attend weekly services that the Cathedral could not accommodate the "innumerable multitude of inhabitants" (Cuvelier and Jadin 1954, 47) and that the king along with the rest of the population usually "stand outside the church in the vast square to hear mass." This Christian community was not limited to Africans, for the Portuguese population had grown as well. Many of the one thousand Portuguese in the kingdom had a residence in the city.[13] By 1645, the mixed African-Portuguese residents in the city had also increased and numbered a total of four hundred people, several of whom were priests.

The expenses that went to maintain this Atlantic Creole center increased as well, although it is impossible to come up with a detailed accounting of the percentage of the kings' revenue that went into building and maintaining the institutions. Nevertheless, a range of descriptive evidence suggests that the kings did not spare any resources. In the early years they spent liberally to pay in kind for the satin and velvet and other clothes, books, bed canopies, door curtains, and religious and cultural items that came from Portugal, as well as for the wages of the skilled Portuguese workmen who worked in the various construction projects. These in-kind payments included slaves and a wide variety of Kongo products and animals such as silver and copper manilas, leopard skins, parrots, civet cats, and the like. They also covered the upkeep of the churches and their personnel. Because Kongo had an actual currency before the Portuguese arrived, some of the payment was made in it. In Kongo the people used zimbu shells fished from the shallow waters off the island of Luanda, and the kings and nobles used it to assess taxes and to pay for the goods and services they received. The highest unit of account was the cofu, which was worth twenty thousand zimbu shells, while the lefuco was worth ten thousand zimbu shells (Cuvelier 1946, 307–10). The Portuguese workers who came during Afonso's time were not only paid in the local currency, but were paid in kind. Over the years, the kings sent thousands of slaves, ivory, manilas, local cloths, and the like to their Portuguese counterparts (and at times to Rome) to help cover the cost for priests, the religious icons, and other items that came from Portugal and Rome. They also set up accounts in Portugal and Kongo to allow transfers of money from one to the other.

[13] For the activities of the Portuguese in Kongo, see Heywood and Thornton (2007, 139).

Some idea of the expenses that went into the building projects in the early years of the city's transformation comes from a letter that Afonso wrote to King Manuel of Portugal in 1514 in which he complained that the masons who came from Portugal refused to work and instead "demand pay all the time [for] building the house for me and my queen." Slaves who the king gave to the representatives of the Portuguese as gifts to the Portuguese kings or free Kongo subjects who the Portuguese illegally enslaved also represented part of the payments from the kings' revenues because slaves were valuable commodities among both the Kongolese and the Portuguese. The various complaints that Afonso and later kings made against the Portuguese who came to work in the city but who often found it more profitable to use their income to unlawfully enslave or purchase Kongo subjects also represented part of the cost connected with the physical layout and cultural life of the city.[14]

Part of the revenues that the Kongo kings used to cover the Christian project also came in the form of the labor hours that Kongo workers put into the building projects. These laborers gathered the stones from several miles outside the city and transported them to the city center where the churches were built. Kings also handed over large amounts of land and the laborers on them to the priests who managed the churches. Afonso and the kings after him often referred in their letters to the thousands of laborers they recruited to work on the building projects.

The resources that Kongo kings plowed into the building projects represented only a part of the expenses they invested to transform Mbanza Kongo into an Atlantic Creole city. Over the years, as they deepened their cultural ties with fellow Christian monarchs in Portugal and with the Papacy, Kongo kings allocated a part of their revenues to cover the cost of the recruitment and upkeep of the European experts – mainly priests and other religious personnel who they believed were essential to implement their vision. All of the foreign experts along with the many Kongolese they trained lived at one time or another in the city and were in part supported by funds that the kings and nobles provided.

During Afonso's time when few institutions existed for training members of the local elite, he provided the funds for the travel to and the upkeep of his relatives in Portugal. In fact, in 1540, he actually arranged to have five thousand cruzados on credit from King João in Portugal to cover the cost of his relatives who he had sent to Portugal to study and

[14] King Afonso to Manuel I, October 5, 1514, *MMA* 1:306.

to cover the expenses of an embassy he had sent to Rome.[15] He promised to pay him back in the local currency that the Portuguese agents could use to purchase slaves. As more missionaries traveled to Kongo to manage the churches and to help in the education and training of local men and women, kings and nobles continued to cover the cost. For example, soon after the arrival in the city of a group of missionaries from Europe in 1548, one of them wrote back to his colleagues noting that King Diego I ordered his nobles to "bring us great gifts" to help with their transition.[16] Moreover, Diego also paid for the salary of Portuguese linguist Pedro Alverez and carriers who he supplied to missionary Father George Vas in 1548. Several decades later, Alvaro II, writing to Pope Paulo V in 1613, attempted to outline his efforts to assess the cost of the upkeep of the bishops and the canons at the Cathedral. He insisted that the king of Portugal should bear some of the cost, because "the chaplains and curates instituted by his grandparents are paid each year from his royal income."[17] Similarly Alvaro III, writing to Rome in 1615 to request missionaries, took pains to assure papal officials that he would be able to pay for their upkeep as the "kings my predecessors" did. He noted that earlier kings always gave the royal chapel to their confessors "with lands, rents, vassals and Lordship ... which renders a good 2,000 cruzados," and promised that this amount would apply "from now for ever to that dignitary." Later kings made similar financial commitments. In the 1623 invitation that King Pedro II made to the Jesuits in his attempt to encourage them to return to the city to work, he took pains to remind them of the many churches that his predecessors had built, noting that they had "instituted and endowed the church of St. James ... to serve as a royal chapel." He also spelt out the funding he planned to spend on the mission, agreeing to set aside "400 *cofus* of zimbo" in perpetuity for a chaplain major and for "successors in the office" to run the operation.[18] Likewise, in 1632, King Alvaro IV reminded the head of the Jesuits in Rome that the kings of Kongo had funded the college that they had established and that he himself had given them "not only the site for the college but also other lands for farms for the rearing and producing of animals and for planting."[19] Later kings also did not waver when it came to the financial upkeep of the churches and

[15] King Afonso I to João III, April 4, 1540, *MMA* 2:100–2.

[16] Christvão Ribiero, August 1, 1548, *MMA* 15:162–3.

[17] Alvaro II to Pope Paulo V, February 27, 1613, *MMA* 6:128–32.

[18] "Instructions of King Pedro II, King of Congo..." July 5, 1623, *MMA* 7:33–8.

[19] Alvaro IV to General of the Company of Jesus, October 25, 1632, *MMA* 8:199–200.

Figure 11.4. Garcia II welcoming the Capuchins. This is from Cavazzi (1687) p. 336.

their personnel. In 1652, King Garcia blamed some of his immediate predecessors for allowing four of the churches built in the early years to fall into ruins and vowed to "restore them and rebuild them from their foundation." In fact, he impressed Father Giacinto da Vetralla, the Capuchin prefect, with his commitment, even though the missionary concluded that "this would cost a lot, because it would be necessary to make them and then transport them here." At the same time, Garcia employed a large number of laborers to rebuild the Church of St. Michael for the use of the Capuchins.[20] Unfortunately, by the 1660s, because of the disastrous civil war many more churches fell into ruin as tensions among the elite led to the neglect of the churches. A 1660 Capuchin report reflecting on the several ruined churches blamed the Portuguese in Angola, who they accused of preventing the Kongos from importing "lime" and other materials used to repair the churches and other buildings because of the fear they would use them to build "fortifications." In 1678, when the city was temporarily abandoned, São Salvador's status as a showpiece of architecture and social engineering was doomed as the city was already a shell of what it was during its heyday (Figure 11.4).

[20] Giacinto da Vatralla ao Procurador Geral, 20 August, 1652, *MMA* X1:221–3.

11.3 ATLANTIC CREOLE CULTURE IN MBANZA KONGO

Despite all their efforts (Afonso even at one point wrote that he had sufficient numbers of Kongolese trained as carpenters and masons who could work on repairing the church buildings), Kongo kings and nobles were never able to train enough local experts to have a cadre of professionals who could maintain the physical and cultural infrastructure and the cultural knowledge so necessary to maintain Mbanza Kongo's place as a vibrant Atlantic Creole city. Throughout the period when the city flourished they continued to rely on foreign experts. Kings and nobles did all they could to provide financial support not only to the churches and the many chapels, but also to defray the cost of the several dozen European and Afro-European priests, the bishop, canons, and other church officials who came to the city from Europe. They also paid the cost for the training of the thousands of Kongo-born lay ministers (*mestres de escola*) who performed the crucial work of bringing the new religious ideas to the population in the city and elsewhere. Afonso's commitment to the churches and the very pious life he lived laid the foundations for shaping the Christian character of the city and its inhabitants. Most of the Kongo kings who followed him also worked to maintain the Christian character of the city and to promote it as the Christian capital of the kingdom. Christianity took root in the city with the annual arrival of missionaries from Portugal and Rome who concentrated on teaching the people, from kings and nobles to slaves, the core principles of Christianity. The number of foreign priests and secular clergy was never enough and fluctuated from as high as fifty to as low as five (in 1649, there were sixteen European missionaries in the entire kingdom). To offset the shortfall, Kongo maintained a system that trained a great number of Kongolese as lay teachers. The kings provided the resources for the training of this local laity who carried out the day-to-day teaching and other duties of priests, even though they did not do baptisms. Although the kings and nobles and members of their households were the first people in the city to be baptized, over the years the majority of the city's residents, whether slave or free, were baptized. In fact, Inquisition accounts from the 1570s suggest that most Kongos who lived in the city (and indeed the entire kingdom) were being instructed in the teachings of the church.[21] In the early years the baptisms were mostly mass conversions, as occurred in 1548 when on March 17 the Jesuit Father Vas reported that he had baptized

[21] Arquivo Nacional de Torre do Tombo (ANTT),Inquisição de Lisboa, Processo 2522, fol. 144, Testimony of Francisco de Medeiros, 1584.

twenty-seven hundred people who attended the several churches, some of them elderly Kongos between sixty and eighty years old. All twenty-seven hundred who received baptism lived in or immediately around the city. By the 1650s, missionaries were baptizing as many as four thousand to five thousand babies per year, and by the 1670s, most people who lived in the city in fact were baptized and considered themselves Christians.[22] By the 1640s, although there were still mass baptisms in the city, most people who were baptized would have received some form of religious education from the many priests who officiated at masses in the city's several churches or from the lay Kongo and mixed Kongo-Europeans who served as their teachers. By the early seventeenth century, as the city grew in population and social complexity, its layout and social makeup made Mbanza-Kongo very different not only from Luanda, but also from the capitals of other African kingdoms of the time. Seventeenth-century residents and visitors often commented on the layout and makeup of São Salvador. For example, in 1609, Antonio Viera, the confessor of King Alvaro II, testified in Lisbon that the city had ten thousand houses and that the bishop's residence was located next to the Cathedral, which had a parish church, a college, and a hospital attached to it (Cuvelier and Jadin 1954, February–April 1609). By the mid-1620s, when Jesuit missionary João de Paiva arrived in São Salvador, he described the Portuguese quarter of the city, noting that the city was surrounded by "villages and neighboring hamlets" (Franco 1627, 249, paragraph 17). Descriptions from the early 1630s noted that the Jesuits had their own quarters in the city as well. Olfert Dapper, describing the city as it was when the Dutch embassy arrived in 1645, noted that it contained streets and pointed out that the public square (*mabzi*), which was located between the enclosed court of the king and the Portuguese enclosure, had become a central place for celebrations. Even when the number of residents began to decline in the 1650s, the city kept its status as a center of Christianity in the kingdom. Antonio Cavazzi, writing about the city in the early 1670s, put the population at a mere five thousand people. Even by the late 1670s, when most of the remaining population fled because of the increased fighting among royal factions, the city remained the symbolic religious center of the kingdom and was eventually reoccupied in 1705 (Cavazzi 1965, 80).

[22] "Carta do Padre Jorge Vaz ao Padre Simão Rodrigues," August 1, 1548, *MMA* XV:151–2; Giacinto da Vetralla ao Procurador Geral di Capucini, August 20, 1652, *MMA* X1:221–3; "Descrição das necessidades do reino do Congo," Instituto Historico e Geografico Brasileiro, DL 846, 16.

Mbanza Kongo's culture was dominated by the religious and secular culture that developed around the kings and nobles. In the early years the pious Christian demeanor of King Afonso stood out against the Portuguese experts, who he felt disrespected him, and the nobles, who were still deeply attached to the old pre-Christian ways and rituals even though they had converted. In time, however, as the Kongo nobility blended the Christianity that the Europeans brought with elements from their pre-Christian rituals and beliefs, life in the city comprised the vibrant cultural mixture that characterized Mbanza Kongo's Atlantic Creole character. The most important aspects of this culture were the celebrations that were connected with the coronation of kings, religious services that the churches, convents, and lay brotherhoods organized on Sundays and other religious days in the Catholic calendar, the new burial rites that included a mixture of Kongo and Christian rituals, and the central place of religion in Kongo politics. The city was the center of all of these developments. For example, the city served as the venue for the coronation of every new king following Afonso as the elaborate ceremony had to take place in the Cathedral with the participation of the bishop or a European priest. In fact, throughout this period no king was considered legitimate unless he came to the city to be crowned. During the coronation ceremony, the new king was required to take an elaborate oath in front of the thousands of city residents and Kongo notables and their followers who traveled to the city from the provinces to witness the event. Because European religious authorities played such a crucial role in proclaiming the king's legitimacy, reigning kings or nobles who were eligible to be elected as king made a point of staging elaborate public ceremonies in the city to welcome European missionaries. Furthermore, the king, his nobles, and members of their households always attended the weekly masses held in front of the Cathedral, led the many public penances that the churches encouraged, and participated in the religious celebrations to honor the feast days of various saints. Because the Cathedral was built on lands used as the burial site during the pre-Christian period, burials in the Cathedral were as important as coronations. Burials of kings and nobles were major public events, as all kings and nobles, no matter where they died, were brought back to the Cathedral to be buried in elaborate Christian ceremonies (Thornton 1992, 57–63). As important as the burials were the annual Christian celebration of All Souls' Day and celebrations honoring the ancestors (pre-Christian and Christian), which also took place in the Cathedral. The detailed descriptions of the burials of Pedro II and the coronation of Garcia I, which both occurred in 1624 with the mix of the knights of the Order of Christ as well as the presence of people carrying the traditional blacksmith whistle, spoke to the unique European and Kongo cultural mix (Thornton 1992, 57).

The experience of the first Carmelite mission, which arrived on the outskirts of the city on October 28, 1583, provides an excellent example of how important it was to the kings to use the city as a center of grandiose political and religious pageantry. When Alvaro I, who was reigning at the time, received the news that the members of the mission had arrived, he ordered them to spend the night outside the city while he prepared a great procession to welcome them and to receive the statue of the Virgin Mary and other relics that they had brought from Rome. The missionaries duly complied, and waited until the following day with "some relics of the Eleven Thousand Virgins, and a bone of one of the Ten Thousand Martyrs."[23] During that time Alvaro was able to assemble more than thirty thousand persons, who formed a grand procession to lead the group into the city. This all took place without the king being present, because he had an ailment that prevented him from walking, although he was able to view the procession and image from his palace.[24] Such public gatherings to welcome new missionaries or to attend religious festivals became commonplace for the residents of Mbanza Kongo. In 1619, for example, when missionaries arrived from Rome bringing an altar and "the ten thousand medals, crown and similar things," the crowd that gathered to witness the blessing of the medals was so large that most people had to remain outside the Cathedral. In fact, by the first decades of the 1600s, the Cathedral did not have enough space to accommodate the large crowds that attended regular Sunday services, and these took place in the square in front of the Cathedral. In 1631, for example, missionary Francisco de Soveral reported that Sunday services and religious festivals were always held outdoors.[25] Again in 1651 King Garcia II was so pleased that Pope Innocent X had sent him an official letter granting him several indulgences that he had requested that he "decreed that there be great celebration in the city, which lasted three months, all to show how pleased he was for the great extraordinary favors he received from the Pope."[26]

23 Diego del Sanctissimo Sacarmento, "Relation del viage de Gvinea que hiço el Padre Fray D d S," 1583, *MMA* 4:365.

24 "Relatione di quello che occorse, videro nel Regno di Congo tre Religiosi Carmelitani Scalzi...," *MMA* 4:395.

25 [Francisco do Soveral] Infra scriptam relationem de statu Cathedralis ecclesiae Sancti Saluatoris ... April 1, 1631, *MMA* 8:13–18.

26 "Interrogatorio de Statu Regni Congensis Facta Ulissipone. Anno Domini 1591," *MMA*, III:502–3.

Another interesting development that made Mbanza Kongo different from other Atlantic Creole cities was the important place of the various religious brotherhoods in the city's religious and political life. During this period, every Kongo king and male member of the nobility belonged to one of the various lay religious brotherhoods that missionaries established in the city. The first brotherhood in Mbanza Kongo was founded sometime before 1585, and the numbers dramatically increased in the early 1600s when several groups of Jesuit and Dominican missionaries arrived and the king honored their request to open more brotherhoods. By 1609, Antonio Viera noted that six confraternities operated in the city and the king and nobles supported them and that "every day masses are celebrated for the souls of the dead."[27] In fact, in 1612 King Alvaro II was so eager to show the newly arrived Dominicans that he was a devoted Christian that he agreed to their suggestion to found "the Brotherhood of the Rosary," and actually oversaw the first procession of nobles and people in the city who paraded in a way similar to the "way it was done in Portugal." In time, the activities of the various religious brotherhoods were intimately connected to royal politics as rival factions of the nobility attached themselves to one or another of the brotherhoods. The experience of the Jesuits provides a telling commentary on how the kings and nobles used the brotherhoods to settle political rivalries. In the early 1620s King Pedro invited the Jesuits to return to work in the city because, as he explained, he needed to strengthen Christian morality, which he believed was necessary to protect the kingdom from the Portuguese, who were sending armies into Kongo's southern provinces. One of these invasions had proven disastrous to the Kongo province of Mbamba, where the invaders had killed and enslaved thousands of Kongo subjects. According to Jesuit João de Paiva, who later became the rector of the college the Jesuits built, "King Pedro ... [believed] that only men of the Society of Jesus could placate God for the Congo people.... [And] he gave letters to our rector at Luanda, to send him some of the Society in order that they erect a stable home in the royal city."[28]

Pedro and the kings after him gave their full support to the Jesuits, but they soon realized that Pedro had an ulterior motive as he intended to use their presence to support his rather weak claims to the Kongo throne. In fact, when the Jesuits sent some of members of the order to the city to start construction of the college, Pedro insisted that he should be considered the founder of the college. He not only selected the best site, but offered the

[27] Ibid.

[28] Franco, *Synopsis*, 1726, paragraph 4, p. 235.

brothers food and supplies and "was often present so that by seeing him the workers might be urged in their work."[29] The first church that the Jesuits built in São Salvador was dedicated to "Jesus and King Garcia" who succeeded his father Pedro and provided the funds to continue the construction.[30]

By the late 1620s, the Jesuits had erected their own residence, opened schools for children of the nobility, and opened brotherhoods in almost all eight churches that were functioning in the city. The presence of the Jesuits actually led to more intense political divisions among members of the Kongo elite, the Portuguese, and the rest of the city's population. One such fraternity was the Brotherhood of the Holy Trinity, which restricted its membership to twelve-year-old unmarried "noble adolescents" and Portuguese, while another Jesuit-supported brotherhood located in the Church of the Holy Trinity was dedicated to St. Ignatius and restricted membership to the nobility "either married or bereaved of a spouse." Fraternities proved an excellent way of spreading the Atlantic Creole culture of the nobility to the rest of the population as the members of the brotherhoods were required to take a vow "to teach the Christian doctrine to uncultured and ignorant men especially to the members of their own household," to take communion once a month, and to "engage in other practices of Christian piety."[31] Not to be outdone, noblewomen in the city pressed their husbands and sons to organize a brotherhood for them, and by 1628 Mbanza Kongo boasted a brotherhood whose members consisted of "whatever matrons are more illustrious by birth ... queens and wives of former kings of these and the rest were moved to virtue and holy morals."[32] In time, the religious festivals that the brotherhoods organized to honor their patron saints attracted large crowds to the city center.

There was an underside to the crucial role that brotherhoods came to have in the city. By the 1630s, Kongo members of the brotherhoods divided themselves not only according to the various religious orders that funded their brotherhoods (Jesuits, Dominicans, and Capuchins), but also according to their political allegiance. During wars and other periods of political infighting, members of the brotherhoods often took political sides, and might support one or another contender for the throne. Moreover, at times the religious and political affiliations of leading members of the brotherhoods led to open warfare in the city.[33] For example, in 1628 members of

[29] Ibid., paragraph 10, p. 235.
[30] Ibid., paragraph 23, p. 242.
[31] Ibid., paragraph 17, p. 249.
[32] Ibid., paragraph 20, p. 249.
[33] For an overview of the competition between Rome and Portugal, see Thornton (1984). For a general treatment of European missionaries in Kongo, see Saccardo (1982–3, vol. 1).

one brotherhood whose members were suspected of plotting against the king were chained and dragged through the city streets, while a member of another brotherhood was among fifty conspirators executed for plotting against the king.[34] Despite the political intrigues, the religious activities of the brotherhoods contributed to the social fabric of the city.

The financial support that Kongo kings put into the physical transformation of the city during more than a century and a half of transformation gave rise to two social groups. The city boasted a population made up of European missionaries, other European residents (mostly Portuguese), and members of the Kongo ruling elite, many of them descendants of past kings, as well as a mixed race population. The Kongo members of the group were literate in Portuguese and even in Latin, bore Portuguese and African names that indicated their noble status, owned and sold slaves, dressed in a mixture of European and Kongo clothing, and devoted a lot of their time and resources to activities connected to the church. The members of the other group, comprising the bulk of the city's population, were the Kongo commoners, both free and enslaved. They provided the labor on which the other groups relied, but were officially excluded from the social and other privileges that the members of the elite enjoyed.

Despite their differences, both groups shared a common Atlantic Creole Christian identity. City residents, whether they were noble or enslaved, called themselves *Moxicongo*, a term that distinguished them from most of their non-noble rural counterparts (*mubhata*) who lived beyond the city or in the provinces. The markers of noble Moxicongo status were literacy in Portuguese as well as the use of Kikongo, Christian baptism, regular church attendance, church burials, and opportunities to participate in the several celebrations that took place. Familiarity with these aspects of city life separated Moxicongos from their rural and provincial counterparts (Thornton 1983).

The urban environment that nurtured this Moxicongo identity was largely owing to the financial investment that Kongo kings and nobles put into the project to attract European secular and religious experts to Mbanza Kongo. Their investment did not create a city that was a copy of its European counterparts as the foreign missionaries hoped or that Afonso and some of the other kings imagined. By the 1640s, the churches and other buildings in the city represented a blend of Kongo and European elements, constructed with stones and mortar but with thatched roofs. Moreover, the services held in the Cathedral and other places of worship did not replicate services in

[34] Franco, *Synopsis*, 1726, paragraph 22, p. 253 and paragraph 16, 1726, p. 256.

Europe. In fact, on many occasions European priests substituted palm wine for imported wine during communion, and candles made from palm oil often took the place of imports from Europe. The choirs that sung hymns in Latin might be accompanied by musicians who played both European and African musical instruments. Furthermore, more Kongolese in the city learned church doctrine from Kongo lay preachers who were speaking Kikongo than from the lips of the foreign religious experts as the Kongolese served as interpreters when priests were around or as lay ministers for the long years when the people saw no priests (Heywood and Thornton 2007).

This cultural blend was most visible in the celebrations that took place in the city. On St. James Day, the most important religious and cultural celebration in the city, thousands of Kongos from the provinces flocked to the city eager to participate in the public celebrations to honor St. James, Kongo's patron saint, who they believed helped King Afonso defeat his pagan brother in 1509. Despite its religious origin, the day was also one when people paid respect to the kings by bringing the traditional tribute and performing the *ensanga/sangamento*, the pre-Christian military dance, and otherwise engaging in non-Christian rituals.[35] Furthermore, on All Souls' Day when Kongo Christians gathered in the Cathedral and in the many churches or went to outdoor localities with candles and other ritual objects to honor the dead in Christ, they also honored the non-Christian ancestors as the Cathedral and some of the churches were built on pre-Christian burial sites.

The slave trade and slaveholding that became a part of the city's economic and social fabric slavery never dominated Mbanza Kongo as it did the Atlantic port cities of Quidah and Lagos. Although slavery predated the physical and cultural transformation of the city, between 1491 and the 1670s slavery in the city had more in common with the slaveholding patterns found in other Atlantic Creole cities. Whereas in the early days of the city's transformation most of the slaves held there were captives brought in from conquests, by the seventeenth century, slave trading and slaveholding were commonplace. Most members of the elite – Kongos, Portuguese, missionaries, and merchants – sold and owned slaves. Many commoners also owned a slave or two. Slaves did not comprise a separate class in the city and many found creative ways to participate in the city's culture (da Roma 1648, 69, 78). The inequalities associated with social transforma-

35 For a discussion of an eighteenth-century celebration of St. James Day, see Thornton (1998, 31–5).

Figure 11.5. Ruins of the Episcopal See, Mbanza Kongo, 1940. (Antonio Brásio, Monumenta Missionaria Africana, (1954) vol. IV, p. 192).

tion, however, were more pronounced in the 1670s than in 1491 when the Portuguese arrived (Figure 11.5).

11.4 CONCLUSION

Although Afonso and the kings who followed him imagined and partially succeeded in transforming Mbanza Kongo/São Salvador into their own version of a Kongo Christian city, by the 1670s most of the stone structures they had built and some of the cultural institutions they had supported were disappearing from the landscape. In fact, modern critics of the Kongo experiment often dismiss the early initiatives of the Kongo elite, even arguing that the Portuguese duped Afonso to such an extent that they turned Kongo into one of the major emporiums for the slave trade in central Africa. In fact, they often regard the resources the rulers expended on the infrastructural and cultural projects as early examples of Africa's foreign dependency, as a city such as Mbanza Kongo was not organic and could not be sustained without the constant presence of foreign experts. This kind of critique has been leveled at many postcolonial governments whose foreign experts built many white elephants that now litter the landscape of many countries. This thinking has been encouraged since Portuguese colonial control, which began in the 1880s, also led to the physical erasure of the experiment as stones forming the ruined buildings (except the Cathedral) were removed to build new colonial structures. Despite the disappearance of the city, however, the Mbanza Kongo experiment does provide early lessons for the *longue durée* understandings of wealth and poverty in the Atlantic. The most remarkable impact of the experiment was not its eventual failure but what it tells us about the imaginings of the Kongo nobility to finance and spearhead a cultural revolution even as the slave trade, conflicts among the nobility, and Portuguese conquest would obliterate their vision. Perhaps the one lasting by-product of the Mbanza Kongo experiment was that it gave rise to a new Kongo identity based on notions of kingship and Christianity. The hundreds of thousands of Kongos who were enslaved and carried to places such as Brazil brought this Kongo identity with them. This Kongo identity survives as folklore in contemporary Brazil in the *congada*, which has as its central activity the crowning of the Kongo king. Furthermore, an even more politically important legacy of the Mbanza Kongo experiment is the pride that modern Kongos, who are citizens of independent Angola, place in their Kongo identity and the place of Mbanza Kongo in their history. These Kongos are proud of Mbanza Kongo's Atlantic Creole past, are conscious of where the ruined churches used to be located, and would certainly disagree with the idea that the resources that the kings invested into transforming Mbanza Kongo were misplaced.

References

Cavazzi da Montecuccolo, Giovanni Antonio. (1687). *Istorica Descrizione de' tre Regni Congo, Matamba ed Angola*. Bologna.

(1965). *Descrição Histórica dos Três Reinos do Congo, Matamba e Angola*. Lisbon.

Cuvelier, Jean. (1934). *Nkutuma a Mvila za Makanda*. Tumba, Congo: Diocèse de Matadi.

(1946). *L'ancien royaume de Congo; fondation, découverte, première évangélisation de l'ancien royaume de Congo, règne du grand roi Affonso Mvemba Nzinga (1541)*. Bruges: Desclée de Brouwer.

Cuvelier, Jean and Louis Jadin. (1954). *Le ancien Congo d'après les archives romaines (1518–1640)*. Brussels: Visita ad Limina, 1619.

da Roma, Giovanni Francesco. (1648). *Breve relatione del svuccesso della missione de Frati Minori Capuccini del Serafico P.S. Francesco al Regno del Congo....* Rome: Sacra Congregatione de Propagande Fide.

Franco, R. P. Antonio. (1726). *Synopsis Annalium...in Lusitania, 1540–1725*. Augustae: Veith, 1726.

Heywood, Linda and John Thornton. (2007). *Central Africans, Atlantic Creoles and the Foundation of the Americas, 1585–1660*. Cambridge: Cambridge University Press.

Mann, Kristin. (2007). *Slavery and the Birth of an African City: Lagos, 1760–1900*. Bloomington: Indiana University Press.

Law, Robin. (2004). *Quidah, the Social History of a West African Slaving "Port," 1729–1892*. Athens: Ohio University Press.

Ogilby, John. (1670). *Africa*. London: Thomas Johnson.

Pigafetta, Filippe, Duarte Lopes, and Bartolomeo Grassi. (1591). *Relatione del Reame di Congo e delle Circonvicine Contrade*. Rome: Grassi.

Saccardo, Graziano. (1982–3). *Congo e Angola con la storia del antica missione dei cappuccini*, 3 volumes. Milan: Curia Curia Provinciale dei Cappuccini.

Thornton, John K. (1983). *Kingdom of Kongo: Civil War and Transition, 1641–1718*. Madison: University of Wisconsin Press.

(1984). "The Development of an African Catholic Church in the Kingdom of the Kongo." *Journal of African History* 25: 147–67.

(1992). "The Regalia of the Kingdom of Kongo, 1491–1895." In *Kings of Africa: Art and Authority in Central Africa, Collection Museum für Völkerkunde Berlin*, edited by Ema Beumers and Hans-Joachim Koloss, 57–64. Berlin: Maastricht: Foundation Kings of Africa.

(1998). *The Kongolese Saint Anthony: Dona Beatriz Kimpa Vita and the Antonion Movement*. Cambridge: Cambridge University Press.

(2000). "Mbanza Kongo/São Salvador: Kongo's Holy City." In *Africa's Urban Past*, edited by David M. Anderson and Richard Rathborne, 67–84. Portsmouth, NH: Heinemann.

(2001). "The Origins and Early History of the Kingdom of Kongo, c. 1350–1550." *International Journal of African Historical Studies* 34(1): 112–19.

PART III

INSTITUTIONS

12

The Fragile Revolution: Rethinking War and Development in Africa's Violent Nineteenth Century

Richard Reid

12.1 INTRODUCTION

The central concern of this chapter is sub-Saharan Africa's nineteenth century, and its place in the continent's long-term development. I argue that although war had long been both a driver and a product of innovation and consolidation in African history, the nineteenth century is of particular importance because it witnessed a major transformation in the organization and deployment of violence. Much of the new warfare involved imported technology, expanded strategic horizons, new tactical formations, and new forms of organization, with significant political and economic implications. This was tantamount to a revolution in military affairs, which also had political and economic facets. It was, in sum, a golden age of extraordinary vitality and creativity, as well as a markedly violent one. Scholars have increasingly neglected this period, however, placing ever greater emphasis on modern conflict at the expense of deeper understanding of the role and impact of warfare in Africa's past. Popular notions endure surrounding Africa's violent savagery in some imagined precolonial past, and have prevented a reconsideration of the role of war in African development over the long term, as well as of the links between past and present conflict. This chapter aims to make a contribution to that debate. I suggest that in the course of the nineteenth century – in different places at different times, and for a variety of reasons – there were indications that this transformation in military affairs was moving in the direction of new and enlarged forms of political cohesion, increased economic capacity and diversification, and heightened levels of social mobility. In other words, the revolution in violence involved development, according to the most basic definition of the term.

However, this developmental process did not go far enough, especially politically – political reform usually lagged behind military advances – while economic systems remained fragile and vulnerable to both endogenous and exogenous pressures. In part, this must be seen in the context of certain perennial limitations – notably, environmental and economic challenges and uneven demographic spread – on the scope and scale of revolutionary warfare in Africa that slowed the rate of change, and indeed prevented wholesale internal reform in some cases. Ultimately, European imperial incursions – facilitated in large part, ironically, by Africa's own violent transformation in the course of the preceding century – engendered further instability, and sharpened, indeed institutionalized, internal conflict.

12.2 DECOLONIZING WARFARE

In many respects, the history of African warfare is one of the last frontiers of decolonization: the study of the role and impact of organized violence in Africa's deeper past, certainly over *la longue durée*, remains a minority sport. While scholars have carried out fine work over the past forty years or more on various aspects of precolonial war,[1] it has never represented the academic mainstream. There are various reasons for this, no doubt. One leftist tendency of the generation responsible for the establishment of African history as a professional discipline during the 1960s and 1970s – against the backdrop of an unpopular war in Southeast Asia – was its disinclination to foreground violence and the military in its work. The shift toward "history from below," moreover, militated against the history of war, with its emphasis – at least before its 1980s relaunch as "war studies" – on great men and decisive battles, and African studies was in the cockpit of this new historiography. But perhaps most important of all – and certainly most germane to the argument in this chapter – was that to study war in African history was to push against the developmental agenda in academic and policy circles, already building in momentum in the course of the 1960s and 1970s. A concentration on violence was inappropriate vis-à-vis more mainstream work on political dynamism, social innovation and creativity, and economic development – while at the same time, from the 1970s onward, most of this kind of work was being done not on the precolonial past at all, but rather on the colonial era, which increasingly dominated the scholarly

[1] A very basic reading list would include Ogot (1972), Mazrui (1977), Thornton (1999), Smith (1976), and Reid (2007). For a representative sample, see also Lamphear (2007).

horizon. Historians were more interested in heroic economies than military heroism. This is not to say that no one worked on it: a number did, for a while, as even a cursory glance at the first decade of the *Journal of African History* reveals. But it was not sustained. In the end, few self-respecting historians of Africa could ponder warfare without the odorous associations of nineteenth-century missionaries and humanitarians lingering about them, for after all, to look seriously at war would mean, presumably, having to concur that sometimes nineteenth-century Africa was really rather violent. That is what the racialists of the 1880s and 1890s had emphasized, and so it would not do.

Moreover, warfare, it seemed, was the one realm of activity on which the European Scramble for Africa had imposed itself decisively: industrial-era armaments swept aside an array of African armies and militias, and dancing and painted warriors were thus consigned to distant and quaintly tribal memory. In certain circles, some of them survived – the Zulu, for example, or the Sudanese "Dervishes" – as examples of savage but somehow honorable warriors bravely but foolishly waving their spears in the direction of modernity. There was something compelling in this image, for military history buffs, but not for most Africanists, who had long since left that particular battlefield behind. They were now increasingly interested in what came after, in those aspects of creeping anticolonial protest and identity that, some believed, were central to understanding Africa's own modernity, and that, not coincidentally, involved "history from below."

Not only has this development privileged the period of the Scramble for Africa as a military moment, positioning it as a point of departure between the past and the present in terms of African violence, but it also, by implication, denies the broader developmental role of warfare in Africa's earlier past. Those scholars who have worked on the subject have done enough to indicate how important war was to African states and societies seeking to accumulate people, create broader pools of factor endowments, access commerce, and enhance social cohesion – in sum, to build stronger and more competitive economies and polities. Often, it was bloody and messy, and it did not work, but sometimes it did, and either way it needs and deserves much closer and more sustained attention. Meanwhile, the veritable explosion of literature on modern African wars since the mid-1990s[2]

[2] In recent years, see, for example, Clapham (1998), Reno (1998), Ali and Matthews (1999), Richards (2005), Kaarsholm (2006), Boas and Dunn (2007), Derman, Odgaard, and Sjaastad (2007), and Nhema and Zeleza (2008a, 2008b).

is notable in one significant respect, namely the strikingly ahistorical, foreshortening approach of much of this material to the subject. A great deal of it, indeed, appears to be driven by solution-oriented, presentist research agendas. The overwhelming focus on the modern has enabled scholars to restrict themselves to thinking in terms of specifically postcolonial malaise. They do so at the expense of a long-term approach – in other words, a consideration of the role of war in Africa's deeper past and of the links between past and present. To be sure, this is a risky strategy, for it will inevitably involve highlighting African failures as well as achievements, and the destructive as well as the creative in Africa's history. But without it, our understanding of the recent past is at best one-dimensional. A pervasive presentism in intellectual culture is much in evidence across the disciplines, but it is perhaps tautological to point out that it is in history that it does the most damage.

The central focus of this chapter is the nineteenth century, an era of extraordinary vitality in political, economic, and military affairs, which has nonetheless suffered from a certain scholarly neglect in recent years.[3] The nineteenth century was, in the 1960s, the centerpiece of much of the new African historiography; since then, it has gradually become mere prologue to the main action – namely, that of the colonial period and beyond. My purpose here is to contribute to its rehabilitation as the foundational era of modern African history, and also to resuscitate and develop the idea of a nineteenth-century African military revolution, first proposed, in a somewhat different form and context, by Nigerian historian Godfrey Uzoigwe more than thirty years ago (Uzoigwe 1977). That argument quickly fizzled out – the trend was against both military history and indeed the study of the precolonial period – but a wealth of evidence supports it.

Inspiration can be drawn from European models, in particular the ongoing debate surrounding the nature of the putative "revolution in military affairs" and its relationship with the rise of European statehood and attendant economic development.[4] A cursory glance at the literature on European warfare reveals a deeply embedded and widely accepted thesis that a dynamically reciprocal relationship existed between state formation, economic development, and organized violence in European history. It

[3] A notable, though somewhat disappointing, exception in recent times is Coquery-Vidrovitch (2009).

[4] For example: McNeill (1982), Tilly (1992), Parker (1996), Howard (2009), Kennedy (1988).

may ultimately be considered a successful combination, with the predictable caveat that of course success is always relative, and its measurement debatable. The notion of the military revolution in European history has long been the subject of debate among scholars;[5] the precise details of that debate need not detain us in the course of this chapter, but only those key aspects – particularly in terms of the relationship between war and state formation – that appear to have relevance for the African experience. The dangers of Eurocentrism in drawing on this body of scholarship are clear enough; I hope they have been avoided here. The most obvious risk is that in keeping the European experience in view, we think of war and political and economic development in terms of linear progression, and consider therefore that something has gone wrong in Africa – in other words, the European experience becomes the template. Sometimes, war is simply not a matter of linear progression (or at least it does not yet appear to be); moreover, one of the central points of this chapter is that Africa has had its own particular set of problems and issues, and the African experience needs to be understood within distinctive parameters.

Finally, it is worth noting that work on African economic development in historical context frequently neglects the role of war whether as cause or as consequence.[6] This chapter is not about economics – but it is about the contexts within which economic change takes place, the drivers of such change, and the economic aspirations of key actors. Suffice to note here that the picture is a patchwork: at times, organized violence is clearly the outcome of economic decline or catastrophe and seeks to rectify the latter; at others, war itself is the central driver of economic change, either bringing about economic growth or being inimical, ultimately, to such growth. It is certainly evident in nineteenth-century Africa that it could be both simultaneously – with war driving certain types of economic expansion, but not others; facilitating particular trajectories of political development, but not others.

5 A useful summary can be found in Henniger (2006).

6 Forty years ago, Jack Goody began to consider the comparative history of African and Eurasian societies with respect to the means of both production and destruction, but little came of the debate (Goody 1971). In John Iliffe's otherwise superb history of African poverty, the index contains no entry for *warfare*, *violence*, *conflict*, *militarization*, or any other term suggesting an analytical link between war and economic depravation (Iliffe 1987). Ralph Austen's grand survey of African economic history does discuss "warfare and raiding" at various junctures, but in a way that only suggests the need for a great deal more work (Austen 1987). As Tony Hopkins's survey article shows, warfare scarcely features in recent analyses of African economic history (Hopkins 2009).

12.3 NINETEENTH-CENTURY TRANSFORMATIONS IN VIOLENCE

The beginnings of our putative revolution – or, perhaps more accurately, revolutions – are not easy to nail down with any great precision. A number of the key features of the transformations in violence most closely associated with the nineteenth century were already in place in the eighteenth in some areas – most notably along those stretches of Atlantic Africa most intensely involved in the slave trade. Between ca. 1500 and ca. 1800, the violence of the slave trade drove the formation of new states and societies: the instability of the Atlantic zone destroyed some communities – Kongo was an early victim – yet others thrived on the opportunities for violent entrepreneurialism, for example Dahomey, Oyo, Asante. The human tragedy notwithstanding, this was an era of remarkable political, economic, and ultimately military dynamism, leading to the formation of durable states with vigorous military cultures. Alongside territorial monarchies, there were mobile associations of professional warriors, such as the Imbangala, who thrived on – indeed manufactured – much of the violent disorder around them. These would be key features of the nineteenth century, already present in the seventeenth and eighteenth. But the claim made for the revolutionary nature of the nineteenth century is based on the dramatic proliferation of such highly militarized states and communities; on the transformative effects of firearms, which had a muted impact in most places before the early and mid-eighteenth century; and above all, perhaps, on the widespread emergence of armed entrepreneurs and adventurers responsible for the creation of an array of new communities – some relatively durable, others less so, but almost always on the frontiers of contest and exchange – characterized by military professionalism, material ambition, and, in many cases, ideological ardor.

This was a *long* nineteenth century in many places, reaching from the last third of the eighteenth century to the 1910s and 1920s, when colonial rule engendered a temporary *pax* across much of the continent, and change occurred throughout this era, coming later in some places than in others, and at times more intense than at others. Nonetheless, the period between the 1780s and the 1820s can be seen as a transitional moment, when a series of events and processes signified dramatic change. The Ngoni conflagration in southeast Africa, which would give rise to the Zulu state; the disintegration of the Oyo Empire; the Fulani-Hausa jihad; Buganda's apogee as driver of regional military and economic change; the collapse of the Solomonic state in Ethiopia: these developments were mostly unconnected, but they each clearly encapsulated issues germane to much of Africa as a whole in the century to come. Violence was deployed in ever more innovative and concentrated ways in pursuit of political and economic objectives. Soldiery was becoming increasingly professionalized; war provided new opportunities to young men for the achievement of socioeconomic and indeed political status. In this sense, broad comparisons can be drawn with Europe's early modernization process from the late fifteenth century into the sixteenth, involving the transition from the feud of chivalry to more professional, salaried armies and the attendant rise, in the sixteenth century, of the powerful prince, embodying – and carving out by force – sovereignty. Africa's nineteenth-century warlords were doing much the same thing, in the process frequently articulating ideas about just and legal war – again, as in sixteenth- and seventeenth-century Europe.

New military organization appeared, including new forms of politico-military leadership, while firearms became increasingly common and drove a range of tactical and structural innovations. Guns had been present along the Atlantic coast, and in the Ethiopia Highlands, since the early sixteenth century, but their impact on tactics and organization was minimal for at least two hundred years. Across the West African savannah and in the deeper sub-Saharan interior, meanwhile, guns had little or no impact whatsoever. Only from the early eighteenth century, with the arrival in increasing numbers of more effective flintlock muskets, did firearms become important, and only in the course of the nineteenth century did they become weapons of revolutionary change across the continent. In this context, indeed, a useful comparison can be made with the European experience between the mid-sixteenth and mid-seventeenth centuries, during which time the use of portable firearms by the Dutch and the Swedes meant the need for more professional, better trained soldiers – one of the central planks of the European military revolution thesis (Black 2009, 64–5, Henniger 2006, 8).

It is impossible to provide detail from across the entire continent; instead, examples may be selected to illustrate the central idea. To begin with, developments in coastal West Africa and in the East African interior – among the Yoruba and the Nyamwezi respectively – encapsulate some of the core themes. In the first instance, it was the collapse of an *ancien regime* – the Oyo Empire – as well as the local impact of more gradual shifts in the global economy that led to a transformation in the nature and structure of warfare. In the second, external commercial pressures likewise played a key role; but rather than the destruction of an older state system – which had been notably absent in the early history of the Tanzanian interior – there were novel attempts at state building and the militarization of political culture as a result. Oyo's hegemony in the region of the Benin Gap dated to the late seventeenth century; by the early years of the nineteenth century, however, diminishing profits from the slave trade – Oyo's major source of revenue for the better part of two centuries – meant the inability to buy horses from the north, which meant in turn increased internal taxation to meet the shortfall. But a weakened military and restive centrifugalism fundamentally destabilized the Oyo polity, which was dealt a further blow by the advance of Sokoto's jihadist forces from the north (Law 1977). The consequence of Oyo's collapse in the 1820s and 1830s was a century of violent reform (Smith and Ajayi 1971). The product and then the engine of much of this change was the Yoruba city-state, self-contained, fortified, and linked together by a complex and periodically shifting network of alliances and antagonisms. Between the 1830s and the 1870s, Ibadan was the dominant force in Yoruba politics, and its rise came at the expense of Ijaye in particular, which was largely destroyed in the early 1860s. From the late 1870s, an alliance crystallized around opposition to Ibadan – now positioning itself as the successor of Oyo – and included the Egba, centered on Abeokuta, and the Ijebu, situated close to the coast near Lagos and a key commercial power in the region. These prolonged wars facilitated the rise of military leaders – warlords, in modern parlance – who sometimes had links with the old Oyo system, but who were often self-made men who established new military aristocracies; and they were at the head of increasingly professional forces, comprising young men – the "war boys" – equipped with both matchlocks and more potent flintlocks. Significantly, too, these forces were often professional mercenaries, hiring themselves out to the highest bidder and fighting on behalf of their chosen city-state until better material rewards were offered elsewhere. War had become a career choice, and often a highly lucrative one; and the skills in battlefield maneuver and, in particular, use of firearms were both sharpened and increasingly in demand. Commercial upheaval – the expansion of the illegal slave trade and the more general widening of commercial opportunities – loosened the bonds of older loyalties and conventions and unleashed new generations of armed youth onto political and economic markets in search of adventure, material improvement, and social standing.

It was this explosion of novel forces for change – frequently driven by, and certainly involving, a younger generation eager for new opportunities – that also defined eastern Africa in the mid- and late nineteenth century. The expansion of the slave and ivory trades from the early nineteenth century onward prompted new ways of organizing violence and heightened levels of militarization. Between Lake Victoria and the Zambezi valley, the

Nyamwezi and the Yao were in the vanguard of these violent transformations, of both political and commercial change, between the 1850s and the 1890s: among these groups, new forms of military leadership emerged, around which new communities coalesced – often highly mobile, certainly fluid, and frequently transient.[7] As with the Yoruba "war boys," young men were becoming an increasingly professionalized soldiery – known among the Nyamwezi as *ruga ruga* – ever more adept in the arts of flintlock musketry and noted for their speed of deployment and maneuver. The *ruga ruga* were often little better than thugs and criminals, but more broadly they formed part of a self-perpetuating cycle of sociopolitical reform, for military states both created the disorder that released young manpower from more traditional obligations and then utilized that manpower in the quest for economic profit and political development. They formed part of a new generation of aggressive and displaced youth – often joined by slaves similarly armed with guns and with loyalty to a new class of entrepreneurs of violence with enlarged visions of what was economically and politically possible. Nyungu-ya-Mawe among the Kimbu; Msiri in Katanga; Tippu Tip to the west of Lake Tanganyika: these were restlessly brilliant military leaders who traded and raided simultaneously, overthrowing old political structures and processes and seeking to build new polities designed to take advantage of the commercial opportunities opening up around them (Bennett 1971; Reid 2007; Roberts 1968). There was no better illustration of the turbulence of the age than Mirambo, whose Nyamwezi state had emerged by the end of the 1860s and dominated much of the Tanzanian interior down to his death in 1884. Mirambo harnessed the youthful, violent exuberance of his *ruga ruga* and pursued larger political and economic objectives, including those of unity and stability. He partially and temporarily achieved the former, but never the latter, and his state – Urambo – collapsed soon after his death. Nonetheless, these experiments in political and economic reform, highly militarized and underpinned by the novel utilization of violence, were symptomatic of developmental shifts across nineteenth-century eastern Africa. The fortified towns that grew up across the eastern African interior – in themselves a striking innovation, given the previous pattern of dispersed settlement in an underpopulated region – were for protection in the first instance, but they became centers of trade and industry and political business, too. Even Tippu Tip's rough-hewn empire in the eastern Congo – based on slave militias doing the business of ivory trading and slave trading – represented an advance, if an unsteady

[7] Alpers (1975); Reid (2007).

and profoundly unattractive one, in economic organization, and certainly embodied a new kind of aggressive, dynamic entrepreneurialism.

Such privatized violence – under personal leadership and increasingly involving mercenary professionals – was in evidence elsewhere, too. In west-central Africa and along the southern Atlantic coast, the Ovimbundu and Chokwe created entrepreneurial militarisms similar to those in the eastern region, for which military professionalism and commercial adventurism (the export of slaves) were the twin elements in a process of sociopolitical transformation – even if, again, the roots of that process were in the pre-1800 era. In the Zambezi valley, groups of guns for hire coalesced into a series of mercenary armies centered on leaders who were merchants and warlords simultaneously. One common theme of particular significance was the harnessing and organization of armed youth with larger aims in view; this was also discernible separately, among, for example, the Turkana and Maasai (Lamphear 1998; Spear and Waller 1993). Here, age-grade structures signified the growing militarization of youth – in the dry grasslands of the Rift Valley, it may have been driven in the nineteenth century by environmental shifts – under the direction of new forms of charismatic centralizing leadership, often provided by prophets and diviners. Neighboring Somali and Oromo had used age regimentation to good effect for some time.

Developments in the southeast of the continent also fit with the dynamic model discernible in the Atlantic and eastern zones. During the 1790s and 1800s, competition for land among the Ngoni chiefdoms was escalating following a period of population growth. Increased levels of warfare prompted the use of age regimentation as a means of both sociopolitical and military organization among the key centralized states of the region, and by the mid-1810s, a commander named Shaka – from the comparatively unimportant Zulu clan – came to the fore as the most prominent exponent of the new systems and tactical formations. Under Shaka's leadership, the Zulu state emerged as the key driver of sociopolitical and above all military change in the region. The Zulu fought in close formation using short stabbing spears, deployed with fearsome speed, and were noted for their deadly use of flanking maneuvers to crush opponents. The new state, in place by the beginning of the 1820s, was based on the skillful and brutally disciplinarian management of youthful male aggression; the regiments, the *amabutho*, were used to tend cattle while not actively deployed in war. Defeated opponents were absorbed into the regimental system (or were killed in the attempt), breaking down older patterns of loyalty and underpinning a novel style of militarized kingship. The *mfecane* – a term referring loosely to the era of violent upheaval – led to the migration of a number of groups out of the area for safety, and thus military transformation was exported beyond the immediate area.[8] New polities and societies – some at more than one remove from the original Ngoni upheaval – emulated Zulu organization and tactics: the Ndebele, the Sotho, the Bemba. Other Ngoni groups wandered north through Malawi and into Tanzania by the 1840s and 1850s, and the communities they encountered frequently copied their military structures and ethos: the Hehe, the Bena, the Sangu. The Ngoni – or more accurately groups that were the product of contact with the Ngoni – almost certainly inspired the young Mirambo, as such itinerant and armed communities entered northern Tanzania in the course of the 1850s. Firearms became increasingly important to these polities after the mid-nineteenth century.

Some of these groups at length settled down, demilitarized to some extent, and took up agriculture alongside the keeping of cattle; others maintained a more or less predatory way of life down to the 1890s. The Zulu state itself struggled for stability through much of the nineteenth century following Shaka's assassination in 1828, both in terms of external relations – specifically with European settlers, present in the area from the second half of the 1830s, as well as with increasingly well-armed African neighbors – and internal political arrangements, especially as succession was rarely uncontested, while restless regiments remained a headache for the kingship. There was therefore enormous variation in terms of local flavor and direction of travel; nevertheless, taken in the round, a veritable revolution in military affairs had unfolded across an enormous swathe of southern, central, and eastern Africa between the 1790s and the 1850s – and this rolling revolution had intersected with separate, equally explosive, developments in central eastern Africa in mid-century. It amounted to a stunning patchwork of violence across a wide area, creative and brutally destructive in equal measure. This was a military transformation, moreover, that involved economic consolidation and diversification and social stratification, as polities of various hues were driven by material objectives and aimed to maximize internal productive and external commercial opportunities.

So far, we have dealt – by and large – with wholly novel political forms, new creations born of transformative violence. In other cases, states of long standing – that is, with their roots in an earlier era – also experienced dramatic military change in the course of the nineteenth century, their

[8] It might be noted in passing here that some twenty years ago there was debate over whether the *mfecane* happened at all, at least in the manner traditionally depicted: see Cobbing (1988). For a more consensual approach, see Hamilton (1992, 1998), Wylie (2006).

innovations in violence taking place within broadly preexisting political and territorial parameters. Dahomey, rooted in the seventeenth-century slave trade, was one such polity – and indeed one of the most successful precolonial militarisms anywhere in Africa (Law 1991; Smith 1976). It expanded considerably its range of military operations in the course of the nineteenth century – including westward, into Yoruba country, following the collapse of Oyo – and was one of the worst offenders in the illegal slave trade down to the 1850s, whereupon it turned increasingly to the export of agricultural produce. Its strikingly martial culture was arguably more monolithic than that of Asante, another monarchical state with its roots in the seventeenth century. Asante was more dextrous in its balancing of commerce and war, and its military success was at least matched by its highly effective diplomatic machine – although Europeans, particularly the British, continued to see Asante, as they did Dahomey, as the embodiment of the archetypically savage, bloodthirsty African empire, particularly in the later nineteenth century (Adjaye 1996; Wilks 1975).

On the other side of the continent, Buganda reached the apex of its military strength between the 1780s and the 1820s, from which position it sought to dominate the wider lacustrine region as well as the commercial system encroaching on it. The Ganda innovated accordingly, militarizing aspects of the political establishment – explicitly military chieftaincies were created and a martial culture was further underpinned – and importing firearms in increasing numbers. As the limitations of war on land became ever clearer, the Ganda developed a fleet of canoes with a view to rendering Lake Victoria a Ganda sea, thus increasing their military and commercial reach (Reid 2002). In terms of internal military reform, Bunyoro was at least the equal of its old rival Buganda, for in the 1870s new regiments of riflemen – the *barusura* – aided the kingdom's resurgence in the 1880s and 1890s, a resurgence only crushed by British arms (Doyle 2006). Bunyoro's deployment of firepower was more effective than that of the Ganda – the *barusura* bear comparison with the *ruga ruga* and the Yoruba "war boys," including their brutality and the license to ravage granted them by their founder, Kabalega – for in Buganda a gun culture at the royal court served to undermine the professional military ethos as firearms became more symbols of sociopolitical standing than indications of new military skill. Nonetheless, militarization in both Buganda and Bunyoro served to heighten their mutual antagonism on the eve of colonial rule; this was a conflict into which the British would be co-opted in the 1890s, with profound implications for the wider region (Low 2009). Important, too, both Buganda and Bunyoro sought economic expansion as part of their programs of military transformation – internally, through the development of existing resources, and externally, through the capture of commercial opportunities.

A further variation on the theme of state building through war in the nineteenth century can be discerned in the western African savannah and in the Ethiopian Highlands; for here, new states were formed through violence that laid claim to ancient ideological and religious inheritances, thus rendering their violence righteous. Revivalist Islam had long facilitated political and military innovation in the Saharan world; as recently as the early and mid-eighteenth century, jihads in Futa Toro and Futa Jalon had demonstrated the possibilities violent theocracy offered for the creation of new communities. But the Sokoto Caliphate – founded as a result of jihadist war among the Hausa states in the first decade of the nineteenth century – was the most remarkable manifestation of armed Islam to date (Roberts 1987; Smaldone 1977). Sokoto's infantry ranks were soon joined by cavalry forces to great effect, and by the late 1810s the armies of the faithful were pressing in on Yoruba territory to the south and exporting both tactics and ideology across the savannah. Bornu, notably, reformed its military to check the advance of Hausa and Fulani forces. By the mid-nineteenth century, firearms – long eschewed by the highly mobile warriors of savannah and desert – were common and were deployed with considerable success by Umar Tal's armies during the Tukolor jihad of the 1850s. Samori Ture's Mandinke forces used both horses and guns in the 1880s and 1890s, and were serviced by craftsmen who learned how to repair and modify firearms and to make ammunition (Legassick 1966). Sokoto, meanwhile, had become a major economic power, in addition to a political and ideological presence, across the wider region.

The violent renewal of Islam drove political, military and economic change in the region – Sokoto became a major economic power as well as a religious one – and a broadly comparable set of processes were at work in the Ethiopian Highlands. Here, however, it was ancient Christian nationalism that was at work in the formation of the highly militarized neo-Solomonic state between the 1850s and the 1890s. The polity claimed to be the recreation of an older Christian empire in the region, the original Solomonic state founded in the late thirteenth century that finally collapsed amidst violent regionalism in the 1760s and 1770s. As with the aftermath of the fall of Oyo among the Yoruba – and indeed the jihadist challenge to the Hausa states – the disintegration of an *ancien regime* would produce new forms of strident militarism and the innovative organization of violence as ethno-regional units, albeit often porous, consolidated and competed over both trade and ideological inheritance. This was the period known in

Ethiopian historiography as the *zemene mesafint* – the "era of the princes." The "new" Ethiopia that eventually emerged from these conflicts was largely the work of a triumvirate of leaders in the second half of the nineteenth century, namely Tewodros, Yohannes, and Menelik, each of whom, in different ways, understood the transformative power of violence and the political and economic possibilities in its usage. The Ethiopian empire that was created by the 1880s and 1890s – encompassing the agricultural and mineral wealth of newly conquered lands to the south – was the outcome of several decades of military reform, expansionist violence, and a dynamic military culture that lauded righteous Christian violence in the face of Muslim enemies who pressed in on the kingdom's flanks (Reid 2011). Ethiopian armies, moreover, made arguably more effective use of firearms – some of which were the best Europe had to offer, imported via Djibouti – than any on the continent. The Sokoto Caliphate and Solomonic Ethiopia were the products of ideological revolutions inspired by ancient faith, but they were underpinned by innovative violence and involved transformations in the rather more secular realms of economy and polity.

Let us pause briefly and consider the degree to which comparisons between Africa and Europe make for something of a mixed bag. Debates are perhaps to be had over whether Tewodros or Mirambo or Shaka embodied much of the same skill and ambition of, say, Maurice of Nassau or Gustav Adolphus or (Shaka's exact contemporary) Napoleon, in terms of military reorganization; whether the Zulu or the Amhara in the nineteenth century were like the Prussians of the seventeenth. Indeed, nineteenth-century European commentators were keen to establish the same points of reference, witness Henry Morton Stanley's description of Mirambo as the region's Frederick the Great (Stanley 1899, 386, although he was probably more of an Oliver Cromwell, militarily if not politically). Whether such debates are ultimately of any use is another issue, while the question might reasonably be asked (and indeed has been asked): Why do any of them have to be compared to *any* European figure? But, as one of the aims of this chapter is comparative history, the niceties of historical relativism can be dispensed with and broad contours noted. The African experience of military professionalization, not least owing to the widespread adoption of modern firearms, is broadly comparable to that of Europe, as are the proliferation of mercenary forces and the rise of military overlords who were armed sovereignty incarnate. But while firepower demanded discipline and control, not all African societies had quite perfected this by the 1880s or 1890s. In Europe, state systems ultimately provided order, but in Africa, political mobility persisted in many areas. Much of nineteenth-century Africa looks not unlike Europe during the Thirty Years' War in the first half of the seventeenth century, in terms of complex regional relations, prolonged and brutal levels of violence, and attendant political and military innovation. But there had been few "Westphalia moments" in Africa by the late nineteenth century, even if the trajectory of violence in many areas suggested that such political settlements were within reach. And few of Africa's wars were as crushingly expensive. In the aftermath of Westphalia, Europe's "wars of mercenaries" became the "wars of merchants": funds from business and commerce were needed desperately to pay for armies and enlarged military systems (Howard 2009). While there is evidence of this in Africa – among the Yoruba, the Nyamwezi, the Amhara, in Sokoto – this process was far from completion by century's end, although again there was a clear movement in this direction. Arguably, too, mobility and instability across Africa – not least in terms of succession and territory – prevented something similar to Europe's eighteenth-century shift from mercenaries and privateers to patriotism and mass revolutionary war. We return to some of these contrasts a little later. The final point to note here, however, is that both Europe and Africa had become highly militarized by the late nineteenth century. The European "nation" was a military beast indeed, its roots in war, its outlook bellicose, its sense of self markedly martial; and it now intersected with not dissimilar, but nonetheless distinctive, processes of militarization further south.

12.4 THE VORTEX OF VIOLENCE: EUROPE AND THE REVOLUTION

Much of the discussion of late nineteenth-century European imperialism has rested on technological advances, understandably; but care is needed to avoid technological determinism, namely the belief that technical innovation in itself proffers battlefield superiority on the innovator. The second half of the twentieth century has repeatedly demonstrated the fallacy of that notion; and it is demonstrable for a much earlier period, too. As Black points out, for example, there was no fundamental shift in the military balance between the West and the rest much before the mid-nineteenth century; Europe's innovations in firepower frequently floundered in African and Asian settings in the seventeenth and eighteenth centuries (Black 2009, 65). Yet Bayly makes the more generally accepted point succinctly: that in the course of the eighteenth century, Europe became "generally more mobilised for warfare and more ruthless in prosecuting it than Asians, Africans, and Polynesians." In part this could be explained by the particular demands of war in the modern European context – the need to adapt rapidly between land and sea, cramped spaces requiring ever more investment in technical innovations to achieve success. More efficient systems of tax, again, were needed to finance this kind of organized violence, and those systems underpinned modern state formation (Bayly 2004, 81). Yet it was not that Africans were any less mobilized for warfare; rather, as Bayly himself puts it, more effective linkages between war and finance meant that "Europeans became much better at killing people" (Bayly 2004, 62).

In the latter years of the nineteenth century – and rather earlier in some areas – the looming external threat drove further military innovation across the continent. Amhara, Ganda, Nyoro, Nyamwezi, Zulu, Yoruba, and Fulani leaders saw in the advance of the European imperial frontier both danger – though some came to this position rather later than others – and inspiration, in terms of organization of firepower, order, and discipline, and the economic systems that underpinned the military. North Africa provides the most dramatic examples of so-called defensive modernization, in which elites sought to emulate the military-industrial model provided by Europe in order to ward off the threat posed by it. The perils of succeeding too well were clear enough, however: witness the case of Muhammad Ali, who between the 1810s and the 1840s transformed Egypt into a major military and economic power – using European expertise, finance, and inspiration as appropriate – but who was subsequently cut down to size by a European coalition that considered that he had become rather *too* powerful. Flattery, in the form of imitation, was not enough to prevent European intervention – as a host of African leaders would discover in the decades that followed. Few were as effective as Muhammad Ali, but most would come to appreciate that the attempt to modernize militarily – in reality, representing only the latest stage in Africa's ongoing process of military reform – only elicited an aggressive response from a Europe determined to manage Africa's modernity on its own terms.

The great irony is that the innovation across Africa in the nineteenth century, as well as the traumas and turbulence of the age, provided Europe with a critical point of entry and considerable leverage across the continent. Without Africa's violent transformation, there would likely have been no "scramble" – or at least there would have been a greatly modified form of European intervention and influence. As it was, European imperialism was drawn into a series of vortices of violence; and while the details of the ironic outcome known as the Scramble for Africa need not detain us here,[9] a brief explanation is required as to how Africa's military revolution facilitated

[9] There is no more stimulating analysis of the era than Lonsdale (1985).

Europe's colonial moment. A century of violent upheaval between the 1780s and the 1880s produced across the continent floating populations – the displaced and the rootless, as well as armed predatory bands representing the detritus of rapid social change and political reformation – which meant manpower for European imperial projects. Without this manpower, most of Europe's late-century adventures into Africa would have been impossible – the obvious exceptions being those areas where European troops were used in large numbers, as in South Africa and Sudan. Further, not only did these traumatized and militarized communities lend their muscle to a multitude of European armed incursions, but such incursions were not infrequently dependent on Africans' martial skills, as well as their local knowledge. The European contribution was clearly critical – in terms of modern firepower (although this is in itself often exaggerated) and, more important, organization, discipline, and drill. But European officers were able to work with some fine raw material, including a swell of young men well versed in the martial arts, while the continual flux of sociopolitical conditions in late-century Africa had produced mercenary cultures – or, perhaps more appropriately, mercenary markets. Individuals and entire groups were willing and able to attach themselves to new leadership in exchange for security, adventure, and material reward. Loyalty was entirely contingent and negotiable. Many of the new states and societies that had arisen in the course of the nineteenth century had been founded on the same principles, and thus were the military foundations of the colonial state laid.

Much has been made, correctly, of the fact that there was no internal unity within Africa – indeed "Africa" itself did not exist, except as a European geographical and cultural concept – and that there was therefore no capacity for more concerted resistance. But this needs to be taken a little further, for it is in itself neither adequate nor appropriate. The nineteenth century witnessed a particularly explosive upsurge in interstate and intercommunity violence, which involved the opening up of especially deep fissures between states and societies, particularly between centers and their armed frontier lands. The militarization of African political culture provided the adventuring agents of European imperialism with ready-made points of leverage. One interpretation of this would be Europeans skillfully (but also rather luckily) positioning themselves between proverbial petty warring tribes and fighting and overcoming each of these one by one. There is no doubt that comparatively small European forces – comprising a handful of European officers in charge of an African rank and file – were able to insert themselves into the contested places between states and societies, exploiting local antagonisms to their own ends. Yet in fact Europeans were frequently co-opted into local wars, unwittingly becoming actors in local struggles, often of long standing. Africa's own military revolution in many ways facilitated the European partition and ushered in the colonial moment. Struggles for local material and political dominance that had escalated throughout the nineteenth century now drew external agents into them; many a beleaguered European company official, army officer, and missionary in the 1880s and 1890s was uncomfortably aware of the fact, indeed, and it was only some time after – certainly by the 1920s – that a rather grander narrative was constructed around the purposefulness and inevitable success of the civilizing military mission. The reality had been altogether messier.

Nonetheless, the "Western way of war" was demonstrated to deadly effect in the second half of the nineteenth century, when European states engaged in a process of imperial expansion, which was in many respects the natural outflow of the state-war vortex inside Europe itself. The wars Europe waged on Africans in the late nineteenth century were often more brutally efficient than anything most of the latter had ever before encountered (Vandervort 1998). Although Douglas Porch is right to remind us that the margin of victory in many of Europe's so-called small wars of imperial expansion was rather narrower than was often supposed (Porch 2001), there is no question that nineteenth-century Europe was armed to the teeth, with greatly improved military resources and more muscular state apparatuses following Europe's own wars of the 1780–1820 period (Bayly 2004, 266*ff*). The comparative ease, with one or two exceptions, with which African resistance was crushed in the 1890s and 1900s – especially in eastern and southern Africa – further contributed to the twin notions that, first, Africa's precolonial past had been bloodily tribal and inimical to change, still less to development; and, second, that a rightful moral monopoly had been established on the use of force. Europe mobilized ideas about race and culture to depict African violence as perpetual and as symptomatic of a deep-rooted savagery, and in so doing put in place a remarkably enduring set of misconceptions about the role of warfare in Africa's past. In their essentials, they endure still, and because precolonial violence had been radicalized, so now was the development that would supposedly follow it – for the colonial state had stamped out atavistic savagery and would now facilitate, in a range of ways, Africa's halting first steps into modernity. In fact the colonial state represented only the latest stage in an ongoing process of violent transformation, and had been co-opted – if at times almost imperceptibly – into African contours of change. But this is not to dismiss the colonial moment as largely irrelevant in the grand flow of African history – even if its significance has indeed been greatly exaggerated – for the net outcome, as far as we can assess it from the standpoint of our own era, has been long-term destabilization. Europe was indeed drawn into African conflicts, but the colonial state in many cases crystallized particular patterns of violence – even if the temporary colonial *pax* concealed this for a generation or so – and heightened the potential for continued violence among particular groups enclosed within and straddling colonial territories. The colonial era greatly restricted Africans' room for maneuver in terms of indigenous resolution and prevention of conflict, and ultimately sustained material development. This has been the lasting colonial legacy – alongside the perpetuation of misapprehensions about the role of violence in Africa's deeper past, for much contemporary analysis, especially in the world of policy, is not much more (or perhaps just as) sophisticated as that of the late nineteenth century. And so the nineteenth-century revolution has been prolonged, although it is manifest in new ways – in modern coups d'état, in popular ideological insurrection, in the privatized violence of warlordism

12.5 WHAT WAS ACHIEVED, WHAT WAS NOT, AND "WHAT IF...?"

The nineteenth century can be seen as something of a golden age of military and political creativity, of social mobility, and of economic dynamism. Some of the perennial limitations on African warfare described earlier began to be overcome, and the capacity for change was greatly heightened. The revolution proposed here did not happen everywhere (nor did it, indeed, in Europe), but it was widespread. It unfolded in different places at different times, and there was some variation in the drivers involved, but broad, linking themes are clearly discernible between the late eighteenth and early twentieth centuries. What we see, in sum, are ever more innovative ways of organizing and utilizing violence in pursuit of political, economic, and social objectives.

Important political, economic, and social changes attended military reformation. Greatly enhanced social mobility was the defining feature of many of the new communities that came into being; intergenerational struggle, moreover, involved the rejection of older systems of authority by young men with access to guns and other commodities. These were entrepreneurs of violence, to be sure, but they were also representative of new economies, closely bound up with long-distance commerce and underpinned by new and aggressive forms of aspiration. War and material advancement were indelibly intertwined – as in many ways they would remain – for individuals as well as larger communities. War itself often involved the creation of new economic centers or the reinforcement of existing ones; these were places of production and exchange that were part of the broader phenomenon of urbanization across the continent resulting from prolonged violence. As people moved together for protection, settlements – often fortified or with a fortified core – became larger, and new ones were carved out of the bush. Towns themselves meant new socioeconomic and political forms, new identities, new stresses – and populations that were somewhat easier to control, vis-à-vis earlier dispersed patterns of settlement, and therefore urban settlements were in many areas the building blocks of new and enhanced political systems. More broadly, communities sought to defend or enlarge their factor endowment bases, very often at the expense of neighbors and rivals, and thus involved the further refinement of total war, long a feature of African warfare. As for those communities themselves, states were often the outcome of the violence of the nineteenth century – new forms of political centralization that sought cohesion and unity. Older states likewise sought to enhance internal cohesion and pursued external security through cultures of militarism and violence respectively, innovating on the battlefield in the process. In many respects, the nineteenth century saw the culmination of state-building processes in motion since the fourteenth and fifteenth centuries. Where statehood in the conventionally defined sense was absent, there were enlarged systems of identity and mobilization – most obviously among pastoral groups – and many of the same features witnessed in state creation, namely new forms of leadership, and the use of violence in pursuit of larger political and economic goals.

And yet this was a fragile, halting revolution in which, for all the advances made, there were serious failings. This can be explained in several ways. Certain perennial limitations on the scope and scale of warfare – economic, environmental, and demographic – lessened its potential to completely transform African polity and economy. Notably, for example, underpopulation was one of the defining features of African history (Iliffe 2007). Low levels of population governed styles of both war and military organization, and within the continent itself there was differentiation between land-rich and relatively densely populated areas. This clearly had implications for social stratification and hierarchy, as well as capacity for mobilization of available manpower, and, indeed, tactics. In addition, environmental and climatic challenges were clearly critical. Fragile economies and resource systems had a direct impact on the nature and meaning of organized violence, and had implications for the very nature of militarism and military organization and for the needs of defense and aggression. In sum, states and societies continually struggled to maintain stability and cohesion at the center, and were vulnerable to overextension – in terms of both limited resources and limited people. These perennial struggles produced politically fertile, mobile frontiers[10] characterized by the episodic production and reproduction of societies and cultures, and on the frontier, war represented part of a creative vortex: in the eastern and central Great Lakes; across the semiarid grasslands of West Africa; on the escarpments of the Ethiopian Highlands; on the South African Highveld. This continual process of fission and fusion – manifest in the armed frontier in opposition to the ambitious center – facilitated enormous political creativity and military adventurism, but otherwise prevented long-term growth and even consolidation, politically as well as economically, although of course significant advances were made in this direction even prior to the nineteenth century.

Contrast this with the European experience: during the early modern period, the era of mounted nobility was drawing to a close and infantry was becoming more important. The increasing power of infantry over cavalry was pushed along with technological innovation, the latter manifest in the arquebus, the individually portable firearm introduced in the fifteenth century. This was part of a larger sequence of sociopolitical changes, namely the increasing incorporation into the political and military system of urban bourgeoisies and rural peasantries. The arming of infantries was potentially dangerous, of course, representing as it did the militarization of segments of the population not previously regarded as part of the political order. Therefore states needed to co-opt and control the process. This could be done either through the gradual expansion of parliamentary political systems (as in England), or through the expansion of the centralized monarchical system (as in France and Spain). Thus the military revolution is seen to have had a symbiotic relationship with the rise of the European state system. Only states, moreover, were able to bear the costs of large military forces, and indeed of that other key aspect of the revolution on land, artillery, which could be deployed against enemies at home as well as further away. States and enhanced military power, in sum, went hand in hand, and this was ever more in evidence in the course of the eighteenth century. The state, in the simplest of terms, emerged from the need on the part of princes to raise the sums from their subjects to pay for war (Howard 2002, 13–14).

While in Africa there is evidence for what can be described as "campaigning war" – involving structured campaigns and set-piece battles – "raiding war" was probably more common (Lamphear 2003), as indeed

[10] I owe much in the way of inspiration here to Kopytoff (1987).

it has remained, in various forms, throughout the modern era across the continent. The distinction between the two may not, in fact, always have been particularly pronounced – a single war, as it might be defined in Europe, could stretch out over several years and involve a combination of the occasional large-scale pitched battle but more commonly cycles of smaller-scale attacks. The target was frequently the resource base of the enemy – people, livestock, and materials. This was highly skilled and sophisticated war, if apparently more limited in its destructive power compared to Europe in the seventeenth and eighteenth centuries (and beyond); a similar limitation has been noted for native North American warfare – described as a "skulking way of war" – with native Americans in the seventeenth century apparently expressing shock and horror at the level of violence European colonists unleashed when they went to war (Malone 1991, 78). In the African context, the struggle for control of resources – productive and reproductive – gave rise to, and doubtless was often driven by, more abstract and intellectual ideas about identity, territory, and history, and underpinned by cultures of militarism and violence that framed the righteousness of war in both spatial and temporal terms. This was cyclical war that was shaped by relations between shifting frontier and center, with cultures developed to justify actions and unify communities. But the scale and reach of such war was limited by the mobility of the frontier itself – facilitated, again, by relatively low population densities and the availability of land – which made cultures richly complex but also prevented large-scale political and economic transformation. In that sense, arguably, the most successful – that is, enduring and cohesive – states and societies were those that remained compact, territorially but also culturally and ideologically, for to stretch beyond approximate boundaries was to risk unleashing and ultimately losing control of frontiers that then became an armed threat. More practically, terrain remained inhibitive across sub-Saharan Africa, where most African armies were infantries with no access to pack animals. Movement during particular seasons and over particular terrain was extremely difficult, and impossible over large distances. The economic constraints on communities rendered the transition from what we might broadly term "conservative" war to revolutionary violence extremely difficult to achieve; it was an elusive take-off point for many.

Africa's revolution was also rendered fragile by the very nature of its dependence on imported commodities. War over control of commerce was frequently self-defeating – presenting us with a kind of "golden goose" scenario – for it led to the destruction of trade itself, as was the case across the eastern African interior, for example. One of the key elements in military change, moreover – the firearm, used increasingly effectively across Africa in the nineteenth century – was imported, and thus polities ever more dependent on it were fundamentally weakened by that dependency. More specifically, exports – used to pay for guns and to meet the costs of enlarged warfare and political organization – were intrinsically ill suited to developing internal economies in such a way as to fund further military and political transformation. In fact, some societies did remarkably well to use the proceeds as skillfully as they did, and again advances were made, but export commodities – slaves, palm oil, groundnuts, ivory – were inimical to long-term development, as their modern equivalents have generally remained. The colonial moment exacerbated this trend: the restrictive nature of the export trade, which in the end benefited particular groups in a narrow range of ways, locked much of Africa into a spiral of violent competition, leading to escalating militarization with little or none of the maneuverability – in sum, the capacity to fight to the point of local, indigenous resolution – characteristic of the nineteenth century.

It is also the case that the era of Africa's revolutionary violence coincided with that of European imperial expansion. Europe was in a position to take advantage of turbulence in Africa, inserting itself into heightened competition between societies and states at a critical moment, and harnessing such violence for its own ends – even if a measure of good fortune was also frequently involved. Europe willfully or otherwise misread what was happening in Africa in the nineteenth century, justifying its intervention through the creation of a series of myths about a universal political, economic, and, indeed, moral order. Africa was detained developmentally for several decades, its revolution becoming diverted, its violence becoming all the more destabilizing and uncompromising, and therefore its ability to negotiate and ultimately compete in global economic and political terms seriously compromised. The resurgence of violence in the mid-twentieth century is testament to this fact. War in Africa, both past and present, was racialized; so too was discourse around development, if covertly, which is profoundly ironic, given that much modern violence in Africa has been about economic access and opportunity, as indeed it was in the nineteenth century.

Nevertheless, innovation and development – again, assuming certain universal criteria, Eurocentric in origin – were much in evidence; and it is proposed here, counterfactually, that such processes would have produced, in many respects, a somewhat different Africa in the twentieth century. We must be careful at this juncture, for just as no pristine precolonial Africa is depicted in this chapter, nor is Africa's twentieth century imagined as some glorious and inexorable march toward peace, prosperity, and stability in the absence of colonial rule. It is quite likely that even without European colonialism much of Africa would have experienced a high level of violent instability until well into the twentieth century, probably – if we allow ourselves a few moments of conjecture – into at least the 1920s and 1930s. And it would in all likelihood have involved avaricious Western companies competing aggressively for influence and access, while Western governments made moral-sounding noises about the need for peace, stability, and good governance. In other words, it would have looked much like today, except perhaps – for a while – a little worse. However, the direction of travel would have been toward local resolution, accommodation, and stabilization, with a much greater potential for economic and political development and a natural – if gradual – tendency toward demilitarization. Much greater levels of violence in the early to mid-twentieth century would have been followed – more confidently in some areas than in others – by consolidated political and economic systems, and above all a much greater capacity for maneuver and for equitable negotiation on the part of African actors.

Of course, struggles over external linkages – and over how to manage external relationships – would have continued and would probably have produced new forms of conflict: this had been the case since the early sixteenth century, and is demonstrable elsewhere in the world, notably in China and Japan. Low-level conflict would have persisted in many parts of the continent as state systems struggled to impose themselves on troublesome frontiers, although levels of Western concern – moral or otherwise – over this would clearly have depended on how distracting were Europe's own internal problems.[11] Slavery, too, would presumably have persisted across Africa throughout the twentieth century (rather more widespread and overt, perhaps we should add, than is currently the case), and would, as in the nineteenth century, have underpinned much of Africa's economic activity. But, notwithstanding a continued moral outcry, Western economic systems in general and consumers in particular would have proven rather more tolerant of slavery elsewhere in the world than one might imagine – witness the hegemony of the sweatshop underpinning much of the global economy today. The key question for our purposes, however, is how prevalent, therefore, would slaving violence have been, and how inhibitive would

[11] In our imaginary world, for example, would there have been a Second (or even a First) World War without the Scramble for Africa? How important *was* the partition and subsequent administration of Africa to Europe's own political, economic, and, indeed, cultural development in the twentieth century? These are questions to make the head throb – and the undergraduate heart sink.

such low-level war have been regarding African economic growth: one is tempted to suggest it would have been manageable, and that violence would have easily coexisted with very successful entrepreneurialism – whether in state or nonstate settings.

In other words, according to this interpretation, the first half of the twentieth century would have looked a lot more violent, and the second half a lot less. Even in the late twentieth century, Africa might well have looked pretty violent, but there would have been more stable markets, and across the continent more consolidated political and economic authority at the local level, as well as more stable indigenous authorities. The latter would probably have been more accountable, too, as decades of violent upheaval would have been, in the loosest sense, democratizing: soldiers and their wars required popular support and popular participation.[12] Whether the particular forms of government that emerged would have won wholesale approval from Western powers is another question; it seems safe to assume that many would not, and that some – monarchical autocracies, say, or (at the other end of the spectrum) pastoral heterarchies – would have been deemed incompatible with concepts of political modernity. Important, however, external powers would have had, in the long run, somewhat less leverage over them. There is every reason to suppose that a map of Africa in, say, 1920 would have displayed a number of prominent, relatively stable polities – Sokoto, Dahomey, Asante in West Africa; Buganda, Bunyoro and neo-Solomonic Ethiopia in the east and northeast of the continent; a Zulu state of some description in the south. Extrapolating forward from nineteenth-century trends, these are polities with the capacity to develop, or indeed which had already developed, professional administrative bureaucracies that would be importers of modern military and economic technologies with a view to political and economic growth and that would be seeking – through various external linkages, no doubt – to manage their economic systems to best advantage. Many African states and societies had been doing precisely this for the previous century or more.

Again, however, there would have been a fair amount of political and military instability; in the frontiers between the stable polities, political and economic conditions would have been rather more in flux. There was clearly enormous sociopolitical and economic diversity across late nineteenth-century Africa, and clearly some communities were more likely to succeed than others: as a rule, compact territorial states as opposed to sprawling

[12] There is some evidence to suggest this for nineteenth-century eastern Africa (Reid 2007, 150).

and inefficient ones; effectively centralized hierarchies rather than more dispersed, stateless groups. But although pastoral-sedentary conflict had long been a key dynamic, the historic relationship was characterized by a marked degree of accommodation and reciprocity: more flexible, organic relationships between socioeconomic forms would have reduced marginalization, and indeed as the Somali – and large African diasporas – have demonstrated, states are not necessary to thriving commerce. Even so, entire regions would have lacked overarching authority, even in the 1920s and 1930s – much of west-central Africa, for instance, and on either side of Lake Tanganyika. Would the Nyamwezi or the Yoruba have had their "Westphalia moment," for example? On the evidence of the nineteenth century, the answer would seem to be yes – eventually. This was already the direction of travel in many areas, although it needs to be emphasized that parts of the continent would have remained fairly violent for quite some time – and many of the states with an air of permanence in the late nineteenth century might not have made it to the mid-twentieth. Buganda was under great pressure from Bunyoro, as well as undergoing major internal strains; significant internal tensions had also undermined the Zulu state; Ethiopia's spectacular expansion might easily have been reversed without the props of neighboring European colonial administrations. Africa's alternative twentieth century would have been messy – Europe's was hardly otherwise – and the map would have been a dazzling and doubtless (to the European eye) discombobulating arrangement of zones of transition, and greater or lesser spheres of jurisdiction. But the capacity for indigenous agency to make mistakes, and then to resolve and build, would have been all the greater.

12.6 CONCLUSION

We can be sure that the factors prompting a particular path of development as opposed to another will remain the focus of considerable debate. The divergent paths of Europe and Africa are the product of countless different determinants – some dramatic, others minuscule, but no less important for all that. In Europe, there was an intricate and symbiotic relationship between technology, economic might, military power, and state formation. As with the "revolution in military affairs," debates continue on the precise relationship between war and the emergence of the state in European history;[13] but certainly key themes have endured. Especially germane is the

[13] For example, see James (2006).

thesis William H. McNeill placed on the relationship between economic and military expansion, and the stabilization (and professionalization) of the states that were able to facilitate both. As McNeill put it, by the seventeenth century Europe had "launched itself on a self-reinforcing cycle in which its military organisation sustained, and was sustained by, economic and political expansion at the expense of other peoples and polities of the earth" (McNeill 1982, 143). This was the transformative power of violence writ large. Paul Kennedy reiterated the idea that "great power" status depended as much on "the more or less efficient utilisation of the state's productive economic resources in wartime" as on events on the battlefield, and indeed on economic performance relative to other powers in peacetime (Kennedy 1988, xv). Economic might (or at least *relative* economic might) underpinned military success, while military success had the potential (no more than that) to feed economic performance and enhance economic capacity. Ultimately, much depended on the powers of coercion of the state, and the efficiency with which the state could marshal resources. This was the concern of Charles Tilly, who aimed to explain the various routes by which the nation-state had become the dominant form of human organization (Tilly 1992). In essence, he argued that early modern military innovations (mass infantry, gunpowder, fortification) were expensive, and could only be supported by states with large populations and that were able to accumulate sufficient amounts of capital and financial resources – not least in terms of tax revenue. The modern state thus came about because of the needs of waging war.

Ultimately, what differentiates Africa from Europe in the context of the nineteenth-century revolution in military affairs proposed here is the nature of Africa's *internal* struggle. This struggle is exemplified by the African frontier – itself the product of distinctive environmental challenges, limited and uneven demographic spread, and the fierce introspection demanded by close economic management. The possibilities for expansion, whether territorial or in terms of internal resource bases, were limited, as centrifugalism and strains at the center restricted the reach of even the most successful states. This meant that African societies were less able to capitalize – literally and figuratively; to consolidate and accumulate political and economic resources with a view to enlargement of scale. Timing, moreover, is indeed critical, and most African societies were certainly unable to achieve a level of political and economic stability in time to see off (or render unnecessary) European intervention; ironically, indeed, the very violence driving much of the continent's development in the nineteenth century attracted detrimental outside interference. Major change was afoot in the nineteenth century, but it ultimately intersected with a rampant European militarism, which in many ways prolonged and distorted it.

The issue of cost is ultimately crucial, moreover. African warfare moved relatively rapidly into the realm of professional entrepreneurialism, even – arguably – compared to Europe; in so doing it avoided the kind of long, drawn-out, and enormously expensive wars Europe experienced during the sixteenth and seventeenth centuries. This meant, in addition to the longer-term prohibitive dynamics noted earlier, that Africa did not *need* to develop comparably elaborate fiscal, administrative, and governmental systems to pay for its wars – at least, again, not on the scale of Europe's experience. African warfare contained often enormous internal costs, as it were – but these were (outside the horse zone, at any rate) *relatively* low and required few of the political as well as technical innovations of Europe's wars. The African frontier involved highly destructive economic war; but in general, even long wars allowed for periods of recovery (a key element of the North American "skulking war" model), and thus these were, as a rule, wars of short, intense bursts involving comparatively low levels of capital investment, and therefore reducing the need for the kind of political, economic, and technological innovations of Europe's later seventeenth and eighteenth centuries.

By this logic, of course, it might be argued that had Africa's violent transformation run its natural course (in other words, with a minimal level of outside interference), it would have proceeded in a manner more akin to that of Europe: war would have involved capital accumulation; political reform would have followed to reflect economic shifts; and a clearer path of endogenous development would have ensued. Again, this is what the events of the nineteenth century suggest: Africa's military revolution – the most visible manifestation of internal transformation – may be considered the prerequisite for the kind of wholesale reform and consolidation witnessed in northwest Europe, the first wave of a multifaceted set of changes. This first wave of reform was unquestionably violent, but it was also marked by a trajectory suggestive of an alternative future involving rather more effective economic management, political restructuring, and ultimately demilitarization. It may yet prove to be just that, although further violence will certainly attend the process; there is every reason to hope, given the lessons contained in Africa's *longue durée*, that the colonial experience has merely postponed, not cancelled, organic solutions to seemingly intractable problems.

The "perennial limitations" noted earlier would have continued to operate well into our imaginary twentieth century, and would likely still be operating at the time of writing; and it is foolish to think in terms of African societies transforming themselves into European clones. Again, no "merrie Africa" is proposed here, but rather one characterized by a great deal of violence with developmental potential. The central point here is that Africans would have done no worse, and probably altogether better, in terms of management and distribution of material and political resources, than recent postcolonial elites. The processes of the nineteenth century suggest that this was possible, however violent the process was – as it was, too, in Europe – and might still have been, along the way. As it was, the notion of Africa's military defeat in the late nineteenth century, and the mythology subsequently developed around ideas about development – principally that violence was inimical to it, when Europe's own historical experience demonstrated the exact opposite – generated profound distaste for what African warfare had supposedly represented, and in turn deep misunderstanding of it.

References

Adjaye, Joseph K. (1996). *Diplomacy and Diplomats in 19th Century Asante*. 1st edition 1984. Trenton, NJ: Africa World Press.

Ali, Taisier Mohamed Ahmed and Robert O. Matthews, eds. (1999). *Civil Wars in Africa: Roots and Resolution*. Montreal: Montreal & Kingston.

Alpers, Edward A. (1975). *Ivory and Slaves in East Central Africa*. London: Heinemann.

Austen, Ralph A. (1987). *African Economic History: Internal Development and External Dependency*. London: James Currey.

Bayly, C. A. (2004). *The Birth of the Modern World 1780–1914: Global Connections and Comparisons*. Oxford: Blackwell Publishers.

Bennett, Norman Robert. (1971). *Mirambo of Tanzania, 1840?–1884*. New York: Oxford University Press.

Black, Jeremy. (2009). *War: A Short History*. London: Continuum.

Boas, Morten and Kevin C. Dunn, eds. (2007). *African Guerrillas: Raging against the Machine*. Boulder, CO: Lynne Rienner Publishers.

Clapham, Christopher S. (1998). *African Guerrillas*. Oxford: James Currey.

Cobbing, Julian. (1988). "The Mfecane as Alibi: Thoughts on Dithakong and Mbolompo." *Journal of African History*, 29(3): 487–519.

Coquery-Vidrovitch, Catherine. (2009). *Africa and the Africans in the Nineteenth Century: A Turbulent History*. London.

Derman, William, R. Odgaard, and E. Sjaastad, eds. (2007). *Conflicts over Land and Water in Africa*. Oxford: James Currey.

Doyle, Shane. (2006). *Crisis and Decline in Bunyoro: Population and Environment in Western Uganda, 1860–1955*. Oxford: James Currey.

Goody, Jack. (1971). *Technology, Tradition and the State in Africa*. London: Oxford University Press.

Hamilton, Carolyn Anne. (1992). "'The Character and Objects of Chaka': A Reconsideration of the Making of Shaka as 'Mfecane' Motor." *Journal of African History*, 33(1): 37–63.

(1998). *Terrific Majesty: The Powers of Shaka Zulu and the Limits of Historical Invention*. Cape Town: David Philip.

Henniger, Laurent. (2006). "Military Revolutions and Military History." In *Modern Military History*, edited by Matthew Hughes and William James Philpott. Basingstoke: Palgrave Macmillan.

Hopkins, Anthony G. (2009). "The New Economic History of Africa." *Journal of African History*, 50: 155–77.

Howard, Michael. (2002). *The Invention of Peace and the Reinvention of War*. London: Profile.

(2009). *War in European History*. Oxford: Oxford University Press (new update of 1st edition, 1976).

Iliffe, John. (1987). *The African Poor: A History*. Cambridge: Cambridge University Press.

(2007). *Africans: The History of a Continent*, second edition; first edition 1995. Cambridge: Cambridge University Press.

James, A. (2006). "Warfare and the Rise of the State." In *Modern Military History*, edited by Matthew Hughes and William James Philpott. Basingstoke: Palgrave Macmillan.

Kaarsholm, Preben, ed. (2006). *Violence, Political Culture and Development in Africa*. Oxford: James Currey.

Kennedy, Paul Michael. (1988). *The Rise and Fall of the Great Powers: Economic Change and Military Conflict from 1500 to 2000*. London: Unwin Hyman.

Kopytoff, Igor, ed. (1987). *The African Frontier: The Reproduction of Traditional African Societies*. Bloomington & Indianapolis: Indiana University Press.

Lamphear, John. (1998). "Brothers in Arms: Military Aspects of East African Age-Class Systems in Historical Perspective." In *Conflict, Age and Power in North East Africa*, edited by Eisei Kurimoto and Simon Simonse. Oxford: James Currey.

(2003). "Sub-Saharan African Warfare." In *War in the Modern World*, edited by Jeremy Black. London: Routledge.

Lamphear, John, ed. (2007). *African Military History*. Aldershot: Ashgate Publishing Company.

Law, Robin. (1977). *The Oyo Empire, c.1600–c.1836: A West African Imperialism in the Era of the Atlantic Slave Trade*. Oxford: Clarendon Press.

(1991). *The Slave Coast of West Africa, 1550–1750: The Impact of the Atlantic Slave Trade on an African Society*. Oxford: Clarendon Press.

Legassick, Martin. (1966). "Firearms, Horses and Samorian Army Organisation 1870–1898." *Journal of African History*, 7(1): 95–115.

Lonsdale, J. (1985). "The European Scramble and Conquest in African History." In *Cambridge History of Africa, Vol 6: From 1870 to 1905*, edited by R. Oliver and G. N. Sanderson. Cambridge: Cambridge University Press.

Low, D. A. (2009). *Fabrication of Empire: The British and the Uganda Kingdoms, 1890–1902*. Cambridge: Cambridge University Press.

Malone, Patrick M. (1991). *The Skulking Way of War: Technology and Tactics among the New England Indians*. Lanham, MD: Madison Books.

Mazrui, Ali Al'Amin, ed. (1977). *The Warrior Tradition in Modern Africa*. Leiden: Brill.

McNeill, William Hardy. (1982). *The Pursuit of Power: Technology, Armed Force and Society since AD 1000*. Chicago: University of Chicago Press.

Nhema, Alfred G. and P. Tiyembe Zeleza, eds. (2008a). *The Roots of African Conflicts: The Causes and Costs*. Oxford: James Currey.

Nhema, Alfred G. and P. Tiyembe Zeleza, eds. (2008b). *The Resolution of African Conflicts: The Management of Conflict Resolution and Post-conflict Reconstruction* Oxford: James Currey.

Ogot, Bethwell A., ed. (1972). *War and Society in Africa*. London: F. Cass.

Parker, Geoffrey. (1988). *The Military Revolution: Military Innovation and the Rise of the West, 1500–1800*. 2nd edition 1996. Cambridge: Cambridge University Press.

Porch, Douglas. (2001). *Wars of Empire*. London: Cassell Military.

Reid, Richard J. (2002). *Political Power in Pre-colonial Buganda: Economy, Society and Warfare in the Nineteenth Century*. Oxford: James Currey.

(2007). *War in Pre-colonial Eastern Africa: The Patterns and Meanings of State-level Conflict in the Nineteenth Century*. Oxford: James Currey.

(2011). *Frontiers of Violence in Northeast Africa: Genealogies of Conflict since 1800*. Oxford: Oxford University Press.

Reno, William. (1998). *Warlord Politics and African States*. Boulder, CO: Lynne Rienner Publishers.

Richards, Paul, ed. (2005). *No Peace, No War: An Anthropology of Contemporary Armed Conflicts*. Oxford: James Currey.

Roberts, Andrew D., ed. (1968). *Tanzania before c.1900*. Nairobi.

Roberts, Richard L. (1987). *Warriors, Merchants and Slaves: The State and the Economy in the Middle Niger Valley, 1700–1914*. Stanford. CA: Stanford University Press.

Smaldone, Joseph P. (1977). *Warfare in the Sokoto Caliphate: Historical and Sociological Perspectives*. Cambridge: Cambridge University Press.

Smith, Robert Sydney. (1976). *Warfare and Diplomacy in Pre-colonial West Africa*. 2nd edition 1989. London: James Currey.

Smith, Robert Sydney and Jacob F. Ade Ajayi. (1971). *Yoruba Warfare in the Nineteenth Century*. Cambridge: Cambridge University Press.

Spear, Thomas T. and Richard Waller, eds. (1993). *Being Maasai: Ethnicity and Identity in East Africa*. London: James Currey.

Stanley, Henry M. (1899). *Through the Dark Continent*. 1st edition 1878. London: George Newnes.

Thornton, John. (1999). *Warfare in Atlantic Africa, 1500–1800*. London: University College of London.

Tilly, Charles. (1992). *Coercion, Capital and European States, AD 990–1992*. Oxford.

Uzoigwe, G. N. (1977). "The Warrior and the State in Pre-colonial Africa." In *The Warrior Tradition in Modern Africa*, edited by Ali Al'Amin Mazrui. Leiden: Brill.

Vandervort, Bruce. (1998). *Wars of Imperial Conquest in Africa, 1830–1914*. Bloomington & Indianapolis: Indiana University Press.

Wilks, Ivor. (1975). *Asante in the Nineteenth Century: The Structure and Evolution of a Political Order*. London: Cambridge University Press.

Wylie, Dan. (2006). *Myth of Iron: Shaka in History*. Scottsville: University of KwaZulu-Natal Press.

13

The Imperial Peace

Robert H. Bates

When praised at all, imperialism is most often commended for the peace it bestowed. By demobilizing armies, deposing marauding princes, and subduing war-like states, European powers fashioned a half century of political order. The question nonetheless arises: Should they be lauded for doing so? In this chapter, I view Africa's history through the lens of comparative history[1] and argue that the imperial peace may have retarded Africa's development.

Those addressing the rise of the West often highlight the contribution of the state. The Western state has inflicted untold misery, they acknowledge; but they also stress its importance for development. An important school of thought argues that the two faces of power – the one destructive and the other developmental – share common origin: the Western state became developmental the better to finance its wars (Brewer 1988; Gilbert 1975; Roberts 1956; Tilly 1985). Driven by insecurity abroad, states become developmental at home, these scholars argue: heads of state employ power to foster economic growth and thereby finance their militaries. If the threat of war thus rendered European states developmental, then the possibility arises that imperial peace may have contributed to the underdevelopment of Africa (but see Centeno 1997). Viewed against this background, the imperial peace assumes a new guise: rather than conferring a blessing, it may have imposed a cost; it may have stilled the impulse to development that originates from the search for security in a hostile political environment.

Throughout this chapter, I focus on the relationship between wealth and power. Power can be used to secure wealth, either by forcefully seizing it or by safeguarding its creation (see, for example, Hirshleifer 1994). The latter promotes growth; the former, mere redistribution. In probing the political

[1] As was attempted by Warner (1999). For a skeptical response, see Hopkins (2000).

foundations of development, it thus becomes critical to understand how power is exercised and to explore the factors that shape its use. It is my argument that through purposeful behavior on the one hand and physical extinction on the other, international insecurity selects for the developmental use of power. It is for this reason that the imperial peace may have therefore been costly.

I begin this chapter by contending that the state is essential for development, an argument I advance by recounting a recent reappraisal of the logic of Evans-Pritchard's classic study of the Nuer: a society without a state (Evans-Pritchard 1940).

13.1 KINSHIP SOCIETIES

Africa is attractive to scholars in part because of the diversity of its political institutions. Some polities are based on kinship; they are societies without states. In others, centralization and hierarchy shape political life. In such polities, kinship ties may remain powerful, but they now lie imbedded within political structures that they influence but do not control: political hierarchies and bureaucratic offices that may be filled by appointment rather than succession or descent.

From the study of Africa's political forms, we learn many lessons. One of the most important is that political order can prevail even in societies that lack states. Even in the absence of centralized and hierarchical institutions, life and property can be secure. A second is that such order is fragile and, worse yet, susceptible to breakdown in response to development.

13.2 PEACE IN THE FEUD

As Gluckman (1955) argued, order in kinship societies rests on the fear of revenge. Should a person in one family transgress against a member of another, then she faces the prospect of retaliation by her victim and his kin. In such societies, no third party preserves the peace, then. Rather, it is the "shadow of the future," in Axelrod's (1985) phrasing; it is the certainty of future losses at the hands of a vengeful neighbor that stays the hand of those who might be tempted to transgress. Even in the absence of formal institutions, property can therefore be secure and people safe in stateless societies; thus, the argument of Evans-Pritchard (1940), Gluckman (1955), and others (e.g., Fallers 1966) who have studied such societies. More recently, however, political scientists and economists have revisited this argument and cautioned against its claims. In so doing, they highlight the link between the state and development.

As noted in Bates, Greif, and Singh (2002), Gluckman's claim – that there can be "peace in the feud" – follows from the "folk theorem" of repeated games, which states (roughly) that the first best – here, peace and prosperity – can be sustained as an equilibrium in games wherein people can adopt punishment strategies, ensuring that future losses offset the prospect of short-term gains. Once the parallel to game theory is recognized, then so too are its implications. Among the most relevant is that the first best equilibrium is not robust; in particular, it is vulnerable to the temptations increased prosperity spawns. As society becomes wealthier and riches mount, the level of temptation increases as well. As a result, punishments that once served to underpin peace may no longer deter.

13.3 NO STATE, NO DEVELOPMENT?

Note the implication: if development requires both security and wealth, then, by requiring that prosperity be sacrificed to secure peace, kinship societies may remain underdeveloped. Another implication is that while their polities might be able to protect and sustain some kinds of economic activities, such as commerce, they might not be able to protect others, such as those that require fixed investments. Commercial relations are likely to involve repeated interactions; fixed investments, by contrast, require but a single move. Unlike merchants, investors therefore lack the ability to make credible threats. A kinship economy might therefore benefit from markets and trade; but, lacking investment, it may fail to secure an industrial base. Because of the nature of their political institutions, such polities may therefore achieve but a low level of development.

It is therefore not surprising to encounter evidence that suggests that stateless societies seek to alter their political institutions, some going so far as to import political specialists from neighboring societies. Well-known cases would include the Aro in southern Nigeria (Northrop 1978), the Atyak in northern Uganda (Southall 1999), and the Lunda in Congo and Zambia (Vansina 2004), each of whom exported their political services to neighboring stateless societies, thereby introducing political hierarchy into previously egalitarian cultures.

13.4 PRECOLONIAL DYNAMICS

In this section, we focus on the formation – and the destruction – of states in precolonial Africa. Figure 13.1 illustrates the population of states in West Africa, from 1400 (just before European states began to form empires) to

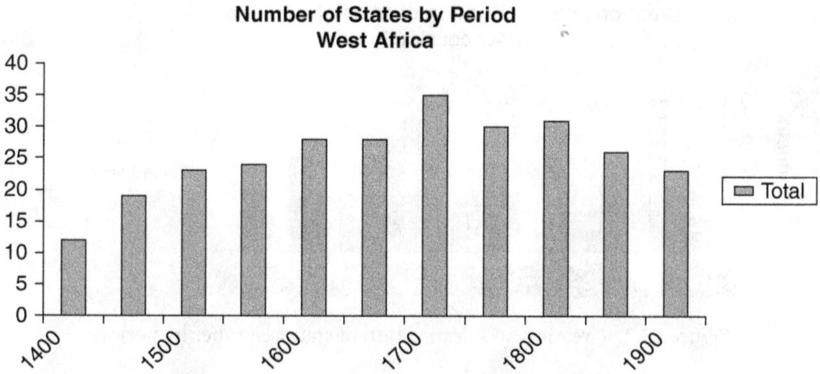

Figure 13.1. Number of states by period, West Africa.

1900 (the end of the Scramble for Africa).[2] While the scholars from whose work it was compiled concur in their definition of West Africa,[3] they count as states a wide variety of political forms, ranging from city-states to empires. Despite this heterogeneity, where their accounts intersect, they tend to include the same polities, which increases our confidence in inferences drawn from these data.

Prior to the fifteenth century, state formation in West Africa, these sources remind us, was largely confined to the margins of the Sahel, where polities formed astride the trade routes linking West Africa's commercial centers with North Africa. With the arrival of Europeans along the coast, commerce shifted southward and states began to form in the interstices between the interior and the coast. The narrative accounts then portray the rise of Oyo, Bono, Nupe, and the Hausa city-states. Later comes the rise of states along the coast: Wadyah, Warri, Bonny, Allada, Grand Popo, and others.

More important for the argument of this chapter, however, is the demise rather than the creation of states. As shown in Figure 13.2, by the mid-eighteenth century, more states depart than enter the panel, thus making possible the process of selection. The question is: Did "developmental" states

[2] Sources include: Forde and Kaberry (1967), Stevenson (1968), Colson (1969), Gray and Birmingham (1970), Southall (1970), Fage (1974), Ajayi and Crowder (1976), Oliver (1977), Law (1978), Fortes and Evans-Pritchard (1987), Southall (1988), Morrison, Mitchell, and Paden (1989), Curtin et al. (1995), Kwamena-Poh et al. (1995), S. K. McIntosh and R. McIntosh (1996), McIntosh (1999), Thornton (1999), and Banton ([1965] 2004).

[3] That it extends from the Chad basin to the Atlantic coast and from the coast northward to the Sahel.

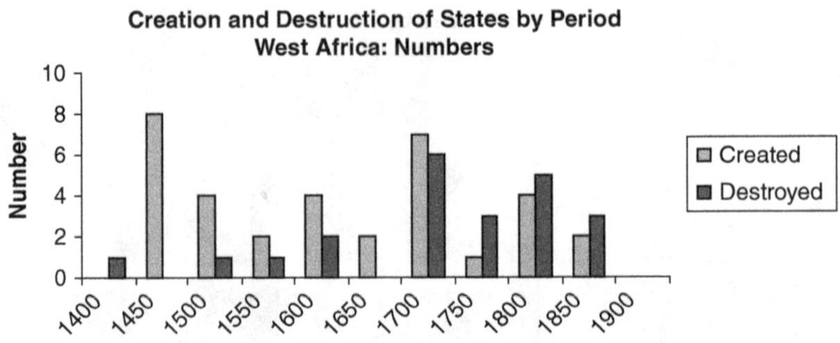

Figure 13.2. Creation and destruction of states: number by period.

prove more fit than those that were not? Did the demise of polities select for states in which power was used to promote the creation of wealth? If the response to these questions is yes, then the imperial peace may have decoupled the search for security from the creation of wealth.

13.5 COLONIAL CROSS-SECTIONS

To address this possibility, we turn our attention to the colonial period. When doing so, we make use of three cross-sections of data: *Ethnographic Atlas* (Murdock 1967), the Standard Cross-Cultural Sample (SCCS) (Divale 2000), and the Human Relations Area Files (HRAF) (Bates 1983). Each data set exhibits major weaknesses. Both the SCCS and HRAF samples contain few African cases: twenty-eight in the first and thirty-six in the latter. *Ethnographic Atlas* contains data from many more polities (more than 400); but its utility is reduced by the limited range of the characteristics it reports, most of which are irrelevant to our purposes. Each provides insight into the cross-section of cases bequeathed to the colonial order. If our argument is correct, we should expect this cross-section to suggest a positive relationship between measures of state formation and indicators of prosperity.

Addressing the primary question posed in this chapter requires that I classify the societies according to their political institutions. Scholars such as Southall (1999), Yoffee (1993), and McIntosh (1999) have insisted that African polities cannot be crudely classified as stateless or not; nor can they be arrayed along a scale of "state-likeness." The first underestimates their heterogeneity, while the second opens the door to cultural triumphalism, they argue, as notions of modernity or civilization might easily inform

Table 13.1. *Data from the Human Relations Area Files*

Society	Pages of documentation	Society	Pages of documentation
Bambara	1127	Chagga	1986
Dogon	1132	Ngondo	1474
Mossi	942	Pygmies	1350
Mande	605	Azande	3264
Tallensi	964	Mongo	773
Ashanti	3523	Rundi	1314
Katab	352	Mbundu	847
Nupe	856	Bemba	830
Tiv	2891	Ila	998
Yoruba	1637	Lozi	1635
Fang	1117	Tonga	1616
Nuer	1541	Ngoni	1123
Shilluck	1073	Thonga	1231
Ganda	2261	Yao	555
Dorobo	354	Bushmen	1259
Kikuyu	1950	Hottentot	1339
Luo	463	Lovedu	455
Masai	2085	Tanala	354

Note: The names are those chosen by the Human Relations Area Files.
Source: Bates 1983, 57.

placement on the scale. In conformity with their counsel, I therefore make but qualitative judgments, determining whether the reports indicated the existence of chiefs and whether there was a monarch. I also note the existence of a bureaucracy or a national army (Table 13.1).

Recall the discussion of political order: kinship societies, I argued, were vulnerable to internal disruption. Suggestive, therefore, is the relationship between markers of political centralization and incidence of feuding: it is negative and the relationship is one of the most pronounced in the data. Whereas the HRAF records attest to feuding in 89 percent of the societies governed by kinship, they report it in but 23 percent of those governed by monarchs (Table 13.2). The data thus suggest that polities based on rulers and bureaucracies are associated with higher levels of political order.[4]

[4] Supportive are data from the SCCS, which indicate that chieftaincies and centralized states are more likely to have "enforcement specialists," such as police, than are stateless societies; the source fails to note the impact of this innovation on the level of conflict, however.

Table 13.2. *Feuding and political structure (percent "yes")*

	Kinship	Chiefs	Monarch	Central bureaucracy	
				Present	Absent
Report of Feuds?	89	78	23	27	72

Note: N = 28.
Source: Data from Human Relations Area Files (Bates 1983, 45).

Table 13.3. *Economic activity and political structure (percent "yes")*

	Kinship	Chiefs	Monarch	Central bureaucracy	
Presence of:				Present	Absent
Market Centers?	15	31	54	58	42
Long-distance Trade?	0	45	55	56	44
Craft Specialists?	21	25	54	57	60
Private Investors?	0	33	67	50	48

Note: N = 31–3.
Source: Data from Human Relations Area Files (Bates 1983, 44, 46).

While enhancing the level of political order, do such institutions assure greater prosperity? Do they thereby provide a corrective to the fragility of kinship systems? Keeping in mind the poor quality of the data, as seen in Table 13.3, the answer appears to be yes. Studies of societies with chiefs and monarchs were far more likely to report the presence of market centers than were studies of societies ruled through kinship. They were also more likely to report participation in long-distance trade, the production of crafts, and the presence of private investors.

Further evidence is contained in Table 13.4. Insofar as possessing a national army, as opposed to one recruited at the village or household level, provides an index of military power, the data suggest that wealth and military power covary.

Turning briefly to *Ethnographic Atlas*, we note its data on craft specialists. According to this source, this kind of economic activity was observed in but a third of Africa's stateless societies but in nearly three-quarters of its centralized states. Similar differences characterize the incidence of leather working, ceramics, and metalworking. These data suggest that occupational

Table 13.4. *Military forces and economic activity*

	Local	National
Presence of:		
Market Centers?		
% Yes	15	31
Long-distance Trade?		
% Yes	13	40
Craft Specialists?		
% Yes	12	42
Private Investors?		
% Yes	15	46

Note: *N* = 31–3.
Source: Data from Human Relations Area Files (Bates 1983, 44, 46).

Table 13.5. *Public goods and political structure (percent "yes")*

	Kinship	Chiefs	Monarch	Central Bureaucracy	
Presence of:				Present	Absent
Roads?	0	20	75	88	14
Bridges?	0	0	22	40	0
Pontoons?	0	0	50	50	10
Canals?	0	11	33	40	5

Note: *N* = 26–30.
Source: Data from Human Relations Area Files (Bates 1983, 50).

specialization more frequently occurs in states than in stateless societies. The reports archived in the Human Relations Area Files also indicate (Table 13.5) that when ruled by chiefs, monarchs, and bureaucracies, polities were more likely to contain roads, bridges, pontoons, and canals. When sufficiently "state-like" to maintain a national army, African polities, once again, were more likely to invest in such public goods (Table 13.6).

In this instance, neither *Ethnographic Atlas* nor SCCS provide useful information; they simply fail to record the relevant data.

While scanty and highly imperfect, the data suggest that the competition among the states in precolonial Africa may have given rise to a cross-section of polities in which state formation and economic development covaried. Either because they responded to external threats by seeking to strengthen

Table 13.6. *Military forces and public goods*

	Local	National
Presence of:		
Roads?		
% Yes	27	50
Bridges?		
% Yes	0	20
Pontoons?		
% Yes	7	33
Canals?		
% Yes	13	20

Note: N = 29–30.
Source: Data from Human Relations Area. Files (Bates 1983, 44).

Table 13.7. *Political structures and warfare (percent)*

External warfare	Stateless	Chieftaincies	Centralized states
Yearly	33	60	60
Common/ Occasional	33	40	40
Rare	33	0	0
N	5	5	5

Source: Standard Cross-Cultural Sample.

their economic base, or because interstate competition winnowed from the sample polities that were weak and poor, we find that "state-like" societies also appear to have been developmental.

Before concluding this section, I turn to two additional pieces of data from the Standard Cross-Cultural Sample (SCCS) (Divale 2000). While missingness reduces the sample from twenty-eight to sixteen observations, the data suggest a relationship between rates of warfare and degrees of political centralization in Table 13.7.

The data also indicate that more centralized polities were more likely to fight their neighbors (Table 13.7). Of equal relevance are the data on increases or decreases in the size of the polities. As seen in Table 13.8, the data from SCCS suggest that chieftaincies and centralized states were increasing in size whereas most stateless societies were shrinking.

Table 13.8. *Political structures and political trajectory (percent)*

Boundaries and population	Stateless	Chieftaincies	Centralized states
Expanding	20	56	60
Stable	20	11	20
Decreasing	60	33	20
N	10	9	5

Source: Standard Cross-Cultural Sample.

The small size of the sample and uncertainty as to the era to which the coding applies attenuate the impact of these findings. They remain suggestive at best.

13.6 POLITICAL RESTRAINT AND POLITICAL STRUCTURE

Thus far I have focused on the external relations of African states. I now turn to their internal politics. Doing so we see that those who governed states presided over a surplus: they could have extracted the rents that lay before them. But the data also highlight the presence of internal checks. Those with power might use it to limit feuding among powerful families and groups of kin; to construct public works, to fight, and to tax; but given the institutions that encompassed them, they found it costly to use this power to seize the assets of those they governed.

The data from the HRAF suggest that states tended to form in locations that contained relatively rich soils, abundant water supplies, and valuable resources – gold, copper, salt, and iron. People found such locations attractive; more important, once settled in them, they were reluctant to depart. As a result, those who exercised power could extract rents from them without fear that they would defect, as did their counterparts. Differentials in productivity thus created the possibility of taxation. Thus could states exist in deserts, if located in the mountains (as were the Fur); or in the Sahel, if located in inland deltas (as were Ghana, Mali, and Songhay); or in the savannah, if located in lakes or swamplands (as were the Lozi and Lunda). In such locations, a surplus existed that could be appropriated without fear of political breakdown.

If states arose in such environments, why then would not their rulers exploit their power to secure private advantages? The reports archived by the HRAF suggest that to some degree they did, thus their possession of superior homes or clothing and their possession of larger numbers of cattle

Table 13.9. *Economic inequality and political structure (percent "yes") Do monarchs or chiefs possess?*

Superior		More numerous	
Houses?	Clothing?	Livestock?	Slaves
66	59	58	59

Note: $N = 32–5$.
Source: Data from Human Relations Area Files (Bates 1983, 56).

Table 13.10. *Political checks and political structure (percent)*

Are there:		Is there an Aristocracy?	
Policy Councils?		Yes	No
	Yes	60	15
	No	40	15
Independent Courts?			
	Yes	93	31
	No	7	69

Note: $N = 28$.
Source: Data from Human Relations Area Files (Bates 1983, 57).

or slaves (Table 13.9). But the data also suggest that rulers faced political checks. Kin groups, they suggest, remained jealous of their power and kept important offices under their control: that of the "linguist," among the Akan; of the war chief and "prime minister," among the Yoruba; or of the ritualist and diviner, among the Lunda. As have others, those who were rich or powerful claimed the standing of aristocrats and dominated key councils. The monarch then had to gain their approval before introducing new policies, imposing new levies, or declaring new wars. From their position of power, commoners and aristocrats defended the independence of the courts, thus imposing yet another limit on the power of the state (Table 13.10).

In the cross-section of societies bequeathed to the colonial era by the pre-colonial state system, then, those who ruled were often limited in their ability to exercise power. Ritualists could call their legitimacy into question and threaten divine retribution should monarchs abuse their power. Councils dominated by the heads of powerful families could oppose their policies. In some, courts could limit their ability to bring the power of the judicial system to bear on their political enemies. In settings where exit constituted a costly option, internal checks nonetheless limited the use of power.

13.7 FURTHER REFLECTIONS

It is dangerous to invoke particular cases in support of a general argument. It is impossible to prove that the cases were not selected simply to bolster the argument; the selection, moreover, may imply that its author concurs with the argument when he may not do so. Despite these dangers, I conclude by drawing on two works by eminent historian Jan Vansina.

In *How Societies are Born*, Vansina (2004) studies the history of societies in south central Africa: a region that runs from the Congo in the north to Botswana in the south and from the Atlantic in the west to the Lualaba in the east. These societies, he contends, initially consisted of small aggregates of kin who foraged to survive. Over time, their populations increased and technologies changed. Two changes proved pivotal: the domestication of cattle and the invention of the iron hoe. Of necessity, foragers travel light; what they need, they consume. The domestication of plants and animals – that is, the Neolithic transformation – facilitated accumulation, however, and notions of private property. Cattle and cultivation, he writes, "widened the concept of individual ownership, fostered a novel notion of material wealth, and made the emergence of classes based on wealth possible" (Vansina 2004, 99). Economic growth thus gave rise to government, Vansina argues, by creating private property. Vansina thus sketches out a causal path that, while differing from the one advanced here, runs parallel to it. To reconcile the two, we need only add the emergence of conflict and the demand for adjudication and the termination of disputes: conditions that could lead to the demand for order and the means of enforcing it.

Also suggestive is Vansina's study of the Kuba,[5] a people who dwell in Congo near the junction of the Kasai and Sankuru. His account begins with the migration of kin groups from the north, the crossing of the Sankuru, and their settlement in the lands wherein they now reside. Once again, Vansina links the growth of population and the transition to permanent cultivation to the formation of chiefdoms. Distinctive of this work, however, is his study of the emergence of a monarch capable of collecting taxes, providing public services, and making war.

Focusing on the most celebrated monarchs – Syaam and his two immediate successors, MboMboosh and Mboong a Leeng – Vansina notes how they transformed the Kuba into a powerful and prosperous people. In discussing this transition, Vansina stresses that "the call for a surplus came

[5] Also known by the name of their ruling clan, the Bushong. J. Vansina (1978). *The Children of Woot: A History of the Kuba Peoples*. Madison, University of Wisconsin Press.

from above, from the political authorities" (Vansina 1978, 184). Syaam and his royal lineage forged a central bureaucracy consisting of supervisors of public works; judges, police, and messengers; inspectors and tax collectors; and attendants to the king, his wives, and offspring. The expansive growth of the public sector, in turn, inspired the search for the resources from which to pay for it. Taking advantage of the arrival of new crops from the Americas – maize, tubers, and tobacco, for example – the government promoted their widespread adoption.[6] In addition, it promoted multiple cropping. The government then began not only to extract wealth, but also to create it. The result was the growth of public revenues and private incomes.

To account for the behavior of this government, we need make use of hints that lay scattered in Vansina's account. It is clear that in "the Age of Chief" – as he calls the era prior to the formation of the monarchy – the Kuba competed for territory with others who had crossed the Sankuru such as the Ngongo, the Ngoonde, the Shoowa, and the Kel. Vansina implies, but does not boldly claim, that the competition for territory lent impetus to political centralization and the formation of chieftaincies. When turning to "the Age of Kings," Vansina notes that MboMboosh and Mboong a Leeng led the Kuba in wars against the Pyaang, Kote, Cwa, and Luba; he never places warfare at the center of his analysis, however. A close reading of his account suggests a possible reason: so rich and powerful were the Kuba that they had little need to fight.

The Kuba established a "large kingdom that was generally peaceful contrasted with the insecurity that became more and more prevalent elsewhere" (Vansina 1978, 165). The kingdom grew, Vansina notes, not only because its borders expanded, but also because people migrated to it. The "ascendancy" of the Kuba, he adds, "was due in large part to the continuing process of fission in other kingdoms" (Vansina 1978, 164). The Pyaang did not long remain a serious threat, he notes; rather they "fell apart" (Vansina 1978, 162). Perhaps, one might think, the enemies of the Kuba fractured because they could not compete.

Those who held power among the Kuba thus devised strategies that proved winning in the contested terrain of Central Africa. They secured themselves politically, in part by promoting their nation's prosperity. Their polity endured while others collapsed.

[6] While not made explicit in Vansina's account, it would appear that cultivation was prescribed rather than encouraged. This certainly would be the case in the slave villages that provisioned the residents of the capital.

While Vansina's depiction of interstate conflict is muted, his description of the internal politics of the Kuba is not. He makes clear the extent to which the monarchs faced internal checks to their use of power. Powerful lineages lay claim to the status of aristocrats, he states; and the aristocrats dominated key councils, where they could, if united, check the king's power and shape his choice of policies. The monarch, Vansina makes clear, sought to penetrate and control these councils. Through intermarriage and favoritism, he sought support from their members. But the aristocrats had interests that differed from his and were often unwilling to be suborned. The monarch's use of power was thus checked. Willing to back policies that provided security and prosperity, those who populated the state councils were able to resist any effort by the king to use public power for private gain.

Historians of Europe have noted that interstate conflict selected for societies in which power was deployed to foster the creation of wealth. We have seen that in precolonial Africa, interstate conflict also led to the extinction of polities: between 1700 and 1900, the number of states in West Africa declined by more than a third. We have also seen that in postcolonial Africa, societies with states were more likely to foster markets, long-distance trade, and craft production and more likely as well to create public goods, such as roads, bridges, and canals than were those that lacked centralized political institutions. Taken together, these observations suggest that while traditional states may well have been violent, they also were developmental.

13.7.1 Discussion

During the nineteenth century, Africa was invaded, conquered, and occupied. The conquerors were few in number and, to a great degree, reliant on those whom they had conquered for information, cooperation, and resources. Whatever their theory of rule, most found it useful to rule through established elites. As in the times before the conquest, Africa's elites sought wealth and power. But now they could better satisfy those desires by providing political service than by preparing for war. As a consequence, they no longer had to promote development to survive. Following the partition of Africa, the impulse that earlier and elsewhere had driven those with power to generate growth had been stilled.

13.8 COUNTERARGUMENTS

But then, why did Africa fail to develop? What checked the developmental impulse of the African state? Clearly, it was stilled by conquest, something that was not achieved as readily as is commonly assumed. People appear to have forgotten the defeat of the Italians by the Ethiopians in East Africa or of the British by the Zulu in South Africa. They have forgotten as well that the British held the Ashanti military in such high regard that the commanders who defeated the Ashanti became known as the "Ashanti Ring," and moved rapidly into leading positions in Britain's military. As for their putative technological superiority, pace Hilaire Belloc, European forces in Africa often abandoned their Maxim guns, rather than having to lug them through Africa's challenging terrain, and Africans were able to purchase and import modern weapons – breach loading rifles, for example – soon after their adoption by armies in Europe. The closeness of the contest provides an indication of the power of indigenous states.

Other factors were clearly at play, however. One was slavery; a second was the lack of modern technology. The presence of the first made it profitable to use power to compel rather than to encourage effort while the absence of the second lowered the returns that effort would yield.

Elementary reasoning suggests that under most circumstances, slave economies will be less productive than those based on free labor.[7] Not only are the incentives to expend effort low, given that labor is highly taxed, so too are incentives to innovate, given that the majority of those engaged in production will fail to secure the benefits. Empirical confirmation comes from the work of economic historians, in particular those who compare the economies of the northern portions of North America, where labor was free, and those of the Caribbean, South America, and the southern states of North America, where slavery prevailed (Acemoglu, Johnson et al. 2001; Acemoglu, Robinson et al. 2001; Engerman and Sokoloff 1997; Nunn 2008).

As documented by Lovejoy (1983), Thornton (1999), Manning (1982), and others, monarchs, princes, and heads of state in Africa presided over polities that not only promoted commerce and produced public goods, but also seized and enslaved numerous human beings. Some they shipped abroad; others they sold domestically or settled on plantations, compelling them to feed and provision the royals, officials, soldiers, bureaucrats, and political hangers-on. Precolonial African states may have mobilized power to promote economic development, but, in labor markets at least, they employed it to extract and forcefully to redistribute.

7 Where teams are more productive than isolated individuals, however, a given quantity of labor may yield greater output when closely – and coercively – supervised. R. Fogel and S. Engerman (1974). *Time on the Cross: The Economics of American Negro Slavery*. New York, W. W. Norton.

When probing the reasons for the absence of industry, it is useful to turn to Mokyr's (2008) discussion of the institutional and cultural setting for scientific innovation in eighteenth-century England. In contrast to the patterns of exclusion that characterized many British institutions, those engaged in the natural sciences created societies that were open; in pursuit of knowledge, people from different social classes met to discuss, to demonstrate, and to appraise. Their efforts focused on fields that promised human improvement: botany, soil and animal sciences, navigation, medicine, and astronomy. As important as the technical innovations that they fostered, Mokyr (2008) argues, were the principles that they adopted. Knowledge, they recognized, was best pursued socially. By the eighteenth century, where there were Englishmen, there were societies that held public meetings where new findings were reported and correspondence with other societies read and discussed.

In a brilliant essay, Mudimbe and Appiah (1993) probe the creation of knowledge within African societies. There they too find skepticism, interrogation, and experimentation: key steps in the scrutiny of arguments and the testing of hypotheses. What is missing, they argue, is verification. Drawing on Goody (1986), Mudimbe and Appiah stress the significance of literacy; without writing, they argue, it is impossible to stake a claim or to record a method such that it could be verified. In the absence of literacy, it is therefore difficult to prove oneself right and someone else wrong. Innovation, competition, and destruction – that is, economic progress – is therefore slowed.

As Mudimbe and Appiah note, some artisans in Africa in fact achieved high levels of technical proficiency. Among them numbered the ironworkers, who refined and smelted ores to a degree that matched or exceeded what had been achieved in the West prior to the Industrial Revolution. Rather than publicly exhibiting their technologies and subjecting them to investigation, however, the ironworkers jealously hoarded their knowledge. Ritually, they set themselves apart; often, they married endogamously, forming a separate caste. Rather than broadcasting their knowledge, they clothed it in mystery. Theirs was the code of the guild rather than of the scientific society.

When the Europeans conquered Africa, then, they encountered societies that, while willing and able to fight, lacked an industrial base and the cultural practices that would might have fostered its creation.

13.9 CONCLUSION

The arguments just discussed resonate with many of the standard accounts of Africa's underdevelopment. There is truth in both of them, of course. But

Table 13.11. *Slave trading and political structure (percent "yes")*

	Kinship	Chiefs	Monarch	Central bureaucracy	
				Present	Absent
Engaged in slave trade?	0	22	78	75	17

Note: N = 31–4.
Source: Data from Human Relations Area Files (Bates 1983, 51).

here I have advanced a new claim. The imperial peace is commonly viewed as offering a respite from the misery of warfare and slavery. It is held to be one of Europe's principal contributions to Africa's development. I have argued the contrary. The imperial peace dismantled relationships that in other times and places tempered the use of power, rendering those who possessed it economically productive. Imperial rule left ample opportunities in place for political elites to employ power for self-aggrandizement. If power can be employed to protect or to prey on the creation of wealth, then the imperial peace may have tipped the balance in favor of the latter. When security does not depend on prosperity, the developmental impulse is stilled among those who rule (Table 13.11).

References

Acemoglu, Daron., James. A. Robinson et al. (2001). "The Colonial Origins of Comparative Development." *American Economic Review*, 91(1369–1401).

Ajayi, J. F. Ade and Michael Crowder, eds. (1976). *History of West Africa*. London: Longman, second edition.

Axelrod, Robert. (1985). *The Evolution of Cooperation*. New York, Basic Books.

Banton, Michael, ed. (2004). *Political Systems and the Distribution of Power*. London: Taylor and Francis, first published 1965.

Bates, Robert H. (1983). *Essays on the Political Economy of Rural Africa*. Cambridge: Cambridge University Press.

Bates, Robert H., Karen Ferree, A. J. Robinson, Smita Singh, and Anne Wren. (1996). "Toward the Systematic Study of Transitions." *Development Discussion Paper No. 256*. Cambridge, MA: Harvard Institute for International Development.

Bates, Robert H., Avner Greif, and Smita Singh. (2002). "Organizing Violence." *Journal of Conflict Resolution*, 46(5): 599–628.

Brewer, John. (1988). *The Sinews of Power: War Money and the English State, 1688–1783*. New York: Knopf.

Centeno, Miguel Angel. (1997). "Blood and Debt: War and Taxation in Nineteenth Century Latin America." *The American Journal of Sociology*, 102(6): 1565–1605.

Colson, Elizabeth. (1969). "African Society at the Time of the Scramble." In *Colonialism in Africa, 1870–1960*, edited by Lewis H. Gann and Peter Duignan, 27–65. New York: Cambridge University Press.

(1974). *Tradition and Contract: The Problem of Orer*. Chicago: Aldine Publishing Company.

Crowder, Michael. (1977). *West Africa: An Introduction to Its History*. London: Longman.

Curtin, Phillip, Steven Feierman, Leonard Thompson, and Jan Vansina. (1995). *African History*. Harlow: Longman.

Divale, William. (2000). "Standard Cross-Cultural Sample." *World Cultures*, 14: 1–2.

Elvers, T. M. S. and D. Handelman, eds. (2006). *Defining the Manchester School*. New York: Berghahn.

Engerman, Stanley and Kenneth Sokoloff (1997). "Factor Endowments, Institutions, and Differential Paths of Growth among New World Economies." In *How Latin America Fell Behind*, edited by Steven Haber, 260–304. Stanford, CA: Stanford University Press.

Evans-Pritchard, E. E. (1940). *The Nuer: A Description of the Modes of Livelihood and Political Institutions of a Nilotic People*. Oxford: The Clarendon Press.

Fage, J. D. (1974). *States and Subjects in Sub-Saharan African History*. Johannesburg: Witwatersrand University Press.

Fallers, Lloyd A. (1966). *Bantu Bureaucracy*. Chicago: University of Chicago Press.

Fogel, Robert William and Stanley L. Engerman. (1974). *Time on the Cross: The Economics of American Negro Slavery*. New York: W. W. Norton.

Forde, Cyril Daryll and Phyllis Mary Kaberry, eds. (1967). *West African Kingdoms in the Nineteenth Century*. Oxford: Oxford University Press.

Fortes, Meyer and E. E. Evans-Pritchard, eds. (1987). *African Political Systems*. New York: KPI in association with the International African Institute.

Gilbert, F., ed. (1975). *The Historical Essays of Otto Hintze*. New York, Oxford University Press.

Gluckman, Max. (1955). *Custom and Conflict in Africa*. Oxford: Blackwell.

Goody, Jack. (1986). *The Logic of Writing and the Organization of Society*. New York: Cambridge University Press.

Gray, Richard and David Birmingham, eds. (1970). *Pre-colonial Trade*. London: Oxford University Press.

Hintze, Otto. (1975). *The Historical Essays of Otto Hintze*, edited by Felix Gilbert. New York: Oxford University Press.

Hirshleifer, Jack. (1994). "The Dark Side of the Force." *Economic Inquiry*, 32(1–10).

(2001). "The Dark Side of the Force: Economic Foundation of Conflict Theory." *Economic Inquiry*, 32: 1–10.

Hopkins, Anthony. (2000). "Quasi-states, Weak States and the Partition of Africa." *Review of International Studies*, 26: 311–20.

Kwamena-Poh, Michael, John Tosh, Richard Waller, and Michael Tidy. (1995). *African History in Maps*. Harlow: Longman.

Law, Robin. (1978). "Slaves, Trade and Taxes." In *Research in Economic Anthropology*, edited by George Dalton, 37–42. Greenwich, CT: JAI Press.

Lovejoy, Paul. (1983). *Transformations in Slavery*. New York, Cambridge University Press.

Manning, Patrick (1982). *Slavery, Colonialism, and Economic Growth in Dahomey, 1640–1960*. New York, Cambridge University Press.

McIntosh, Susan Keech. (1999). *Beyond Chiefdoms: Pathways to Complexity in Africa*. New York: Cambridge University Press.

McIntosh, Susan Keech and Robert J. McIntosh. (1996). "West African Savanna Kingdoms." In *The Oxford Companion to Archaeology*, edited by Brian Fagan, 748–50. New York: Oxford University Press.

Mokyr, Joel. (2008). "The Institutional Origins of the Industrial Revolution." In *Institutions and Economic Performance*, edited by Elhanan Helpman, 64–119. Cambridge, MA: Harvard University Press.

Morrison, Donald George, Robert Cameron Mitchell, and John N. Paden. (1989). *Black Africa: A Comparative Handbook*. New York: Paragon House, revised edition.

Mudimbe, V. Y. and Kwame A. Appiah. (1993). "The Impact of African Studies on Philosophy." In *Africa and the Disciplines*, edited by Robert H. Bates, V. Y. Mudimbe, and J. O'Barr, 113–38. Chicago: University of Chicago Press.

Murdock, George Peter. (1967). *Ethnographic Atlas*. Pittsburgh: University of Pittsburgh Press.

Northrop, David. (1978). *Trade without Rulers*. Oxford: The Clarendon Press.

Nunn, Nathan. (2008). "The Long-Term Effects of Africa's Slave Trades." *The Quarterly Journal of Economics*, 123(1): 139–76.

Oliver, Roland A., ed. (1977). *The Cambridge History of Africa*. New York: Cambridge University Press.

Parker, Geoffrey. (1991). *The Military Revolution: Military Innovation and the Rise of the West, 1500–1800*. New York: Cambridge University Press.

Roberts, Michael. (1956). *The Military Revolution 1560–1660*. Belfast: M. Boyd.

Southall, Aidan W. (1970). "The Illusion of Tribe." In *The Passing of Tribal Man in Africa*, edited by Peter Claus Wolfgang Gutkind, 28–51. Leiden: Brill.

(1988). "Segmentary State in Africa and Asia." *Comparative Studies in Society and History*, 30(1): 52–82.

(1999). "The Segmentary State and the Ritual Phase in Political Economy." In *Beyond Chiefdoms: Pathways to Complexity in Africa*, edited by Susan Keech McIntosh, 31–8. Cambridge: Cambridge University Press.

Stevenson, Robert F. (1968). *Population and Political Systems in Africa*. New York: Columbia University Press.

Thornton, John K. (1999). *Warfare in Atlantic Africa, 1500–1800*. London: UCL Press.

Tilly, C. (1975). "Reflections on the History of State Making. In *The Formation of Nation States in Western Europe*, edited by C. Tilly, 3–83.Princeton, NJ: Princeton University Press.

(1985). "War Making and State Making as Organized Crime." In *Bringing the State Back*, edited by P. Evans, D. Rueschemeyer, and T. Skocpol, 169–91. Cambridge: Cambridge University Press.

Turner, Victor W. (1957). *Schism and Continuity in an African Society*. Manchester: Manchester University Press on Behalf of the Rhodes-Livingstone Institute.

Vansina, Jan. (1978). *The Children of Woot: A History of the Kuba Peoples*, Madison: University of Wisconsin Press.

(2004). *How Societies Are Born: Governance in West Central Africa.* Charlottesville and London: University of Virginia Press.

Warner, Carolyn M. (1999). "The Political-Economy of 'Quasi-statehood' and the Demise of 19th Century African Politics." *Review of International Studies*, 25: 233–55.

Yoffee, Norman. (1993). "Too Many Chiefs?" In *Archeological Theory: Who Sets the Agenda?*, edited by Norman Yoffee and Andrew Sherratt, 60–78. New York: Cambridge University Press.

PART IV

EXTERNAL FORCES

14

Dahomey in the World: Dahomean Rulers and European Demands, 1726–1894

John Thornton

The Kingdom of Dahomey has a bad reputation. When the debate concerning the slave trade broke out in Europe during the late eighteenth century, Dahomey was defined as the classic example of either a pariah state dedicated to the capture and sale of people to European slavers, or of a state so addicted to violence that sale of its victims was an act of mercy. Yet there is always another side to this story, and that is of a Dahomey forced by one motive or another into the slave trade. One of the earliest writers on Dahomey's history, Robert Adams, whose work was published in 1735, argued that Dahomey opposed the slave trade but that foreign pressure compelled the kingdom to participate in it. Two influential books about Dahomey, however, written by Europeans who claimed to be eyewitnesses, one by Robert Norris in 1789 and the other by Archibald Dalzel in 1793, both published in the thick of the debate, presented Dahomey in a different light, and indeed challenged factual data from Adams's book, to reinforce the close association between Dahomey and the slave trade (Adams and Norris 1789; Dalzel 1793).[1]

When abolitionists won the day, and the British decided that they needed to end the slave trade, Dahomey was widely regarded as an uncooperative holdout. Reports of untrammeled slave dealing and defiance of international pressure to stop enslaving people joined continued reports of Dahomey's violence against its neighbors and practice of human sacrifice. Ultimately these claims against Dahomey and its rulers justified the colonial occupation of the kingdom by France at the end of the nineteenth century.

Modern historians have also struggled with Dahomey and its historical legacy. Isaac Akinjogbin strove to reverse the model of Dahomey as a state devoted entirely to the slave trade by arguing that during its formative

[1] See on this general point, Law (1986).

years, under King Agaja, Dahomey actually sought very hard to limit and control the slave trade in the interest of regional harmony, and only became devoted to the trade when it failed (Akinjogbin 1967). But Akinjogbin's work was criticized by a number of other historians, and the most significant of these, Robin Law, viewed Dahomey as being at the very least an enthusiastic supporter of the slave trade, a product, he argued of its origin (according to some traditions) from bandit gangs (Henige and Johnson 1976; Law 1986, 246–7; Ross 1982). Werner Peukert, in contrast, challenged what he called the "Atlantic theory" of Dahomey's history, that the state was largely organized around the slave trade. He pointed out that although Dahomey had a reputation for military prowess, and repeated successful military attacks on its neighbors were the source of its slaves, Dahomey was not, in fact, particularly successful as a military state, losing a good number of its wars. Instead, he argued that Dahomey's religious system, which relied on human sacrifice, was more important in explaining Dahomey's wars (Peukert 1978).

In addition to wrestling with Dahomey's reputation as a state devoted to the slave trade, historians have pointed to it as an example of a state-dominated society, perhaps because the state grew out of the warfare needs of the slave trade. K. Madhu Pannikar, an early scholar of dependency theory, argued that Dahomey's role in the slave trade led to an all-powerful state, and indeed thwarted growth in more positive directions (Panikkar 1963). Along the same lines, Karl Polanyi used Dahomey as a model of a state-dominated economy, with administered trade and a classic type of the nonmarket substantive economy (Polanyi 1968). Here again, Robin Law has entered the discussion by challenging the idea that Dahomey's kings held a monopoly on the slave trade, and indirectly also that Dahomey was the sort of absolutist state Polanyi and others had argued it was (Law 1977). At the very least, Law argued, Dahomey had a private sector, both during the slave trade and afterward. In fact, in my own study of Dahomey's military system, I was able to demonstrate that the army itself was at least in part privately controlled, though the state's share in raising and supplying the army increased considerably over time, especially in the late eighteenth century and beyond (Thornton 1998, 88–93). In fact, one could make a fairly solid case that the idea of a totally dominant Dahomean state was based on observations from the middle of the nineteenth century onward, at the very end of the slave trade and even beyond the end.

It may well be best to think of Dahomey as a fiscal-military state, a term that has recently come into use for early modern Europe. In the European model, most effectively elaborated by John Brewer for England after 1688, the fiscal-military state existed to fight (Brewer 1990). It built its taxation policies and indeed even its commercial policies around maximizing the fighting potential of its armies, and then used the armies for military adventure. Brewer's model has been subsequently expanded and employed for a wide variety of other European states in the same period (Glete 1992).

Dahomey can be seen in the same light. It was a military state, to be sure, for it fought nearly constant war, and although we know much less about its internal taxation and expenditure mechanisms than we do for European states, it clearly sent out large armies virtually every year. But these armies, which surely captured slaves in large numbers and exported them in exchange for munitions and luxury goods, may not have simply been economic instruments destined to shape the development of the state. In short, the truncation of nineteenth-century development in Africa in general, and Dahomey in particular, the "reversal of fortune" that moved Africa back in the pack of countries in the development of the nineteenth century, may not be so simply blamed on the slave trade, for all its horrible impact on demography and politics. Africa was not alone in a reversal of fortune, and the slave trade cannot be so simple an explanation.

In some measure, the nature of the source material that all modern historians must use to write Dahomey's history has determined how it is interpreted. Much of the most available historical material was written in the polemic accounts of the late eighteenth century. While modern historians have had access to and made a lot of use of archival materials, mostly records of the British, French, and Dutch African Companies and Portuguese records from Portugal's fort at Whydah, the most important port in the area, these records do not give the same sort of information about political history that the larger narrative histories do. They are good for checking and establishing chronology and sometimes for fleshing out details of events mentioned in the narratives, but they provide relatively little information about Dahomey's politics.

There are other sources, however, that have not been as systematically studied that can provide us with much more information about Dahomey and its politics. These are letters written by the Dahomean monarchs themselves. A few of these have been known for a fairly long time; one letter, written by Agaja in 1728 and sent to King George II of England, was published in 1789, and French researcher Pierre Verger discovered and published several others. However, until Robin Law republished the first letter, it was largely regarded as a forgery, and the letters published by Verger, while known since the early 1960s, had not been studied on their own merits, as important insights into royal thinking as presented by the rulers themselves.[2] To these I must add the six letters that I uncovered, by singular good fortune, in the archives of the Instituto Histórico e Geografico Brasileiro in Rio de Janeiro in 1998. These letters, written by King Adandozan between 1810 and 1812, are by far the longest and most detailed letters written by any Dahomean monarch. One of them is eleven folios (22 sides) long and another is seven folios (14 sides) long. Taken with a few other royal letters I located in Bahia in 2003, we now have a substantial collection of letters from Dahomey monarchs.[3]

This body of letters sheds some light on the single most important source for the lengthy narrative accounts of Dahomey written in the late eighteenth century, Norris's *Memoires of Bossa Ahadee* and Dalzel's *History of Dahomey*, which declare their dependence for the historical portions of what they wrote on the diary of Lionel Abson, the English factor at Whydah from 1767 to 1803 (Adams 1789; Dalzel 1793). Abson was close to the Dahomey court, spoke Fon (Dahomey's language), and married into the Dahomean elite. According to another visitor, Robert Adams, Abson was the best informed European on the coast (Adams 1823, 52). However, Abson's diary has not survived aside from its quotation and summarization by Norris and Dalzel, and it is not always easy to determine what in the diary as Norris and Dalzel reported it belongs to Abson, and what portion represents commentary by the Englishmen to prove their polemical points.

The royal letters also help in the critical understanding of Abson's account. Abson's chronicle has many of the same traits and interests as those found in the long letter that Adandozan wrote to the king of Portugal outlining his attacks on the coastal kingdoms before 1811. While one cannot be certain, the flavor of the royal letters and Abson's accounts matches enough that we can be somewhat reassured that Abson spoke, at least in some ways, with the voice that was typical of Dahomean monarchs, or at least the royal family. While this voice is muted and sometimes overwritten by its English commentators and editors, it allows us to reconsider the matters dealt with in his version of Dahomey's history.

[2] The original French version of this book was published in 1966 and is widely cited. In the Portuguese edition, the texts in Portuguese are transcriptions of the original texts, not retranslations from the French. See Law (1990) and Verger (1987, 289).

[3] These documents are found in the Instituto Historico e Geografico Brasileiro (henceforward IHGB), Lata 137, pasta 62, and Arquivo Público do Estado de Bahia (henceforward APEB), Secção Colonial, Correspondência Recebida de Autoridades Diversas, Maço 197, Cx 76. Now republished in Luis Parés, ed. "Cartas do Daomé," *Afro-Ásia*, 47 (2013): 295–395.

These letters have some important characteristics that also need to be discussed. It is fairly clear that no Dahomean ruler was personally literate, and so the letters were written by secretaries in Portuguese, from dictation in Fon. The language of the letters is complex Portuguese, perhaps the work of a nonnative speaker or even one whose first language was a Creole language. One of the authors, who declared himself the "scribe of this cruel king," added an unofficial note to the bottom of an 1804 letter that he had been a prisoner for twenty-three years in Dahomey, was innocent of any wrongdoing, and was uncomfortable in being forced to write letters.[4] Undoubtedly the other letters were written by similar sorts of people, and in fact, King Agongolo, writing in 1791, mentioned sending "all the necessary governors and commissioners and white boys who know how to read and write to respond with the captains," to greet ships.[5] It is possible that these "white boys," clerks in the employ of the Kingdom of Dahomey, might subvert letters and thus misrepresent the actual intentions of the authors; we have to assume as well that the king had reasonable checks in place to ensure that letters were accurate, even if we do not know what they were. This seems especially reasonable if we consider that the custom of using "white boys" as secretaries and literate go-betweens was well established.

A second point to consider is that the letters were written for fairly specific reasons to particular parties in Brazil (or the Portuguese court, then residing in Brazil), and thus cover only the business that needed to be done. They might not take too many asides to address questions that would be of greater interest to modern historians. In his longest letter, however, Adandozan took the opportunity to console the king of Portugal, then residing in exile in Rio de Janeiro, about the loss of his country, and to describe in considerable detail several of his military campaigns as a means of revealing to his Lusitanian brother that he might have been able to help him against his enemies. The detailed description of a military campaign seems to have been an obsession of the Dahomey kings, and not surprisingly is the central theme of Norris and Dalzel's chronicles as well.

A third and important point is that these letters were not written against the backdrop of the polemic in Britain at the time concerning the slave trade. The speeches of Dahomean rulers reported by writers like Norris or Dalzel have always to be taken with a grain of salt, given their use in the debates

4 Biblioteca Nacional de Rio de Janeiro, (henceforward BNRJ) MS 846 Adandozan to João Carlos da Bragança, November 20, 1804, published in Verger (1987, 289). Now republished in Pares, "Cartas do Daomé," 359.

5 APEB, Secção Colonial, Correspondência Recebida de Autoridades Diversas, Maço 197, Cx 76, doc. 1, Agonglo to unknown, March 31, 1790. In Pares, "Cartas do Daomé," 330.

over the slave trade. But Portugal was certainly not interested in suppressing the slave trade, and the Dahomean kings felt no compunction in writing to its leaders honestly about the role of the trade in their country.

The fact that the language of the letters was Portuguese and that the addressees were living in Portugal or Brazil and thus not participants in the polemics of the slave trade allows us to introduce two rarely used sources of Dahomean history that can provide an independent perspective. The first of these is the long report of a more or less failed religious mission from Brazil to Dahomey led by Vicente Ferreira Pires in 1800 (Pires 1957). Ferreira Pires, like the kings of Dahomey, was not particularly interested in the slave trade or its suppression. He did have religious interests of course, and it is not surprising that his report is the fullest account of Dahomean religion written during the era of the slave trade. But it is also rich in anecdotal information about the functioning of the Dahomean state.

The other source is also in Portuguese and thus equally free from the polemic of the English sources. Found in the same Brazilian institute where the cache of royal letters now lies, and published only in 2002, this 1806 document was written by Luís Antonio de Oliveira Mendes, a Brazilian who had never been to Dahomey. He was, however, a sugar planter and slave owner, and had learned the Fon language to communicate with his slaves, and, by his report, had also learned of their country from them. He also interviewed the Dahomean ambassador to Brazil, and while visiting Portugal, he happened to meet another long-term resident in Dahomey. The text is interesting for its insider and occasionally rural details (Oliveira Mendes 2002).

These new sources, some insider accounts of Dahomey, others from visitors or students of the kingdom, allow us to move beyond the polemical and sometimes misleading accounts of its English-speaking historians.

There is no doubt from the body of royal letters that the rulers of Dahomey considered their trade with Europe as normal and that the slave trade was a fundamental part of it. Agongolo, in a letter of 1790, noted the care he took to repopulate and secure his ports and reassured the Portuguese of their trading status, and then noted in a letter of 1795 that they would be paying for their tobacco imports in "good captives," as in ancient times.[6] When writing to Brazil in 1795, Agongolo again reassured his Brazilian customers that they could trade in precious materials such as silk or worked precious

[6] APEB, Secção Colonial, Correspondência Recebida, Maço 197, Cx 76, doc. 1, Agongolô to unknown, March 31, 1790 and doc. 2, Agongolô to Fernando José, n. d. ca. 1791 [dated in the archive]. In Pares, "Cartas do Daomé," 330–2.

metals in security, "for this there are captives in excess there, and more of them that can be sold against tobacco and aguardente."[7]

There can be little doubt that Dahomey's commercial interests were not restricted to the luxury goods the king sought from his Brazilian correspondents. They were also important components of his military activities, in that they supplied munitions. The link between warfare and captives was made very clear in Adandozan's letter of 1800 in which he asked Prince João de Bragança to "do me the favor of sending two hundred or three hundred barrels of powder, for which I will make good payment in excellent captives."[8]

While there can be little doubt that Dahomey waged numerous wars, indeed they can be documented in fair detail in a plethora of sources, the origin and rationality of these wars is more problematic. Certainly no Dahomean monarch claimed that his wars were simply to capture people. Lionel Abson recorded, famously, the statement Agongolo made in 1789 when, as Abson was reading to him about the parliamentary debates on the slave trade in England, the question of the origin of wars came up. Agongolo did not accept the idea of war for slaves at all, chiding his English visitor that he did not understand Africans very well. He noted that England was protected by the sea and had commerce everywhere, while Dahomey was on a large continent, hedged in by other nations, "of the same complexion, but speaking different languages," and in this situation, "we must defend ourselves by the sharpness of our swords to defend ourselves from their incursions, and punish the depredations they make on us." This, he averred, was the cause of "incessant wars." He went on to declare, "Your countrymen, therefore, who allege that we go to war for the purpose of supplying your ships with slaves, are grossly mistaken." Continuing in this vein, he asserted that "in the name of my ancestors and myself I aver, that no Dahoman man ever embarked in war merely for the sake of procuring wherewithal to purchase your commodities."

But Agongolo's wars were not just for defense, they also had judicial dimensions. He went on to describe how he, who had not ruled the country for long, had already killed thousands of people whom he could have sold, but who deserved death for their actions or for other reasons. "When policy or justice require that men be put to death, neither silk, nor brandy, nor coral nor cowries, can be substituted for the blood that must be spilt, for

[7] BNRJ MS 552, Angongolô to D Maria I, March 20, 1795 in Verger (1987, 287).

[8] APEB Ordens Regias, 89, fol. 345, Adandozan to Prince D. João de Bragança, undated, ca. 1800, in Verger (1987).

examples sake." He continued further that wars would not stop just because merchants from Europe no longer visited Africa, and moreover that he did not need guns to fight, pointing out that when he dressed as the third king of Dahomey, Weebaigh, he carried a bow, the traditional weapon of the time, and asserting that "Prisoners in those days were killed to a man." Finally he challenged assertions made in Europe that Dahomeans sold their wives and children, but that they only sold "a part of our prisoners." After all, "are not all prisoners at the disposal of their captors?" (Dalzel 1793, 218–19).

The quotation has been challenged, largely because of the use to which Dalzel put it to, that is, to assert that in some ways the slave trade rescued those who would be killed, and that Dahomey was addicted to war. But in the book, Dalzel set it aside as a direct quotation, and perhaps did so from Abson's own notes. While there is no question that it was and remains potentially a self-serving statement that might support the proslavery position in the debate, it is also possible that it reflects the genuine attitude of Agongolo and his colleagues.

Subtle confirmation of this exists in the correspondence with Portugal/Brazil. Although it is not clear, it would seem that Agongolo waged a war to secure the trade of the port of Jaquin about 1790; he wrote to Brazil to inform Portuguese authorities that he had secured the area from wars and robberies, and that for that reason trade was safe for Portuguese vessels.[9]

In a letter of 1804, Adandozan gave as his motive for an attack on the beaches of Allada and Porto Novo "some palavers we had among us," in this instance meaning simply disagreements and disputes. He continued that it was "our custom" to seize everything in such a war, including, it turns out, three Portuguese ships, hence the need for the letter.[10] By far the most important statement on war from Adandozan, however, came in his long letter to the king of Portugal in 1810, in which he noted that had he known in a timely manner, he would have sent an army to aid him in his defeat by Napoleonic forces. He then went on to say that he had waged a number of wars himself, "here in my land I have fought many wars in the interior both against the nation of Magiunas and the Nagos and that in all of these I had victory, as I also have participated in many wars that I have had to make because I have a small country," a sentiment that echoes his predecessor's complaint that he was surrounded by enemies.

[9] APEB Secção Colonial, Correspondência Recebida de Autoridades Diversas, Maço 197, Cx 76, doc. 1, Agonglo to unknown, March 31, 1790.

[10] BNRJ MS 846 Adandozan to João Carlos de Bragança, November 20, 1804, in Verger (1987). Adandozan gives the date of the action as September 7, 1804.

Indeed, he mentioned specifically a war waged with Oyo because, in his opinion, that ruler came against him to take captives.[11] He also described a war against an island on the coast called "aGomça" as a defensive war, waged to protect his interests, for he took many heads and did many executions, including some 703 killed or beheaded, to terrorize the ruler so that he would not attack again.[12] He also waged a war of vengeance against a king "who was an enemy of my father's" named Sapî Maquino, who had killed or mistreated a female relative he had married. He intervened in a war that Sapî Maquino had fought against the country of Aê, and as a result of his victory, he "destroyed all the land and killed the said king and burned the place where his sons, daughters and brothers were."[13]

Thus, the correspondence of Agongolo and Adandozan does in fact lend support to Agongolo's description of his motivations for war. Indeed, from his point of view, the acquisition of slaves was truly a secondary factor, a given in any war, but rarely the reason for waging it. It also tends to undermine the contention, made by the English writers, that the kings of Dahomey waged specific wars solely to acquire slaves. None of this means that the slave trade was not a major portion of the income of Dahomey, though it must also be said that no national income accounting has ever been done to calculate how much of Dahomey's national wealth or royal revenues flowed directly from the slave trade.

There is little doubt that the kings of Dahomey regarded the enslavement of people captured in war as their right, and they had strict laws against the enslavement of their own people. But of course, this does not mean that Dahomey did not suffer from the slave trade. In Dahomey, or rather the Bight of Benin region of which Dahomey was a part, enslavement took place as a result of wars more than raids. Dahomey suffered losses from the incursions of its neighbors, just as Adandozan and Agongolo contended. For example, the neighboring polities of Porto Novo and other coastal countries routinely raided the south coast of Dahomey using the intercoastal waterway. Adandozan's attacks along those routes were in fact in response to such raids, and Agongolo's writings about the disruption to trading ports were specific references to this (Thornton 1998, 76–9, 94–6).

While the kings' letters make it appear that they were always victorious in restoring security and overcoming their enemies, they also reveal that there had been prior raids and attacks, which presumably had captured

[11] IHGB, Lata 137, pasta 62, fol. 1, Adandozan to João Carlos de Bragança, October 9, 1810.

[12] Ibid., fols. 1v–2.

[13] Ibid., fols. 2v–3.

Dahomean subjects and enslaved them. Similarly, at an earlier period, Werner Peukert used Abson's detailed account of Dahomey's campaigns against its neighbors during the reigns of Kpengla and Tegbesu, rectified by more detailed and chronologically ordered commercial records, to show that Dahomey waged important wars and suffered defeats (Peukert 1978). In fact, Dahomey's armies, in spite of their reputation for being warlike and efficient, were frequently defeated by their enemies. In these cases, Dahomey suffered losses and no doubt its people were enslaved as well. There was, after all, a sufficiently large population of Dahomeans in Brazil that they dominated the lay brotherhood of Santo Elesbão and Santa Efigênia in Rio de Janeiro until the 1760s when the fraternity split, in part over their excessive claims over other groups from the region (de Carvalho Soares 2004).

The letters of the kings do not entirely bear out the idea of an overly powerful Dahomean state, created by war and standing in the way of private enterprise. Adandozan was constantly aware of foreign technology and the possibility of using it in his country. Of course, he was interested in military equipment; in 1811 he asked specifically about different types of rifles and explosive shells for his army.[14] But his interest went beyond these. He was also interested in obtaining firefighting equipment for his town, for example.

Perhaps Adandozan's most interesting request in this regard came about because of his observation that the Napoleonic wars had driven both French and English slave trades out of business. He noted that there was therefore a shortage of the sorts of commodities that European shippers brought in, mentioning a wide range of supplies, luxury goods, cloth, and of course tobacco and alcohol. He suggested that this presented a business opportunity for Portugal, or rather more exactly for Portugal now in Brazil. He suggested that the king give him a ship of his own to carry goods, in which he would be the captain and he would bear the responsibility for profit and loss. He was confident that he would succeed in shipping and would show them what blacks could do.[15]

We do not know if any of Adandozan's requests were met, or what he might have done with them. In 1818 he was overthrown by his brother Guezo, whose letter announcing his usurpation of the throne and declaring his intention to continue good relations with Brazil is the last one of the Rio de Janeiro series.[16] However, Dahomey did make a transition to addressing

[14] IHGB, Lata 137, pasta 62, Adandozan to João Carlos Bragança, October 9, 1810, fol. 5.

[15] Ibid., Adandozan to king of Portugal, no date (ca. 1811), fol. 7.

[16] Ibid., Guezo to king of Portugal, no date.

the challenges of the nineteenth century. Dahomey was no more free of warfare than it had been before; indeed, Guezo and his successors continued to press to expand Dahomean influence, to shake the country free of the nominal dependence it had on Oyo, and to fill the vacuum in power created by the collapse of Oyo after 1823. As these wars, like the earlier ones, continued to bring in slaves, Dahomey continued to export them, and likewise to expand its access to foreign technology. Dahomey never failed to keep up with the latest developments in weapons technology; in fact, by 1894 when France conquered the country, its soldiers were equipped with rapid-firing magazine rifles, machine guns, and Krupp artillery (Garcia 1988).

At the same time, Dahomey also moved into alternate products when the slave trade was clearly ending, but using slaves captured from the wars as its labor force. State-managed, slave-worked palm oil plantations provided Dahomey with the foreign exchange it needed to keep the military moving and to support the management of Dahomey's expanding state apparatus.

The failure of Dahomey, or indeed of any other African state, to develop into an industrial society is a problem that needs to be addressed. The participation of the Africans in the slave trade provides a useful, but I believe limited answer. European states also engaged in the sort of destructive militarism that characterized Dahomey in the same period, and developed industrial capacity anyway, and at least in some analysts' opinion, warfare helped develop technology. It is fairly clear that the Industrial Revolution was not a state-run enterprise in Europe, but came out of the private sector, often in spite of state interference and monopoly concessions.

It is probably safe to say that in the minds of its leaders, the function of the state in Dahomey was to wage war, in many respects like the European fiscal-military states. The wars need not simply be to feed the slave trade, but in fact, the revenue of the slave trade was invested in war and perhaps made more wars or bigger wars possible. The objectives of the wars, however, were generally not simply to get slaves, but to achieve a variety of other goals, to centralize Mahi country, to finish the conquest of the coast, to avenge insults, and to take over strategic positions, often to further military objectives.

This is important to keep in mind when considering Dahomey in the post–slave trade era. The state in nineteenth-century Dahomey did participate strongly in the economy, primarily to expand exports of palm oil, but even then primarily to meet the goals of a fiscal-military state, to continue to offset the costs of war and material. Furthermore, it is quite clear that Dahomey did have a private sector, in fact quite a strong one, though precisely how the private-public competition may have worked is problematic in the current state of research. Robin Law, in particular, has pointed out that both small-scale producers and large plantations tapped palm oil for the international market. The state controlled many of these plantations and used war captives as labor, but such captives may have also been in private hands or farmed out by the state to private farmers (Law 1977).

It is difficult to determine if the costs of war, especially the depopulation elements of the type of war waged in Africa, where casualties were inflated by exported captives, overwhelmed productive potentials. Demographic research has not focused on Dahomey, and in any case, nineteenth-century Dahomey may well have benefited from importing labor forcibly, and offset military losses. The internal slave trade of the post-abolition period presented a transfer of labor within Africa with labor going by force, often to the most productive regions.

It is, perhaps more worthwhile to focus on the late nineteenth century and even the colonial period to see the true locus of the reversal of fortune in Dahomey. The nineteenth century was a highly dynamic period, when improvements in oceanic transportation, a product of the Industrial Revolution, made low-cost, high-bulk exports possible. It is in the process of deindustrialization, where, for example, textile producers moved into importing cloth rather than making it, and attempts to create a local textile industry, such as that missionaries attempted at Abeokuta, failed, that we might seek the origins of the reversal, rather than in the earlier slave trade.

References

Adams, Robert. (1823). *Remarks on the Country Extending from Cape Palmas to the River Congo*. London. Reprinted, Frank Cass, 1966.

Akinjogbin, I. A. (1967). *Dahomey and Its Neighbours 1708–1818*. Cambridge: Cambridge University Press.

Brewer, John. (1990). *The Sinews of Power: War, Money, and the English State, 1688–1783*. Cambridge, MA: Harvard University Press.

Dalzel, Archibald. (1793). *A History of Dahomey, an Inland Kingdom in Africa*. London: Spilsbury and Son.

de Carvalho Soares, Mariza. (2004). "A nação que se tem e a 'terra'de onde se vem: categorias de inserção social de africanos no império português, século XVIII." *Estudos Afro-Asiáticos*, 26: 303–30.

de Oliveira Mendes, Luís Antônio de. (2002). "Memoria histórica sobre os costumes particulares dos Africanos..." in "A Memoria histórica sobre os costumes particulares dos Africanos com relação privitiva ao Reino da Guiné e nele ao respeito ao Rei de Daomé," edited by Alberto da Costa e Silva. *Afro-Ásia*, 28: 253–94.

Garcia, Luc. (1988). *Le royaume du Dahomé: Face à la penetration colonial: affrontements et incomprehension, 1875–1894*. Paris: Karthala.

Glete, Jan. (1992). *War and the State in Early Modern Europe: Spain, the Dutch Republic and Sweden as Fiscal-military States, 1500–1660*. London: Routledge.

Henige, David and Marion Johnson. (1976). "Agaja and the Slave Trade: Another Look at the Evidence." *History in Africa*, 3: 57–67.

Law, Robin. (1977). "Royal Monopoly and Private Enterprise in the Atlantic Trade: The Case of Dahomey." *Journal of African History*, 18: 555–77.

(1986). "Dahomey and the Slave Trade: Reflections on the Historiography of the Rise of Dahomey." *Journal of African History*, 27: 237–67.

(1990). "Further Light on Bulfinch Lambe and the 'Emperor of Pawpaw': King Agaja of Dahomey's Letter to George I of England, 1726." *History in Africa*, 17: 211–26.

Norris, Robert. (1789). *Memoires of the Reign of Bossa Ahadee, King of Dahomey*. London: Printed for Frank Lowndes, 1789. Reprinted Frank Cass, 1968.

Ross, David. (1982). "The Anti-Slave Trade Theme in Dahomean History: An Examination of the Evidence." *History in Africa*, 9: 263–71.

Panikkar, K. Madhu. (1963). *The Serpent and the Crescent: A History of the Negro Empires of Western Africa*. Bombay: Asia Publishing.

Parés, Luis ed. (2013). "Cartas do Daomé." *Afro-Ásia*, 47: 295–395.

Peukert, Werner. (1978). "Der Atlantische Skavenhandel von Dahomey 1740–1797." *Wirtschaftsanthropologie und Sozialgeschichte*. Wiesbaden: Spengler.

Pires, Vicente Ferreira. (1957). *Viagem de África em o Reino de Dahomé*. Claudo Ribeiro de Lessa, ed. São Paulo: Editora Nacional.

Polanyi, Karl. (1968). *Dahomey and the Slave Trade: An Analysis of an Archaic Economy*. Seattle: University of Washington Press.

Thornton, John. (1998). *Warfare in Atlantic Africa, 1500–1800*. London: University College of London.

Verger, Pierre. (1987). *Fuxo e refluxo do tráfico de escravos entre o Golfo de Benin e a Bahia de Todos os Santos do séculos XVII a XIX*. 2nd edition. São Paulo: Curropio.

15

The Transatlantic Slave Trade and the Evolution of Political Authority in West Africa

Warren C. Whatley

Since the publication of Douglas North's *Structure and Change in Economic History* (1981), social scientists have accumulated an abundance of new evidence showing how institutions shape the structures and performance of economies as they move through time. African economies are no exception. The term *patrimonial* (or *neo-patrimonial*) is controversial, but it is often used to describe a class of postcolonial African nation-states where a weak federal authority attempts to rule over ethnically based local authorities. Political stability often rests on an unstable coalition of patrons and clients who extract large amounts of national income through personal networks, intimidation, corruption, and bribes.[1] In these kinds of "failed states," public policy is influenced more by a political calculation to retain the privileges of power than by the political authorities' credibly committed to improve growth and welfare. The recent spread of democratic institutions like multiparty politics has improved accountability, but stability and violence are often more pressing concerns. It is difficult for people to prosper under this kind of uncertainty, unless of course they have access to a personal network of patrons and clients that defines the resources available to them.

Department of Economics, University of Michigan, Ann Arbor, 48109. This chapter has benefited from seminars at Washington University in St. Louis, the University of Michigan, and Harvard University. I thank Nathan Nunn for very helpful editorial comments and Rob Gillezeau for research assistance. Remaining errors are mine.

1 See Pitcher, Moran, and Johnston (2009) for a critical discussion of the term *patrimonial*. They argue against the use of the term. I agree with their critique, especially the charge that as a Weberian concept patrimonialism is inappropriately applied. I use the term to characterize a historically specific solution to a political problem faced by many emerging postcolonial nation-states in Africa. My meaning is similar to the political formations described in Van de Walle (2001), Boone (2003), Chabal and Daloz (1999), and Bates (2008), and is similar in many ways to Greif's (1994) description of medieval Genoa before the Podesta, except the clients here are customary local authorities.

What are the historical origins of this type of political system? The traditional view links it to the era of colonial rule and how it birthed a disjointed and decentralized nation-state. Mamdani (1996) is perhaps the best-known proponent of this view. He sees the most important political outcome of colonial rule to be a kind of dual legal system – European laws for colonial rulers and a variety of "customary" laws for colonial "subjects." In a very real sense, the postcolonial nation-state is the colonial state adjusted to new political realities like democratic elections, new global economic forces, stronger internal challenges, and mounting international debt.

In this chapter, I argue that the historical roots go deeper than colonialism and can be found in the absolutist authority structures that emerged out of the slave trade era. To make my case, I link the data on slave exports found in the *Transatlantic Slave Trade Database* with data on authority structures found in *Ethnographic Atlas* (Murdock 1967). My purpose is to see if the transatlantic slave trade transformed local political authority in Africa prior to colonial occupation. I find that it did. I then suggest ways in which indirect colonial rule institutionalized these authority structures and transformed them into a kind of local rule of law that continues to extract surplus and challenge federal authority today.

15.1 THE SEARCH FOR ORIGINS AND PATH DEPENDENCE

In his book *States and Power in Africa*, Jeffrey Herbst (2000) advances the idea that African political authority is ancient in origin and rooted in Africa's harsh physical environment, an environment that has always constrained population growth and elites' capacity to broadcast political power. Herbst argues that low population density constrained the reach of political authority long before colonial rule. In fact, colonial authorities wrestled with the same physical constraints and failed, leaving behind a state apparatus too weak to govern effectively over its exogenously created political territories.

Herbst is not the only scholar to invoke labor scarcity to explain an African institution. Anthony Hopkins (1973), in his widely read economic history of Africa, uses labor scarcity to explain technological choices and the institution of slavery. John Iliffe (2007), the renowned historian of Africa, uses labor scarcity to explain the institution of polygyny. Gareth Austin (2008) revises and extends the application of the idea and James Fenske (2010) applies it to property rights.

I believe there is a fundamental truth in this idea. Following the showing of the film *Eve*, which argues that ancient Africans migrated out of

Africa and populated the world, I ask my class: "If Africans could populate the world, then why couldn't they populate Africa?" If Africa was labor scarce, then certainly it was because of the environment and not the people. The major problem with this view is not consistency but lack of evidence. There are no census counts of an Africa population prior to the nineteenth century, and the widely used estimates for earlier times found in McEvedy and Jones (1978) are educated guesses and the extrapolations of current estimates back in time. These types of exercises rely on a variety of counterfactual assumptions regarding historical rates of population growth and the impact of the slave trades on African populations (see Manning 1990).

Here I take a different approach. I use the fact that slave exports reduced African population. I then look to see if cross-sectional variations in slave exports can explain cross-sectional variations in institutions that others have attributed to environmentally induced labor scarcity. Thanks to the *Trans-Atlantic Slave Trade Database*, some slave exports can now be measured with a high degree of precision. In a very real sense, a focus on the slave trade opens the door to an empirically grounded assessment of the population hypothesis, albeit a door with a slightly different view. Rather than seeing labor scarcity as the result of a steadfast environmental constraint, a focus on the slave trade emphasizes an economic shock to Africa.[2]

This shock certainly reduced population, but it also set off a chain reaction of warfare and raiding among African societies that "changed the way wars were waged at the lowest level" (Thornton 1999, 151). Robin Law, in his study of the Slave Coast, concludes that "by the end of the seventeenth century, the European demand for slaves had brought about a profound transformation of African societies of the Slave Coast. Although this was primarily an economic transformation, it had dramatic effects in the political sphere also, in the collapse of political order leading to the rise of the new state of Dahomey" (Law 1991, 345). One finds similar conclusions in Barry's (1998) study of the Senegambia region and Daaku's (1970) study of the Gold Coast. Inikori (1982, 2003) argues that the slave trade encouraged the formation and spread of banditry and small militarized states. And in a review of Herbst's *States and Power in Africa*, James Robinson argues that we should "hypothesize that slavery-induced predatory institutions had significant adverse influence on development paths not just in the Americas where the slaves were used, but also in Africa where the slaves

[2] For two estimates of this shock, see Whatley and Gillezeau (2011a) and Gemery and Hogendorn (1979).

originated.... Nonetheless, this is ultimately an empirical issue" (Robinson 2002, 517–18).

A decade later, and with a few notable exceptions, the idea that the slave trade altered African political institutions remains largely untested. Whatley and Gillezeau (2011a) model both effects mentioned previously. They treat the slave trade as an increase in the market value of anyone who can be enslaved. The shock alters factor prices in a way that mimics labor scarcity, but it also turns political incentives to build states into economic incentives to raid for slaves. The model predicts decentralized and militarized absolutist political authorities more interested in raiding for slaves than growing citizens. Nunn and Wantchekon (2011) present evidence showing that centuries of slaving in Africa fomented mistrust among people and toward their institutions, and that this slavery-induced mistrust persists to today. Whatley and Gillezeau (2011b) present evidence that the slave trade increased ethnic fragmentation in Africa and that this too persists to today. Nunn (2008) finds that slaving hampered long-term economic progress. Among the many possible channels is its impact on economic and political institutions.

In this chapter, I follow these leads and ask if the slave trade influenced the institutions of authority in Africa and whether these influences persist over the long term. I am not concerned with assessing the relative importance of environment versus shock. It could very well be the case that the slave trade merely tightened a labor constraint that had been binding for millennia. I do not offer a way to distinguish between these two views, nor am I particularly concerned to. My goal is more limited: to trace the long-term effects of the slave trade on the evolution of political authority in Africa.

As such, the effects, if any, must pass through colonialism. Did slavery-induced precolonial authority structures survive colonialism? The literature is surprisingly silent on this question. Herbst devotes an entire chapter of *States and Power* to a discussion of authority in precolonial Africa, but he never mentions the transatlantic slave trade (Herbst 2000, 35–57). Recent econometric studies of African political economy show how remnants of precolonial authority continue to influence local outcomes in Africa, but none of these studies considers the possibility that the precolonial legacies they identify are traditions of authority that date back to the slave trade (Englebert 2000; Gennaioli and Rainer 2007; Michalopoulos and Papaioannou 2010, 2011). Historians consider the link between the slave trade and African politics, but, with the exception of a few radical historians like Walter Rodney (1972) and Basil Davidson (1992), they are not particularly interested in the long-term impact on development.

Causal history is. It is an empirical project expressly designed to statistically identify and estimate causal relationships between past events and subsequent outcomes (see Nunn 2009 and Fenske 2010 for recent reviews). This line of research often produces the first salvo in the search for historical legacies, and institutions often take center stage as carriers of legacies.[3] Like a pulling guard on the gridiron, causal history suggests that some paths forward are more likely than others. The actual play, however, unfolds on the ground. As Paul David put it in his classic article on the economics of QWERTY, "it is sometimes not possible to uncover the logic (or illogic) of the world around us except by understanding *how* it got that way" (David 1985, 332). Avner Grief (2006) has theorized on the concept "path of play" in historical settings and has focused attention on how self-enforcing institutions of social cooperation (the shared playbook in our football analogy) can order how the play unfolds.

In the remainder of this chapter I follow the leads of this causal history of Africa and trace the impact of participation in the transatlantic slave trade on the evolution of political authority. I present econometric evidence showing how the transatlantic slave trade caused the spread of absolutism in sub-Saharan West Africa. I argue that slavery-induced absolutism also influenced the way politics were played in the colonial era and beyond. I present aggregate evidence that British colonies that exported more slaves were ruled less directly by colonial administrations. I argue that indirect colonial rule instead institutionalized these slavery-induced absolutist authority structures and transformed them into a kind of rule of law at the local level. The postcolonial nation-state, like the colonial state before it, lacks the administrative apparatus or the political clout to govern effectively over these local authorities, even when it wants to. From this perspective, the structure of many postcolonial nation-states in Africa is rooted in a political history that is unique to Africa in many respects, a history that stretches at least as far back as the era of the transatlantic slave trade.

15.2 THE TRANSATLANTIC SLAVE TRADE AND POLITICAL AUTHORITY IN AFRICA

Slave trading in Africa has a long and nuanced history. How are we to think of it as a shock to Africa? It is best to begin with the position of Africa in medieval Mediterranean civilization. Italian city-states, Arab caliphates, and European kingdoms all used conquest and trade to obtain

[3] On path dependence as legacy in competitive equilibrium, see Arrow (2004).

treasure, land, and slaves. Muslim and Christian armies fought "just" war that justified the enslavement of nonbelievers. Roman and Islamic law contained well-developed civil codes regulating the legal status of slaves (Patterson 1982).

The southern frontier of this system was Africa, down its east coast by sea and across the Sahara desert by camel. By the middle of the fifteenth century, lateen sails enabled Portuguese caravels to sail down the west coast of Africa as well. Then came the discovery of the Americas, the decimation of American populations, and the transplantation of slave codes across the Atlantic. In the hands of the emerging capitalist nations of Europe, the proximity of cheap African labor was an opportunity to profit from and defend their American colonies. By the beginning of the eighteenth century an old sporadic long-distance African trade in slaves had become *the* export engine of growth (Bean 1974; Eltis 1994; Eltis and Jennings 1994; Gemery and Hogendorn 1990). The real price of slave exports rose 500 percent during the eighteenth century (Eltis and Richardson 2004; Richardson 1991). Exports increased by 1,000 percent (Eltis 2009).

Asking about the effects of these slave trades on the evolution of political authority in Africa might seem farfetched, but we can focus the question and break it down into stages. Nunn (2008) asks if there is a correlation between the numbers of slaves coming out of different regions of Africa and the economic performance of those regions today. His is an ambitious attempt to locate and count up all of the slaves taken by the trans-Saharan, Indian Ocean, Red Sea, and transatlantic trades. He then looks to see if slave exports in the past correlate with GDP levels today. After controlling for a variety of other factors that might explain the correlation, including reverse causality, he concludes that slaving and slave trading depressed long-term economic growth. His estimates of slave exports have been used by Nunn and Wantchekon (2011), Whatley and Gillezeau (2011b), and others.

Here I adopt a slightly different empirical approach, one designed to better isolate the slave trade as a shock to Africa. First, I limit the analysis to the transatlantic slave trade because these data are much more reliable than data on the trans-Saharan, Red Sea, or Indian Ocean trades. The transatlantic slave trade evolved as a core component of European mercantile systems operating in the Atlantic. Records of ship manifests, government agencies, insurance companies, and newspapers have been digitized into the widely used *Trans-Atlantic Slave Trade Database*. Estimates of the Muslim-based trades are much less reliable in terms of volume, dates, and places (Austen 1979, 1987).

Second, I confine my analysis to the transatlantic slave trade on the west coast of Africa. After 1807 the transatlantic slave trade expanded on the east coast of Africa to avoid British efforts to suppress the trade on the west coast. I exclude the east coast extension because East African societies had previously been influenced by the Indian Ocean and Red Sea trades, for which slave export data are much less precise.

Third, there is little evidence of slave trading along the west coast of Africa prior to the transatlantic slave trade. Evidence on West African slave trading in the fifteenth and early sixteenth centuries is very thin (Fage 1980). Most of the slave trading in the Upper Guinea Coast and in the Western Sudan were southern extensions of the Muslim-based Mediterranean systems, and were centered on Lake Chad and the interior delta of the Niger River (Fisher 2001; Lovejoy 2004). Rodney (1966) surveys evidence for the Upper Guinea Coast and finds slaves as servants in the households of elites, as elsewhere in the Mediterranean world, but little evidence of the kind of systematic slave raiding and slave marketing that would become the norm centuries later.

True, by the time the Portuguese arrived on the Lower Guinea Coast in the late fifteenth century the Muslim-based network had extended as far south as the Gold Coast of present-day Ghana. Wilks (1993) documents how Muslim traders from the north supplied the gold-mining Akan of Ghana with the slave workforce they needed to clear their rainforests for agriculture. Not to be outdone, Portuguese traders stimulated a second slave trade into the Akan gold fields. They sailed yachts back and forth along the Lower Guinea Coast, purchasing war captives from Benin's political expansion further down the coast and selling them to the Akan for their gold. (Graham 1965; Ryder 1969; Wilks 1982). These are certainly slave trades and they certainly predate the eighteenth-century explosion in the transatlantic trade, but they are long-distance slave trades and precisely because societies along the west coast of Africa were much less predatory than they would become by the eighteenth century (Daaku 1970; Law 1991; Thornton 1999).

Finally, not only is the magnitude of the shock and its timing better measured on the west coast of Africa, so too is its location. Most of the thirty-four thousand voyages found in the *Trans-Atlantic Slave Trade Database* have some information on the location of slave purchases. Sometimes location is by port. I use GIS software to merge the locations of ports with the locations of societies found in Murdock's *Ethnographic Atlas*. Murdock's goal was to code the ethnographic features of societies prior to substantial European influence. I look to see if slaving influenced these authority structures, so in a sense I am testing Murdock too.

Figure 15.1 depicts how I merged the two data sets. The mapping of subnational societies comes from the digitized version of the map found in Murdock's (1967) *Ethnographic Atlas*. I overlay on top of this the locations of the slave ports found in the *Transatlantic Slave Trade Database*. These are denoted by the stars along the coast. I then construct two hundred observations from the merged spatial data. I divide the west coast of Africa into two hundred evenly spaced points, each fifty kilometers apart, running from Tunis, Tunisia to Cape Town, South Africa. The dependent and independent variables are constructed from spatial data that fall within predefined buffers around these points. These are depicted by the circles in Figure 15.1.

The treatment variable is the numbers of slaves exported from ports in these buffers (SLAVES). Environmental controls are the average values of environmental features inside these buffers (X): forest and desert coverage, elevation, local agricultural suitability as measured by climate and terrain slope, and population density in 1960 (UNESCO 2010; USGS 2010; IIASA 2010). The dependent variables are three authority types derived from variable V72 in *Ethnographic Atlas* called "Succession to the Office of Local Headman." This variable is dichotomized three different ways. ABSOLUTIST = 1 for Murdock's code 1 = "patrilineal heir," and code 2 = "matrilineal heir;" ABSOLUTIST = 0 otherwise. LIBERAL = 1 for Murdock's code 5 = "influence, wealth or social status, nonhereditary;" LIBERAL = 0 otherwise. DEMOCRATIC = 1 for Murdock's code 6 = "election or other formal consensus, nonhereditary;" DEMOCRATIC = 0 otherwise.

Table 15.1 reports unweighted means. The first three columns report means for the Western sample, the full 200 buffer sample covering the western half of the continent of Africa from Tunis, Tunisia to Cape Town, South Africa. The top panel is for buffers with a 250 km radius. The bottom panel is for buffers with a 500 km radius. On average, 316,050 slaves were exported from each of the 200 buffers with a 250 km radius.[4] One

[4] This implies more than 100 million slave exports, but the *Transatlantic Slave Trade Database* contains information on approximately 13 million slave exports. The discrepancy is due to the overlap of buffers causing each port's slave exports to be recorded more than one time. The center of each buffer is 50 kms away from the next center. With a radius of 250 km (or a diameter of 500 km) the ports are canvassed once if we take the average exports of every tenth buffer: 200/10=20, which yields 20 x 316,050 = 6,321,000 slave exports. The *Transatlantic Slave Trade Database* has specific port information for approximately 6,494,200 West African slave exports, so our ports pick up the vast majority of slave exports that have information on port.

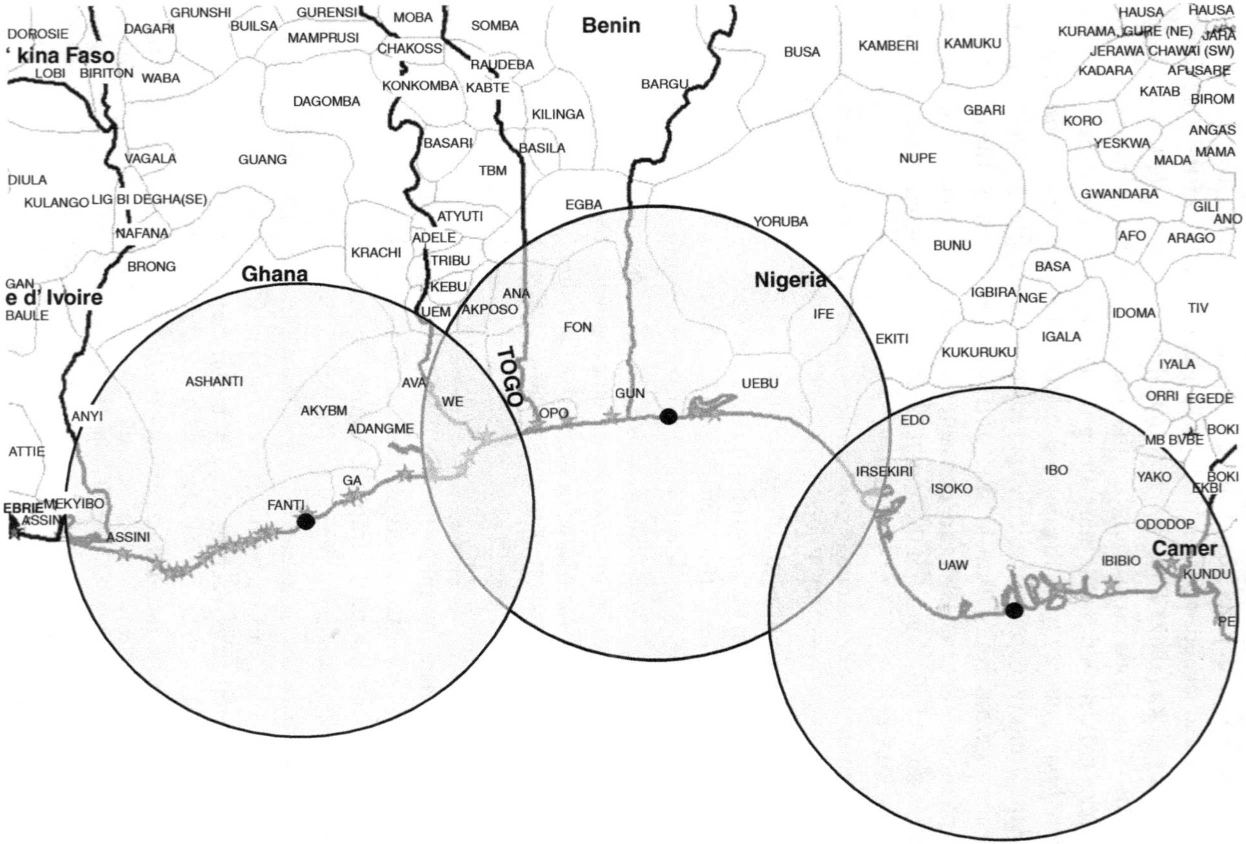

Figure 15.1. Merging the *Transatlantic Slave Trade Database* and *Ethnographic Atlas*.

Table 15.1. *Sample means*

	Western sample			Atlantic sample			Sub-Saharan sample		
	N	Mean	SD	N	Mean	SD	N	Mean	SD
250 km radius buffers									
Slave Exports (000)	200	316.05	225.62	169	374.02	238.34	131	482.52	255.32
Absolute Authority	117	0.62	0.41	86	0.84	0.20	48	0.88	0.18
Democratic Authority	117	0.16	0.30	86	0.07	0.17	48	0.04	0.13
Liberal Authority	117	0.03	0.13	86	0.03	0.10	48	0.00	0.00
Agricultural Suitability	200	2.89	1.10	169	2.99	1.11	131	2.83	0.99
Population in 1960	200	10.73	15.36	169	9.36	15.81	131	9.91	16.74
Elevation	200	12.56	6.58	169	11.95	6.31	131	12.12	6.18
Forest	200	0.15	0.24	169	0.16	0.26	131	0.19	0.28
Desert	200	0.54	0.65	169	0.53	0.69	131	0.34	0.59
500 km radius buffers									
Slave Exports (000)	200	632.1	392.70	169	748.05	407.97	131	965.04	424.58
Absolute Authority	180	0.59	0.39	149	0.71	0.31	111	0.80	0.21
Democratic Authority	180	0.17	0.26	149	0.13	0.24	111	0.06	0.09

(*continued*)

Table 15.1. (*continued*)

	Western sample			Atlantic sample			Sub-Saharan sample		
	N	Mean	SD	N	Mean	SD	N	Mean	SD
Liberal Authority	180	0.03	0.11	149	0.04	0.12	111	0.02	0.03
Agricultural Suitability	200	2.89	1.30	169	2.90	1.29	131	2.71	1.17
Population in 1960	200	7.00	8.66	169	6.20	8.56	131	6.56	9.04
Elevation	200	13.09	7.64	169	12.80	7.37	131	12.87	7.54
Forest	200	0.27	0.47	169	0.30	0.50	131	0.36	0.55
Desert	200	1.10	1.45	169	1.02	1.51	131	0.60	1.34

Notes: *N* is the number of observations or buffers with non-missing data. Means are the unweighted averages of observations in the sample. SD is sample standard deviation.

Sources: I divide the west coast of Africa into 200 evenly spaced points starting at the northernmost point of Tunisia and ending at the middle of South Africa. Variables are constructed from spatial data falling within a radius of 250 km or 500 km around these points. The Western sample contains all 200 buffers, from Tunis, Tunisia to Cape Town, South Africa. The Atlantic sample runs from Gibraltar to Cape Town. The sub-Saharan sample runs from Cape Blanc to Cape Town. SLAVES are in thousands (0,000) of slaves exported from ports that fall within a buffer (Eltis 2009). Environmental controls are forest and desert coverage, elevation, local agricultural suitability as measured by climate and terrain slope, and population density in 1960 (UNESCO 2010; USGS 2010; IIASA 2010). Authority code variable V72 in the *Ethnographic Atlas* (Murdock 1967) called "Succession to the Office of Local Headman." V72 is dichotomized three different ways. ABSOLUTIST = 1 for Murdock's code 1 = "patrilineal heir," and category 2 = "matrilineal heir;" ABSOLUTIST = 0 otherwise. LIBERAL = 1 for Murdock's code 5 = "influence, wealth or social status, nonhereditary;" LIBERAL = 0 otherwise. DEMOCRATIC = 1 for Murdock's category 6 = "election or other formal consensus, nonhereditary;" DEMOCRATIC = 0 otherwise.

hundred seventeen of the 200 buffers have at least one ethnic group with information on authority type. The unweighted average shows 62 percent of the societies being governed by absolutist authority, 16 percent being governed by democratic authority, and only 3 percent with liberal or wealth-based access to authority. One hundred eighty of the 500 km buffers have information on authority type. The number of hits is larger because the larger buffers cover more territory and have a higher probability of containing at least one ethnic group with information on authority type.

The next three columns report means for the Atlantic sample, which begins at approximately Gibraltar and runs to Cape Town. This sample covers the African coastline that faces the Atlantic Ocean and the Americas. It excludes the African coast that faces the Mediterranean. The number of observations falls to 169. The average number of slaves per observation increases to 374,020. Absolutism increases to 84 percent.

The third sample is the sub-Saharan sample, and begins near Cape Blanc on the southern edge of the Sahara desert. The number of observations declines to 131, slave exports increase to 482,520, and absolutism increases to 88 percent. All of the slaves in all of the samples were captured and exported from sub-Saharan Africa. The sample on authority type gets small (48 observations), but it serves as a check on the others by making sure the estimated impact of exports on authority are not being identified off of unobserved regional heterogeneity.

The null hypothesis is loosely derived from Whatley and Gillezeau (2011a), where slaving is modeled as a violent production process – what Patterson (1982) calls "social death." The increased violence increases individuals' demands for protection – a public good best provided by political authorities who have the power to authorize and coordinate a defense (or offense). Like all individuals in times of war, individuals subject to slave capture will pay more for protection, including relinquishing freedoms and rights that might otherwise be cherished in times of peace. It is not inconceivable that centuries of slaving created an environment where peace had become a distant memory – where a state of war seemed like a natural state of affairs. A rough calculation reported in Whatley and Gillezeau (2011a) estimates that between 1700 and 1850 a West African person faced a one in five chance of being swept up in the transatlantic slave trade sometime in his life. Under these conditions it is not inconceivable that individuals will relinquish political rights and accept absolute rulers (Bates, Grief, and Singh 2002). It is not inconceivable for political authority to become more absolutist in nature where previously there had been some semblance of democratic or liberal influence on authority.

I look for evidence of this by performing the following OLS regressions:

$$\text{AUTHORITY TYPE}_{ji} = \alpha + \beta \text{ SLAVES}_i + \Omega \text{ X}_i + v_i$$

Observations are buffers. AUTHORITY TYPE_{ji} is the average value of AUTHORITY TYPE_j (ABSOLUTE, LIBERAL OR DEMOCRATIC) for ethnic groups whose centroid falls in buffer *i*. SLAVES_i is the total number of slaves exported from the slave ports in buffer *i*. Environmental variables are mean values for spaces in buffers. X_i is the vector of environmental control variables. v_i is the error term. The larger circular buffers reach farther inland, but they overlap more along the coast. I calculate Conley standard errors to account for spatial correlation in the errors across observations.

OLS results are reported in the columns labeled OLS in Table 15.2. In the 250 km samples, slave exports are positively and statistically significantly correlated with absolutist authority. All of the estimated coefficients are positive and significant at the 99 percent confidence level. The correlation is also large. Mean slave exports explain between 16 and 40 percent of the absolutism recorded in *Ethnographic Atlas*. In the sub-Saharan sample the correlation is also significant and large, so the relationship between slaving and absolutism is not due to unobserved regional heterogeneity.

I interpret these correlations as if the direction of causality ran from slaving to absolutism, but there could be some reverse causation in the estimated relationship. Absolutist authority, for example, could have been a more efficient way to organize slave raids, giving rise to a reverse correlation running from absolutism to slave exports. Also, Whatley and Gillezeau (2011a) discuss conditions under which absolutist rulers might authorize halfhearted defenses of their people. Coalition building across ethnic groups required some degree of power sharing among elites, but if elites can insulate themselves from capture, and if they care little about the welfare of their people, then they may prefer to leave their people exposed to capture so long as they themselves are safe. This outcome is more likely where authority is inherited and absolute, and less likely in democratic systems where leaders are held accountable.

In an effort to identify a causal relationship that runs from slaving to absolutism I perform a two-stage instrumental variables estimation of the relationship between slaving and absolutism. In the first stage I seek a set of exogenous predictors of slave exports that are uncorrelated with the error terms $v_{i.}$. Here I make use of the instruments developed by Nunn

Table 15.2. *The impact of the transatlantic slave trade on absolutist authority in West Africa*

	Western sample		Atlantic sample		Sub-Saharan sample	
	OLS	IV	OLS	IV	OLS	IV
	250 km radius for buffer					
(β) Est. coefficient on slave exports (000,000)	0.0779***	0.0590	0.0380***	0.0755***	0.0412***	0.0636***
Conley standard errors	0.0230	0.1367	0.0116	0.0197	0.0133	0.0156
Environmental controls	YES	YES	YES	YES	YES	YES
Number of observations	117	117	86	86	48	48
Adjusted R-squared	0.4393		0.1833		0.4236	
Hansen-Sargan test of overid. restrictions		4.07		0.01		4.76
($\bar{X}$) Mean slave exports (000,000)	3.260	3.260	3.740	3.740	4.825	4.825
($\bar{Y}$) Mean pct. with Absolute Authority	62.19	62.19	84.02	84.02	88.1	88.1
$\beta^*\bar{X}^*100$	25.40	19.23	14.20	28.24	19.87	30.67
Pct. of Absolutism ($\bar{Y}$) explained by ($\bar{X}$)	40.84	30.92	16.90	33.61	22.56	**34.81**
	500 km radius for buffer					
(β) Est. coefficient on slave exports (000,000)	0.0225*	0.177***	0.0040	0.0342	0.0080	0.0134
Conley standard errors	0.0157	0.0079	0.0105	0.0431	0.0082	0.0129
Environmental controls	YES	YES	YES	YES	YES	YES
Number of observations	180	180	149	149	111	111
Adjusted R-squared	0.2234		0.0535		0.3781	
Hansen-Sargan test of overid. restrictions		10.03		6.16		1.91
($\bar{X}$) Mean slave exports (000,000)	6.321	6.321	7.480	7.480	9.650	9.650
($\bar{Y}$) Mean pct. with Absolute Authority	58.72	58.72	70.94	70.94	79.78	79.78
$\beta^*\bar{X}^*100$	14.21	11.2	3.00	25.56	7.68	12.91
Pct. of Absolutism ($\bar{Y}$) explained by ($\bar{X}$)	24.19	190.82	4.23	36.03	9.62	16.19

Notes: Dependent variable = Pct. of societies with ABSOLUTIST authority; the coefficients in the columns labeled "OLS" are estimated OLS. The two-stage estimates in the column labeled "IV" were estimated GMM. *** denotes 99 percent confidence level. ** denotes 95 percent confidence level. * denotes 90 percent confidence level. All two-tail tests. The Hansen-Sargan test statistic of over-identification restrictions is distributed Chi-Square with two degrees of freedom. The critical value for the 90 percent confidence level is 4.61. Conley standard errors allowed for spatial correlation over five contiguous buffers for the 250 km buffers and over ten contiguous buffers for the 500 km buffers.

Sources: See Table 15.1.

(2008), which in this case are the distances between the center of each buffer and the nearest destination in the Americas and North Africa.[5] These distances, plus the environmental controls, capture variations in slave exports that are not likely to be correlated with authority type. In the second stage I look for correlations between estimated slave exports and absolutism. In the second stage I also control for the impact of environment on the adoption of absolutist authority. I rely on Hansen-Sargan tests of over-identification restrictions to test for the absence of correlations with the error terms v_i.

In Table 15.3 I report first-stage regressions of slave exports on distance and environmental controls. These are reduced form equations, so it is difficult to interpret coefficients, but the F-statistics and the R-squares show that the exogenous regressors capture a significant amount of the variation in slave exports. In general, distance to the Americas offered some protection against capture. Also, fewer slaves were exported from desert regions and from higher elevations. This could be due to fewer people living in these regions, but some of the population effect is already captured by the variables measuring agricultural suitability and 1960 population, so desert and elevated regions may have also provided some refuge from slavers (Nunn and Puga 2012).

The second-stage results are reported in the columns labeled IV in Table 15.2. In the Western sample of 250 km buffers, the coefficient on slave exports loses statistical significance, but as we move toward sub-Saharan Africa the estimated coefficients get larger and tighter. In the sub-Saharan sample, 16.9–34.8 percent of average observed absolutism is explained by average slave exports. The relationship between slave exports and absolutism is less apparent in the 500 km samples. All of the coefficients are still positive, but they fail to achieve significance, except in the Western sample. It is not clear why this is the case. One possibility is that the impact of slaving is less direct farther inland. Most of the slaves pulled into the orbit of the transatlantic slave trade originated within 250–300 kilometers of the coast, although after the late eighteenth century higher slave prices covered longer treks to the coast. There are forty-eight observations in the sub-Saharan sample that have both 250 km and 500 km buffers. Absolutism is 88 percent in the smaller buffer but declines to 72 percent in the larger buffers that reach farther inland. The student-t statistic on difference in means is 3.46.

5 The American destinations are Virginia, Havana, Haiti, Kingston, Dominica, Guyana, Salvador, and Rio de Janeiro; and the North African destinations are Algiers, Tunis, Tripoli, Benghazi, and Cairo.

Table 15.3. *First-stage IV regressions*

	250 km radius buffer			500 km radius buffer		
	Western sample	Atlantic sample	Sub-Saharan sample	Western sample	Atlantic sample	Sub-Saharan sample
Distance to American destinations	−4.38***	−3.04*	−5.74	−7.46***	−5.84**	10.81
	(1.23)	(2.10)	(8.76)	(2.26)	(3.06)	(17.39)
Distance to N. African destinations	−2.23	3.80	0.74	−5.20	3.93	30.93
	(2.95)	(8.39)	(16.79)	(4.50)	(14.68)	(35.26)
Agricultural suitability	32.57***	50.19**	18.97	152.76***	181.57***	142.95*
	(1.23)	(30.71)	(37.96)	(51.63)	(60.40)	(82.21)
Population in 1960	4.24***	3.92	4.74*	10.17**	11.45**	6.94
	(1.60)	(4.88)	(2.47)	(5.65)	(6.91)	(5.97)
Elevation	−10.01***	−14.19***	−13.23***	−24.45***	−31.75***	−21.75
	(3.73)	(4.88)	(6.44)	(7.50)	(9.97)	(16.00)
Forest	165.77	140.03	164.67	297.00*	275.11*	283.91*
	(169.24)	(177.82)	(182.24)	(157.91)	(160.36)	(159.08)
Desert	−88.67**	−114.67**	−132.72**	−105.47***	−113.82**	−113.60**
	(35.56)	(51.61)	(56.86)	(39.76)	(53.62)	(53.75)
Constant	540.60**	154.63	538.73	884.87***	316.41	−2061.30
	(223.24)	(536.71)	(1378.22)	(324.80)	(881.03)	(2792.58)
Number of observations	200	169	131	200	169	131
Adjusted R-Squared	0.3515	0.3367	0.2865	0.6037	0.5941	0.5286
F-statistic	16.41	13.18	8.46	44.31	36.13	21.82

Notes: Dependent variable = slave exports in thousands; coefficients estimated OLS. Conley standard errors in parentheses. *** denotes 99 percent confidence level. ** denotes 95 percent confidence level. * denotes 90 percent confidence level. All two-tail tests. Conley standard errors allow for spatial correlation over five contiguous buffers for the 250 km buffers and over ten contiguous buffers for the 500 km buffers.
Sources: See Table 15.1.

Not finding significant effects farther inland does not necessarily mean the impact of the slave trade was limited to the coast, although it does mean the issue deserves further investigation. The relationship could have becomes less direct and more complex as the process moved inland. Also, the inland areas were subject to slave raiding for shorter periods of time, so inland peasants might have been more successful at resisting extreme revolutions in authority. The empirical strategy in this essay captures only revolutionary changes across categories of authority, from non-absolutist to absolutist. It does not capture increases in the degree of absolutism within authority types, something that was undoubtedly occurring as well.

This interpretation finds some support in the regression for democracy and liberalism. These are reported in Tables 15.4 and 15.5. First note that all of the estimated coefficients have negative signs. Slaving tended to reduce liberalism and democracy. There are no liberal societies in the 250 km sub-Saharan sample, but there are some in the sample that reaches 500 km inland. Slaving reduced liberalism, even in the interior of sub-Saharan Africa. The results for democracy are also negative, but they never achieve statistical significance in the sub-Saharan sample. Perhaps the designation "democratic" is flexible enough to absorb elements of absolutism while retaining some degree of accountability, like in the case of the Asante kingdom situated inland from the Gold Coast (Rattray 1929; Wilks 1975).

Patriarchy is another form of authority, and George Murdock (1949, 1967) claims to have theoretically proven that much of the patriliny in precolonial West Africa was of recent historical origin. His proof is based on the observation that many precolonial West African societies with patrilineal rules of descent retained legacy kinship terms more appropriate for other lineage systems. Not being a historian, and having never set foot in Africa, Murdock never claimed that the slave trade transformed lineage rules, but his list of possible causes could have easily included it. Basil Davidson, the preeminent historian of Africa who chronicled Africa's history from slavery to the present, does highlight slaving. He states, "As the slaving state became increasingly a predator, kinship systems were strengthened and elaborated as a means of providing protection against the dangers of the violence created by the slave trade" (Davidson 1992, 266). Predation not only shifted more power onto already powerful men but it may have also, as Ekeh argues, increased the "entrenchment of kinship corporation" (1990, 660).

Table 15.4. *The impact of the transatlantic slave trade on LIBERAL authority in West Africa*

	Western sample		Atlantic sample		Sub-Saharan sample	
	OLS	IV	OLS	IV	OLS	IV
	250 km radius for buffer					
(β) Est. coefficient on slave exports (000,000)	−0.0084	−0.0247	−0.0068*	−0.0044	NA	NA
Conley standard errors	0.0063	0.0269	0.0041	0.0063		
Environmental controls	YES	YES	YES	YES		
Number of observations	117	117	86	86		
Adjusted R-squared	0.0313		0.11			
Hansen-Sargan test of overid. restrictions		0.83		3.363		
	500 km radius for buffer					
(β) Est. coefficient on slave exports (000,000)	−0.0037*	−0.0084	−0.0057**	−0.0125**	−0.0031**	−0.0070**
Conley standard errors	0.0022	0.0087	0.0024	0.0056	0.0016	0.0031
Environmental controls	YES	YES	YES	YES	YES	YES
Number of observations	180	180	149	149	111	111
Adjusted R-squared	0.1671		0.1759		0.2823	
Hansen-Sargan test of overid. restrictions		1.66		0.0010		2.37

Notes: Dependent variable = Pct. of polities with LIBERAL authority; the coefficients in the columns labeled "OLS" are estimated OLS. The two-stage estimates in the columns labeled "IV" were estimated GMM. *** denotes 99 percent confidence level. ** denotes 95 percent confidence level. * denotes 90 percent confidence level. All two-tail tests. The Hansen-Sargan test statistic of over-identification restrictions is distributed Chi-Square with two degrees of freedom. The critical value for the 90 percent confidence level is 4.61. Conley standard errors allowed for spatial correlation over five contiguous buffers for the 250 km buffers and over ten contiguous buffers for the 500 km buffers.

Sources: See Table 15.1.

Table 15.5. *The impact of the transatlantic slave trade on democratic authority in West Africa*

	Western sample		Atlantic sample		Sub-Saharan sample	
	OLS	IV	OLS	IV	OLS	IV
	250 km radius for buffer					
(β) Est. coefficient on slave exports (000,000)	−0.0456**	−0.0357	−0.0081	−0.0210*	−0.0067	−0.0044
Conley standard errors	0.0196	0.1211	0.0057	0.0126	0.0053	0.0071
Environmental controls	YES	YES	YES	YES	YES	YES
Number of observations	117	117	86	86	48	48
Adjusted R-squared	0.1129		0.2174		0.6961	
Hansen-Sargan test of overid. restrictions		3.04		0.1483		1.52
	500 km radius for buffer					
(β) Est. coefficient on slave exports (000,000)	−0.0185**	−0.0935***	−0.0072	−0.0193	−0.0020	−0.0095
Conley standard errors	0.0083	0.0341	0.0064	0.0259	0.0041	0.0066
Environmental controls	YES	YES	YES	YES	YES	YES
Number of observations	180	180	149	149	111	111
Adjusted R-squared	0.1618		0.1188		0.2238	
Hansen-Sargan test of overid. restrictions		3.17		7.83		0.0820

Notes: Dependent variable = Pct. of polities with DEMOCRATIC authority; The coefficients in the columns labeled "OLS" are estimated OLS. The two-stage estimates in the column labeled "IV" were estimated GMM. *** denotes 99 percent confidence level. ** denotes 95 percent confidence level. * denotes 90 percent confidence level. All two-tail tests. The Hansen-Sargan test statistic of over-identification restrictions is distributed Chi-Square with two degrees of freedom. The critical value for the 90 percent confidence level is 4.61. Conley standard errors allowed for spatial correlation over five contiguous buffers for the 250 km buffers and over ten contiguous buffers for the 500 km buffers.
Sources: See Table 15.1.

15.3 FROM PREDATION TO RULE OF LAW

What about colonialism? How did colonialism interact with these new slavery-induced predatory political customs? Over the past decade a series of influential articles has laid the empirical foundation for approaching this type of question. One strand of this literature searches for the long-term impact of legal customs transplanted around the world by European colonizing authorities, contrasting primarily the experiences of common law countries and civil law countries (Glaeser and Shleifer 2002; La Porta 2008). Another series of articles by Acemoglu, Johnson, and Robinson (2001, 2002) emphasizes the long-run impact of colonial property rights laws laid down by European colonial authorities. In colonies where the colonizer's strategy (or capability) was to settle and produce, one tends to find property rights systems that constrain states' rights to expropriate surplus from producers. Where incentives to settle and produce were not so great, the colonial authority tended to establish institutions that facilitated resource extraction, and often by force. Over the long term, settler institutions encouraged economic development while extractive institutions did not.

These are useful perspectives, but one needs to be careful when applying them to Africa. Incorporating the transatlantic slave trade can help. First, Albouy (2013) argues that thus far the settler data are not good enough to test for the long-term effects of extraction versus settlement in Africa. The slave trade was definitely an extractive institution, and the numbers on exports are good measure of how extractive it was across time and space.

Second, it is important to note that prior to the Berlin Conference of 1885 the official colonization of Africa was confined to a few coastal protectorates. Most of Africa was officially colonized for less than seventy-five years, contrasting sharply with other areas of the world like the Americas, the Caribbean, India, and many parts of Asia. Acemoglu, Johnson, and Robinson (2001, footnote 1) interpret the slave trade as an extractive colonial institution, but others do not. Olsson (2009), for example, presents evidence that the length of colonial rule encouraged the development of democratic institutions over the long term, but they define colonialism in Africa as formal colonial occupation. Given the impact of the slave trade on political customs in Africa, incorporating the slave trade as a phase of colonialism might help explain why African democracy differs from democracy in other former colonies around the world.

Finally, Acemoglu and Johnson (2005) argue that property rights institutions have had a greater impact on structure and performance than have legal origins because inefficient legal rules can be circumvented by the private ordering of contracts (Grief 1989). There are a number of studies, however, documenting the lasting impact of legal origin in Africa, although the channels are not always clear. Colonies under British rule, and therefore administered by common law traditions, tend to exhibit higher postcolonial incomes per capita, more investments in education, and higher rates of school enrollment than do colonies administered by French civil codes (Bertocchi and Canova 2002; Grier 1999; Price 2003).

One possible explanation has to do with the way the legal customs of colonizer and colonized interacted to shape the institutions of colonial rule. Sir Frederick Lugard, first governor-general of the Colony and Protectorate of Nigeria, is generally considered the architect of the British policy of indirect rule, but Mamdani and Herbst argue that the policy evolved on the ground, as a solution to the problem of controlling colonial subjects. Mamdani (1996) argues that indirect colonial rule grew out of a recognition that direct rule, a single legal system encompassing colonizer and colonized but peppered with racial distinctions, was untenable in the long term because it encouraged class-based and race-based protests against injustices. Gradually colonial authorities moved toward a sharing of power with real or imagined local chiefs controlling real or imagined "customary" lands. Herbst (2000) argues that indirect rule evolved out of a colonial recognition that broadcasting centralized authority over African territory was too costly to be effective.

Here the legal customs of colonizers can matter in reshaping the political landscape. Firmin-Sellers (2000), for example, compares the institutions of French and English colonial rule among the ethnically similar Akan peoples who straddled the colonial border between the Ivory Coast and Ghana. Consistent with civil law tradition, the French colonial system was designed to achieve a clear directive from above: maximize tax collection. The French undermined the authority of paramount chiefs, chose lower-order divisional chiefs as their agents, took periodic censuses of the population to estimate potential tax revenue, paid chiefs a share of the taxes they collected, and monitored chiefs' performance by checking collected taxes against expected taxes.

The British, in contrast, careful not to undermine local custom (read common law), chose the higher-order paramount chiefs as their agents and allowed them to rule over the divisional chiefs and lineages below them. They paid chiefs a fixed salary and deposited tax collections in a public treasury for the development of public works. The British did not monitor chiefs' tax collection like the French did, but instead monitored chiefs' performance as public servants and administrators of justice. Based on this case study one would conclude that the French system was a more efficient

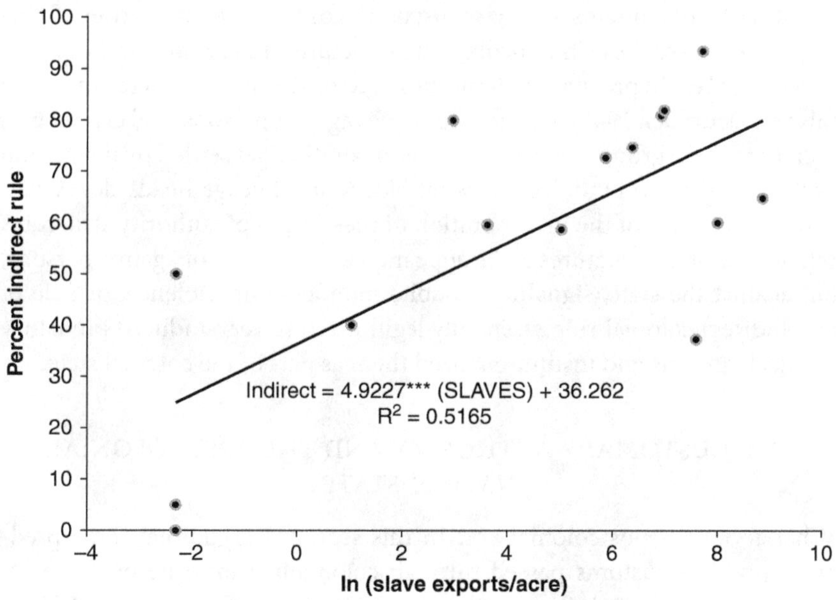

Figure 15.2. The slave trade and indirect rule.

system of resource extraction but perhaps less developmental than the British system.

One could also conclude that the colonial authorities, both French and British, empowered slavery-induced absolutist power structures. Figure 15.2 presents aggregate evidence that indirect colonial rule relied on the kind of absolutism that I estimated in the previous section. The figure graphs the relationship between slave exports and the degree of indirect rule among British colonies. The unit of analysis is the postcolonial nation-state. The sample is former British colonies in Africa. The measure of indirect rule is taken from Lange (2004, 2009) and is the percentage of legal cases adjudicated in African customary courts. Slave exports per acre are taken from Nunn (2008). The figure shows that indirect rule is positively and significantly correlated with past slave exports.

This is understandable. The colonial goal is to control population and extract surplus. The political objective of indirect colonial rule is to take the overlapping authorities that kin, clans, patriarchs, and elders previously used to adjudicate local conflict and invest them in a chief who now has the authority to rule over his people on behalf of the colonizer. Enlisting a powerful local authority was probably easier where the slave trade had already entrenched absolutist authority structures.

Bates (2010) contains a concise discussion of how the integration of kinship systems like these into formal state structures transforms local customs into rule of law. In pre-state systems the heads of kin and clan mete out justice (also see Murdock 1949). Crimes are crimes against persons, and crimes by a member of one group against a member of another get settled by intergroup exchange of some kind. This is what elders and lineage heads do. A reasonable indicator of the incorporation of these types of authority structures into formal state structures is the appearance of crimes, not against persons, but against the state, signaling a public monopoly on violence, or rule of law. Indirect colonial rule essentially legitimized slavery-induced predatory political customs and institutionalized them as part of the colonial state.[6]

15.4 CUSTOMARY AUTHORITY AND THE POSTCOLONIAL NATION-STATE

What about the postcolonial era? In this section I argue that these predatory political customs passed through colonialism into the postcolonial era and continue to influence the structure and performance of African political economies today. At the federal level is the disjointed postcolonial nation-state facing difficulty with broadcasting power. At the local level is absolutist customary authority. The poor governance, ethnic conflict, and corruption observed in many postcolonial African states are unstable equilibrium outcomes on the path of play among these parties (Bates 2008; Chabal and Daloz 1999; Herbst 2000; Lange 2009; Van de Walle 2001).

At the federal level, the path begins with the Berlin Conference of 1885 where European powers agreed to cooperate in carving Africa into territories that would become postcolonial nation-states. The process was swift, surgical, and haphazard, with colonial powers often drawing straight-line borders inland from the coast, and taking possession of real estate as quickly and as easily as they would eventually relinquish it. Davidson recounts the random and haphazard nature of colonial occupation on the Gold Coast. Noting that in the 1880s the king of Asante offered the British authorities monopoly control of all Asante trade, Davidson writes, "Now one might think that the British government, eager to acquire a monopoly of commercial control over West African lands, but far less eager to meet the almost certain high cost of conquest, would have jumped at this

6 Contrast these legal origins with the legal origins of common law in England, where custom came to rely on a judiciary independent of the king and lords, and based on trial by juries of peers. See Glaeser and Shleifer (2002) for an insightful discussion.

offer. But the British ministers in charge at home now wanted more than monopolistic commercial control; they wanted territorial ownership. Partly in order to keep out the French ..., but even more, as most evidence seems to show, because a demand for territorial ownership had become an imperial obsession and even a popular cause ... " (Davidson 1992, 70–1). But "no more than 60 years or so after preferring to invade ... British imperial government found that it had little to gain, after all, from territorial possession and reverted to the policy of withdrawal" (Davidson 1992, 72).

Lange (2004, 2009) tracks the evolution of federal authority from colonialism to the present among the former British colonies. He focuses on the disjointed postcolonial nation-state that emerged out of the dual legal systems of indirect rule. Lange shows how country-level measures of indirect rule (measured by the percent of legal cases adjudicated in customary courts) are highly correlated with poor governance structures today. Indirect colonial rule produced a postcolonial nation-state crippled by ineffective bureaucracy, restrictions on private contracting, weak rule of law, and widespread corruption.

Of course, indirect colonial rule could be correlated with poor postcolonial outcomes for other reasons. Iyer (2010), for example, shows how in British India colonial authorities indirectly ruled the poorer regions and directly ruled the richer ones. This kind of occupation strategy could produce the same correlation between indirect colonial rule and poor postcolonial governance that Lange finds in British Africa. As a preliminary check on this I take country-level population density in 1900 (from Nunn 2008) as a proxy for country income in 1900. A simple regression of indirect rule on population density has an insignificant and positive coefficient, not the significantly negative coefficient one would expect if indirect rule chased poor lands in Africa too.[7]

Given weak federal authority in postcolonial Africa, one should expect precolonial authorities to continue to assert themselves. Michalopoulos and Papaioannou (2010) use satellite light density at night to proxy for local economic development and find that the borders of precolonial authorities explain more cross-sectional variations in economic activity than do the borders of postcolonial nation-states. Gennaioli and Rainer (2007) show that regions in Africa that had concentrated authority structures in the precolonial era are better able to secure public goods for their constituents today.

Patron-clientism is the glue that holds this system of authority together. It need not be deadly, but the cost in terms of political stability can be

[7] Indirect Rule = 0.9092 * ln(POP DENSITY 1900) + 47.024, SE = .802, R^2 = 0.1429.

extremely high. Greif (1994) attributes the civil wars of medieval Genoa to this kind of political gamesmanship. Van de Walle (2001) argues that the fiscal crises of the postcolonial nation-state in Africa are not due to excessive government spending, but to states' inability to collect revenues from local authorities. Michalopoulos and Papaioannou (2011) find that much of the postcolonial political violence and civil war in Africa is located near precolonial ethnic homelands that were divided by the haphazard drawing of colonial borders. Divided ethnicities need not lead to conflict, but a history of slaving and the mistrust it engenders might be a fuel that feeds the flame (Nunn and Wantchekon 2011).

15.5 CONCLUSION

I have argued in this chapter that the lens of the transatlantic slave trade provides a useful perspective on contemporary politics in Africa. First, my main point is that the precolonial authority structures of West Africa that are recorded in the *Ethnographic Atlas* are not traditional in the sense of being old, but are more recent in origins and closely tied to the ways African societies responded to the shock of the transatlantic slave trade. The image of a decentralized, absolutist, isolated village exploiting women is not an image of ancient Africa. It is a modern one.

Second, I have nothing invested in the term *patrimonial*, but I do want to suggest that the postcolonial nation-state in Africa is rooted in African history – a history fundamentally altered by the slave trade and colonialism. This path dependence is seen in all of the empirical studies linking precolonial authority structures to postcolonial political and economic outcomes. My contribution to this literature is a reinterpretation of what it means to be precolonial in the African context.

Finally, I do not mean to suggest that history determined postcolonial political outcomes in Africa, or that the political problem to be solved was as simple as I suggested. I do, however, want to suggest that viewing customary authority as something of recent origin can encourage change. "You sometimes cannot understand the logic (or illogic) of the world without knowing how it got that way." Radelet (2010) identifies seventeen emerging countries in Africa. Four of the five reasons he cites for their success have to do with improvements in policy and governance. What Ekeh (1975) calls the "two publics" in Africa, and what Van de Walle (2001) calls "permanent crisis," and what Chabal and Daloz (1999) call "disorder as political instrument" need not be permanent nor disorderly. The first order of business, however, is to understand how it got that way.

References

Acemoglu, Daron and Simon Johnson. (2005). "Unbundling Institutions." *Journal of Political Economy*, 113(5): 949–95.

Acemoglu, Daron, Simon Johnson, and James A. Robinson. (2002). "Reversal of Fortune: Geography and Institutions in Making of Modern World Income Distribution." *Quarterly Journal of Economics*, 117: 1231–94.

(2001). "The Colonial Origins of Comparative Development: An Empirical Investigation." *American Economic Review*, 91(5): 1369–1401.

Albouy, David. (2013). "The Colonial Origins of Comparative Development: An Empirical Investigation: A Comment." *American Economic Review*, 102(6): 3059–76.

Arrow, Kenneth J. (2004). "Path Dependence and Competitive Equilibrium." In *History Matters: Essays in Economic Growth, Technology and Demographic Change*, edited by Timothy W. Guinnane, William A. Sundstrom, and Warren C. Whatley, 23–35. Stanford, CA: Stanford University Press.

Austen, Ralph A. (1979). "The Trans-Saharan Slave Trade: A Tentative Census." In *The Uncommon Market: Essays in the Economic History of the Atlantic Slave Trade*, edited by Henry. A. Gemery and Jan. S. Hogendorn, 23–75. New York: Academic Press.

(1987). *African Economic History: Internal Development and External Dependency*. London: James Curry.

Austin, Gareth. (2008). "Resources, Techniques, and Strategies South of the Sahara: Revising the Factor Endowments Perspective on African Economic Development, 1500–2000." *Economic History Review*, 61: 587–624.

Barry, Boubacar. (1998). *Senegambia and the Atlantic Slave Trade*. Cambridge: Cambridge University Press.

Bates, Robert. (2008). *When Things Fell Apart: State Failure in Late-Century Africa*. New York: Cambridge University Press.

(2010). *Prosperity and Violence: The Political Economy of Development*. New York: W. W. Norton.

Bates, Robert, Avner Greif, and Smita Singh. (2002). "Organizing Violence." *Journal of Conflict Resolution*, 46(5): 599–628.

Bean, Richard. (1974). "A Note on the Relative Importance of Slaves and Gold in West African Exports." *The Journal of African History*, 5(3): 351–56.

Bertocchi, G. and F. Canova (2002). "Did Colonization Matter for Growth? An Empirical Exploration into the Causes of Africa's Underdevelopment." *European Economic Review* 46(10): 1851–1871.

Boone, C. (2003). *Political Topographies of the African State: Territorial Authority and Institutional Choice*. Cambridge, Cambridge University Press.

Chabal, Patrick and Jean-Pascal Daloz. (1999). *Africa Works: Disorder as Political Instrument*. Bloomington: Indiana University Press.

Daaku, Kwame Yeboa. (1970). *Trade and Politics on the Gold Coast, 1600–1720: A Study of the African Reaction to European Trade*. London: Clarendon.

David, Paul. (1985). "Clio and the Economics of Qwerty." *American Economic Review*, 76: 332–7.

Davidson, Basil. (1992). *The Black Man's Burden: Africa and the Curse of the Nation-State*. New York: Three Rivers Press.

Ekeh, Peter P. (1975). "Colonialism and the Two Publics in Africa: A Theoretical Statement." *Comparative Studies in Society and History*, 17(1): 91–112.

(1990). "Social Anthropology and Two Contrasting Uses of Tribalism in Africa." *Comparative Studies in Society and History*, 32(4): 660–700.

Eltis, David. (1994). "The Relative Importance of Slaves and Commodities in the Atlantic Trade of Seventeenth-Century Africa." *Journal of African History*, 35(2): 237–49.

(2009). Voyages Database. Voyages: The Transatlantic Slave Trade Database. http://www.slavevoyages.org (accessed October 1, 2010).

Eltis, David, Stephen D. Behrendt, David Richardson, and Herbert S. Klein. (1999). *The Trans-Atlantic Slave Trade: A Database on CD-Rom*. London: Cambridge University Press.

Eltis, David and Lawrence C. Jennings. (1988). "Trade between West Africa and the Atlantic World in the Pre-Colonial Era." *American Historical Review*, 9(4): 936–59.

Eltis, David and David Richardson. (2004). "Prices of African Slaves Newly Arrived in the Americas, 1673–1865: New Evidence on Long-Run Trends and Regional Differentials." In *Slavery in the Development of the Americas*, edited by David Eltis, Frank. D. Lewis, and Kenneth. L. Sockoloff, 181–218. Cambridge: Cambridge University Press.

Englebert, Pierre. (2000). "Pre-Colonial Institutions, Post-Colonial States, and Economic Development in Tropical Africa." *Political Science Research Quarterly*, 53(1): 7–36.

Fage, John. (1980). "Slaves and Society in Western Africa C.1445-C.1700." *Journal of African History*, 21(3): 289–310.

Fenske, James. (2010). "The Causal History of Africa: A Response to Hopkins." *Economic History of Developing Regions*, 25(2): 177–212.

Firmin-Sellers, Kathryn. (2000). "Institutions, Context, and Outcomes: Explaining French and British Rule in West Africa." *Comparative Politics*, 32(3): 253–72.

Fisher, Humphrey. (2001). *Slavery in the History of Muslim Black Africa*. London: Hurst and Company.

Gemery, Henry A. and Jan S. Hogendorn. (1979). "The Economic Cost of West African Participation in the Atlantic Slave Trade: A Preliminary Sampling for the Eighteenth Century." In *The Uncommon Market: Essays in the Economic History of the Atlantic Slave Trade*, edited by H. A. Gemery and J. S. Hogendorn. New York: Academic Press.

Gemery, Henry and Jan Hogendorn. (1990). "Evidence on English/African Terms of Trade and 18th Century." *Explorations in Economic History*, 27: 157–77.

Gennaioli, Nicola and Ilia Rainer. (2007). "The Modern Impact of Precolonial Centralization in Africa." *Journal of Economic Growth*, 12: 185–234.

Glaeser, Edward L. and Andrei Shleifer. (2002). "Legal Origins." *Quarterly Journal of Economics*, 117(4): 1193–1229.

Graham, James. (1965). "The Slave Trade, Depopulation and Human Sacrifice in Benin History: The General Approach." *Cahiers d'Etudes Africaines*, 5(18): 317–34.

Grief, Avner. (1989). "Reputation and Coalition in Medieval Trade: Evidence on the Maghribi Traders." *Journal of Economic History*, 49(4): 857–82.

(1994). "On the Political Foundations of the Late Medieval Commercial Revolution: Genoa during the Twelfth and Thirteenth Centuries." *Journal of Economic History*, 54(4): 217–87.

(2006). *Institutions and the Path to the Modern Economy: Lessons from Medieval Trade*. Cambridge: Cambridge University Press.

Herbst, Jeffrey. (2000). *States and Power in Africa: Comparative Lessons in Authority and Control*. Princeton, NJ: Princeton University Press.

Hopkins, Anthony. (1973). *An Economic History of West Africa*. New York: Columbia University Press.

IIASA. (2010). "Global Agro-Ecological Assessment for Agriculture in the 21st Century: Methodology and Results." http://www.iiasa.ac.at/research/luc/gaez/index.html (Accessed October 1, 2010).

Iliffe, John. (2007). *Africans: The History of a Continent*. New York: Cambridge University Press.

Inikori, J., Ed. (1982). *Forced Migration: The Impact of the Slave Trade on African Societies*. New York, Africana Publishing Company.

Inikori, J. (2003). "The Struggle Against the Transatlantic Slave Trade: The Role of the State." In *Fighting the Slave Trade: West African Strategies*. S. A. Diouf, (ed.). Athens, Ohio University Press.

Grier, R. M. (1999). "Colonial Legacy and Economic Growth." *Public Choice* 98(3): 317–335.

Iyer, Lakshmi. (2010). "Direct Versus Indirect Colonial Rule in India: Long-Term Consequences." *Review of Economics and Statistics*, 90(4): 693–713.

La Porta, Rafael, Florencio Lopez-de-Silanes, and Andrei Shleifer. (2008). "The Economic Consequences of Legal Origin." *Journal of Economic Literature*, 46(2): 285–332.

Lange, Matthew. (2004). "British Colonial Legacy and Political Development." *World Development*, 32(6): 905–22.

(2009). *Lineages of Despotism and Development: British Colonialism and State Power*. Chicago: University of Chicago Press.

Law, R. (1991). *The Slave Coast of West Africa, 1550–1750 : The Impact of the Atlantic Slave Trade on an African Society*. Oxford, Oxford University Press.

Lovejoy, Paul E. (2004). *Slavery on the Frontiers of Islam*. Princeton, NJ: Markus Wiener Publishers.

Mamdani, Mahmood, ed. (1996). *Citizen and Subject: Contemporary Africa and the Legacy of Late Colonialism*. Princeton, NJ: Princeton University Press.

Manning, Patrick. (1990). *Slavery and African Life: Occidental, Oriental, and African Slave Trades*. Cambridge: Cambridge University Press.

McEvedy, Colin and Richard Jones. (1978). *Atlas of World Population History*. Harmondsworth: Penguin.

Michalopoulos, Stelios and Elias Papaioannou. (2010). "Divide and Rule or the Rule of the Divided? Evidence from Africa." *Discussion Paper Series No. 8088*. Center for Economic Policy Research.

(2011). "The Long-Run Effects of the Scramble for Africa." NBER Working Paper No. 17620.

Murdock, G. P. (1949). *Social Structure*. New York, Macmillan Co.

(1967). *Ethnographic Atlas*. Pittsburgh: University of Pittsburgh Press.

North, Douglas. (1981). *Structure and Change in Economic History*. New York: Norton.

Nunn, Nathan. (2008). "The Long Term Effects of Africa's Slave Trades." *Quarterly Journal of Economics*, 123(1): 139–76.

(2009). "The Importance of History for Economic Development." *Annual Review of Economics*, 1: 65–92.

Nunn, Nathan and Diego Puga. (2012). "Ruggedness: The Blessings of Bad Geography in Africa." *Review of Economics and Statistics*, 94(1): 20–36.

Nunn, Nathan and Leonard Wantchekon. (2011). "The Slave Trade and the Origins of Mistrust in Africa." *American Economic Review*, 111(7): 3221–52.

Olsson, Ola. (2009). "On the Democratic Legacy of Colonialism." *Journal of Comparative Economics*, 37: 534–51.

Patterson, Orlando. (1982). *Slavery and Social Death: A Comparative Study*. Cambridge, MA: Harvard University Press.

Pitcher, Anne, Mary H. Moran, and Michael Johnston. (2009). "Rethinking Patrimonialism and Neopatrimonialism in Africa." *African Studies Review*, 52(1): 125–56.

Price, G. N. (2003). "Economic Growth in a Cross-Section of Nonindustrial Countries: Does Colonial Heritage matter for Africa?" *Review of Development Economics* 7: 478–495.

Radelet, Steven. (2010). *Emerging Africa: How 17 Countries Are Leading the Way*. Washington, DC: Center for Global Development.

Rattray, Capt. R. S. (1929). *Ashanti Law and Constitution*. Oxford University Press.

Richardson, David. (1991). "Prices of Slaves in West and West Central Africa: Towards an Annual Series, 1698–1807." *Bulletin of Economic Research*, 43(1): 21–56.

Robinson, J. A. (2002). "States and Power in Africa by Jeffrey I. Herbst: A Review Essay." *Journal of Economic Literature* 40(2): 510–519.

Rodney, Walter. (1966). "African Slavery and Other Forms of Social Oppression on the Upper Guinea Coast in the Context of the Atlantic Slave Trade." *Journal of African History*, 7(3): 431–43.

(1972). *How Europe Underdeveloped Africa*. London: Bogle-L'Ouverture Publications.

Ryder, Alan F. (1969). *Benin and the Europeans, 1485–1897*. New York: Humanities Press.

Thornton, John K. (1999). *Warfare in Atlantic Africa, 1500–1800*. London: UCL Press.

UNESCO. (2010). "Unep Sioux Falls Clearninghouse." http://Na.Unep.Net/Datasets/Datalist.Php. (Accessed October 1, 2010).

USGS. (2010). "Usgs Geographic Data Download." http://Edc2.Usgs.Gov/Geodata/Index.Php. (Accessed October 1, 2010).

Van de Walle, Nicolas. (2001). *African Economies and the Politics of Permanent Crisis, 1979–1999*. Cambridge: Cambridge University Press.

Whatley, Warren and Rob Gillezeau. (2011a). "The Fundamental Impact of the Slave Trade on African Economies." In *Economic Evolution and Revolution in Historical Time*, edited by Paul Rhode, Joshua Rosenbloom, and David Weiman, 86–110 . Stanford, CA: Stanford University Press.

(2011b). "The Impact of the Slave Trade on Ethnic Stratification in Africa." *American Economic Review*, 101(3): 571–6.

Wilks, Ivor. (1975). *Asante in the Nineteenth Century: The Structure and Evolution of a Political Order*. London, New York: Cambridge University Press.

(1982). "Wangara, Akan and Portuguese in the 15th and 16th Centuries, II: The Struggle for Trade." *The Journal of African History*, 23(4): 463–72.

(1993). *Forests of Gold: Essays on the Akan and the Kingdom of Asante*. Athens: Ohio University Press.

16

Gender and Missionary Influence in Colonial Africa

Nathan Nunn

16.1 INTRODUCTION

Increasingly, evidence has emerged showing that the historical presence of European missionaries is an important factor affecting economic development across the globe today. The causal mechanism that has received the most attention, and the most empirical support, is education. The presence of Christian missionaries, particularly Protestant missionaries, has been shown to be strongly correlated with increased educational attainment, and the effects appear to persist for many generations (Bai and Kung 2011; Grier 1997; Woodberry 2004, 2009).[1] The education-promoting influence of Protestant missionaries is not surprising given the evidence that the rise of Protestantism within Europe had long-term education (and economic growth) promoting effects (Becker and Woessmann 2009, 2008, 2010; Schaltegger and Torgler 2009).

This study provides evidence for the long-term impact of colonial missionary activity within Africa. The analysis uses data on the location of Protestant and Catholic missions from a map titled "Ethnographic Survey

I thank Robert Barro, Oeindrila Dube, Rachel McCleary, Murat Iyigun, and Robert Woodberry for valuable comments, as well as Sayon Deb and Eva Ng for excellent research assistance. I also thank seminar participants at Harvard University, ERSA's Conference on Slavery, Colonial History and the New Economic History of Southern Africa, ASSA Annual Meetings, New Technologies and Interdisciplinary Research in Religion Conference, African Poverty over the Longue Durée Conference, Mellon Foundation Sawyer Seminar on Ethnicity in Africa Conference, and Before and Beyond Europe: Economics Change in Historical Perspective Conference.

Department of Economics, Harvard University, 1805 Cambridge Street, Cambridge, MA 02138, U.S.A. (e-mail: nnunn@fas.harvard.edu; Web site: http://www.economics.harvard.edu/faculty/nunn). Also affiliated with the NBER and BREAD.

[1] Also see Barro and McCleary (2003), as well as the review article by McCleary and Barro (2006).

of Africa: Showing the Tribes and Languages; also the Stations of Missionary Societies" published by William Roome (1924). This information, combined with data on the locations of ethnic groups from Murdock (1959), is used to calculate estimates of the exposure of African ethnic groups to missionary activity.

I then link this information to the 2005 Afrobarometer survey using reported information about the ethnicity of each respondent. With this, I am able to test whether survey respondents with ancestors living closer to missions during the colonial period are today more educated. I find a positive effect of both Protestant and Catholic missions on the educational attainment of descendants, although the effect of Protestant missions tends to be stronger and more robust than the effect of Catholic missions. When I examine the effects by gender, an interesting pattern emerges. While the impact of Protestant missions on education is strongest for females, the impact of Catholic missions is strongest for males. This is consistent with the Protestant belief that both men and women had to read the Bible to go to heaven. It also supports previous findings that the Protestant religion had a particularly important impact on female education (Becker and Woessmann 2008). The finding is also consistent with the arguments of Woodberry and Shah (2004) and Woodberry (2009), who assert that because Protestant missionary activity was open to educating minorities and women, it had a particularly positive effect for these groups.

16.2 HISTORICAL BACKGROUND

A number of factors determined the locations chosen for mission stations. The three most important appear to have been access to a clean water supply, a high altitude with as temperate a climate as possible, and the ability to establish an external trade route with Europe to import needed supplies (Johnson 1967). Access to water was crucial for the European missionaries, high altitude and temperate climate reduced the likelihood of disease, and access to supplies from Europe were necessary for the establishment and continued functioning of the mission stations.

Other factors like population density also mattered, but the general effect is ambiguous. Some missionaries and societies intentionally built missions in more remote locations, where the word of God would not have reached otherwise, while others recognized the benefits and efficiencies associated with dense populations, and targeted these groups.

Another potential determinant of the location of missionary activity is based on path dependence. The routes taken by the first missionary explorers determined which areas of Africa became relatively more well known to Europe, and this may have affected the locations of subsequent missions.

In the analysis, I control for these determinants. If these factors had a direct long-term effect on the outcomes of interest, not properly accounting for this effect will result in biased estimates of the effects of missionary activity.

Historical accounts indicate that missionaries had significant impacts. William Brown, writing about missionary efforts in Southern Africa in the mid-nineteenth century, notes that "the success of the mission was, on the whole, highly pleasing. The congregations were considerable; numbers of the natives baptized, many were also admitted as communicants. The influence of the mission extended far beyond the stations; it was felt in a great part of the surrounding country" (Brown 1864, 532).

A large part of this success arose from the provision of education, training, and health care as incentives for conversion. With increased European influence, it became clear that a new era had arrived, and with education came power and influence. Robin Horton writes: "With the advent of the twentieth century … Europeans came to be seen as symbols of power, and Christianity itself came to be seen as part of a larger order, comprising Western education, colonial administration, commerce and industry, with which everyone had henceforth to reckon. These changes created a much more favourable climate for conversion" (Horton 1971, 86).

William Brown, the secretary of the Scottish Missionary Society, described the benefits to conversion experienced by the Bechuana of southern Africa: "The people under the care of the missionaries made considerable advances in some of the more common and necessary arts of civilized life. Many of them built themselves convenient houses, some of them of stone, instead of their old smoky unhealthy huts. In place of the skins of animals which they used to throw over their bodies, the men adopted in part the European dress, while the women who had learned to sew made decent clothes for themselves and their daughters. Though they were previously not simply a pastoral people, but cultivated millet and other produce, yet now their husbandry was considerably extended. They obtained ploughs and other agricultural implements, and many of them occupied themselves in the culture of corn, which they sold to the Dutch farmers for cattle, clothing, soap, salt, and other useful articles" (Brown 1864, 534).

Education was so central to the conversion strategy of missionaries that education was almost exclusively provided by missions during the colonial period. In the 1940s, 97 percent of the student population in Ghana and

Nigeria were from missionary schools. In South Africa during this period, there were 5,360 mission-sponsored schools and only 230 state-sponsored schools (Berman 1974, 527).

16.3 DATA AND THEIR SOURCES

The data used in the analysis are built around the third round (2005) of the Afrobarometer surveys. These nationally standardized questionnaires measure a host of characteristics among a random sample of either twelve hundred or twenty-four hundred individuals in each country. The questionnaire provides a variety of information, including individuals' education, religion, age, gender, and their views about female equality.

The 2005 Afrobarometer covers the following seventeen sub-Saharan African countries: Benin, Botswana, Ghana, Kenya, Lesotho, Madagascar, Malawi, Mali, Mozambique, Namibia, Nigeria, Senegal, South Africa, Tanzania, Uganda, Zambia, and Zimbabwe. It is clear that this is not a random sample. The countries tend to be concentrated in West Africa, eastern Africa, and southern Africa. All of west central Africa is not included, as well as countries inland of the Red Sea. Therefore, it is important to keep in mind that all of the results in this chapter apply only to the seventeen sub-Saharan African countries included in our sample. The relationships that I identify in the data may be very different within the African countries not included in our sample.

Information on the historical influence of Christianity within Africa is taken from a map created by Roome (1924). The map provides the exact location of all Protestant and Catholic missions in Africa in 1924. A *foreign mission* is defined as a location foreign missionaries established with the intention to convert, educate, and/or assist in other ways the foreign indigenous populations. Therefore, churches foreigners developed for their own populations are not included in the data, as are churches meant to serve the immigrant (e.g., white) populations living in Africa. The analysis only includes individuals belonging to ethnic groups indigenous to Africa.

The map Roome produced was highly regarded by experts in the area, who confirmed that the locations of the mission stations are accurate.[2] The only criticisms of the map involved disagreements about the exact spellings of the tribes' names and of their locations on the maps. For my analysis here, I do not rely on the spellings or locations of ethnic groups from Roome's map. Roome's map is shown in Figure 16.1. Superimposed on the map are

[2] See, for example, E. W. S. (1925).

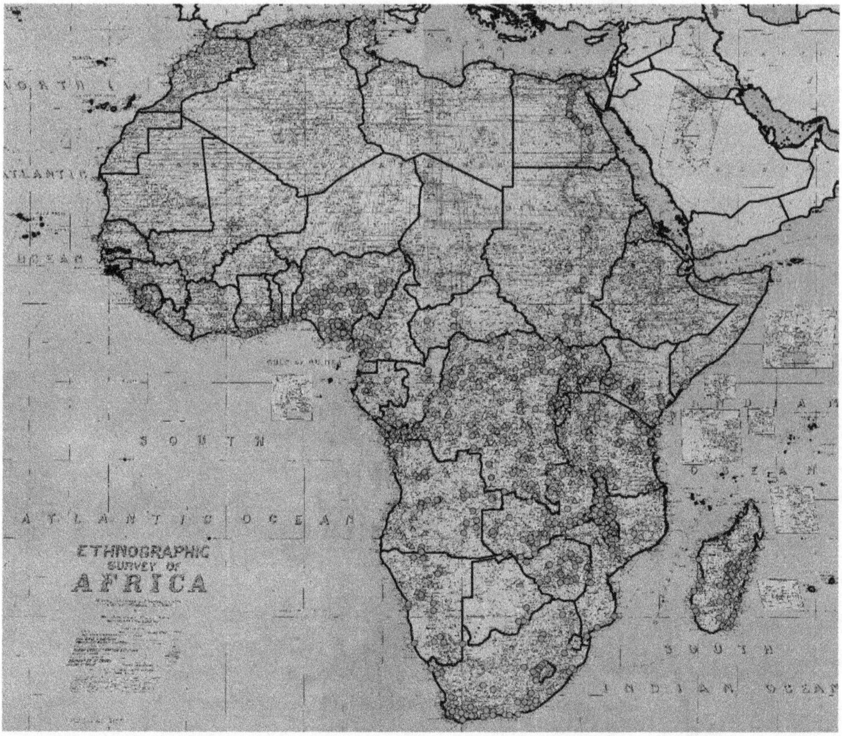

Figure 16.1. Map displaying the location of Catholic missions (triangles) and Protestant missions (circles) in Africa in 1924.

circles showing the location of each Protestant mission and triangles showing the locations of Catholic missions.

Although there is a clear clustering of Protestant and Catholic missions, there is also a fair amount of mixing. Many locations contain missions of both types, closely mixed together. This fact can be explained in part by the General Act of the Conference of Berlin, which guaranteed freedom of religion throughout Africa.[3]

I undertake two strategies to trace the impacts of missions on individuals today. The first is to use an individual's ethnic identity to construct a

[3] Article 6 of Chapter I mandated that each of the European powers "shall, without distinction of creed or nation, protect and favour all religious, scientific, or charitable institutions, and undertakings created and organized for the above ends, or which aim at instructing the natives and bringing home to them the blessings of civilization. Christian missionaries, scientists, and explorers, with their followers, property, and collections, shall likewise be the objects of especial protection" (Keith 1919, 304).

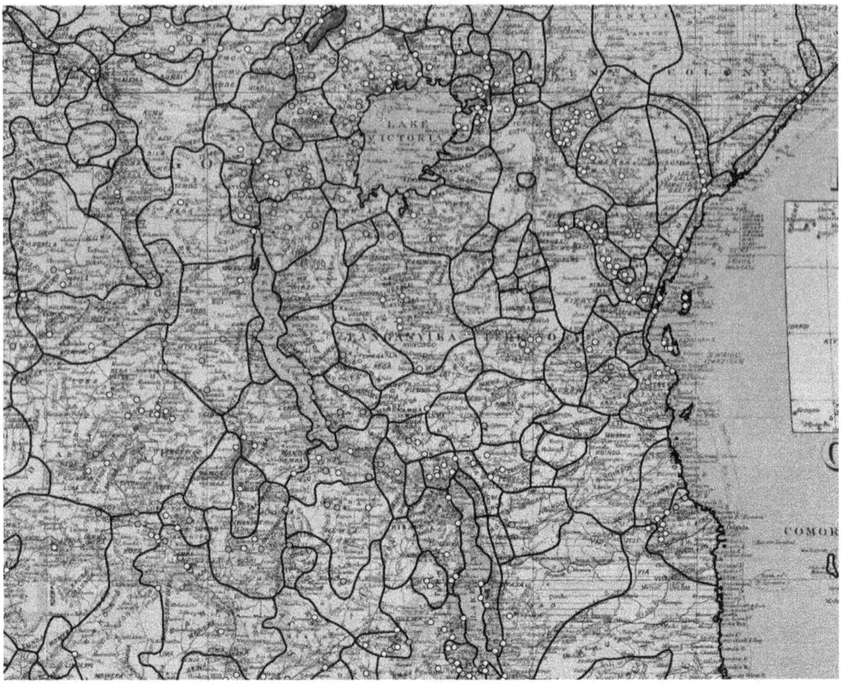

Figure 16.2. Constructing ethnicity-level mission measures.

measure of historical exposure to missionaries. The second is to use an individual's current location to construct a measure of past missionary activity.

In the first strategy, I examine the reported ethnicities from the Afrobarometer survey and calculate the intensity of missionary activity in the 1920s within the area inhabited by the ethnic group at the time. Information on the location of ethnicities during the colonial period is taken from a map from Murdock (1959) showing the approximate borders of ethnic groups in early nineteenth-century Africa. Superimposing Murdock's information over Roome's map, I construct a measure of the density of Catholic and Protestant mission in the area traditionally inhabited by each ethnic group.

This procedure is illustrated by Figure 16.2. The figure shows the locations of Catholic and Protestant mission stations in eastern Africa. It also shows, as black polygons, the boundaries of ethnic groups (in the nineteenth century) as mapped by Murdock (1959). For each ethnic group I calculate the number of missions (total, Protestant, or Catholic) per one thousand kilometers of land area. This variable is my measure of the exposure a respondent's ethnic group had to religion in the early twentieth century.

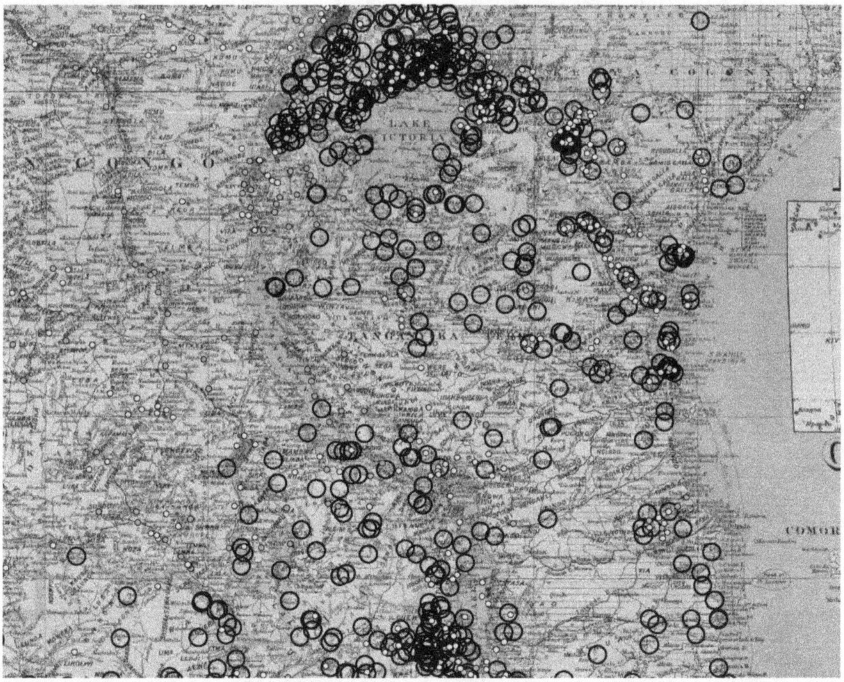

Figure 16.3. Constructing village-level mission measures.

In the second strategy, I also construct a geography-based measure of the historical intensity of missionary activity. Unlike the first variable, which is measured at the ethnicity level, this is measured at the village level.[4] The construction of the variable is illustrated in Figure 16.3, which shows the location of Catholic and Protestant mission stations, as well as a number of circles, indicating 25 km radii around the locations of each individual from the Afrobarometer surveys.[5]

The second measure calculates the number of missions (total, Catholic, and Protestant) that lie within each circle. Therefore, the variable measures the number of missions that the village where the individual is currently living was exposed to in 1924.

In the analysis, I control for a number of variables. These include the existence of a colonial railway line, and of early explorer contact, both

4 For individuals living in larger cities, the variable is actually measured at the neighborhood level.

5 Twenty-five kilometers is chosen arbitrarily. The results are similar using larger radii, such as 50 or 100 kilometers.

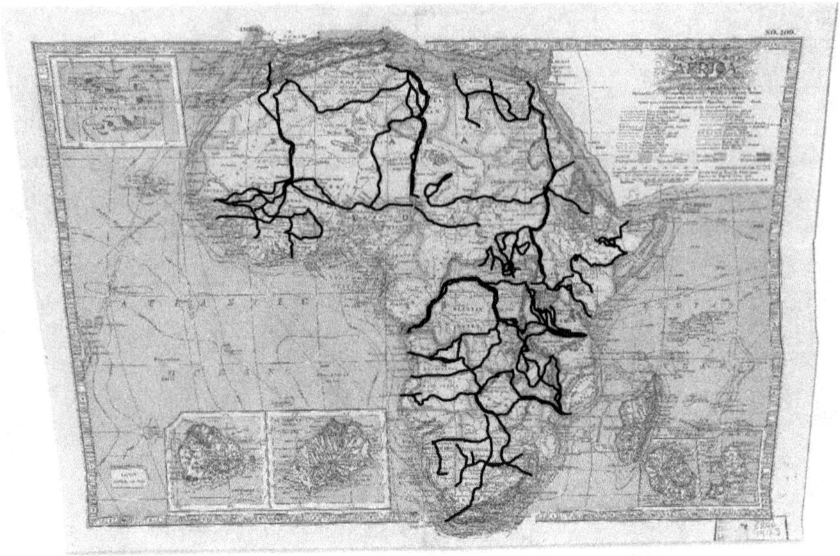

Figure 16.4. Explorer routes.

measured at the ethnicity and village levels. Data on the location of rail lines (as of 1897) and explorer routes (prior to 1895) are from a map created by The Century Company (1897). The original map is shown in Figures 16.4 and 16.5. In Figure 16.4, the expedition routes are superimposed over the map. Figure 16.5 illustrates the colonial railway lines.

The procedure used for the missions is also used to construct analogous measures for the control variables. For each village and ethnic group, I construct an indicator variable that equals one if a railway contacted the town or group, and zero otherwise. I also construct ethnicity- and village-level indicator variables that equal one if a European explorer contacted the ethnic group or town.

The railway variable is meant to capture ease of access that villages or ethnic groups had to supplies from Europe, an important factor affecting the choice of mission stations. The explorer variable captures the proximity of villages and ethnic groups to the routes of early missionaries and other explorers. This may have affected European knowledge about an area, which may have affected the likelihood of missions being developed there.

The set of controls also includes three geographic measures: the suitability of climate and land for the cultivation of crops; the amount of land

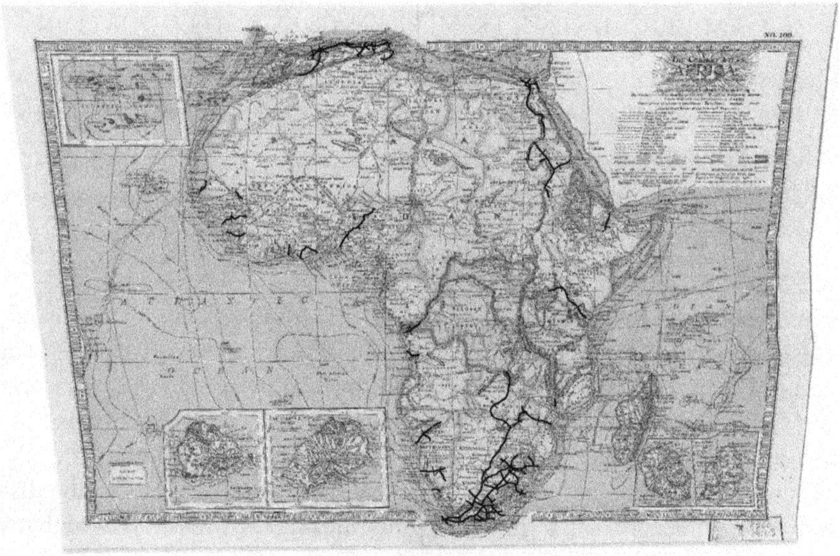

Figure 16.5. Colonial railway lines.

within ten kilometers of a fresh water source; and average altitude. Again, the three controls are measured at both the ethnicity and village levels.

Data on suitability for agriculture are from the FAO's GAEZ 2002 database. The FAO provides a suitability index for five arc minute by five arc minute (approx. 56 km by 56 km) grid cells globally. Data on the location of fresh water sources and elevation are from Global Mapping International's (GMI) Seamless Digit Chart of the World Version 3.2.

The final control variable included is a measure of the intensity of the slave trade; given that the goal of many missionaries, particularly Protestant missionaries, was to end slavery, missions may have been intentionally located in areas with a history of slavery (Johnson 1967). The measures of the intensity of the Atlantic and Indian Ocean slave trade are taken from Nunn and Wantchekon (2011). The study provides both ethnicity- and village-level measures. The ethnicity-level variable measures the number of slaves taken from the ethnic group, normalized by the size of the ethnic group, which is measured by the amount of land it inhabited during the early twentieth century. To construct a village-level measure, the authors use the location of each village as well as Murdock's map to determine which ethnic group traditionally inhabited the location of the village. The village is then given the slave export measure of the ethnic group, thereby providing an estimate of the intensity of the slave trade in that location historically.

16.4 EMPIRICAL RESULTS: MISSIONARIES AND EDUCATION

I begin by examining the relationship between historical missionary activity and educational attainment today. I first examine the average effect of all Christian mission stations (both Protestant and Catholic) on educational attainment. The estimating equation is:

$$Y_{i,e,v,c} = \alpha_c + \beta M_e + \gamma M_v + X_i\Gamma + X_e\Lambda + X_v\Phi + \varepsilon_{i,e,v,c} \qquad (16.1)$$

where i indexes individuals, e ethnic groups, v villages, and c countries. The dependent variable measures individual i's educational attainment (in years). The variable M_e measures the exposure of ethnic group e to Protestant and Catholic missions in 1924. It is measured as the log number of missions per one thousand kilometers of land area historically inhabited by the ethnic group. I take the natural log to remove the skew that exists in the distribution otherwise. M_v is the analogous measure of missionary activity, but measured at the village level. It is measured by the number of missions (Catholic and Protestant) in the village of the respondent. More precisely, the measure is calculated by identifying the number of missions within a twenty-five kilometer radius of the geographic location of the respondent. α_c denotes country fixed effects, which are included in all regressions.

These capture country-level characteristics, including colonial policies, which may be correlated with average education and missionary activity.

Equation (16.1) also includes a host of control variables that vary at either the individual, ethnicity, or village levels. $\mathbf{X}_i$ denotes a vector of individual-level control variables that include a gender indicator variable, age, and an indicator variable that equals one if he or she is living in an urban location. $\mathbf{X}_e$ denotes a vector of ethnicity-level control variables, including an indicator that equals one if the ethnic group was contacted by early European explorers, an indicator that equals one if a railway was built on the land inhabited by the ethnic group, the proportion of the ethnic group's historical land that is arable, the proportion that was within ten kilometers of a fresh water source, and the normalized number of slaves exported in the Atlantic and Indian Ocean slave trades. $\mathbf{X}_v$ includes the same covariates, but measured at the village level, rather than the ethnicity level.

OLS estimates of Equation (16.1) are reported in Table 16.1. Column (1) reports estimates with the ethnicity-level mission variable and ethnicity-level controls. Column (2) includes the village-level mission variable and village-level controls, while column (3) includes the village-level and ethnicity-level variables together. All three specifications also include individual-

Table 16.1. *OLS estimates of the relationship between colonial missionary activity and educational attainment today*

	Dependent variable: years of education		
	(1)	(2)	(3)
Mission stations among ethnic group, M_e	0.102**		0.098**
	(0.046)		(0.044)
Mission stations in village, M_v		0.143***	0.119***
		(0.033)	(0.042)
Individual-level controls	Yes	Yes	Yes
Ethnicity-level controls	Yes	No	Yes
Village-level controls	No	Yes	Yes
Country fixed effects	Yes	Yes	Yes
Number of observations	20,914	20,914	20,914
Number of clusters	185	2,693	185 / 2,693
R-squared	0.337	0.336	0.342

Notes: The table reports OLS estimates. The unit of observation is an individual. The individual control variables are for age, age squared, a gender indicator variable, and an indicator variable for whether the respondent lives in an urban location. The ethnicity-level controls include the log number of slaves exported per land area during the Atlantic and Indian Ocean slave trades, an indicator variable equal to one if the ethnicity was contacted by a European explorer prior to colonial rule (1885), an indicator variable equal to one if a railway line dissected the region in which the ethnicity was living during colonial rule, the proportion of the ethnic group's land that is suitable for agriculture, the proportion of land that is within ten kilometers of a fresh water source, and average elevation. The village-level controls include an indicator variable equal to one if the inhabitant's current village was contacted by a European explorer prior to colonial rule (1885), an indicator variable equal to one if a railway line dissected the village, the log number of slaves exported per land area during the Atlantic and Indian Ocean slave trades among the ethnic group that historically inhabited the village, the fraction of the land within the village (twenty-five kilometer radius of the centroid) that is suitable for cultivation, the fraction of the village land that is within ten kilometers of a fresh water source, and the average elevation of the village. Coefficients are reported, with clustered standard errors in brackets. ***, ** and * indicates significance at the 1 percent, 5 percent, and 10 percent levels.

level controls and country fixed effects. The estimates show a positive and statistically significant effect of missionary activity, measured either at the ethnicity or village level, on educational attainment.

This finding provides added support for the arguments and cross-country evidence of Woodberry (2004) that missionary activity (his analysis focuses on Protestants) had long-term impacts on the level of education.

These effects could occur through a variety of channels. First, missionaries may have altered people's views about the importance of education. If individuals transmitted their new attitudes and beliefs to their children, then the descendants of those in contact with Protestant missions would also value education more and therefore be better educated today. This explanation is consistent with the positive estimates for the ethnicity-level missionary variable. The positive and significant coefficients in columns (1) and (3) show that ethnicities that had closer contact to missionaries have descendants who are more educated today.

An alternative mechanism is because missionaries valued education, they immediately established schools and universities. In fact, in British colonies, most of the schools in the colonies were established by missionaries rather than by the colonial administration (e.g., Berman 1974, 527).

These investments in educational infrastructure tend to persist over time (e.g., Huillery 2009), so that today, towns and villages that historically had more missionary activity may have more schools, and therefore the equilibrium level of education is higher. This channel, which operates through location and not ethnicity, is captured by the village-level mission variable, which is positive and significant in columns (2) and (3). Villages that had more missions during the colonial period have more educated inhabitants today.

Given that the two sets of mission variables – measured at the village and ethnicity levels – capture different transmission mechanisms, a natural question is which is more important. Because the variables are measured in different units, a direct comparison of their coefficients is inappropriate. Instead, I compare standardized beta coefficients, which are unit-less coefficients that report the number of standard deviation increases in the dependent variable per one-standard-deviation increase in the independent variable. This comparison suggests that the effect of the ethnicity-level measure is approximately three times the magnitude of the effect of the village-level measure. According to the estimates of column (3), the beta coefficient for the ethnicity-based measure is 0.047 and for the village-level measure is 0.036. Therefore, the evidence suggests that both channels are important and of a similar magnitude.

16.5 EMPIRICAL RESULTS: MISSIONARIES AND EDUCATION, DISTINGUISHING BETWEEN CATHOLICS AND PROTESTANTS

Much of the preexisting qualitative and quantitative literature distinguishes between the impact of Protestant and Catholic missions, documenting important differences between the two (Gallego and Woodberry 2010; Woodberry 2004; Woodberry and Shah 2004). The most detailed evidence in the African context is from Gallego and Woodberry (2010), who provide evidence that Protestant missions, relative to Catholic missions, had a greater impact on increased education. They also show that this is most pronounced in Catholic nation-states where there was less competition from Protestant missions.

In this section, I examine whether there is evidence of differential impacts of Protestant and Catholic missions on religious conversion. I construct variables that measure the intensity of Catholic missions and of Protestant missions, at both the ethnicity and the village levels. These are then included in the estimating equation, rather than the measures of missionary activity generally. Doing this allows the impact of missionary activity to differ depending on whether the mission was Catholic or Protestant. The new estimating equation is:

$$\begin{aligned} Y_{i,e,v,c} = \alpha_c + \beta_p M_e^{prot} + \gamma_p M_v^{prot} + \beta_c M_e^{Cath} + \gamma_c M_v^{Cath} \\ + X_i \Gamma + X_e \Lambda + X_v \mathbf{\Phi} + \varepsilon_{i,e,v,c} \end{aligned} \quad (16.2)$$

where i continues to index individuals, e ethnic groups, v villages, and c countries. The variables M_e^{Prot} and M_e^{Cath} are measures of the intensity of exposure of ethnic group e to Protestant and Catholic missions in 1924. They are measured in the same units as M_e. Similarly, M_v^{Prot} and M_v^{Cath} measure the intensity of exposure of village v to Protestant and Catholic missionaries and are given in the same units as M_v. $\mathbf{X}_e$, $\mathbf{X}_v$ and $\mathbf{X}_i$ are the same vectors of covariates as in Equation (16.1).

Estimates of Equation (16.2) are reported in Table 16.2. Column (1) reports estimates with missionary activity measured at the ethnicity level, while column (2) measures missionary activity at the village level. The estimates show a positive and statistically significant impact of Protestant missions on educational attainment today. The estimates for Catholic missions are also positive, but smaller in magnitude and statistically insignificant. The results are consistent with Gallego and Woodberry's (2010) finding that Protestant missionaries had a larger positive impact on long-term education than Catholic missionaries. In column (3), I include both the village- and ethnicity-level variables together. All coefficients remain positive and approximately the same magnitude as in columns (1) and (2). The coefficients for Protestant missions remain statistically significant, while the coefficients for Catholic missions remain insignificant.

In the previous section, we distinguished between location- and ethnicity-based channels of causality. In this section, we undertake an additional exercise to help distinguish between mechanisms. It is possible that the

Table 16.2. *OLS estimates of the relationship between colonial missionary activity and education today, allowing for differences between Catholic and Protestant missions*

	Dependent variable: years of education								
	(1)	(2)	(3)	(4)	(5)	(6)	(7)	(8)	(9)
Ethnicity-based measure:									
Catholic Missions	0.050		0.036				0.046		0.033
	(0.034)		(0.031)				(0.032)		(0.029)
Protestant Missions	0.094*		0.096**				0.068*		0.073*
	(0.049)		(0.045)				(0.040)		(0.037)
Location-based measure:									
Catholic Missions		0.106	0.124					0.131*	0.141*
		(0.072)	(0.082)					(0.069)	(0.080)
Protestant Missions		0.163***	0.104**					0.105**	0.067
		(0.049)	(0.048)					(0.046)	(0.046)
Current Religion Indicator:									
Catholic				1.852***	1.884***	1.810***	1.823***	1.859***	1.764***
				(0.162)	(0.099)	(0.159)	(0.154)	(0.098)	(0.150)
Protestant				1.911***	1.962***	1.870***	1.876***	1.947***	1.828***
				(0.161)	(0.100)	(0.162)	(0.149)	(0.098)	(0.147)
Other Christian				1.665***	1.681***	1.621***	1.652***	1.662***	1.597***
				(0.161)	(0.102)	(0.161)	(0.151)	(0.101)	(0.149)

Country fixed effects	Yes	Yes	Yes	Yes	Yes	Yes	Yes	Yes	Yes
Ethnicity-level controls	Yes	No	Yes	Yes	No	Yes	Yes	No	Yes
Village-level controls	No	Yes	Yes	No	Yes	Yes	No	Yes	Yes
Number of observations	20,914	20,914	20,914	20,836	20,836	20,836	20,836	20,836	20,836
Number of clusters	185	2,692	185/2,692	185	2,692	185/2,692	185	2,692	185/2,692
R-squared	0.337	0.336	0.343	0.355	0.356	0.359	0.356	0.357	0.361

Notes: The table reports OLS estimates. The unit of observation is an individual. The individual control variables are for age, age squared, a gender indicator variable, and an indicator variable for whether the respondent lives in an urban location. The ethnicity-level controls include the log number of slaves exported per land area during the Atlantic and Indian Ocean slave trades, an indicator variable equal to one if the ethnicity was contacted by a European explorer prior to colonial rule (1885), an indicator variable equal to one if a railway line dissected the region in which the ethnicity was living during colonial rule, the proportion of the ethnic group's land that is suitable for agriculture, the proportion of land that is within ten kilometers of a fresh water source, and average elevation. The village level controls include an indicator variable equal to one if the inhabitant's current village was contacted by a European explorer prior to colonial rule (1885), an indicator variable equal to one if a railway line dissected the village, the log number of slaves exported per land area during the Atlantic and Indian Ocean slave trades among the ethnic group that historically inhabited the village, the fraction of the land within the village (twenty-five kilometer radius of the centroid) that is suitable for cultivation, the fraction of the village land that is within ten kilometers of a fresh water source, and the average elevation of the village. Coefficients are reported, with clustered standard errors in brackets. ***, ** and * indicates significance at the 1 percent, 5 percent, and 10 percent levels.

estimated long-term impacts of missions arise because of changes in the perception of the value of education, which have been transmitted through time. Alternatively, if, as documented by Nunn (2010), colonial missions resulted in conversion, even in the long run, then this may cause increased education. According to the second explanation, the persistence is through the transmission of religious values and not through the transmission of beliefs about the importance of education.

I attempt to distinguish between these two hypotheses in columns (4)–(9) of Table 16.2. Columns (4)–(6) report estimates of the three specifications from columns (1)–(3), but with the missionary variables replaced with variables measuring the religion of the respondent. I include three indicator variables that equal one if the respondent is: (i) Catholic, (ii) Protestant, or (iii) another type of Christian. As shown, all three indicator variables are highly correlated with educational attainment. Those belonging to any of the three religions, on average, have 1.6–2.0 years more education.

In columns (7)–(8), I reestimate the specifications from columns (1)–(3), but now include the three religion controls. If the importance of colonial missionary activities, estimated in columns (1)–(3), arises because of the current religious affiliation of the individual, then we would expect the estimated impact of historical missionary activity to be much smaller once we account for the current religion of respondents. Comparing the estimates in columns (1)–(3) to those in columns (7)–(8), I find a small drop in the point estimates of the Protestant mission variables after the inclusion of the religion controls. The decrease ranges from 24–35 percent. This suggests that a sizable part of the long-term impact of Protestant missions on education may arise due to the persistence of religious values. Interesting, controlling for religion does not attenuate the estimated impacts of Catholic missions. The point estimates tend to stay constant or even increase after the inclusion of the religion controls. This suggests that the estimated impact of Catholic missions on long-term education is not due to the persistence of a belief in Catholicism. This is consistent with the fact that the Catholic religion places much less importance on education and literacy than Protestantism.

16.6 EMPIRICAL RESULTS: MISSIONARIES, EDUCATION, AND GENDER

A number of existing studies examine how the Protestant religion may be responsible for reducing the gender gap in education by emphasizing the importance of educating women. In Europe, Martin Luther urged the education of women so that they too would be able to read the Bible. Becker and Woessmann (2008) empirically test for this effect of the Protestant religion. Examining fifteen village-level data from the Prussian Census of 1816, they identify a negative relationship between the prevalence of the Protestant religion and the educational gender gap, measured as average male education minus average female education.

Motivated by Becker and Woessmann's finding, I examine whether, within the African context, the effect of colonial missions on current education is different for males relative to females. This is done by estimating a specification that allows the effect of missions on current education to differ, depending on the gender of the respondent. In practice, this is done by interacting the baseline mission variables with an indicator variable that equals one if the respondent is female, I_i^{female}. The updated estimating equation is given by:

$$Y_{i,e,v,c} = \alpha_c + \beta_p M_e^{prot} + \theta_p M_e^{prot} \cdot I_i^{female} + \beta_c M_e^{Cath} + \theta_c M_e^{Cath} \cdot I_i^{female} + X_i \Gamma + X_e \Lambda + X_v \Phi + \varepsilon_{i,e,v,c} \quad (16.3)$$

Estimates of Equation (16.3) are reported in columns (1) and (2) of Table 16.3. Column (1) reports estimates using the ethnicity-level Catholic and Protestant mission variables and column (2) reports estimates using the village-level variables. The findings show that for Protestant missions, the coefficient for the mission variable itself is positive, but not statistically different from zero, while the mission variable interacted with the female indicator variable is positive and highly significant. This suggests that historical missionary activity is associated with no long-term impact on the education of men, but a positive and statistically significant long-term impact on female education. As reported in columns (3) and (4), the results are very similar even when controlling for the current religion of the respondent. This suggests that the long-term education effect primarily works through mechanisms other than the current religion of the respondent. Protestant missions may have created a persistent belief in the importance of female education.

For Catholic missions, the baseline mission variables in columns (1) and (2) are both positive and statistically significant, while the coefficients for the mission variables interacted with the female indicator variable are negative and statistically significant. The sum of the two coefficients, which gives the total effect of Catholic missions on the long-run educational attainment of women, is very close to zero. Again, the results are similar when religion

Table 16.3. *OLS estimates of the relationship between missionaries and education, allowing for differential effects by gender*

	Dependent variable: Years of education			
	(1)	(2)	(3)	(4)
Ethnicity-based measure:				
Catholic missions	0.102**		0.095**	
	(0.042)		(0.040)	
Catholic missions x Female	−0.108*		−0.102*	
	(0.057)		(0.055)	
Protestant missions	0.016		−0.003	
	(0.053)		(0.046)	
Protestant missions x Female	0.158***		0.145***	
	(0.052)		(0.050)	
F-test for Catholic females = 0 (p-value)	0.902		0.885	
F-test for Protestant females = 0 (p-value)	0.003		0.004	
Location-based measure:				
Catholic missions		0.228***		0.248***
		(0.088)		(0.086)
Catholic missions x Female		−0.244***		−0.234***
		(0.087)		(0.086)
Protestant missions		0.086		0.022
		(0.057)		(0.055)
Protestant missions x Female		0.154***		0.165***
		(0.050)		(0.050)
F-test for Catholic females = 0 (p-value)		0.841		0.852
F-test for Protestant females = 0 (p-value)		0.000		0.000
Religion indicator variables	No	No	Yes	Yes
Individual-level controls	Yes	Yes	Yes	Yes
Ethnicity-level controls	Yes	Yes	No	No
Village-level controls	No	No	Yes	Yes
Country fixed effects	Yes	Yes	Yes	Yes
Number of observations	20,914	20,914	20,836	20,836
Number of clusters	185	185	2,692	2,692
R-squared	0.338	0.337	0.357	0.358

Notes: The table reports OLS estimates. The unit of observation is an individual. The individual control variables are for age, age squared, a gender indicator variable, and an indicator variable for whether the respondent lives in an urban location. The ethnicity-level controls include the log number of slaves exported per land area during the Atlantic and Indian Ocean slave trades, an indicator variable equal to one if the ethnicity was contacted by a European explorer prior to colonial rule (1885), an indicator variable equal to one if a railway line dissected the region in which the ethnicity was living during colonial rule, the proportion of the ethnic group's land that is suitable for agriculture, the proportion of land that is within ten kilometers of a fresh water source, and average elevation. The village-level controls include an indicator variable equal to one if the inhabitant's current village was contacted by a European explorer prior to colonial rule (1885), an indicator variable equal to one if a railway line dissected the village, the log number of slaves exported per land is controlled for (reported columns (3) and (4)). These findings, which are in stark contrast to the findings for Protestants, suggest that a history of Catholic missionary activity increased education in the long run, but only for males.

The findings of Table 16.3 raise an interesting possibility. It may be that the historical presence of Protestant missionaries also altered not only individuals' beliefs about the importance of female education, but also of the role of women in society more generally. That is, the Protestant religion may have resulted in a stronger belief about the equality of men and women more generally.

To explore this possibility, I consider two questions about the perceived role of women relative to men from the Afrobarometer survey. The first question asks the respondent whether they agree with the following two statements: (A) In our country, women should have equal rights and receive the same treatment as men, (B) Women have always been subject to traditional laws and customs and should remain so. The respondent can choose to "agree very strongly" with (A), "agree strongly" with (A), "agree strongly" with (B), or "agree very strongly" (B). The second question asks the respondent their view on the following two statements: (A) Women should have the same chance of being elected to political office as men, (B) Men make better political leaders than women, and should be elected rather than women. Again, the respondents were given the same choices.

Using the responses, I code a variable that takes on the value 1, 2, 3, or 4, and is increasing in their agreement with statement (A) over statement (B). In other words, the variable is increasing in the respondent's belief that women and men should have equal rights.

I then estimate variants of Equation (16.2) with the two gender beliefs variables as dependent variables. The estimates, which are reported in Table 16.4, fail to provide consistent evidence that historical Protestant missionary activity promoted attitudes reflecting gender equality. For six of the eight Protestant variables, the coefficient is not statistically different from zero. As

Notes: (*continued*)

area during the Atlantic and Indian Ocean slave trades among the ethnic group that historically inhabited the village, the fraction of the land within the village (twenty-five kilometer radius of the centroid) that is suitable for cultivation, the fraction of the village land that is within ten kilometers of a fresh water source, and average elevation of the village. Coefficients are reported, with clustered standard errors in brackets. ***, ** and * indicates significance at the 1 percent, 5 percent, and 10 percent levels.

Table 16.4. *OLS estimates of the relationship between colonial missionary activity and gender role attitudes today*

	Dep var: belief in females equality generally			Dep var: belief in females as equal leaders		
	(1)	(2)	(3)	(4)	(5)	(6)
Ethnicity-based measure:						
Catholic Missions	−0.010		−0.009	0.014**		0.015**
	(0.009)		(0.009)	(0.007)		(0.007)
Protestant Missions	0.005		0.004	−0.004		−0.006
	(0.009)		(0.009)	(0.008)		(0.008)
Location-based measure:						
Catholic Missions		−0.025*	−0.018		−0.028**	−0.032*
		(0.015)	(0.017)		(0.013)	(0.017)
Protestant Missions		0.024**	0.016		0.023**	0.014
		(0.011)	(0.011)		(0.010)	(0.012)
Country fixed effects	Yes	Yes	Yes	Yes	Yes	Yes
Ethnicity-level controls	Yes	No	Yes	Yes	No	Yes
Village-level controls	No	Yes	Yes	No	Yes	Yes
Number of observations	19,533	19,533	19,533	20,603	20,603	20,603
Number of clusters	185	2,691	185/2,691	185	2,691	185/2,691
R-squared	0.108	0.103	0.109	0.106	0.099	0.107

Notes: The table reports OLS estimates. The unit of observation is an individual. The individual control variables are for age, age squared, a gender indicator variable, and an indicator variable for whether the respondent lives in an urban location. The ethnicity-level controls include the log number of slaves exported per land area during the Atlantic and Indian Ocean slave trades, an indicator variable equal to one if the ethnicity was contacted by a European explorer prior to colonial rule (1885), an indicator variable equal to one if a railway line dissected the region in which the ethnicity was living during colonial rule, the proportion of the ethnic group's land that is suitable for agriculture, the proportion of land that is within ten kilometers of a fresh water source, and average elevation. The village level controls include an indicator variable equal to one if the inhabitant's current village was contacted by a European explorer prior to colonial rule (1885), an indicator variable equal to one if a railway line dissected the village, the log number of slaves exported per land area during the Atlantic and Indian Ocean slave trades among the ethnic group that historically inhabited the village, the fraction of the land within the village (twenty-five kilometer radius of the centroid) that is suitable for cultivation, the fraction of the village land that is within ten kilometers of a fresh water source, and average elevation of the village. Coefficients are reported, with clustered standard errors in brackets. ***, ** and * indicates significance at the 1 percent, 5 percent, and 10 percent levels.

well, the coefficients for the Catholic mission variables are not consistently positive or negative and many are not statistically different from zero.[6]

[6] It is possible that only the attitudes of males were affected by missionary activity, and this is the reason for the weak results. However, I have checked for this by restricting the sample to include males only and continue to find similar results (not reported in the table).

Therefore, although the evidence is consistent with Protestant missionary activity affecting long-term female educational attainment, I do not find evidence of an effect on attitudes about gender equality. This finding is not surprising given the nature of missionary education. Although women were educated in reading, writing, and even arithmetic, the greatest emphasis was typically placed on teaching women practical domestic skills, like laundry, housework, and cooking, rather than providing them with the highest levels of education. It was believed that African women should be taught how to prepare a suitable Christian home for their husbands who were to be more highly educated and serve in positions of responsibility and authority.[7]

16.7 CONCLUSIONS

Combining information on the locations of Catholic and Protestant missions in colonial Africa, I have examined the long-term impacts of Protestant and Catholic missionary activity during the colonial period on educational attainment. Using variation across villages and ethnicities from seventeen sub-Saharan African countries, I have provided evidence that Protestant missionary activity had a positive long-term impact on educational attainment. Catholic missions are estimated to have a quantitatively much smaller impact on education that is not statistically different from zero. The finding of a much larger impact of Protestant missions relative to Catholic missions on education is consistent with the previous findings of Gallego and Woodberry (2010). Interestingly, these findings, which are an average across the full Afrobarometer sample, mask stark differences of the impacts by gender. The positive impact of Protestant missions is concentrated almost solely among females. Protestant missions are estimated to have a small positive and insignificant effect on male education, and a large significant positive effect on female education. The positive but insignificant impact of Catholic missions on education is composed of a large and significant positive impact on male education, but a precisely estimated zero effect on female education. These findings are consistent with the greater importance placed on the education of women by Protestants relative to Catholics.

[7] See Labode (1993) for a discussion of this aspect of missionary education within southern Africa and Kanogo (1993) for a description for Kenya.

DATA APPENDIX

Contemporaneous Individual-Level Data

All information at the individual level, such as age, gender, education, religion, occupation, and so forth are from the third round of the Afrobarometer surveys, conducted in 2005. The data are publicly available and can be downloaded at: www.afrobarometer.org. The Afrobarometer is an independent and nonpartisan research project conducted by the Center for Democratic Development (CDD), Institute for Democracy in South Africa (IDASA), and Michigan State University (MSU).

Data on Missionary Activity

Data on the location of Catholic and Protestant mission stations in the 1920s are from Roome (1924). The mission location data are combined with information about the boundaries of Africa's ethnic groups in the late nineteenth century from Murdock (1959) to calculate the number of Catholic and Protestant mission stations in the area inhabited by each ethnic group. This is the ethnicity-based measure of missionary activity. The information is also combined with information about the location of each respondent in the Afrobarometer surveys to construct a measure of the number of Catholic and Protestant mission stations within a twenty-five kilometer radius of the location where the respondent is currently living. This is the village-based measure of missionary activity.

Ethnicity- and Village-Level Control Variables

The information of the exploration routes of early European explorers is from The Century Company (1897). The map includes the routes of twenty-seven expeditions occurring before 1895. Information of the location of colonial rail lines is also from the same map.

Data on the suitability of a location for agricultural cultivation are from the FAO's GAEZ 2002 database. The FAO provides a suitability index for five arc minute by five arc minute (approx. 56 km by 56 km) grid cells globally. Data on the location of fresh water sources and on elevation is from Global Mapping International's (GMI) Seamless Digit Chart of the World Version 3.2.

The data used to control for the number of slaves taken from each ethnicity during the transatlantic and Indian Ocean slave trade are from

Nunn and Wantchekon (2011), and the primary sources are described in Nunn (2008).

References

Bai, Ying and James Kai-sing Kung. (2011). "Diffusing Knowledge While Spreading God's Message: Protestantism and Economic Prosperity in China, 1840–1920," Mimeo, Hong Kong University of Science and Technology.

Barro, Robert J. and Rachel McCleary. (2003). "Religion and Economic Growth across Countries." *American Sociological Review*, October, 68(5): 760–81.

Becker, Sascha O. and Ludger Woessmann. (2008). "Luther and the Girls: Religious Denomination and the Female Education Gap in 19th Century Prussia." *Scandinavian Journal of Economics*, 110: 777–805.

(2009). "Was Weber Wrong? A Human Capital Theory of Protestant Economic History." *Quarterly Journal of Economics*, May, 124(2): 531–96.

(2010). "The Effect of Protestantism on Education before Industrialization: Evidence from 1816 Prussia." *Economics Letters*, 107(2): 224–8.

Berman, Edward H. (1974). "African Responses to Christian Mission Education." *Africa Studies Review*, December, 17(3): 527–40.

Brown, William (1864). *The History of Christian Missions, Volume II*. London: Thomas Baker.

E. W. S. (1925). "Review of: An Ethnographic Map of Africa." *Journal of the Royal African Society*, April, 24(95): 263.

Gallego, Francisco A. and Robert Woodberry. (2010). "Christian Missionaries and Education in Former Colonies: How Competition Mattered." *Journal of African Economies*, 19(3): 294–329.

Grier, Robin. (1997). "The Effect of Religion on Economic Development: A Cross-National Study of 63 Former Colonies." *Kyklos*, 50(1): 47–62.

Horton, Robin. (1971). "African Conversion." *Africa: Journal of the International African Institute*, 41(2): 85–108.

Huillery, Elise. (2009). "History Matters: The Long-Term Impact of Colonial Public Investments in French West Africa," *American Economic Journal: Applied Economics*, 1(2): 176–215.

Johnson, Hildegard Binder. (1967). "The Location of Christian Missions in Africa." *Geographical Review*, 57(2): 168–202.

Kanogo, Tabitha. (1993). "Mission Impact on Women in Colonial Kenya." In *Women and Missions: Past and Present*, edited by Fiona Bowie, Deborah Kirkwood, and Shirley Ardener, 165–86. Oxford: Berg.

Keith, Arthur Berriedale. (1919). *The Belgian Congo and the Berlin Act*. Oxford: Clarendon Press.

Labode, Modupe. (1993). "From Heathen Kraal to Christian Home: Anglican Mission Education and African Christian Girls, 1850–1900." In *Women and Missions: Past and Present*, edited by Fiona Bowie, Deborah Kirkwood, and Shirley Ardener, 126–44. Oxford: Berg.

McCleary, Rachel and Robert J. Barro. (2006). "Religion and Economy." *Journal of Economic Perspectives*, 20(2): 49–72.

Murdock, George. (1959). *Africa: Its Peoples and Their Cultural History*. New York: McGraw-Hill Book Company.

Nunn, Nathan. (2008). "The Long-Term Effects of Africa's Slave Trades." *Quarterly Journal of Economics*, 123(1): 139–76.

(2010). "Religious Conversion in Colonial Africa." *American Economic Review Papers and Proceedings*, 100(2): 147–52.

Nunn, Nathan and Leonard Wantchekon. (2011). "The Slave Trade and the Origins of Mistrust in Africa." *American Economic Review*, 101(7): 3221–52.

Roome, William R. M. (1924). "Ethnographic Survey of Africa: Showing the Tribes and Languages; Also the Stations of Missionary Societies [map]," 1:5,977,382.

Schaltegger, Christoph A. and Benno Torgler. (2009). "Was Weber Wrong? A Human Capital Theory of Protestant Economic History: A Comment on Becker and Woessmann," Mimeo, Queensland University of Technology.

The Century Company. (1897). "The Century Atlas, Africa [map]."

Woodberry, Robert D. (2004). "The Shadow of Empire: Christian Missions, Colonial Policy, and Democracy in PostColonial Societies," PhD Dissertation in Sociology, University of North Carolina at Chapel Hill.

(2009). "Dividing Elites: Religious Liberty, Protestant Competition, and Democracy in the Global South," Working Paper 002, Project on Religion and Economic Change. March.

Woodberry, Robert D. and Timothy S. Shah. (2004). "The Pioneering Protestants." *Journal of Democracy*, 15(2): 47–61.

Index

For EU product safety concerns, contact us at Calle de José Abascal, 56–1°,
28003 Madrid, Spain or eugpsr@cambridge.org.

www.ingramcontent.com/pod-product-compliance
Lightning Source LLC
Chambersburg PA
CBHW031407180625
28321CB00019B/13
* 9 7 8 1 1 0 7 0 4 1 1 5 8 *